1760	1800	1820	1840	1860
Ram Mohan Roy (1772–1833) Ottoman sultan Selim III (1789–1807)	Ottoman sultan Mahmud II (1808–1839)	Chinese cholera epidemic (1822–1824) Thomas Raffles founds Singapore (1824) Empress Dowager Cixi (1835–1900) Tanzimat era (1839–1876) Opium War (1839–1842)	Reforms of Mizuno Tadakuni (1841–1843) Ito Hirobumi (1841–1909) Treaty of Nanjing (1843) Taiping rebellion (1850–1864) Kang Youwei (1852–1927) Vietnam, Cambodia, and Laos fall to France (1859–1893)	Meiji restoration (1868) Liang Qichao (1873–1929) Japan sends warships to Korea (1876) Promulgation of the Ottoman constitution (1876)
Publication of Olaudah Equiano's autobiography (1789) Napolean Bonaparte invades Egypt (1798)	Slave trade ends: Great Britain (1807), United States (1808), France (1814), Netherlands (1817) Fulani conquer Hausa city-states Muhammad Ali becomes ruler of Egypt (1805)	Slavery abolished: Great Britain (1833), France (1848), United States (1865), Cuba (1886)	Construction of Suez Canal (1859–1869)	King Leopold II establishes Congo Free State Exploration under Stanley, Livingston, Speke, and Burton Discovery of diamonds in South Africa (1866) Scramble for Africa (1875–1900)
James Cook's exploration of Australia, New Zealand, and Hawai`i (1768–1780) American revolution (1775–1783) *Declaration of Independence* (1776) British surrender at Yorktown (1781) Peace of Paris (1783) and American independence Slave revolt in Saint-Domingue (1791) Simón Bolívar (1783–1830)	Louisiana Purchase (1803) Independence of Haiti (1804) War of 1812 (1812–1814) John A. McDonald (1815–1891)	Independence of Brazil Brazilian emperor Pedro I (1822–1834) Monroe Doctrine (1823) Central American Federation(1824–1838) splits	Treaty of Waitangi (1840) Mexican-American War (1845–1848) Seneca Falls Convention (1848)	U.S. Civil War (1861–1865) Annexation of Tahiti (France), Fiji (Britain), and Marshall Islands (Germany) Battle of Little Big Horn (1876) Juan Perón (1895–1974)
James Watt invents the steam engine (1765) French revolution begins (1789) *Declaration of the Rights of Man and the Citizen* (1789) Olympe de Gouges's *Declaration of the Rights of Woman and the Female Citizen* (1791) Mary Wollstonecraft's *A Vindication of the Rights of Women* (1792) Klemens von Metternich (1773–1859)	Congress of Vienna (1814–1815) Napoleon's final defeat at Waterloo (1815) George Stephenson invents the steam locomotive (1815) Giuseppe Garibaldi (1807–1882) Count Camillo di Cavour (1810–1861) Otto von Bismarck (1815–1898)	Russo-Turkish war (1828–1829) Origins of utopian socialism Cecil Rhodes (1835–1902) Queen Victoria (1837–1901)	Rebellions of 1848 Karl Marx's *Manifesto of the Communist Party* (1848) Crimean War (1853–1856) Alexander II (1855–1881)	Italian unification (1866) German unification (1871)

ENCOUNTERS IN WORLD HISTORY

ENCOUNTERS IN WORLD HISTORY

Sources and Themes from the Global Past, Volume Two: From 1500

FIRST EDITION

THOMAS SANDERS
United States Naval Academy

SAMUEL H. NELSON
United States Naval Academy

STEPHEN MORILLO
Wabash College

NANCY ELLENBERGER
United States Naval Academy

Boston   Burr Ridge, IL   Dubuque, IA   Madison, WI   New York
San Francisco   St. Louis   Bangkok   Bogotá   Caracas   Kuala Lumpur
Lisbon   London   Madrid   Mexico City   Milan   Montreal   New Delhi
Santiago   Seoul   Singapore   Sydney   Taipei   Toronto

Mc Graw Hill | Higher Education

ENCOUNTERS IN WORLD HISTORY: SOURCES AND THEMES FROM THE GLOBAL
PAST, VOLUME 2: FROM 1500
Published by McGraw-Hill, an imprint of The McGraw-Hill Companies, Inc., 1221 Avenue of the
Americas, New York, NY 10020. Copyright © 2006. All rights reserved. No part of this publication
may be reproduced or distributed in any form or by any means, or stored in a database or retrieval
system, without the prior written consent of The McGraw-Hill Companies, Inc., including, but not
limited to, in any network or other electronic storage or transmission, or broadcast for distance
learning.

This book is printed on acid-free paper.

1 2 3 4 5 6 7 8 9 0 DOC/DOC 0 9 8 7 6 5

ISBN 0-07-245103-3

Editor-in-chief: Emily G. Barrosse
Publisher: Lyn Uhl
Sponsoring editor: Jon-David Hague
Marketing manager: Katherine Bates
Developmental editor: Kristen Mellitt
Project manager: Carey Eisner
Manuscript editor: Elaine Kehoe
Design manager: Kim Menning
Interior and cover design: Glenda King
Art editor: Ayelet Arbel
Photo editor: Alexandra Ambrose
Photo researcher: Judy Mason

Production supervisor: Randy Hurst
Composition: 10/12 Galliard by
    Thompson Type
Printing: 45# New Era Plus by R. R. Donnelley
Cover: The Battle of Isandhlwana: The Last
    Stand of the 24th Regiment of Foot (South
    Welsh Borders) during the Zulu War, 22nd
    January 1879 (oil on canvas) by Charles
    Edwin Fripp (1854–1906)/National
    Army Museum, London, UK
    www.bridgeman.co.uk

Credits: The credits section for this book begins on page 523 and is considered an extension of the
copyright page.

Library of Congress Cataloging-in-Publication Data
Encounters in world history : sources and themes from the global past / Thomas Sanders . . .
  [et al.].—1st ed.
    p. cm.
  Contents: v. 1. To 1500 — v. 2. From 1500.
  ISBN 0-07-245101-7 (softcover : v. 1) — ISBN 0-07-245103-3 (softcover : v. 2)
    1. History—Examinations, questions, etc.   2. World history.   3. World history—Sources.
  4. Historiography.   5. History—Philosophy.   I. Sanders, Thomas, 1951–

D21.E575 2005
907'.6—dc22   2005041590

The Internet addresses listed in the text were accurate at the time of publication. The inclusion of a
website does not indicate an endorsement by the authors or McGraw-Hill, and McGraw-Hill does not
guarantee the accuracy of the information presented at these sites.

http://www.mhhe.com

To Jolene, Brooke, Joseph, and Jose for their love and support,
and to my mentors, colleagues, and students
for all that they taught me.—TS

To my family.—SHN

To Lynne, Robin, Dione, and Raphael:
you can have the computer back now.
And to Velazquez, Vermeer, and Georgia,
missed but not forgotten.—SRM

About the Authors

THOMAS SANDERS received his doctorate in Russian history from Stanford University. He has taught at a variety of colleges and universities, including Stanford, Georgia Southern, the University of Dayton, Oberlin College, and since 1990 at the United States Naval Academy. His most recent book is a collaborative translation and commentary entitled *Against the Mountains: Qarakhi's Shining Swords and Tolstoy's Hadji Murat Depict Russian-Muslim Conflict in the Caucasus* (Routledge-Curzon, 2004). He has just begun a biography of the Soviet composer Vladimir Shainskii.

SAMUEL H. NELSON's interest in world cultures began during his service in the Peace Corps, when he taught secondary school in a small town in the Congo. Afterwards, he studied African history and anthropology at Stanford University, where he received his PhD. He joined the faculty of the United States Naval Academy in 1987 and created courses on African history, comparative world cultures, and illness and therapy. He has conducted fieldwork in central and southern Africa, and is the author of a history of the Congo basin and, more recently, articles on the HIV/AIDS epidemic in Africa.

STEPHEN MORILLO grew up in New Orleans, received his AB from Harvard and his DPhil from Oxford. He has taught at Loyola (New Orleans), the University of Georgia, and since 1989 at Wabash College, with a year at Hawai'i Pacific University as their NEH Distinguished Visiting Professor in 2003–04. He is the author of several books and numerous articles on various combinations of medieval, military, and global history.

NANCY ELLENBERGER received a BA in political science from Wellesley College, an MA in International Relations from the University of Chicago, and a PhD in British history from the University of Oregon. Her interest in global history grew out of this eclectic background and was reinforced by her teaching of the history of the British Empire at the United States Naval Academy, where she has been on the faculty since 1983. Her research interests center around the British social and political elites of the late-Victorian and Edwardian generation.

BRIEF CONTENTS

Preface   *xxv*

PART ONE   EXPANDING HORIZONS, 1500–1750
1   Expanding Global Encounters in the Fourteenth
   through Sixteenth Centuries   3
2   Cross-Cultural Perceptions in the New World   36
3   Perspectives on the Atlantic Slave Trade   70
4   Paths to Enlightenment   101
5   "Great Men" and Virtues of Leadership   123

PART TWO   THE AGE OF REVOLUTION, INDUSTRIALIZATION,
AND NATIONALISM, 1750–1898
6   Liberty and Revolution in the Atlantic World,
   1776–1850   155
7   The Industrial Revolution and Its Impact on Work,
   Wealth, and Power   197
8   The Frontier Experience and Cultural Self-Images   237
9   The World Encounters the West   283
10   Nationalism and Nation Building in the Nineteenth
   Century   317

PART THREE   THE TWENTIETH-CENTURY WORLD AND
FUTURE PROSPECTS
11   Collectivist Ideologies in the Twentieth Century   359
12   Confronting Human Aggression in
   the Twentieth Century   396
13   Perspectives on the Cold War, Decolonization, and
   the Vietnam War   427
14   Shifting Identities of Ethnicity, Race, Gender, and
   Sexuality   460
15   Perspectives on Globalization   495

CONTENTS

Preface xxv

PART ONE
EXPANDING HORIZONS, 1500–1750

CHAPTER 1   **EXPANDING GLOBAL ENCOUNTERS IN THE FOURTEENTH THROUGH SIXTEENTH CENTURIES** 3

INTRODUCTION   3
    Chapter Questions   8

IBN BATTUTA'S TRAVELS IN THE ISLAMIC WORLD   8
    Questions to Consider   10
    READING: *Ibn Battuta, My Travels* (1355)   11

THE CHINESE NAVAL EXPEDITIONS OF ZHENG HE   14
    Questions to Consider   16
    READING: *Zheng He,* Inscription of World Voyages   16

VASCO DA GAMA'S VOYAGE TO AFRICA AND INDIA   19
    Questions to Consider   20
    READING: *A Journal of the First Voyage of Vasco da Gama* (1497–1499)   21

COLUMBUS'S FIRST VOYAGE TO THE "NEW WORLD"   27
    Questions to Consider   29
    READING: *Christopher Columbus,* Prologue to the Logbook of the First Voyage (1492)   30
    READING: *Christopher Columbus,* Letter Describing His First Voyage (1493)   31
    Notes   34

CHAPTER 2   **CROSS-CULTURAL PERCEPTIONS IN THE NEW WORLD   36**

INTRODUCTION   36
Chapter Questions   39

AN AZTEC ACCOUNT OF THE CONQUEST OF MEXICO   40
Questions to Consider   42
READING: *Bernardino de Sahagún, The General History of New Spain* (1577)   43

A SPANISH ACCOUNT OF THE CONQUEST OF MEXICO   48
Questions to Consider   49
READING: *Bernal Díaz del Castillo, The True History of the Conquest of New Spain* (1568)   49

IMAGES OF THE CONQUEST   65
Questions to Consider   66
Notes   68

CHAPTER 3   **PERSPECTIVES ON THE ATLANTIC SLAVE TRADE   70**

INTRODUCTION   70
Chapter Questions   74

THE PERSPECTIVE OF A SLAVE TRADER   74
Questions to Consider   75
READING: *Jacques Barbot,* The Slaving Voyage of the *Albion-Frigate* (1698–1699)   77

THE PERSPECTIVE OF A SLAVE   84
Questions to Consider   85
READING: *Olaudah Equiano, The Interesting Narrative of the Life of Olaudah Equiano* (1789)   86

THE PERSPECTIVE OF A SLAVE OWNER   95
Questions to Consider   96
READING: *Thomas Jefferson, Notes on the State of Virginia* (1781)   96
Notes   100

CHAPTER 4   **PATHS TO ENLIGHTENMENT   101**

INTRODUCTION   101
Chapter Questions   103

RENÉ DESCARTES' DEDUCTIVE METHOD OF INQUIRY   104
Questions to Consider   105

READING: *René Descartes, Discourse on Method* (1637) 105

THE EMPIRICAL REASONING OF JOHN LOCKE 109
Questions to Consider 110
READING: *John Locke,* "An Essay Concerning Human Understanding"
(1690) 111

THE ENLIGHTENED PATH OF WANG YANG-MING 115
Questions to Consider 117
READING: *Wang Yang-ming,* "Inquiry on *The Great Learning*"
(1525) 117
Notes 121

CHAPTER 5   "GREAT MEN" AND VIRTUES
OF LEADERSHIP 123

INTRODUCTION 123
Chapter Questions 125

SUNDIATA: FOUNDER OF THE MALIAN EMPIRE 126
Questions to Consider 127
READING: *Sundiata: An Epic of Old Mali* 127

AKBAR OF MUGHAL INDIA 132
Questions to Consider 134
READING: *Barnī,* "Rulings on Temporal Government"
(1358) 134
READING: *Father Antonio Monserrate, Commentary on
His Journey to the Court of Akbar* (1582) 135

EMPEROR KANGXI OF THE QING DYNASTY IN CHINA 138
Questions to Consider 140
READING: *Kangxi,* "On Ruling" 140
READING: *Kangxi,* "Valedictory" (1717) 143

PETER THE GREAT OF RUSSIA 145
Questions to Consider 146
READING: "Decree on the Invitation to Foreigners" (1702) 146
READING: "Decrees on the Building of St. Petersburg"
(1714) 147
READING: "Prohibition on Kneeling" 148
READING: "Order to the Army Before the Battle of Poltava"
(1709) 148
READING: "Peter's Conception of Imperial Authority" 149
READING: "An Old Believer Manuscript from
Solovetsky Monastery" 149
READING: "A Nineteenth-Century Assessment of
Peter the Great" 150
Notes 151

PART TWO

THE AGE OF REVOLUTION, INDUSTRIALIZATION, AND NATIONALISM, 1750–1898

CHAPTER 6   **LIBERTY AND REVOLUTION IN THE ATLANTIC WORLD, 1776–1850**   155

INTRODUCTION   155
Chapter Questions   159

THE AMERICAN REVOLUTION   160
The Revolutionary Ideals of Jefferson   160
Questions to Consider   161
READING: *Thomas Jefferson,* Declaration of Independence (1776)   161
The Fears of the Founding Fathers   162
Questions to Consider   163
READING: *James Madison,* Federalist No. 10 (The Union as a Safeguard Against Domestic Faction and Insurrection) (1787)   164
An Argument for Democratic Reform   167
Questions to Consider   168
READING: *George Bancroft,* "The Office of the People in Art, Government, and Religion" (1835)   169
A Critique of American Liberty from a Former Slave   171
Questions to Consider   172
READING: *Frederick Douglass,* "What to the Slave Is the 4th of July?" (1852)   173

THE FRENCH REVOLUTION   176
A Declaration of the Rights of Man   176
Questions to Consider   177
READING: Declaration of the Rights of Man and Citizen (1789)   177
A Feminist Perspective on the Revolution, 1791   179
Questions to Consider   179
READING: *Olympe de Gouges,* Declaration of the Rights of Woman and the Female Citizen (1791)   180
Terror in Defense of Liberty   183
Questions to Consider   184
READING: *Maximilien Robespierre,* "The Moral and Political Principles of Domestic Policy" (1794)   184

REVOLUTIONS IN THE CARIBBEAN AND LATIN AMERICA   186
The Haitian Revolution   186
Questions to Consider   187
READING: *Toussaint L'Ouverture,* Speeches and Letters on the Haitian Revolution (1793–1800)   187
The Liberator of South America, 1815   191

Questions to Consider 192
READING: Simón Bolívar, "The Jamaican Letter" (1815) 192
Notes 196

CHAPTER 7 **THE INDUSTRIAL REVOLUTION AND ITS IMPACT ON WORK, WEALTH, AND POWER 197**

INTRODUCTION 197
Chapter Questions 201

THE RATIONALITY AND BENEFITS OF INDUSTRIAL CAPITALISM AND ECONOMIC LIBERALISM 202
Questions to Consider 202
READING: Adam Smith, *Wealth of Nations* (1776) 203

TWO PERSPECTIVES ON THE FACTORY SYSTEM IN ENGLAND 208
Questions to Consider 209
READING: Testimony of Matthew Crabtree from the Sadler Committee Report (1832) 209
READING: Andrew Ure, *The Philosophy of Manufactures* (1835) 211

THE MARXIST CRITIQUE OF CAPITALISM AND THE COMMUNIST ALTERNATIVE 213
Questions to Consider 215
READING: Karl Marx and Friedrich Engels, *The Communist Manifesto* (1848) 215

ANDREW CARNEGIE'S GOSPEL OF WEALTH 220
Questions to Consider 221
READING: Andrew Carnegie, "Wealth" (1889) 221

WEALTH, POWER, AND CONSPICUOUS CONSUMPTION IN AMERICA 224
Questions to Consider 225
READING: Thorstein Veblen, *Theory of the Leisure Class* (1899) 226

INDUSTRIALIZATION IN IMPERIAL RUSSIA 229
Questions to Consider 231
READING: Sergei Witte, *Secret Memorandum on Industrialization* (1899) 232
Notes 235

CHAPTER 8 **THE FRONTIER EXPERIENCE AND CULTURAL SELF-IMAGES 237**

INTRODUCTION 237
Chapter Questions 241

THE FRONTIER IN AMERICAN HISTORY 241
The Frontier and American Identity 241

Questions to Consider 243
READING: *Frederick Jackson Turner, "The Significance of the Frontier in American History"* (1893) 243
READING: *Chief Joseph of Nez Percé,* Selected Statements, Speeches, and Letters (1877–1879) 249
Myths of the American West 253
Questions to Consider 254
READING: *Owen Wister, The Virginian: A Horseman of the Plains* (1902) 255
The Frontier Remembered 260
Questions to Consider 261
READING: *Ronald Reagan,* Remarks at the Completion of the Fourth Mission of the Space Shuttle *Columbia* (1982) 262

THE FRONTIER IN SOUTH AFRICAN HISTORY 263
Frontier Wars and the Rise of the Zulu 263
Questions to Consider 265
READING: *Jantshi ka Nongila, The History of Shaka* (recorded 1903) 267
READING: *Izibongo: A Shaka Praise Poem* 268
Shaka Remembered: A Different Story 270
Questions to Consider 271
READING: *Mazisi Kunene, Emperor Shaka the Great* (1979) 271
The Frontier and the Afrikaner "Great Trek" 273
Questions to Consider 275
READING: *Piet Retief,* "Manifesto of the Emigrant Farmers" (1837) 275
READING: *Sarel Cilliers, The Battle of Blood River* (1871) 277
The Trek Remembered 278
Questions to Consider 279
READING: *Daniel Malan,* "The Second Great Trek" (1938) 280
Notes 281

CHAPTER 9 THE WORLD ENCOUNTERS THE WEST 283
INTRODUCTION 283
Chapter Questions 287

CHINESE RESPONSES TO IMPERIALISM 287
An Imperial Response to the British King, 1793 287
Questions to Consider 289
READING: *The Qianlong Emperor,* Letters to George III (1793) 289
The Antiforeigner Boxer Uprising, 1900 291
Questions to Consider 292
READING: Proclamation of the Boxers United in Righteousness 292

INDIAN RESPONSES TO IMPERIALISM 294
The View of an Indian Modernizer 294

Questions to Consider 295
READING: *Ram Mohun Roy,* Letter to Lord Amherst on Education (1823) 295
A Critique of British Exploitation, 1904 297
Questions to Consider 298
READING: *Ramesh Dutt, India in the Victorian Age* (1904) 299

AFRICAN RESPONSES TO IMPERIALISM 302
An African Missionary Promotes Christian Conversion 302
Questions to Consider 303
READING: *Samuel Crowther,* Letter to the Rev. H. Venn (1854) 304
A View of Village Life in British Kenya, 1920s 306
Questions to Consider 306
READING: *Oginga Odinga,* "At the Feet of the Village Elders" (1967) 307

A BRITISH VIEW OF THE PARADOXES OF EMPIRE 309
Confessions of a British Administrator, 1936 309
Questions to Consider 310
READING: *George Orwell,* "Shooting an Elephant" (1936) 310
Notes 315

CHAPTER 10 **NATIONALISM AND NATION BUILDING IN THE NINETEENTH CENTURY 317**

INTRODUCTION 317
Chapter Questions 321

AMERICAN NATIONALISM IN THE NINETEENTH CENTURY 321
States' Rights Versus the Union 321
Questions to Consider 323
READING: *John C. Calhoun,* On Nullification and the Force Bill (1833) 323
READING: *Abraham Lincoln,* First Inaugural Address (1861) 325
The Question of Immigration and "Americanization" in the 1890s 327
Questions to Consider 329
READING: *Josiah Strong, Our Country* (1891) 329
READING: *Theodore Roosevelt,* "What 'Americanism' Means" (1894) 331

JAPANESE NATIONALISM IN THE NINETEENTH CENTURY 333
Initial Responses to the West 333
Questions to Consider 335
READING: *Tokugawa Nariaki,* "Memorandum to the Bakufu" (1853) 336
Japanese National Identity and the Meiji Restoration 337
Questions to Consider 339

READING: *Ito Hirobumi,* Reminiscences on the Drafting
of the New Constitution   339
READING: "Imperial Proclamation on the Constitution of the Empire
of Japan" (1889)   341
Japanese Nationalism and Imperialism   342
Questions to Consider   342
READING: *Fukuzawa Yukichi,* "Good-Bye Asia" (1885)   343

GERMAN NATIONALISM IN THE NINETEENTH CENTURY   345
A Call for German Unity   345
Questions to Consider   346
READING: *Johann Gottlieb Fichte, Addresses to the German Nation*
(1807–1808)   346
Unification through "Blood and Iron"   348
Questions to Consider   349
READING: *Otto von Bismarck, Memoirs* (1899)   349
A German "Place in the Sun"   351
Questions to Consider   352
READING: *Heinrich Treitschke, German History in the Nineteenth
Century* (1915–1919)   353
Notes   355

PART THREE

THE TWENTIETH-CENTURY WORLD AND FUTURE PROSPECTS

CHAPTER 11   COLLECTIVIST IDEOLOGIES IN THE TWENTIETH CENTURY   359

INTRODUCTION   359
Chapter Questions   362

SOVIET MARXISM   363
Questions to Consider   364
READING: *Nikolai Bukharin and Evgeny Preobrazhensky,
The ABC of Communism* (1919)   365

GERMAN FASCISM   370
Questions to Consider   372
READING: *Adolph Hitler, Mein Kampf* (1923)   372

DEBATES ON COLLECTIVISM IN AMERICA   378
Questions to Consider   379
READING: *Herbert Hoover,* Presidential Campaign Speech
(1928)   380

THE GREAT DEPRESSION AND ROOSEVELT'S CALL
TO ACTION   383
  Questions to Consider   385
  READING: *Franklin Delano Roosevelt*, First Inaugural Address
  (1933)   385

COLLECTIVISM AND DEVELOPMENT IN TANZANIA   388
  Questions to Consider   390
  READING: *Julius Nyerere*, "Socialism and Rural Development"
  (1967)   390
  Notes   394

CHAPTER 12   **CONFRONTING HUMAN AGGRESSION
IN THE TWENTIETH CENTURY**   396

INTRODUCTION   396
  Chapter Questions   399

TWO SOLDIERS VIEW THE GREAT WAR   400
  Questions to Consider   401
  READING: *Herbert Asquith*, "The Volunteer" (1915)   402
  READING: *Wilfred Owen*, "Dulce et Decorum Est" (1917)   402

PSYCHOLOGY AND THE INSTINCT FOR DESTRUCTION   403
  Questions to Consider   404
  READING: *Sigmund Freud, Civilization and Its Discontents*
  (1931)   404

A COMMUNIST ASSESSMENT   407
  Questions to Consider   408
  READING: *Mao Zedong*, Fighting for Perpetual Peace (1938)   409

A WOMAN WRITER'S PERSPECTIVE   410
  Questions to Consider   411
  READING: *Virginia Woolf, Three Guineas* (1938)   412

THE BANALITY OF EVIL   416
  Questions to Consider   417
  READING: *Hannah Arendt, Eichmann in Jerusalem* (1963)   418

AN ISLAMIC VOICE   421
  Questions to Consider   422
  READING: *Ruhollah Khomeini*, "Message to the Pilgrims" (1980)   422
  Notes   425

CHAPTER 13   **PERSPECTIVES ON THE COLD WAR,
DECOLONIZATION, AND THE VIETNAM WAR**   427

INTRODUCTION   427
  Chapter Questions   430

SOVIET VIEWS OF THE UNITED STATES AND THE COLD WAR   431
  Questions to Consider   432
  READING: *Josef V. Stalin,* "On the Tasks of Workers in the Economy"
  (1931)   433
  READING: *Nikolai Novikov,* "Telegram to Moscow" (1946)   434

AMERICAN VIEWS OF THE SOVIET UNION AND
THE COLD WAR   437
  Questions to Consider   440
  READING: *X [George F. Kennan],* "The Sources of Soviet Conduct"
  (1947)   440
  READING: *Harry S. Truman,* The Truman Doctrine (1947)   444
  READING: *J. Edgar Hoover,* "The Threat of Communism"
  (1946)   445

VIETNAMESE VIEWS ON DECOLONIZATION
AND THE VIETNAM WAR   447
  Questions to Consider   449
  READING: *Ho Chi Minh,* The Vietnamese Declaration
  of Independence (1945)   449
  READING: *Vo Nguyen Giap,* "The People's War" (1961)   450
  READING: *Nguyen Tan Thanh,* "Why I Joined the Vietcong"
  (1961)   452

AMERICAN VIEWS ON DECOLONIZATION
AND THE VIETNAM WAR   453
  Questions to Consider   454
  READING: *Lyndon B. Johnson,* "Why Americans Fight in Vietnam"
  (1965)   455
  READING: *John Kerry,* "Why I Oppose the Vietnam War"
  (1971)   456
  Notes   458

CHAPTER 14   **SHIFTING IDENTITIES OF ETHNICITY, RACE,
            GENDER, AND SEXUALITY   460**

INTRODUCTION   460
  Chapter Questions   463

SELF-IDENTITY, SELF-RULE, AND DECOLONIZATION   463
  Questions to Consider   465
  READING: *Mohandas K. Gandhi, Hind Swaraj (Self-Rule)*
  (1909)   465

WOMEN AS "THE OTHER"   469
  Questions to Consider   471
  READING: *Simone de Beauvoir, The Second Sex* (1949)   471

CIVIL RIGHTS, RACIAL IDENTITY, AND BLACK NATIONALISM
IN AMERICA 476
  Questions to Consider 478
  READING: Malcolm X, Address to a Meeting in New York
  (1964) 479

BLACK CONSCIOUSNESS IN SOUTH AFRICA 481
  Questions to Consider 483
  READING: Steve Biko, "Black Consciousness and the Quest
  for a True Humanity" (1973) 483

SEXUAL IDENTITY, SELF-OPPRESSION, AND GAY RIGHTS 488
  Questions to Consider 490
  READING: The London Gay Liberation Front, "Manifesto"
  (1970) 490
  Notes 493

CHAPTER 15   PERSPECTIVES ON GLOBALIZATION   495

INTRODUCTION 495
  Chapter Questions 497

THE GLOBAL ENVIRONMENT 497
  Questions to Consider 498
  READING: J. R. McNeill, "Peculiarities of a Prodigal Century"
  (2000) 499

DATA ON ENVIRONMENTAL AND SOCIAL CHANGE 501
  Questions to Consider 501
  Demographic Data 501
  Technology and Lifestyle 502

HUMAN RIGHTS 506
  Questions to Consider 506
  READING: "Righting Wrongs" (2001) 507
  UNDP, Human Development Balance Sheet 510
  READING: The Human Development Balance Sheet (2002) 510

TOWARD A GLOBAL CULTURE? 513
  Questions to Consider 513
  READING: Globally Speaking: Global Culture 514
  Picture Gallery of Global Culture 518
  Questions to Consider 519
  Notes 522

Credits 523

PREFACE

༄༅

History is an encounter with the past, and the past is a history of encounters. This book is designed to introduce students to both of these sorts of encounters.

APPROACH

The past as a history of encounters is the organizing theme of this book. Each chapter consists of primary sources illustrating various encounters between and within civilizations and cultures. Some encounters involved one group of humans meeting another group of humans, and so encountering different ways of life, modes of thought, and ambitions. Some of these sorts of encounters produced violent confrontations: the meeting of settled farming-based societies with nomadic herding-based societies, or the encounter of industry-based imperial powers with nonindustrial peoples in the nineteenth century, often resulted in warfare. But many, as in the encounters different peoples had with practitioners of new religions, were peaceful, resulting in exchanges of ideas, goods, and populations. Sometimes such encounters produced both peaceful and violent outcomes. The variety of human encounters is one of the things that makes studying history so interesting.

Another sort of encounter this book presents is more abstract, involving not the meeting of separate groups of people, but the encounter of groups of people with their environment, and even more abstractly, the encounter of groups of people with the problems of living together in a functioning society. People encountered nature and their need to explain it; they encountered the conflict between the need for social order and the need for individual freedom and generated codes of behavior; and they encountered divisions in their society, whether based on gender, class, or other sorts of divisions.

We strove to put before the student substantive selections that present the historical evidence for cultural encounters as directly as possible, but in a context that makes the problems the sources address comprehensible. The problem of context and comprehension is a perennial issue in World Civilization courses; we believe the "encounter" format will be effective both in enriching students' understanding and in helping to provide unity and coherence to the ideas that instructors are trying to get across.

In presenting not a finished narrative of world history, but a selection of sources on which such a narrative could be based, this book shows students some of the evidence that historians use and invites them to interpret that evidence themselves and come to their own conclusions. In other words, it invites them to become historians and to join the constant work in progress that is history.

GENERAL ORGANIZATION AND PRIMARY SOURCES

While "encounters" serves as our overall conceptual device, the book is organized in a broadly chronological fashion, and each chapter is organized around a particular theme. In this way, we have been able to introduce general concepts such as authority, violence, gender, transcendent spirituality, and so on, concepts that are useful in the analysis of concrete historical situations from global human history. We hope by means of the encounters idea and the thematic elements integrated into the various chapters to participate productively in the current effort to present world civilization and history in an integrated and meaningful fashion. We aspire, as well, to assist instructors in providing students not merely with new information, but also with new ways of thinking about the human historical experience.

To provide instructors flexibility in their assignments, we have sought to incorporate a range of civilizations and to rely on as diverse a set of "texts"—including various nonwritten materials—as possible. The encounters themselves were chosen according to criteria of (1) cross-cultural interest or significance, (2) appropriateness to the chronological periods of world history, and (3) applicability to classroom instruction. It is our desire that instructors in all areas of specialization, research interest, and pedagogical approach find in our reader materials that suit their purposes and help them communicate their interpretations of world civilization to their students. To that end, the selections have been judiciously edited to be manageable for students, while retaining enough length to provide a fuller feel for the civilizations that produced these sources and allow students to formulate their own opinions.

We have tried to arrive at a useful mix of new materials and of "classic," well-established sources. In many cases, even when we have included well-known sources, we have used nontraditional selections or edited the material in novel ways consistent with the perspective of a given chapter's theme. The inclusion of both new materials and new approaches to traditional sources makes this book unique.

CHAPTER ORGANIZATION

Each chapter begins with a general introduction, providing students with the context and background required to appreciate the sources that follow. For example, we attempt to connect particular historical encounters with modern versions of the same sorts of encounters. Comparing how different societies have handled similar problems again shows the variety of human experience, but also offers lessons (if only, at times, in what not to do!) The possibility of learning from the past is another valuable outcome of studying history.

A set of general questions follows the chapter introduction, to orient readers and help them make connections among all of the sources in the chapter. Brief Introductions to each group of related sources outline the cultural and historical context in which the encounter occurred and, just as importantly, seek to locate the encounter conceptually for readers without telling them what to think or what they will discover in exploring the sources themselves. Similarly, a set of Questions to Consider precedes each group of sources, guiding students' reading without telling them what to think or burdening them with a theoretical apparatus. It is our intention that the dialogue established between the documents will (1) give the students a richer information source on which to base their judgments and (2) by focusing on perceptions and ways of "seeing" the other, allow for student assessments even in the absence of extensive background information on the specific cultures.

ACKNOWLEDGMENTS

Many people contributed to making this book both possible and better than it otherwise would have been. The authors would like to thank the following reviewers, who read the manuscript and offered helpful feedback:

Thomas Callahan
Rider University

Douglas B. Chambers
University of Southern Mississippi

Denise Z. Davidson
Georgia State University

Paul B. Goodwin, Jr.
University of Connecticut

Russell A. Hart
Hawai'i Pacific University

Scott W. Howlett
Saddleback College

Jonathan Judaken
University of Memphis

Eric C. Rust
Baylor University

William A. Wood
Point Loma Nazarene University

Sanders, Nelson, and Ellenberger would like to thank those Naval Academy colleagues who so generously shared their scholarly expertise and their teaching experience during many lunchtime teaching seminars and corridor chats. They note with particular gratitude the patient advice rendered by Larry Thompson, Dan Masterson, Mary DeCredico, David Peeler, Ernie Tucker, Maochun Yu, Brian VanDeMark, Lori Bogle, and Allison Mellis. In addition to his erudition and collegial assistance, Rich Abels put us in touch with Stephen Morillo. They also express their deep appreciation to Barbara Manvel of Nimitz Library, who chased down our obscure references and rare sources with unflagging energy and resourcefulness.

Morillo thanks Wabash College, Hawai'i Pacific University, and the National Endowment for the Humanities for jointly funding the sabbatical year during which much of his work was accomplished; his colleagues, especially in the History Department and the Cultures and Traditions Program at Wabash, for suggestions and ongoing communal discussions about teaching primary sources (with special thanks to David Blix and Joe Day); and Judy Oswalt for valuable technical assistance. Finally, all the authors would like to express our appreciation to Lyn Uhl, who has been a patient, supportive, and knowledgeable editor throughout this long process, and to Kristen Mellitt and the rest of the McGraw-Hill staff, who skillfully picked up the project and steered it through the final shoals to completion.

Thomas Sanders
Samuel H. Nelson
Stephen Morillo
Nancy Ellenberger

PART ONE

EXPANDING
HORIZONS,
1500–1750

CHAPTER 1

Expanding Global Encounters in the Fourteenth through Sixteenth Centuries

INTRODUCTION

Beginning in the mid-fifteenth century, European nations began to send explorers, merchants, missionaries, and colonizers throughout the rest of the world. Historians have often called this the "Age of Discovery," in which enterprising Portuguese and Spanish explorers took the lead in developing new sailing skills to traverse the unknown seas, discovering new lands and peoples, and initiating a new phase of global encounters that was unprecedented and unmatched in human history. In other words, the so-called Age of Discovery has commonly been portrayed as exclusively European and historically unique. But such accounts of world history are misleading and incomplete. It was certainly not a unique event, for exploration and expansion are as old as the history of mankind.[1] It was also not uniquely European. Centuries before Columbus set out from Spain in 1492, Muslim and Chinese explorers and traders had pioneered routes overland and by sea that served to link together the peoples, goods, and ideas of Asia, Arabia, and Africa. Moreover, such historical accounts do not reveal much about the essence of these voyages—the motivations, attitudes, and cross-cultural perceptions that were to have long-term consequences far beyond the initial period of "discovery."

This chapter explores the theme of exploration through the voyage diaries and chronicles of four of the most widely traveled men of the fourteenth through sixteenth centuries: Ibn Battuta, whose journeys in the mid-fourteenth century took him throughout the vast extent of the Islamic world; Zheng He, a Chinese admiral who sailed as far as the coast of east Africa in the mid-fifteenth century; Vasco da Gama, the Portuguese sea captain who was the first European to reach India by sea in 1498; and Christopher Columbus, who inadvertently "discovered" the Americas as he sought a western sea route to the spice markets of Asia. The accounts of these travelers are fascinating and useful for the detailed historical information they convey about different civilizations and cultures in the fourteenth through sixteenth centuries.[2] Moreover, they allow us to examine and assess the personal motives and actions of explorers, the nature of their experiences and contacts, and, most important, the formation of cross-cultural perceptions and attitudes.

The first voyager we shall examine is Ibn Battuta (1304–1369), a Muslim from Morocco, who was so enthralled by the sights he witnessed on his way to complete the *hajj*[3] in Mecca that he afterward devoted his life to traveling throughout most of the Muslim world, covering an estimated 75,000 miles. Such distances should not be too surprising, for the Islamic world had grown to be one of the largest, wealthiest, and most dynamic civilizations in the world by the fourteenth century. In the years following Muhammad's proclamation of the new faith in Arabia during the seventh century, Islam had spread quickly westward across north Africa and into Iberia (Spain and Portugal) and eastward into Syria and Persia (Iran). In subsequent centuries, Islam continued to expand into northern India and Asia, along the coast of east Africa, and even across the Sahara Desert into west Africa.

Although the Islamic world was rarely unified politically, Muslims were partially bound by religion and commerce. Islam offered a set of common laws and values to its adherents that helped to provide a bond of unity and common identity that transcended ethnic and regional differences. Equally important, the establishment of long-distance trading networks linked Muslim producers and consumers from different regions, as well as with peoples of different religions. In their quest for spices, gold, and other luxury commodities, Muslim traders organized camel caravans to the frontiers of India and across the Sahara in Africa, while organizing equally profitable trade routes by sea across the Indian Ocean. By the time of the first European arrivals in the late fifteenth century, most of the lands bordering the Indian Ocean were linked together in a dynamic and prosperous trade that was under the near monopolistic control of Muslim traders and businessmen.

Such extensive trade networks had important consequences for world history. First, it promoted a parallel development in industry and export production throughout the Islamic world. By the fourteenth century, for example, Persia was renowned for its exquisite glassware, jewelry, and pottery; Morocco for its finely-worked leather goods; and Syria for its durable cotton fabrics. Trade and industry also helped to create an urban, cosmopolitan society. The hub of Islamic civilization lay in its great cities, such as Cairo, Damascus, Baghdad, Timbuktu, and Zanzibar, that straddled major trade routes. The commercial opportunities and sophisticated culture found in these cities attracted residents from far-flung regions, resulting in a rich intermingling of different cultures. Finally, the expansion of trade and cultural contacts helped to spread Islam and elements of Islamic culture to more distant regions, such as the Delhi Sultanate (India) and the west African kingdom of Mali. In fact, some scholars suggest that one of Ibn Battuta's primary goals in his travels was to observe and record the successful expansion of Islam in much of the known world.

In terms of wealth, advanced industry, and technology, China was at least the equal of the Islamic world. But whereas Islam was expanding along with its commerce in the mid-fourteenth century, China was just emerging from a period of foreign conquest and occupation by the Mongols.[4] Eager to assert its power and influence, the first emperors of the new Ming dynasty (1368–1644) launched an ambitious new foreign policy based on sea power. Although China has tradition-ally been viewed as a land power, it has had a long seafaring tradition, and Chinese vessels had sailed to India as early as the Han dynasty (202 BCE–200 CE). China also possessed important maritime technologies to make long-distance travel possible, including the compass, large multimasted ships, and shipboard rockets. Under the early Ming emperors, China organized seven major expeditions between 1405 and 1422, which were led by the capable and daring Chinese admiral Zheng He.

In sheer scope and scale, Zheng He far surpassed the European maritime voyages that occurred later. His armada was several times the size of the fleets commanded by Columbus, and his ships were more than six times bigger. With approximately 300 vessels and 27,000 sailors, Zheng He visited ports in southeast Asia, India, Persia, Arabia, and east Africa. His primary mission was political: to display Chinese might, to collect tribute from subordinate "barbarians" in other lands, and to ferry foreign diplomats to the Chinese emperor's court. In exchange for tribute, Zheng He delivered gifts of fine porcelain dishes, silks, gold and silver, and manufactured goods. But as his travel record also shows, he was prepared and able to use military force to demand deference and to assert his superiority.

After 1422, the great maritime expeditions of China ended abruptly. Historians have proposed several different theories to explain this sudden halt, suggesting that the voyages were too costly, that funds were needed for the construction of the Great Wall, or that the expeditions were seen as counter to Confucian ideals.[5] Nonetheless, the seven voyages of Zheng He had long-term impact. They extended China's political hegemony overseas, promoted the emigration of Chinese into regions of southeast Asia, and reinforced an international tribute system that continued into the nineteenth century.

In comparison with Chinese and Islamic civilizations, Europe was relatively poor, undeveloped, and isolated during much of the fourteenth and fifteenth centuries. The economy was still small, largely agricultural, and organized to meet local needs. Although the Crusades had created a new demand for spices and luxury items from Asia, Europeans remained mostly dependent on Muslim merchants and middlemen. Europe was also politically fragmented, and scarce resources and manpower were spent in innumerable wars and conflicts. And finally, beginning in the mid-fourteenth century, the Black Death (bubonic plague) struck Europe, killing millions, further weakening economies, and creating a widespread climate of fear and xenophobia.[6] From a global perspective, Europe was insular, backward, and unsophisticated.

The initial European drive to explore and expand began in Iberia, and it was fueled by a mixture of political, religious, and commercial motives. For centuries, Portuguese and Spanish Christians had struggled to expel the Moors (Muslim Arabs) who had ruled their lands ever since the eighth century. The *Reconquista*[7] of Iberia by Christian armies created an intense religious fervor and missionary zeal among the warring Christians, and it also generated a new sense of unity and national identity. With the successful expulsion of Muslims from Iberia in the fourteenth and fifteenth centuries, Spain and Portugal emerged as strong, dynamic, and consolidated monarchies, eager to continue the offensive against the hated Moors.

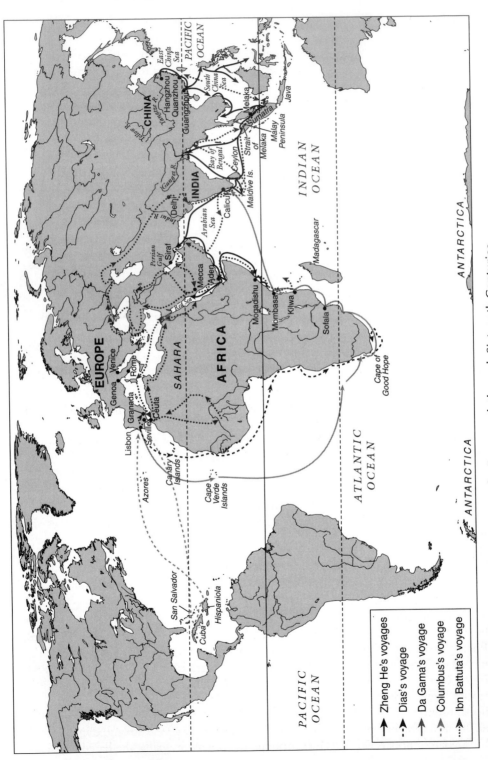

Map 1.1 Global Expeditions and Encounters in the Fourteenth through Sixteenth Centuries

One of the major proponents and patrons of expansion was Prince Henry the Navigator (1394–1460), the third son of King John I of Portugal. Under Henry's auspices, the Portuguese improved ship designs and sailing technologies that allowed voyages to venture farther from their home ports, which culminated in the 1488 voyage of Bartholomeu Dias around Africa's southern Cape of Good Hope (South Africa). Equally important, Henry provided a grand strategy to gain profit and fight the Muslim enemy at the same time by outflanking their trade routes and establishing direct European contact with the rich markets and producers of Africa and Asia. It was also Henry's goal that Europeans discover and make alliances with long-lost Christian monarchs such as Prester John, a wayward Crusader who was believed to have established a large Christian kingdom somewhere in the east. Although Prester John proved to be a myth, such intense religious ideals profoundly shaped European attitudes and actions in their initial encounters with peoples from distant lands.

Less than four decades after Prince Henry's death, Vasco da Gama departed from Portugal in 1497, determined to find a direct sea route to India and Asia. After rounding the Cape of Good Hope in four medium-sized boats with only 168 men, his first stops were at several wealthy city-states situated along the east coast of Africa in what is now Mozambique, Tanzania, and Kenya. Here he found cosmopolitan cities and a thriving trading network controlled by Muslims, but no Christians, and his stay was marked by mutual suspicion and violence. Da Gama then sailed on to India, but here his efforts to conclude commercial treaties with rulers were largely unsuccessful because European trade goods were not highly desired. Still, he returned to Portugal with his ships filled with spices and precious stones, inspiring more commercial ventures and a greater determination than ever to seize control of the Indian Ocean trade from the Muslims.

While the Portuguese were exploring eastern trade routes to India and Asia, Christopher Columbus was determined to find a western route. In 1492, after winning the patronage and financial support of the Spanish monarchy, Columbus set sail from Europe in three small ships with only 120 men. After a voyage of just over thirty days, Columbus sighted the Bahamas and then found and explored Cuba and Haiti, which he initially confused with Japan and China. Although Columbus remained disappointed that he did not find the western route to Asia (and he tried again on three more subsequent voyages), he declared himself "enchanted" with the land and peoples he "discovered," which he described in great detail in a letter to the Spanish monarchs King Fernando and Queen Ysabel.

The early voyages of the Portuguese and Spanish had immediate and long-term consequences for world history. By the sixteenth and seventeenth centuries, these initial European travelers were joined (and eventually overshadowed) by explorers and merchants from the Netherlands, Britain, and France, who joined in the conquest and colonization of the Americas and in the establishment of trading routes and depots elsewhere. With superior military might, as well as the willingness to use it, Europeans were eventually able to extend their commercial and political influence over large parts of the world. This age of expansion also initiated a process of biological exchange, whereby plants, animals, and various diseases were able to migrate beyond their original ecological environments into new areas.

Historical research has shown that the so-called Columbian Exchange[8] has had a very uneven historical impact. Although the introduction of crops such as corn and the potato from the Americas to Europe may have initiated a dramatic increase in population by the eighteenth century, the global dispersion of diseases such as smallpox, syphilis, and bubonic plague decimated entire regional populations.

The readings included in this chapter provide the opportunity to explore the process of exploration and expansion in greater depth and to make comparisons between the four case studies. One of the most important themes to keep in mind is the formation and impact of cross-cultural perceptions and attitudes. Are there any commonalities in the ways people first viewed "others"? What are the most important factors that shape opinions, beliefs, and behaviors? How does one's own culture and values shape one's view of the world? What lasting impact might these initial encounters have had on subsequent meetings?

CHAPTER QUESTIONS

1. When the four travel accounts are compared, what were the most important motivations that underlay the age of expansion? How did explorers see themselves and their mission? How did their expressed motives compare with the ones that are revealed in their descriptions of their discoveries and experiences?

2. What kinds of observations and experiences were recorded by the explorers? What do they tell us about different cultures? Existing trade routes? What kind of information seems to be missing from these accounts?

3. What role did religion play in the motives and experiences of the explorers? How were beliefs used to justify actions? What are the implications?

4. How were cross-cultural ideas formed? Were they the result of actual experiences and observations? Or were they the result of preexisting values and cultural biases? What general conclusions can be made?

5. In what ways, if any, were the European voyages of exploration unique? Examine the relationship between motives, experiences, attitudes, and long-term consequences. Do you think world history would have been radically different if China and Zheng He had "discovered" Europe in the early fifteenth century?

IBN BATTUTA'S TRAVELS IN THE ISLAMIC WORLD

Even by our modern measures, the travels of Abu Abdullah Muhammad Ibn Battuta (1304–1369) are extraordinary. Over a period of nearly thirty years, he is estimated to have traveled 75,000 miles and visited regions that now comprise over forty modern nations (see Map 1.2). Born in 1304 at Tangier, Morocco, to a family of legal scholars, Ibn Battuta initially planned to become a judge, and he pursued a legal education. But his journey to Mecca for the *hajj* when he was

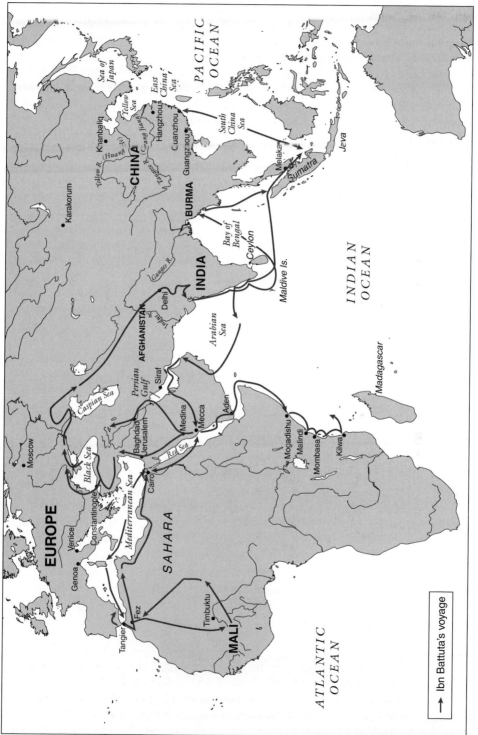

Map 1.2 Ibn Battuta's Travels

twenty-one forever changed his life. Fascinated by his long journey across north Africa, he determined to devote his entire life to traveling in different lands and observing different cultures. He reportedly had only two rules: to visit only Muslim countries, and never to travel the same road twice.

For the most part, Ibn Battuta followed his own rules. He first traveled the lands of the Middle East, crossed the Arabian desert, and visited the cities of present-day Iraq and Iran. In 1330, he changed directions and sailed down the Red Sea to the Indian Ocean, stopping along the way at trading towns situated along the coast of east Africa. Two years later, he journeyed through southern Russia and Afghanistan to India, where he was appointed a regional judge by the Sultan of Delhi. After five years' service, he recommenced his journeys and traveled to China, Burma, and Sumatra (Indonesia). After a short return home to Tangier, he departed on his last major trip in 1349, a trek across the Sahara Desert to visit the kingdom of Mali in west Africa. Upon his return, he finished writing his travel accounts while residing as an honored guest at the court of Sultan Abu Inan of Morocco. Unfortunately, little is known about the final two decades of his life before he died in 1369.

Some historians contend that Ibn Battuta's chronicles are occasionally fictional and sometimes prone to errors. Yet his record of observations and experiences provides a wealth of information about the social structures and cultural values of many different lands in the fourteenth century. In some regions of the world, such as the interior regions of Africa, his account of different African societies is one of the few remaining recorded sources for this time period. Although he focused most of his attention on the ruling classes in the areas he visited, he also recorded a wide range of human activities, from the royal ceremonies of the Malian king to farming techniques in imperial China. Indeed, some biographers of Ibn Battuta contend that it was his deep personal interest in people and their customs that led him to record and assess in such great detail the practices, beliefs, and daily life of different societies.

The reading that follows provides brief excerpts from three of Ibn Battuta's trips. The first excerpt recounts his visit to the holy sites of Medina and Mecca[9] in 1326, early in his career as a world traveler. Here his account is very favorable, focusing on the kindness and cleanliness of residents. The second excerpt includes his observations while visiting China around 1340, one of the few non-Muslim areas that he visited. Although he was impressed with the prosperity found in China, he ultimately judged that the country "did not attract me" because of its "heathendom." The final excerpt focuses on Ibn Battuta's journey to the Kingdom of Mali in west Africa, where he finds cultural attributes to praise and to condemn.

QUESTIONS TO CONSIDER

1. Compare and contrast Ibn Battuta's descriptions of Mecca, China, and Mali. What commonalities are found in each description? What does he find to praise? What does he condemn?

2. Using his descriptions as evidence, what were some of the underlying motives that inspired his travels? In what ways might these motives shape or distort his observations?

3. Identify the most important assumptions, values, or attitudes that helped shape his assessments about other cultures. Is it possible to be an "objective" world traveler?

4. Given his selective observations and value judgments, can Ibn Battuta's travel accounts be used as a reliable source of historical information?

5. Imagine that Ibn Battuta had been able to visit France or England during his travels. What kind of observations do you think he might have made? Would he have had a favorable impression of Europe during this time period? Why?

MY TRAVELS (1355)

Ibn Battuta

I left Tangier, my birthplace, on June 14, 1325, being at that time twenty-one years of age with the intention of making the Pilgrimage to the Holy House [at Mecca] and the Tomb of the Prophet [at Medina].

I set out alone, finding no companion to cheer the way with friendly intercourse, and no party of travelers with whom to associate myself. Swayed by an overmastering impulse within me, and a long-cherished desire to visit those glorious sanctuaries, I resolved to quit all my friends and tear myself away from my home. As my parents were still alive, it weighed grievously upon me to part from them, and both they and I were afflicted with sorrow. . . .

Visiting the Holy Sites of Medina & Mecca

[One] evening . . . we entered the holy sanctuary and reached the illustrious mosque, halting in salutation at the Gate of Peace; then we prayed in the illustrious garden between the tomb of the Prophet and the noble pulpit, and reverently touched the fragment that remains of the palm-trunk against which the Prophet stood when he preached. Having paid our respects to the lord of men from first to last, the intercessor for sinners, the Prophet of Mecca, Muhammad . . . we returned to our camp, rejoicing at this great favor bestowed upon us, praising God for our having reached the former abodes and the magnificent sanctuaries of His Holy Prophet, and praying [to] Him to grant that this visit should not be our last and that we might be of those whose pilgrimage is accepted.

On this journey, our stay at Medina lasted four days. We used to spend every night in the illustrious mosque, where the people, after forming circles in the courtyard and, lighting large numbers of candles, would pass the time either in reciting the

Source: Ibn Battuta, *Travels in Asia and Africa, 1325–1354,* trans. H. A. R. Gibb (London: Routledge, 1929), 43, 74–76, 282–84, 292, 321–25, 329.

Koran from volumes set on rests in front of them, or in intoning litanies, or in visiting the sanctuaries of the holy tomb. . . . We departed at night . . . with hearts full of joy at reaching the goal of our hopes, and in the morning arrived at the City of Surety, Mecca (may God ennoble her!), where we immediately entered the holy sanctuary and began the rites of pilgrimage.

The inhabitants of Mecca are distinguished by many excellent and noble activities and qualities, by their beneficence to the humble and weak, and by their kindness to strangers. When any of them makes a feast, he begins by giving food to the religious devotees who are poor and without resources, inviting them first with kindness and delicacy. The majority of these unfortunates are to be found by the public bakeries, and when anyone has his bread baked and takes it away to his house, they follow him and he gives each one of them some share of it, sending away none disappointed. Even if he has but a single loaf, he gives away a third or a half of it, cheerfully and without any ill-feeling.

Another good habit of theirs is this. The orphan children sit in the bazaar, each with two baskets, one large and one small. When one of the townspeople comes to the bazaar and buys cereals, meat and vegetables, he hands them to one of these boys, who puts the cereals in one basket and the meat and vegetables in the other and takes them to the man's house, so that his meal may be prepared. Meanwhile the man goes about his devotions and his business. There is no instance of any of the boys having ever abused their trust in this matter, and they are given a fixed fee of a few coppers.

The Meccans are very elegant and clean in their dress, and most of them wear white garments, which you always see fresh and snowy. They use a great deal of perfume and kohl and make free use of toothpicks of green arak-wood. The Meccan women are extraordinarily beautiful and very pious and modest. They too make great use of perfumes to such a degree that they will spend the night hungry in order to buy perfumes with the price of their food. They visit the mosque every Thursday night, wearing their finest apparel; and the whole sanctuary is saturated with the smell of their perfume. When one of these women goes away the odor of the perfume clings to the place after she has gone.

Voyage to China

The land of China is of vast extent, and abounding in produce, fruits, gold, and silver. In this respect there is no country in the world that can rival it. It is traversed by the river called the "Water of Life."* It is bordered by villages, fields, fruit gardens, and bazaars, just like the Egyptian Nile, only that [China] is even more richly cultivated and populous. . . . All of the fruits we have in our country are to be found here, either the same or better quality. . . . [As for Chinese pottery], it is exported to India and other countries, even reaching us as far as our own lands in the West, and it is the finest of all makes of pottery.

The Chinese themselves are infidels, who worship idols and burn their dead like the Hindus. The king of China is a Tatar [Mongol], one of the descendants of Genghis Khan. In every Chinese city there is a quarter for Muslims, in which they live by them-

---

*Most scholars believe that Ibn Battuta is referring to China's "Grand Canal," one of the world's oldest (begun in 486 BCE) and largest (over 1,000 miles long) man-made waterways.

selves, and in which they have mosques both for Friday services and for other religious purposes. The Muslims are honored and respected. The Chinese infidels eat the flesh of swine and dogs, and sell it in their markets. They are wealthy folk and well-to-do, but they make no display [of wealth] in their food or their clothes. You will see a principal merchant, a man so rich that his wealth cannot be counted, wearing a coarse cotton tunic. But one thing that the Chinese do take a pride in is gold and silver plate. Everyone of them carries a stick, on which they lean in walking, and which they call the third leg. . . .

. . . The land of China, in spite of all that is agreeable in it, did not attract me. On the contrary, I was sorely grieved that heathendom had such a strong hold over it. Whenever I went out of my house I used to see any number of revolting things, and that distressed me so much that I used to keep indoors and go out only in case of necessity. When I met Muslims in China, I always felt just as though I were meeting with my own faith and kin. . . .

Travels to the Kingdom of Mali in West Africa

When I decided to make the journey to Mali, which is reached in twenty-four days from Walata [an oasis in the Sahara] if the traveler pushes on rapidly, I hired a guide . . . for there is no necessity to travel in a company on account of the safety of that road, and set out with three of my companions. . . .

A traveler in this country carries no provisions, whether plain food or seasonings, and neither gold nor silver. He takes nothing but pieces of salt and glass ornaments, which the people call beads, and some aromatic goods. When he comes to a village the womenfolk of the blacks bring out millet, milk, chickens, pulped fruit, rice . . . and pounded beans. The traveler buys whatever of these foods he wants. . . .

Thus I reached the city of Mali, the capital of the king of the blacks. I stopped at the cemetery and went to the quarter occupied by the whites [Arab merchants], where I asked for Muhammad ibn al-Faqih. I found that he had hired a house for me and went there. His son-in-law brought me candles and food, and next day Ibn al-Faqih himself came to visit me, with other prominent residents. I met the judge of Mali, Abd ar-Rahman, who came to see me; he is a Negro, a devout Muslim, and a man of fine character. I met also the interpreter Dugha, who is one of the principal men among the blacks. All these persons sent me hospitality gifts of food and treated me with the utmost generosity. May God reward them for their kindnesses! . . .

The sultan of Mali is Mansa Sulayman, "mansa" meaning [in Mandingo*] sultan, and Sulayman being his proper name. He is a miserly king, not a man from whom one might hope for a rich present. It happened that I spent these two months without seeing him, on account of my illness. Later on he held a banquet . . . to which the commanders, doctors, judges, and preachers were invited, and I went along with them. Reading desks were brought in, and the Koran was read through, then they prayed for . . . Mansa Sulayman.

When the ceremony was over I went forward and saluted Mansa Sulayman. The judge, the preacher, and [my host] Ibn al-Faqih told him who I was, and he answered

---

*Mandingo is an African language spoken by the Malinke people who reside in the grasslands south of the Sahara Desert.

them in their tongue. They said to me, "The sultan says to you 'Give thanks to God,'" so I said, "Praise be to God and thanks under all circumstances." When I withdrew, the [sultan's] welcoming gift was sent to me. . . . Ibn al-Faqih came hurrying out of his house barefooted, and entered my room saying, "Stand up; here comes the sultan's gift to you." So I stood up, thinking that it would consist of robes of honor and money, and behold! It was three cakes of bread, and a piece of beef fried in native oil, and a calabash of sour curds. When I saw this I burst out laughing, and thought it a most amazing thing that they could be so foolish and make so much of such a paltry matter. . . .

The Negroes possess some admirable qualities. They are seldom unjust, and have a greater abhorrence of injustice than any other people. Their sultan shows no mercy to anyone who is guilty of the least act of it. There is complete security in their country. Neither traveler nor inhabitant in it has anything to fear from robbers or men of violence. They do not confiscate the property of any white man who dies in their country, even if it be uncounted wealth. On the contrary, they give it into the charge of some trustworthy person among the whites, until the rightful heir takes possession of it. They are careful to observe the hours of prayer, and assiduous in attending them in congregations, and in bringing up their children to them. On Fridays, if a man does not go early to the mosque, he cannot find a corner to pray in, on account of the crowd. It is a custom of theirs to send each man his boy [to the mosque] with his prayer-mat; the boy spreads it out for his master in a place befitting him [and remains on it] until he comes to the mosque. Their prayer-mats are made of the leaves of a tree resembling a date-palm, but without fruit.

Another of their good qualities is their habit of wearing clean white garments on Fridays. Even if a man has nothing but an old worn shirt, he washes it and cleans it, and wears it to the Friday service. Yet another is their zeal for learning the Koran by heart. They put their children in chains if they show any backwardness in memorizing it, and they are not set free until they have it by heart. I visited the *qadi* [judge] in his house on the day of the festival. His children were chained up, so I said to him, "Will you not let them loose?" He replied, "I shall not do so until they learn the Koran by heart."

Among their bad qualities are the following. The women servants, slave-girls, and young girls go about in front of everyone naked, without a stitch of clothing on them. Women go into the sultan's presence naked and without coverings, and his daughters also go about naked. Then there is their custom of putting dust and ashes on their heads, as a mark of respect, and the grotesque ceremonies we have described when the poets recite their verses. Another reprehensible practice among many of them is the eating of carrion, dogs, and asses.

THE CHINESE NAVAL EXPEDITIONS OF ZHENG HE

In 1935, a Chinese official in Fujian province found a long-forgotten stone tablet that recounted one of the greatest series of naval expeditions in world history. The tablet briefly describes the seven voyages of the Chinese admiral, explorer, and diplomat Zheng He (1371–1435), who traveled as far as Arabia and the east coast of Africa and visited more than thirty present-day countries. Born in 1371 in Yunnan (Kunyang) province, he was drafted at age ten to serve as an orderly in the army, which had just succeeded in overthrowing the Mongols and reestablishing Chinese authority under the Ming dynasty. Under the command of the Prince of Yen, Zheng He rose rapidly in rank, proving himself strong, loyal, ambitious, and a skilled junior officer. In 1403, when the Prince of Yen seized the Celestial Throne from a rival, Zheng He fought bravely on his behalf and was rewarded with an administrative position within the royal household. Two years later, he was promoted to commander in chief of one of the largest flotillas in world history

From 1405 to 1422, Zheng He led six different expeditions that took him as far as Java, Sumatra, Vietnam, India, and Arabia and to trading centers in east Africa (see Map 1.3). For the most part, these were diplomatic missions, centered on the exchange of ambassadors, presents, and tribute. Among the gifts he brought back to China for the Yongle Emperor[10] were giraffes and lions. In exchange for tribute, Zheng He presented gifts from the emperor that included finely made porcelain dishes, rare silks, precious metals, and manufactured goods. But in places where the local "barbarians" did not adequately show deference and respect to representatives of the Celestial Empire, Zheng He and his crew used their power to impose their will on others.

When the Yongle Emperor died in 1424, Zheng He lost his most important ally and benefactor. Although he made one last great voyage in 1431, subsequent Ming emperors turned their primary attention to overland ventures and defense, most notably the construction of the Great Wall. To underscore their change in foreign policy, court officials destroyed the official travel logs of Zheng He, leaving us with only the stone tablet inscriptions and some notes kept by his crew as evidence of his achievements. The last years of his life also remain shrouded in mystery, and it is believed that he died in 1435 at the age of sixty-five.

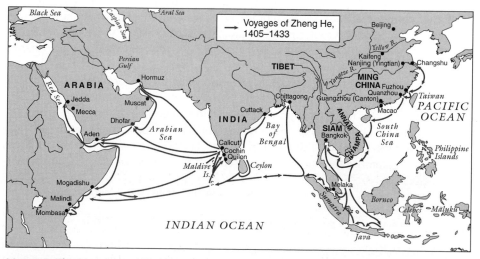

Map 1.3 The Voyages of Zheng He

QUESTIONS TO CONSIDER

1. According to the inscription, what were the goals of the voyages? In what ways might the Ming dynasty have hoped to benefit from these expeditions?
2. What role was played by the Celestial goddess? How did religious beliefs shape Zheng He's perceptions of his mission and his relations with others? How did it motivate him to leave a record of his voyages?
3. What kinds of interactions did Zheng He have with the peoples he encountered? What factors explain his different experiences and reactions?
4. In his voyage to China, Ibn Battuta was impressed with the economy and society but criticized their "heathen" practices. How might Zheng He, himself a Muslim, have responded?
5. After 1431, the Chinese abruptly stopped their overseas voyages. Based on Zheng He's account, what might have happened if they had continued into the next century? Would they have altered world history in a significant manner? What might have been different if China had "discovered" Europe, instead of Europe "discovering" China?

INSCRIPTION OF WORLD VOYAGES

Zheng He

A record of the miraculous answer [to prayer] to the goddess the Celestial Spouse.*

The Imperial Ming Dynasty unifying seas and continents, surpassing the three dynasties even goes beyond the Han and Tang dynasties. The countries beyond the horizon and from the ends of the earth have all become subjects and to the most western of the western or the most northern of the northern countries, however far they may be, the distance and the routes may be calculated. Thus the barbarians from beyond the seas, though their countries are truly distant . . . have come to audience bearing precious objects and presents.

The Emperor, approving of their loyalty and sincerity, has ordered us, Zheng He and others at the head of several tens of thousands of officers and flag-troops to ascend more than one hundred large ships to go and confer presents on them in order to make manifest the transforming power of the (imperial) virtue and to treat distant people with kindness. From the third year of Yongle[†] [1405] till now we have seven times received the commission of ambassadors to countries of the western ocean. The barbar-

---

Source: Teobaldo Filesi, *China and Africa in the Middle Ages*, trans. David Morison, 1972, 61–65. Reprinted by permission of Frank Cass Publishers.

*The Celestial Spouse was a goddess in Taoism, one of the major religions of China. She was considered to be the protector of travelers on the sea.

[†]In these inscriptions, years are measured by the emperor's reign.

ian countries which we have visited are Zhancheng [Vietnam], Zhaowa [Java, Indonesia], Sanfoqi [Sumatra, Indonesia], and Xianlo [Siam] crossing straight over to Xilanshan [Sri Lanka] in South India, Calicut [India], and Kezhi [India], we have gone to the western regions of Hulumosi [Ormuz], Aden [Yemen], Mogadishu [Somalia], altogether more than thirty countries large and small. We have traversed more than one hundred thousand *li** of immense water spaces and have beheld in the ocean huge waves like mountains rising sky-high, and we have set eyes on barbarian regions far away hidden in a blue transparency of light vapors, while our sails loftily unfurled like clouds day and night continued their course rapidly like that of a star, traversing those savage waves as if we were treading a public thoroughfare. Truly this was due to the majesty and the good fortune of the Imperial Court and moreover we owe it to the protecting virtue of the divine Celestial Spouse.

The power of the goddess having indeed been manifested in previous times has been abundantly revealed in the present generation. In the midst of the rushing waters it happened that, when there was a hurricane, suddenly there was a divine lantern shining in the mast, and as soon as this miraculous light appeared[†] the danger was appeased, so that even in the danger of capsizing one felt reassured that there was no cause for fear. When we arrived in the distant countries we captured alive those of the native kings who were not respectful and exterminated those barbarian robbers who were engaged in piracy, so that consequently the sea route was cleansed and pacified and the natives put their trust in it. All this is due to the favors of the goddess.

It is not easy to enumerate completely all the cases where the goddess has answered [my prayers]. Previously in a memorial to the Court we have requested that her virtue be recognized . . . and a temple be built at Nanking on the bank of the river where regular sacrifices should be made forever. We have respectfully received an Imperial commemoration exalting her miraculous favors, which is the highest recompense and praise indeed. However, the miraculous power of the goddess resides wherever one goes. . . .

We have received the high favor of a gracious commission from our sacred Lord [the Yongle Emperor], we carry to the distant barbarians the benefits of respect and good faith [on their part]. Commanding the multitudes on the fleet and being responsible for a quantity of money and valuables in the face of the violence of the winds and the nights, our one fear is not to be able to succeed. How, then, dare we not to serve our dynasty with . . . all our loyalty and the gods with the utmost sincerity? How would it be possible not to realize what is the source of the tranquillity of the fleet and the troops and the salvation on the voyage both going and returning? Therefore, we have inscribed the virtue of the [Celestial Spouse] on stone and have also recorded the years and months of the voyages to the barbarian countries . . . in order to leave the memory forever.

---

*Scholars estimated that Zheng He traveled over 35,000 miles during his seven voyages.

†Scholars believe that this miraculous light may have been St. Elmo's fire, static electricity that is not an uncommon sight to seafarers. Because the sailors had prayed to the Taoist goddess, they believed that the light was a sign of her beneficent protection. This helps explain why Zheng He later placed a pillar of thanksgiving at the Temple of the Celestial Spouse in Fujian province.

I. In the third year of Yongle [1405] commanding the fleet we went to Calicut [India] and other countries. At that time the pirate Chen Zuyi had gathered his followers in the country of Sanfoqi [island of Sumatra], where he plundered the native merchants. When he also advanced to resist our fleet, supernatural soldiers secretly came to the rescue so that after one beating of the drum he was annihilated. In the fifth year [1407] we returned.

II. In the fifth year of Yongle [1407] commanding the fleet we went to Zhaowa [Java], Calicut, Kezhi [India], and Xianle [Siam]. The kings of these countries all sent as tribute precious objects, precious birds and rare animals. In the seventh year [1409] we returned.

III. In the seventh year of Yongle [1409] commanding the fleet we went to the countries (visited) before and took our route by the country of Xilanshan [Sri Lanka]. Its king Alagakkonara was guilty of a gross lack of respect and plotted against the fleet. Owing to the manifest answer to prayer of the goddess, [the plot] was discovered and thereupon that king was captured alive. In the ninth year [1411] on our return the captured king was presented [to the throne as a prisoner]; subsequently he received the Imperial [forgiveness and] favor of returning to his own country.

IV. In the eleventh year of Yongle [1413] commanding the fleet we went to Hulumosi [Ormuz] and other countries. In the country of Samudra [northern tip of Sumatra] there was a false king [named Sekandar] who was marauding and invading his country. The [true] king [Zaynu-'l-Abidin] had sent an envoy to the Palace Gates in order to lodge a complaint. We went there with the official troops under our command and exterminated some and arrested [other rebels], and owing to the silent aid of the goddess, we captured the false king alive. In the thirteenth year [1415] on our return he was presented [to the Emperor as a prisoner]. In that year the king of the country of Manlajia [Malacca, Malaysia] came in person with his wife and son to present tribute.

V. In the fifteenth year of Yongle [1417] commanding the fleet we visited the western regions. The country of Ormuz presented lions, leopards with gold spots and large western horses. The country of Aden [Yemen] presented [giraffes], as well as the long-horned [oryx]. The country of Mogadishu [Somalia] presented [zebras] as well as lions. The country of Brava [Somalia or Kenya] presented camels which run one thousand *li*, as well as camel-birds [ostriches]. The countries of Zhaowa [Java] and Calicut [India] presented animal *miligao* [hides] They all vied in presenting the marvelous objects preserved in the mountains or hidden in the seas and the beautiful treasures buried in the sand or deposited on the shores. Some sent a maternal uncle of the king, others a paternal uncle or a younger brother of the king in order to present a letter of homage written on gold leaf as well as tribute.

VI. In the nineteenth year of Yongle [1421] commanding the fleet we escorted the ambassadors from Ormuz and the other countries who had been in attendance at the capital for a long time back to their countries. The kings of all these countries prepared even more tribute than previously.

VII. In the sixth year of Exeunt* [1431] once more commanding the fleet we have left for the barbarian countries in order to read to them [an Imperial edict] and to confer presents.

We have anchored in this port awaiting a north wind to take the sea, and recalling how previously we have on several occasions received the benefits of the protection of the divine intelligence we have thus recorded an inscription in stone.

VASCO DA GAMA'S VOYAGE TO AFRICA AND INDIA

Vasco da Gama's (1460–1524) two voyages to India (1497–1498; 1502–1503) are significant because they initiated direct and profitable trading routes between Europe and Asia that marked the beginning of a new phase of global commerce. Equally important, they foreshadow the use of European military power to assert its economic and political interests in new areas of the world. In both regards, Vasco da Gama played a central and pivotal role.

Born into the Portuguese nobility in 1460, da Gama received an education in mathematics and navigation and then followed his father (and most aristocrats) into the military, where he proved himself an effective officer. In the mid-1490s, when King John of Portugal ordered a naval expedition to India to open up trade, outflank the Muslims, and find new Christian allies, Vasco da Gama was placed in command of the fleet. In stark contrast to the large armada led by Zheng He more than a century earlier, da Gama had only four ships and less than two hundred men under his command when he left Lisbon in July 1497 (Map 1.4).

Five months later, as the ships rounded the tip of southern Africa, two of his vessels were leaking and many of the crew were sick with scurvy.[11] He therefore stopped along the coast of east Africa for fresh food and repairs and took the opportunity to visit some of the wealthy Swahili city-states (Mozambique, Mombasa [Kenya], Mylanta [Kenya]) that had been engaged in maritime trade with Arabia, Persia, and India for centuries.[12] But as the journal describes in great detail, the Portuguese visit to these city-states was not entirely successful nor amicable, and da Gama was frustrated in his failure to locate the lost Christian kingdom of Prester John. After a 23-day voyage across the Indian Ocean, da Gama became the first European to reach Calicut, one of the most important commercial ports of India. But his efforts to arrange a business pact with the local Hindu ruler proved unsuccessful because of mutual suspicions, the hostility of local Muslim government advisors and merchants, and, most interestingly, the general lack of interest in European trade goods. Misfortune followed da Gama after his departure from India: bad winds caused a very slow return, and many of his crew died of scurvy. Despite these setbacks, his return to Portugal in 1499 was accompanied

---

*The Emperor Zhu Zhang ordered one final voyage planned for 1431, the sixth year of his reign.

by a hero's welcome, and his prized and profitable cargoes of spices and jewels encouraged additional commercial ventures and investments.

In 1502, Vasco da Gama returned to east Africa and India with a larger, better armed fleet at his disposal. His primary mission was to avenge the murder of several Portuguese seamen who had visited Calicut in the intervening years, but his subsequent actions suggest that he was equally intent upon establishing Portuguese supremacy in the Indian Ocean. Arriving back at the east African city-state of Mombasa, da Gama threatened to burn the town and destroy its Muslim inhabitants if they did not submit to Portuguese authority (which they promptly did). The fleet then sailed to Calicut, where the Portuguese admiral demanded that all Muslims be banished from the port. To demonstrate his determination and strength, he then bombarded the city with cannon fire and routed the Muslim ships that tried to put up a fight. Following his return to Portugal in 1503, he seems to have lived in relative obscurity until called to duty again in 1524 to become a diplomat at one of the permanent outposts that the Portuguese had established in India in the meantime. But shortly after his arrival in India, he died suddenly and unexpectedly.

The original written sea logs of Vasco da Gama disappeared and are lost. Consequently, the only detailed account we possess was written by a crew member of the expedition. Although his exact identity remains somewhat a mystery, his account has been mostly verified by comparison with some of da Gama's letters and Portuguese government documents from that era. The excerpts that follow describe da Gama's experiences in the city-states of east Africa, as well as his misadventures in India. In both instances, it is valuable to examine Portuguese motives and perceptions of others, and how these shaped their particular experiences.

QUESTIONS TO CONSIDER

1. What kinds of observations and impressions are recorded in the journal? Are these shaped more by Vasco da Gama's motives and preexisting cultural values or by actual experiences? How important is physical appearance in making cultural judgments?

2. What role did religion play in shaping Portuguese motives and their views of others? How were religious beliefs used to justify their actions?

3. Why did the Swahili and Indians show such little interest in Portuguese trade goods and gifts? What dilemma did this cause? What might have been a solution to this problem?

4. In Africa and Asia, the Portuguese encountered both hospitality and hostility. What might have explained the varying reaction? To what degree, if any, did the Portuguese bring this hostility upon themselves?

5. How would you describe the cross-cultural attitudes formed during da Gama's first voyage? What kind of future relations did they portend?

Map 1.4 Vasco da Gama's First Voyage to Africa and India

A JOURNAL OF THE FIRST VOYAGE OF VASCO DA GAMA (1497–1499)

In the name of God. Amen. In the year 1497, King Dom Manuel . . . despatched four vessels to make discoveries and go in search of spices. Vasco da Gama was the captain of these vessels. . . .

1497. Mozambique. The people of this country are of ruddy complexion and well made. They are Muhammadans [Muslims], and their language is the same as

Source: A Journal of the First Voyage of Vasco da Gama, 1497–1499, trans. E. Ravenstein, Hakluyt Society Series 1, vol. 99 (London: The Hakluyt Society, 1898), 22–25, 28–30, 34–36, 37–38, 48–68.

that of the Moors.* Their dresses are of fine linen or cotton stuffs, with variously colored stripes, and of rich and elaborate workmanship. They all wear robes with borders of silk embroidered in gold. They are merchants, and have transactions with white Moors,† four of whose vessels were at the time in port, laden with gold, silver, cloves, pepper, ginger, and silver rings, as also with quantities of pearls, jewels, and rubies, all of which are used by the people of this country. We understood them to say that all these things, with the exception of the gold, were brought thither by these Moors; and that further on to where we were going, they abounded, and that precious stones, pearls and spices were so plentiful that there was no need to purchase them as they could be collected in baskets. All this we learned through a sailor the Captain [Vasco da Gama] had with him, and who, having formerly been a prisoner among the Moors, understood their language.

These Moors, moreover, told us that along the route which we were about to follow we should meet . . . many cities along the coast, and also an island, where one half the population consisted of Moors and the other half of Christians, who were at war with each other. This island was said to be very wealthy. We were told, moreover, that Prester John resided not far from this place; that he held many cities along the coast, and that the inhabitants of those cities were great merchants and owned big ships. The residence of Prester John was said to be far in the interior, and could be reached only on the back of camels. . . . This information, and many other things which we heard, rendered us so happy that we cried with joy, and prayed God to grant us health, so that we might behold what we so much desired.

In this place and island of Mozambique, there resided a chief who had the title of Sultan. He often came aboard our ships attended by some of his people. The Captain gave him many good things to eat, and made him a present of hats, shirts, corals and many other articles. He was, however, so proud that he treated all we gave him with contempt, and asked for scarlet cloth, of which we had none. We gave him, however, of all the things we had. . . . During our stay here the Sultan of Mozambique sent word that he wanted to make peace with us and to be our friend. His ambassador was a white Moor and a nobleman, and at the same time a great drunkard. . . .

One evening, as we left the ship for the mainland to obtain drinking water, we saw about twenty men on the beach. They were armed with spears, and forbade our landing. After the Captain heard this, he ordered three bombards [small cannon] to be fired upon them, so that we might land. Having effected our landing, these men fled into the bush, and we took as much water as we wanted. [The next day], a Moor rowed out to our ships, and told us that if we wanted more drinking water, that we should go for it, suggesting that we would encounter more trouble and be forced to turn back. The Captain no sooner heard this [threat] than he resolved to go, in order to show that we were able to do them harm if we desired it. We then armed our boats, placing bombards in their poops, and started for the shore. The Moors had constructed [a defensive wall] by lashing planks together . . . [but as we approached] they were at the time walking along the beach, armed with spears, knives, bows, and slingshots,

---

*The Portuguese are describing the Swahili people of east Africa.
†"White Moors" was a term used to identify Muslim Arabs.

with which they hurled stones at us. But our bombards soon made it so hot for them that they fled behind their walls, but this turned out to their injury rather than their profit. During the three hours that we were occupied in this manner [bombarding the beach] we saw at least two men killed, one on the beach and the other behind the wall. When we were weary of this work we retired to our ships to dine. . . .

[Vasco da Gama and his fleet left Mozambique shortly thereafter and arrived two weeks later at the Swahili city-state of Mombasa.]

On Saturday, we cast anchor off Mombasa, but did not enter the port. . . . In front of the city there lay numerous vessels, all dressed in flags.* And we, anxious not to be outdone, also dressed our ships, and we actually surpassed their show. . . . We anchored here with much pleasure, for we confidently hoped that on the following day we might go on land and hear [Catholic] mass jointly with the Christians reported to live there in a neighborhood separate from that of the Moors. . . .

But those who had told us [about the Christians] had said it [to trap us], for it was not true. At midnight there approached us a *dhow* with about a hundred men, all armed with cutlasses and shields. When they came to the vessel of the Captain they attempted to board her, armed as they were, but this was not permitted, only four or five of the most distinguished men among them being allowed on board. They remained about a couple of hours, and it seemed to us that they paid us this visit merely to find out whether they might not capture one or the other of our vessels. . . .

[The next day] the King of Mombasa sent the Captain a sheep and large quantities of oranges, lemons and sugar-cane, together with a ring, as a pledge of safety, letting him know that in case of his entering the port he would be supplied with all he stood in need of. . . . The Captain sent the king a string of coral-beads as a return present, and let him know that he planned to enter the port on the following day. . . . Two men were sent by the Captain to the king, still further to confirm these peaceful assurances. . . . The king received them hospitably, and ordered that they should be shown the city. . . . When they had seen all, the king sent them back with samples of cloves, pepper and sorghum, articles he would allow us to purchase and load on our ships. . . .

That evening, the Captain questioned two Moors whom we had captured, by dropping boiling oil upon their skin, so that they might confess to any treachery intended against us. They said that orders had been given to capture us as soon as we entered the port, and thus to avenge what we had done at Mozambique. And when this torture was being applied a second time, one of the Moors, although his hands were tied, threw himself into the sea, whilst the other did so during the morning watch.

About midnight two *dhows*, with many men in them, approached. The *dhows* stood off whilst the men entered the water, swimming in the direction of our ships. . . . Our men on watch thought at first that they were fish, but when they perceived their mistake they shouted to the other vessels. They [Moors] had already boarded one ship and got hold of the rigging of the mizzen-mast, but seeing themselves discovered,

---

*The Swahili traditionally "dress" their vessels with flags and pennants to mark the feast that ends the month-long fast of Ramadan. Ramadan is an important Islamic holiday that commemorates Allah's gift of the Qur'an to mankind, a time when Muslims fast and spend more time concentrating on their faith.

they silently slipped down and fled. These and other wicked tricks were practiced upon us by these dogs, but our Lord did not allow them to succeed, because they were unbelievers.

[After a 23-day voyage across the Indian Ocean, aided by a Muslim navigator lent by the Sultan of Mozambique, the Portuguese arrived at Calicut, one of the most prosperous and important trading centers in southern India. Although the local ruler and much of the population were Hindu, there were also many merchants, traders, and government officials who were Muslims.]

After we were at anchor, four boats approached us from the land, and they asked of what nation we were. We told them, and they then pointed out Calicut to us. . . . The city of Calicut is inhabited by Christians.* They are of tawny complexion. Some of them have big beards and long hair, whilst others clip their hair short or shave the head, merely allowing a tuft to remain on the crown as a sign that they are Christians. They also wear moustaches. They pierce the ears and wear much gold in them. They go naked down to the waist, covering their lower extremities with very fine cotton stuffs. But it is only the most respectable who do this, for the others manage as best they are able.† The women of this country, as a rule, are ugly and of small stature. They wear many jewels of gold round the neck, numerous bracelets on their arms, and rings set with precious stones on their toes. All these people are well-disposed and apparently of mild temper. At first sight they seem covetous and ignorant. . . .

When we arrived at Calicut the king was away. The Captain sent two men to him with a message, informing him that an ambassador had arrived from the King of Portugal with letters. . . . [The king] sent word to the Captain bidding him welcome [and sent] a pilot . . . with orders to take us to [an anchorage] in front of the city of Calicut. We were told that the anchorage at the place to which we were to go was good . . . and that it was customary for the ships which came to this country to anchor there for the sake of safety. We ourselves did not feel comfortable . . . and we did not anchor as near the shore as the king's pilot desired. . . .

On the following morning . . . the Captain set out to speak to the king, and took with him thirteen men. We put on our best attire, put bombards [small cannon] in our boats, and took with us trumpets and many flags. On landing, the Captain was received by government officials, along with a crowd of many men, armed and unarmed. The reception was friendly, as if the people were pleased to see us, though at first appearances looked threatening, for they carried naked swords in their hands. A palanquin‡ was provided for the captain, such as is used by men of distinction in that country. . . . When we arrived [at the king's palace], men of much distinction and great lords came out to meet the Captain, and joined those who were already in attendance upon him. . . .

---

*With no prior knowledge of Indian culture or religion, Vasco da Gama and his crew mistook Hindus for Christians.

†The differences in dress witnessed by the Portuguese were most likely related to the caste system prevalent in Indian society.

‡A palanquin is a mode of transportation consisting of a chair mounted on poles and carried on the shoulders of four to six men.

The king was in a small court, reclining upon a couch covered with a cloth of green velvet, above which was a good mattress, and upon this again a sheet of cotton stuff, very white and fine, more so than any linen. . . . The Captain, on entering, saluted in the manner of the country: by putting the hands together, then raising them towards Heaven, as is done by Christians when addressing God, and immediately afterwards opening them and shutting fists quickly. . . .

And the Captain told him he was the ambassador of the King of Portugal, who was Lord of many countries and the possessor of great wealth of every description, exceeding that of any king of these parts; that for a period of sixty years his people had annually sent out vessels to make discoveries in the direction of India, as they knew that there were Christian kings there like themselves. This, he said, was the rea son which induced them to order this country to be discovered, not because they sought for gold or silver, for of this they had such abundance that they needed not what was to be found in this country. . . . There reigned a king now whose name was Dom Manuel, who had ordered [da Gama] to build three vessels, of which he had been appointed Captain, and who had ordered him not to return to Portugal until he should have discovered this King of the Christians, on pain of having his head cut off. That two letters had been intrusted to him to be presented in case he succeeded in discovering him . . . and, finally, he had been instructed to say by word of mouth that he [the King of Portugal] desired to be his friend and brother.

In reply to this the king said that he was welcome; that, on his part, he held him as a friend and brother, and would send ambassadors with him to Portugal. . . . These and many other things passed between the two in this chamber, and as it was already late in the night, the king asked the Captain with whom he desired to lodge, with Christians or with Moors? And the Captain replied, neither with Christians nor with Moors, and begged as a favor that he be given a lodging by himself. The king said he would order it thus, upon which the Captain took leave of the king and came to where his men were. . . .

By that time four hours of the night had already gone . . . and the time occupied in passing through the city was so long that the captain at last grew tired, and complained to the king's advisor, a Moor of distinction, who attended him to the lodgings. The Moor then took him to his own house, and we were admitted to a court within it. . . . Many carpets had been spread, and there were two large candlesticks like those at the Royal palace. . . .

[The next morning], the captain got ready the following gifts to be sent to the king: twelve pieces of *lambel,** four scarlet hoods, six hats, four strings of coral, a case containing six wash-hand basins, a case of sugar, two casks of oil, and two of honey. And as it is the custom not to send anything to the king without the knowledge of the Moor [his financial advisor], and other officials, the Captain informed them of his intention. They came, and when they saw the present they laughed at it, saying that it was not a thing to offer to a king, that the poorest merchant from Mecca, or any other part of India, gave more, and that if he wanted to make a present it should be in gold, as the king would not accept such things. When the Captain heard this he grew

---

*Striped cotton cloth.

sad, and said that he had brought no gold, that, moreover, he was no merchant, but an ambassador; that he gave of that which he had, which was his own private gift and not the king's; that if the King of Portugal ordered him to return he would intrust him with far richer presents; and that if the king would not accept these things he would send them back to the ships. Upon this they [the government officials] declared that they would not forward his presents, nor consent to his forwarding them himself. When they had gone there came certain Moorish merchants, and they all mocked the presents which the Captain desired to be sent to the king.

When the Captain saw that they were determined not to forward his presents, he [asked] to speak to the king, and would then return to the ships. [The officials] approved of this, and told [the Captain] that if he would wait a short time they would return and accompany him to the palace. And the Captain waited all day, but they never came back. The Captain was very angry at being among so phlegmatic and unreliable a people, and intended, at first, to go to the palace without them. On further consideration, however, he thought it best to wait until the following day. . . .

On Wednesday morning the Moors returned, and took the captain to the palace. The palace was crowded with armed men. Our Captain was kept waiting . . . for fully four long hours, outside a door, which was only opened when the king sent word to admit him. . . . The king said that he [the Captain] had claimed that he came from a very rich kingdom, and yet had brought him nothing; that he had also told him that he was the bearer of a letter, which had not yet been delivered. To this the Captain rejoined that he had brought nothing, because the object of his voyage was merely to make discoveries, but that when other ships came he would then see what they brought him; as to the letter, it was true that he had brought one, and would deliver it immediately.

The king then asked what it was he had come to discover: stones or men? If he came to discover men, as [the Captain] had claimed, why had he brought nothing? Moreover, he had been told that [the ships] carried . . . the golden image of a Santa Maria. The Captain said that the Santa Maria was not of gold, and that even if she were he would not part with her, as she had guided him across the ocean, and would guide him back to his own country. . . .

The king then asked what kind of merchandise was to be found in [Portugal]. The Captain said there was much corn, cloth, iron, bronze, and many other things. The king asked whether he had any merchandise with him. The Captain replied that he had a little of each sort, as samples, and that if permitted to return to the ships he would order it to be landed, and that meantime four or five men would remain at the lodgings assigned them. The king refused [and was not interested]. The Captain might take all his people with him, securely moor his ships, land his merchandise, and attempt to sell it himself to the best advantage. Having taken leave of the king, the Captain returned to his lodgings, and we with him. As it was already late no attempt was made to depart that night.

[After two days of waiting], the Captain again asked for boats to take him to his ships. [The king's advisors] began to whisper among themselves, and said that we should have them if we would order our vessels to come nearer the shore. The Captain replied that if he ordered his vessels to approach his brother* would think that

---

*Vasco da Gama's younger brother was second in command of the fleet.

he was being held a prisoner, and would hoist the sails and return to Portugal. They said that if we refused to order the ships to come nearer we should not be permitted to leave . . . [and] they immediately closed all the doors, and many armed men entered to guard us, none of us being allowed to go outside without being accompanied by several of these guards. . . .

The Captain and we others felt very down-hearted, though outwardly we pretended not to notice what they did. . . . The Captain did not wish the ships to come within the port, for it seemed to him—as it did to us—that once inside they could easily be captured, after which they would first kill him, and us others, as we were already in their power. We passed all that day most anxiously. At night more people surrounded us than ever before, and we were no longer allowed to walk in the compound, within which we were, but confined within a small tiled court, with a multitude of people around us. We quite expected that on the following day we should be separated, or that some harm would befall us, for we noticed that our jailers were much annoyed with us. This, however, did not prevent our making a good supper off the things found in the village. Throughout that night we were guarded by over a hundred men, all armed with swords, two-edged battle-axes, shields, and bows and arrows. Whilst some of these slept, others kept guard, each taking his turn of duty throughout the night.

On the following day, these gentlemen [the Moors and government officials] came back, and this time they wore better faces. They told the Captain that . . . as it was the custom of the country that every ship on its arrival should at once land the merchandise it brought, as also the crews, and that the sellers should not return on board until the whole of it had been sold. The Captain consented, and said he would . . . see to its being done. They said this was well, and that immediately after the arrival of the merchandise he would be permitted to return to his ship. . . . At this there was great rejoicing, thanks being rendered to God for having extricated us from the hands of people who had no more sense than beasts. . . .

The merchants whom the king had sent . . . instead of buying our merchandise merely ridiculed it. The Moors no longer visited the house where the merchandise was, but they bore us no good-will, and they spat on the ground, saying "Portugal, Portugal." Indeed, from the very first they had sought to take and kill us. . . .

COLUMBUS'S FIRST VOYAGE TO THE "NEW WORLD"

Christopher Columbus (1451–1506) is probably the most famous—and infamous—explorer in world history. He has long been viewed as a heroic figure, a master navigator whose four voyages (1492–1504) across the Atlantic Ocean paved the way for the triumphant European exploration and colonization of the Americas, and his exploits have been celebrated with a national holiday, monuments and parades, and innumerable place names. But more recently, Columbus has been seen in a different, more critical perspective. He was a man driven by flawed and selfish motives, whose personal actions and ambitions opened the way for the European exploitation of the resources and peoples of the New World.

Unlike his contemporary Vasco da Gama, Columbus began life with humble origins. He was born in Genoa (Italy) in 1451, the eldest son of a Genoese wool-worker and small-time trader. He began his career on the seas in the Portuguese merchant marine, which took him as far as Iceland to the north and the coast of west Africa to the south. These experiences gave him invaluable navigation and sailing experience, and they fueled his curiosity and desire to find a western route to Asia. In 1484, he began seeking financial support for an Atlantic crossing, and he was rebuffed at least three times by the Portuguese and Spanish monarchs before he finally received support from King Fernando and Queen Ysabel in early 1492. In the initial contract, Columbus bargained to win promotion to admiral, admittance to the Spanish nobility, and a 10 percent claim to the riches of new lands discovered upon successful completion of the first voyage.

On August 3, 1492, Columbus set sail in three small ships with 120 crewmen. After a relatively uneventful voyage of thirty-three days, the fleet sighted the Bahama islands and then landed and explored parts of Cuba and Hispaniola (the island currently divided between Haiti and the Dominican Republic). With assistance of a local leader, he established a fort on Hispaniola called *Villa de Navidad* and left about forty crewmen there to guard it until his return. The Spanish monarchs were so impressed with Columbus's gifts of gold, spices, exotic birds, and human captives that he secured the financial backing for a second voyage. In 1493, Columbus left with a much larger flotilla of seventeen ships, filled with colonists, investors, and a small troop of cavalry. But his return to the fort at *Villa de Navidad* was too late, for he discovered the fort ruined and all of the crew gone.

Altogether, Columbus made four voyages across the Atlantic under the sponsorship of Fernando and Ysabel. By the end of the second voyage (1493–1496), he had sighted most of the Caribbean islands, and he rebuilt his base in Hispaniola. During the third and fourth trips (1498–1500; 1502–1504), Columbus explored the coasts of Central and South America, from present-day Honduras to Venezuela. But his last trip was marred by his difficulties with Spanish colonists, increased hostility from indigenous peoples, and his frustrating inability to discover the westward route to Asia. Back in Spain, his attempts to join the nobility and to recover his governorship of the "Indies" from King Fernando were unsuccessful. By many accounts, Columbus died a disappointed man.

The outcome of Columbus's voyages are open to interpretation and debate. His discoveries undoubtedly brought Europe and the Americas into sustained contact with each other and ultimately led to European immigration and the transplantation of their culture and values. But others might add that it also led to the exploitation and genocide of native Americans. On the island of Hispaniola, for example, Spanish actions against the indigenous population dramatically reduced their population from an estimated 250,000 in 1492 to under 500 by 1538. Moreover, the genocide of native Americans throughout the Caribbean, by conquest or disease, was one of the principal factors behind the importation of African slave labor in subsequent centuries.

We possess two accounts of Columbus's first voyage to the Americas, and excerpts from each are included in this chapter. The first source is the logbook kept by Columbus during the trip and presented in 1493 to the Spanish monarchs.

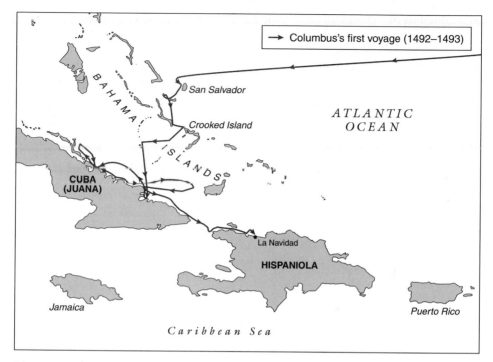

Map 1.5 Columbus's First Voyage to the "New World"

The prologue to the log highlights his stated motives and objectives prior to his departure. The second source is a letter written by Columbus prior to his return, in which he summarized his discoveries and assessments, with the goal of securing additional financial support for a second voyage. The letter describes his enchantment with the natural beauty of the islands and his impressions of the "innocent" inhabitants. But it is also evident that Columbus was somewhat disappointed and remained uncertain whether he had discovered anything of great importance. He found neither great cities nor civilized peoples, and although the islands might hold potential wealth, they were not his intended object of discovery.

QUESTIONS TO CONSIDER

1. What were Columbus's primary motives, as declared in the prologue to his logbook? How do these compare with the ones revealed in his descriptions of Hispaniola and Cuba? How might one account for the differences?
2. Columbus portrays most of the island inhabitants as "innocent" and "timid." What led him to these conclusions? What impact did this perception have on his behavior? In your estimation, did Columbus take advantage of the innocence and generosity of the inhabitants?

3. Columbus says of Hispaniola, "It is a land to be desired, and when seen, never to be left." What did he consider to be the attractions on Hispaniola? Did these portend future relationships between Europeans and the indigenous islanders?

4. At the end of his letter, Columbus made a direct appeal for more financial assistance from the Spanish monarchy. Might this request have affected the way in which he described his discoveries?

5. Columbus specifically noted two distinct future policies in the New World: the conversion of the indigenous peoples to Christianity and the pursuit of wealth from the accumulation of gold and other resources. Based on his own explanations, were these two goals compatible? Why or why not?

PROLOGUE TO THE LOGBOOK OF THE FIRST VOYAGE (1492)

Christopher Columbus

Most Christian and most exalted and most excellent and most mighty princes, King and Queen of the Spains* and of the islands of the sea, our sovereigns. . . . [In] this present year of 1492, your Highnesses concluded a [successful] end of the war with the Moors who reigned in Europe . . . and as Catholic Christians and as princes devoted to the holy Christian faith and its propagators, and enemies of the sect of Mahomet [Muhammad] and of all idolatries and heresies, took thought to send me, Christopher Columbus, to India, to see the princes and peoples and lands and . . . the manner which should be used to bring about their conversion to our Holy Faith. . . . I shall not go [to India] to the eastward, by which way it was the custom to go, but by way of the west, by which down to this day we do not know certainly that any one has passed. . . . [This voyage] has accorded me great rewards and ennobled me so that from that time henceforward I might style myself *Don*† and be high admiral of the Ocean Sea and [become] perpetual governor of the islands and [lands] which I should discover. . . . To this end, I thought to write all this journey very carefully . . . in which I will set all the seas and lands of the Ocean Sea in their true places. . . . And all these things will be a great enterprise.

Source: Christopher Columbus, *The Voyages of Christopher Columbus, Being the Journals of his First and Third, and the Letters Concerning his First and Last Voyages,* trans. and ed. Cecil Jane (London: Argonaut Press, 1930), 135–36.
*The marriage of King Fernando and Queen Ysabel united the formerly separate Spanish kingdoms of Aragon; Castile, and Leon.
†A title of nobility.

LETTER DESCRIBING HIS FIRST VOYAGE (1493)

Christopher Columbus

Since I know that you will be pleased at the great victory with which Our Lord has crowned my voyage, I write this to you, from which you will learn how in thirty-three days I passed from the Canary Islands to the Indies, with the fleet which the most illustrious king and queen, our sovereigns, gave to me. There I found very many islands, filled with people innumerable, and of them all I have taken possession for their Highnesses, by proclamation made and with the royal standard unfurled, and no opposition was offered to me.

To the first island which I found I gave the name "San Salvador," in remembrance of the blessed Savior, who had marvelously bestowed all this; the Indians call it "Guanahani." To the second island, I gave the name "Santa Maria de Concepcion" [Rum Cay]; to the third, "Fernandina"; to the fourth, "Isabella" . . . and so each island received a new name from me.*

When I came to Juana [Cuba], I followed its coast to the westward, and I found it to be so extensive that I thought that it must be the mainland, the province of Cathay [China]. And since there were neither towns nor villages on the seashore, but only small villages whose residents all fled immediately, I continued along the coast, thinking that I could not fail to find great cities and towns. At the end of many miles, seeing that there was no change . . . I retraced my path back to a remarkable harbor known to me. From that point, I sent two men inland to learn if there were a king or great cities. They traveled three days' journey, finding many small villages and numerous people, but nothing of importance, and so they returned.

I understood sufficiently from other Indians, whom I had previously seized there, that this land was nothing but an island, and I therefore followed its coast eastward for over three hundred miles to the point where it ended. From that point, I saw another island to the east, distant about fifty miles, and I gave it the name "Hispana" [Hispaniola].† I sailed there and followed its northern coast eastward for over five hundred miles.

This island and all the others are very fertile. . . . [Along the coast of Hispaniola] are many harbors, beyond comparison with others that I know in Christendom, and many rivers, good and large. Its lands are high, and there are many sierras and very lofty mountains. . . . [All the islands] are most beautiful, of a thousand shapes; all are accessible and are filled with trees of a thousand kinds, and so tall that they seem to touch the sky. I am told that they never lose their foliage, and this I can believe, for I

Source: Christopher Columbus, *The Voyages of Christopher Columbus, Being the Journals of his First and Third, and the Letters Concerning his First and Last Voyages,* trans. and ed. Cecil Jane (London: Argonaut Press, 1930), 259–64.

*All of these islands are part of the present-day Bahamas.

†The large island of Hispaniola is now divided between the nations of Haiti and the Dominican Republic. It is believed that Columbus's first voyage took him to the north coast of Haiti.

saw them as green and lovely as they are in Spain in May, and some of them were flowering, some bearing fruit. . . . There are six or eight kinds of palm, which are a wonder to behold on account of their beautiful variety, but so are the other trees and fruits and plants. There are also marvelous pine groves, very wide and smiling plains, birds of many kinds, and fruits and honey in great diversity. In the interior, there are mines of metals, and the population is without number.

Hispana [Hispaniola] is a marvel. The sierras and the mountains, the plains, the arable and pasture lands, are so lovely and so rich for planting and sowing, for breeding cattle of every kind, and for building towns and villages. The harbors of the sea here are such as cannot be believed to exist unless they have been seen, and so with the rivers, many and great, and of good water, the majority of which contain gold. In the trees, fruits and plants, there is a great difference from those of Juana [Cuba]. In this island, there are many spices and great mines of gold and of other metals.

The people of this island, and of all the other islands which I have found and of which I have information, all go naked, men and women, as their mothers bore them, although some of the women cover a single place with the leaf of a plant or with a net of cotton which they make for the purpose. They have no iron or steel or weapons, nor are they inclined to use them. This is not because they are not well built and of handsome stature, but because they are very timid. They have no other arms than spears made of reeds, to which they fix a small sharpened stick. They do not dare to make use of these weapons against us, for many times it has happened that I have sent ashore two or three men to some town to have speech with them, and countless people have come out to them, and as soon as they have seen my men approaching, they have fled, a father not even waiting for his son. This is not because we have done them any harm; on the contrary, at every place where I have been and have been able to have speech with them, I have given gifts to them, such as cloth and many other things, receiving nothing in exchange. But they remain by nature incurably timid.

It is true that, once they have been reassured and have lost their fear of us, they are so innocent and so generous with all that they possess, that no one would believe it who has not seen it. They refuse nothing that they possess if it be asked of them. On the contrary, they invite any one to share it and display as much love as if they would give their hearts. They are content with whatever trifle or gift that is given to them, whether it be of value or valueless. I forbade that they should be given things so worthless as fragments of broken crockery, scraps of broken glass and ends of straps, although when they were able to get them, they fancied that they possessed the best jewel in the world. A sailor once received gold equal to the weight of two and a half coins for a little piece of strap, and others received much more for other things which were worth less. . . . They took even the pieces of the broken hoops of the wine barrels and, like savages, gave what they had, but this seemed to me to be wrong and I forbade it. I gave them a thousand handsome good things, which I had brought, in order that they might conceive affection for us and, more than that, might become Christians and be inclined to the love and service of your Highnesses and of the whole Spanish nation, and strive to aid us and to give us of the things which they have in abundance and which are necessary to us.

They do not hold any creed nor are they idolaters; they only believe that power and good are in the heavens. . . . This belief is not the result of ignorance, for they are actually of a very acute intelligence, they know how to navigate the seas, and it is amazing how good an account they give of everything. [Instead], this belief is because they have never seen people clothed or ships such as ours.

As soon as I arrived in the Indies, I took by force some natives at the first island that I found in order that they might give me information about these places. And so it was that they soon understood us, and we them, either by speech or signs, and they have been very helpful. I still have them with me, and they are always assured that I come from Heaven, despite all the discussions which they have had with me. They were the first to announce this wherever I went in the islands, and others went running from house to house, and to neighboring towns, crying loudly "Come! Come! See the men from Heaven!" So all, men and women alike, once their fear was set at rest, came out to welcome us, and they all brought something to eat and drink, which they gave with extraordinary affection and generosity.

In all the islands, they have very many canoes, which are like our rowboats, except they are not so broad, because they are made of a single log of wood. But a rowboat would not be able to keep up with them, since their speed is incredible. In these they navigate among all the islands, and carry their goods and conduct trade. In one of these canoes I have seen with seventy and eighty men, each one with his oar.

In all these islands, I saw no great diversity in the appearance of the people or in their manners and language. On the contrary, they all understand one another . . . and if their Highnesses assent, this will [assist] their conversion to our holy faith of Christ, to which they are very ready and favorably inclined.

I have already said how I went three hundred miles in a straight line from west to east along the seashore of the island of Juana [Cuba], and as a result of this voyage I can say that this island is larger than England and Scotland together. . . . There remains to the westward on this island two provinces to which I have not gone. One of these provinces they call "Avan," and I am told that the people here are born with tails. . . . The other island, Hispana [Hispaniola], has a circumference greater than all Spain. . . . It is a land to be desired and, when seen, never to be left. I have taken possession of this island and all others for their Highnesses so that they may dispose of them as they wish, and all are more richly endowed than I know how or am able to say. Hispana [Hispaniola] is the most conveniently located, and it has the greatest potential for gold mines and all other trade. I have taken possession of a large town, to which I gave the name "Villa de Navidad" [located on the north coast of Haiti], and in it I have made a fort, which by now will be entirely completed. At this fort, I have left enough men as seemed necessary, with arms and artillery and provisions for more than a year, as well as one of our ships and enough skilled men to build others. I also established great friendship with the king of that land, so much so that he was proud to call me "brother" and to treat me as such. And even were the king to change his attitude to one of hostility towards the men left behind, he does not have the power to hurt us. As I have already related, the natives go naked and they are the most timid people in the world, so that the few men whom I have left there alone could destroy them all. The island is without danger if our men follow the regulations and orders that we gave them.

In all these islands, it seems to me that each man is content with one wife, except the chiefs or kings who may have as many as twenty wives. It appears to me that the women work more than the men. I have not been able to learn if they hold private property, but it seemed to me that they all shared what they had, especially of eatable things. In these islands I have so far found no human monstrosities, as many expected . . . on the contrary, the whole population is very well formed. They are not black like the people in Guinea [West Africa], but their hair is flowing. . . .

And so I have found no monsters, nor have I heard of any, except on an island called Charis. . . . This island is inhabited by a people* who are regarded in all the islands as very fierce, and they are cannibals who eat human flesh. They have many canoes with which they range through all the islands of India and pillage and take whatever they can. They are no more malformed than are the others, except that they have the custom of wearing their hair long like women, and they use bows and arrows. . . . They are ferocious towards these other people who are excessively cowardly, but I regard them as no more fearsome than the others. . . . I have also been told of another island, which they assure me is larger than Hispana, where the people have no hair. In this place there is reportedly incalculable amounts of gold. . . .

To conclude this report . . . their Highnesses can see that I can supply them as much gold as they may need if their Highnesses will continue to assist [my voyages]. Moreover, I will provide them spices and cotton, as much as their Highnesses shall command; and mastic and aloe, as much as they shall order to be shipped; and slaves, as many as they shall order to be shipped and who will be from the idolaters. I believe also that I have found rhubarb and cinnamon, and I shall find a thousand other things of value. . . .

Our thanksgiving must be directed the most to the eternal God, Our Lord, Who gives to all those who walk in His way triumph over things which appear to be impossible, and this was one such glorious example. For although men have talked or have written of these distant lands, all was conjectural and without evidence. . . . It is our Redeemer who has given the victory to our most illustrious king and queen, and to their renowned kingdom . . . and all Christendom ought to feel delight and make great feasts and give solemn thanks to our Lord and Savior Jesus Christ, with many solemn prayers for the great exaltation which they shall have in the turning of so many pagan peoples to our Holy Faith, and afterwards for the temporal benefits, because not only Spain but all Christendom will have hence refreshment and gain.

These deeds that have been accomplished are thus briefly recorded while aboard ship, off the Canary Islands, on the fifteenth of February, in the year one thousand four hundred and ninety-three. I remain, at your orders and your service.

The Admiral

NOTES

1. Exploration and expansion have been constants in human history and can be seen in the early evolution of migration patterns, the creation of long-distance trade, and, in many cases, the formation of states and empires.

---

*Columbus is referring to the Caribs, from whom the "Caribbean" gets its name. Scholars believe the Caribs emigrated to the islands of the Caribbean from South America and took advantage of their warrior skills to raid and prey upon the indigenous peoples of the islands, the Arawaks.

2. In some cases, such as the remote interior regions of Africa, these accounts are among the few written sources available for this time period.

3. The *hajj* is the annual pilgrimage to Mecca to worship and visit the holy sites of Islam. It is one of the five "Pillars of Faith," a duty that devout Muslims are expected to undertake once in their lifetimes, if possible. Some scholars have suggested that the ritual and celebration of the *hajj* has created a stimulus for travel that surpasses the rite of Christian pilgrimages during the Middle Ages.

4. In 1279, the Mongols had successfully invaded China and created their own dynasty (Yuan dynasty), the first instance when foreigners ruled over China. But the Mongols were mostly content to impose their rule only in the highest positions of authority, and they actually succeeded in linking China more closely with the outside world via Mongol-controlled overland trade networks in central Asia. Nonetheless, the rule of foreign "barbarians" over the illustrious "Middle Kingdom" proved intolerable to the Chinese, and in 1368, Chinese armies defeated the Mongols and reestablished their authority.

5. Some scholars suggest that the Confucian virtues of cultivating family and ancestral bonds were perceived by later Ming emperors to be in disharmony with the motives and actions inherent in exploration.

6. See the readings in chapter 14 that focus on cultural reactions to disease and bubonic plague.

7. Literally translates as the "Reconquest" and refers to the period of Christian holy war against Muslim control of Spain and Portugal that began as early as the tenth century but that culminated in the expulsion of Muslims (and Jews) from Spain in 1492.

8. The *Columbian Exchange* is a broad term used by historians to refer to the global spread of plants, animals, and diseases following the voyages of Christopher Columbus.

9. Mecca and Medina are both located in the mountainous regions along the Red Sea in the Arabian peninsula. Mecca was the birthplace of Muhammad, and it is the prime site for pilgrimages in Islam (the *hajj*). Medina was the city where Muhammad built a following, and it remains his burial place. Together, they represent two of the most holy sites in Islam.

10. Zhu Di, also known as the Yongle Emperor (1403–1424), was the third Ming emperor, whose great ambition was to rebuild Chinese power following the rule of the Mongols.

11. Scurvy is a painful and life-threatening disease caused by a deficiency in vitamin C (ascorbic acid). It was once a widespread malady among crewmen of sailing ships on long voyages due to the lack of fresh fruits and vegetables.

12. Beginning sometime in the ninth or tenth century, Muslim traders from Arabia moved to coastal towns in east Africa to facilitate their commercial activities. They frequently settled down and married African women, and their future progeny, language, and society became known as Swahili, a mixing of African and Arab blood-lines and cultures. By the time of da Gama's visit, generations of Swahili governed prosperous independent city-states along the coast from present-day Mozambique to Somalia.

CHAPTER 2

Cross-Cultural Perceptions in the New World

INTRODUCTION

On April 22, 1519, Hernan Cortés (1485–1547), captain of a Spanish armada, disembarked from his ship along the Yucatan coast, near the present-day city of Vera Cruz, Mexico. Because it was Good Friday, the day that Christians believe Jesus died on the cross, Cortés wore black. According to one of his men, Cortés's face "had little color and was inclined to be greyish. . . . His hair and beard were black and rather thin."[1] Unbeknownst to Cortés, it was also the year "One Reed" of the Aztec[2] calendar, and the day was a "9 Wind day," according to their recurring, 52-year dating system. It was part of the Aztec belief system that their Feathered Serpent god Quetzalcoatl would return on this date to reclaim his land from the Aztec emperors who were ruling in his absence. Moreover, Quetzalcoatl was to return from the direction the Spaniards had come, and he was thought to have light skin, a beard, and dark clothing. In other words, when Cortés stepped off his ship, he also stepped into the middle of the Aztec belief system.

The expedition led by Cortés consisted of 11 ships, 508 swordsmen, 32 crossbow men, 13 musketeers, 14 cannon, 16 horses, and several large war dogs. With this minuscule force, he set out to conquer an empire of some 25 million people.[3] He vowed to his emperor, Charles V of Spain, that he would go to Tenochtitlan, the capital of the Aztec emperor Mocteuzma II (commonly rendered Montezuma) and "have him prisoner or dead or subject to Your Majesty."[4] Although Cortés was motivated by rumors of Aztec treasure, his actions also demonstrated his belief that he was on a divinely sanctioned mission. As the first formal report of his expedition says, of one of his early clashes with a Mesoamerican army, "Surely this battle was won by the will of God rather than by our forces, for we were four hundred against forty thousand warriors."[5] No less than the Aztecs, the Spanish were equally motivated and influenced by their own fervently held belief system.

The Aztec–Spanish encounter is one of the most dramatic and tragic interactions in human history. Although much historical attention has focused on Cortés and Mocteuzma, the Spanish–Aztec conflict involved much more than the personal interactions between those two leaders. Rather, they embodied the values and visions of the civilizations that produced them, so that their dramatic encounter represents the coming together of two vividly different cultures, value systems, and understandings of the world. Hence, the Aztec–Spanish encounter allows us to explore deeply the workings of cross-cultural perceptions (and misperceptions). Furthermore, the historical recordings they have left behind both reflect and preserve these differential worldviews. As a result, by presenting two opposed interpretations of what actually occurred, the sources enable us to engage in one of the primary tasks of the historian: the critical analysis of sources and the evaluation of their accuracy and utility. The issues of cross-cultural perceptions and the critical skills necessary to assess them are the twin topics of this chapter.

In the historical encounter between the Spanish and the Aztecs, it was not just two civilizations that came into conflict, but two powerful, confident imperial structures that also clashed. It was only in 1492, the year of Columbus's first voyage, that the Spaniards had completed their centuries-long *reconquista* (reconquest) of the Iberian peninsula from the control of the Islamic Moors. The Spaniards' religion was a militant, aggressive Catholicism, forged in the long, hard centuries of their political and religious crusade against the Muslim Moors. By 1519, the Spanish had nearly thirty years of exploration and expansion in the Caribbean basin. They had conquered both Hispaniola[6] and Cuba, and they had established towns and estates on each island. Moreover, they had sent expeditions along the northern coast of South America, and Balboa had even crossed the isthmus of Panama to the Pacific. They had not, however, encountered any large, militarily powerful states until 1517, when the first of three exploratory expeditions westward from Cuba made contact with Mesoamerican civilization. Here they encountered sophisticated civilizations with large towns, thriving trade, and a seemingly ample supply of gold and precious stones. It was the wealth of the region that most impressed the Spaniards, and together with their religious fervor, it fueled their advance into the heartland of Mexico. As Cortés himself was to say to Mocteuzma, "We Spaniards have a disease of the heart that only gold can cure."[7]

The Aztecs, meanwhile, had themselves been relative latecomers to the central valley of Mexico and had experienced their own uphill climb to the summit of power. They had founded their capital Tenochtitlan in 1325 on an island in the swamps of the valley's main lake because all other land was already taken. From that modest beginning, their diligent efforts and fighting prowess had allowed them by 1428 to become the major power of the central valley. Like the Romans, the Aztecs conquered an area in which highly advanced agricultural civilization had already developed. In the case of the Aztecs, many of their social institutions and cultural traditions were adopted from earlier empires (the earlier Mayan and Teotihuacan, ca. 450–750, as well as Tula of the Toltecs, ca. 950–1150). Common cultural attributes, for example, included their maize-based agriculture, their writing and calendar systems, step pyramids, the ritual of human sacrifice, and the belief in a feathered serpent god.

One of the most striking features of Aztec culture was human sacrifice, which was deeply entwined in Mesoamerican cosmology.[8] As in many other cultures, ritual sacrifice was perceived as a means to propitiate the gods and to seek their continued blessings and good fortune. The Aztecs were particularly concerned with appeasing Huitzilopochtli (the god of war to whom they attributed their success and rise to power) with the ultimate sacrifice of human beings. But in their lore, the god Quetzalcoatl (the god of wind who brought rain clouds) had opposed human sacrifice and fought with Huitzulopochtli over the issue. Although Quetzalcoatl had lost and had been driven off, he promised one day to return and to reclaim his lands and his throne. The Aztec rulers believed themselves to be reigning in his absence.[9]

Hence the appearance of Cortés/Quetzalcoatl had enormous significance for the Aztec leaders and their people, and it profoundly shaped the character of Aztec–Spanish interactions. The Aztecs feared the arrival of Cortés/Quetzalcoatl but also remembered that the god had been banished once before and perhaps could be exiled again. How that would best be achieved—by bribes, by magic, or by force (if at all)—was the central focus of Aztec policy debates concerning the Spanish. In the eyes of the Spanish, human sacrifice was a shock and an abomination, contrary to all of their religious beliefs and values. Such views undoubtedly shaped their cross-cultural perceptions of the Aztecs and may help explain some of their subsequent actions and behaviors. We are fortunate to have two extraordinary written sources to use in evaluating the Aztec–Spanish encounter. After the conquest, the Spanish systematically destroyed much of Aztec history and culture, and as a result, the records we have of events from the Aztec perspective generally come to us through a Spanish filter. This is true even of the most comprehensive single account of Aztec culture and history at the time of the Conquest, *The General History of New Spain* (also known as the *Florentine Codex*),[10] written in 1575–1577. *The History of New Spain* was compiled under the supervision and at the behest of the Spanish Franciscan friar Bernardino de Sahagún, who had come to New Spain (Mexico) in 1529. Sahagún became deeply interested in the history and culture of the Aztecs, and he ultimately mastered the Nahuatl (Aztec) language. As a result, his encyclopedic account of Aztec society and daily life has a scope and rigor that other sources cannot approach.

The Spanish text we use was also prepared some time after the events. In Bernal Díaz del Castillo's work *The True History of the Conquest of New Spain,* we have a great rarity: the historical record of the views of an insider who had participated in one of history's momentous undertakings. He had been born in Spain in the fateful year of 1492. Like many young Spaniards, he journeyed to the New World to seek his fortune, and through relatives he was included in the expedition to Mexico. A common soldier, he nonetheless fought in many engagements as part of Cortés's forces. He composed the work in the 1560s, because he had read inaccurate accounts written by people who had no direct knowledge of the events. He was present at most of the events he discusses, and he describes what happened from a firsthand, eyewitness perspective. Although he was not a great writer, he writes with clarity. While Cortés himself wrote a series of dispatches to Emperor Charles V of Spain from Mexico, his reports have always been considered suspect, because they are thought by many to include a lot of special pleading by Cortés and therefore to be untrustworthy. This makes Díaz's record all the more valuable.

Three pictorial images of the conquest complete this chapter. Drawings, illustrations, paintings, and photographs can frequently serve as important historical documents. They recount events and people in a visual format, providing additional information to augment written sources. But images are also products of human culture, and they often express or reinforce political ideologies, social institutions, and cultural values. The three images included in this chapter help to illustrate these points. In the Tlaxcalan drawing, *Massacre at Cholula,* and in the Aztec *Massacre of the Mexican Nobility,* cross-cultural perceptions and power relations are powerfully expressed in an abstract and culturally defined manner. The final image, a European painting titled *Battle for Tenochtitlan,* portrays Cortés's final assault on the Aztec capital in a strikingly different manner. Comparing the stories told in these different images—as well as their unique styles of composition and expression—illustrates how visual images can be used to deepen our understanding of history.

The very complex cultural maps that both the Spanish and the Aztecs brought to their encounter make this an ideal instance for studying the way that cross-cultural perceptions are shaped by preexisting belief systems. Thus we can assess the degree to which, in cross-cultural interaction, it is not so much a matter of "seeing is believing" but rather that "believing is seeing." Moreover, the cultural backgrounds influenced the ways that these historic events were recorded, illustrated, and remembered by the two sides. Therefore, we have a "twice-told tale" that comes out very differently in the two narrations. Consequently, we can also perform the fundamental work of historical assessment by critiquing the sources and weighing their respective strengths, limitations, and inherent biases.

CHAPTER QUESTIONS

1. What were the most important factors shaping the vision that each side had of the other? How did this vision affect their behavior? Did the image that either side had of the other change over time? If so, why?

2. How do the pictorial images affect your understanding of this cross-cultural encounter? Do they impart information different from that in the texts?

3. These sources were produced specifically to explain or to represent this encounter from the point of view of one of the two groups. Can you identify instances in which the circumstances under which these sources were produced might have affected the way each side told the story?

4. Historians use primary sources to reconstruct the past. Using the sources provided here, what different stories can be told?

5. Human religious beliefs and rituals have meaning in terms of the cultural context that produced them. Should we then avoid all value judgments when studying other societies? Or are there some human behaviors—for example, the human sacrifice of the Aztecs or the convert-or-die practices of the Spanish—that ought to be condemned, even though they are highly valued in the societies that practice them?

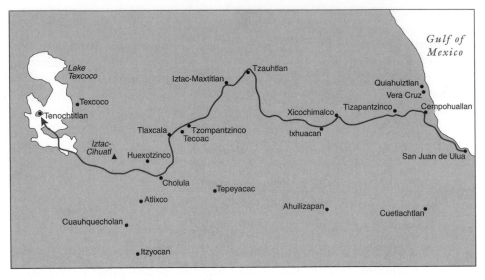

Map 2.1 Cortés's Route to Tenochtitlan

AN AZTEC ACCOUNT
OF THE CONQUEST OF MEXICO

The epic saga of the Spanish–Aztec encounter has been recounted elsewhere in sufficient detail, and only a brief account needs repeating here. Following the landing of Cortés and his forces in 1519, the first peoples they encountered were either unhappy subjects or outright enemies of the Aztec empire. Nonetheless, they opposed the Spanish in a number of military engagements. Although the native forces were more numerous and fought bravely, the Spanish overcame them, owing to the technological and psychological advantage of their weapons, especially their cavalry, which gave them an enormous advantage in speed and power. Those advantages were multiplied by the terror the horse and rider inspired, because the largest domesticated animal among the Mesoamericans was the dog.[11]

Once they were convinced that the Spanish could not be defeated, a number of these peoples allied themselves with Cortés against the Aztecs. The most significant allies were the Tlaxcalans, who provided soldiers to fight their longtime Aztec adversaries. Cortés also benefited from the assistance of a captive Aztec woman known to the Spanish as "Doña Marina." She informed Cortés about Mesoamerican and Aztec ways, and she helped the Spaniards more than once to escape ambush and other very dangerous situations.[12] By mid-October, the conquistadores were in Cholula, where they attacked and massacred a large number of warriors. The circumstances surrounding this event are unclear: According to Aztec sources, the massacre was a violent and unprovoked attack on unarmed men, whereas Spanish sources claim it was a necessary preemptive strike against Cholulans, who were planning their own massacre of the Spanish. Such discrepancies are not unusual and illustrate some of the difficulties faced by historians in the reconstruction of Mexican history.

By early November, the steady advance of the Spanish brought them to the outskirts of Tenochtitlan. The Aztec capital was built on an island in the middle of a lake, with three causeways leading to it and the massive temple complex in the middle. The city was densely populated, and its neighborhoods were connected by both streets and canals. The causeways were built of stone, but they had gaps in them that were bridged over with wooden constructions that could be removed in case of attack. They also had a vast number of war canoes that could attack a foe from the sides. It is difficult to estimate the population of the city, but it was at least 200,000, and perhaps much higher. It was greater than European cities of that era, and the Spanish were duly impressed.

Mocteuzma had been kept well informed on the advance of the foreigners, and he had sent numerous emissaries to present gifts and to gather information about the god's intentions. With his advisors divided on the best course of action, Mocteuzma personally greeted Cortés at his arrival, gave him numerous gifts, and housed him in a palace. Among other things, the Spaniards found a room filled with an incredible treasure of gold and jewelry, and Cortés dispatched survey parties to explore other sources of wealth. To ensure cooperation, Cortés placed Mocteuzma and other notables under his supervision and control in a form of house arrest. The situation remained tense but relatively peaceful until May 1520, when Cortés learned that a force of 1,300 men had been sent out by the governor of Cuba to arrest him and take over the expedition because of his failure to obey orders. Cortés had a great deal at stake. On the one hand, whoever won royal recognition would receive one-fifth of the treasure taken. On the other hand, if he did not win royal recognition, he could be arrested as a traitor and rebel. As it turned out, the leader of the second expedition was no match for Cortés, who boldly marched back to Vera Cruz, captured the other leader, won over his forces, and merged them with his own small force.

On arriving back in Tenochtitlan, Cortés found a much changed environment. The man he had left in charge in the capital, Pedro de Alvarado, had attacked and massacred a group of Aztec nobles, who were dancing unarmed in the plaza of the main temple in celebration of a major feast (this event is the subject of the Aztec painting included here as Figure 2.2 on page 67). After the massacre, the Spanish force had been attacked and cut off from almost all supplies. The city seethed with anger toward the Spanish, and fighting flared up again immediately after Cortés returned. It was at this point that Mocteuzma died. Once again, sources are not clear on the death of the Aztec leader. Some assert that he was struck down by a rock thrown by an Aztec warrior, others contend that he was killed by the Spanish, and still others maintain that he committed suicide. Whatever occurred, on June 30, 1520, Cortés led his forces out of the city in a desperate breakout that came to be known as the *Noche Triste,* or the "Night of Sorrows." Many Spaniards were killed or captured, and the captives were sacrificed. Others drowned in the canals surrounding the city, weighed down by gold and their greed.

When Cortés returned in January 1521, he brought an army of 500 Spaniards and tens of thousands of native allies, especially the Tlaxcalans. With the aid of

Tlaxcalan laborers, they constructed thirteen sloops and mounted cannon on them, effectively cutting off both food and fresh water supplies to Tenochtitlan. Nonetheless, the city proved incredibly difficult to conquer, and the Spaniards suffered heavy losses. In addition, a smallpox epidemic broke out in October 1520 that lasted more than two months and claimed thousands of victims. Despite this, the Aztecs refused to surrender. On August 13, 1521, the last Aztec leader was captured, and the Tlaxcalan allies massacred many of the survivors in the city.

The first documents in this chapter contain descriptions of these monumental and agonizing events from the Aztec perspective. They were compiled at the behest and under the supervision of a Franciscan friar, Bernardino de Sahagún. Sahagún had arrived in New Spain, as the territory had been designated by Cortés, in 1529 at the age of thirty. He soon acquired a sophisticated mastery of Nahuatl, the Aztec language, and over the years he collected an invaluable mass of material relating to preconquest life of the native peoples. Beginning in 1547, the material was acquired by native Americans who were taught to write and who recorded the memories of elderly nobles who had witnessed the events. Later, Sahagún put the material together and edited it, finishing his *General History of New Spain* in 1577. Although the text was compiled under Spanish auspices and given final form by a Spanish Franciscan priest, it nonetheless imparts a sense of how the events of the conquest were perceived by the Aztecs themselves. In the view of most scholars, it remains the best and fullest native account of the conquest.

QUESTIONS TO CONSIDER

1. How did the Aztec belief system shape the Aztecs' perception of the Spanish and Cortés? What characteristics of the Spanish worked to reinforce Aztec perceptions?

2. How did the Spanish belief and value systems affect the Spaniards' perception of the Aztecs? How did subsequent Aztec and Spanish actions and reactions affect their mutual understanding?

3. Identify the different means which Mocteuzma sought to deal with Cortés and the Spanish. Does the text indicate that other Aztecs who shared his belief system might have reacted differently to the Spanish forces? If so, identify passages that give that impression.

4. Characterize the way the Spanish are depicted in this document. Based on what you know, is this an accurate portrayal of Cortés and his forces?

5. How might the circumstances in which the *Florentine Codex* was compiled have affected the interpretation of events presented in it? Would those circumstances make it more or less likely to present an accurate view of the Aztec understanding of the encounter?

THE GENERAL HISTORY OF NEW SPAIN (1577)

Bernardino de Sahagún

The year 13-Rabbit* now approached its end. And when it was about to end, they [the Spaniards] appeared, they were seen again. The report of their coming was brought to Mocteuzma, who immediately sent out messengers. It was as if he thought the new arrival was our prince Quetzalcoatl.

This is what he felt in his heart: *He has appeared! He has come back! He will come here, to the place of his throne and canopy, for that is what was promised when he departed!*

Mocteuzma sent five messengers to greet the strangers and to bring them gifts. . . . He said to them: "Come forward, my Jaguar Knights, come forward. It is said that our lord has returned to this land. Go to meet him. Go to hear him. Listen well to what he tells you; listen and remember."

Mocteuzma also said to his messengers: "Here is what you are to bring our lord. This is the treasure of Quetzalcoatl." This treasure was the god's finery: a serpent mask inlaid with turquoise, a decoration for the breast made of quetzal feathers, a collar woven in the *ptatillo* style with a gold disk in the center, and a shield decorated with gold and mother-of-pearl and bordered with quetzal feathers with a pendant of the same feathers.

There was also a mirror like those which the ritual dancers wore. . . . The reverse of the mirror was a turquoise mosaic: it was encrusted and adorned with turquoise. And there was a spear-thrower inlaid with turquoise, a bracelet hung with little gold bells. . . .

Mocteuzma also gave them the finery of Tezcatlipoca† . . . : a helmet in the shape of a cone, yellow with gold and set with many stars, a number of earrings adorned with little gold bells. . . .

These were the many kinds of adornments that were known as "divine adornments." They were . . . to be taken as gifts of welcome along with many other objects. . . ."

Then Mocteuzma gave the messengers his final orders. He said to them: "Go now, without delay. Do reverence to our lord the god. Say to him: 'Your deputy, Mocteuzma, has sent us to you. Here are the presents with which he welcomes you home to Mexico.'" . . .

Source: Excerpted from *The Broken Spears: The Aztec Account of the Conquest of Mexico,* edited and with an introduction by Miguel Leon-Portilla (Boston: Beacon Press, 1962), 22–31, 33–35, 40–41, 51–52, 63–68. Copyright © 1962 Beacon Press. Reprinted by permission.

*The Aztecs had a repeating fifty-two-year calendar. The cycle was broken up into four signs (e.g., "Wind" and "Rabbit"), each with thirteen years. The Spanish arrived at the end of the thirteenth year designated by the sign of the Rabbit.

†The Aztec god of "Here and Now," who rules the everyday life of earth.

One by one they did reverence to Cortés by touching the ground before him with their lips. They said to him: "If the god deign to hear us, your deputy Mocteuzma has sent us to render you homage. He has the City of Mexico in his care. He says: 'The god is weary.'"

Then they arrayed the Captain in the finery they had brought him as presents. . . . The Captain asked them: "And is this all? Is this your gift of welcome? Is this how you greet people?" . . .

Then the Captain gave orders, and the messengers were chained by the feet and by the neck. When this had been done, the great cannon was fired off. The messengers lost their senses and fainted away. They fell down side by side and lay where they had fallen. But the Spaniards quickly revived them: they lifted them up, gave them wine to drink and then offered them food. . . .

While the messengers were away, Mocteuzma could neither sleep nor eat, and no one could speak with him. He thought that everything he did was in vain, and he sighed almost every moment. He was lost in despair, in the deepest gloom and sorrow. Nothing could comfort him, nothing could calm him, nothing could give him any pleasure.

He said: "What will happen to us? Who will outlive it? Ah, in other times I was contented, but now I have death in my heart! My heart burns and suffers, as if it were drowned in spices . . . ! But will our lord come here?"

[He was told] "The messengers have come back from the sea."

Then he . . . gave this order: "Two captives are to be painted with chalk."

The messengers went down to the House of the Serpent, and Mocteuzma arrived. The two captives were then sacrificed before his eyes: their breasts were torn open, and the messengers were sprinkled with their blood. This was done because the messengers had . . . seen the gods, their eyes had looked on their faces. They had even conversed with the gods!

When the sacrifice was finished, the messengers reported to the king. They told him how they had made the journey, and what they had seen and what food the strangers ate. Mocteuzma was astonished and terrified by their report, and the description of the strangers' food astonished him above all else.

He was also terrified to learn how the cannon roared, how its noise resounded, how it caused one to faint and grow deaf. The messengers told him: "A thing like a ball of stone comes out of its entrails: it comes out shooting sparks and raining fire. The smoke that comes out with it has a pestilent odor, like that of rotting mud. The odor penetrates to the brain and causes the greatest discomfort. If the cannon is aimed against a mountain, the mountain splits and cracks open. If it is aimed against a tree, it shatters the tree into splinters. This is a most unnatural sight, as if the tree had exploded from within."

The messengers also said: "Their trappings and arms are all made of iron. They dress in iron and wear iron casques on their heads. Their swords are iron; their bows are iron; their shields are iron; their spears are iron. Their deer carry them on their backs wherever they wish to go. The deer, our lord, are as tall as the roof of a house.

"The strangers' bodies are completely covered, so that only their faces can be seen. Their skin is white, as if it were made of lime. They have yellow hair, though some of them have black. Their beards are long and yellow, and their mustaches are yellow. Their hair is curly, with very fine strands.

"As for their food, it is like human food. It is large and white, and not heavy. It is something like straw, but with the taste of a cornstalk, of the pith of a cornstalk. It is a little sweet, as if it were flavored with honey; it tastes of honey, it is sweet-tasting food.

"Their dogs are enormous, with flat ears and long dangling tongues. The color of their eyes is a burning yellow; their eyes flash fire and shoot off sparks. Their bellies are hollow, their flanks long and narrow. They are tireless and very powerful. They bound here and there, panting, with their tongues hanging out. And they are spotted like an ocelot."

When Mocteuzma heard this report, he was filled with terror. It was as if his heart had fainted, as if it had shriveled. It was as if he were conquered by despair. . . .

Mocteuzma sent out . . . his most gifted men, his prophets and wizards, as many as he could gather. He also sent out his noblest and bravest warriors. . . .

Mocteuzma also sent captives to be sacrificed, because the strangers might wish to drink their blood. The envoys sacrificed these captives in the presence of the strangers, but when the white men saw this done, they were filled with disgust and loathing. They spat on the ground, or wiped away their tears, or closed their eyes and shook their heads with abhorrence. They refused to eat the food that was sprinkled with blood, . . . it sickened them, as if the blood had rotted.

Mocteuzma ordered the sacrifice because he took the Spaniards to be gods; he believed in them and worshiped them as deities. That is why they were called "Gods who have come from heaven." . . .

Mocteuzma had sent the magicians to learn what sort of people the strangers might be, but they were also to see if they could work some charm against them, or do them some mischief. They might be able to direct a harmful wind against them, or cause them to break out in sores, or injure them in some way. Or they might be able to repeat some enchanted word, over and over, that would cause them to fall sick, or die, or return to their own land.

The magicians carried out their mission against the Spaniards, but they failed completely. They could not harm them in any way. . . .

When the Spaniards left their ships and began to march here . . . Mocteuzma was distraught and bewildered; he was filled with terror, not knowing what would happen to the city. The people were also terrified, debating the news among themselves. There were meetings and arguments and gossip in the street; there was weeping and lamenting. The people were downcast; they went about with their heads bowed down and greeted each other with tears.

At this time the Tlaxcaltecas* were enemies of Cholula. They feared the Cholultecas; they envied and cursed them; their souls burned with hatred for the people of

---

*The Tlaxcalans (called Tlaxcaltecas in the *Florentine Codex*) were enemies of the Aztecs. They had at first opposed Cortés, but, after they had lost a battle to the Spaniards, they became Cortés's most reliable allies.

Cholula. This is why they brought certain rumors to Cortés, so that he would destroy them. They said to him: "Cholula is our enemy. It is an evil city. The people are as brave as the Aztecs and they are the Aztecs' friends."

When the Spaniards heard this, they marched against Cholula. . . . When they arrived, . . . an assembly was held in the courtyard of the god, but when they had all gathered together, the entrances were closed, so that there was no way of escaping.

Then the sudden slaughter began: knife strokes, and sword strokes, and death. The people of Cholula . . . had not suspected it. They faced the Spaniards without weapons, without their swords or their shields. The cause of the slaughter was treachery. They died blindly, without knowing why, because of the lies of the Tlaxcaltecas.

And when this had taken place, word of it was brought to Mocteuzma. . . . The common people were terrified by the news; they could do nothing but tremble with fright. It was as if the earth trembled beneath them, or as if the world were spinning before their eyes, as it spins during a fit of vertigo. . . .

When the massacre at Cholula was complete, the strangers set out again toward the City of Mexico. They came in battle array, as conquerors, and the dust rose in whirlwinds on the roads. Their spears glinted in the sun, and their pennons fluttered like bats. They made a loud clamor as they marched, for their coats of mail and their weapons clashed and rattled. Some of them were dressed in glistening iron from head to foot; they terrified everyone who saw them.

Their dogs came with them, running ahead of the column. They raised their muzzles high; they lifted their muzzles to the wind. They raced on before with saliva dripping from their jaws.

Then Mocteuzma dispatched various chiefs. . . . They gave the "gods" ensigns of gold, and ensigns of quetzal feathers, and golden necklaces. And when they were given these presents, the Spaniards burst into smiles; their eyes shone with pleasure; they were delighted by them. They picked up the gold and fingered it like monkeys; they seemed to be transported with joy, as if their hearts were illumined and made new.

The truth is that they longed and lusted for gold. Their bodies swelled with greed, and their hunger was ravenous; they hungered like pigs for gold. They snatched at the golden ensigns, waved them from side to side and examined every inch of them. They were like one who speaks a barbarous tongue; everything they said was in a barbarous tongue.

The Spaniards arrived. . . . Thus Mocteuzma went out to meet them. . . . He presented many gifts to the Captain and his commanders, those who had come to make war. He showered gifts upon them and hung flowers around their necks. . . . Then he hung the gold necklaces around their necks and gave them presents of every sort as gifts of welcome. . . .

And the king . . . stood up to welcome Cortés; he came forward, bowed his head low and addressed him in these words: "Our lord, you are weary. The journey has tired you, but now you have arrived on the earth. You have come to the city, Mexico. You have come here to sit on your throne, to sit under its canopy.

"The kings who have gone before, your representatives, guarded it and preserved it for your coming. The kings . . . ruled for you in the City of Mexico. The people were protected by their swords and sheltered by their shields." . . .

"No, it is not a dream. I am not walking in my sleep. I am not seeing you in my dreams. I have seen you at last! I have met you face to face! I was in agony for five days, . . . and now you have come out of the clouds and mists to sit on your throne again.

"This was foretold by the kings who governed our city, and now it has taken place. You have come back to us; you have come down from the sky. Rest now, and take possession of your royal houses. Welcome to your lands, my lords!" . . .

Cortés replied in his strange and savage tongue, . . . "Tell, Mocteuzma that we are his friends. There is nothing to fear. We have wanted to see him for a long time, and now we have seen his face and heard his words. Tell him that we love him well and that our hearts are contented." . . .

[A]nd the Spaniards grasped Mocteuzma's hands and patted his back to show their affection for him. . . .

When the Spaniards entered the Royal House, they placed Mocteuzma under guard. . . . Then the Spaniards fired one of their cannons, and this caused great confusion in the city. The people scattered in every direction; they fled without rhyme or reason; they ran off as if they were being pursued. It was as if they had eaten the mushrooms that confuse the mind, or had seen some dreadful apparition. They were all overcome with terror, as if their hearts had fainted. And when night fell, the panic spread through the city and their fears would not let them sleep. . . .

When the Spaniards were installed in the palace, they asked Mocteuzma about the city's resources and reserves and about the warriors' ensigns and shields. They questioned him closely and then demanded gold.

Mocteuzma guided them to it. They surrounded him and crowded close with their weapons. He walked in the center, while they formed a circle around him.

When they arrived at the treasure house . . . , the riches of gold and feathers were brought out to them: ornaments made of quetzal feathers,* richly worked shields, disks of gold, the necklaces of the idols, gold nose plugs, gold greaves[†] and bracelets and crowns.

The Spaniards immediately stripped the feathers from the gold shields and ensigns. They gathered all the gold into a great mound and set fire to everything else, regardless of its value. Then they melted down the gold into ingots. As for the precious green stones, they took only the best of them; . . . The Spaniards searched through the whole treasure house, questioning and quarreling, and seized every object they thought was beautiful.

Next they went to Mocteuzma's storehouse, . . . where his personal treasures were kept. The Spaniards grinned like little beasts and patted each other with delight.

When they entered the hall of treasures, it was as if they had arrived in Paradise. They searched everywhere and coveted everything; they were slaves to their own greed. All of Mocteuzma's possessions were brought out: fine bracelets, necklaces with large stones, ankle rings with little gold bells, the royal crowns and all the royal

---

*Some of the Aztecs' most valued ornaments were feathers.

[†]A piece of armor that covered the shin.

finery—everything that belonged to the king and was reserved to him only. They seized these treasures as if they were their own, as if this plunder were merely a stroke of good luck.

A SPANISH ACCOUNT OF THE CONQUEST OF MEXICO

The best Spanish source on the Aztec–Spanish encounter was written by Bernal Díaz del Castillo, an old campaigner from Cortés's army. Born and raised in a poor family in Spain, Díaz began his military career as a common soldier. In 1514, he went to America to serve with the Spanish forces opening up the "New World," and he made two previous expeditions to the Yucatan prior to the one led by Hernando Cortés in 1519. According to his own accounts, he took part in over one hundred battles and was present at the surrender of Tenochtitlan in 1521. As a reward for services he received a commission as *regidor*, or governor, of Santiago de los Caballeros in Guatemala, where he was also awarded a minor, relatively unproductive grant of land and native labor (*encomienda*).[13] Unhappy with this grant, Díaz even traveled once to Spain to argue for a better reward for his services. Charles V and his government in Spain, who had no real appreciation for the caliber of foe that Cortés and company had bested, quickly grew weary of the conquistadores and their clamor for greater reward. After having read a published account of the conquest that he considered a distortion, Díaz set about writing his own account during the 1560s, when he was already an old man. He finished it when he was seventy-six years old. Though he had sent a copy to Spain, the work was not published until the next century, well after his long and eventful life had ended in 1581. The drama of the events and the intimacy and novelty of his observations make this a remarkable historical source.

Though many years had passed, Díaz seemed to have vivid memories of both the events and the personages he had witnessed. His memory for names failed him in only a few instances. For example, there was one native leader whose name he had forgotten, and whom he always referred to simply as "the fat lord." Such lapses are remarkably few and far between. Though he was not a polished writer, his style is clear and his voice confident, and he has left us an extraordinary and intimate recording of these epochal events from the Spanish point of view. The selections include Díaz's reconstruction of the events at Cholula, the Spaniards' entry into Tenochtitlan, the initial interactions between Cortés and Mocteuzma, and the Spanish decision to make the Aztec ruler a captive. These readings provide us with insights into the events that transpired, as well as giving us information on perceptions and attitudes of the participants.

QUESTIONS TO CONSIDER

1. Compare the Aztec explanation for the events at Cholula with explanations provided by Díaz. How do they differ? Whose version is more convincing to you? Why?

2. List the things about Aztec civilization that Díaz admires and then put them into categories (for example, technology, economics, culture, and so on).

3. What does Díaz reject about Aztec civilization? Categorize what he rejects and then compare that with what he admires. What general conclusions can you draw? How did the Spanish make value judgments?

4. How do the overall representations of the Spanish and the Aztecs provided by Díaz compare with the impressions that emerge from the *Florentine Codex*? How do you explain the differences?

5. How do the religious beliefs and practices of the Spanish and the Aztecs affect their behavior, as described by Díaz? Are any of their behaviors surprising?

THE TRUE HISTORY OF THE CONQUEST OF NEW SPAIN (1568)

Bernal Díaz del Castillo

[The excerpt begins with Díaz's account of the massacre at Cholula.]

After the people of Cholula had received us in the festive manner already described, and most certainly with [a show of] good will, it presently appeared that Mocteuzma sent orders to his ambassadors, who were still in our company, to negotiate with the Cholulans that an army of 20,000 men which Mocteuzma had sent and equipped, should on entering the city, join with them in attacking us by night or by day, get us into a hopeless plight, and bring all of us that they could [capture] bound to Mexico. And he sent grand promises together with many presents of jewels and cloths, also a golden drum, and he also sent word to the priests of the city that they were to retain twenty of us to sacrifice to their idols.

All was in readiness and the warriors whom Mocteuzma quickly sent were stationed in some ranchos and some rocky thickets about half a league from Cholula and some were already posted within the houses, and all had their arms ready for use, and had built up breastworks . . . and had dug holes and ditches in the streets so

Source: Bernal Díaz del Castillo, *The True History of the Conquest of New Spain,* vol. 1, Hakluyt Society, Second Series, XXIII (London, 1908), 132–35; vol. 2, Hakluyt Society, Second Series, XXIV (London, 1910), 4–18, 37–38, 39–40, 44, 55–58, 59–60, 69–79, 84–88. Some passages have been taken out of their original order without changing the sense. Díaz's spelling of two gods' names, Tescatepuca and Huichilobos, have been changed to their modern spellings—Tezcatlipoca and Huitzilopochtli, respectively—to avoid confusion.

as to impede the horsemen, and they had already filled some houses with long poles and leather collars and cords with which they were to bind us and lead us to Mexico; but our Lord God so ordained that all their plots should be turned against them. . . .

[T]hey had taken us to our quarters, they fed us very well for the first two days, and although we saw them so peacefully inclined, we never gave up our good custom of keeping fully prepared, and on the third day they neither gave us anything to eat nor did any of the *Caciques** or priests make their appearance, and if any Indians came to look at us, they did not approach us, but remained some distance off, laughing at us as though mocking us. When our Captain saw this, he told our interpreters Doña Marina and Jeronimo de Aguilar to tell the Ambassadors of the Great Mocteuzma, who remained with us, to order the *Caciques* to bring some food, but all they brought was water and fire wood, and the old men who brought it said that there was no more maize.

That same day other Ambassadors arrived from Mocteuzma, and joined those who were already with us and they said to Cortés, very impudently, that their Prince had sent them to say that we were not to go to his city because he had nothing to give us to eat, and that they wished at once to return to Mexico with our reply. When Cortés saw that their speech was unfriendly, he replied to the Ambassadors in the blandest manner, that he marveled how such a great Prince as Mocteuzma should be so vacillating, and he begged them not to return to Mexico, for he wished to start himself on the next day, to see their Prince, and act according to his orders, and I believe that he gave the Ambassadors some strings of beads and they agreed to stay.

When this had been done, our Captain called us together, and said to us, "I see that these people are very much disturbed, and it behooves us to keep on the alert, in case some trouble is brewing among them," and he at once sent for the principal chief, whose name I now forget, telling him either to come himself or to send some other chieftains. The chief replied that he was ill and could not come.

When our Captain heard this, he ordered us to bring before him, with kindly persuasion, two of the numerous priests who were in the great Cue [step-pyramid temple] near our quarters. We brought two of them, without doing them any disrespect, and Cortés ordered each of them to be given a *chalchihuite*,† which are held by them to be as valuable as emeralds, and addressing them with friendly words he asked them what was the reason that the chief and chieftains and most of the priests were frightened, for he had sent to summon them and they did not want to come. It seems that one of these priests was a very important personage among them, who had charge of or command over all the Cues in the City, and was a sort of Bishop among the priests and was held in great respect. He replied that they, who were priests, had no fear of us, and if the chief and chieftain did not wish to come, he would go himself and summon them, and that if he spoke to them he believed they would do as he told them and would come.

Cortés at once told him to go, and that his companion should await his return. So the priests departed and summoned the chief and chieftains who returned in his com-

---

*Leaders or chiefs.

†Jade ornaments.

pany to Cortés' quarters. Cortés asked them, through our interpreters, what it was they were afraid of, and why they had not given us anything to eat, and said that if our presence in their city were an annoyance to them, we wished to leave the next day for Mexico to see and speak to the Lord Mocteuzma, and he asked them to provide carriers for the transport of the baggage and *tepusques* (which are the cannon) and to send us some food at once.

The chief was so embarrassed that he could hardly speak; he said that they would look for the food, but their Lord Mocteuzma had sent to tell them not to give us any, and was not willing that we should proceed any further.

While this conversation was taking place, three of our friends, the Cempoala Indians,* came in and said secretly to Cortés, that close by where we were quartered they had found holes dug in the streets, covered over with wood and earth, so that without careful examination one could not see them, that they had removed the earth from above one of the holes and found it full of sharp pointed stakes to kill the horses when they galloped, and that the *Azoteas*† had breastworks of adobes and were piled up with stones, and certainly this was not done with good intent for they also found barricades of thick timbers in another street. At this moment eight Tlaxcalans arrived, from the Indians whom we had left outside in the fields with orders that they were not to enter Cholula, and they said to Cortés, "Take heed, Malinche;‡ for this City is ill disposed, and we know that this night they have sacrificed to their Idol, which is the God of War, seven persons, five of them children, so that the God may give them victory over you, and we have further seen that they are moving all their baggage and women and children out of the city." When Cortés heard this, he immediately sent these Tlaxcalans back to their Captains, with orders to be fully prepared if we should send to summon them, and he turned to speak to the *Cacique,* priests and chieftains of Cholula and told them to have no fear and show no alarm, but to remember the obedience which they had promised to him, and not to swerve from it, lest he should have to chastise them. That he had already told them that we wished to set out on the morrow and that he had need of two thousand warriors from the city to accompany us, just as the Tlaxcalans had provided them, for they were necessary on the road. They replied that the men would be given, and asked leave to go at once to get them ready, and they went away very well contented, for they thought that between the warriors with whom they were to supply us, and the regiments sent by Mocteuzma, which were hidden in the rocky thickets and *barrancas* [canyons] we could not escape death or capture, for the horses would not be able to charge on account of certain breastworks and barricades which they immediately advised the troops to construct, so that only a narrow lane would be left through which it would be impossible for us to pass. They warned the Mexicans to be in readiness as we intended to

---

*The Cempoala were a coastal people held in tributary status by the Aztecs, and they were the first people Cortés's forces overcame and won as allies.

†A rooftop garden.

‡The name that the Aztecs applied to Cortés. The exact meaning of the name is open to debate. Bernal Díaz said that because Doña Marina was always with Cortés, he was called "Malinche,"which Díaz translated as "Marina's Captain." Others have defined "Malinche" as "Captain," and have interpreted "La Malinche" (or Doña Marina) as "the captain's woman."

start on the next day and told them that they were going to give us two thousand war-riors to accompany us, so that as we marched along, off our guard, between the two forces our capture would be sure and they would be able to bind us, and this they might look on as a certainty, for they [the Cholulans] had made sacrifices to their War Idols who had promised them victory.

Let us cease speaking of this which they looked on as a sure thing and return to our Captain who, as he wished to be more thoroughly informed about the plot and all that was happening, told Doña Marina to take more *chalchihuites* to the two priests who had been the first to speak, for they were not afraid, and to tell them with friendly words that Malinche [Cortés] wished them to come back and speak to him, and to bring them back with her. Doña Marina went and spoke to the priests in the manner she knew so well how to use, and thanks to the presents they at once accompanied her. Cortés addressed them and asked them to say truly what they knew, for they were the priests of Idols and chieftains and ought not to lie, and that what they should say would not be disclosed in any manner, for we were going to leave the next morning, and he would give them a large quantity of cloth. They said the truth was that their Lord Mocteuzma knew that we were coming to their city, and that every day he was of many minds and could not come to any decision on the matter, that sometimes he sent to order them to pay us much respect when we arrived and to guide us on the way to his city, and at other times he would send word that it was not his wish that we should go to Mexico, and now recently his [gods] Tezcatlipoca* and Huitzi-lopochtli, to whom he paid great devotion, had counseled him that we should either be killed here in Cholula or should be sent, bound, to Mexico. That the day before he had sent out twenty thousand warriors, and half of them were already within this city and the other half were stationed nearby in some gullies, and that they already knew that we were about to start tomorrow; they also told us about the barricades which they had ordered to be made and the two thousand warriors that were to be given to us, and how it had already been agreed that twenty of us were to be kept to be sacri-ficed to the Idols of Cholula.

Cortés ordered these men to be given a present of richly embroidered cloth, and told them not to say anything [about the information they had given us] for, if they disclosed it, on our return from Mexico we would kill them. He also told them that we should start early the next morning and he asked them to summon all the *Caciques* to come then so that he might speak to them.

That night Cortés took counsel of us as to what should be done, for he had very able men with him whose advice was worth having, but as in such cases frequently happens, some said that it would be advisable to change our course and go by Huex-otzingo, others that we must manage to preserve the peace by every possible means and that it would be better to return to Tlaxcala, others of us gave our opinion that if we allowed such treachery to pass unpunished, wherever we went we should be treated to worse [treachery], and that being there in the town, with ample provisions, we ought to make an attack, for the Indians would feel the effect of it more in their own homes than they would in the open, and that we should at once warn the Tlax-

---

*One of the Aztecs most powerful gods, associated with the sun and rebirth. Literally translated it means "Smoking Mirror."

calans so that they might join in it. All thought well of this last advice. As Cortés had already told them that we were going to set out on the following day, for this reason we should make a show of tying together our baggage, which was little enough, and then in the large courts with high walls, where we were lodged, we should fall on the Indian warriors, who well deserved their fate. As regards the Ambassadors of Mocteuzma, we should dissemble and tell them that the evil-minded Cholulans had intended treachery and had attempted to put the blame for it on their Lord Mocteuzma, and on themselves as his Ambassadors, but we did not believe Mocteuzma had given any such orders, and we begged them to stay in their apartments and not have any further converse with the people of the city, so that we should not have reason to think they were in league with them in their treachery, and we asked them to go with us as our guides to Mexico.

They replied that neither they themselves nor their Lord Mocteuzma knew anything about that which we were telling them. Although they did not like it, we placed guards over the Ambassadors, so that they could not go out without our permission, and Mocteuzma should not come to know that we were well aware how it was he who had ordered it to be done.

All that night we were on the alert and under arms with the horses saddled and bridled, and with many sentinels and patrols, although indeed it was always our custom to keep a good watch, for we thought that for certain all the companies of the Mexicans as well as the Cholulans would attack us during the night.

There was an old Indian woman, the wife of a *Cacique*, who knew all about the plot and trap which had been arranged, and she had come secretly to Doña Marina our interpreter, having noticed that she was young and good looking and rich, and advised her, if she wanted to escape with her life, to come with her to her house, for it was certain that on that night or during the next day we were going to be killed, for the Great Mocteuzma had so arranged, and commanded that the Mexicans and the people of the city were to join forces, and not one of us was to be left alive, except those who would be carried bound to Mexico. Because she knew of this, and on account of the compassion she felt for Doña Marina, she had come to tell her that she had better get all her possessions together and come with her to her house, and she would there marry her to her son, the brother of a youth who was with another old woman who accompanied her.

When Doña Marina understood this (as she was always very shrewd) she said to her, "O mother, thank you much for this that you have told me, I would go with you at once but that I have no one here whom I can trust to carry my clothes and jewels of gold of which I have many, for goodness sake, mother, wait here a little while, you and your son, and tonight we will set out, for now, as you can see, the *Teules* [gods] are on the watch and will hear us."

The old woman believed what she said, and remained chatting with her, and Doña Marina asked her how they were going to kill us all, and how and when and where the plot was made. The old woman told her neither more nor less than what the two priests had already stated, and Doña Marina replied, "If this affair is such a secret, how is it that you came to know about it?" and the old woman replied that her husband had told her, for he was a captain of one of the parties in the city, and as captain he was now away with his warriors giving orders for them to join the squadrons of Mocteuzma in the *barrancas,* and she thought that they were already assembled waiting for us to set out, and that they would kill us there; as to the plot she had known about it for three days, for a gilded drum had been sent to her husband from Mexico, and rich cloaks and jewels of gold had been sent to three other captains to induce them to bring us bound to their Lord Mocteuzma.

When Doña Marina heard this she deceived the old woman and said, "How delighted I am to hear that your son to whom you wish to marry me is a man of distinction. We have already talked a good deal, and I do not want them to notice us, so Mother you wait here while I begin to bring my property, for I cannot bring it all at once, and you and your son, my brother, will take care of it, and then we shall be able to go." The old woman believed all that was told her, and she and her son sat down to rest. Then Doña Marina went swiftly to the Captain and told him all that had passed with the Indian woman. Cortés at once ordered her to be brought before him, and questioned her about these treasons and plots, and she told him neither more nor less than the priests had already said, so he placed a guard over the woman so that she could not escape.

When dawn broke, it was a sight to see the haste with which the *Caciques* and priests brought in the warriors, laughing and contented as though they had already caught us in their traps and nets, and they brought more Indian warriors than we had asked for, and large as they are (for they still stand as a memorial of the past) the courtyards would not hold them all.

Early as it was when the Cholulans arrived with the warriors, we were already quite prepared for what had to be done. The soldiers with swords and shields were stationed at the gate of the great court so as not to let a single armed Indian pass out. Our Captain was mounted on horseback with many soldiers round him, as a guard, and when he saw how very early the *Caciques* and priests and warriors had arrived, he said, "How these traitors long to see us among the *barrancas* so as to gorge on our flesh, but Our Lord will do better for us." Then he asked for the two priests who had let out the secret, and they told him that they were at the gate of the courtyard with the other *Caciques* who wished to come in, and he sent our interpreter, Aguilar, to tell them to go to their houses, for he had no need of their presence now. This was in order that, as they had done us a good turn, they should not suffer for it, and should not get killed. Cortés was on horseback and Doña Marina near to him, and he asked the *Caciques,* why was it, as we had done them no harm whatever, that they had wished to kill us on the previous night? and why should they turn traitors against us, when all we had said or done was to warn them against certain things of which we had already warned all the towns that we had passed through, namely, that they should not be wicked and sacrifice human beings, nor worship Idols, nor eat the flesh of their neighbors, nor commit unnatural crimes, but that they should live good lives; and to tell them about matters concerning our holy faith, and this without compulsion of any kind. To what purpose then had they quite recently prepared many long and strong poles with collars and cords and placed them in a house near to the Great Temple, and why for the last three days had they been building barricades and digging holes in the streets and raising breastworks on the roofs of the houses, and why had they removed their children and wives and property from the city? Their ill will however had been plainly shown, and they had not been able to hide their treason. They had not even given us food to eat, and as a mockery had brought us firewood and water, and said that there was no maize. He knew well that in the *barrancas* nearby, there were many companies of warriors and many other men ready for war who had joined the companies that night, laying in wait for us, ready to carry out their treacherous plans, thinking that we should pass along that road towards Mexico. So in return for our having come to treat them like brothers and to tell them what Our Lord God and the King have ordained, they wished to kill us and eat our flesh, and had already prepared the pots with salt and peppers and tomatoes. If this was what they wanted it would have been better for them to make war on us in the open field like good and valiant warriors, as did their neighbors the Tlaxcalans. He knew for certain all that had been planned in the city and that they had even promised to their Idol, the patron of warfare, that twenty of us should be sacrificed before it, and that three nights ago they had sacrificed seven Indians to it so as to ensure victory, which was promised them; but as the Idol was both evil and false, it neither had, nor would have power against us, and all these evil and traitorous designs which they had planned and put into effect were about to recoil on themselves. Doña Marina told all this to them and made them understand it very clearly, and when the priests, *Caciques,* and captains had heard it, they said that what had been stated was true but that they were not to blame for it, for the Ambassadors of Mocteuzma had ordered it at the command of their Prince.

Then Cortés told them that the royal laws decreed that such treasons as those should not remain unpunished and that for their crime they must die. Then he ordered a musket to be fired, which was the signal that we had agreed upon for that purpose, and a blow was given to them which they will remember for ever, for we killed many of them, so that they gained nothing from the promises of their false Idols.

Not two hours had passed before our allies, the Tlaxcalans, arrived, whom I have already said we had left out in the fields, and they had fought very fiercely in the streets where the Cholulans had posted other companies to defend the streets and prevent their being entered, but these were soon defeated. They [the Tlaxcalans] went about the city, plundering and making prisoners and we could not stop them, and the next day more companies from the Tlaxcalan towns arrived, and did great damage, for they were very hostile to the people of Cholula, and when we saw this, both Cortés and the captains and the soldiers, on account of the compassion that we had felt for them, restrained the Tlaxcalans from doing further damage, and Cortés ordered Cristobal de Olid to bring him all the Tlaxcalan captains together so that he could speak to them, and they did not delay in coming; then he ordered them to gather together all their men and go and camp in the fields and this they did, and only the men from Cempoala remained with us.

Just then certain *Caciques* and priests of Cholula who belonged to other districts of the town, and said that they were not concerned in the treasons against us (for it is a large city and they have parties and factions among themselves), asked Cortés and all of us to pardon the provocation of the treachery that had been plotted against us for the traitors had already paid with their lives. Then there came the two priests who were our friends and had disclosed the secret to us, and the old woman, the wife of the captain, who wanted to be the mother-in-law of Doña Marina, as I have already related, and all prayed Cortés for pardon.

When they spoke to him, Cortés made a show of great anger and ordered the Ambassadors of Mocteuzma, who were detained in our company, to be summoned. He then said that the whole city deserved to be destroyed, but that out of respect for their Lord Mocteuzma, whose vassals they were, he would pardon them, and that from now on they must be well behaved, and let them beware of such affairs as the last happening again, lest they should die for it.

Then, he ordered the Chiefs of Tlaxcala, who were in the fields, to be summoned, and told them to return the men and women whom they had taken prisoners, for the damage they had done was sufficient. Giving up the prisoners went against the grain with them [the Tlaxcalans], and they said that the Cholulans had deserved far greater punishment for the many treacheries they had constantly received at their hands. Nevertheless as Cortés ordered it, they gave back many persons, but they still remained rich, both in gold and mantles, cotton cloth, salt and slaves. Besides this Cortés made them and the people of Cholula friends, and, from what I have since seen and ascertained, that friendship has never been broken.

Furthermore Cortés ordered all the priests and *Caciques* to bring back the people to the city, and to hold their markets and fairs, and not to have any fear, for no harm would be done to them. They replied that within five days the city would be fully peopled again, for at that time nearly all the inhabitants were in hiding. They said it was necessary that Cortés should appoint a *Cacique* for them, for their ruler was one of those who had died in the Court, so he asked them to whom the office ought to go, and they said to the brother [of the late *Cacique*] so Cortés at once appointed him to be Governor, until he should receive other orders.

In addition to this, as soon as he saw the city was reinhabited, and their markets were carried on in safety, he ordered all the priests, captains and other chieftains of that city to assemble, and explained to them, very clearly the matters concerning our holy faith, and told them that they must cease worshiping idols, and must no longer sacrifice human beings or eat their flesh, nor rob one another, nor commit the offences which they were accustomed to commit, and that they could see how their Idols had deceived them, and were evil things not speaking the truth; let them remember the lies which they told only five days ago when seven persons had been sacrificed to them and they promised to give them victory, therefore all [that] they tell to the priests and to them is altogether evil, he begged them to destroy the Idols and break them in pieces. That if they did not wish to do it themselves we would do it for them. He also ordered them to whitewash a temple, so that we might set up a cross there.

They immediately did what we asked them in the matter of the cross, and they said that they would remove their Idols, but although they were many times ordered to do it, they delayed. Then the Padre de la Merced said to Cortés that it was going too far, in the beginning, to take away their Idols until they should understand things better, and should see how our expedition to Mexico would turn out and time would show us what we ought to do in the matter, that for the present the warnings we had given them were sufficient, together with the setting up of the Cross.

[The Entry into Tenochtitlan, Description of the City and the Seizure of Mocteuzma]

The next day, in the morning, we arrived at a broad causeway,* and continued our march towards Iztapalapa, and when we saw so many cities and villages built in the water and other great towns on dry land and that straight and level causeway going towards Mexico, we were amazed and said that it was like the enchantments they tell of in the legend of Amadis,† on account of the great towers and cues and buildings rising from the water, and all built of masonry. And some of our soldiers even asked whether the things that we saw were not a dream? . . . And then when we entered that city of Iztapalapa, the appearance of the palaces in which they lodged us! How spacious and well built they were, of beautiful stone work and cedar wood, and the wood of other sweet scented trees, with great rooms and courts, wonderful to behold, covered with awnings of cotton cloth.

When we had looked well at all of this, we went to the orchard and garden, which was such a wonderful thing to see and walk in, that I was never tired of look-ing at the diversity of the trees, and noting the scent which each one had, and the paths full of roses, and the pond of fresh water. There was another thing to observe, that great canoes were able to pass into the garden from the lake through an opening that had been made so that there was no need for their occupants to land. And all was cemented and very splendid with many kinds of stone [monuments] with pic-tures on them, which gave much to think about. Then the birds of many kinds and breeds which came into the pond. I say again that I stood looking at it and thought that never in the world would there be discovered other lands such as these. . . . [Of all these wonders that I then beheld] today all is overthrown and lost, nothing left standing.

Early next day we . . . proceeded along the causeway which is here eight paces in width and runs so straight to the City of Mexico that it does not seem to turn either much or little, but, broad as it is, it was so crowded with people that . . . we were hardly able to pass . . . and the towers and cues were full of people as well as the canoes from all parts of the lake. It was not to be wondered at, for they had never before seen horses or men such as we are.

Gazing on such wonderful sights, we did not know what to say, or whether what appeared before us was real, for on one side on the land there were great cities, and in the lake ever so many more, and the lake itself was crowded with canoes, and in the causeway were many bridges at intervals and in front of us stood the great City of Mexico, and we, —we did not even number four hundred soldiers! . . .

The Great Mocteuzma who was approaching in a rich litter . . . got down from his litter and those great *Caciques* supported him with their arms beneath a mar-velously rich canopy of green colored feathers with much gold and silver embroidery and with pearls and *chalchihuites*, . . . which was wonderful to look at. . . . [T]here were many other Lords who walked before the Great Mocteuzma, sweeping the

---

*The Causeway of Cuitlahuac separating the lake of Chalco from the lake of Xochimilco.

†Amadis was a legendary knight in well-known Iberian tales. Cervantes parodies him in his famous work *Don Quixote.*

ground where he would tread. . . . Not one of these chieftains dared even to think of looking him in the face, but kept their eyes lowered with great reverence. . . .

The Great Mocteuzma was about forty years old, of good height and well proportioned, slender, and spare of flesh, not very swarthy, but of the natural color and shade of an Indian. He did not wear his hair long, . . . his scanty black beard was well shaped and thin. His face was somewhat long, but cheerful, and he had good eyes and showed in his appearance and manner both tenderness and, when necessary, gravity. He was very neat and clean and bathed once every day in the afternoon. When Cortés was told that the Great Mocteuzma was approaching, . . . he dismounted and simultaneously they paid great reverence to one another. Cortés thanked Mocteuzma through our interpreters, and Mocteuzma replied—"Malinche, you and your brethren are in your own house, rest awhile," and then he went to his palaces . . . not far away, and we divided our lodgings by companies, and placed the artillery pointing in a convenient direction, and the order which we had to keep was clearly explained to us, and that we were to be much on the alert, both the cavalry and all of us soldiers. A sumptuous dinner was provided for us according to their use and custom, and we ate it at once. So this was our lucky and daring entry into the great city of Tenochtitlan Mexico on the 8th day of November the year of our Savior Jesus Christ 1519.

The next day Cortés decided to go to Mocteuzma's palace, . . . Cortés and he paid the greatest reverence to each other and then they took one another by the hand and Mocteuzma made him sit down on his couch on his right hand, and he also bade all of us to be seated. . . .

Then Cortés began to make an explanation through Doña Marina . . . (Doña Marina was a person of the greatest importance and was obeyed without question by the Indians throughout New Spain. . . . Doña Marina knew the language common to Mexico . . . without the help of Doña Marina we could not have understood the language of New Spain and Mexico. As Doña Marina proved herself such an excellent woman and good interpreter throughout the wars in New Spain, Cortés always took her with him.)* [Cortes] said . . . That in coming to see and converse with such a great Prince as he was, we had completed the journey and fulfilled the command which our great King and Prince had laid on us. But what he chiefly came to say on behalf of our Lord God had already been brought to his [Mocteuzma's] knowledge . . . that we were Christians and worshiped one true and only God, named Jesus Christ, who suffered death and passion to save us, and we told them that a cross . . . was a sign of the other Cross on which our Lord God was crucified for our salvation, and that the death and passion . . . was for the salvation of the whole human race, which was lost, and that this our God rose on the third day and is now in heaven, and it is He who made the heavens and earth, the sea and the sands, and created all the things there are in the world, and . . . nothing happens in the world without His holy will. That we believe in Him and worship Him, but that those whom they look upon as gods are not so, but are devils . . . and if their looks are bad their deeds are worse, and they could see that they were evil and of little worth, for where we had set up crosses . . .

---

*The excerpt in parentheses is inserted here from Bernal Díaz del Castillo, *The True History of the Conquest of New Spain, Vol. 1*, Hakluyt Society, Second Series, XXIII (London: Hakluyt Society, 1908), 132–35.

they dared not appear . . . through fear. . . .

The favor he now begged of him was his attention to the words . . . then he explained to him very clearly about the creation of the world, and how we are all brothers, sons of one father and one mother who were called Adam and Eve, and how such a brother as our great Emperor, grieving for the perdition of so many souls, such as those that their idols were leading to Hell, where they burn in living flames, had sent us, so that after what he [Mocteuzma] had now heard he would put a stop to it and they would no longer adore these Idols or sacrifice Indian men and women to them, for we were all brethren, nor should they commit sodomy or thefts. He also told them that, in course of time, our Lord and King would send some men who among us lead very holy lives, much better than we do, who will explain to them all about it, for at present we merely came to give them due warning, and so he prayed him to do what he was asked and carry it into effect. . . .

Mocteuzma replied, Senor Malinche, I have understood your words and arguments very well before now, from what you said to my servants at the sand dunes, this about three Gods and the Cross, and all those things that you have preached in the towns through which you have come. We have not made any answer to it because here throughout all time we have worshiped our own gods, and thought they were good, as no doubt yours are, so do not trouble to speak to us any more about them at present. Regarding the creation of the world, we have held the same belief for ages past, and for this reason we take it for certain that you are those whom our ancestors predicted would come from the direction of the sunrise. As for your great King, I feel that I am indebted to him, and I will give him of what I possess. . . .

While this conversation was going on Mocteuzma secretly sent a great *Cacique,* one of his nephews who was in his company, to order his stewards to bring certain pieces of gold, which it seems must have been put apart to give to Cortés, and ten loads of fine cloth, which he apportioned, the gold and mantels between Cortés and the four captains, and to each of us soldiers he gave two gold necklaces, each necklace being worth ten pesos, and two loads of mantles. The gold that he then gave us was worth in all more than a thousand pesos and he gave it all cheerfully and with the air of a great and valiant prince. As it was now past midday, so as not to appear importunate, Cortés said to him, "Senor Mocteuzma, you always have the habit of heaping load upon load in every day conferring favors on us, and it is already your dinner time." Mocteuzma replied that he thanked us for coming to see him, and then we took our leave with the greatest courtesy and we went to our lodgings.

And as we went along we spoke of the good manners and breeding which he showed in everything, and that we should show him in all ways the greatest respect, doffing our quilted caps when we passed before him, and this we always did, but let us leave this subject here, and pass on.

As we had already been four days in Mexico [City] and neither the Captain nor any of us had left our lodgings . . . , Cortés said to us that it would be well to go to the great Plaza and see the great Temple of Huitzilopochtli,* and that he wished to consult the Great Mocteuzma. . . . When we arrived at the great market place, called

---

*The Aztec god of war and their main deity.

Tlaltelolco, we were astounded at the number of people and the quantity of merchandise that it contained, and at the good order and control that was maintained, for we had never seen such a thing before. The chieftains who accompanied us acted as guides. Each kind of merchandise was kept by itself and its fixed place marked out . . . the dealers in gold, silver, and precious stones . . . , and embroidered goods. Then there were other wares consisting of Indian slaves both men and women: and I say that they bring as many of them to that great market for sale as the Portuguese bring negroes from Guinea; and they brought them along tied to long poles, with collars round their necks so that they could not escape, and others they left free. Next there were other traders who sold great pieces of cloth and cotton, and articles of twisted thread, and there were *cacahuateros* who sold cacao. In this way one could see every sort of merchandise that is to be found in the whole of New Spain, placed in arrangement in the same manner as they do in my own country . . . where they hold the fairs, where each line of booths has its particular kind of merchandise. . . . There were those who sold cloths . . . and ropes and the *cotaras** . . . and sweet cooked roots, and other tubers. . . . In another part of the market there were skins of tigers and lions, of otters and jackals, deer and other animals and badgers and mountain cats, and other classes of merchandise. . . .

[There were] those who sold beans and sage and other vegetables and herbs in another part, and those who sold fowls, cocks . . . rabbits, hares, deer, mallards, young dogs and other things of that sort in their part of the market, and . . . the fruiterers, and the women who sold cooked food . . . then every sort of pottery made in a thousand different forms from great water jars to little jugs, . . . then those who sold honey and honey paste and other dainties like nut paste, and those who sold lumber, boards, cradles, beams, blocks and benches . . . and the venders of *ocote*† . . . I must furthermore mention, asking your pardon, that they also sold many canoes full of human excrement, and these were kept in the creeks near the market, and this they use to make salt or for tanning skins, for without it they say that they cannot be well prepared. I know well that some gentlemen may laugh at this, but I say that it is so, and I may add that on all the roads it is a usual thing to have places made of reeds or straw or grass, so that they may be screened from the passers by, into these they retire when they wish to purge their bowels so that even that filth should not be lost. . . .

Now let us leave the great market place, and not look at it again, and arrive at the great courts and walls where the great Cue stands. Before reaching the great Cue there is a great enclosure of courts, it seems to me larger than the plaza of Salamanca, with two walls of masonry surrounding it and the court itself all paved with very smooth great white flagstones. And where there were not these stones it was cemented and burnished and all very clean, so that one could not find any dust or a straw in the whole place.

When we arrived near the great Cue and before we had ascended a single step of it, the Great Mocteuzma sent down from above, where he was making his sacrifices, six priests and two chieftains to accompany our Captain. On ascending the steps, which are one hundred and fourteen in number, they attempted to take him by the

---

*Sandals.

†Pine pitch for torches.

arms so as to help him ascend, (thinking that he would get tired) as they were accustomed to assist their lord Mocteuzma, but Cortés would not allow them to come near him. When we got to the top where there was a space like a platform and some large stones placed on it, on which they put the poor Indians for sacrifice, there was a bulky image like a dragon and other evil figures and much blood shed that very day.

When we arrived there Mocteuzma came out of an oratory where his cursed idols were, at the summit of the great Cue, and two priests came with him, and after paying great reverence to Cortés and to all of us he said, "You must be tired, Senor Malinche, from ascending this our great Cue," and Cortés replied through our interpreters who were with us that he and his companions were never tired by anything. Then Mocteuzma took him by the hand and told him to look at his great city and all the other cities that were standing in the water, and the many other towns on the land round the lake, and that if he had not seen the great market place well, that from where they were they could see it better.

So we stood looking about us, for that huge and cursed temple stood so high that from it one could see over everything very well, and we saw that the three causeways which led into Mexico, that is the causeway of Iztapalapa by which we had entered four days before, and that of Tacuba, along which later on we fled on the night of our great defeat, when Cuitlahuac the new prince drove us out of the city, as I shall tell later on, and that of Tepeaquilla, and we saw the fresh water that comes from Chapultepec which supplies the city, and we saw the bridges on the three causeways which were built at certain distances apart through which the water of the lake flowed in and out from one side to the other, and we beheld on that great lake a great multitude of canoes, some coming with supplies of food and others returning loaded with cargoes of merchandise; and we saw that from every house of that great city and of all the other cities that were built in the water it was impossible to pass from house to house, except by drawbridges which were made of wood or in canoes; and we saw in those cities Cues and oratories like towers and fortresses and all gleaming white, and it was a wonderful thing to behold; then the houses with flat roofs and on the causeways other small towers and oratories which were like fortresses.

After having examined and considered all that we had seen we turned to look at the great market place and the crowds of people that were in it, some buying and others selling, so that the murmur and hum of their voices and words that they used could be heard more than a league off. Some of the soldiers among us who had been in many parts of the world, in Constantinople, and all over Italy, and in Rome, said that so large a market place and so full of people, and so well regulated and arranged, they had never beheld before.

Let us leave this and return to our Captain, who said to Fray Bartolomé de Olmedo, who has often been mentioned by me, and who happened to be nearby him: "It seems to me, Senor Padre, that it would be a good thing to throw out a feeler to Mocteuzma, as to whether he would allow us to build our church here"; and the Padre replied that it would be a good thing if it were successful, but it seemed to him that it was not quite a suitable time to speak about it, for Mocteuzma did not appear to be inclined to do such a thing.

Then our Cortés said to Mocteuzma through the interpreter Doña Marina, "Your Highness is indeed a very great prince and worthy of even greater things. We are rejoiced to see your cities, and as we are here in your temple, what I now beg as a favor is that you will show us your gods and idols." Mocteuzma replied that he must first speak with his high priests, and when he had spoken to them he said that we might enter into a small tower and apartment, a sort of hall, where there were two altars, with very richly carved boardings on the top of the roof. On each altar were two figures, like giants with very tall bodies and very fat, and the first which stood on the right hand they said was the figure of Huitzilopochtli their god of War; it had a very broad face and monstrous and terrible eyes, and whole of his body was covered with precious stones, and gold and pearls, and with seed pearls stuck on with a paste that they make in this country out of a sort of root, and all the body and head was covered with it, and the body was girdled by great snakes made of gold and precious stones, and in one hand he held a bow and in the other some arrows. And another small idol that stood by him, they said was his page, and he held a short lance and a shield richly decorated with gold and stones. Huitzilopochtli had round his neck some Indians' faces and other things like hearts of Indians, the former made of gold and the latter of silver, with many precious blue stones.

There were some braziers with incense which they call copal, and in them they were burning the hearts of the three Indians whom they had sacrificed that day, and they had made the sacrifice with smoke and copal. All the walls of the oratory were so splashed and encrusted with blood that they were black, the floor was the same and the whole place stank vilely. Then we saw on the other side on the left hand there stood the other great image the same height as Huitzilopochtli, and it had a face like a bear and eyes that shone, made of their mirrors which they call *Tezcat,* and the body plastered with precious stones like that of Huitzilopochtli, for they say that the two are brothers; and this Tezcatepuca* was the god of Hell and had charge of the souls of the Mexicans, and his body was girt with figures like little devils with snakes' tails. The walls were so clotted with blood and the soil so bathed with it that in the slaughter houses of Spain there is not such another stench.

They had offered to this Idol five hearts from that day's sacrifices. In the highest part of the Cue there was a recess of which the woodwork was very richly worked, and in it was another image half man and half lizard, with precious stones all over it, and half the body was covered with a mantle. They say that the body of this figure is full of all the seeds that there are in the world, and they say that it is the god of seed time and harvest, but I do not remember its name, and everything was covered with blood, both walls and altar, and the stench was such that we could hardly wait the moment to get out of it.

They had an exceedingly large drum there, and when they beat it the sound of it was so dismal and like, so to say, an instrument of infernal regions, that one could hear it a distance of two leagues, and they said that the skins it was covered with were those of great snakes. In that small place there were many diabolical things to be seen, bugles and trumpets and knives, and many hearts of Indians that they had

---

*Tezcatlipoca—"the Giver of Life."

burned in fumigating their idols, and everything was so clotted with blood, and there was so much of it, that I curse the whole of it, and as it stank like a slaughter house we hastened to clear out of such a bad stench and worse sight. Our Captain said to Mocteuzma through our interpreter, half laughing, "Senor Mocteuzma, I do not understand how such a great Prince and wise man as you are has not come to the conclusion, in your mind, that these idols of yours are not gods, but evil things that are called devils, and so that you may know it and all your priests may see it clearly, do me the favor to approve of my placing a cross here on the top of this tower, and that in one part of these oratories where your Huitzilopochtli and Tezcatepuca stand we may divide off a space where we can set up an image of Our Lady (an image which Mocteuzma had already seen) and you will see by the fear in which these Idols hold it that they are deceiving you."

Mocteuzma replied half angrily, (and the two priests who were with him showed great annoyance,) and said: "Senor Malinche, if I had known that you would have said such defamatory things I would not have shown you my gods, we consider them to be very good, for they give us health and rains and good seed times and seasons and as many victories as we desire, and we are obliged to worship them and make sacrifices, and I pray you not to say another word to their dishonor."

When our Captain heard that and noted the angry looks he did not refer again to the subject, but said with a cheerful manner: "It is time for your Excellency and for us to return," and Mocteuzma replied that it was well, but that he had to pray and offer certain sacrifices on account of the great *tatacul,* that is to say sin, which he had committed in allowing us to ascend his great Cue, and being the cause of our being permitted to see his gods, and of our dishonoring them by speaking evil of them, so that before he left he must pray and worship. Then Cortés said "I ask your pardon if it be so," and then we went down the steps. . . .

When we were all assembled in those chambers, as it was our habit to inquire into and want to know everything, while we were looking for the best and most convenient site to place the altar, two of our soldiers, one of whom was a carpenter, named Alonzo Yañes, noticed on one of the walls marks showing that there had been a door there, and that it had been closed up and carefully plastered over and burnished. Now as there was a rumor and we had heard the story that Mocteuzma kept the treasure of his father Axayacatl in that building, it was suspected that it might be in this chamber which had been closed up and cemented only a few days before. Yañes spoke about it to Juan Velásquez de Leon and Francisco de Lugo, who were Captains and relations of mine, and Alonzo Yañes had attached himself to their company as a servant, and those Captains told the story to Cortés, and the door was secretly opened. When it was open and Cortés and some of his Captains went in first, and they saw such a number of jewels and slabs and plates of gold and *chalchihuites* and other great riches, that they were quite carried away and did not know what to say about such wealth. The news soon spread among all the other Captains and soldiers, and very secretly we went in to see it. When I saw it I marveled, and as at that time I was a youth and had never seen such riches in my life before, I took it for certain that there could not be another such store of wealth in the whole world. It was decided by all our captains and soldiers, that we should not dream of touching a particle of it, but that the stones should immediately be put back in the doorway and it should be sealed up and cemented just as we found it, and that it should not be spoken about, lest it should reach Mocteuzma's ears, until times should alter.

Let us leave this about the riches, and say that as we had such valiant captains and soldiers of good counsel and judgement, (and first of all we all believed for certain that our Lord Jesus Christ held his Divine hand over all our affairs,) four of our captains took Cortés aside in the church, with a dozen soldiers in whom he trusted and confided, and I was one of them, and we asked him to look at the net and trap in which we found ourselves, and to consider the great strength of that city, and observe the causeways and bridges, and to think over the words of warning that we had been given in all the towns we had passed through, that Mocteuzma had been advised by his Huitzilopochtli to allow us to enter into the city, and when we were there, to kill us. That he [Cortés] should remember that the hearts of men are very changeable, especially those of Indians, and he should not repose trust in the good will and affection that Mocteuzma was showing us, for at some time or other, when the wish occurred to him, he would order us to be attacked, and by the stoppage of our supplies of food or of water, or by the raising of any of the bridges, we should be rendered helpless. Then, considering the great multitude of Indian warriors that Mocteuzma had as his guard, what should we be able to do either in offence or defense? and as all the houses were built in the water, how could our friends the Tlaxcalans enter and come to our aid? He should think over all this that we had said, and if we wished to safeguard our lives, that we should at once, without further delay, seize Mocteuzma and should not wait until the next day to do it. He should also remember that the gold that Mocteuzma had given us and all that we had seen in the treasury of his father Axayaca, and all the food which we ate, all would be turned to arsenic poison in our bodies, for we could neither sleep by night nor day nor rest ourselves while these thoughts were in our minds, and that if any of our soldiers should give him other advice short of this, they would be senseless beasts who were dazed by the gold, incapable of looking death in the face.

When Cortés heard this he replied, "Don't you imagine, gentlemen, that I am asleep, or that I am free from the same anxiety, you must have felt that it is so with me; but what possibility is there of our doing a deed of such great daring as to seize such a great prince in his own palace, surrounded as he is by his own guards and warriors, by what scheme or artifice can we carry it out, so that he should not call on his warriors to attack us at once?" Our Captains replied, (that is Juan Velásquez de Leon and Diego de Ordás, Gonzalo de Sandoval and Pedro de Alvarado,) that with smooth speeches he should be got out of his halls and brought to our quarters, and should be told that he must remain a prisoner, and if he made a disturbance or cried out, that he would pay for it with his life; that if Cortés did not want to do this at once, he should give them permission to do it, as they were ready for the work, for, between the two great dangers in which we found ourselves, it was better and more to the purpose to seize Mocteuzma than to wait until he attacked us; for if he began the attack, what chance should we have? Some of us soldiers also told Cortés that it seemed to us that Mocteuzma's stewards, who were employed in providing us with food, were insolent and did not bring it courteously as during the first days. Also two of our Allies [from] the Tlaxcalan Indians said secretly to Jerónimo de Aguillar, our interpreter, that the Mexicans had not appeared to be well disposed towards us during the last two days. So we stayed a good hour discussing the question of whether or not we should take Mocteuzma prisoner, and how it was to be done, and to our Captain this last advice seemed opportune, that in any case we should take him prisoner, and we left it until the next day. All that night we were praying to God that our plan might tend to His Holy service.

The next morning after these consultations, there arrived, very secretly, two Tlaxcalan Indians with letters from Villa Rica and what they contained was the news that Juan do Escalante, who had remained there as Chief Alguacil, and six of our soldiers had been killed in a battle against the Mexicans, that his horse had also been slain, and many Totonacs who were in his company. Moreover, all the towns of the Sierra and Cempoala and its subject towns were in revolt, and refused to bring food or serve in the fort. They [the Spaniards] did not know what to do, for as formerly they had been taken to be Teules, that now after this disaster, both the Totonacs and Mexicans were like wild animals, and they could hold them to nothing, and did not know what steps to take.

When we heard this news, God knows what sorrow affected us all, for this was the first disaster we had suffered in New Spain. The interested reader may see how evil fortune came rolling on us. No one who had seen us enter into that city with such a solemn and triumphant reception, and had seen us in possession of riches which Mocteuzma gave every day both to our Captain and to us, and had seen the house that I have described full of gold, and how the people took us for *Teules,* that is for Idols, and that we were conquerors in all our battles, would have thought that now such a great disaster could have befallen us, namely that they no longer attributed to us our former repute, but looked upon us as men liable to be conquered, and that we should have to feel their growing insolence towards us.

As the upshot of much argument it was agreed that, by one means or another, we should seize Mocteuzma that very day, or we would all die in the attempt.

IMAGES OF THE CONQUEST

Pictorial images can greatly add to our understanding of history. As briefly discussed in the introduction, paintings, drawings, photographs, and other visual representations can augment historical texts, giving us a richer sense of time and place than can be achieved by the written word alone. Images not only provide us with additional information about "what happened," but they also have an immediate and powerful impact on our senses, emotions, and feelings.

When pictures are used in the reconstruction of history, they should be analyzed and appreciated on several different levels. The first thing to remember is that a picture is a form of storytelling, and that in any story, it is important to comprehend what is happening and who is involved. In this regard, it is frequently interesting to compare the stories told by visual images and written texts on the same subject. Second, images often provide glimpses into popular culture and details about everyday life in past societies. Pictures may provide important and interesting clues on manners of dress, types of food, important rituals, architectural

Figure 2.1 *Massacre of Cholula*

styles, and so on. And lastly, images and pictures must be examined and understood as artistic human creations. The image maker has a story to tell, and he or she may use color, composition, and various cultural symbols to evoke specific responses on the part of the viewer. In other words, historical images are frequently a form of theater, consciously composed and represented to elicit a particular interpretation and reaction.[14]

The three images included in this section embody different interpretations of the conquest of Mexico. The first two images come from native sources depicting armed encounters with the Spanish. The last painting is a European interpretation of Cortés's final assault on Tenochtitlan in 1521. As you view these images, keep the following questions in mind.

QUESTIONS TO CONSIDER

1. What role does Doña Marina seem to play in the *Massacre of Cholula* (Figure 2.1)? Why might she be represented in this manner?
2. In *Massacre of the Mexica Nobility* (Figure 2.2), Alvarado was incensed by the Aztec dancing because it accompanied a festival that included human sacrifice. Does this information affect the way you interpret the painting?
3. What information is highlighted in the *Battle for Tenochtitlan* (Figure 2.3)? What historical data seem conspicuously absent? How might you account for this?
4. What cultural symbols can be found in each of these images? How important are they in understanding the meaning of the picture?
5. In what ways do these images contribute to your understanding of the conquest of Mexico? What are the limitations or problems associated with these images?

Figure 2.2 *Massacre of the Mexica Nobility*

The image in Figure 2.1 shows Spanish soldiers and their Tlaxcalan allies attacking the Cholulans. Cortés claimed that the Cholulans had prepared a trap for the conquistadores and that they were warned in advance by Doña Marina (standing at the right). But Aztec sources claim that the attack was an unjustified slaughter of unarmed men, women, and children. There are several cultural symbols to note in this picture. The serpent at the top of the temple is likely a depiction of Huitzilopochtli (the god of war), and the Cholulan falling from the temple roof may represent a suicide. According to scholars, this picture is from a Tlaxcalan source.

The image in Figure 2.2 is an Aztec representation of the attack by Pedro de Alvarado on noble Aztecs who were dancing in the temple opposite the Spanish quarters in Tenochtitlan in connection with a religious celebration. Alvarado, always one of the most impetuous and headstrong of Cortés's captains, unleashed the attack on the unarmed dancers. This occurred while Cortés was marching back to Vera Cruz to defeat the second force sent by Velazquez to capture Cortés. After this, the Aztecs attacked the Spanish. When Cortés returned, he was allowed to enter the city, but then had to fight his way out on the so-called *Noche Triste,* or "Night of Sorrows."

Figure 2.3 shows a European painting that portrays Cortés's final assault on the Aztec capital in 1521. The Spanish attack included charges up the causeways leading to the island city, as well as the construction of thirteen sloops to fight the Aztec war canoes. The elevated structure at center is the main temple of Tenochtitlan. Note how the style, composition, and sentiments of this painting compare with the Tlaxcalan and Aztec images.

Figure 2.3 *Battle for Tenochtitlan*

NOTES

1. Noted by Bernal Díaz and cited in Maurice Collis, *Cortés and Montezuma* (New York: Harcourt Brace, 1954), 34.

2. "Aztec" is really a misnomer. The people themselves was Nahua (speakers of the Nahuatl language), and the dominant group at the time of conquest was the Mexica. Aztlan referred to the territory, somewhere in the contemporary American southwest, from which the peoples had migrated to the central valley of Mexico.

3. Collis, 39, 60. Cortés first scuttled his ships so that his troops had no way to escape.

4. Harry Rosen, ed., *Conquest: Dispatches of Cortes from the New World* (New York: Grosset & Dunlap, 1962), 22.

5. Ibid., 12.

6. The name of the island now divided between Haiti and the Dominican Republic.

7. Cited in Stephen Greenblatt, *Marvellous Possessions: The Wonder of the New World* (Oxford, UK: Clarendon Press, 1991), 170, n.36.

8. A people's understanding of the universe and of their place in it. There is a current academic debate over Aztec mythology and the figure of Quetzalcoatl, but such issues lie outside of the main purposes of this chapter.

9. See the general discussion in Maurice Collis, *Cortés and Montezuma* (London: Faber, 1954).

10. *The General History* acquired the name the *Florentine Codex* because it was long stored in Florence, Italy.

11. Another reason for Spanish victories was that the Mesoamerican warrior sought first and foremost to capture, rather than to kill, an opponent. Senseless death in battle was seen as far less valuable than sacrificial death, which had religious and cosmic significance.

12. According to sources, Doña Marina was offered, along with twenty other slave girls, as a gift to Cortés. The Spanish baptized her "Marina" (she who came from the sea), but her people called her *"La Malinche,"* a term that has come to mean a traitor to his or her country or people. She ultimately played an important role in the conquest for Cortés, who took her as his interpreter, advisor, and lover. When she bore a child, she became, at least symbolically, the mother of the first Mexican, the first infant born of Indian and Spanish ancestry. Later, when Cortés brought his own wife from Spain to Mexico, Marina was married off to one of his soldiers, and she died in relative obscurity at the age of twenty-four.

13. An *encomienda* was a grant of land, together with authority over the native populations inhabiting that land. The natives were required to provide labor services to the holder of the *encomienda*. It guaranteed a supply of cheap labor to the Spanish overlords.

14. Ideally, the historian also seeks to investigate the artist in question and the circumstances behind this particular creation. At the same time, care must be taken when assigning "meaning" to images, for modern-day values and symbols may be quite different from those of the past or from different cultures.

CHAPTER 3

Perspectives on the Atlantic Slave Trade

INTRODUCTION

In the mid-fifteenth century, Europeans began to arrive along the shores of west Africa. Led by the Portuguese, their initial motive was trade, particularly in the valuable gold and ivory that came from the African interior. In return, African traders received brass, copper, liquor, manufactured goods, and cloth. In the Kongo kingdom of central Africa, the initial level of cross-cultural contact went much deeper. In the 1490s, Portuguese missionaries were invited to establish schools and churches in the kingdom, resulting in the conversion of the Kongo king to Catholicism and the establishment of diplomatic ties with Lisbon and the Vatican.

The rise of the Atlantic slave trade in the sixteenth through nineteenth centuries dramatically altered the character and impact of African–European encounters. For nearly three centuries, the Europeans' predominant interest in Africa centered on the enslavement and removal of its strongest and most productive people. Most historians estimate that between 10 and 12 million Africans were imported to the New World, in addition to the many more that died during capture and transport to the slave ships.[1] The Atlantic slave trade was the largest forced migration in world history, and for approximately 300 years, more Africans than Europeans crossed the Atlantic bound for the Americas. This chapter studies slavery and the slave trade from the differing perspectives of three participants— a slave trader, a slave, and a slave owner—to better understand the organization of the trade and the attitudes and behaviors that it inspired.

The main reason behind it all was sugar, a valuable but labor-intensive commodity. The planting and harvesting of vast acres of sugar cane, together with the processing of sugar juice into molasses and rum, required a large labor force engaged in difficult and tiring work. The use of slave labor on sugar plantations had proved so profitable in the Mediterranean as early as the thirteenth century that

Europeans were inclined to reestablish the same system on a much larger scale in the Americas. But whereas the soil and climate of Brazil and the islands of the Caribbean were ideal for the cultivation of sugar, labor supply was a problem. The indigenous Amerindians had been decimated by diseases, such as smallpox and measles, brought by the initial explorers; indentured servants were too few in number; and Europeans were generally reluctant to enslave other Europeans. Faced with these difficulties, Africans soon became the prime choice for slave labor. They had better immunity to tropical diseases than either Amerindians or Europeans, they were readily available and relatively inexpensive, and their cultural distinctiveness helped Europeans to contrive racial justifications for their enslavement.

For the most part, European slave merchants purchased their human cargoes from African chiefs or traders or from European middlemen residing in forts erected along the African coast. Africans had long practiced their own form of slavery, but in most societies, individuals who had lost their freedom as a result of crime, debt, or defeat in war had opportunities for assimilation and social advancement. Once the international trade in slaves began, however, the enslavement of people in Africa via warfare and kidnapping grew dramatically, and captives were increasingly perceived and treated as marketable commodities. In many parts of Africa, slaves were captured hundreds of miles from the coast and were brought to slave ships by long-distance traders. In exchange for their captives, African chiefs or traders bargained for and received metal bars, cloth, manufactured goods, liquor, and guns from European slave merchants.

Firearms played a particularly important and coercive role in the history of the slave trade. Some African leaders, such as the kings of Benin and Dahomey, eagerly sought commerce with European slave traders in order to obtain the new weapons that provided the military superiority to expand and protect their kingdoms, to gain new forms of wealth, and to produce even more slaves. Other African leaders who tried to resist the slave trade often found it impossible because of the new arms race. When the king of the Kongo initially refused to sell slaves, for example, Portuguese traders provided firearms to his rivals and enemies, forcing the king to either "slave or be enslaved." Ultimately, the Kongo kingdom was torn apart by civil war, and large numbers of war captives were sold into slavery in exchange for more guns, which perpetuated a cycle of violence and enslavement that continued for much of the sixteenth and seventeenth centuries.

Slave imports into the Americas peaked in the late eighteenth century, reaching approximately 80,000 a year in the 1780s. This great demand for slaves was partly due to the vast extension of the plantation system to tobacco, rice, sugar, and other commodities. But equally important, new slaves were needed to replace those that died so quickly. Approximately one-third of slaves perished within the first three years of captivity, and few survived beyond ten years. Such high mortality rates were most commonly the result of poor treatment and disease. Most slave owners found that it was more profitable to work their slaves to death and purchase fresh supplies from Africa than to provide them with the food, shelter, and rest required to promote longer, healthier lives. The tragic consequences can be witnessed in demographic statistics from the British colony of Jamaica. Of the approximate 750,000 slaves imported to the small sugar island over the course of nearly two centuries, there remained only 350,000 Africans at the date of emancipation in 1808.

A year earlier, in 1807, Britain had become the first western nation to permanently terminate the African slave trade, followed by the United States in the following year.[2] The end of the legal importation of slaves from Africa, however, did not immediately end the practice of slavery itself. In the United States, slavery remained legal in many states until passage of the Thirteenth Amendment to the Constitution in 1865,[3] while in Brazil, slavery remained legal until 1888. But the enslavement of Africans was generally in decline in the nineteenth century, and historians have identified several factors crucial to the ultimate success of the abolitionist movement. Christian reformers, often assisted by former African slaves, successfully aroused public opinion in England and America by highlighting the apparent contradiction between Christian morality and slavery. In addition, the rise and spread of eighteenth-century Enlightenment ideas about the natural rights of people to life and liberty also played a role in changing attitudes about human bondage. But many historians also link the abolitionist movement to changing economic conditions in Europe and America. Beginning first in England, a new industrial class, with growing political power, was superseding the old planter aristocracy. In congruence with their own financial interests, they wished to keep Africans in Africa, producing the raw materials for their factories and purchasing the finished goods. But whereas Parliament formally ended slavery in the British Empire in 1833 and sent squadrons of the Royal Navy to west Africa to suppress the slave trade, smuggling and commerce by other nations continued well into the mid-nineteenth century.

The Atlantic slave trade had a tremendously important, yet often underappreciated, impact on world history. It helped to create a great circuit of international trade and commodity exchange that linked the agricultural exports of the Americas to the finished goods of Europe and the uprooted labor from Africa. Some historians believe that the profits derived from the sugar trade provided the much-needed capital to finance England's industrial revolution. Other historians have argued that the export of millions of African workers, together with the import of destructive guns, helped to lay the foundations for Africa's current state of underdevelopment. In the Americas, African slaves provided much of the agricultural skills and manual labor that significantly contributed to the prosperity of European settlers and their colonies. The slave trade also led to the creation of multicultural nations whose histories have long been marked by racial and ethnic disparities in wealth, opportunity, and power.

The three readings in this chapter provide deeper insights into the organization, ideas, and impact of the Atlantic slave trade. Each reading also provides a unique perspective from a firsthand participant in the trade. The first selection is from the journal of Jacques Barbot, a European maritime trader who recounted a slaving voyage to Africa and the West Indies in 1698–1699. His account describes the character of trade along the coast, his negotiations with African traders, and his advice concerning the "Middle Passage," or the long and perilous voyage from

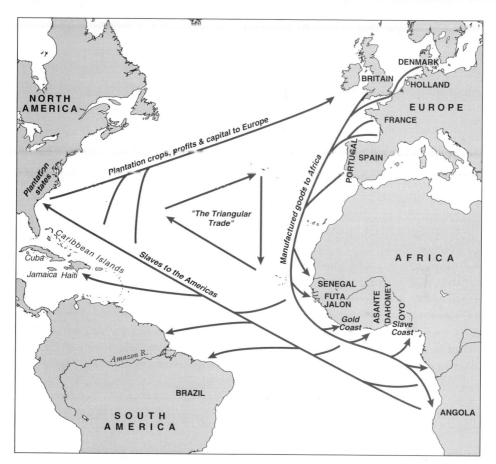

Map 3.1 General Patterns in Atlantic Slave Trade, Sixteenth through Eighteenth Centuries

Africa to America. The second selection is excerpts from the autobiography of Olaudah Equiano (1745–1797), an Igbo youth taken from his village in present-day Nigeria and sent to the West Indies and Virginia. Equiano's experience as a slave was exceptional, for with persistence and good fortune, he was able to obtain an education, convert to Christianity, and purchase his freedom, after which he became a prominent voice in the English abolitionist movement. His detailed and moving account provides rich information about the organization of the trade, the condition of slavery in the Caribbean, and cross-cultural attitudes. The final reading is from Thomas Jefferson (1743–1826), a leading American patriot, author of the Declaration of Independence, and third president of the United States (1801–1809). Jefferson was a proclaimer of the "natural rights" of mankind, an advocate of human liberty, and a slave owner. In the final reading, taken from his *Notes on the State of Virginia* (1781), Jefferson's ambiguous position on freedom and slavery becomes clearer, and it provides greater insights into his character, as well as the debate over slavery that troubled the American republic in its early history.

CHAPTER QUESTIONS

1. All three readings either directly or indirectly make an argument for or against slavery. How does each side use evidence and reasoning to support its case? What are the beliefs and assumptions inherent in each argument? What role do cultural perceptions play? When viewed in a comparative way, what insights or conclusions can be made?

2. Using the material in all three sources, trace the impact of slavery and the slave trade on the various parties directly affected. What different impacts can be identified? Despite the divergent perspectives of the sources, are there any commonalities in their assessments of impacts?

3. As described by Equiano, slavery in the Americas was brutal and violent. What can you find in each of the three readings that helps to explain the reasons why?

4. Jacques Barbot and Thomas Jefferson both assume the inherent inferiority of Africans. Imagine that they were able to meet Equiano at the time he wrote his memoirs. Do you think this meeting would change their opinions?

5. Using the readings as your sources of evidence, which factors (or combination of factors) most contributed to the slave trade? (a) European technological and military power, (b) economic incentives, (c) African cooperation, (d) racist attitudes.

THE PERSPECTIVE OF A SLAVE TRADER

Jacques Barbot (also known as James Barbot) was born around 1650 to a Protestant family in Saint-Martin on the Ile de Re, near the French seaport of La Rochelle. Little is known about his early life, but it is likely that he was engaged in commerce at an early age. The Barbot family had a long history in maritime trade, and Jacques' younger brother Jean (or John) became involved in slave trading at an early age, organizing voyages for the Royal Africa Company, one of the largest slave trading companies in Europe. In 1685, both Barbot brothers emigrated to England following the revocation of the Edict of Nantes, which had granted religious toleration of Protestantism in France. Once settled in England, they started their own commercial firm, assisted by additional investors and speculators.

Their first slaving expedition in 1697 ended in a disastrous shipwreck. The next year they tried again, purchasing the *Albion-Frigate* and refitting it for slaving operations. Jacques accompanied the *Albion-Frigate* on its maiden African voyage to New Calabar, along what was then known as the "Slave Coast." The ship left England in 1698, carrying 24 guns, 60 men, and a cargo of manufactured goods worth 2,600 pounds sterling. In little more than three months' time they purchased 648 slaves and enough food and provisions for the "middle passage," or the trip across the Atlantic. The trip was not entirely successful: midway through the passage, the slaves found an opportunity to revolt, and in the ensuing fight three sailors and twenty-eight captives were killed before Europeans regained control. The *Albion* arrived safely in Barbados, but ill fortune continued to follow the Barbot family. In the following year, Jacques Barbot's son joined the family business and undertook his first slave voyage, but he contracted a fever and died en route to the West Indies.

Slave journals such as this were written primarily to instruct future travelers and traders about Africa, so they are a very useful historical source for understanding the organization and operation of the slave trade, although from one perspective. Barbot's journal reveals that slave trading was a dangerous but potentially very lucrative enterprise. Tropical fevers, competition from European rivals, profit-seeking African sellers, and the perilous "middle passage" made slave trading a risky business but one worth pursuing when one compares the purchase costs with the sale prices. It is also interesting to note the character of African–European relations as portrayed by Barbot and his attitudes concerning Africans and their culture. His account of African involvement in the trade, particularly the special role played by local leaders, also provides a glimpse into the impact of the slave trade on African society.

QUESTIONS TO CONSIDER

1. Examine the process and outcome of the negotiations between Barbot and the king of Bonny. What do they tell us about the organization of the trade? What do they say about cross-cultural relations?
2. In addition to slaves, what else is traded along the west African coast? Who benefits most from this trade? What impact might this have on African society?
3. In one instance, Barbot wishes that the king's brother, Pepprell, was "out of the way" in order to "facilitate trade." In Barbot's eyes, why was Pepprell an obstacle?
4. Examine the way the "slave mutiny" is portrayed by Barbot. What insights can be gained from his description of events and conditions?
5. What are Barbot's views about Africans? What are they based on? In what ways might they explain or justify his role in the slave trade?

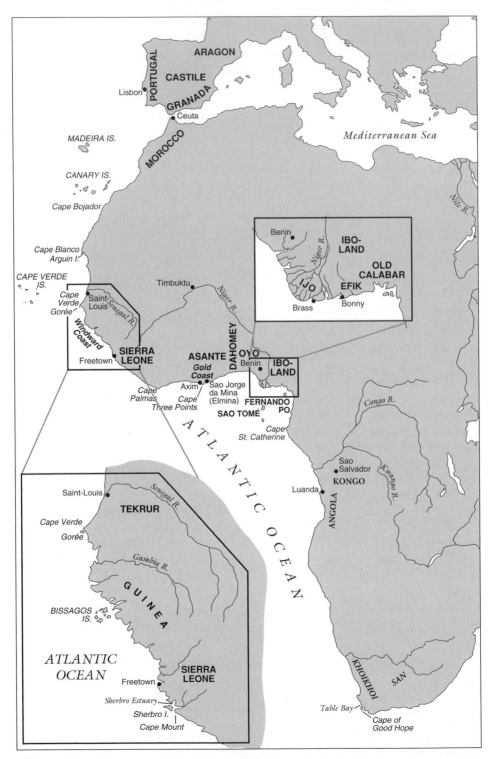

Map 3.2 West Africa, Seventeenth through Eighteenth Centuries

THE SLAVING VOYAGE
OF THE *ALBION-FRIGATE* (1698–1699)

Jacques Barbot

This narrative of a voyage to New Calabar River, or Rio Real, on the Coast of Guinea,* is taken from the journal kept by Mr. Jacques Barbot, the supercargo, and part owner with other adventurers of London, in the *Albion-Frigate*, of 300 tons and 24 guns, a 10 percent ship.†

We sailed from the Downs,‡ on the thirteenth of January, 1698–9, and arrived before Madeira island, the third of February, whence we proceeded immediately after we had got some wine and refreshments aboard. . . . On the 25th of February, we anchored before Sestro river where we stayed for nearly a month getting in wood, water, rice, fowls and other refreshments and provisions. King Peter§ was still alive and well, but we got few elephant's teeth because they were held very dear.

On the 7th of April we came before Axim, the first Dutch fort on the Gold Coast and the next day anchored before the Prussian fort, Great Fredericksburgh, where the Prussian general received us very civilly, but told us he had no occasion for any of our goods. Trade everywhere on that coast was at a standstill by reason of the vast number of interlopers and other trading ships and also because of the wars among the natives. The fort was a very handsome fortress mounted with about forty guns. The general told me that six weeks before he had been assaulted by a pirate, who was forced to let him go, being too warmly received; and that there were two or three other pirates cruising about that Cape. . . . We had abundance of our men sick and several already dead, the weather being intolerably scorching hot, and we could get hardly any provisions save a few goats, very dear.

On the 17th of April, we were before Mina castle and found seven sail in the road, three or four of them tall ships, among which, two frigates, each of about thirty guns and a hundred and thirty men, cruisers at the coast, who had taken three

---

Source: Jacques Barbot's account has been preserved in his brother Jean Barbot's English account of his voyages, published in 1732. The selections in this reading come from P. E. H. Hair, Adam Jones, and Robin Law, eds., *Barbot on Guinea: The Writings of Jean Barbot on West Africa, 1678–1712, Vol. 2* (London: The Hakluyt Society, 1992), 681–98, and George Francis Dow, ed., *Slave Ships and Slaving* (Salem, MA: Marine Research Society, 1927), 73–87.

*"Guinea" was a generic term used to describe sub-Saharan Africa, particularly the coastal forest regions of west Africa.

†Following an act of 1698 that modified the commercial monopoly of the Royal Africa Company, independent traders could operate in west Africa as long as they paid a duty to the company of 10 percent of the value of their trade goods.

‡The Downs was an important anchorage and pilot station located off the East Kent coast. In the days of sail, ships would wait here for favorable winds before making their way out of the English Channel.

§It was common for European slave traders to give Africans western names, but it does not suggest these leaders were westernized or Christian. It is also nearly impossible to identify any of these chiefs by their African names.

interlopers of Zealand,* one of which carried thirty-six guns, who having made a brave resistance, the commander was to be tried for his life. One of the frigates having been already two years at the Coast, was ready to return home, with a thousand marks of gold. . . .

On the fifteenth, we arrived at Accra and anchored about a league and a half from shore. Here we stayed for eleven days, trading for gold, slaves and some few teeth; diverting ourselves by turns, with the English, Dutch and Danish commanders of the forts, but more intimately with Mr. Trawne, the Danish chief, who had his lady with him. On making sail, as we worked our small bower aboard, both cable and buoy-rope breaking, we were forced to sail, leaving the anchor behind, which was hitched among the rocks at the bottom. We had purchased sixty-five slaves along the Gold Coast, besides gold and elephants' teeth and after saluting the three European forts, each with nine guns, we steered for New Calabar to buy more slaves, being followed by our small sloop under sail. . . .

At last, at three o'clock in the afternoon of the 17th of June, we came to an anchor off New Calabar river, on five and a half fathom muddy sand, by guess north and south of Foko point, and the next morning, by day-break, we sent our longboat with three men to sail to land for intelligence and to bring some black to pilot us into Calabar, together with samples of some merchandise. We spied a ship lying in Bandy [Bonny] river, as much as we could see it, and the next day sent one of the pilots in the pinnace to sound the bar. He returned at seven at night, with much trouble, the wind and sea being so high. Our long-boat not returning, as expected, by the 22d we began to be much concerned. The weather all the while was very cold and it blowing very hard from south-south-west.

At eleven o'clock on the morning of the 23d, we spied a boat near the bar [and] found it was a great canoe with nine black rowers, besides other blacks, and the master of our long-boat. . . . The King of Bandy [Bonny], William, had sent us two or three of his pilots, in the canoe, with certificates of several English masters of ships they had piloted formerly safe in, some of them drawing thirteen foot of water. Our frigate then drew fourteen foot and a half water.

Our man reported that the ship we could see within the river was English, commanded by Captain Edwards, who had got his complement of slaves, being five hundred, in three weeks time, and was ready to sail for the West Indies. He also reported, that as soon as the blacks could see our ship off at sea, they immediately went up the river to buy slaves, besides a hundred and fifty that were in the town when he left it; and that King William had assured him, he would engage to furnish five hundred slaves for our loading, all lusty and young. Upon which we consulted aboard with the officers and unanimously agreed to carry up the ship, if possible, for the greater expedition. . . .

The next morning we saluted the black king of Great Bandy, with seven guns; and soon after fired as many for Captain Edwards, when he got aboard, to give us the most necessary advice concerning the trade we designed to drive there. At ten he returned ashore, being again saluted with seven guns. We also went ashore to compliment the King and make him overtures of trade, but he gave us to understand that he

---

*The "interlopers of Zealand" were private Dutch traders encroaching upon the monopoly of the Dutch West India Company.

Figure 3.1 Barbot Presents Himself to the King of Sestro, 1681

expected one bar of iron for each slave, more than Edwards had paid for his; and he also objected much against our basins, tankards, yellow beads, and some other merchandise, as being of little or no demand there at that time.

On the 26th we had a conference with the King and principal natives of the country, about trade, which lasted from three o'clock till night, without any result, they insisting to have thirteen bars of iron for a male and ten for a female slave; objecting that they were now scarce, because of the many ships that had exported vast quantities of late. The King treated us at supper and we took leave of him. The next morning he sent for a barrel of brandy, at two bars of iron per gallon and at ten o'clock we went ashore and renewed our conference but concluded nothing. Four days later we had a new conference at which the King's brother made us a discourse, saying he was sorry we would not accept his proposals; that it was not his fault, he having a great esteem and regard for the whites, who had much enriched him by trade; that what he so earnestly insisted on, thirteen bars for males, and ten for female slaves, came from the country people holding up the price of slaves at the inland markets, seeing so many large ships resort to Bandy for them; but to moderate matters and encourage trading with us, he would be content with thirteen bars for males and nine bars and two brass rings for females, and the next day the trade was concluded on these terms and the King promised to come aboard and be paid his duties.

There was a heavy rain all the morning, the next day, and at two o'clock in the afternoon, we fetched the King from the shore. He came with all of his attendants and officers, in three large canoes, and was saluted with seven guns. He had on an old-fashioned scarlet coat, laced with gold and silver, very rusty, with a fine hat on his head, but was bare-footed. His brother, Pepprell, came with him and was a sharp blade and a mighty talking black, always making sly objections against something or other, and teasing us for this or that present, as well as for something to drink. It were to be wished that such a one as he were out of the way, to facilitate trade.

We filled them with drinks of brandy and bowls of punch, till night, at such a rate that they all being about fourteen, with the King, had such loud clamorous tattling and discourses among themselves, as were hardly to be endured. With much patience, however, all our matters were at last adjusted indifferently, after their way, who are not very scrupulous to find excuses or objections for not keeping literally to any verbal contract, for they have not the art of reading and writing, and therefore we are forced to stand to their agreement, which often is no longer than they think fit to hold it themselves. The King ordered the public crier to proclaim permission of trade with us, with the noise of his trumpets, made of elephant's teeth, we paying sixteen brass rings to the fellow for his fee. The blacks objected much against our wrought pewter and tankards, green beads, and other goods, which they would not accept.

We gave the usual presents to the King and his officers. To the King, we gave a hat, a firelock [musket], and nine bunches of beads; to his officers, we gave two firelocks, eight hats and nine narrow Guinea stuffs.* We also advanced to the King, by way of loan, the value of 150 bars of iron, in sundry goods, in order to repair forthwith to the inland markets to buy yams.

All the regulations having been agreed upon, supper was served, and it was comical, as well as shocking, to observe the behavior of the blacks, both King and subjects making a confused noise, and all of them talking together and emptying the dishes as soon as set down; everyone filling his pockets with meat as well as his belly, especially of hams and neat's tongues;† falling on all together, without regard to rank or manners, as they could lay their hands on food, and having drank and eaten till they were ready to burst, they returned ashore receiving a salute of seven guns as they went.

Two days afterwards the King sent aboard thirty slaves, men and women, out of which we picked nineteen and returned him the rest, and so from day to day, either by means of our armed sloop making voyages to New Calabar town or by our contract with the King, by degrees we had aboard 648 slaves of all sexes and ages, including the sixty-five we purchased at the Gold Coast, all very fresh and sound, very few exceeding forty years of age. The King supplied us with yams and bananas, and plantains, which are a sort of banana dried, yet somewhat green, a food well liked by the natives. . . .

The town of Great Bandy [Bonny] is built on a little island much as that of Calabar, it being marshy, swampy ground, and somewhat larger, but like it in buildings, and its people employ themselves in trade, and some at fishing, by means of long and large canoes, some of them sixty foot long and seven broad, rowed by sixteen, eighteen or twenty paddlers, carrying European goods and fish to the upland blacks and bringing back to the coast, by way of exchange, a vast number of slaves and some

---

*Lengths of cotton cloth.

†Pickled ox tongue.

large elephant's teeth. The principal thing that passes as current money among the na-tives is brass rings, for the arms and legs, which they call *bochie;* and they are so par-ticular in the choice of them that they will often turn over a whole cask before they find two to please their fancy.

The English and Dutch also trade a great deal of copper in small bars, about three feet long and weighing about a pound and a quarter each, which the blacks of Cal-abar work with much art, splitting the bar into three parts, which they polish as fine as gold and twist the three pieces together very ingeniously, like cords, to make into arm rings. But the most current goods for trade are iron bars, striped Guinea clouts of many colors, horse-bells, hawks-bells, rangoes, pewter basins of one, two, three and four pounds weight, tankards of pewter, small glazed beads, yellow, green, purple and blue, and copper armlets or arm rings, of Angola make, the latter being peculiar to the Portuguese.

Their large canoes are made of the trunks of big trees and framed much like the canoes at the Gold Coast, but much longer, sometimes being seventy feet in length. They are very sharp pointed at each end and are fitted with benches, for the conven-ience of the paddlers who sit as near the sides of the canoes as possible. They com-monly hang at the head of the canoe two shields and along the sides, bundles of spears. Every canoe also has a hearth in the head of it, on which they dress their vict-uals and they also have a contrivance by which they can set up an awning made of mats. Some have a sort of quarter-deck made of strong reeds, but the slaves, when they carry any, lie exposed to all weathers. Such canoes are navigated with eighteen to twenty hands and when armed for war commonly carry seventy or eighty men, with all necessary provisions, generally yams, bananas, chickens, hogs, goats or sheep and palm wine and palm oil. . . .

It is customary here for the king of Bandy to treat the officers of every trading ship, at their first arrival, and the officers return the treat to the king, some days before they have their compliment of slaves and yams aboard. Accordingly, on the twelfth of August we treated the king and his principal officers, with a goat, a hog, and a barrel of punch; and that is an advertisement to the Blacks ashore, to pay in to us what they owe us, or to furnish with all speed, what slaves and yams they have contracted to supply us with, else the king compels them to it. At that time also such of the natives as have received from us a present, use to present us, each with a boy or girl slave in requital. According to this custom we treated the Blacks ashore on the fifteenth of August . . . as also the Black ladies; the king lending us his music, to the noise of which we had a long diver-sion of dances and sports of both sexes, some not unpleasing to behold.

On the 22d of August, 1699, we let fly our colors and fired a gun, for a signal to the blacks of our being near ready to sail and to hasten aboard with the rest of the slaves and the yams contracted for. . . . As to the management of the slaves aboard, we lodged the two sexes apart, by means of a strong partition at the main-mast. The fore part was set apart for the men and behind the mast for the women. In large ships, carrying five or six hundred slaves, the deck ought to be at least five and a half or six foot high, making it the more airy and convenient and consequently far more healthy for them. We built a sort of half deck along the sides, with deals and spars brought from England, which extended no farther than the side of our scuttles, and so the slaves lay in two rows, one above the other, and as close together as they could be crowded. . . .

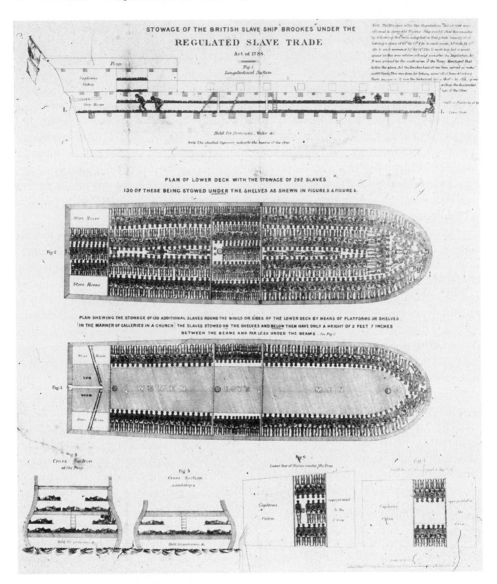

Figure 3.2 Diagram of a Slave Ship

We were very nice in keeping the places where the slaves lay clean and neat, appointing some of the ship's crew to do that office constantly and several of the slaves themselves to be assistants to them and thrice a week we perfumed between decks with a quantity of good vinegar in pails, and red-hot iron bullets in them, to expel the bad air, after the place had been well washed and scrubbed with brooms; after which the deck was cleaned with cold vinegar, and in the daytime, in good weather, we left the scuttles open and shut them again at night.

It has been observed that some slaves fancy they are being carried away to be eaten, which makes them desperate, and others are so on account of their captivity, so that if care be not taken, they will mutiny and destroy the ship's crew in hopes to get away. One day, about one in the afternoon, after dinner, according to custom we caused them, one by one, to go down between decks, to have each his pint of water. Most of them were yet above deck and many of them were provided with knives which we had indiscreetly given them two or three days before, not suspecting the least attempt of this nature from them. It afterwards appeared that others had pieces of iron which they had torn off the forecastle door, having premeditated this revolt. They had also broken off the shackles from the legs of several of their companions, which also served them. Thus armed they suddenly fell upon our men and stabbed one of the stoutest, who received fourteen or fifteen wounds from their knives so that he expired shortly. Next they assaulted our boatswain and cut one of his legs so round the bone that he could not move, the nerves being cut through.

Others cut the cook's throat to the windpipe and yet others wounded three of the sailors and threw one of them overboard from the fore-castle, who, however, by good providence, got hold of the bowline of the foresail and saved himself, along the lower wale of the quarter-deck, where we stood in arms, firing on the revolted slaves, of whom we killed some and wounded many, which so terrified the rest that they gave way and dispersed themselves. Many of the most mutinous leaped overboard and drowned themselves with much resolution, showing no manner of concern for life. Thus we lost twenty-eight slaves and having mastered them, caused all to go between decks, giving them good words. The next day however we had them all again upon deck and caused about thirty of the ringleaders to be severely whipped by all our men.

To prevent a recurrence of such misfortune we used to visit them daily, narrowly searching every corner between decks, and taking care not to leave any tools or nails or other things in the way, which, however, cannot always be so exactly observed, where so many people are in the narrow compass of a ship. We had as many of our men as convenient to lie in the quarter-deck, and gun-room, and our principal officers in the great cabin, where we kept all our small-arms in readiness with sentinels constantly at the door and avenues to it, being thus ready to disappoint any further attempts our slaves might make on a sudden. These precautions contributed much to keep them in awe and if all those who carry slaves duly observed them, we should not hear of so many revolts as have happened.

It is true, we allowed them much more liberty and used them with more tenderness than most other Europeans would think prudent, as we had them all on deck, every day in good weather. . . . We took care they did wash from time to time, to prevent vermin, which they are subject to. Towards evening the blacks would divert themselves on the deck, as they thought fit; some conversing together, others dancing, singing or sporting after their manner, which often made us pastime, especially the females, who, being apart from the males and on the quarter deck and many of them young sprightly maidens, full of jollity and good humor, afforded us abundance of recreation. . . .

As for the sick and wounded, our surgeons, in their daily visits between decks, finding any indisposed, caused them to be carried to a room reserved for a sort of hospital, where proper remedies could be applied. This could not leisurely be done between decks because of the great heat that is there continually, which is sometimes so excessive that the surgeons would faint away and the candles would not burn, and besides, in such a crowd of brutish people there are many so greedy that they will snatch from the sick the fresh meat or liquor that is given them. Nor is it advisable to put sick slaves into the long-boat upon deck for being thus exposed in the open air and lying there in the cool of the nights after coming out of the excessively hot hold, they are soon taken with violent cholics and bloody fluxes and die in a few days time. . . .

The slaves of New Calabar are a strange sort of brutish creatures, very weak and slothful, but cruel and bloody in their temper, always quarreling, biting and fighting and sometimes choking and murdering one another without mercy, and whoever carries such slaves to the West Indies, has need to pray for a quick passage, that they may arrive there alive and in health. . . .

As soon as a slave ship arrives at port in the West Indies, the planters and other inhabitants flock aboard to buy as many slaves as they have occasion for. The price being agreed upon, they search every slave, limb by limb, to see whether they are sound and strong and it is diverting enough to see the examining even of those parts which are not to be named. This done, every buyer carries away his slaves and provides them with nourishment, clothing and health. We sold off all our slaves briskly at about seven thousand pounds weight of brown sugar, a piece, the Indian pieces, as they term it there, and set sail on our return voyage deeply laden with sugar, cotton and other goods. The frigate was very leaky but we continued our voyage without any remarkable accident, only our leaks increased very much so that we had much toil to keep up the ship to the end of our voyage, our two pumps going without intermission day and night, which extremely fatigued our crew, though numerous, and made us all very uneasy.

At length, by God's providence, we spied land to leeward of us, being part of the English coast near Dartmouth and four days later we came to an anchor in the river Thames and so ended our voyage.

THE PERSPECTIVE OF A SLAVE

In 1789, Olaudah Equiano published his autobiography, titled *The Interesting Narrative of the Life of Olaudah Equiano, or Gustavus Vassa the African, written by himself.* The title is most appropriate, for there is little doubt that he did indeed live a very interesting and exceptional life. Born around 1745 in what is now southeastern Nigeria, he was only eleven years old when he and his sister were kidnapped by African slave traders, brought to the coast, and sold to a European slave merchant. He was then shipped across the Atlantic to the West Indies, enduring and surviving a horrific experience during the "middle passage." He was subsequently sent to a plantation in Virginia, where he was purchased by Captain Michael Pascal, an officer in the Royal British Navy. Equiano served Pascal well for several years, acting as a shipboard powder boy during several campaigns of the Seven Years' War. While living in England, he was able to receive some schooling, and he converted to Christianity.

His next master, a Philadelphia businessman named Robert King, returned Equiano to the West Indies and employed him as a shipping clerk. Equiano took advantage of his tolerant Quaker master and his commercial travels to engage in some petty trading of his own, and he eventually saved enough to purchase his freedom in 1766. He continued his maritime voyages as a free man for several years, joining expeditions to the Mediterranean, Central America, and a near-fatal exploratory voyage to the Arctic. He later joined the British abolitionist movement and became a popular speaker against slavery and the slave trade in England. In 1787, he was briefly involved with an ill-fated project to repatriate free blacks to Sierra Leone,[4] but he was forced to resign after he complained about corruption and mismanagement within the organization. He returned to his speaking tours across England and wrote his autobiography, which sold very well in Great Britain and the United States. By most accounts, he died in 1797, his final wish to return to Africa as a missionary unfulfilled.

The reading is excerpts taken from Equiano's autobiography. Although originally written to promote the abolitionist cause, his accounts of his experiences seem mostly accurate. His story begins with his description of village life in Africa prior to his capture. Here he acknowledges that Africans had their own institution of slavery, but he strives to make a clear distinction between it and the slavery that he experienced and witnessed in the Caribbean. He then recounts the manner in which he was captured, brought to the coast, and transported to the West Indies. His detailed and moving description clearly conveys the shock and subsequent demoralization that accompanied the loss of freedom and removal from one's ancestral home. It is also interesting to compare his story with the account found in Jacques Barbot's journal and to identify, analyze, and explain the ways in which they are similar and different. The next section focuses on Equiano's experiences in the Caribbean, his views on African–European relations, and his unceasing efforts to win his freedom. Through his own example, he illustrates the behaviors and attitudes required for slaves to make the most of their situation. The reading ends with his final plea for abolition, in which he crafts an argument that blends both moral and economic factors in support of ending the trade in slaves.

QUESTIONS TO CONSIDER

1. According to Equiano, how were most slaves obtained? What goods did Africans receive in exchange for slaves? Is there a connection between the two that helps explain why Africans may have participated in the slave trade?

2. How does Equiano distinguish between African slavery and the slavery practiced in the West Indies? Why do you think he felt it so important to include this in his autobiography?

3. In what ways does Equiano's description of the "middle passage" differ from the account of Jacques Barbot? How do they differ on the depiction of slave suicides?

4. What are the moral and economic arguments proposed by Equiano to arouse public opinion against the slave trade? How would he view the ideal relationship between Africa and England?

Figure 3.3 Olaudah Equiano

5. Despite his condition, Equiano was a confident individual who never lost sight of his goal to win his freedom. Identify the behaviors and attitudes that Equiano found necessary to achieve his goal. What do these tell you about the nature of African–European relations during this era?

THE INTERESTING NARRATIVE OF THE LIFE OF OLAUDAH EQUIANO (1789)

Olaudah Equiano

Life in Africa

That part of Africa known by the name of Guinea to which the trade for slaves is carried on extends along the coast about 3,400 miles, from the Senegal to Angola, and includes a variety of kingdoms. Of these the most considerable is the kingdom of Benin, both as to extent and wealth, the richness and cultivation of the soil, the power of its king, and the number and warlike disposition of the inhabitants. It is situated nearly under the line and extends along the coast about 70 miles, but runs back into

Source: Olaudah Equiano, *The Interesting Narrative of the Life of Olaudah Equiano, or Gustavus Vassa the African, written by himself,* in *Equiano's Travels,* ed. Paul Edwards (Oxford: Heinemann Press, 1996), 1–3, 6–9, 13–14, 22–28, 57–67, 143–46. Copyright © 1996 Heinemann Publishers. Reprinted with permission.

the interior part of Africa to a distance hitherto I believe unexplored by any traveler, and seems only terminated at length by the empire of Abyssinia, near 1,500 miles from its beginning. This kingdom is divided into many provinces or districts, in one of the most remote and fertile of which, called Eboe, I was born in the year 1745, situated in a charming fruitful vale, named Essaka.* The distance of this province from the capital of Benin and the sea coast must be very considerable, for I had never heard of white men or Europeans, nor of the sea. . . .

As we live in a country where nature is prodigal of her favors, our wants are few and easily supplied; of course, we have few manufactures. They consist for the most part of calico cloth, earthenware, ornaments, and instruments of war and husbandry. . . . We have also markets, at which I have been frequently with my mother. These are sometimes visited by stout mahogany-colored men from the south-west of us: we call them *Oye-Eboe,* which term signifies red men living at a distance. They generally bring us fire-arms, gunpowder, hats, beads, and dried fish. The last we esteemed a great rarity as our waters were only brooks and springs. These articles they barter with us for odoriferous woods and earth, and our salt of wood ashes. They always carry slaves through our land, but the strictest account is exacted of their manner of procuring them before they are suffered to pass. Sometimes indeed we sold slaves to them, but they were only prisoners of war, or such among us as had been convicted of kidnaping, or adultery, and some other crimes which we esteemed heinous. This practice of kidnaping induces me to think that, notwithstanding all our strictness, their principal business among us was to entrap our people. I remember too they carried great sacks along with them, which not long after I had an opportunity of fatally seeing applied to that infamous purpose.

Our land is uncommonly rich and fruitful, and produces all kinds of vegetables in great abundance. We have plenty of Indian corn, and vast quantities of cotton and tobacco. . . . All our industry is exerted to improve those blessings of nature. Agriculture is our chief employment, and everyone, even the children and women, are engaged in it. Thus we are all habituated to labor from our earliest years. Everyone contributes something to the common stock, and as we are unacquainted with idleness we have no beggars.

Our tillage is exercised in a large plain or common, some hours walk from our dwellings, and the neighbors resort thither in a body. . . . This common is often the theater of war and therefore when our people go out to till their land they not only go in a body, but generally take their arms with them for fear of a surprise, and when they apprehend an invasion they guard the avenues to their dwellings by driving sticks into the ground, which are so sharp at one end as to pierce the foot and are generally dipped in poison. From what I can recollect of these battles, they appear to have been irruptions of one little state or district on the other to obtain prisoners or booty. Perhaps they were incited to this by those traders who brought the European goods I mentioned amongst us. Such a mode of obtaining slaves in Africa is common, and I believe more are procured this way and by kidnaping than any other. When a trader wants slaves he applies to a chief for them and tempts him with his wares. It is not extraordinary if on this occasion he yields to the temptation with as little firmness, and accepts the price of his fellow creature's liberty with as little reluctance as the enlightened

---

*Located in present-day Nigeria.

merchant. Accordingly he falls on his neighbors and a desperate battle ensues. If he prevails and takes prisoners he gratifies his avarice by selling them, but if his party be vanquisher and he falls into the hands of the enemy, he is put to death: for as he has been known to foment their quarrels it is thought dangerous to let him survive, and no ransom can save him, though all other prisoners may be redeemed. We have firearms, bows and arrows, broad two-edged swords and javelins: we have shields also which cover a man from head to foot. All are taught the use of these weapons; even our women are warriors and march boldly out to fight along with the men. . . . Those prisoners which were not sold or redeemed we kept as slaves: but how different was their condition from that of the slaves in the West Indies! With us they do no more work than other members of the community, even their master; their food, clothing and lodging were nearly the same as theirs, (except that they were not permitted to eat with those who were freeborn), and there was scarce any other difference between them than a superior degree of importance which the head of a family possesses in our state, and that authority which, as such, he exercises over every part of his household. Some of these slaves have slaves under them as their own property and for their own use.

Captured

My father, besides many slaves, had a numerous family of which seven lived to grow up, including myself and a sister who was the only daughter. As I was the youngest of the sons I became, of course, the greatest favorite with my mother and was always with her; and she used to take particular pains to form my mind. I was trained up from my earliest years in the art of war, my daily exercise was shooting and throwing javelins, and my mother adorned me with emblems after the manner of our greatest warriors. In this way I grew up until I turned the age of eleven, when an end was put to my happiness in the following manner. Generally when the grown people in the neighborhood were gone far in the fields to labor, the children assembled together in some of the neighbors' premises to play, and commonly some of us used to get up a tree to look out for any assailant or kidnapper that might come upon us, for they sometimes took those opportunities of our parents' absence to attack and carry off as many as they could seize. One day, as I was watching at the top of a tree in our yard, I saw one of those people come into the yard of our next neighbor to kidnap a child, there being many stout young people in it. Immediately I gave the alarm, and the rogue was surrounded by the stoutest of the youth, who entangled him with cords so that he could not escape till some of the grown people came and secured him. But alas! Before long it was my fate to be thus attacked and to be carried off when none of the grown people were nigh.

One day, when all our people were gone out to their works as usual and only I and my dear sister were left to mind the house, two men and a woman got over our walls, and in a moment seized us both, and without giving us time to cry out, or make resistance, they stopped our mouths and ran off with us into the nearest wood. Here they tied our hands and continued to carry us as far as they could till night came on, when we reached a small house where the robbers halted for refreshment and spent the night. We were then unbound but were unable to take any food, and being quite overpowered by fatigue and grief, our only relief was some sleep, which allayed our misfortune for a short time. The next morning we left the house and continued traveling all the day. For a long time we kept to the woods, but at last we came into a road which I believed I knew. I had now some hopes of being delivered, for we had advanced but a little way before I discovered some people at a distance, on which I began to cry out for their assistance: but my cries had no other effect than to make them tie me faster and stop my mouth, and then they put me into a large sack. They also stopped my sister's mouth and tied her hands and in this manner we proceeded till we were out of the sight of these people. When we went to rest the following night they offered us some food, but we refused it, and the only comfort we had was in being in one another's arms all that night and bathing each other with our tears. But alas! We were soon deprived of even the small comfort of weeping together. The next day proved a day of greater sorrow than I had yet experienced, for my sister and I were then separated while we lay clasped in each other's arms. It was in vain that we besought them not to part us; she was torn from me and immediately carried away, while I was left in a state of distraction not to be described. I cried and grieved continually, and for several days I did not eat anything but what they forced into my mouth. . . .

The Middle Passage

The first object which saluted my eyes when I arrived on the coast, was the sea, and a slave ship, which was then riding at anchor, and waiting for its cargo. These filled me with astonishment, which was soon converted into terror, when I was carried on board. I was immediately handled, and tossed up to see if I were sound, by some of the crew; and I was now persuaded that I had gotten into a world of bad spirits, and that they were going to kill me. Their complexions, too, differing so much from ours, their long hair, and the language they spoke, (which was very different from any I had ever heard) united to confirm me in this belief. Indeed, such were the horrors of my views and fears at the moment, that, if ten thousand worlds had been my own, I would have freely parted with them all to have exchanged my condition with that of the meanest slave in my own country. When I looked round the ship too, and saw a large furnace of copper boiling, and a multitude of black people of every description chained together, every one of their countenances expressing dejection and sorrow, I no longer doubted of my fate; and, quite overpowered with horror and anguish, I fell motionless on the deck and fainted. When I recovered a little, I found some black people about me, who I believed were some of those who had brought me on board, and had been receiving their pay; they talked to me in order to cheer me, but all in vain. I asked them if we were not to be eaten by those white men with horrible looks, red faces, and long hair. They told me I was not: and one of the crew brought me a small portion of spirituous liquor in a wine glass, but, being afraid of him, I would not take it out of his hand. One of the blacks, therefore, took it from him and gave it to me, and I took a little down my palate, which, instead of reviving me, as they thought it would, threw me into the greatest consternation at the strange feeling it produced, having never tasted any such liquor before. Soon after this, the blacks who brought me on board went off, and left me abandoned to despair.

I was not long suffered to indulge my grief; I was soon put down under the decks, and there I received such a salutation in my nostrils as I had never experienced in my life: so that, with the loathsomeness of the stench, and crying together, I became so sick and low that I was not able to eat, nor had I the least desire to taste any thing. I now wished for the last friend, death, to relieve me; but soon, to my grief, two of the white men offered me eatables; and, on my refusing to eat, one of them held me fast by the hands, and laid me across, I think the windlass, and tied my feet, while the other flogged me severely. I had never experienced any thing of this kind before, and although not being used to the water, I naturally feared that element the first time I saw it, yet, nevertheless, could I have got over the nettings, I would have jumped over the side, but I could not; and besides, the crew used to watch us very closely who were not chained down to the decks, lest we should leap into the water; and I have seen some of these poor African prisoners most severely cut, for attempting to do so, and hourly whipped for not eating. This indeed was often the case with myself. In a little time after, amongst the poor chained men, I found some of my own nation, which in a small degree gave ease to my mind. I inquired of these what was to be done with us? They gave me to understand, we were to be carried to these white peo-ple's country to work for them. I then was a little revived, and thought, if it were no worse than working, my situation was not so desperate; but still I feared I should be put to death, the white people looked and acted, as I thought, in so savage a manner; for I had never seen among any people such instances of brutal cruelty; and this not only shown towards us blacks, but also to some of the whites themselves. One white man in particular I saw, when we were permitted to be on deck, flogged so unmerci-fully with a large rope near the foremast, that he died in consequence of it; and they tossed him over the side as they would have done a brute. This made me fear these people the more; and I expected nothing less than to be treated in the same manner. . . .

At last, we came in sight of the island of Barbados, at which the whites on board gave a great shout, and made many signs of joy to us. We did not know what to think of this; but as the vessel drew nearer, we plainly saw the harbor, and other ships of different kinds and sizes, and we soon anchored amongst them, off Bridgetown. Many merchants and planters now came on board, though it was in the evening. They put us in separate parcels, and examined us attentively. They also made us jump, and pointed to the land, signifying we were to go there. We thought by this, we should be eaten by these ugly men, as they appeared to us; and, when soon after we were all put down under the deck again, there was much dread and trembling among us, and nothing but bitter cries to be heard all the night from these apprehensions, insomuch, that at last the white people got some old slaves from the land to pacify us. They told us we were not to be eaten, but to work, and were soon to go on land, where we should see many of our country people. This report eased us much. And sure enough, soon after we were landed, there came to us Africans of all languages.

We were conducted immediately to the merchant's yard, where we were all pent up together, like so many sheep in a fold, without regard to sex or age. . . . We were not many days in the merchant's custody, before we were sold after their usual man-ner, which is this: On a signal given, (as the beat of a drum) the buyers rush at once into the yard where the slaves are confined, and make choice of that parcel they like best. The noise and clamor with which this is attended, and the eagerness visible in the countenances of the buyers, serve not a little to increase the apprehension of ter-rified Africans, who may well be supposed to consider them as the ministers of that destruction to which they think themselves devoted. In this manner, without scruple, are relations and friends separated, most of them never to see each other again. I re-member, in the vessel in which I was brought over, in the men's apartment, there were several brothers, who, in the sale, were sold in different lots; and it was very moving on this occasion, to see and hear their cries at parting. O, ye nominal Christians! might not an African ask you, "Learned you this from your God, who says unto you, 'Do unto all men as you would men should do unto you?' Is it not enough that we are torn from our country and friends, to toil for your luxury and lust of gain? Must every tender feeling be likewise sacrificed to your avarice? Are the dearest friends and relations, now rendered more dear by their separation from their kindred, still to be parted from each other, and thus prevented from cheering the gloom of slavery, with the small comfort of being together; and mingling their sufferings and sorrows? Why are parents to lose their children, brothers their sisters, husbands their wives?" Surely, this is a new refinement in cruelty, which, while it has no advantage to atone for it, thus aggravates distress; and adds fresh horrors even to the wretchedness of slavery.

[After a short stay in Barbados and then in Virginia, Equiano was sold to a British seaman, who took him back to England. Seizing every opportunity to improve his condition, he learned to read and write, and converted to Christianity and was baptized Gustavus Vassa (a name given to him by his owner). But although Equiano continued to serve his master well at home and at sea (where he served as a powder boy during naval engagements with the French in the Seven Years' War), he was eventually sold to another master named Mr. King, and taken back to the Caribbean.]

Life as a Slave

Mr King dealt in all manner of merchandise and kept from one to six clerks. He loaded many vessels in a year, particularly to Philadelphia, where he was born and was connected with a great mercantile house in that city. He had besides many vessels of different sizes which used to go about the island and others, to collect rum, sugar, and other goods. I understood pulling and managing these boats very well, and this hard work, which was the first that he set me to, in the sugar season used to be my constant employment. . . . I had the good fortune to please my master in every department in which he employed me, and there was scarcely any part of his business or household affairs in which I was not occasionally engaged. I often supplied the place of a clerk in receiving the delivering cargoes to the ships, in tending stores, and delivering goods: and besides this I used to shave and dress my master when convenient, and take care of his horse, and when it was necessary, which was very often, I worked likewise on board of different vessels of his. By these means I became very useful to my master, and saved him, as he used to acknowledge, above a hundred pounds a year. Nor did he scruple to say I was of more advantage to him than any of his clerks, though their usual wages in the West Indies are from sixty to a hundred pounds current a year. . . .

I have sometimes heard it asserted that a negro cannot earn his master the first cost, but nothing can be further from the truth. I suppose nine-tenths of the mechanics throughout the West Indies are negro slaves, and I well know the coopers among them earn two dollars a day, the carpenters the same and oftentimes more, as also the masons, smiths, and fishermen, etc. and I have known many slaves whose masters would not take a thousand pounds current for them. But surely this assertion refutes itself, for if it be true, why do the planters and merchants pay such a price for slaves? And, above all, why do those who make this assertion exclaim the most loudly against the abolition of the slave trade? So much are men blinded, and to such inconsistent arguments are they driven by mistaken interest! I grant, indeed, that slaves are some-times, by half-feeding, half-clothing, over-working and stripes, reduced so low that they are turned out as unfit for service and left to perish in the woods or expire on a dunghill. . . .

It was very common in several of the islands, particularly at St. Kitt's, for the slaves to be branded with the initial letters of their master's name; and a load of heavy iron hooks hung about their necks. Indeed, on the most trifling occasions, they were loaded with chains; and often instruments of torture were added. The iron muzzle, thumb-screws, etc., are so well known, as not to need a description, and were some-times applied for the slightest faults. I have seen a negro beaten till some of his bones were broken, for only letting a pot boil over. Is it surprising that usage like this should drive the poor creatures to despair, and make them seek a refuge in death from those evils which render their lives intolerable. . . . They frequently do [commit suicide]. A negro man, on board a vessel of my master, while I belonged to her, having been put in irons for some trifling misdemeanor, and kept in that state for some days, being weary of life, took an opportunity of jumping overboard into the sea; however, he was picked up without being drowned. Another, whose life was also a burden to him, resolved to starve himself to death, and refused to eat any victuals. This procured him a severe flogging; and he also, on the first occasion which offered, jumped overboard at Charleston, but was saved.

Nor is there any greater regard shown to the little property [of slaves], than there is to the persons and lives of the negroes. I have already related an instance or two of particular oppression out of many which I have witnessed; but the following is fre-quent in all the islands. The wretched field-slaves, after toiling all the day for an un-feeling owner, who gives them but little food, steal sometimes a few moments from rest or refreshment to gather some small portion of grass, according as their time will admit. This they commonly tie up in a parcel; either a bit's worth (sixpence) or half a bit's worth, and bring it to town, or to the market, to sell. Nothing is more common than for the white people on this occasion to take the grass from them without paying for it. . . . Other [whites] have committed acts of violence on the poor, wretched, and helpless females, whom I have seen for hours stand crying to no purpose, and get no redress or pay of any kind. . . .

The small account in which the life of a negro is held in the West Indies, is so universally known, that it might seem impertinent to quote the following extract, if some people had not been hardy enough of late to assert that negroes are on the same footing in that respect as Europeans. By the [laws] of the Assembly of Barbados, it is enacted "That if any negro, or other slave, under punishment by his master, or his order, for running away, or any other crime or misdemeanor towards his said master, unfortunately shall suffer in life or member, no person whatsoever shall be liable to a fine; but if any person shall, out of wantonness, or only of bloody-mindedness, or cruel intention, wilfully kill a negro, or other slave, of his own, he shall pay into the public treasury fifteen pounds sterling." And it is the same in most, if not all, of the West India islands. . . .

I have often seen slaves, particularly those who were meager, in different islands, put into scales and weighed, and then sold from three pence to six pence or nine pence a pound. My master, however, whose humanity was shocked at this mode, used to sell such by the lumps. And after a sale, it was not uncommon to see negroes taken from their wives, wives taken from their husbands, and children from their parents, and sent off to other islands, and wherever else their merciless lords choose; and probably never more during life see each other! Oftentimes my heart has bled at these partings, when the friends of the departed have been at the water side, and with sighs and tears, have kept their eyes fixed on the vessel, till it went out of sight. . . .

Nor was such usage as this confined to particular places or individuals; for, in all the different islands in which I have been, (and I have visited no less than fifteen,) the treatment of the slaves was nearly the same; so nearly, indeed, that the history of an island, or even a plantation, with a few such exceptions as I have mentioned, might serve for a history of the whole. Such a tendency has the slave trade to debauch men's minds, and harden them to every feeling of humanity! For I will not suppose that the dealers in slaves are born worse than other men—No; it is the fatality of this mistaken avarice,* that it corrupts the milk of human kindness and turns it into gall. And, had the pursuits of those men been different, they might have been as generous, as tenderhearted and just, as they are unfeeling, rapacious, and cruel. Surely this traffic cannot be good, which spreads like a pestilence, and taints what it touches! [It] violates that first natural right of mankind, equality and freedom, and gives one man a dominion over his fellows which God could never intend! For it raises the owner to a state as far above man as it depresses the slave below it; and, with all the presumption of human pride, sets a distinction between them, immeasurable in extent, and endless in duration!

Yet how mistaken is the avarice even of the planters. Are slaves more useful by being thus humbled to the condition of brutes, than they would be if suffered to enjoy the privileges of men? The freedom which diffuses health and prosperity throughout Britain answers "No." When you make men slaves, you deprive them of half their virtue, you set them, in your own conduct, an example of fraud, rapine, and cruelty, and compel them to live with you in a state of war; and yet you complain that they are not honest or faithful! You stupify them with whippings and brandings, and think it necessary to keep them in a state of ignorance. And yet you assert that they are incapable of learning; that their minds are such a barren soil or moor, that culture would be lost on them; and that they come from a climate, where nature, though prodigal of her bounties in a degree unknown to yourselves, has left man alone scant and unfinished, and incapable of enjoying the treasures she has poured out for him! An assertion at once impious and absurd. Why do you use those instruments of torture? Are they fit to be applied by one rational being to another? And are you not struck with shame and mortification, to see the partakers of your nature reduced so low? But, above all, are there no dangers attending this mode of treatment? Are you not hourly in dread of an insurrection? But by changing your conduct, and treating your slaves as men, every cause of fear would be banished. They would be faithful, honest, intelligent, and vigorous; and peace, prosperity, and happiness would attend you.

---

*Greed.

Plea to End Slavery

Such were the various scenes which I was a witness to and the fortune I experienced until the year 1777. Since that period my life has been more uniform and the incidents of it fewer than in any other equal number of years preceding; I therefore hasten to the conclusion of a narrative, which I fear the reader may think already sufficiently tedious.

I hope to have the satisfaction of seeing the renovation of liberty and justice resting on the British government, to vindicate the honor of our common nature. . . . It is upon these grounds that I hope and expect the attention of gentlemen in power. These are designs consonant to the elevation of their rank and the dignity of their stations: they are ends suitable to the nature of a free and generous government; and, connected with views of empire and dominion, suited to the benevolence and solid merit of the legislature. . . . May Heaven make the British senators the givers of light, liberty, and science, to the uttermost parts of the earth: then will be glory to God on the highest, on earth peace, and goodwill to men. . . . May the blessings of the Lord be upon the heads of all those who commiserated the cases of the oppressed negroes, and the fear of God prolong their days; and may their expectations be filled with gladness. . . !

As the inhuman traffic of slavery is to be taken into the consideration of the British legislature, I doubt not, if a system of commerce was established in Africa, the demand for manufactures would most rapidly augment, as the native inhabitants will insensibly adopt the British fashions, manners, customs, etc. In proportion to the civilization, so will be the consumption of British manufactures. . . . A commercial intercourse with Africa opens an inexhaustible source of wealth to the manufacturing interests of Great Britain, and to all which the slave trade is an objection. . . .

If I am not misinformed, the manufacturing interest is equal, if not superior, to the landed interest, as to the value, for reasons which will soon appear. The abolition of slavery, so diabolical, will give a most rapid extension of manufactures, which is totally and diametrically opposite to what some interested people assert. . . . [Similarly], the manufactures of [England] must and will, in the nature and reason of things, have a full and constant employ by supplying the African markets. . . .

[The] population [and resources] of Africa abound in valuable and useful returns; the hidden treasures of centuries will be brought to light and into circulation. Industry, enterprise, and mining, will have their full scope, proportionably as they civilize. In a word, it lays open an endless field of commerce to the British manufacturer and merchant adventurer. The manufacturing interest and the general interests are synonymous. The abolition of slavery would be in reality a universal good. Tortures, murder, and every other imaginable barbarity and iniquity, are practiced upon the poor slaves with impunity. I hope the slave trade will be abolished. I pray it may be an event at hand. The great body of manufacturers, uniting in the cause, will considerably facilitate and expedite it; and as I have already stated, it is most substantially their interest and advantage, and as such the nation's at large, (except those persons concerned in the manufacturing of neck-yokes, collars, chains, handcuffs, leg bolts, thumb-screws, iron muzzles . . . and other instruments of torture used in the slave trade). In a short time one sentiment alone will prevail, from motives of interest as well as justice and humanity. Europe contains one hundred and twenty millions of inhabitants. Query: how many millions does Africa contain? . . . If the blacks were permitted to remain in their own country, they would double themselves every fifteen years. In proportion to such increase, will be the demand for manufactures. Cotton and indigo grow spontaneously in most parts of Africa; thus a consideration this of no small consequence to the manufacturing towns of Great Britain. It opens a most immense, glorious, and happy prospect—the clothing, etc. of a continent ten thousand miles in circumference, and immensely rich in productions of every denomination in return for manufactures.

I have only therefore to request the reader's indulgence and conclude. I am far from the vanity of thinking there is any merit in this narrative: I hope censure will be suspended when it is considered that it was written by one who was as unwilling as unable to adorn the plainness of truth by the coloring of imagination. My life and fortune have been extremely checkered and my adventures various. Even those I have related are considerably abridged. If any incident in this little work should appear uninteresting and trifling to most readers, I can only say as my excuse, for mentioning it that almost every event of my life made an impression on my mind and influenced my conduct. I early accustomed myself to look for the hand of God in the minutest occurrence and to learn from it a lesson of morality and religion, and in this light every circumstance I have related was to me of importance. After all, what makes any event important, unless by its observation we become better and wiser, and learn 'to do justly, to love mercy, and to walk humbly before God'? To those who are possessed of this spirit there is scarcely any book of incident so trifling that does not afford some profit, while to others the experiences seem of no use; and even to pour out to them the treasures of wisdom is throwing the jewels of instruction away.

THE PERSPECTIVE OF A SLAVE OWNER

In 1781, while recovering from a fall from his horse, Thomas Jefferson (1743–1826) penned his *Notes on the State of Virginia,* a wide-ranging critical assessment of conditions in his home state in the successful aftermath of the American victory at Yorktown. At age thirty-eight, he already had a distinguished career, having served as a colonial legislator, a member of Virginia's House of Delegates, and governor of Virginia. He was also widely known and respected for the drafting of the Declaration of Independence in 1776 (see chapter 6). In this document, Jefferson clearly expressed the Enlightenment era's concern for the natural rights of mankind, which Jefferson identified as the rights of life, liberty, and happiness for all. But in his *Notes on the State of Virginia,* Jefferson's views on Africans and slavery seem to conflict with his earlier stated beliefs. This is more understandable when one considers the ambiguities and contradictions within Jefferson's own life. Although he drafted legislation to end the slave trade in Virginia in 1778, Jefferson remained a slave owner until the day he died.[5] And although he clearly regarded Africans as an inferior people, there is widespread evidence that he had an amorous affair with Sally Hemings, one of his slaves.

Such contradictions were not unique in American history, for slavery set American ideals of liberty and equality in direct conflict with American racial prejudices. Nor was the contradiction ever resolved for Jefferson. In 1789, Jefferson entered national politics once again, serving as George Washington's secretary of state, John Adams's vice president, and finally as president from 1801 to 1809. As a national leader, Jefferson did little to resolve the issue of slavery or the slave trade. Although he recognized the immorality of slavery, he was unable to envision a workable remedy. As Jefferson explained the dilemma in 1820, "We have the wolf by the ears; and we can neither hold him, nor safely let him go. Justice is in one scale, and self-preservation in the other."

The following excerpts from Jefferson's *Notes on the State of Virginia* center on his arguments against the abolition of slavery. As a man of the Enlightenment era, he endeavored to present a rational argument, based on compelling logic and specific evidence that focus on racial differences. As you read his account, examine carefully his use of logic, data, and historical comparisons. Jefferson concludes his remarks with a consideration of the moral impact of slavery. Do these remarks conflict with his earlier conclusions? How do they compare with Equiano's discussion on the impact of slavery?

QUESTIONS TO CONSIDER

1. In what ways does Jefferson assert that whites are superior to blacks? What is his evidence and reasoning? What assumptions are implicit in his judgments?

2. In his efforts to explain why Africans are inferior, Jefferson argues that it cannot merely be attributed to the conditions in which slaves live. How does he attempt to use history to prove his point? What are the flaws in his argument? Why do you think Jefferson seemed to ignore individuals like Olaudah Equiano in his assessments and conclusions?

3. In Jefferson's view, the United States could never become a successful, peaceful multiracial nation. Why? What solution does Jefferson suggest? What might be some of the obstacles in his ideal plan?

4. Compare and contrast Jefferson's depiction of African society and culture with the description provided by Equiano. What are the implications of the differing accounts?

5. At the end of his essay, Jefferson concedes that slavery is immoral and an evil to all associated with it. What evils concern him the most? What issues does he ignore?

NOTES ON THE STATE OF VIRGINIA (1781)

Thomas Jefferson

It will probably be asked [by those who support abolition], "Why not retain and incorporate the blacks into the state, and thus save the expense of supplying, by im-

Source: Thomas Jefferson, *Notes on the State of Virginia,* ed. William Peden, 138–43, 162–63. Copyright © 1982 University of North Carolina Press. Reprinted with permission. Some editorial changes have been made for clarity.

portation of white settlers, the vacancies they will leave?" Deep rooted prejudices entertained by the whites; ten thousand recollections, by the blacks, of the injuries they have sustained; new provocations; the real distinctions which nature has made; and many other circumstances, will divide us into parties, and produce convulsions, which will probably never end but in the extermination of the one or the other race.

To these objections, which are political, may be added others, which are physical and moral. The first difference which strikes us is that of color. Whether the black of the negro resides in the membrane between the skin,   or the color of the blood, the color of the bile, or from that of some other secretion, the difference is fixed in nature, and is as real as if its seat and cause were better known to us. And is this difference of no importance? Is it not the foundation of a greater or less share of beauty in the two races? Are not the fine mixtures of red and white, the expressions of every passion by greater or less suffusions of color in the one, preferable to that eternal monotony, which reigns in the countenances, that immovable veil of black which covers all the emotions of the other race? Add to these, flowing hair, a more elegant symmetry of form. . . . The circumstance of superior beauty, is thought worthy of attention in the propagation of our horses, dogs, and other domestic animals; why not in that of man? Besides those of color, figure, and hair, there are other physical distinctions proving a difference of race. They have less hair on the face and body. They secrete less by the kidneys, and more by the glands of the skin, which gives them a very strong and disagreeable odor. This greater degree of transpiration renders them more tolerant of heat, and less so of cold than the whites. . . . They seem to require less sleep. A black after hard labor through the day, will be induced by the slightest amusements to sit up till midnight, or later, though knowing he must be out with the first dawn of the morning. They are at least as brave, and more adventuresome. But this may perhaps proceed from a want of forethought, which prevents their seeing a danger till it be present. . . .

[African slaves] are more ardent after their female: but love seems with them to be more an eager desire, than a tender delicate mixture of sentiment and sensation. Their griefs are transient. Those numberless afflictions . . . are less felt, and sooner forgotten with them. In general, their existence appears to participate more of sensation than reflection. To this must be ascribed their disposition to sleep when abstracted from their diversions, and unemployed in labor. An animal whose body is at rest, and who does not reflect, must be disposed to sleep of course. Comparing them by their faculties of memory, reason, and imagination, it appears to me that in memory they are equal to the whites; in reason much inferior, as I think one could scarcely be found capable of tracing and comprehending the investigations of Euclid;* and that in imagination they are dull, tasteless, and anomalous. It would be unfair to follow them to Africa for this investigation.

We will consider them here, on the same stage with the whites, and where the facts are not apocryphal on which a judgement is to be formed. It will be right to make great allowances for the difference of condition, of education, of conversation, of the sphere in which they move. Many millions of them have been brought to, and

---

*Euclid was a classical Greek geometer who established a mathematical school at Alexandria around 300 BCE.

born in America. Most of them indeed have been confined to tillage, to their own homes, and their own society: yet many have been so situated, that they might have availed themselves of the conversation of their masters; many have been brought up to the handicraft arts, and from that circumstance have always been associated with the whites. Some have been liberally educated, and all have lived in countries where the arts and sciences are cultivated to a considerable degree, and have had before their eyes samples of the best works from abroad.

The Indians, with no advantages of this kind, will often carve figures on their pipes not destitute of design and merit. They will crayon out an animal, a plant, or a country, so as to prove the existence of a germ in their minds which only wants cultivation. They astonish you with strokes of the most sublime oratory; such as prove their reason and sentiment strong, their imagination glowing and elevated. But never yet could I find that a black had uttered a thought above the level of plain narration; never saw even an elementary trait of painting or sculpture. In music they are more generally gifted than the whites with accurate ears for tune and time, and they have been found capable of imagining a small catch [melody].* Whether they will be equal to the composition of a more extensive run of melody, or of complicated harmony, is yet to be proved. . . .

The improvement of the blacks in body and mind, in the first instance of their mixture with the whites, has been observed by every one, and proves that their inferiority is not the effect merely of their condition of life. We know that among the Romans, about the Augustan age especially, the condition of their slaves was much more deplorable than that of the blacks on the continent of America. . . . Yet notwithstanding these and other discouraging circumstances among the Romans, their slaves were often their rarest artists. They excelled too in science, insomuch as to be usually employed as tutors to their masters' children. Epictetus, Terence, and Phaedrus, were slaves.† But they were of the race of whites. It is not their condition then, but nature, which has produced the distinction. Whether further observation will or will not verify the conjecture, that nature has been less bountiful to them in the endowments of the head, I believe that in those of the heart she will be found to have done them justice. That disposition to theft with which they have been branded, must be ascribed to their situation, and not to any depravity of the moral sense. The man, in whose favor no laws of property exist, probably feels himself less bound to respect those made in favor of others. . . .

The opinion, that they are inferior in the faculties of reason and imagination, must be hazarded with great diffidence. To justify a general conclusion, requires many observations, even where the subject may be submitted to the anatomical knife, to optical classes, to analysis by fire, or by solvents. How much more then where it is a faculty, not a substance, we are examining; where it eludes the research of all the Senses; where the conditions of its existence are various and variously combined; where the effects of those which are present or absent bid defiance to calculation; let

---

*Note by Jefferson: "The instrument proper to them is the Banjar [banjo], which they brought hither from Africa, and which is the original of the guitar. . . ."

†Epictetus was a famous Roman teacher and philosopher; Terence was a major playwright; and Phaedrus penned a collection of popular fables and short stories.

me add too, as a circumstance of great tenderness, where our conclusion would degrade a whole race of men from the rank in the scale of beings which their Creator may perhaps have given them. To our reproach it must be said, that though for a century and a half we have had under our eyes the races of black and of red men, they have never yet been viewed by us as subjects of natural history. I advance it therefore as a suspicion only, that the blacks, whether originally a distinct race, or made distinct by time and circumstances, are inferior to the whites in the endowments both of body and mind. It is not against experience to suppose, that different species of the same genus, or varieties of the same species, may possess different qualifications. Will not a lover of natural history then, one who views the gradations in all the races of animals with the eye of philosophy, excuse an effort to keep those in the department of man as distinct as nature has formed them?

This unfortunate difference of color, and perhaps of faculty, is a powerful obstacle to the emancipation of these people. Many of their advocates, while they wish to vindicate the liberty of human nature are anxious also to preserve its dignity and beauty. Some of these, embarrassed by the question "What further is to be done with them?" join themselves in opposition with those who are actuated by sordid avarice only. Among the Romans emancipation required but one effort. The slave, when made free, might mix with, without staining the blood of his master. But with us a second is necessary, unknown to history. When freed, he is to be removed beyond the reach of mixture.

. . . There must doubtless be an unhappy influence on the manners of our people produced by the existence of slavery among us. The whole commerce between master and slave is a perpetual exercise of the most boisterous passions, the most unremitting despotism on the one part, and degrading submissions on the other. Our children see this, and learn to imitate it; for man is an imitative animal. This quality is the germ of all education in him. From his cradle to his grave he is learning to do what he sees others do. If a parent could find no motive either in his philanthropy or his self love, for restraining the intemperance of passion towards his slave, it should always be a sufficient one that his child is present. But generally it is not sufficient. The parent storms, the child looks on, catches the lineaments of wrath, puts on the same airs in the circle of smaller slaves, gives a loose to the worst of passions, and thus nursed, educated, and daily exercised in tyranny, cannot but be stamped by it with odious peculiarities. The man must be a prodigy who can retain his manners and morals undepraved by such circumstances. And with what denunciations should the statesman receive, who, permitting one half the citizens thus to trample on the rights of the other, transforms those into despots, and these into enemies, destroys the morals of the one part, and the love of country of the other? For if a slave can have a country in this world, it must be any other in preference to that in which he is born to live and labor for another; in which he must lock up the faculties of his nature, contribute as far as depends on his individual endeavors to the disappearance of the human race, or entail his own miserable condition on the endless generations proceeding from him. With the morals of the people, their industry also is destroyed. For in a warm climate, no man will labor for himself who can make another labor for him. This is so true, that of the proprietors of slaves a very small proportion indeed are ever seen to labor.

And can the liberties of a nation be thought secure when we have removed their only firm basis, a conviction in the minds of the people that these liberties are of the gift of God? That they are not to be violated but with his wrath? Indeed I tremble for my country when I reflect that God is just: that his justice cannot sleep forever: that considering numbers, nature and natural means only, a revolution of the wheel of fortune, an exchange of situation is among possible events: that it may become probable by supernatural interference! The Almighty has no attribute which can take side with us in such a contest. But it is impossible to be temperate and to pursue this subject through the various considerations of policy, of morals, of history natural and civil. We must be contented to hope they will force their way into every one's mind. I think a change already perceptible, since the origin of the present revolution. The spirit of the master is abating, that of the slave rising from the dust, his condition mollifying, the way I hope preparing, under the auspices of heaven, for a total emancipation, and that this is disposed, in the order of events, to be with the consent of the masters, rather than by their extirpation.

NOTES

1. Slave trade statistics from David Eltis, Stephen D. Behrendt, David Richardson, and Herbert S. Klein, *The Trans-Atlantic Slave Trade: A Database on CD-ROM* (Cambridge and New York: Cambridge University Press, 1999).

2. During the French Revolution, radical reformers in 1794 were the first Europeans to abolish slavery in their colonial possessions until slavery was reinstated by Napoleon from 1802 to 1815. (See the readings on Haiti in chapter 6.)

3. President Lincoln's Emancipation Proclamation (1863) was a war measure that did not free slaves in the border states or in areas of the Confederacy already under Union occupation and control.

4. Sierra Leone was a slave trading outpost until the late eighteenth century, when it became a new homeland for freed slaves. Between 1790 and 1800, approximately 1,500 freedmen, under the leadership of British abolitionists, were returned to Africa to establish the settlement of Freetown. The new colony was controlled by the Sierra Leone Company, which forcefully held off resistance from local inhabitants while the settlers supported themselves by farming. After Britain outlawed the slave trade in 1808, it took over from the financially troubled company, using it as a naval base for antislavery patrols. Between 1808 and 1864, an additional 50,000 liberated slaves settled at Freetown, and their descendants, known as Creoles, became active as Christian missionaries and traders along the coast of west Africa, as well as the ruling elites of the region.

5. Because of his poor business practices and money problems, Jefferson was unable to free his slaves upon his death. Instead, they were sold off to new masters to pay off the debt.

CHAPTER 4

Paths to Enlightenment

INTRODUCTION

What do we know? And how do we know it? Is knowledge based on verifiable data and experimentation? Or is it purely subjective and limited to the parameters of the human mind? These are issues central to epistemology, a branch of philosophy that examines how knowledge is defined, obtained, and validated at different times and in different cultures. Most of us take the issue of knowledge for granted, assuming that it consists of facts and information that are supported and proved by evidence and examples. But how do we define "evidence" or "proof," or even "knowledge"? Can an opinion be evidence? Is a belief knowledge? Can there exist multiple truths, even when they are founded on conflicting logic and evidence? These philosophical questions reveal how our conceptions of knowledge can provide us with a fundamental blueprint for interpreting our daily experiences, creating values, and making sense of the world around us.

Conceptions of knowledge can also tell us a great deal about human history and its ongoing encounters with nature and the cosmos. All societies have their own systems and theories of knowledge, which commonly serve as a foundation for many of their religious and cultural values. In many regions of traditional Africa, for example, it was believed that knowledge was acquired both from daily experience and from the spirits of deities and ancestors and that these twin factors helped to give elders special respect and authority in society. In the Islamic world of the sixteenth century, scholars conducted sophisticated scientific experiments while simultaneously acknowledging the truth and wisdom of the Qur'an. This chapter focuses on three historically important yet considerably different philosophies of knowledge that originated in Europe and Asia during the sixteenth and seventeenth centuries. The first two readings come from René Descartes and John Locke, two western philosophers who offered new concepts and methods of knowledge during the age of Europe's scientific revolution. The third reading is from Wang Yang-ming, a renowned Chinese philosopher who offered a revisionist interpretation of Confucian philosophy during the sixteenth-century Ming dynasty. Although each of these philosophers proposed distinct modes of acquiring knowledge, they shared a common fundamental goal: to find a better path to human understanding and enlightenment.

In the western tradition, philosophers have engaged in epistemological discussions since the time of ancient Greece, when Socrates, Plato, and Aristotle debated the source and validity of ideas. With the fall of Greece and Rome, rational pursuits of knowledge gave way to a medieval reliance on revelation, faith, and the authority of Scripture and Church. But although Thomas Aquinas attempted to synthesize logic and faith into one unified system of belief in the thirteenth century,[1] it was not until the scientific revolution in the sixteenth and seventeenth centuries that the west fully reembraced rational modes of inquiry. The heliocentric[2] theories of Copernicus and Galileo, together with the mathematically precise law of gravity proposed by Newton, inspired a revolutionary change in the western understanding of both humankind and nature. If human logic and reason could unlock the mysteries of the universe, then surely the human intellect could be used to launch a new "age of enlightenment" that would bring unparalleled social progress and prosperity. And, as concisely expressed by the German philosopher Immanuel Kant, progress and prosperity would all depend and center on a new approach to knowledge and learning:

> "Enlightenment" is man leaving his self-imposed childhood. This childhood is the inability to make use of one's own understanding without the guidance of another. This is caused by one's . . . lack of resolution and courage to use one's own understanding without another's supervision. "Dare to know!" This is the slogan of the Enlightenment.[3]

Two of the leading and most influential contributors to the European Enlightenment were the philosophers René Descartes and John Locke. Born in France, Descartes (1596–1650) may be considered one of the pioneers of Europe's scientific revolution, for his theoretical work in mathematics, physics, and astronomy advanced these fields in radically new ways. More important, Descartes established a systematic process for scientific analysis and intellectual thought that was ultimately based on the power of human reason and deductive reasoning.[4] An alternative theory of knowledge was proposed by John Locke (1632–1704), the noted English philosopher, scientist, and political theorist. Like his French counterpart, Locke's intellectual interests and achievements were extraordinary, none more so than his theory of knowledge. But whereas Descartes placed his full trust in the power of reason, Locke trusted careful observation, the collection of data, careful analysis, and inductive reasoning. Taken together, Descartes and Locke proposed new strategies for the attainment of knowledge that revolutionized western epistemology and set the foundations for the great surge in modern analysis and scientific discovery.

The history of epistemology in China is at least as old as it is in the west, but it has evolved quite differently. The successive introduction of Confucianism, Taoism, and Buddhism each brought new ideas about the goals and methods of human knowledge, as well as new beliefs about man's proper relationship with each other and the external world. One of the most creative synthesizers of Chinese philosophical traditions was Wang Yang-ming (1472–1529), who combined elements of Confucianism and Buddhism into a philosophy that has become known as the Neo-Confucian "School of the Mind." Wang believed that the purpose of knowledge was to acquire a "clear character," or an awareness of the fundamental unity of all things, both animate and inanimate. This knowledge was not obtained by the study of great texts, nor by the scientific study of nature; instead, it was already inborn in each individual and only required recognition. Awareness was the ultimate key to self-perfection, "clear character," and proper ethical behavior. Wisdom and happiness lay in following one's innate essence, including one's inborn sense of right and wrong. Although Wang Yang-ming's ideas never gained official status in Ming China, they were nonetheless quite influential, particularly in the formulation of Ch'an (Zen) Buddhism in China and Japan.

The epistemological theories of Descartes, Locke, and Wang Yang-ming reflect very different conceptions of and paths to enlightenment. In their pursuit of greater understanding, they all share a common goal, but each one adopts a different path and thus proceeds in a separate direction. Both Descartes and Locke saw the world as a giant repository of knowledge and information that could be objectively studied, assessed, and ultimately controlled by the use of human logic and reason, a philosophy that launched Europe's scientific revolution and Age of Enlightenment. But whereas Descartes sought to understand the external world through a mathematically precise method of rational deduction, Locke stressed the importance of empirical observation and experimentation. A more divergent path was taken by Wang Yang-ming, who saw a unity of man with nature. In his view, enlightenment was not achieved by a rational or scientific analysis of the external world but from an intuitive awareness of the fundamental harmony of all things.

As you read the following selections, compare how each philosopher states his goals and defines his concept of knowledge. Identify the underlying assumptions and cultural values that shape each interpretation, and assess the coherency and logic of each argument. Also, consider the implications of each philosophy, particularly how each envisions the power and potential of humankind, as well as humankind's relationship to nature and the universe. How might the differing philosophies help explain the divergent historical paths followed by Europe and China after the seventeenth century?

CHAPTER QUESTIONS

1. As stated by Wang Yang-ming, "When things are investigated, true knowledge is extended." Compare and contrast how Descartes, Locke, and Wang pursued knowledge. How do their methods suggest very different conceptions of mankind's relationship with nature and the cosmos?

2. Are people born with some form of innate understanding or knowledge? Or are people born "blank"? What is the position of each philosopher, and how does each make his argument in support of his hypothesis? Which position do you find the most persuasive?

3. Consider the literary style of each source. Descartes' account is in the form of a personal recollection; Locke provides an expository outline complete with topic headings; and Wang Yang-ming expresses his ideas in the form of a question–answer dialogue. How might the various styles reflect or reveal meaningful differences in their philosophical positions?

4. How would Descartes, Locke, and Wang define "enlightenment"? How might these definitions reflect the historical events or cultural values of their respective regions? In what ways might they explain or foreshadow different paths of development between the east and the west?

5. Which of these philosophical approaches to knowledge is closest to that employed in contemporary America? Is it possible for each of the differing viewpoints to have validity and usefulness? If so, what does that suggest about knowledge?

RENÉ DESCARTES' DEDUCTIVE METHOD OF INQUIRY

René Descartes (1596–1650) is often called the "father of modern philosophy" because his systematic method of radical doubt led to a questioning of all forms of knowledge based on revelation. Born in La Haye, France, to a modest yet respected family of the nobility, he received a Jesuit education in classical studies, Scholastic philosophy,[5] and mathematics, and he later earned a degree in law from the University of Poitiers in 1616. But Descartes never practiced law, for in his early twenties he suffered a crisis of confidence that led him to question the validity and relevance of all knowledge he had acquired in school. Seeking to gain wisdom from personal experience, he joined the army of Prince Maurice of Nassau, leader of the United Provinces of the Netherlands, during the tumultuous era of the Thirty Years' War. But while stationed in the small town of Ulm during the winter of 1620, Descartes had a sudden revelation of a new investigative method that was to form the basis of an entire new system of rational thought.

After leaving the army in 1623, Descartes traveled to Italy and France, continuing his study of philosophy and experimenting with new theories concerning optics. He then returned to the Netherlands and began work on his *Philosophical Essays* (1637), a four-part collection of essays that examined geometry, optics, meteors, and his philosophy of knowledge. Following the publication of two additional works on philosophy in the 1640s, Descartes accepted an invitation from Queen Christina of Sweden to join her court as a distinguished philosopher and intellectual. But the bitter Swedish winter proved detrimental to his health, and he died of pneumonia in 1650.

Descartes outlined the origins, components, and significance of his new mode of inquiry in the final part of his *Philosophical Essays,* in a section aptly titled "Discourse on Method of Rightly Conducting Reason and Seeking Truth in Sciences." Frustrated by the uncertainties spawned by his Scholastic education and travel experiences, Descartes decided to reject all of his assumptions and beliefs until he had established rational grounds for believing something was true. In doing so, he ultimately came to the issue of his own existence, which he resolved with his famous dictum, *"Cogito ergo sum,"* or "I think, therefore I am." Arguing that a clear consciousness of his own thinking irrefutably and logically proved his own existence, Descartes developed a method of deductive reasoning that he claimed could unlock many mysteries of the world, including the existence of God. Moreover, by expressing in philosophical terms the consequences of the scientific revolution, he provided a new conception of man as an autonomous being distinct and separate from the world that he endeavors to examine and control.

QUESTIONS TO CONSIDER

1. Why did Descartes decide to make himself the initial object of his study? What were his complaints with his education?
2. What are the four major precepts to Descartes' mode of investigation? Where did he get these precepts? According to his argument, what is the problem with relying upon our senses for knowledge?
3. Descartes' famous dictum, "I think, therefore I am," is offered as proof of his own existence. Summarize the logic of his proof. Why does he conclude that this must be the first principle of philosophy? How does he know that his existence is not merely a dream?
4. How does Descartes determine that God exists? What are the strengths and possible flaws in his argument? Despite Descartes' independent intellectual thought, why does he suggest that humans are still dependent upon God?
5. Descartes argued that it was necessary to abandon all preconceptions, beliefs, and assumptions before beginning his quest for knowledge. In your final analysis, do you think he was successful, or not?

DISCOURSE ON METHOD (1637)

René Descartes

Good sense is, of all humanly attributes, the most equally distributed, for every one thinks himself so abundantly provided with it, that even those who are the most difficult to please in everything else usually do not desire a larger measure [of good sense] than they already possess. And it is not likely that they are mistaken; but instead, it is evidence that the power of judging right and distinguishing truth from error (which is properly called good sense or reason) is by nature equal in all men. Consequently, the diversity of our views does not arise from some being more endowed with reason

Source: René Descartes, *A Discourse on Method,* trans. John Veitch (London: Dent; New York: Dutton, 1912), 3, 5, 8–9, 14–18, 26–32.

than others, but because we conduct our thoughts along different ways, and do not view the same objects [in the same ways]. For to be possessed of a vigorous mind is not enough; the prime directive is to use it correctly. The greatest minds are capable of the highest virtues, but are also open to the greatest vices, and those who travel very slowly may yet make far greater progress, provided they keep always to the straight road, than those who, while they run, take the wrong road. . . .

From my childhood, I have been familiar with letters,* and since I was given to believe that by their help a clear and certain knowledge of all that is useful in life might be acquired, I had a deep desire for instruction. But as soon as I had finished my entire course of study (at the close of which it is customary to be admitted into the order of the learned), I completely changed my opinion. For I found myself embarrassed by so many doubts and errors that I was convinced that my education had no effect other than to highlight my own ignorance. And yet I was studying in one of the most celebrated schools in Europe, in which I thought there must be learned men, if such were to be found anywhere in the world. I had learned everything that others had learned at the school, and I also had read additional books on subjects considered the most advanced and interesting. I knew the judgment which other [students] had formed of me, and I did not feel that I was considered inferior, although there were some among them who were already marked out to fill the places of our instructors. And finally, I saw that our century was flourishing, and as fertile in great minds as any preceding one. All this encouraged me to judge all other men by myself, and I therefore concluded that there was no learning in the world of the type I had previously been led to believe existed. . . .

For these reasons, as soon as my age permitted me to pass from the control of my instructors, I entirely abandoned the study of letters, and resolved no longer to seek any other science than the knowledge of myself, or of the great books of the world. I spent the remainder of my youth traveling, visiting courts and armies, holding discussions with men of different backgrounds, dispositions and ranks, collecting varied experiences, overcoming difficulties, and, above all, thinking about my experiences in order to improve myself. For it occurred to me that I should find much more truth from the thoughts and beliefs of ordinary people on matters that concern them personally. . . than in the theories conducted by a scholar in his study. . . . In addition, I always had a most earnest desire to know how to distinguish the true from the false in order that I might be able clearly to discriminate the right path in life, and proceed in it with confidence.

[But] while learning the views of different people, I found as many contradictions as I had among the opinions of the philosophers and scholars. So much was this the case that the greatest benefit which I derived from their study was . . . [that] I learned to believe in nothing too certainly until I had been persuaded by example and custom . . . and I gradually avoided many errors powerful enough to darken our natural intelligence and incapacitate us from listening to reason. But after I had been occupied several years in studying the world and gathering experiences, I finally decided to make myself the object of my study, and to employ all the powers of my mind in

---

*Learning based on reading and writing.

choosing the paths I ought to follow. This endeavor [eventually] brought me greater success than if I had never left my country or my books.

But like one walking alone and in the dark, I resolved to proceed slowly and with great care, so that if I did not much progress, I would at least guard against making too many errors. . . . First of all, I took sufficient time to satisfy myself of the nature of my task, and to determine the true method to acquire knowledge. . . . Among the branches of philosophy I had learned earlier [at school], I gave some attention to the logic of mathematics, geometrical analysis, and algebra, three sciences which I believed might contribute to my task. But I discovered that logic . . . is more useful in communicating what we already know . . . than in the investigation of the unknown. . . . This caused me to seek some other method which would have the advantages of these sciences without their limitations. . . . Believing that a few clear laws are preferable to a multitude of laws . . . I found that the following four basic rules [of logic] would prove sufficient for me, provided I took a firm and unwavering resolution never in a single instance to fail in observing them.

The first [basic rule] was never to accept anything for true which I did not clearly know to be such; that is to say, carefully to avoid haste and prejudice, and to accept nothing as true except what was presented to my mind so clearly and distinctly as to exclude all ground of doubt.

The second [rule] was to divide each of the difficulties under examination into as many parts as possible, and as might be necessary for its adequate solution.

The third [rule] was to conduct my thoughts in such order that, by commencing with objects the simplest and easiest to know, I might advance step by step to the knowledge of more complex things; assigning in thought a certain order even to those objects which in their own nature do not show a natural progression.

And the last [rule] was that in every case to make enumerations so complete, and reviews so general, that I might be assured that nothing was omitted.

The long chains of simple and easy reasoning by which geometers* are accustomed to reach the conclusions of their most difficult problems had led me to imagine that all things . . . are mutually connected in the same way. And that there is nothing so far removed from us as to be beyond our reach, or so hidden that we cannot discover it, provided we abstain from accepting the false for the true, and always preserve in our thoughts the order necessary for the deduction of one truth from another. . . . And, as a matter of fact, the exact usage of these few precepts gave me . . . such ease in solving problems in these sciences [geometry and algebra] that in two or three months . . . not only did I reach solutions of questions that I had formerly deemed exceedingly difficult, but I also determined the means to solve other problems I had not yet considered. . . .

But the chief ground of my satisfaction with this [analytical] method was the assurance I had of exercising my intellect in all matters, if not with absolute perfection, at least as well as possible. And besides, I was conscious that by its use my mind was becoming gradually accustomed to clearer and more distinct thinking, and I hoped . . . to apply [my analytical skills] to the difficulties of the other sciences. . . . I should

---

*A specialist in geometry.

not, however, have ventured at once in examining all the difficulties of all the sciences, for this would have been contrary to the order prescribed in my method. Observing that such knowledge is dependent on principles borrowed from philosophy, in which I found nothing certain, I found it necessary to begin by establishing the principles [of philosophy]. And because I knew that such an inquiry was of the greatest importance . . . I thought that I ought not to attempt it until I had reached a more mature age (being at that time only twenty-three years of age). [Instead], I decided that I should first use my time in preparation for the work, and begin by erasing from my mind all the erroneous opinions I had acquired up to that moment. . . .

I decided to reject as absolutely false all beliefs that contained the least bit of doubt, in order to determine afterward whether any of my beliefs were wholly certain. Accordingly, understanding that our senses sometimes deceive us, I was willing to suppose that nothing existed precisely as it might appear. And because some men err in their reasoning . . . I also rejected all of the reasonings that I had formerly taken as proofs. And finally, when I considered that the very same thoughts which we experience when we are awake may also be experienced when we are asleep, without any one of them being true, I imagined that all of my thoughts . . . had no more reality than the illusions of my dreams. . . . But while I began to think that all was false, it was absolutely necessary that I, who was thinking, must be something. And when I observed this truth, *I think, therefore I am,* I was so certain that no reason of doubt could be presented by the sceptics to shake it. Therefore, I concluded that I might, without hesitation, accept this as the first principle of the philosophy I was searching for.

Next, I carefully examined what I was, and I observed that I could imagine having no body, and that there was no world nor any place in which I might exist. But I could not imagine that I *was not;* on the contrary, from the very fact that I doubted the truth of all things meant that I *was.* . . . From this I concluded that I was a substance whose whole essence or nature consists only in thinking, which has need of no place, nor is dependent on any material thing, so that I (that is to say, the mind) remains entirely distinct from the body . . . and if the [body] did not exist, the mind would still continue to be all that it is.

After this, I inquired into what is essential to the truth and certainty of a proposition, for after discovering one which I knew to be true, I thought that I must likewise be able to discover the basis of this certainty. And I observed that in the words *I think, therefore I am* that there is nothing which gives me assurance beyond this: that it is clearly evident that in order to think it is necessary to exist. I therefore concluded that I might take, as a general rule, the principle that all thoughts and things which we very clearly and distinctly conceive are true, even if there is some difficulty in correctly determining which objects we distinctly conceive.

Next, after thinking about the fact that I doubted, and that I was not wholly perfect (for I clearly saw that it was a greater perfection to know than to doubt), I was led to inquire from where I had learned to imagine something more perfect than myself, and I clearly recognized that I must hold this idea from some nature which really was more perfect. As for the thoughts which I had of other objects external to me, such as the sky, the earth, light, heat, and a thousand more, I had less difficulty knowing from where these came, for nothing in them seemed to render them [perfect or] superior to myself. . . . But this could not be the case with the idea of a nature more perfect than myself, for to receive it from nothing was a thing manifestly impossible . . . The only possibility was that it had been placed in me by a nature which was in reality more perfect than I was, and which even possessed within itself all the perfections of which I could form any idea; that is to say, in a single word, God. And also, since I knew of some perfections that I did not possess, I was not the only being in existence. . . . On the contrary, there was the necessity of some other more perfect Being upon whom I was dependent, and from whom I had received all that I possessed. . . .

The reason why so many people find it difficult to know this truth [the existence of God] . . . is that they never raise their thoughts above material objects. They are so accustomed to consider nothing except by way of visualization, which is a mode of thinking limited to material objects, and so all things that cannot be visualized are considered non-existent. . . . But it seems to me that [such people] who only make use of their visualization to comprehend these ideas do exactly the same thing as if, in order to hear sounds or smell odors, they try to only make use of their eyes. . . .

If there are still individuals who are not sufficiently persuaded of the existence of God by the reasons I have given, I want them to know that all of the other truths that they know, such as having a body, and the existence of stars and an earth . . . are all much less certain. For although we have a moral assurance of these things . . . no one, unless his intellect is impaired, can deny that when the question relates to a metaphysical certainty, there remains sufficient doubts to exclude complete assurance. [For example], when we are asleep we can imagine ourselves possessed of another body and that we see other stars and another earth, when there is nothing of the kind. For how do we know that the thoughts which occur in dreaming are false rather than those which we experience when awake, since the former are often not less vivid and distinct than the latter? And though men of the highest intelligence may study this question as long as they please, I do not believe that they will be able to give any sufficient reason to remove this doubt, unless they presuppose the existence of God. For . . . if all things which we clearly and distinctly conceive are true, it is only because God is or exists, and because he is a Perfect Being, and because all that we possess is derived from him. From this it follows that our ideas or notions, which to the extent of their clearness and distinctness are real, and proceed from God, must to that extent be true. Accordingly, [when] we have frequent ideas or notions which contain some falsity, this can only occur with [ideas] that are to some extent confused and obscure . . . and not wholly perfect. . . . But if we did not know that all which we possess of real and true proceeds from a Perfect and Infinite Being, however clear and distinct our ideas might be, we should not be able to be assured that they possess the perfection of being true.

THE EMPIRICAL REASONING OF JOHN LOCKE

John Locke (1632–1704), the noted English philosopher, scientist, and political theorist, was one of the leading intellectuals of his age and one of the most influential architects of the modern western world. Like his French counterpart René

Descartes, Locke came from a respected family and did well in school, directing his studies at Oxford University for a career as a physician. But Locke's interests were much broader than medicine, and with the assistance of influential friends such as Lord Shaftesbury, he was appointed to a series of governmental positions following the English Civil War and the Glorious Revolution of 1688–1689 that brought William of Orange and Mary to the throne. In his *Two Treatises of Civil Government* (1690), Locke argued against the Divine Right Theory and began to formulate and espouse a liberal political philosophy based on the notions of natural rights, limited government, and the legitimate right of people to rebel against tyranny.

But although Locke may be best known for his political theories, he was also deeply interested in epistemology and the ways in which people acquire knowledge. In his "Essay Concerning Human Understanding" (1690), Locke expressed frustration with overly abstract forms of thought, which he believed only yielded meaningless and futile discussions of truth and reality. Instead, Locke argued that all knowledge was based on data acquired by the dual process of sensory experience (what he called "sensation") and subsequent mental thought and analysis ("reflection"). By stressing the importance of observation, the collection of evidence, and inductive reasoning, Locke defined a mode of inquiry called empiricism,[6] which became the foundation for the scientific method so important to the discoveries and technological innovations of the modern world.[7] Moreover, by claiming that babies were born "blank" without innate knowledge or precepts, Locke revolutionized the understanding of human nature in much the same manner that Isaac Newton revolutionized the understanding of the physical universe. Locke's claim that people were solely the products of their environment conflicted with the Christian belief in the inheritance of original sin and gave human beings a new power to shape their own destiny. Indeed, Locke's theory helped to stimulate the development of the social sciences (political science, economics, psychology, and so on), whose common goal was to use modes of rational, scientific inquiry to construct the most beneficial social environments for human development.

In the reading that follows, Locke carefully advances his new theory of human understanding. He begins with his statement of purpose, which he claims is to know and understand the limits of human knowledge. He then proceeds to explain his ideas of "sensation" and "reflection," as well as his assertion that people are born lacking all innate ideas. It is left to the reader to assess the logic of Locke's argument and to identify the assumptions on which it is based. Also, it is important to consider the full implications of his views and what they suggest about human potential, and mankind's relationship with nature and with God.

QUESTIONS TO CONSIDER

1. How does Locke describe the purpose of knowledge? How do his goals compare with those of René Descartes?
2. By initially assuming that human knowledge has its limits, does Locke impose restraints on his investigation? What kind of knowledge is he suggesting lies beyond man's full comprehension?

3. Locke argues that the human mind is born a blank slate, without any inherent ideas. How does he arrive at the assessment? If this is true, what are some of the implications? How does it compare with Christian theology?

4. According to Locke, "a fetus in the mother's womb differs not much from the state of a vegetable." Why? How might this view shape one's definition of life?

5. If knowledge is ultimately based on "sensation" and "reflection," how can people best develop and increase their knowledge? What might be the links between Locke's epistemology and his political theories?

"AN ESSAY CONCERNING HUMAN UNDERSTANDING" (1690)

John Locke

An inquiry into understanding, pleasant and useful. Since it is the understanding that sets man above the rest of sensible beings, and gives him all the advantage and dominion which he has over them, it is certainly a subject . . . worth our labor to investigate. Like our eyes that allow us to see and perceive all things, understanding takes no notice of itself, and it requires art and pains to set it at a distance, and make it its own object.* But whatever are the difficulties that lie in the way of this inquiry, whatever it is that keeps us so much in the dark to ourselves, I am sure that all the light we can let in upon our own minds, all the acquaintance we can make with our own understandings, will not only be very pleasant, but bring us great advantage in directing our thoughts in the search of other things. . . .

Useful to know the extent of our comprehension. If, by this inquiry into the nature of the understanding, I can discover its powers, how far they reach, to what things they are in any degree proportionate, and where they fail us, I suppose it may . . . persuade the mind of man to be more cautious in meddling with things exceeding his comprehension, to stop when it is at the utmost extent of its tether, and to sit down in a quiet ignorance of those things, which, upon examination, are found to be beyond the reach of our capacities. . . . If we can find out how far the understanding can extend its view, how far it has faculties to attain certainty, and in what cases it can only judge and guess, we may learn to content ourselves with what is attainable by us in this state.

Knowledge of our capacity, a cure of scepticism and idleness. When we know our own strength, we shall better know what to undertake with hopes of success. When we have surveyed the powers of our own minds, and made some estimate what we may expect from them, we should not therefore be inclined to sit still and not set our thoughts on work at all in the hopelessness of knowing nothing. Nor [should we]

Source: John Locke, *The Works of John Locke, a New Edition, Corrected, Vol. 1* (London: Thomas Tegg, 1823), 1–2, 13, 82–84, 86–87, 90–91, 96–98, 99–103, 153–54.
*Meaning an objective analysis of the operation of the mind.

question every thing and disclaim all knowledge because some things are not to be understood. It is of great use to the sailor to know the length of his line,* [even] though he cannot use it to fathom all the depths of the ocean. It is sufficient that he knows [the line] is long enough to reach the bottom, at such places as are necessary to direct his voyage, and caution him against running upon shoals that may ruin him. Our business here is not to know all things, but those which concern our conduct. If we can find out those measures, whereby a rational creature, put in that state in which man is in this world, may and ought to govern his opinions and actions depending thereon, we need not to be troubled that some other things escape our knowledge.

The way shown how we come by any knowledge, sufficient to prove it not innate. It is an established opinion among some men that there are in the understanding certain innate [inborn] principles, some primary notions† . . . stamped upon the mind of man, which the soul receives in its very first being and brings into the world with it. It would be sufficient to convince unprejudiced readers of the falseness of this supposition, if I should only show (as I hope I shall in the following parts of this discourse) how men . . . may attain all the knowledge they have without the help of any inborn impressions . . . [or] original notions or principles. . . .

Idea is the object of thinking. Every man being conscious that he thinks, and that which his mind is applied to while thinking being the ideas that are there, it is past doubt that men have in their minds several ideas, such as are those expressed by the words whiteness, hardness, sweetness, thinking, motion, man, elephant, army, drunkenness, and others. It is in the first place then to be inquired, how he comes by them? I know it is an accepted doctrine that men have innate ideas, stamped upon their minds in their very first being. This opinion I have at large examined already, and I suppose what I have already said earlier will be much more easily admitted when I have shown where the understanding may get all the ideas it has, and by what ways and degrees they may come into the mind, for I shall appeal to every one's own observation and experience.

All ideas come from sensation or reflection. Let us then suppose the mind to be white paper, void of all characters, without any ideas. How comes it to be furnished? From where comes that vast store of ideas which the busy and boundless fancy of man has painted on it with an almost endless variety? From where has it all the materials of reason and knowledge? To this I answer, in one word, from experience. From [experience] all of our knowledge is founded and ultimately derived. Our observation, turned upon either external objects, or upon the internal operations of our minds, is that which supplies our understanding with all the materials of thinking. These two are the fountains of knowledge, from where all the ideas we have, or can naturally have, do spring.

The objects of sensation one source of ideas. First, our senses, familiar with particular material objects, convey to the mind several distinct perceptions of things, according to those various ways wherein those objects do affect them. And thus we come by those ideas we have of yellow, white, heat, cold, soft, hard, bitter, sweet, and all those

---

*A cord or rope used to measure water depths.

†Ideas that are not based on evidence or reason.

which we call sensible qualities. . . . This great source of most of the ideas we have, depending wholly upon our senses, and derived by them to the understanding, I call SENSATION.

The operations of our minds the other source of ideas. Secondly, the other fountain from which experience furnishes the [mind] with ideas is the perception of the operations of our own mind within us. . . . These operations [occur] when the mind comes to reflect and consider, [and they] furnish the [mind] with another idea that could not come from external things. And [examples] are perception, thinking, doubting, believing, reasoning, knowing, willing, and all the different notions of our own minds, which we . . . receive into our understandings as distinct ideas. . . . This source of ideas every man has wholly in himself, and though it be not sense, as having nothing to do with external objects, yet it is very like it and might properly be called internal sense. But as I call the other sensation, so I call this REFLECTION . . . [meaning] that understanding which the mind takes of its own operations. . . .

All our ideas are of the one or the other of these. The understanding seems to me not to have the least glimmering of any ideas which it does not receive from one of these two [sensation and reflection]. External objects furnish the mind with the ideas of sensible [material] qualities, which are all those different perceptions they produce in us; and the mind furnishes the understanding with ideas of its own operations. When we have taken a full survey of them . . . we shall see . . . that we have nothing in our minds which did not come in one of these two ways. Let anyone examine his own thoughts, and thoroughly search into his understanding, and then let him tell me, whether all the original ideas he has there, are any other than of the objects of his senses, or of the operations of his mind, considered as objects of his reflection. . . .

The soul begins to have ideas when it begins to perceive. To ask, at what time a man has first any ideas, is to ask, when does he begin to perceive, for having ideas, and perception are the same thing. I know it is an opinion that the soul always thinks, and that it has the actual perception of ideas in itself constantly, as long as it exists; and that actual thinking is as inseparable from the soul as actual extension is from the body; which if true, to inquire about the beginning of a man's ideas is the same as to inquire after the beginning of his soul. For, by this account, soul and its ideas, as body and its extension, will begin to exist both at the same time. . . .

State of child in the mother's womb. [Anyone] willing . . . to be informed by observation and experience . . . will find few signs of a soul accustomed to thinking in a newborn child, and much fewer [signs] of any reasoning at all. . . . I say, [anyone] who considers this, will perhaps find reason to imagine that a fetus in the mother's womb differs not much from the state of a vegetable. [The fetus] passes the greatest part of its time without perception or thought, doing very little in a place where it need not seek food, and is surrounded by liquid, always equally soft, and nearly of the same temperature. There the eyes have no light and the ears, so shut up, are not susceptible of sounds, and where there is little or no variety or change of objects to move the senses.

The mind thinks in proportion to the matter it gets from experience to think about. Follow a child from its birth, and observe the alterations that time makes, and you shall find, as the mind by the senses comes more and more to be furnished with ideas, it comes to be more and more awake. It thinks more, the more it has matter to think on. After some time it begins to know the objects which, being most familiar with it, have made lasting impressions. Thus it comes by degrees to know the persons it daily converses with, and distinguishes them from strangers, which are instances and effects of it coming to retain and distinguish the ideas the senses convey to it. And so we may observe how the mind, by degrees, improves and advances to the exercise of those other faculties by enlarging, compounding, and abstracting its ideas, and of reasoning about them, and reflecting upon all these, of which I shall have occasion to speak more hereafter. . . .

Of simple ideas and uncompounded appearances. The better to understand the nature, manner, and extent of our knowledge, one thing is carefully to be observed concerning the ideas we have: some of them are simple, and some are complex. Though the qualities that affect our senses are, in the things themselves, so united and blended, that there is no separation, no distance between them; yet it is plain, the ideas they produce in the mind enter by the senses simple and unmixed. For though the sight and touch often take in from the same object, at the same time, different ideas—as a man sees at once motion and color, [or] the hand feels softness and warmth in the same piece of wax—yet the simple ideas thus united in the same subject are as perfectly distinct as those that come in by different senses. The coldness and hardness which a man feels in a piece of ice are as distinct ideas in the mind as the smell and whiteness of a lily, or as the taste of sugar, or smell of a rose. And nothing can be plainer to a man than the clear and distinct perception he has of those simple ideas, which, being each in itself uncompounded, contains in it nothing but one uniform appearance in the mind, and is not distinguishable into different ideas.

The mind can neither make nor destroy them. These simple ideas, the materials of all our knowledge, are suggested and furnished to the mind only by those two ways above mentioned, namely sensation and reflection. When the understanding is once stored with these simple ideas, it has the power to repeat, compare, and unite them, even to an almost infinite variety, and so can make at pleasure new complex ideas. But it is not in the power of the most exalted wit, or enlarged understanding, by any quickness or variety of thought, to invent or frame even one new simple idea in the mind, which is not taken in by the ways aforementioned; nor can any force of the understanding destroy those that are there. The dominion of man, in this little world of his own understanding, is much the same as it is in the great world of visible things, whereby his power, however managed by art and skill, reaches no farther than to compound and divide the materials that are at his hand. He can do nothing toward making the least particle of new matter, or destroying one atom of what is already in existence. The same inability everyone will find in himself, if he tries to fashion in his understanding one simple idea, not received by his senses from external objects, or by reflection from the operations of his own mind about them. I would have anyone try to imagine any taste which had never touched his palate; or frame the idea of a scent he had never smelled. If he can do this, I will also conclude that a blind man has ideas of colors, and a deaf man true distinct notions of sounds.

Of complex ideas made by the mind out of simple ones. We have hitherto now considered those ideas, in the reception of which the mind is only passive, and which come from sensation and reflection, and which the mind can neither make nor destroy. But as the mind is wholly passive in the reception of all its simple ideas, so it exerts several acts of its own, whereby out of its simple ideas, as the materials and foundations of the rest, the others are framed. The acts of the mind, wherein it exerts its power over its simple ideas, are chiefly these three. (1) Combining several simple ideas into one compound one, and thus all complex ideas are made. (2) The second is the bringing together of two ideas, whether simple or complex, and setting them by one another, so as to take a view of them at once, without uniting them into one; by which way it gets all its ideas of relations. (3) The third is separating them from all other ideas that accompany them in their real existence: this is called abstraction, and thus all its general ideas are made. This shows man's power, and its ways of operation, to be much the same in the material and intellectual world. For the materials in both being such as he has no power over, either to make or destroy, all that man can do is either to unite them together, or to set them by one another, or wholly separate them. I shall here begin with the first of these in the consideration of complex ideas, and come to the other two in their due places. As simple ideas are observed to exist in several combinations united together, so the mind has the power to consider several of them united together as one idea; and that not only as they are united in external objects, but as the mind has joined them together. Ideas thus made up of several simple ones put together, I call complex; such as are beauty, gratitude, a man, an army, the universe; which, though consisting of various simple ideas, or complex ideas made up of simple ones, yet are, when the mind pleases, considered each, by itself, as one entire thing, and signified by one name.

Made voluntarily. In this ability for repeating and joining together its ideas, the mind has great power in varying and multiplying the objects of its thoughts infinitely beyond what sensation or reflection furnished it with; but all this is still confined to those simple ideas which it received from those two sources, and which are the ultimate materials of all its compositions. For simple ideas are all from things themselves, and of these the mind can have no more, nor other than what are suggested to it. It can have no other ideas of sensible qualities than what come from without by the senses, nor any ideas of other kind of operations of thinking than what it finds in itself. But when it has once got these simple ideas, it is not confined barely to observation, and what offers itself from without; it can, by its own power, put together those ideas it has, and make new complex ones, which it never received so united.

THE ENLIGHTENED PATH OF WANG YANG-MING

Over the course of many centuries, China has embraced many different intellectual traditions, including Confucianism, Taoism, and Buddhism, which have made significant contributions to the Chinese worldview. As the oldest and most important philosophy, Confucianism promoted and extolled a system of ethical principles designed to promote social stability and order in all social relationships, particularly those of the family. These principles, in turn, were based on the concept of *jen*,[8] or a belief in a fundamental essence of mankind—a core humanness—that underlay individual differences and served to unite and link all people. Taoism added the belief that individuals could gain power, strength, and longer life if they acted in harmony with the nature of the universe. And the adoption of Buddhism from India introduced a new emphasis on the power of the individual to attain harmony and peace based on his or her own meditative insights and proper moral conduct. Although each of these philosophies has offered its own unique contributions to Chinese thought, they have frequently merged and blended at different times in Chinese history to create a dynamic and flexible philosophical tradition.

By the era of the Ming dynasty (1368–1644), the prevailing orthodox philosophy was Neo-Confucianism,[9] and its master was Chu Hsi (1130–1200). Neo-Confucianism held that there was an underlying, immaterial principle (*li*) inherent in all things, which gave all things (including human beings) their essence, form, and meaning. Chu Hsi taught that knowledge of this principle could be achieved through a critical analysis of nature and the classic texts, using the powers of observation, analysis, and reflection. Known as the "School of Principle," Chu Hsi's philosophy became the official interpretation of Confucianism in China, and its precepts were a central component on the imperial civil service examinations.

A radically different interpretation of *li* was proposed by Wang Yang-ming (1472–1529), whose philosophy became known as the "School of the Mind." Born in the village of Yu-yao in the Chekiang province, Wang Yang-ming shocked his tutor at age eleven by declaring that the purpose of learning was not to pass an exam or to win an official government post but to become a sage. Wang was initially a fervent believer in the teachings of Chu Hsi, but his faith was broken when he attempted to follow Chu's methods of investigation. According to legend, Wang sat down in a bamboo grove determined to discover the *li* (essence) of bamboo, but after seven days and nights of observation and thought, he only succeeded in making himself ill through exhaustion. This defeat threw him into a deep spiritual crisis, which continued until he experienced a sudden flash of insight into the cause of his failure. Because the immaterial essence of *li* is found in humans as well as in all things, it was this essence that united mankind to all of nature. Moreover, Wang realized that this essence was best recognized and understood not from the study of bamboo or other objects in the external world but in one's awareness of one's *jen* (humanness) that resided within each person. An awareness of *jen* was the ultimate key to understanding the unity of all things, an awareness that created a "clear character" and a code of ethical behavior based on one's innate knowledge of right and wrong. Consequently, the path to knowledge and self-perfection was attainable by all, for it was based entirely on self-awareness without the need for external study or rational thought. Although Wang Yang-ming's teachings never gained official status in China, they were important in the philosophical development of Ch'an (Zen) Buddhism in China and Japan. More recently, Wang's ideas on self-awareness and harmony have become increasingly popular in the Western world, as seen in growing numbers of people who practice daily meditation, mind–body medicine, sports visualization, and *feng shui*.[10]

The following reading by Wang Yang-ming comes from his work, "Inquiry on *The Great Learning*," a commentary on the original *Great Learning* written by Confucius around 500 BCE. It is written in the form of a question-and-answer dialogue, with the questions referring to themes and ideas originally raised by Confucius centuries earlier. Wang begins by asserting that the goal of learning is the manifestation of "clear character," which comes from an intuitive understanding that "Heaven and earth and all things" are fundamentally and inextricably united. Of particular importance is his discussion of *jen*, or the humanity that unites in one body the individual with the universe. He further explains that this awareness is not attained by external study but by a unity of knowledge and action that encompasses "loving the people" and attaining the "highest good." As you read his argument, carefully consider and assess his ideas and objectives, as well as his underlying assumptions about the relationship of man with his world.

QUESTIONS TO CONSIDER

1. Wang asserts that the prime goal of learning should be to "manifest clear character." What is clear character, and how is it expressed? How is it related to knowledge?

2. According to his philosophy, there is an underlying essence that unites all things, both animate and inanimate. What is this essence? What evidence or argument does Wang propose to prove its existence? Why is it not more widely recognized?

3. How would Wang Yang-ming criticize John Locke's empirical method? Why does he assert that tranquility is more important than experimentation in the pursuit of knowledge?

4. Examine the doctrine of the unity between knowledge and action. How is "loving" related to the acquisition of knowledge?

5. In your assessment, is Wang's philosophy practical? Is it based on logic or emotion?

"INQUIRY ON *THE GREAT LEARNING*" (1525)

Wang Yang-ming

QUESTION: *The Great Learning* was considered by a former scholar [Chu Hsi] to be the learning of the great man. I venture to ask why [you believe that] the learning of the great man should consist in "manifesting the clear character"?

Source: Wang Yang-ming, "Inquiry on *The Great Learning*," in *Sources of Chinese Tradition*, ed. William de Bary, Wing-tsit Chan, and Burton Watson (New York: Columbia University Press, 1960), 571–81. Copyright © Columbia University Press. Reprinted with permission.

MASTER WANG'S RESPONSE: The great man regards Heaven and earth and the myriad things as one body. He regards the world as one family and the country as one person. As to those who make a cleavage between objects and distinguish between the self and others, they are small men. That the great man can regard Heaven, earth, and the myriad things as one body is not because he deliberately wants to do so, but because it is natural with the humane nature of his mind that he should form a unity with Heaven, earth, and the myriad things. This is true not only of the great man. Even the mind of the small man is no different. Only he himself makes it small. Therefore when he sees a child about to fall into a well, he cannot help a feeling of alarm and commiseration. This shows that his humanity (*jen*) forms one body with the child.

It may be argued that the child belongs to the same species [as he]. Yet when he observes the pitiful cries and frightened appearance of birds and animals to be slaughtered, he cannot help feeling their suffering. This shows that his humanity forms one body with birds and animals. It may be stated that birds and animals are sentient beings* [as he is]. But when he sees plants broken and destroyed, he cannot help a feeling of pity. This shows that his humanity forms one body with plants. It may be said that plants are living things [as he is]. Yet even when he sees tiles and stones shattered and crushed he cannot help a feeling of regret. This shows that his humanity forms one body with tiles and stones. This means that even the mind of the small man necessarily has the humanity that forms one body with all.

Such a mind is rooted in his Heaven-endowed nature, and is naturally intelligent, clear, and not obscured. For this reason it is called the "clear character." Although the mind of the small man is divided and narrow, yet his humanity that forms a unity can remain free from darkness like this. This is due to the fact that his mind has not yet been aroused by desires and blinded by selfishness. When it is aroused by desires and blinded by selfishness, compelled by the greed for gain and fear of harm, and stirred by anger, he will destroy things, kill members of his own species, and will do everything to the extreme, even to the slaughtering of his own brothers, and the humanity that forms a unity will disappear completely. Hence if it is not blinded by selfish desires, even the mind of the small man has the humanity that forms a unity with all as does the mind of the great man. As soon as it is obscured by selfish desires, even the mind of the great man will be divided and narrow, like that of the small man. Thus the learning of the great man consists entirely in getting rid of the blindness of selfish desires in order by one's own efforts to make manifest his clear character, so that the original condition of the unity of Heaven, earth, and the myriad things may be restored, that is all. Nothing can be added to this original nature from outside.

QUESTION: Why, then, does the learning of the great man consist also in loving the people?

RESPONSE: To manifest the clear character is to bring about the substance of the unity of Heaven, Earth, and the myriad things, whereas loving the people is to

---

*Having sense perception and consciousness.

put into universal operation the function of that unity. Hence manifesting the clear character must lie in loving the people, and loving the people is the way to manifest the clear character. Therefore, only when I love my father, the fathers of others, and the fathers of all men, can my humanity really form one body with my father, the fathers of others, and the fathers of all men. When it truly forms one body with them, then the clear character of filial piety will be manifested. Only when I love my brother, the brothers of others, and the brothers of all men, can my humanity really form one body with my brother, the brothers of others, and the brothers of all men. When it truly forms one body with them, then the clear character of brotherly respect will be manifested. Everything from ruler, minister, husband, wife, and friends to mountains, rivers, heavenly and earthly spirits, birds, animals, and plants, should be truly loved in order to realize my humanity that forms a unity, and then my clear character will be completely manifested, and I will really form one body with Heaven, earth, and the myriad things. This is what is meant by "manifesting the clear character throughout the empire." This is what is meant by "regulating the family ordering the state," and "pacifying the world." This is what is meant by "fully developing one's nature."

QUESTION: Then why does the learning of the great man consist in seeking "the highest good"?

RESPONSE: The highest good is the ultimate principle of manifesting character and loving people. The nature endowed in us by Heaven is pure and perfect. The fact that it is intelligent, clear, and not obscured is evidence of the emanation and revelation of the highest good. It is the original nature of the clear character which is called innate knowledge [of the good]. As the highest good emanates and reveals itself, one will consider right as right and wrong as wrong. Things of greater or less importance and situations of grave or light character will be responded to as they act upon us. In all our changes and activities, we will entertain no preconceived attitude; in all this we will do nothing that is not natural. This is the normal nature of man and the principle of things. There can be no suggestion of adding to or subtracting anything from them. If any such suggestion is entertained, it means selfish purpose and shallow wisdom, and cannot be said to be the highest good. Naturally, how can anyone who does not watch over himself carefully when alone, and who has no refinement and singleness of mind, attain to such a state of perfection? Later generations fail to realize that the highest good is inherent in their own minds, but each in accordance with his own ideas gropes for it outside the mind, believing that every event and every object has its own definite principle. For this reason the law of right and wrong is obscured; the mind becomes concerned with fragmentary and isolated details, the desires of man become rampant and the principle of Heaven is at an end. And thus the education for manifesting character and loving people is everywhere thrown into confusion. . . .

QUESTION: [It has been said that] only after knowing what to abide in can one be calm. Only after having achieved calm can one be tranquil. Only after having achieved tranquillity can one have peaceful repose. Only after having peaceful repose can one begin to deliberate. Only after deliberation can the end be attained. How do you explain this?

RESPONSE: People fail to realize that the highest good is in their minds and seek it outside. As they believe that everything or every event has its own definite principle, they search for the highest good in individual things. Consequently, the mind becomes fragmented and isolated; mixed and confused, it has no definite direction. Once it is realized that the highest good is in the mind and does not depend on any search outside, then the mind will have definite direction and there will be no danger of its becoming fragmented and isolated, mixed, or confused. When there is no such danger, the mind will not be foolishly perturbed but will be tranquil. Not being foolishly perturbed but tranquil, in its daily functioning it will be unhurried and at ease and will attain peaceful repose. Being in peaceful repose, whenever a thought arises or whenever an event acts upon it, the mind with its innate knowledge will thoroughly sift and carefully examine whether or not the thought or event is in accord with the highest good, and thus the mind can deliberate. With deliberation, every decision will be excellent and every act will be proper, and in this way the highest good will be attained. . . .

Now the original substance of the mind is man's nature. Human nature being universally good, the original substance of the mind is correct. How is it that any effort is required to rectify the mind? The reason is that, while the original substance of the mind is correct, incorrectness enters when one's thoughts and will begin to emanate and become active. Therefore he who wishes to rectify his mind must rectify it in connection with the emanation of his thoughts and will. If, whenever a good thought emanates, he loves it as he loves beautiful colors, and whenever an evil thought emanates, he hates it as he hates bad odor, then his will will always be sincere and the mind can be rectified.*

However, what emanates from the will may be good or evil, and unless there is a way to make clear the distinction between good and evil, there will be a confusion of truth and untruth. In that case, even if one wants to make his will sincere, he cannot do so. Therefore he who wishes to make his will sincere must extend his knowledge. By extension is meant to reach the limit. . . . Extension of knowledge is not what later scholars understand as enriching and widening knowledge. It means simply extending my innate knowledge of the good to the utmost. . . . The sense of right and wrong requires no deliberation to know, nor does it depend on learning to function. This is why it is called innate knowledge. It is my nature endowed by Heaven, the original substance of my mind, naturally intelligent, clear, and understanding.

Whenever a thought or a wish arises, my mind's faculty of innate knowledge itself is always conscious of it. Whether it is good or evil, my mind's innate knowing faculty itself also knows it. It has nothing to do with others. Therefore, although an inferior man may have done all manner of evil, when he sees a gentleman he will surely try to disguise this fact, concealing what is

---

*To set right, correct, amend, or repair.

evil and displaying what is good in himself. This shows that innate knowledge of the good does not permit any self-deception. Now the only way to distinguish good and evil in order to make the will sincere is to extend to the utmost the knowledge of the innate faculty. Why is this? When [a good] thought or wish arises, the innate faculty of my mind already knows it to be good. Suppose I do not sincerely love it but instead turn away from it. I would then be regarding good as evil and obscuring my innate faculty which knows the good. When [an evil] thought or wish arises, the innate faculty of my mind already knows it to be evil. If I did not sincerely hate it but instead carried it out, I would be regarding evil as good and obscuring my innate faculty which knows evil. In such cases what is supposed to be knowledge is really ignorance. How then can the will be made sincere? If what the innate faculty knows to be good or evil is sincerely loved or hated, one's innate knowing faculty is not deceived and the will can be made sincere. Now, when one sets out to extend his innate knowledge to the utmost does this mean something merely apparent, hazy, vacuous, and without substance? No, it means something concrete.

Therefore, the extension of knowledge must consist in the investigation of things. . . . To investigate is to rectify. It is to rectify that which is incorrect so as to return to its original correctness. To rectify that which is not correct is to remove evil, and to return to correctness is to do good. This is what is meant by investigation. . . . If one sincerely loves the good known by the innate faculty but does not in reality act on the thing to which the will is directed, it means that the thing has not been investigated and that the will to love it is not yet sincere. If one sincerely hates the evil known by the innate faculty but does not in reality repel the thing to which the will is directed, it means that the thing has not been investigated and that the will to hate it is not sincere. If within what is good as known by the innate faculty one acts to the utmost degree on the thing to which the will is directed, and if within what is evil as known by the innate faculty one really repels to the utmost degree the evil to which the will is directed, then everything will be investigated and what is known by one's innate faculty will not be deficient or obscured but will extend to the utmost. Then the mind will be joyous in itself, happy and without regret, the emanation of the will shall carry with it no self-deception and sincerity may be said to have been attained. Therefore it is said, "When things are investigated, true knowledge is extended; when knowledge is extended, the will becomes sincere; when the will is sincere, the mind is rectified; and when the mind is rectified, the personal life is cultivated. . . ."

NOTES

1. It should be noted that Thomas Aquinas (1225–1274) was heavily indebted to Muslim philosophers who had kept alive the Greek and Roman classics after the fall of the Roman Empire. One of the most important of these was Ibn Rushd (1126–1198; also

known as Averroës), a Muslim philosopher who (like Aquinas) argued that there was no incompatibility between faith and reason, nor religion and philosophy, if they are all correctly understood (see volume one, chapter 13).

2. The heliocentric, or "sun-centered," theory proposed that the planets, including Earth, revolved around the sun. This stood in sharp contrast to medieval Christian theology that held that the Earth was the center of God's creation, and, therefore, all bodies revolved around it.

3. Immanuel Kant, "What Is the Enlightenment?" (1784) in *Perpetual Peace and Other Essays*, transl. Ted Humphrey (Indianapolis: Hackett, 1983), 41.

4. In logic, there are two broad categories of reasoning. *Deductive reasoning* generally begins with a broad theory and moves to a testing of more specific possible hypotheses in order to confirm or refute the original theory. *Inductive reasoning* moves in the opposite direction, beginning with a collection of specific data in order to make broader generalizations or theories.

5. Medieval European education was centered on Scholasticism, which was the study and memorization of the great works of renowned scholars in the past.

6. Empiricism is a mode of inquiry that relies on observation, data, and experimentation; it is also a theory that all knowledge originates in experience.

7. Locke's personal dedication to experimental science led to his founding of the Royal Society, Britain's oldest scientific organization.

8. *Jen* is commonly defined as "humanity" or "humanness"—the core essence of an individual, as well as the human species.

9. Neo-Confucianism incorporated various elements of China's philosophical legacy, particularly elements of Confucianism and Buddhism (see volume one, chapter 13).

10. The "new age" movement of the 1970s and 1980s borrowed heavily from well-established Eastern practices and traditions, including Zen Buddhism. Mind–body medicine (sometimes called "holistic medicine") is based on the premise that the mind and body are inextricably united and that the mind has the power to affect and heal ailments of the body. *Feng shui* attempts to promote greater harmony between man and his physical environment by redirecting energy flows to achieve ultimate balance and well-being.

CHAPTER 5

"Great Men" and Virtues of Leadership

INTRODUCTION

In a famous formulation, Thomas Carlyle (1795–1881), a prominent writer and historian of nineteenth-century England, asserted that "in all epochs of the world's history, we shall find the Great Man to have been the indispensable savior of his epoch; the lightning, without which the fuel never would have burnt."[1] Carlyle's interpretation of the motive force in history is known as the "Great Man Theory," and his work, fittingly titled *On Heroes, Hero-Worship, and the Heroic in History,* is considered the strongest assertion of that theory. In that work, he explained that

> Universal History, [or] the history of what man has accomplished in this world, is at bottom the History of the Great Men who have worked here. They were the leaders of men, these great ones; the modelers, patterns, and in a wide sense creators, of whatsoever the general mass of men contrived to do or to attain; all things that we see standing accomplished in the world are properly the outer material result, the practical realization and embodiment, of Thoughts that dwelt in the Great Men sent into the world: the soul of the whole world's history, it may justly be considered, were the history of these.[2]

Though few would go as far as Carlyle, leadership—especially political leadership—is widely recognized to be a significant aspect of human society and history. Political leadership is deemed important because leaders occupy prominent positions and are thought to wield power. If any individual is capable of making a profound impact on human social and historical life, surely a political leader ought to have that capability. Hence, an examination of prominent historical leaders will enable us to explore the workings of authority in human society and also to test the "Great Man" theory in historical experience. We shall address these issues in this chapter by examining four extraordinary political leaders who ruled in the thirteenth to early eighteenth centuries: Sundiata of old Mali, Akbar of Mughal India, Kangxi of Qing China, and Peter the Great of Russia.

One of the most famous political axioms is Machiavelli's advice to leaders that "it is better to be feared than loved," and this statement may serve as a useful starting point for examining and assessing the virtues of leadership. Are the most successful leaders the ones who are aligned most closely with the wants and needs of their followers? Or is political greatness the property of those who boldly carve out new trails, using force when necessary to bring others along behind? Are there fundamental precepts of good governance that fit all times and places, or are leadership virtues inextricably linked to specific social situations and cultural values? Does the "Great Man" theory illuminate world history or does it obscure it? These are some of the most important issues and questions that concern us in this chapter on great leaders of the past.

The first reading excerpted here comes from the *Sundiata,* one of the best-known recorded oral histories of traditional Africa. Like Homer's *Iliad* and the medieval epic of King Arthur, this tale of adventure, hardship, and ultimate triumph of good over evil provides historians with insights into an idealized portrayal of history, society, and culture. Unlike those oral traditions, however, the title character of the west African oral history was an actual historical personage, who lived and ruled in the thirteenth century. The trials and triumphs of Sundiata, founder of the empire of Mali, are particularly useful in exploring early west African conceptions of leadership, justice, and human excellence.

Our second reading relates to the great Mughal emperor Akbar, who from 1556 to his death in 1605 ruled a wide territory that stretched from modern-day Pakistan across northern India and encompassed the area of contemporary Bangladesh. As is still true today, the "subcontinent" of south Asia was at that time the scene of a great and continuous contest between the Islamic and Hindu religious and cultural zones. The Mughal Empire sat astride those two zones, and one of the interesting aspects of Akbar's rule was his attempt to address and bridge those differences. We include excerpts from two sources as a means of examining Akbar's leadership. The first is a statement about ideal royal rule from the Islamic perspective, written in 1358 by the Indo-Muslim historian and scholar Ziā ud-dīn Barnī in his work *Rulings on Temporal Government (Fatāwa-yi-Jahāndāri).* The second is a commentary written by one of the Jesuits Akbar invited to his court to explain Christianity. Like many early Jesuits, Father Antonio Monserrate was educated, intelligent, and intense. He accompanied Akbar on some of his campaigns, as well as discussing religion and ideas with him. From him we get testimony of Akbar's intense interest in religious matters. He also provides us with a general characterization of the man and his rule.

The third leader we examine is Kangxi, the seventeenth-century Manchu Emperor of China. The Manchu had invaded China from the north and established their Qing dynasty in 1644. Kangxi (1661–1722) was the second emperor of this dynasty, and he became the longest serving ruler in Chinese history. The documents we utilize to examine the man and his rule are autobiographical in nature. One selection represents a compilation of various writings by Kangxi relating to his experiences as ruler of China. The second selection is an autobiographical reflection on his life, which he wrote when he was a very old man. By then, his health was poor, his favorite son had proven to be disloyal, and he was subject to fits of melancholy and fatigue. The materials that we are privileged to have at our disposal were never available in China during Manchu rule, which lasted until 1911. Owing to the efforts of the eminent American sinologist Jonathan Spence, we can read Kangxi's original writings and assess his thoughts on the proper exercise of imperial authority.

Finally, we turn to Peter I of Russia (1682–1725), a ruler who combined aspects of old Muscovy with eighteenth-century "enlightened despot" modes of kingship. The Russia that Peter grew up in preserved many traditional cultural and political practices, yet it was also buffeted by winds of change blowing eastward from Europe. In addition, Peter was exposed to violence as a political tool while still a young boy. As a result, his political style was a peculiar melding of rationality and violent force, both to preserve his power and to effect change. Peter introduced widespread social and political changes—best represented by his creation of a new capital at St. Petersburg on the Gulf of Finland—and he transformed Muscovy into the new Russian empire. In the process, he made Russia the dominant force in eastern Europe. There is no single biographical or autobiographical portrait that captures Peter as person and as ruler. Hence, we will use a variety of sources (such as edicts, brief essays by foreigners, and the summation of Peter's influence by a Russian historian of the next century) to provide a sense of his reign.

This collection of documents on various world leaders provides us with a range of leadership experiences and styles, set in distinct cultures and political environments. When studied comparatively, however, they afford us the opportunity to reflect critically about leadership virtues and about the role of the individual in history. As you read the following selections, you may want to keep the following questions in mind.

CHAPTER QUESTIONS

1. What are the virtues of leadership in each of these societies? What roles are leaders expected to fulfill? To what degree are these leaders also role models of human excellence?

2. Once in power, how do leaders consolidate their power and authority? How do they assert legitimacy? How do they use religion? Using Machiavelli's formula, do these leaders believe it is better to be "loved or feared"?

3. What are the opportunities for and constraints on the use of power? Are these leaders "Great Men" who are able to assert their whims on their subjects? Or are they held "hostage" to existing historical and cultural conditions? What might this suggest about the role of the individual in history?

4. The sources about these leaders encompass a variety of forms: oral traditions, visitor accounts, personal testimonies, and so on. How might these various types of sources shape the portrayal of the leaders? What are the strengths and limits of each kind of account?

5. Using all these sources, summarize the character traits that you believe are required in an effective leader. How important are these traits in leadership today?

SUNDIATA: FOUNDER OF THE MALIAN EMPIRE

Beginning in the ninth century, about the time that western Europe was entering its so-called dark ages, the sahel and savannah regions of west Africa were beginning to experience a new period of prosperity and creativity that gave birth to the rise of three successive empires: Ghana (800–1070), Mali (1000–1350), and Songhay (1300–1520). Historians typically attribute the rise of these large, cosmopolitan states to the thriving trans-Saharan caravan trade in salt and gold. Prosperous market towns, such as the legendary Timbuktu, grew up on the edge of the desert to facilitate the exchange of these and other goods, and local leaders taxed the trade in exchange for providing security, law, and order. Over time, the wealth derived from commercial taxes allowed leaders to enlarge their armies, to purchase horses from north Africa to form cavalry, and to launch a series of successful conquests that created huge, tribute-paying empires. Although some leaders converted to Islam to improve their trading relations with Arabs from the north, the majority of the population continued to adhere to their traditional, ancestral religious beliefs. The wealth and prosperity of these kingdoms became well known in the Arab world, and much of our knowledge about the history of the region comes from numerous travelers' accounts of the region (for example, see the description from Ibn Battuta in chapter 1).

Another kind of historical source for this region is African oral histories, which have been handed down from generation to generation for hundreds of years. The task of remembering and recounting oral traditions in west Africa are entrusted to *griots,* who have also served for centuries as the musicians, historians, and trusted advisors and counselors to kings. In a culture that lacked the tradition of literacy, *griots* served a crucial function as the official "memory" of the past. One of the most famous of these *griot*-related histories is the epic of Sundiata, the founder of the empire of Mali around the eleventh century. The account that follows was memorized and passed on by generations of *griots* until it was at last translated and recorded by D. T. Niane less than fifty years ago.

According to the oral history, Sundiata was destined to rise to greatness, but he first had to overcome a long list of personal challenges and adversity, including a self-imposed exile from his home. In his absence, Mali fell under the rule of the evil King Soumaoro, a cruel and despotic leader who resorted to black magic to maintain his power and oppression. When news of Soumaoro's vicious rule reached Sundiata, he returned to Mali to claim his title and to fulfill his destiny. After a prolonged series of military campaigns, Sundiata's forces defeated Soumaoro, and a new reign of justice, peace, and prosperity was restored to Mali.

Clearly, the tale of Sundiata told in the oral history departs from what most westerners would consider "true history." The inclusion of magic, destiny, and superhuman feats seems to suggest that this is a tale based more on fiction than fact. Nonetheless, the tale is an important historical source for what it tells us about Malian cultural history, especially notions of leadership, virtue, and the purpose of remembered history. As you read the following excerpt, keep in mind the following questions.

QUESTIONS TO CONSIDER

1. Fortune-tellers prophesied that Sundiata was destined for greatness, yet it is also clear that he had to earn his exalted position. What is significant about this dual mode of explanation? How does it serve to legitimate his rule? According to this tale, are great leaders born or made?

2. As a youth, Sundiata is tested by a group of witches. Why? How does this episode contribute to the story?

3. What are the virtues that make Sundiata a great leader? What are the vices that make his rival Soumaoro a great villain? How does each of these characters serve as a role model for the listeners to this tale?

4. What does this history tell us about the role of leaders in traditional west African society? According to this account, is it better for leaders to be loved or feared?

5. At the end of this tale, the *griot* reminds his audience that he has taken an oath "to teach only what is to be taught, and to conceal what is to be kept concealed." What kinds of things might the *griot* have kept concealed? What might this tell us about the African conception of history and leadership?

SUNDIATA: AN EPIC OF OLD MALI

Listen then, sons of Mali, children of the black people, listen to my word, for I am going to tell you of Sundiata, the father of the Bright Country, of the savanna land, the ancestor of those who draw the bow, the master of a hundred vanquished kings. . . .

I am going to tell you of Sundiata, he whose exploits will astonish men for a long time yet. He was great among kings, he was peerless among men; he was beloved of God because he was the last of the great conquerors. . . .

[The tale begins with the visit of a fortune-teller to the palace of King Maghan Kon Fetta, announcing the prophecy of the birth of a great leader.]

The soothsayer [fortune-teller] returned to his cowries.* He shook them in his palm with a skilled hand and then threw them out.

"King of Mali, destiny marches with great strides, Mali is about to emerge from the night. Niani[†] is lighting up, but what is this light that comes from the east?"

Source: D. T. Niane, *Sundiata: An Epic of Old Mali* (Essex, UK: Addison Wesley Longman Limited (Longman African Writers, 1994), 2, 5–6, 23–26, 40–42, 47–48, 61–65, 81–82, 84.

*Small white seashells found along the ocean coasts of west Africa. In some African societies, cowrie shells were used in divination practices. The shells were thrown in the air by a fortune-teller, and the pattern of their fall foretold the future.

[†]Capital of Mali and location of the king's palace.

"Hunter," said Gnankouman Doua [the King's *griot*], "your words are obscure. Make your speech comprehensible to us, speak in the clear language of your savanna."

"I am coming to that now, *griot*. Listen to my message. Listen, sire. You have ruled over the kingdom which your ancestors bequeathed to you and you have no other ambition but to pass on this realm, intact if not increased, to your descendants; but, fine king, your successor is not yet born. I see two hunters coming to your city; they have come from afar and a woman accompanies them. Oh, that woman! She is ugly, she is hideous, she bears on her back a disfiguring hump. Her monstrous eyes seem to have been merely laid on her face, but, mystery of mysteries, this is the woman you must marry, sire, for she will be the mother of him who will make the name of Mali immortal forever. The child will be the seventh star, the seventh conqueror of the earth. He will be more mighty than Alexander. But, oh king, for destiny to lead this woman to you a sacrifice is necessary; you must offer up a red bull, for the bull is powerful. When its blood soaks into the ground nothing more will hinder the arrival of your wife. There, I have said what I had to say, but everything is in the hands of the Almighty. . . ."

[The king follows the fortune-teller's advice and took an ugly common woman named Sogolon as his junior wife. Soon, a son named Sundiata was born. Initially ridiculed and scorned because he could neither walk nor talk, the young Sundiata triumphed over these adversities and won favor with his townspeople.]

Sogolon's son was now ten. . . . [Sundiata] was a lad full of strength; his arms had the strength of ten and his biceps inspired fear in his companions. He had already that authoritative way of speaking which belongs to those who are destined to command. . . .

But Sundiata's popularity was so great that the queen mother* became apprehensive for her son's throne. Dankaran Touman [the son and heir-apparent] was the most retiring of men. At the age of eighteen he was still under the influence of his mother and a handful of old schemers. The queen mother wanted to put an end to Sundiata's popularity by killing him and it was thus that one night she received the nine great witches of Mali. They were all old women. The eldest, and the most dangerous too, was called Soumosso Konkomba. When the nine old hags had seated themselves in a semi-circle around her bed the queen mother said:

"You who rule supreme at night, nocturnal powers, oh you who hold the secret of life, you who can put an end to one life, can you help me?"

"The night is potent," said Soumosso Konkomba. "Oh queen, tell us what is to be done, on whom must we turn the fatal blade?"

"I want to kill Sundiata," said Sassouma [the queen mother]. "His destiny runs counter to my son's and he must be killed while there is still time. If you succeed, I promise you the finest rewards. . . ."

"Mother of the king," rejoined Soumosso Konkomba, ". . . [Sundiata] has done us no wrong. It is, then, difficult for us to compass his death."

---

*The first and senior wife of King Maghan Kon Fetta. By rights of age and seniority, senior wives and their children frequently had elevated status and privilege in traditional Africa.

". . . Tomorrow go to Sogolon's vegetable patch and make a show of picking a few *gnougou** leaves," [replied the Queen]. "Sundiata stands guard there and you will see how vicious the boy is. He won't have any respect for your age, he'll give you a good thrashing.". . .

[The next day], Sundiata and his companions came back late to the village [from hunting], but first he wanted to take a look at his mother's vegetable patch as was his custom. It was dusk. There he found the nine witches stealing *gnougou* leaves. They made a show of running away like thieves caught red-handed.

"Stop, stop, poor old women," said Sundiata, "what is the matter with you to run away like this. This garden belongs to all."

Straight away his companions and he filled the gourds of the old hags with leaves, aubergines and onions.

"Each time that you run short of condiments come to stock up here without fear."

"You disarm us," said one of the old crones, and another added, "And you confound us with your bounty."

"Listen, Sundiata," said Soumosso Konkomba, "we had come here to test you. We have no need of condiments but your generosity disarms us. We were sent here by the queen mother to provoke you and draw the anger of the nocturnal powers upon you. But nothing can be done against a heart full of kindness. . . . Forgive us, son of Sogolon."

"I bear you no ill-will," said Djata. "Here, I am returning from the hunt with my companions and we have killed ten elephants, so I will give you an elephant each and there you have some meat!"

"Thank you, son of Sogolon." "Thank you, child of Justice." "Henceforth," concluded Soumosso Konkomba, we will watch over you." And the nine witches disappeared into the night. . . .

[But when Sundiata learns that the Queen is hatching new schemes to hurt his family, he attempts to mollify her anger by choosing self-imposed exile. For several years, he wanders the countryside, learning the skills of the warrior in the service of other leaders.]

We are now coming to the great moments in the life of Sundiata. The exile will end and another sun will arise. It is the sun of Sundiata. *Griots* know the history of kings and kingdoms and that is why they are the best counselors of kings. Every king wants to have a singer to perpetuate his memory, for it is the *griot* who rescues the memories of kings from oblivion, as men have short memories. . . .

At the time when Sundiata was preparing to assert his claim over the kingdom of his fathers, Soumaoro was the king of kings, the most powerful king in all the lands of the setting sun. The fortified town of Sosso was the bulwark of fetishism [black magic] against the word of Allah. For a long time Soumaoro defied the whole world. Since his accession to the throne of Sosso he had defeated nine kings whose heads served him as fetishes [charms] in his macabre chamber. Their skins served as seats and he cut his footwear from human skin. Soumaoro was not like other men, for the *jinn* [spirits] had revealed themselves to him and his power was beyond measure. So his

---

*A green, leafy vegetable used in stews and sauces.

countless sofas [regiments] were very brave since they believed their king to be invincible. But Soumaoro was an evil demon and his reign had produced nothing but bloodshed. Nothing was taboo for him. His greatest pleasure was publicly to flog venerable old men. He had defiled every family and everywhere in his vast empire there were villages populated by girls whom he had forcibly abducted from their families without marrying them. . . .

. . . Soumaoro proclaimed himself king of Mali by right of conquest, but he was not recognized by the populace and resistance was organized in the bush. Soothsayers were consulted as to the fate of the country. The soothsayers were unanimous in saying that it would be the rightful heir to the throne who would save Mali. This heir was "The Man with Two Names." The elders of the court of Niani then remembered the son of Sogolon. The man with two names was no other than Maghan Sundiata. . . .

[When Sundiata learns of the situation back home in Mali, he returns to claim the throne. Because of the skills and generosity he amply demonstrated while in exile, he brings with him an army of loyal soldiers.]

Every man to his own land! If it is foretold that your destiny should be fulfilled in such and such a land, men can do nothing against it. . . . Neither the jealousy of a cruel stepmother, nor her wickedness, could alter for a moment the course of great destiny. The snake, man's enemy, is not long-lived, yet the serpent that lives hidden will surely die old. Sundiata was strong enough now to face his enemies. At the age of eighteen he had the stateliness of the lion and the strength of the buffalo. His voice carried authority, his eyes were live coals, his arm was iron, he was the husband of power.

Moussa Tounkara, king of Mema,* gave Sundiata half of his army. The most valiant came forward of their own free will to follow Sundiata in the great adventure. The cavalry of Mema, which he had fashioned himself, formed his iron squadron. Sundiata, dressed in the Muslim fashion of Mema, left the town at the head of his small but redoubtable army. The whole population sent their best wishes with him. . . . Then [his brother] said to [him], "Djata, do you think yourself able to face Soumaoro now?"

"No matter how small a forest may be, you can always find there sufficient fibers to tie up a man. Numbers mean nothing; it is worth that counts. With my cavalry I shall clear myself a path to Mali. . . ."

Sundiata wanted to have done with Soumaoro before the rainy season, so he struck camp and marched on Krina where Soumaoro was encamped. The latter realized that the decisive battle had come. Sundiata deployed his men on the little hill that dominates the plain. The great battle was for the next day.

In the evening, to raise the men's spirits, Sundiata gave a great feast, for he was anxious that his men should wake up happy in the morning. Several oxen were slaughtered and that evening Balla Fasseke [Sundiata's *griot*], in front of the whole army, called to mind the history of old Mali. He praised Sundiata, seated amidst his lieutenants, in this manner:

"Now I address myself to you, Maghan Sundiata, I speak to you king of Mali, to whom dethroned monarchs flock. The time foretold to you by the *jinn* is now coming.

---

*While in exile, Sundiata won the respect and friendship of the king and served in his regiments.

Sundiata, kingdoms and empires are in the likeness of man; like him they are born, they grow and disappear. Each sovereign embodies one moment of that life. Formerly, the kings of Ghana extended their kingdom over all the lands inhabited by the black man, but the circle has closed and the Cisses of Wagadou are nothing more than petty princes in a desolate land. Today, another kingdom looms up, powerful, the kingdom of Sosso. Humbled kings have borne their tribute to Sosso, Soumaoro's arrogance knows no more bounds and his cruelty is equal to his ambition. But will Soumaoro dominate the world? Are we, the *griots* of Mali, condemned to pass on to future generations the humiliations which the king of Sosso cares to inflict on our country? No, you may be glad, children of the "Bright Country," for the kingship of Sosso is but the growth of yesterday, whereas that of Mali dates from the time of Bilali. Each kingdom has its childhood, but Soumaoro wants to force the pace, and so Sosso will collapse under him like a horse worn out beneath its rider.

"You, Maghan, you are Mali. It has had a long and difficult childhood like you. Sixteen kings have preceded you on the throne of Niani, sixteen kings have reigned with varying fortunes. . . . Sixteen generations have consolidated their power. You are the outgrowth of Mali just as the silk-cotton tree is the growth of the earth, born of deep and mighty roots. To face the tempest the tree must have long roots and gnarled branches. Maghan Sundiata, has not the tree grown? . . .

"You are the son of Nare Maghan, but you are also the son of your mother Sogolon, the buffalo-woman, before whom powerless sorcerers shrank in fear. You have the strength and majesty of the lion, you have the might of the buffalo.

"I have told you what future generations will learn about your ancestors, but what will we be able to relate to our sons so that your memory will stay alive, what will we have to teach our sons about you? What unprecedented exploits, what unheard of feats? By what distinguished actions will our sons be brought to regret not having lived in the time of Sundiata?

"*Griots* are men of the spoken word, and by the spoken word we give life to the gestures of kings. But words are nothing but words; power lies in deeds. Be a man of action; do not answer me any more with your mouth, but tomorrow, on the plain of Krina, show me what you would have me recount to coming generations. Tomorrow allow me to sing the "Song of the Vultures" over the bodies of the thousands of Sossos whom your sword will have laid low before evening."

It was on the eve of Krina. In this way Balla Fasseke reminded Sundiata of the history of Mali so that, in the morning, he would show himself worthy of his ancestors. . . .

[The battle was a great victory for Sundiata and his armies, although Soumaoro cowardly escaped, alive but defeated. At the end of hostilities, Sundiata returned to his native city and received a tumultuous welcome and the sworn allegiances of leaders throughout the new empire.]

After a year Sundiata held a new assembly at Niani. . . . The Kings and notables of all the tribes came. . . . In this way, every year, Sundiata gathered about him all the kings and notables; so justice prevailed everywhere, for the kings were afraid of being denounced at Niani.

Sundiata's justice spared nobody. He followed the very word of God. He protected the weak against the strong and people would make journeys lasting several days to come and demand justice of him. Under his sun, the upright man was rewarded and the wicked one punished.

In their new-found peace the villages knew prosperity again, for with Sundiata happiness had come into everyone's home. Vast fields of millet, rice, cotton, indigo, and fonio surrounded the villages. Whoever worked always had something to live on. Each year long caravans carried the taxes . . . to Niani. You could go from village to village without fear of brigands. A thief would have his right hand chopped off and if he stole again he would be put to the sword. . . .

There are some kings who are powerful through their military strength. Everybody trembles before them, but when they die nothing but ill is spoken of them. Others do neither good nor ill, and when they die, they are forgotten. Others are feared because they have power, but they know how to use it, and they are loved because they love justice. Sundiata belonged to this group. He was feared, but loved as well. He was the father of Mali, and gave the world peace. After him, the world has not seen a greater conqueror, for he was the seventh and last conqueror. He had made the capital of an empire out of his father's village, and Niani became the navel of the earth. . . .

Men of today, how small you are beside your ancestors, and small in mind too, for you have trouble grasping the meaning of my words. . . . Sundiata rests [buried] near Niani, but his spirit lives on. . . .

To acquire my knowledge I [the *griot*] have journeyed all round Mali. At Kita, I saw the mountain where the lake of holy water sleeps; at Segou, I learnt the history of the kings of Do and Kri. . . . Everywhere, I was able to see and understand what my masters were teaching me, but between their hands I took an oath to teach only what is to be taught, and to conceal what is to be kept concealed.

AKBAR OF MUGHAL INDIA

The second leader we consider is the Mughal emperor Akbar (reigned 1556–1605). Akbar ruled northern India, including large parts of present-day Pakistan and Bangladesh, and he is generally considered one of the greatest of Indian kings. The founder of the dynasty, Babur (reigned 1526–1530), and his followers were Muslim Turks from central Asia, who had been driven from their homes by invaders. Called Mughals, because they were mistakenly identified with the Mongols, they were militarily very sophisticated, employing both matchlockmen and field artillery. They needed all that sophistication to hold onto their newly won territory. Akbar's father succeeded Babur after his death, and he first lost the territory and then won it back just a year before he died.

To consolidate his power, Akbar also had to account for the differing beliefs and traditions of the Hindu and Muslim regions of his realm. Akbar devised and put into practice the principles of what proved to be a very effective Mughal administrative system. Probably the single most important aspect of his rule was his tolerance and incorporation of Hindus. Although he evidently started out as a devout Muslim, he eliminated many policies that had made the Hindu population of his empire second-class subjects. His actions included marrying Hindu princesses without requiring them to convert to Islam, naming Hindu nobles to high-ranking positions, and eliminating special taxes that Hindus had to pay. All of this was capped off by his policy of universal toleration of different religions.

Though illiterate himself, Akbar developed a deep knowledge of Hindu and Muslim cultures by having important texts read to him daily. He also sponsored artistic creation and was especially interested in information about different religions. The debates he sponsored among religious scholars apparently distanced him from any of the established religions. Ultimately he attempted to create a syncretic religion called *Din-i Ilahi,* based on worship of the sun and light, that he believed could unify Muslims, Hindus, Christians, and others. Characteristically, Akbar never attempted to force anyone to convert to his religion.

Two primary sources are offered to provide an assessment of Akbar's leadership. The first establishes the political ideal, as elaborated by a Muslim historian of northern India. Ziāud-dīn Barnī (1285–1358) came from a prominent aristocratic family of Indian Muslims. He was a close associate of a sultan of Delhi, but he fell from favor after that sultan's death in 1351, and he was arrested and sent into permanent exile. In 1358, he wrote the work *Rulings on Temporal Government (Fat āwa-yi-Jah ānd āri),* hoping thereby to return to the sultan's favor. It presents his understanding, formulated from an orthodox Sunni Muslim perspective, of how the ideal ruler should govern. Sunni Muslim governmental theory emphasized the role of the ruler in enforcing Muslim holy law (*shari'a*). Unbelievers were not forced to convert or to follow strictly Islamic practices, but they were not allowed to flaunt behaviors that were not in keeping with the religion's core beliefs. Hence, Barnī's writings can be taken as presenting a traditional Muslim understanding of leadership, and they were a well-known and respected portion of the legal and political culture of Muslim India.

The other main source is a commentary written by a Portugese Jesuit, whom Akbar had invited to his court to explain Christianity. Father Antonio Monserrate (1536–1600) was thought to be a humble, God-fearing man. He was chosen as part of a mission sent in 1578 at Akbar's request to instruct him about Roman Catholicism, and he remained in India till 1589. An indication of Akbar's opinion of him is that he asked Monserrate to serve as tutor to the crown prince. The Society of Jesus, or Jesuits, was a Catholic religious order that sought to recapture areas lost to the Reformation and to spread Catholicism to areas that had not benefited, as they saw it, from exposure to the true faith. Like many early Jesuits, Father Antonio Monserrate was intelligent and intense. He accompanied Akbar on some of his campaigns and enjoyed discussing religion and ideas with him. Fortunately, from the point of view of the historical record, Monserrate was instructed by his Jesuit superiors to keep a written account of his experiences, which he did in the form of a diary. Later, he compiled a general account that is the best European appraisal of Akbar. He affords us glimpses of Akbar's enduring interest in religion, and he also provides us with a general characterization of the man and his rule.

QUESTIONS TO CONSIDER

1. According to Barnī, what were the policies and goals that a ruler must pursue in order to fulfill the Muslim ideal of a good ruler?

2. Identify the ways that Akbar strengthened his hold on power. Did he do more to make himself loved by his subjects or feared by them?

3. Describe Akbar's character and assess what aspects of his character made him an effective ruler. Would Barnī have considered Akbar a good ruler?

4. Summarize the different treatment that Akbar meted out to people of different social ranks and religions.

5. The readings on Akbar include a general description of the practices of a good ruler and an eyewitness account of Akbar's actions. Which type of source allows us to assess Akbar's reign? How do the differences in the sources affect our understanding of Akbar as a ruler?

"RULINGS ON TEMPORAL GOVERNMENT" (1358)

Barnī

Whenever the ruler, with truly pious intent, . . . strives with the help of his supporters and followers, and with all the might and power of his office in the conviction that the glory of Muhammad's religion is the most important task of his own faith and dynasty, [then the following consequences follow]: Obedience to the command to do what is lawful and the prohibition of what is unlawful manifests itself in his capital and in the provinces; the banners of Islam are always exalted; virtue and merit grow and good works and obedience to God arise. . . . Those mandates of true religion are enforced and those forbidden by the Holy Law (Shari'a) sink low and become as if they had never been; love of God and of the Prophets is strengthened in the Muslim community and love of the world . . . lessens, and desire for the next world increases and desire for this world becomes wearisome and vexatious. The virtues of the people prevail over their vices; truth and the truthful obtain glory and honor, lying and liars, dishonor.

Descendants of Muhammad, doctors of Shari'a, mystics, ascetics, devotees, recluses appear great, honored, distinguished, and illustrious in the sight and in the minds of men, while the ignorant, the corrupt, the irreligious, the negligent [in performing their prayers], and the shameless appear contemptible, powerless, and unworthy in men's sight. In Holy War sincere zeal is manifested, and the desire for

Source: Barnī, "Rulings on Temporal Government," in *Sources of Indian Tradition,* William Theodore de Bary, Stephen N. Hay, Royal Weiler, and Andrew Yarrow, eds., 503–04. Copyright © 1959 Columbia University Press. Reprinted with permission.

martyrdom graces the warriors and strivers for the faith. Truth and honesty become such; perfidy* and dishonesty are reduced to a sorry plight; the good and the just take up occupations in religion and government; the tyrannical and the wicked are left to roam at large "unwept, unhonored, and unsung," or by a change in their dispositions, to behave justly and well; the rich and propertied discharge their obligations to God, and give alms, and perform charitable good works; the poor and the needy are not left in want and are freed from hunger and nakedness.

[However,] If God Most High views the people of a country and clime with eyes of wrath, and wishes them to remain in toil, trouble, suffering, distress, and disorder, he appoints over them a ruler who is a slave to innate depravity, so that they may be at a loss to know what to do through his evil character and filthy habits, and be utterly confounded through his vicious qualities.

COMMENTARY ON HIS JOURNEY TO THE COURT OF AKBAR (1582)

Father Antonio Monserrate

To return to Akbar, . . . [the] Prince is of a stature and of a type of countenance well-fitted to his royal dignity, so that one could easily recognise, even at the first glance, that he is the King. He has broad shoulders, somewhat bandy legs well-suited for horsemanship, and a light-brown complexion. . . . His forehead is broad and open, his eyes so bright and flashing. . . . He shaves his beard, but wears a moustache like that of a Turkish youth who has not yet attained to manhood (for on reaching manhood they begin to affect a beard). Contrary to the custom of his race, he does not cut his hair; nor does he wear a hat, but a turban, into which he gathers up his hair. He does this, they say, as a concession to Indian usages, and to please his Indian subjects. . . . His body is exceedingly well-built and is neither too thin nor too stout. He is sturdy, hearty and robust. When he laughs, his face becomes almost distorted. His expression is tranquil, serene and open, full also of dignity, and when he is angry, of awful majesty. When the priests first saw him he was thirty-eight years of age. It is hard to exaggerate how accessible he makes himself to all who wish audience of him. For he creates an opportunity almost every day for any of the common people or of the nobles to see him and converse with him; and he endeavours to show himself pleasant-spoken and affable rather than severe toward all who come to speak with him. It is very remarkable how great an effect this courtesy and affability has in

*Treachery.

Source: Taken from *The Commentary of Father Monserrate, S. J. On his Journey to the Court of Akbar*, trans. from Latin by J. S. Hoyland and annotated by S. N. Banerjee (London and Bombay: Oxford University Press, 1922), 196–211. Note: Monserrate refers to Akbar throughout as Zelandinus. For clarity's sake, we have changed every reference to Zelandinus to Akbar, and we have changed the archaic usage "Musalmans" to Muslim.

attaching to him the minds of his subjects. For in spite of his very heterodox* attitude toward the religion of Muhammad, and in spite also of the fact that Muslims regard such an attitude as an unforgivable offence, Akbar has not yet been assassinated. He has an acute insight, and shows much wise foresight both in avoiding dangers and in seizing favourable opportunities for carrying out his designs.

Akbar is greatly devoted to hunting, though not equally so to hawking. As he is of a somewhat morose disposition, he amuses himself with various games. These games afford also a public spectacle to the nobility and the common people, who indeed are very fond of such spectacles. They are the following: Polo, elephant-fighting, buffalo-fighting, stag-fighting and cock-fighting, boxing contests, battles of gladiators, and the flying of tumbler-pigeons. He is also very fond of strange birds, and indeed of any novel object. He amuses himself with singing, concerts, dances, conjurer's tricks, and the jokes of his jesters, of whom he makes much. However, although he may seem at such times to be at leisure and to have laid aside public affairs, he does not cease to revolve in his mind the heavy cares of state. He is especially remarkable for his love of keeping great crowds of people around him and in his sight; and thus it comes about that his court is always thronged with multitudes of men of every type, though especially with the nobles, whom he commands to come from their provinces and reside at court for a certain period each year. When he goes outside the palace, he is surrounded and followed by these nobles and a strong body-guard. They have to go on foot until he gives them a nod to indicate that they may mount. All this adds greatly to the wonderful majesty and greatness of the royal court.

According to the custom of the Muslims, the orthodox must wear a long robe coming down to the calf, together with shoes very low at the ankle. Their dress must be made of wool, linen or cotton: and must be white. The shoes must be of a certain fixed pattern. However, Akbar . . . wears garments of silk, beautifully embroidered in gold. His military cloak comes down only as far as the knee, . . . ; and his boots cover his ankles completely. Moreover, he himself designed the fashion and shape of these boots. He wears gold ornaments, pearls and jewellery. He is very fond of carrying a European sword and dagger. He is never without arms: and is always surrounded, even within his private apartments, by a body-guard of about twenty men, variously armed. He much approves the Spanish dress, and wears it in private. He himself can ride and control elephants, camels and horses. He drives a two-horse chariot, in which his appearance is very striking and dignified. He generally sits, with crossed legs, upon a couch covered with scarlet rugs. However, he has a velvet throne of the Portuguese type carried with him on a journey, and very frequently uses it. . . .

The splendour of his palaces approaches closely to that of the royal dwellings of Europe. They are magnificently built, from foundation to cornice, of hewn stone, and are decorated both with painting and carving. Unlike the palaces built by other Indian kings, they are lofty; for an Indian palace is generally as low and humble as an idol-temple. Their total circuit is so large that it easily embraces four great royal dwellings, of which the King's own palace is the largest and the finest. The second palace belongs to the queens, and the third to the royal princes, whilst the fourth is used as a store house and magazine.

*Unorthodox.

Akbar is so devoted to building that he sometimes quarries stone himself, along with the other workmen. Nor does he shrink from watching and even himself practising, for the sake of amusement, the craft of an ordinary artisan. For this purpose he has built a workshop near the palace, where also are studios and work-rooms for the finer and more reputable arts, such as painting, goldsmith-work, tapestry-making, carpet and curtain-making, and the manufacture of arms. Hither he very frequently comes and relaxes his mind with watching at their work those who practise these arts.

He is a great patron of learning, and always keeps around him erudite men, who are directed to discuss before him philosophy, theology, and religion, and to recount to him the history of great kings and glorious deeds of the past. He has an excellent judgment and a good memory, and has attained to a considerable knowledge of many subjects by means of constant and patient listening to such discussions. Thus he not only makes up for his ignorance of letters (for he is entirely unable either to read or write), but he has also become able clearly and lucidly to expound difficult matters. He can give his opinion on any question so shrewdly and keenly, that no one who did not know that he is illiterate would suppose him to be anything but very learned and erudite. And so indeed he is, for in addition to his keen intellect, of which I have already spoken, he excels many of his most learned subjects in eloquence, as well as in that authority and dignity which befits a King. The wise men are wont every day to hold disputations on literary subjects before him. . . .

Akbar has about twenty Hindu chieftains as ministers and counsellors to assist both in the work of governing the empire and in the control of the royal household. They are devoted to him, and are very wise and reliable in conducting public business. They are always with him, and are admitted to the innermost parts of the palace, which is a privilege not allowed even to the Mongol [Mughal] nobles. However, he is wont to entrust the provincial governorships to chiefs. . . . who are related to him. Some of these chiefs also act not only as tutors but also as guardians to his sons. His object in arranging this is to attach the chiefs to himself by a yet closer bond of affection, and also to provide protectors for his children from the malice of his life-long enemies. . . .

The following is the method the King employs in deliberation—he asks each counsellor privately for his own opinion, and then himself decides upon the course which seems to be supported by the largest number and the most experienced. He asks their advice even about subjects upon which he has already made up his mind, saying to the nobles, "This is what I think should be done, do you agree?" They reply "Salaam, O King;" whereupon he says, "Then let it be carried out." If however any of them do not agree with him, he listens patiently, and sometimes even alters his own opinion. Seven of his chief counsellors are chosen for the following purpose. One of them is on duty each day to attend to the business of those who crave an audience, to bring forward their petitions, and to note down and transmit the King's replies. It is the duty also of these chief counsellors to act as masters of the ceremonies, to usher forward those who are admitted to do homage to the King, to conduct them back again, to station them in the places to which their dignity entitles them, and to present their petitions before the King.

Akbar receives foreigners and strangers in a very different manner to that in which he treats his own fellow-countrymen and subordinates. For he behaves with marked courtesy and kindliness to foreigners, especially to the ambassadors of foreign kings, and to princes who have been driven from their dominions and appeal to him for protection. . . .

When his aunt returned from Mecca, the King had the street-pavements covered with silken shawls, and conducted her himself to her palace in a gorgeous litter, scattering largess meanwhile to the crowds. . . .

Akbar behaves so sternly toward the nobles who are under his proud sway that each one of them believes himself to be regarded not only as a contemptible creature but as the very lowest and meanest of mankind. For instance these nobles, if they commit offences, are punished more severely and relentlessly than the rest of the people, even those of the meanest degree. . . .

The King exacts enormous sums in tribute from the provinces of his empire, which is wonderfully rich and fertile both for cultivation and pasture, and has a great trade both in exports and imports. He also derives much revenue from the hoarded fortunes of the great nobles, which by law and custom all come to the King on their owners' death. In addition, there are the spoils of conquered kings and chieftains, whose treasure is seized, and the great levies exacted, and gifts received, from the inhabitants of newly-subdued districts in every part of his dominions. These gifts and levies are apt to be so large as to ruin outright many of his new subjects. He also engages in trading on his own account, and thus increases his wealth to no small degree; for he eagerly exploits every possible source of profit. . . .

The King's severity toward errors and misdemeanours by officials in the course of government business is remarkable, for he is most stern with offenders against the public faith. Hence all are afraid of his severity, and strive with all their might to do as he directs and desires. For the King has the most precise regard for right and justice in the affairs of government. . . . He is easily excited to anger, but soon cools down again. By nature moreover he is kindly and benevolent, and is sincerely anxious that guilt should be punished, without malice indeed, but at the same time without undue leniency. Hence in the cases in which he himself acts as judge the guilty are, by his own directions, not punished until he has given orders for the third time that this shall be done. . . .

The following are the ways in which the guilty are punished. Those who have committed a capital crime are either crushed by elephants, impaled, or hanged. Seducers and adulterers are either strangled or gibbeted. The King has such a hatred of debauchery and adultery that neither influence nor entreaties nor the great ransom which was offered would induce him to pardon his chief trade commissioner, who although he was already married had violently debauched a well-born Brahman* girl. The wretch was by the King's order remorselessly strangled.

EMPEROR KANGXI OF THE QING DYNASTY IN CHINA

In the autobiographical sketch of Kangxi (reign 1661–1722), we have the self-understanding of a man who melded the new, frontier, warrior culture of the Manchu with the rich intellectual tradition and highly developed political culture

---

*The highest Hindu caste.

of China. The Manchu Qing (pronounced "Ching") dynasty had seized power in 1644 in a China in which the rule of the Ming dynasty (1368–1644) had deteriorated precipitously. Loss of effective control of the bureaucracy and tax revenue combined with ruinous court intrigues to generate corruption, public unrest, and a devastated peasantry. China was in such turmoil that a Chinese rebel army actually seized the capital, Beijing, before the Manchus, causing the last Ming ruler to hang himself in shame.

The Manchus had been organizing and expanding in the region now known as Manchuria for some time. They still retained the martial culture of other nomadic peoples, such as the Mongols. Manchuria had long been a tributary state of China, and the Manchus were heavily influenced by Chinese culture. Despite this strong Chinese imprint on their culture, they were identified by the Chinese as an alien, invading force, and they had to fight for almost three decades to secure their rule in the south and to extinguish the last Ming claimants. Although Kangxi defended the legitimacy of the Manchu conquest, many of their policies were very unpopular. They seized whole areas of land to feed their armies. The Manchu forced Chinese men to shave the front of their heads and wear their hair in a long braided queue in the back. They also required Chinese men to wear the tight, high-collared jacket that fastened at the right shoulder. For all of these reasons, the Qing dynasty had to face anti-Manchu feelings both at the time of the conquest and periodically throughout the centuries until the dynasty finally collapsed in 1911.

Despite these obstacles, the Qing produced some able leaders, and Kangxi is considered by many scholars to be one of the greatest rulers in Chinese history. Kangxi was the second Manchu emperor of China. Whereas his father had had to oversee the elimination of the last Ming claimants to the throne and their supporters, Kangxi had to devote his early energies to consolidating his power. Much power and autonomy had been retained by three noble generals who had led the conquest of southern China. As part of consolidating his rule, Kangxi mastered and then devoted himself with great discipline to the required observances of the "son of Heaven," which were deemed necessary for China to enjoy harmony and prosperity. His extraordinarily long and active reign (1661–1722) gave him time to grow and mature as a ruler and a man, but it also placed a heavy obligation on him. By the end of his life, suffering from ill health and deeply saddened by the betrayal of his favorite son, Kangxi was subject to fits of melancholy and fatigue.

The material included here was excerpted from two distinct sources; one is a compilation of his thoughts on the governance of his realm. We have them in their present form owing to the work of Jonathan Spence, who organized Kangxi's scattered autobiographical reflections on leadership into a coherent narrative. The "On Ruling" excerpt starts out rather dramatically with a discussion of capital punishment, because this is the most serious matter a ruler must deal with. The other text is a valedictory[3] document he produced at the end of his life. He knew the valedictory texts of his predecessors well enough to know that they were heavily edited and shaped documents whose purpose was to inspire future rulers to great acts. The valedictory text was put in its final form by Kangxi himself, and he presented it to his sons and leading officials on December 23, 1717. His purpose in preparing his own valedictory was to present a true picture of the burden and challenges of ruling China. He intended that it warn and assist any man who assumed the mantle of "son of Heaven," but it was not made public by his heir and court officials.

QUESTIONS TO CONSIDER

1. Identify the ways in which Kangxi fulfills his responsibilities as emperor in keeping with Chinese practices. List other ways that he might have made Manchu rule more acceptable to the Chinese.
2. Describe acts or policies of Kangxi that seem to differ from accepted Chinese practices. In your opinion, which way is better, his approach or the accepted practice?
3. Assess Kangxi's use of fear (force) and love (positive policies designed to win loyalty). How and when does he employ different strategies? Would Machiavelli approve of Kangxi's methods of ruling?
4. Characterize Kangxi's conception of leadership in the two sources, "On Ruling" and "Valedictory." How does his understanding of and approach to leadership compare in the two sources? How do you explain the differences?
5. What are the strong points of this sort of autobiographical source? What are its possible weaknesses? How does the view of Kangxi that we get from this source differ from the pictures of Sundiata and Akbar that emerged from the other sources?

"ON RULING"

Kangxi

Giving life to people and killing people—those are the powers that the emperor has. He knows that administrative errors in government bureaus can be rectified, but that a criminal who has been executed cannot be brought back to life any more than a chopped string can be joined together again. He knows, too, that sometimes people have to be persuaded into morality by the example of an execution. . . . [T]he ruler needs both clarity and care in punishing: his intent must be to punish in order to avoid the need for further punishing. . . . I have been merciful where possible. For the ruler must always check carefully before executions, and leave room for the hope that men will get better if they are given the time. In the hunt one can kill all the animals caught inside the circle, but one can't always bear to shoot them as they stand there, trapped and exhausted. . . .

Source: Jonathan D. Spence, *Emperor of China: Self-Portrait of K'ang-Hsi,* 30–59, 143–51. Copyright © 1974 Alfred A. Knopf. Used by permission of Alfred A. Knopf, a division of Random House, Inc.

It's a good principle to look for the good points in a person, and to ignore the bad. If you are always suspicious of people they will suspect you too. . . .

There are too many men who claim to be *ju*—pure scholars—and yet are stupid and arrogant; we'd be better off with less talk of moral principle and more practice of it. Even in those who have been the best officials in my reign there are obvious failings. . . . P'eng P'eng was always honest and courageous—when robbers were in his district he simply put on his armor, rode out, and routed them—but when angry he was wild and vulgar in his speech, and showed real disrespect. Zhao Shen-jiao was completely honest, traveled with only thirteen servants and no personal secretaries at all, but was too fond of litigation and was constantly getting the common people involved in complex cases. Shi Shi-lun was an official of complete integrity, but he swung too much in favor of the poor—in any lawsuit when a commoner was involved with a junior degree holder he'd favor the commoner, and when a junior degree holder was involved with a member of the upper gentry he'd favor the junior degree holder. In the same way Yang Ming-shi kept insisting on failing the rich examination candidates and passing the poor, even if they were really crude at letters. And Zhang Peng-ge, whom I praised so often and kept in the highest offices, could write a memorial so stupid that I ordered it printed up and posted in major cities so that everyone could read it—for he claimed that the drop in the river's level was due to a miracle performed by the spirit of the waters, when the real reason was that no rain had fallen for six months in the upper reaches of the Yellow River. . . .

There is no way the emperor can know every official in the country, so he has to rely on the officials themselves for evaluations. . . . But when they are in cliques, he has to make his own inquiries as well; . . . for example, Governor Wen-pao, who reported that he was so virtuous that the people had begged to be allowed to erect honorary tablets in his name. But I made inquiries and found that most of them were murmuring in fury and would much rather have eaten him. Partly the trouble lies in failure of contact between top and bottom—after I began to make regular tours . . . , then things got better there.

The emperor can get extra information in audience, on tours, and in palace memorials. From the beginning of my reign, I sought ways to guarantee that discussion among great officials be kept confidential. . . . A court audience has the important function of reducing arrogance. Naturally one can't summon all military governors for audiences at the same time, but regular audiences are crucial with military men, especially when they have held power a long time. There might have been no rebellion if [the military governors] . . . had been summoned for regular audiences and made properly fearful. . . .

On tours I learned about the common people's grievances by talking with them, or by accepting their petitions. In northern China I asked peasants about their officials, looked at their houses, and discussed their crops. In the South I heard pleas. . . . But if someone was attacked in an anonymous message, then I refused to take action, for we should always confront a witness directly; and if someone exaggerated too stupidly, then too I would not listen. A man swam toward my boat in Hangchow with a petition tied around his neck, shouting out that he had a certain enemy who was the number-one man in the world for committing evil acts—and I simply had my retainers ask him, "Who then is number two?"

I've tried to be impartial between Manchus and Chinese, and not to separate one from the other in judgments: neither to have the ministers sit in silence like wooden puppets, nor to let them write out enormous memorials on some subject like the granting of an honorary sage's title to a Sung scholar. There are certainly differences in their characters: the Manchus are direct and open, whereas the Chinese think it better not to let any joy or anger show in their faces. And the Manchus are often tougher and braver . . . , and treat both slaves and horses better. But the Manchus' scholarship is often in no ways inferior to that of the Chinese. . . .

In river conservancy work also, though there are only two broad choices—should one speed the flow of water to the sea, or should one heighten the dikes?—it's the constant attention to details that is of the greatest importance. . . .

. . . Talent does not depend on geographical location. Even in the mountain wildernesses how can there be no one with ability? Have the talented ever chosen where they were to be born? . . . When a person is truly good, then one should use him and promote him . . . regardless of whether he has advanced degrees. . . .

"There's an old saying that if the civilian officials don't seek money and the military officials aren't afraid of death, we need never fear that the country won't have Great Peace." How true that is!

The *Doctrine of the Mean* says: "The superior man does what is proper to the station in which he is; he does not desire to go beyond this. In a high situation, he does not treat with contempt his inferiors. In a low situation, he does not court the favor of his superiors. He rectifies himself, and seeks for nothing from others, so that he has no dissatisfactions. He does not murmur against Heaven nor grumble against man. Thus it is that the superior man is quiet and calm, waiting for the appointments of Heaven, while the mean man walks in dangerous paths, looking for lucky occurrences." These are truly wise words, clear as sun or stars.

This is what we have to do: apply ourselves to human affairs to the utmost, while remaining responsive to the dictates of Heaven. . . .

The superior man is firmly resolved.
He walks alone and is caught in the rain.
He is bespattered,
And people murmur against him.
No blame.

And again:

In dealing with weeds,
Firm resolution is necessary.

Things may seem determined in our lives, but there are these and other ways in which man's power can develop Heaven's work. . . . We must urge on Heaven in its work, not just rely upon it. . . . [I]f you do not perform your human part you cannot comprehend Heaven's way. If the fortuneteller says you will be successful, can you then say, "I'm bound to do well and needn't study properly"? If he says you'll be rich, can you sit still and let the wealth come? If he offers you a life without misfortune, can you be reckless without fear? Or be debauched without harm because he says you'll live long without illness? . . .

Once as a youth I was in the mountains, among deep woods, when suddenly there were crashes of thunder and I fled. Moments later the trees among which I had been walking were struck. So we see that though it is hard to fathom Heaven's signs, if you approach them openly you can attain a kind of foreknowledge. . . .

"VALEDICTORY" (1717)

Kangxi

When I was young, Heaven gave me great strength, and I didn't know what sickness was. This spring I started to get serious attacks of dizziness and grew increasingly emaciated. Then I went hunting in the autumn beyond the borders, and the fine climate of the Mongolian regions made my spirits stronger day by day, and my face filled out again. . . . Since there are some things that I have wanted to say to you on a normal day, I have specially summoned you today to hear my edict, face to face with me.

The rulers of the past all took reverence for Heaven's laws and reverence for their ancestors as the fundamental way in ruling the country. To be sincere in reverence for Heaven and ancestors entails the following: Be kind to men from afar and keep the able ones near, nourish the people, think of the profit of all as being the real profit and the mind of the whole country as being the real mind, be considerate to officials and act as a father to the people, protect the state before danger comes and govern well before there is any disturbance, be always diligent and always careful, and maintain the balance between leniency and strictness, between principle and expediency, so that long-range plans can be made for the country. That's all there is to it.

No dynasty in history has been as just as ours in gaining the right to rule. The . . . roving bandit Li Zi-cheng* stormed the city of Peking, the Ming Emperor Zhong-zhen hanged himself,† and the officials and people all came out to welcome us. Then we exterminated the violent bandits and inherited the empire. . . . From this we can tell that all the rebellious officials and bandits are finally pushed aside by truly legitimate rulers.

I am now close to seventy, and have been over fifty years on the throne—this is all due to the quiet protection of Heaven and earth and the ancestral spirits; it was not my meager virtue that did it. Since I began reading in my childhood, I have managed to get a rough understanding of the constant historical principles. Every emperor and ruler has been subject to the Mandate of Heaven. Those fated to enjoy old age cannot prevent themselves from enjoying that old age; those fated to enjoy a time of Great Peace cannot prevent themselves from enjoying that Great Peace.

Source: Jonathan D. Spence, *Emperor of China: Self-Portrait of K'ang-Hsi* (New York: Alfred A. Knopf, 1974), 143–51.

*The leader of one of the two rebel Chinese armies that were formed in the last years of Ming rule because of the chaos in the country.

†In despair over the collapse of his rule and the rebel armies besieging his capital, the last Ming emperor hanged himself in an imperial garden.

Over 4,350 years have passed from the first year of the Yellow Emperor* to the present, and over 300 emperors are listed as having reigned. . . . In the 1,960 years from the first year of Qin Shi Huangdi† to the present, there have been 211 people who have been named emperor and have taken era names. What man am I, that among all those who have reigned long since the Ch'in and Han Dynasties, it should be I who have reigned the longest?

Among the Ancients, only those who were not boastful and knew not to go too far could attain a good end. Since the Three Dynasties, those who ruled long did not leave a good name to posterity, while those who did not live long did not know the world's griefs. I am already old, and have reigned long, and I cannot foretell what posterity will think of me.

With me it is different. I am letting you know what my sincerest feelings are in advance.

When I had been twenty years on the throne I didn't dare conjecture that I might reign thirty. After thirty years I didn't dare conjecture that I might reign forty. Now I have reigned fifty-seven years. The "Great Plan" section of the Book of History says of the five joys:

The first is long life;
The second is riches;
The third is soundness of body and serenity of mind;
The fourth is the love of virtue;
The fifth is an end crowning the life.

The "end crowning the life" is placed last because it is so hard to attain. I am now approaching seventy, and my sons, grandsons, and great-grandsons number over one hundred and fifty. The country is more or less at peace and the world is at peace. Even if we haven't improved all manners and customs, and made all the people prosperous and contented, yet I have worked with unceasing diligence and intense watchfulness, never resting, never idle. . . .

In pacifying the Three Feudatories‡ and clearing out the northern deserts, I made all the plans myself. Unless it was for military matters or famine relief, I didn't take funds from the Board of Revenue treasury, and spent nothing recklessly, for the reason that this was the people's wealth. . . .

I came to the throne at eight, fifty-seven years ago. I've never let people talk on about supernatural influences of the kind that have been recorded in the Histories. . . . Those are all empty words, and I don't presume so far. I just go on each day in an ordinary way, and concentrate on ruling properly. . . .

I wish all of you officials to remember that I have been the peace-bearing Son of Heaven for over fifty years, and that what I have said to you over and over again is really sincere. Then that will complete the fitting end to my life.

---

*The "Yellow Emperor" was Huang-Di, the first of the legendary Five Emperors who were thought to have ruled at the beginning of Chinese history.

†The founder of the Qin dynasty (221–206 BCE) was Shi Huangdi.

‡These were the areas left practically independent under the powerful Manchu military leaders who had completed the conquest of southern China.

I've been preparing this edict for ten years. If a "valedictory edict" is issued, let it contain nothing but these same words.

I've revealed my entrails and shown my guts, there's nothing left within me to reveal.

I will say no more.

PETER THE GREAT OF RUSSIA

Peter I (1672–1725) of Russia was one of the most extraordinary rulers of eighteenth-century Europe. He came to power in a country with a deeply established traditional culture that was changing rapidly in the face of increased contact and competition with western and northern European powers. Under Peter, Russia defeated Sweden to become the single greatest power in eastern Europe. He also instituted an entire range of social, economic, cultural, intellectual, and political changes. So impressive was his remaking of Russia that Daniel Defoe indicated in his notebooks that he had Peter in mind when he wrote about Robinson Crusoe establishing civilized life on the uninhabited and wild island of his shipwreck.

Peter's reforms were not without precedent or consequence. Some reforms had begun under Peter's father, Tsar Alexei—most notably religious changes instituted in 1666–1667 in a belated reaction to the Protestant Reformation. Those changes led to the Great Schism in the Russian Orthodox Church. A sizable minority of the population, known as "Old Believers," refused to accept the changes, and they were persecuted as heretics by the official church and by the state. Despite such changes, Muscovite political culture was still medieval and religious in nature. The tsar's role was thought to be like that of a father in a family, and many of his functions had to do with performing public ceremonies, often related to religious holidays, that would preserve the organic Orthodox Christian unity and well-being of the land. Peter developed a completely different political idea that was an amalgam of Russian doctrines about the personal, autocratic power of the tsar and western ideas about rational, secular rule in service of an abstract, impersonal state. In addition, Peter imported selected parts of western culture and learning, and he imposed them on an often resistant nobility. The most visible sign of Peter's western orientation was the new capital of St. Petersburg that he ordered built.

At 6'7" in height and possessed of incredible energy, Peter towered over his country both figuratively and literally, and his frantic, far-reaching reforms were often instituted at severe costs to the population as a whole. Under Peter the conditions for serfs deteriorated, becoming much more like slavery than like medieval European serfdom. He devised an array of new taxes to pay for the constant warfare of his reign and for such projects as the new capital. Serf labor was conscripted to work on fortifications, shipbuilding, and other crash projects unleashed by Peter's imperial order. In fact, the building of St. Petersburg itself is thought to have taken the lives of 10,000–20,000 serf laborers.

For Peter, we are not blessed with sources of the caliber of Monserrate's report on Akbar or Kangxi's autobiographical writings. As a result, we employ a mixture of different types of documents here. The first source is an imperial edict that invites foreigners to come to Russia and enter Russian government service. It also provides Peter's overall goals. The second set of sources—the decree on building restrictions and the description of a ban on kneeling in the tsar's presence in St. Petersburg—involve Peter's use of "rational" legislation for the public good. Following this, the third set of documents present Peter's view of the ruler's role as first servant of the state and his understanding of the proper behavior of his subjects. The final set of texts present two Russian opinions of Peter. The first represents the widespread contemporary view among the general populace that Peter was the Antichrist. The second is the characterization of Russia's debt to Russia, written by the prominent nineteenth-century conservative historian, Mikhail Pogodin.

QUESTIONS TO CONSIDER

1. On the basis of all of these documents, what were Peter's goals as leader of Russia? In general, are they goals a leader should strive for?
2. What methods did Peter use to attain his goals? Identify places, if there are any, where his methods are not consistent with his goals and explain why.
3. Characterize the opinions of Peter expressed in the final two documents. How can you explain the different opinions of Peter presented in the two texts? In your opinion, does Peter deserve to be called "Great"?
4. How does Peter's understanding of leadership and what is good for his country compare with that of the other leaders discussed in this chapter? How do these sources compare with the types of sources used for the other leaders?
5. How does Peter present a different image of himself to the world than did his father, Tsar Alexei? What impression is imparted by the picture of Peter and the building of St. Petersburg?

"DECREE ON THE INVITATION TO FOREIGNERS" (1702)

It is sufficiently known in all the lands which the Almighty has placed under our rule, that since our accession to the throne all our efforts and intentions have tended to govern this realm in such a way that all of our subjects should, through our care for the general good, become more and more prosperous. For this end we have always

Source: "Decree on the Invitation to Foreigners" (1702), in *Peter the Great*, ed. L. Jay Oliva, 44. Copyright © 1970 Prentice-Hall. Reprinted by permission of Pearson Education, Inc., Upper Saddle River, NJ.

tried to maintain internal order, to defend the State against invasion, and in every possible way to improve and to extend trade. With this purpose we have been compelled to make some necessary and salutary changes in the administration, in order that our subjects might more easily gain a knowledge of matters of which they were before ignorant, and become more skillful in their commercial relations. We have therefore given orders, made dispositions, and founded institutions indispensable for increasing our trade with foreigners, and shall do the same in future. Nevertheless we fear that matters are not in such a good condition as we desire, and that our subjects cannot in perfect quietness enjoy the fruits of our labours, and we have therefore considered still other means to protect our frontier from the invasion of the enemy, and to preserve the rights and privileges of our State, and the general peace of all Christians, as is incumbent on a Christian monarch to do. To attain these worthy aims, we have endeavoured to improve our military forces, which are the protection of our State, so that our troops may consist of well-drilled men, maintained in perfect order and discipline. In order to obtain greater improvement in this respect, and to encourage foreigners, who are able to assist us in this way, as well as artists and artisans profitable to the State, to come in numbers to our country, we have issued this manifesto, and have ordered printed copies of it to be sent throughout Europe. And as in our residence of Moscow, the free exercise of religion of all other sects, although not agreeing with our church, is already allowed, so shall this be hereby confirmed anew in such wise that we, by the power granted to us by the Almighty, shall exercise no compulsion over the consciences of men, and shall gladly allow every Christian to care for his own salvation at his own risk.

"DECREES ON THE BUILDING OF ST. PETERSBURG" (1714)

1. On the City Island and the Admiralty Island in Saint Petersburg, as likewise on the banks of the greater Neva and its more important arms, wooden buildings are forbidden, only adobe houses being allowed. The two above-mentioned islands and the embankments excepted, wood may be used for buildings, the plans to be obtained from the architect Trezzini. The roofs are to be covered either with two thicknesses of turf laid on rafters with cross-ribs (not on laths or boards), or with tiles. No other roof covering is allowed under penalty of severe fines. The streets should be bordered directly by the houses, not with fences or stables.

2. The most illustrious and mighty Peter the Great, Emperor and Autocrat of all Russia, has commanded his imperial decree to be proclaimed to people of all ranks. Whereas stone construction here is advancing very slowly, it being difficult to

Source: "Decrees on the Building of St. Petersburg" (1714), in *Life and Thought in Old Russia*, ed. Marthe Blinoff, 16–17. Copyright © 1961 Pennsylvania State University Press. Reprinted with permission.

obtain stone-masons and other artisans of this craft even for good pay; for this reason all stone buildings of any description are forbidden in the whole state for a few years, until construction has sufficiently progressed here, under penalty of confiscation of the offender's property and exile. This decree is to be announced in all the cities and districts of the Saint Petersburg province, except this city, so that none may plead ignorance as an excuse.

"PROHIBITION ON KNEELING"

Some years after the city of Petersburg was built few streets were paved, and, on the smallest fall of rain, they were very wet and muddy; yet, when the czar appeared in public, every one fell on their knees, according to an ancient custom of the nation. It is easy to conceive the situation of his subjects on rising. The sovereign, little desirous of such useless respect, always made a sign to the people to abstain, and declared several times that this ceremony was by no means flattering to him. But as this declaration had no effect, and as the old custom continued to be kept up, he at last issued a proclamation, forbidding, under penalty of the knout,* any person to kneel before him in the streets, or to cover himself with mud in honor of his sovereign.

"ORDER TO THE ARMY BEFORE THE BATTLE OF POLTAVA" (1709)

Let the Russian soldiers know that the hour has come in which the very existence of the whole fatherland is placed in their hands: either Russia will perish completely, or she will be reborn for the better. They must think that they have been armed and drawn up in battle array, not for the sake of Peter, but for the sake of the state entrusted to Peter, for the sake of their kin and of the whole of the Russian people, which until now, has been protected by their arms, and which today is awaiting from them the final decision of its fortunes. Neither let them be disturbed by the glory of the enemy reputed to be invincible, for they themselves have repeatedly given the lie to this report. In the action to come let them keep only this before their mental eye— that God himself and Justice are fighting with us, of which fact, the Lord, who gives

Source: Account given by John Hosy, the emperor's First Surgeon, in *Original Anecdotes of Peter the Great,* ed. Jakob von Staehlin (New York: Arno Press, 1970), 99–100.

*A knotted-rope whip.

Source: Peter the Great, "Order to the Army Before the Battle of Poltava," June 27, 1709, in *A Source Book for Russian History from Early Times to 1917,* Vol. 2, ed. George Vernadsky, et al., 365. Copyright © 1972 Yale University Press. Reprinted with permission.

strength in battles, has already given them testimony by his aid in many combats: let them rely upon him alone. And as for Peter, let them know for certain that his life is not dear to him, if only Russia and Russian piety, glory, and prosperity survive.

"PETER'S CONCEPTION OF IMPERIAL AUTHORITY"

Peter the Great, conversing in the turner's shop with Bruce and Osterman, told them vehemently, "The foreigners say that I order servitors around like slaves. I order them like subjects who obey my decrees. These decrees contain good and not harm for the state. *English freedom is not relevant here, like a blank wall. One must know the people to rule them.* He who sees the bad and thinks up the good can speak to me directly without fear. You are witnesses to that. I am glad to hear something useful from the least subject; hands, feet, and tongues are not bridled. Access to me is open—if only they do not burden me merely with trifles and do not vainly take up my time each hour of which is dear to me. Ill-wishers and miscreants to me and to the Fatherland cannot be content: their bridle is the law. He is free who does not do evil and obeys the good."

"AN OLD BELIEVER MANUSCRIPT FROM SOLOVETSKY MONASTERY"

The Apostle says first comes a falling away, then is revealed the man of sin, the son of perdition, the Anti-Christ. First came the falling away from the holy faith by the Tsar Alexis in the year 666 [1666], the number of the beast thus fulfilling the prophecy.* And after him there reigned on the throne his first-born son Peter, from his second and unlawful marriage. He was consecrated to the throne of all the Russians by the Jewish laws from head to foot, showing that he is the false Messiah and the false Christ, as the Sibyl prophesied about him that a Jewish Tsar will reign. And that false Christ began to set himself up and be called God by all, persecuting and tormenting all Orthodox Christians, destroying their memory from the face of the earth, spreading

---

Source: In Andrei Nartov, *Razskazy Nartova o Petre Velikom* (Sanktpeterburg: Tip. Imp. akademii nauk, 1891), 82.

Source: In Eugene Schuyler, *Peter the Great,* Vol. 2 (New York: Charles Scribner's Sons, 1884), 153–54.

*This refers to the year of the Church Council that introduced the changes that produced the schism in the Russian Orthodox Church. The first digit was frequently omitted in Old Believer documents, yielding the apocalyptic number 666.

his new Jewish faith throughout all Russia. In the year 1700, to the accomplishment of his wickedness, and on the festival of the Circumcision of Christ, he called together a heathenish court and erected a temple to the heathen god Janus, and before all the people practiced all sorts of magic rites and all called out "vivat! vivat! the New Year," and he sent to all parts of the realm the command to feast for the new year, thus breaking the laws of the Fathers, who in the first Ecumenical Council commanded the feast of the New Year to be on September 1.* In the year 1721 he took upon himself the Patriarchal title, calling himself Father of the Country, Head of the Russian Church, and Autocrat, having no one on an equality with himself, taking craftily to himself not only the power of the Tsar, but also the authority of God, and claiming to be an autocratic pastor, a headless head over all the opponents of Christ, Anti-Christ.[†] Therefore must we conceal ourselves in the deserts just as the Prophet Jeremiah ordered the children of God to flee from Babylon. The years of the Lord have passed; the years of Satan have come.

"A NINETEENTH-CENTURY ASSESSMENT OF PETER THE GREAT"

We wake up. What day is it? 1 January 1841. Peter the Great ordered us to count years from the birth of Christ. Peter the Great ordered us to start the new year with January. It is time to get dressed—our clothing is sewn in a fashion given to us by Peter the First, our uniform according to his pattern. The cloth is woven at a factory that he ordered built, the wool is shorn from sheep that he ordered introduced into Russia. Our glance falls on a book—Peter the Great introduced the script it is written in and he himself carved out the letters. You begin to read it, the language was made into a learned, literary language under Peter the First, pushing aside the earlier church language. Newspapers are delivered—Peter the Great founded them. You need to buy a few things—all of them, from the silk scarf for your neck to the soles of your boots, remind you of Peter the Great. . . . At dinner, from the salted herring to the potatoes that he had ordered planted to the wine that he acquainted us with—all the dishes

---

*Two aspects of Peter's reign are referred to here. Peter held mock processions that blasphemously ridiculed the practices of the Church. He also reformed the Russian calendar, replacing one based on biblical dating with the Julian calendar. Under the old Russian calendar, September 1 was the first day of the New Year. The reference to the Roman god Janus is connected with the month January, which was named after him.

†1721 was an important year in Peter's reign. The Great Northern War (1700–1721) with Sweden ended with Russian victory. In connection with that, Peter took the title of Emperor, in imitation of the Romans. This replaced the customary title of tsar and remained the official title of the rulers until 1917. Also in that year the Church was placed under the supervision of a government office known as the Procurator of the Holy Synod, which also lasted until the Revolutions of 1917.

Source: M. Pogodin, "Petr Velikii" in *Istoriko-Kriticheskie Otryvki* (Moscow, 1846), 341–43. Translation by Thomas Sanders.

will speak to you of Peter the Great. After dinner you go out for a visit—this is Peter the Great's gathering. You meet women there; they were allowed into male social settings by order of Peter the Great. Let's go to the university—the first secular institutions of learning were established by Peter the Great. You receive a [noble service] rank, according to the Table of Ranks of Peter the Great. The rank allows you membership in the nobility, as the system was set up by Peter the Great. You get the idea to travel [in Europe], according to the example set by Peter the Great. You are well accepted there—Peter the Great got Russia a place in the system of European states and began to infuse them with respect for us, and so on and so on and so on.

A place in the European state system, the administration and its divisions, court procedures, the privileges of the estates, the Table of Ranks, the army, the navy, taxes, censuses, recruit levies, factories and workshops, ports, canals, roads, the postal system, agriculture, forestry, animal husbandry, mining, gardening, viniculture, domestic and foreign trade, clothing, external appearance, pharmacies, hospitals, medicine, the system of chronology, language, press, printing, military schools, academies—all are monuments to his tireless activity and to his genius.

He saw everything, thought of everything, and laid his hands on everything—setting everything in motion, giving it either direction or life itself. Everything that is thought, said or done by us now, everything whether difficult or easy, near or far—I repeat—can be traced to Peter the Great.

NOTES

1. Cited in Simon Dixon, *Catherine the Great* (London, 2001), 5.

2. Thomas Carlyle, *On Heroes, Hero-Worship, & the Heroic in History* (Berkeley: University of California Press, 1993), 3.

3. A speech made on leaving somewhere, as in graduation ceremonies.

PART TWO

The Age of Revolution, Industrialization, and Nationalism, 1750–1898

Liberty and Revolution in the Atlantic World, 1776–1850

INTRODUCTION

For much of human history, mankind has lived under various forms of authoritarian political regimes. Possessing magnificent wealth and great power, leaders have frequently ruled over their people with an absolute authority that was sanctioned and justified not by popular assent but by divine will. In most societies, there was very little opportunity for the average person to make his or her voice heard or opinion count at the highest level of decision making. A momentous change occurred during the European Enlightenment of the seventeenth and eighteenth centuries, when political absolutism was challenged by the concept of a government "for the people, by the people." Starting with the premise that people possess basic human rights and liberties, Enlightenment philosophers crafted a new theory called "liberalism"[1] that placed sovereignty in the hands of the people. The consequences have changed world history. Reformers and revolutionaries from around the world have embraced the ideals of liberalism to rebel against unjust authority and to provide a blueprint for their new secular governments and national identities.

The historical documents in this chapter explore the origins, character, and meaning of liberalism within the setting of early revolutionary movements in the Atlantic world during the late eighteenth and early nineteenth centuries. The readings illustrate how liberal ideas served to inspire, motivate, and justify popular rebellions in the United States, France, and South America against authoritarian rule. Yet the readings also highlight the important and complex encounter between theoretical ideals and historical realities, for within each of the revolutionary settings under study, specific events, cultural conditions, and personal perspectives served to redefine and reshape the liberal ideals of liberty, equality, and freedom.

Historians typically trace the roots of modern liberal philosophy to the great political thinkers of the European Enlightenment.[2] One of the most important and influential was John Locke (1632–1704), whose faith in human logic and historical progress was examined in chapter 4. In his *Two Treatises of Government* (1690), Locke postulated that people formed communities and governments to protect their God-given natural rights of life, liberty, and property. If a government attempted to rule absolutely and violate the natural rights of individuals, it reneged on its "contract" and lost legitimacy, freeing the community to form a new government. Another major theorist was Jean-Jacques Rousseau (1712–1778), who agreed with Locke that people enter into a contract with their government to protect liberties. But in *The Social Contract* (1762), Rousseau further argued for a direct democracy, believing that authority could be expressed only in the "general will" of the people, which would serve and promote the common good of the community. In their attack on absolutism, both Locke and Rousseau offered a radical reassessment of human rights and social institutions, and their ideas had a profound influence on the reformers of the French Revolution and the Founding Fathers of the United States.

The American Revolution (1776–1789) began as a rebellion against British colonial rule and evolved into one of the most enduring and influential liberal revolutions. Historians typically view the revolution in two distinct phases: the war for independence (1776–1783) and the crafting of a new government (1783–1789). In the first phase, tensions over British policies toward its American colonies escalated in the mid-eighteenth century, leading to armed skirmishes at Lexington and Concord in 1775 and increased demands for independence. The revolution officially began when the Second Continental Congress adopted the Declaration of Independence (1776), a document written primarily by Thomas Jefferson (1743–1826). A well-read man and avid admirer of Enlightenment philosophy, Jefferson proposed a model of governance that freely borrowed from the work of John Locke. But in the context of revolutionary action, the ideals and principles expressed in the Declaration of Independence have also come to reflect and shape American self-identity. As Jefferson himself explained, the Declaration was "neither aiming at originality of principle or sentiment, nor copied from any particular and previous writing," but was intended to be "an expression of the American mind."

At the successful conclusion of the war in 1783, the newly independent states faced the challenge of establishing a new federal government. Their first attempt, the Articles of Confederation (1781–1787), proved too weak and ineffective for the nation's needs, and in 1787, Congress called for a Constitutional Convention to debate and draft a new national charter. One of the most influential leaders in these debates was James Madison (1751–1836), a 36-year-old delegate from Virginia who advocated a strong national government. In order to sway Congress and public opinion to his model of governance, Madison penned a series of essays known as *The Federalist Papers*[3] that carefully outlined his ideas and proposals. In Federalist Paper No. 10, Madison discussed the issue of "factions," or special interest groups that might infringe upon the rights of others and disregard the public good. Madison's solution was ultimately enshrined in the United States Constitution: a system of political representation to ensure stability by imposing limitations on popular sovereignty.

In 1828, the election of Andrew Jackson from Tennessee as the seventh president (and the first from west of the Appalachian mountains) marked the beginnings of a significant shift in American politics. Campaigning as the candidate of the "common man," Jackson tapped into widespread public discontent with governmental policies that were seen as favoring the plantation elite of the south and the commercial elite of the north. With more citizens and frontiersmen championing the "will of the people," pressure mounted to reform and democratize America's political process. One of the most articulate spokesmen of these changes was George Bancroft (1800–1891), an eminent scholar, ardent Jacksonian democrat, and future founder of the United States Naval Academy. In a speech titled "The Office of the People in Art, Government, and Religion" (1835), Bancroft challenged the views of Madison by advocating an extension of democratic values and institutions in America. "The duty of America," he explained, "is to secure the culture and happiness of the masses by reliance on themselves."

Although the Jacksonian era has been called the age of the "common man," such democratic tendencies clearly had distinct limitations. By law, the "common man" generally referred only to adult white males. Women, minorities, and slaves were denied political power and full citizenship, and to many of them, the promises embedded in Jefferson's Declaration of Independence rang hollow.[4] One of the most vocal and articulate critics was Frederick Douglass, a former slave who had escaped his bondage, bought his freedom, and became one of America's leading abolitionist leaders. In an Independence Day oration titled "What to the Slave Is the 4th of July?" (1852), Douglass condemned American hypocrisy for the glaring contradiction between its ideals of liberty and its continuing practice of slavery. His essay offers an important perspective on the limitations and meaning of liberalism within the context of American history.

The success of the American Revolution excited and inspired liberal thinkers in Europe and especially in France, which was still governed by an absolute monarchy. In 1789, King Louis XVI was forced to convene a rare meeting of the Estates General, France's traditional assembly, to deal with a financial crisis that threatened to bankrupt the state. But the meeting had unintended consequences, as liberal reformers seized the opportunity to dismantle the laws and institutions of the "Old Regime" altogether. Under their leadership, the Estates General was transformed into a National Assembly, which produced a new vision for France in the Declaration of the Rights of Man and Citizen (1789). Insisting that "men are born free and equal," the Declaration attacked the foundations of absolutism and asserted that sovereignty rested on the will of the people.

Although the monarchy and many members of the nobility believed that the liberal reformers had gone too far, there were others who believed the reforms had not gone far enough. Among these were revolutionary women, who sought to extend the principles of liberty and equality to all citizens, regardless of gender. One of the most famous of these early feminists was the writer and activist Olympe de Gouges, who penned the Declaration of the Rights of Women in 1791. Blaming both male chauvinism and female complicity for the inferior status and subjugation of women in France, de Gouges demanded equal participation in the new social order and full rights for women as equal contributors to society. Although her uncompromising stand on controversial issues ultimately led her to the guillotine in 1793, Olympe de Gouges is revered as one of the French Revolution's most dedicated proponents of human rights and a pioneer of the modern feminist movement.

Another group who felt that the revolution had not gone far enough were the Jacobins, a radical political organization led by the dynamic and idealistic Maximilien Robespierre. The Jacobins went beyond the moderate liberals by advocating an end to the monarchy, the extension of political rights beyond the propertied classes, and the abolition of slavery in the French colonies. In the fall of 1792, with the revolution threatened by foreign invasions and domestic plots in support of the monarchy, the Jacobins were able to gain control of the National Assembly and domestic policy. Under the leadership of Robespierre and his Committee of Public Safety, the French Revolution now entered its "radical phase," in which terror and violence were used as instruments of the state. In an address on "The Moral and Political Principles of Domestic Policy" (1794), Robespierre described his utopian revolutionary ideals and justified his use of terror and the guillotine. But the radicals' search for enemies of the revolution became relentless, until at last even the leaders, including Robespierre himself, were sentenced to death. As one enemy of Robespierre gleefully pointed out, the revolution "devoured its own children."

Across the Atlantic, in the European colonies of the Caribbean and South America, discontent with colonial rule, commercial restrictions, and social inequities also grew in the eighteenth century. Inspired by the ideals and successes of the liberal revolutions in the United States and France, some colonial settlers imitated their North American counterparts by demanding political independence. But the situation in the Caribbean and South America was made much more complex by competing national allegiances and racial identities, which imparted unique definitions of "freedom" and "equality."

The first major revolution occurred in Saint-Domingue (now known as Haiti), France's most important and prosperous sugar-producing colony. The Haitian Revolution began in 1789, when white colonists demanded more self-government, better trade policies, and judicial reform consistent with the Declaration of Rights of Man and Citizen. But the ultimate outcome of the Haitian Revolution was not to be decided by whites alone, for in 1791, the slaves of the island (who were not included in the granting of new liberties) revolted against their masters. The slaves were organized and led by Toussaint L'Ouverture, a former slave and skilled politician who successfully battled French, Spanish, and British forces to retain the freedom of blacks. In a series of letters to French authorities, Toussaint explained his goals and strategies using the ideals and rhetoric of liberalism in his defense. But the French were not swayed by his sentiments, and in 1802, he was treacherously seized and deported to France, where he was confined until his death the following year. Facing continued resistance by L'Ouverture's followers, French forces finally withdrew in 1803, and Haiti followed the United States as the second independent colony in the New World.

In the Spanish possessions of South America, colonists fumed under tight imperial control and policies that favored those born in Spain over the *Creoles,* or American-born descendants of Spanish families. Inspired by events in the United

States, the Creoles launched their own independence movement in 1807. Central to their success was Simón Bolívar, proclaimed the "Liberator" by his contemporaries and widely recognized as the hero of South American independence. From 1807 to 1825, he led numerous military expeditions against Spanish rule from Colombia to Peru and later served as the president of Gran Colombia (Colombia, Venezuela, and Equador) and Peru. But although dedicated to the independence of the Spanish colonies, he was not ready or willing to grant full political rights to the people. As he explained in "The Jamaican Letter" of 1815, he believed that South Americans lacked the unity and "virtue" required for such liberal reforms, and he instead advocated a kind of authoritarian republicanism, consisting of a strong central executive and a hereditary legislature. As a consequence, his political philosophy has had the unique legacy of advancing and justifying the competing claims of both democrats and dictators in South America's political history.

The liberty revolutions of the Atlantic world have had profound influence on human history. Many historians conclude that they have provided the model for the modern nation-state, one based on liberal principles, secular authority, and rational institutions. Others claim that they represent the first truly ideological revolutions, for they embraced radically new ideas about human rights and social progress. But the readings in this chapter also reveal significant variances in the definitions of "liberty," "equality," and "freedom," and many of these differences continue to fuel political debates today.

CHAPTER QUESTIONS

1. Among the numerous authors in this chapter, who are the proponents of democracy? How do they defend their views? Who are the opponents of democracy and what is their argument? What factors might account for the different perspectives on democracy? Which perspective do you find the most persuasive?

2. Olympe de Gouges and Frederick Douglass are two individuals who found fault with the limitations of early liberalism. What are the similarities in their complaints and demands? How might liberal political leaders respond to these complaints?

3. Some revolutionaries, such as Robespierre and Toussaint L'Ouverture, employed extreme, antiliberal measures in their attempt to safeguard hard-won liberties. How would you assess their actions? Was their extremism a fundamental betrayal of their liberal ideals? Or is extremism in defense of liberty justified under certain conditions?

4. Many historians contend that there is a close link between the rise of political liberalism and the development of modern nationalism. In what ways might the two forces be related? Did liberals use feelings of nationalism and patriotism to achieve their political reforms? In what ways might patriotism work against liberal goals and values? Does national/group identity threaten individual identity and power?

5. In your perception, how has the definition of liberalism changed since the days of James Madison? In what ways has the philosophy of liberalism remained consistent?

THE AMERICAN REVOLUTION
The Revolutionary Ideals of Jefferson

On July 4, 1826, on the fiftieth anniversary of the Declaration of Independence, Thomas Jefferson died at the age of eighty-three at his home at Monticello, Virginia. On his tombstone, he had engraved the three major achievements for which he wanted to be remembered: "Author of the Declaration of American Independence, of the Statute of Virginia for religious freedom,[5] and Father of the University of Virginia." These three accomplishments share the common ideal of freedom: freedom from colonial rule, freedom of religious belief, and freedom of rational thought and inquiry. Indeed, through much of his life as a public servant—and despite his seemingly contradictory practice of owning slaves[6]—Jefferson remained steadfastly devoted to the Enlightenment ideals of individual liberty that he expressed so eloquently in the Declaration of Independence.

Jefferson was born to a distinguished and wealthy family in Albemarle County, Virginia, in 1743. After attending the College of William and Mary and studying law, he served six years as a representative in Virginia's colonial House of Burgesses before his election to the Second Continental Congress in 1776. After passage of the Declaration of Independence, he returned to Virginia, and as a member of the state legislature, he introduced the statute for religious toleration and other liberal measures. After a brief term as governor of Virginia (1779–1781), he returned to national politics in 1783 and served as a member of Congress, minister to France, and secretary of state in the first Washington administration. After a brief retirement at Monticello, he became the presidential candidate of the Democratic-Republican party in 1796. Jefferson narrowly lost the election to the Federalist candidate John Adams, but under the Constitutional provisions then in effect, he became vice president. In 1800, Jefferson again ran for president and was elected third president of the United States. As president, Jefferson reduced the power of the military and federal government, but he also doubled the size of the nation with the Louisiana Purchase (1803). After completion of his second term in 1809, Jefferson devoted most of the remaining seventeen years of his life to the founding of the University of Virginia.

The Declaration of Independence has three basic sections. It begins with a statement of political ideals, followed by a list of specific grievances against British colonial policies and a concluding final proclamation of independence. In defining the proper relationship between government and the people in the first section, Jefferson borrowed key concepts from the political theories of John Locke and other Enlightenment thinkers. But in his affirmation of political ideals, Jefferson was also creating a much broader definition of what it meant to be American. This is what gives the Declaration of Independence its special place in American history; It is a clear statement of values, a blueprint for governmental institutions and laws, and a bond of unity through a common sense of national identity.

QUESTIONS TO CONSIDER

1. According to Jefferson, what is the purpose of government? Under what circumstances is it justifiable to abolish government? If people are given the right to rebel, why does Jefferson not fear frequent revolutions?
2. Jefferson's theory of government is founded on his belief in human rights and "the laws of nature." What are these rights and laws? In what ways are these beliefs so crucial to his political philosophy?
3. On what occasions does Jefferson make reference to God in this address? How do such references influence his message? Do they seem to reinforce or conflict with his political views?
4. Jefferson states that the Declaration was written out of "decent respect to the opinions of mankind. . . ." Given the contents of the document, might there be other motives as well?
5. Some historians claim that the Declaration of Independence is one of the best expressions of American national identity. What ideas do you believe have been the most significant in shaping American identity? In what areas has American identity most strayed from the ideals of the Declaration?

DECLARATION OF INDEPENDENCE (1776)

Thomas Jefferson

When in the course of human events, it becomes necessary for one people to dissolve the political bands which have connected them with another, and to assume among the powers of the earth, the separate and equal station to which the laws of nature and of nature's God entitle them, a decent respect to the opinions of mankind requires that they should declare the causes which impel them to the separation.

We hold these truths to be self-evident: That all men are created equal; that they are endowed by their Creator with certain unalienable rights; that among these are life, liberty, and the pursuit of happiness; that, to secure these rights, governments are instituted among men, deriving their just powers from the consent of the governed; that whenever any form of government becomes destructive of these ends, it is the right of the people to alter or to abolish it, and to institute new government, laying its foundation on such principles, and organizing its powers in such form, as to them shall seem most likely to effect their safety and happiness. Prudence, indeed, will dictate

Source: The Declaration of Independence is in the public domain.

that governments long established should not be changed for light and transient causes; and accordingly all experience hath shown that mankind are more disposed to suffer, while evils are sufferable than to right themselves by abolishing the forms to which they are accustomed. But when a long train of abuses and usurpations, pursuing invariably the same object, evinces a design to reduce them under absolute despotism, it is their right, it is their duty, to throw off such government, and to provide new guards for their future security. Such has been the patient sufferance of these colonies; and such is now the necessity which constrains them to alter their former systems of government. The history of the present King of Great Britain is a history of repeated injuries and usurpations, all having in direct object the establishment of an absolute tyranny over these states. To prove this, let facts be submitted to a candid world. . . .

[A detailed list of grievances follows]

In every stage of these oppressions we have petitioned for redress in the most humble terms; our repeated petitions have been answered only by repeated injury. A prince, whose character is thus marked by every act which may define a tyrant, is unfit to be the ruler of a free people.

Nor have we been wanting in our attentions to our British brethren. We have warned them, from time to time, of attempts by their legislature to extend an unwarrantable jurisdiction over us. We have reminded them of the circumstances of our emigration and settlement here. We have appealed to their native justice and magnanimity; and we have conjured them, by the ties of our common kindred, to disavow these usurpations which would inevitably interrupt our connections and correspondence. They too, have been deaf to the voice of justice and of consanguinity. We must, therefore, acquiesce in the necessity which denounces our separation, and hold them as we hold the rest of mankind, enemies in war, in peace friends.

We, therefore, the representatives of the United States of America, in General Congress assembled, appealing to the Supreme Judge of the world for the rectitude of our intentions, do, in the name and by the authority of the good people of these colonies solemnly publish and declare, That these United Colonies are, and of right ought to be, *FREE AND INDEPENDENT STATES*; that they are absolved from all allegiance to the British crown and that all political connection between them and the state of Great Britain is, and ought to be, totally dissolved; and that, as free and independent states, they have full power to levy war, conclude peace, contract alliances, establish commerce, and do all other acts and things which independent states may of right do. And for the support of this declaration, with a firm reliance on the protection of Divine Providence, we mutually pledge to each other our lives, our fortunes, and our sacred honor.

The Fears of the Founding Fathers

James Madison (1751–1836) was one of Virginia's leading patriots during the Revolutionary War, was elected fourth president of United States, and led the nation during the War of 1812 with Britain. But he is probably most remembered for his pivotal role in the crafting and ratification of the United States Constitution (ratified in 1789) and its first ten amendments, more commonly known as the Bill of Rights (1791). Known and respected among his contemporaries for his skilled writing and argumentation, Madison was one of the most influential of the Founding Fathers.

Madison was born at Port Conway, Virginia, in 1751, the oldest child of an affluent, plantation-owning family. After studying law and government at the College of New Jersey (Princeton University), he returned to the family estate of Montpelier in Virginia and took up the cause of the American Revolution. Although he served in the Virginia colonial government, he was barred from military service in the Continental Army because of poor health. Chosen by Virginia's governor to represent the state in the Continental Congress from 1780 to 1789, Madison earned fame for crafting a model of government that became the blueprint of the Constitution. Madison believed in the value of a strong federal government whose power was divided among three branches and monitored through a system of "checks and balances." To promote its ratification by the states, Madison joined Alexander Hamilton of New York in penning *The Federalist Papers*, a collection of essays that were intended to explain and justify features of the new government. Following the ratification of the Constitution in 1789, Madison was elected to the new House of Representatives and sponsored the adoption of the Bill of Rights. After serving as secretary of state during the Jefferson administrations (1801–1809), Madison was elected to his own two terms as president from 1809 to 1817. Following his presidency, he retired to his plantation at Montpelier, and he remained interested and engaged in politics until his death in 1836.

The Federalist Papers are considered one of the most significant collection of documents in American political thought. Written primarily by Madison and Hamilton in 1787–1788 under the pseudonym *Publius*,[7] the eighty-five essays promoted the provisions and philosophy of the proposed new Constitution. In Federalist Paper No. 10, Madison discussed the threat of "factions" that could undermine the basic rights and liberties of citizens. Distrustful of democracy, he advocated a representative government made up of wise and propertied male citizens who might better discern "the true interests" of the country. Although some critics have charged that Madison and the other Founding Fathers were more concerned with protecting property than they were with liberty or equality, others credit Madison for establishing a stable and responsive government that has survived the test of time.

QUESTIONS TO CONSIDER

1. How does Madison define factions? Why does he consider them a "mortal disease of popular governments"?

2. According to Madison, what are the primary causes of factions? What role does property play in their formation? Do you agree with his assessment that factions are "sown into the nature of man"?

3. Madison asserts that "democracy offers no cure for the mischiefs of factions." Why? What advantages does he find in a republic?

4. What can be inferred from Federalist Paper No. 10 about Madison's views on human nature and social hierarchy? How central are these views in shaping his political philosophy?

5. Some scholars believe that Madison linked liberty more with property than with democracy. Do you agree? In your assessment, does Madison's anti-democratic sentiment betray the ideals and vision outlined in Jefferson's Declaration of Independence? Why or why not?

FEDERALIST NO. 10 (THE UNION AS A SAFEGUARD AGAINST DOMESTIC FACTION AND INSURRECTION) (1787)

James Madison

Among the numerous advantages promised by a well-constructed Union, none deserves to be more accurately developed than its tendency to break and control the violence of faction. The friend of popular governments never finds himself so much alarmed for their character and fate, as when he contemplates their propensity to this dangerous vice. . . . The instability, injustice, and confusion introduced into the public councils, have, in truth, been the mortal diseases under which popular governments have everywhere perished; as they continue to be the favorite and fruitful topics from which the adversaries to liberty derive their most specious declamations. The valuable improvements made by the American constitutions* on the popular models, both ancient and modern, cannot certainly be too much admired; but it would be an unwarrantable partiality, to contend that they have as effectually obviated the danger on this side, as was wished and expected. Complaints are everywhere heard from our most considerate and virtuous citizens, equally the friends of public and private faith, and of public and personal liberty, that our governments are too unstable, that the public good is disregarded in the conflicts of rival parties, and that measures are too often decided, not according to the rules of justice and the rights of the minor party, but by the superior force of an interested and overbearing majority. . . .

By a faction, I understand a number of citizens, whether amounting to a majority or a minority of the whole, who are united and actuated by some common impulse

---

Source: From *The Federalist, A Commentary on the Constitution of the United States, Being a Collection of Essays Written in Support of the Constitution Agreed upon September 17, 1787, by the Federal Convention.* From the original text of Alexander Hamilton, John Jay, and James Madison. With an introduction by Edward Mead Earle. (New York: The Modern Library), 53–62.

*Referring chiefly to the state governments and to the Articles of Confederation, which provided the separate states some central authority during and immediately after the Revolutionary War from 1781 to 1789.

of passion, or of interest, adverse to the rights of other citizens, or to the permanent and aggregate interests of the community.

There are two methods of curing the mischiefs of faction: the one, by removing its causes; the other, by controlling its effects. There are again two methods of removing the causes of faction: the one, by destroying the liberty which is essential to its existence; the other, by giving to every citizen the same opinions, the same passions, and the same interests.

It could never be more truly said than of the first remedy, that it was worse than the disease. Liberty is to faction what air is to fire, an aliment without which it instantly expires. But it could not be less folly to abolish liberty, which is essential to political life, because it nourishes faction, than it would be to wish the annihilation of air, which is essential to animal life, because it imparts to fire its destructive agency.

The second expedient is as impracticable as the first would be unwise. As long as the reason of man continues fallible, and he is at liberty to exercise it, different opinions will be formed. As long as the connection subsists between his reason and his self-love, his opinions and his passions will have a reciprocal influence on each other; and the former will be objects to which the latter will attach themselves. The diversity in the faculties of men, from which the rights of property originate, is not less an insuperable obstacle to a uniformity of interests. The protection of these faculties is the first object of government. From the protection of different and unequal faculties of acquiring property, the possession of different degrees and kinds of property immediately results; and from the influence of these on the sentiments and views of the respective proprietors, ensues a division of the society into different interests and parties.

The latent causes of faction are thus sown in the nature of man; and we see them everywhere brought into different degrees of activity, according to the different circumstances of civil society. A zeal for different opinions concerning religion, concerning government, and . . . an attachment to different leaders ambitiously contending for pre-eminence and power . . . have, in turn, divided mankind into parties, inflamed them with mutual animosity, and rendered them much more disposed to vex and oppress each other than to co-operate for their common good. So strong is this propensity of mankind to fall into mutual animosities, that where no substantial occasion presents itself, the most frivolous and fanciful distinctions have been sufficient to kindle their unfriendly passions and excite their most violent conflicts. But the most common and durable source of factions has been the various and unequal distribution of property. Those who hold and those who are without property have ever formed distinct interests in society. Those who are creditors, and those who are debtors, fall under a like discrimination. A landed interest, a manufacturing interest, a mercantile interest, a moneyed interest, with many lesser interests, grow up of necessity in civilized nations, and divide them into different classes, actuated by different sentiments and views. . . .

The inference to which we are brought is, that the CAUSES of faction cannot be removed, and that relief is only to be sought in the means of controlling its EFFECTS.

If a faction consists of less than a majority, relief is supplied by the republican principle, which enables the majority to defeat its sinister views by regular vote. It may clog the administration, it may convulse the society; but it will be unable to execute and mask its violence under the forms of the Constitution. When a majority is included in a faction, the form of popular government, on the other hand, enables it to sacrifice to its ruling passion or interest both the public good and the rights of other citizens. . . .

From this view of the subject it may be concluded that a pure democracy, by which I mean a society consisting of a small number of citizens, who assemble and administer the government in person, can admit of no cure for the mischiefs of faction. A common passion or interest will, in almost every case, be felt by a majority of the whole; a communication and concert result from the form of government itself; and there is nothing to check the inducements to sacrifice the weaker party or an obnoxious individual. Hence it is that such democracies have ever been spectacles of turbulence and contention; have ever been found incompatible with personal security or the rights of property; and have in general been as short in their lives as they have been violent in their deaths. Theoretic politicians, who have patronized this species of government, have erroneously supposed that by reducing mankind to a perfect equality in their political rights, they would, at the same time, be perfectly equalized and assimilated in their possessions, their opinions, and their passions.

A republic, by which I mean a government in which the scheme of representation takes place, opens a different prospect, and promises the cure for which we are seeking. Let us examine the points in which it varies from pure democracy, and we shall comprehend both the nature of the cure and the efficacy which it must derive from the Union.

The two great points of difference between a democracy and a republic are: first, the delegation of the government, in the latter, to a small number of citizens elected by the rest; secondly, the greater number of citizens, and greater sphere of country, over which the latter may be extended.

The effect of the first difference is, on the one hand, to refine and enlarge the public views, by passing them through the medium of a chosen body of citizens, whose wisdom may best discern the true interest of their country, and whose patriotism and love of justice will be least likely to sacrifice it to temporary or partial considerations. Under such a regulation, it may well happen that the public voice, pronounced by the representatives of the people, will be more consonant to the public good than if pronounced by the people themselves, convened for the purpose. On the other hand, the effect may be inverted. Men of factious tempers, of local prejudices, or of sinister designs, may, by intrigue, by corruption, or by other means, first obtain the suffrages, and then betray the interests, of the people. The question resulting is, whether small or extensive republics are more favorable to the election of proper guardians of the public weal [well-being]; and it is clearly decided in favor of the latter by two obvious considerations:

In the first place, it is to be remarked that, however small the republic may be, the representatives must be raised to a certain number, in order to guard against the cabals* of a few; and that, however large it may be, they must be limited to a certain number, in order to guard against the confusion of a multitude. Hence, the number of representatives in the two cases not being in proportion to that of the two constituents, and being proportionally greater in the small republic, it follows that, if the propor-

---

*A group of persons secretly united to overturn or usurp an established authority.

tion of fit characters be not less in the large than in the small republic, the former will present a greater option, and consequently a greater probability of a fit choice.

In the next place, as each representative will be chosen by a greater number of citizens in the large than in the small republic, it will be more difficult for unworthy candidates to practice with success the vicious arts by which elections are too often carried; and the suffrages of the people being more free, will be more likely to centre in men who possess the most attractive merit and the most diffusive and established characters.

It must be confessed that in this, as in most other cases, there is a mean, on both sides of which inconveniences will be found to lie. By enlarging too much the number of electors, you render the representatives too little acquainted with all their local circumstances and lesser interests; as by reducing it too much, you render him unduly attached to these, and too little fit to comprehend and pursue great and national objects. The federal Constitution forms a happy combination in this respect; the great and aggregate interests being referred to the national, the local and particular to the State legislatures.

The other point of difference is, the greater number of citizens and extent of territory which may be brought within the compass of republican than of democratic government; and it is this circumstance principally which renders factious combinations less to be dreaded in the former than in the latter. The smaller the society, the fewer probably will be the distinct parties and interests composing it; the fewer the distinct parties and interests, the more frequently will a majority be found of the same party; and the smaller the number of individuals composing a majority, and the smaller the compass within which they are placed, the more easily will they concert and execute their plans of oppression. Extend the sphere, and you take in a greater variety of parties and interests; you make it less probable that a majority of the whole will have a common motive to invade the rights of other citizens; or if such a common motive exists, it will be more difficult for all who feel it to discover their own strength, and to act in unison with each other. Besides other impediments, it may be remarked that, where there is a consciousness of unjust or dishonorable purposes, communication is always checked by distrust in proportion to the number whose concurrence is necessary.

Hence, it clearly appears, that the same advantage which a republic has over a democracy, in controlling the effects of faction, is enjoyed by a large over a small republic—is enjoyed by the Union over the States composing it. . . .

In the extent and proper structure of the Union, therefore, we behold a republican remedy for the diseases most incident to republican government. And according to the degree of pleasure and pride we feel in being republicans, ought to be our zeal in cherishing the spirit and supporting the character of Federalists.

PUBLIUS.

An Argument for Democratic Reform

George Bancroft (1800–1891) was one of the more important, if less famous, political voices in America during the nineteenth century. He was also the nation's leading historian, producing a ten-volume *History of the United States* that took nearly forty years to complete. Both in his scholarly writings and during his career in public service, Bancroft challenged the assumptions of Madison and the Founding Fathers by advocating an extension of democratic values and institutions in America.

Born in 1800 in Worcester, Massachusetts, Bancroft initially seemed destined for a life in academia. Graduating from Harvard University, he founded the innovative Round Hill School for boys and began work on his monumental *History of the United States*. But he also became increasingly devoted to the cause of democratic reform, and his published essays attacking the Bank of the United States and political elites thrilled Jacksonian Democrats. At their urging, he left the Round Hill School in 1831, entered party politics in Massachusetts, lost a race for governor in 1844, but was appointed secretary of the navy a year later by President James Polk, a fellow Democrat. As secretary of the navy (1845–46), Bancroft founded the United States Naval Academy in Annapolis, Maryland, and he helped design military strategy for the Mexican War (1846–47). In the mid-1850s, Bancroft broke with the Democrats over their continued support of slavery and shifted his allegiance to the newly formed Republican Party. He supported Abraham Lincoln in the 1860 election and believed that the Civil War was necessary to preserve the Union.[8] Following the war, Bancroft served as ambassador to Prussia and to the German Empire (1867–74), after which the elderly historian and diplomat retired to work on further editions of his beloved *History* before his death in Washington, D.C., in 1891.

"The Office of the People" was a speech given by Bancroft at Willamstown College (now Williams College) in Massachusetts in August 1835. His oration reflects two significant trends in early-nineteenth-century American history. The first is his high regard for democracy and his assertion that "the best government rests on the people and not on the few." The second trend is Bancroft's spiritualism, a reflection of New England's transcendental movement most frequently associated with Ralph Waldo Emerson.[9] In both regards, Bancroft's reasoning and political philosophy are quite distinct from the logic and perspective of James Madison, and a close comparison of the two provides a fascinating glimpse into American historical and cultural change.

QUESTIONS TO CONSIDER

1. Bancroft believes that all men are imbued with "spirit." How does he conceptualize this "spirit" and why does he view it as so important?

2. Bancroft states that "men cannot agree in an absurdity; neither can they agree in a falsehood." How did he come to this conclusion, and how does it relate to his definition of "truth"? Is his argument convincing? What are the implications, especially to individuals who hold views that conflict with majority opinion?

3. Madison asserted that the election of wise representatives would serve to temper the passions of the masses; in contrast, Bancroft argues that "the people collectively are wiser than the most gifted individual." Which argument do you find more convincing? Why?

4. Bancroft's political philosophy is highly influenced by his religious views. In your assessment, do his spiritual views undermine his political argument? Does it violate the separation of church and state in America?

5. Bancroft argues that the mark of a great civilization is not its might or wealth, but the degree to which it puts its faith "in the intelligence of the common man." Do you agree? If so, what might be the implications to present-day American government organization or domestic policy?

"THE OFFICE OF THE PEOPLE IN ART, GOVERNMENT, AND RELIGION" (1835)

George Bancroft

The material world does not change in its masses or in its powers. The stars shine with no more lustre than when they first sang together in the glory of their birth. The flowers that gemmed the fields and the forests, before America was discovered, now bloom around us in their season. . . . The earth turns on its axis and perfects its revolutions and renews its seasons without increase or advancement.

But a like passive destiny does not attach to the inhabitants of the earth. For them the expectations of social improvement are no delusion; the hopes of philanthropy are more than a dream. The five senses do not constitute the whole inventory of our sources of knowledge. They are the organs by which thought connects itself with the external universe; but the power of thought is not merged in the exercise of its instruments. We have functions which connect us with heaven, as well as organs which set us in relation with earth. We have not merely the senses opening to us the external world, but an internal sense, which places us in connection with the world of intelligence and the decrees of God.

There is *spirit in man*—not in the privileged few; not in those of us only who by the favor of Providence have been nursed in public schools. *It is in man;* it is the attribute of the race. The Spirit, which is the guide to truth, is the gracious gift to each member of the human family.

Reason exists within every breast. I mean not that faculty which deduces inferences from the experiences of the senses, but that higher faculty which from the

Source: From George Bancroft, *Literary and Historical Miscellanies* (New York: Harper & Brothers, 1857), 408–35.

infinite treasures of its own consciousness originates truth and assents to it by the force of intuitive evidence; that faculty which raises us beyond the control of time and space, and gives us faith in things eternal and invisible. There is not the difference between one mind and another which the pride of philosophers might conceive. . . .

If it be true that the gifts of mind and heart are universally diffused, if the sentiment of truth, justice, love, and beauty exists in every one then it follows, as a necessary consequence, that the common judgment in taste, politics, and religion is the highest authority on earth and the nearest possible approach to an infallible decision. . . .

If reason is a universal faculty, the universal decision is the nearest criterion of truth. The common mind winnows opinions; it is the sieve which separates error from certainty. The exercise by many of the same faculty on the same subject would naturally lead to the same conclusions. But if not, the very differences of opinion that arise prove the supreme judgment of the general mind. Truth is one. It never contradicts itself: One truth cannot contradict another truth. Hence truth is a bond of union. But error not only contradicts truth, but may contradict itself; so that there may be many errors, and each at variance with the rest. Truth is therefore of necessity an element of harmony; error as necessarily an element of discord. Thus there can be no continuing universal judgment but a right one. Men cannot agree in an absurdity; neither can they agree in a falsehood.

If wrong opinions have often been cherished by the masses, the cause always lies in the complexity of the ideas presented. Error finds its way into the soul of a nation only through the channel of truth. It is to a truth that men listen; and if they accept error also, it is only because the error is for the time so closely interwoven with the truth that the one cannot readily be separated from the other. . . .

In like manner the best government rests on the people and not on the few, on persons and not on property, on the free development of public opinion and not on authority; because the munificent Author of our being has conferred the gifts of mind upon every member of the human race without distinction of outward circumstances. . . .

The public happiness is the true object of legislation, and can be secured only by the masses of mankind themselves awakening to the knowledge and the care of their own interests. Our free institutions have reversed the false and ignoble distinctions between men; and refusing to gratify the pride of caste, have acknowledged the common mind to be the true material for a commonwealth. . . . The world can advance only through the culture of the moral and intellectual powers of the people. To accomplish this end by means of the people themselves is the highest purpose of government. If it be the duty of the individual to strive after a perfection like the perfection of God, how much more ought a nation to be the image of Deity. . . . The duty of America is to secure the culture and the happiness of the masses by their reliance on themselves.

. . . There may be those who scoff at the suggestion that the decision of the whole is to be preferred to the judgment of the enlightened few. They say in their hearts that the masses are ignorant; that farmers know nothing of legislation; that mechanics should not quit their workshops to join in forming public opinion. But true political science does indeed venerate the masses. It maintains, not as has been perversely asserted, that "the people can make right," but that the people can discern right. Individuals are but shadows, too often engrossed by the pursuit of shadows; the race is immortal. Individuals are of limited sagacity; the common mind is infinite in its experience. . . . Individuals may be false; the masses are ingenuous and sincere. Individuals claim the divine sanction of truth for the deceitful conceptions of their own fancies; the Spirit of God breathes through the combined intelligence of the people. . . .

Thus the opinion which we respect is, indeed, not the opinion of one or of a few, but the sagacity of the many. It is hard for the pride of cultivated philosophy to put its ear to the ground and listen reverently to the voice of lowly humanity; yet the people collectively are wiser than the most gifted individual, for all his wisdom constitutes but a part of theirs. . . .

It is not by vast armies, by immense natural resources, by accumulations of treasure, that the greatest results in modern civilization have been accomplished. . . . The exact measure of the progress of civilization is the degree in which the intelligence of the common mind has prevailed over wealth and brute force; in other words, the measure of the progress of civilization is the progress of the people. . . .

A Critique of American Liberty from a Former Slave

Frederick Douglass (1817–1895) was one of the most exceptional human rights leaders in American history. His fiery speeches and eloquent writing made him an important leader of the nineteenth-century abolitionist movement, and his autobiography, *The Narrative of the Life of Frederick Douglass* (1845), is considered a classic in American history and literature. Douglass devoted his life foremost to the issues of freedom and equality, and his powerful words on these subjects provide another important perspective on the meaning and the limitations of the American Revolution.

Born the son of an unknown white planter and a black slave mother in 1818, Douglass toiled as a slave on a Maryland plantation until he was sent to Baltimore to train as a house servant. But when his new master discovered that Douglass was learning to read and write (with the assistance of the master's wife), he was sent back to the plantation to be "rebroken" through hard work and discipline. When Douglass resisted, he was regularly beaten. Shortly thereafter, at the age of twenty, Douglass fled Maryland and headed north, where he eventually settled in Massachusetts, changed his name,[10] and found part-time work as a laborer.

In 1841, Douglass attended an antislavery meeting, where he was invited to come from the audience to recount his experiences as a slave. His story was so powerful and moving that he was immediately recruited as a speaker by the Massachusetts Anti-Slavery Society. But after the publication of his *Narrative* unmasked his identity and location, he had to flee to Europe to avoid recapture by his former owner. After a two-year speaking tour in Britain, Douglass returned to

Massachusetts in 1847 with enough earnings to purchase his freedom and to establish *The North Star*, a newspaper expressly for blacks. Throughout the next decade, Douglass continued to campaign for abolition, and when the Civil War began in 1861, he advised President Lincoln to make slavery the central moral issue in the war. During Reconstruction, Douglass accepted several governmental posts, including U.S. minister to Haiti (1889–1891), but he continued to work for full civil rights for blacks and for women until his death in 1895.

One of the most vexing challenges faced by Douglass during his long career was public skepticism about his slave background. Many whites in both the north and the south doubted that such an articulate and intelligent man as Douglass could ever have been a lowly and ignorant slave, which in itself reveals much about prevailing racial attitudes and assumptions in America at that time. This skepticism compelled him not only to write his *Narrative* but also to address and challenge white misconceptions in all of his speeches and writings. One of Douglass's most critical speeches occurred on July 5, 1852, at a meeting of the Rochester (N.Y.) Ladies' Anti-Slavery Society. In his address, "What to the Slave Is the 4th of July?" Douglass used "scorching irony" to denounce American slavery, which he claimed showed a shocking disregard for both the Constitution and the Bible. He concluded that Independence Day was a holiday only for whites; for blacks and slaves, it was only a bitter reminder of the fact that they had no freedom or liberty to celebrate.

QUESTIONS TO CONSIDER

1. What are Douglass's main criticisms of America? How does his image of America compare with the values advanced by Jefferson in the Declaration of Independence?

2. Douglass's speech contains an excerpt from one of the biblical Psalms. How is this passage related to his speech? To whom does he compare the plight of the black slaves in America? What might be his purpose in drawing such an analogy?

3. According to Douglass, the question "Is the slave a man?" was already answered satisfactorily. How does Douglass present this issue? Why might this be a crucial issue in the abolitionist debate?

4. In the abolitionist struggle, Douglass claimed that what was needed was "not light but fire." What might this suggest? Do you think he believed that the contradiction between slavery and freedom in America must inevitably lead to conflict?

5. Douglass notes that he and his fellow abolitionists were frequently criticized as having been too radical, militant, and harsh in their denunciations of America. How does Douglass respond to that charge? In your view, was Douglass's "scorching irony" excessively inflammatory?

"WHAT TO THE SLAVE IS THE 4th OF JULY?" (1852)

Frederick Douglass

Fellow-Citizens-pardon me, and allow me to ask, why am I called upon to speak here today? What have I, or those I represent, to do with your national independence? Are the great principles of political freedom and of natural justice, embodied in that Declaration of Independence, extended to us? And am I, therefore, called upon to bring our humble offering to the national altar, and to confess the benefits, and express devout gratitude for the blessings, resulting from your independence to us?

Would to God, both for your sakes and ours, that an affirmative answer could be truthfully returned to these questions! Then would my task be light, and my burden easy and delightful. . . .

But, such is not the state of the case. I say it with a sad sense of the disparity between us. I am not included within the pale of this glorious anniversary. Your high independence only reveals the immeasurable distance between us. The blessings in which you this day rejoice, are not enjoyed in common. The rich inheritance of justice, liberty, prosperity, and independence, bequeathed by your fathers, is shared by you, not by me. The sunlight that brought life and healing to you, has brought stripes and death to me. This Fourth of July is *yours,* not *mine. You* may rejoice, I must mourn. To drag a man in fetters into the grand illuminated temple of liberty, and call upon him to join you in joyous anthems, were inhuman mockery and sacrilegious irony. Do you mean, citizens, to mock me, by asking me to speak today? If so, there is a parallel to your conduct. And let me warn you that it is dangerous to copy the example of a nation whose crimes, towering up to heaven, were thrown down by the breath of the Almighty, burying that nation in irrecoverable ruin! I can today take up the plaintive lament of a peeled and woe-smitten people.

"By the rivers of Babylon, there we sat down. Yea! we wept when we remembered Zion. We hanged our harps upon the willows in the midst thereof. For there, they that carried us away captive, required of us a song; and they who wasted us required of us mirth, saying, Sing us one of the songs of Zion. How can we sing the Lord's song in a strange land? If I forget thee, O Jerusalem, let my right hand forget her cunning. If I do not remember thee, let my tongue cleave to the roof of my mouth."*

Fellow-citizens, above your national, tumultuous joy, I hear the mournful wail of millions, whose chains, heavy and grievous yesterday, are today rendered more

Source: Frederick Douglass, "What to the Slave Is the 4th of July?" in *Narrative of the Life of Frederick Douglass,* David Blight, ed., 141–45. Copyright © 1993 Bedford Books. Reprinted by permission of Bedford/St. Martin's Press. This shortened version of the speech is the one Douglass reprinted in his autobiography, *My Bondage and My Freedom* (1855). The complete speech can be found in John W. Blassingame, ed., *The Frederick Douglass Papers,* series 1, vol. 2 (New Haven: Yale University Press, 1982): 359–88.

*The biblical quote is from Psalms 137:1–6.

intolerable by the jubilant shouts that reach them. If I do forget, if I do not faithfully remember those bleeding children of sorrow this day, "may my right hand forget her cunning, and may my tongue cleave to the roof of my mouth!" To forget them, to pass lightly over their wrongs, and to chime in with the popular theme, would be treason most scandalous and shocking, and would make me a reproach before God and the world. My subject then, fellow-citizens, is AMERICAN SLAVERY. I shall see this day and its popular characteristics from the slave's point of view. Standing there, identified with the American bondman, making his wrongs mine, I do not hesitate to declare, with all my soul, that the character and conduct of this nation never looked blacker to me than on this Fourth of July. Whether we turn to the declarations of the past, or to the professions of the present, the conduct of the nation seems equally hideous and revolting. America is false to the past, false to the present, and solemnly binds herself to be false to the future. Standing with God and the crushed and bleeding slave on this occasion, I will, in the name of humanity which is outraged, in the name of liberty which is fettered, in the name of the Constitution and the Bible, which are disregarded and trampled upon, dare to call in question and to denounce, with all the emphasis I can command, everything that serves to perpetuate slavery—the great sin and shame of America! I will not equivocate; I will not excuse; I will use the severest language I can command; and yet not one word shall escape me that any man, whose judgment is not blinded by prejudice, or who is not at heart a slave-holder, shall not confess to be right and just.

But I fancy I hear some one of my audience say, it is just in this circumstance that you and your brother abolitionists fail to make a favorable impression on the public mind. Would you argue more, and denounce less, would you persuade more and re-buke less, your cause would be much more likely to succeed. But, I submit, where all is plain there is nothing to be argued. What point in the anti-slavery creed would you have me argue? On what branch of the subject do the people of this country need light? Must I undertake to prove that the slave is a man? That point is conceded already. Nobody doubts it. The slave-holders themselves acknowledge it in the enactment of laws for their government. They acknowledge it when they punish disobedience on the part of the slave. There are seventy-two crimes in the state of Virginia, which, if committed by a black man, (no matter how ignorant he be,) subject him to the punishment of death; while only two of these same crimes will subject a white man to the like punishment. What is this but the acknowledgment that the slave is a moral, intellectual, and responsible being. The manhood of the slave is conceded. It is admitted in the fact that southern statute books are covered with enactments for-bidding, under severe fines and penalties, the teaching of the slave to read or write. When you can point to any such laws, in reference to the beasts of the field, then I may consent to argue the manhood of the slave. When the dogs in your streets, when the fowls of the air, when the cattle on your hills, when the fish of the sea, and the reptiles that crawl, shall be unable to distinguish the slave from a brute, then will I argue with you that the slave is a man!

For the present, it is enough to affirm the equal manhood of the negro race. Is it not astonishing that, while we are plowing, planting, and reaping, using all kinds of mechanical tools, erecting houses, constructing bridges, building ships, working in metals of brass, iron, copper, silver, and gold; that, while we are reading, writing, and ciphering, acting as clerks, merchants, and secretaries, having among us lawyers, doctors, ministers, poets, authors, editors, orators, and teachers; that, while we are engaged in all manner of enterprises common to other men—digging gold in California, capturing the whale in the Pacific, feeding sheep and cattle on the hillside, living, moving, acting, thinking, planning, living in families as husbands, wives, and children, and, above all, confessing and worshiping the Christian's God, and looking hopefully for life and immortality beyond the grave—we are called upon to prove that we are men!

Would you have me argue that man is entitled to liberty? That he is the rightful owner of his own body? You have already declared it. Must I argue the wrongfulness of slavery? Is that a question for republicans? Is it to be settled by the rules of logic and argumentation, as a matter beset with great difficulty, involving a doubtful application of the principle of justice, hard to be understood? How should I look today in the presence of Americans, dividing and subdividing a discourse, to show that men have a natural right to freedom, speaking of it relatively and positively, negatively and affirmatively? To do so, would be to make myself ridiculous, and to offer an insult to your understanding. There is not a man beneath the canopy of heaven that does not know that slavery is wrong for him.

What! Am I to argue that it is wrong to make men brutes, to rob them of their liberty, to work them without wages, to keep them ignorant of their relations to their fellow-men, to beat them with sticks, to flay their flesh with the lash, to load their limbs with irons, to hunt them with dogs, to sell them at auction, to sunder their families, to knock out their teeth, to burn their flesh, to starve them into obedience and submission to their masters? Must I argue that a system, thus marked with blood and stained with pollution, is wrong? No; I will not. I have better employment for my time and strength than such arguments would imply.

What, then, remains to be argued? Is it that slavery is not divine; that God did not establish it; that our doctors of divinity are mistaken? There is blasphemy in the thought. That which is inhuman cannot be divine. Who can reason on such a proposition! They that can, may; I cannot. The time for such argument is past.

At a time like this, scorching irony, not convincing argument, is needed. Oh! Had I the ability, and could I reach the nation's ear, I would today pour out a fiery stream of biting ridicule, blasting reproach, withering sarcasm, and stern rebuke. For it is not light that is needed, but fire; it is not the gentle shower, but thunder. We need the storm, the whirlwind and the earthquake.

The feeling of the nation must be quickened; the conscience of the nation must be roused; the propriety of the nation must be startled; the hypocrisy of the nation must be exposed; and its crimes against God and man must be proclaimed and denounced.

What to the American slave is your Fourth of July? I answer, a day that reveals to him, more than all other days in the year, the gross injustice and cruelty to which he is the constant victim. To him, your celebration is a sham; your boasted liberty, an unholy license; your national greatness, swelling vanity; your sounds of rejoicing are empty and heartless; your denunciations of tyrants, brass-fronted impudence; your shouts of liberty and equality, hollow mockery; your prayers and hymns, your sermons and thanksgivings, with all your religious parade and solemnity, are to him mere bombast, fraud, deception, impiety, and hypocrisy—a thin veil to cover up crimes which would disgrace a nation of savages. There is not a nation on the earth guilty of practices more shocking and bloody, than are the people of these United States, at this very hour.

Go where you may, search where you will, roam through all the monarchies and despotisms of the old world, travel through South America, search out every abuse, and when you have found the last, lay your facts by the side of the every-day practices of this nation, and you will say with me, that, for revolting barbarity and shameless hypocrisy, America reigns without a rival.

THE FRENCH REVOLUTION
A Declaration of the Rights of Man

In August 1789, the French National Assembly adopted the Declaration of the Rights of Man and Citizen. Together with Locke's Second Treatise on Government (1690) and the American Declaration of Independence (1776) and the United States Constitution (1789), the Declaration of the Rights of Man and Citizen is considered one of the pivotal documents in the development of political liberalism. In its concise seventeen points, the Declaration of the Rights of Man and Citizen espouses the Enlightenment ideals of human equality, natural rights, and a government that emanates from the will of the people.

The Declaration was also a reaction against royal absolutism and the huge disparities of wealth, status, and power that defined and characterized the three main social classes or "estates" of the Old Regime. The first and second estates, comprising the clergy and nobility, made up less than 10 percent of the population and controlled most of the nation's wealth but were exempt from paying taxes. Consequently, the financial and labor burden of France was borne chiefly by the third estate, a disparate group made up of the professional middle classes[11] (doctors, lawyers, merchants, and so on), the rural peasants, and the urban working class. Political rights were also uneven. Power rested in the person of the king, who ruled in an absolute manner, sanctioned by divine right. But the royal bureaucracy was so intrusive, corrupt, and inefficient that all social classes dreamed of a change.

Consequently, the financial crisis of 1789 that initiated the convening of the Estates General reflected, in large part, the inefficiency and inequities of French society. The representatives from the middle class seized the opportunity to push for liberal reforms and declared their intention to write a constitution for France that would limit the power and privilege of the monarchy, the nobility, and the clergy. Their efforts received crucial support from the urban workers, who stormed and seized the weapons at the Bastille when King Louis XVI tried to quash the revolution. With the king under arrest and the power of the monarchy temporarily checked, the new National Assembly adopted the Declaration of the Rights of Man and Citizen on August 26, 1789, which marked the beginning of the end of the Old Regime.

1. How would you summarize the major principles of the Declaration of the Rights of Man and Citizen? In what ways can the document be seen as a triumph of liberalism?
2. Article 3 states, "The principle of all sovereignty resides essentially in the nation. No body nor individual may exercise any authority which does not proceed directly from the nation." What does this mean? What are the possible implications of this statement?
3. Historians commonly assert that the Declaration of the Rights of Man effectively marked the end of the Old Regime. How does the Declaration fundamentally challenge the foundations of absolutism?
4. In your assessment, who were the winners and the losers in the first phase of the French Revolution?
5. Identify the similarities and differences between the Declaration of the Rights of Man and the American Declaration of Independence.

DECLARATION OF THE RIGHTS OF MAN AND CITIZEN (1789)

The representatives of the French people, organized as a National Assembly, believing that the ignorance, neglect, or contempt of the rights of man are the sole cause of public calamities and of the corruption of governments, have determined to set forth in a solemn declaration the natural, unalienable, and sacred rights of man, in order that this declaration, being constantly before all the members of the Social body, shall remind them continually of their rights and duties; in order that the acts of the legislative power, as well as those of the executive power, may be compared at any moment with the objects and purposes of all political institutions and may thus be more respected, and, lastly, in order that the grievances of the citizens, based hereafter upon simple and incontestable principles, shall tend to the maintenance of the constitution and redound to the happiness of all. Therefore the National Assembly recognizes and proclaims, in the presence and under the auspices of the Supreme Being, the following rights of man and of the citizen:

1. Men are born and remain free and equal in rights. Social distinctions may be founded only upon the general good.
2. The aim of all political association is the preservation of the natural and imprescriptible rights of man. These rights are liberty, property, security, and resistance to oppression.

Source: From James H. Robinson and Charles A. Beard, eds., *Readings in Modern European History*, Vol. 1 (Boston: Ginn and Co., 1908), 260–62.

3. The principle of all sovereignty resides essentially in the nation. No body nor individual may exercise any authority which does not proceed directly from the nation.

4. Liberty consists in the freedom to do everything which injures no one else; hence the exercise of the natural rights of each man has no limits except those which assure to the other members of the society the enjoyment of the same rights. These limits can only be determined by law.

5. Law can only prohibit such actions as are hurtful to society. Nothing may be prevented which is not forbidden by law, and no one may be forced to do anything not provided for by law.

6. Law is the expression of the general will. Every citizen has a right to participate personally, or through his representative, in its foundation. It must be the same for all, whether it protects or punishes. All citizens, being equal in the eyes of the law, are equally eligible to all dignities and to all public positions and occupations, according to their abilities, and without distinction except that of their virtues and talents.

7. No person shall be accused, arrested, or imprisoned except in the cases and according to the forms prescribed by law. Any one soliciting, transmitting, executing, or causing to be executed, any arbitrary order, shall be punished. But any citizen summoned or arrested in virtue of the law shall submit without delay, as resistance constitutes an offense.

8. The law shall provide for such punishments only as are strictly and obviously necessary, and no one shall suffer punishment except it be legally inflicted in virtue of a law passed and promulgated before the commission of the offense.

9. As all persons are held innocent until they shall have been declared guilty, if arrest shall be deemed indispensable, all harshness not essential to the securing of the prisoner's person shall be severely repressed by law.

10. No one shall be disquieted on account of his opinions, including his religious views, provided their manifestation does not disturb the public order established by law.

11. The free communication of ideas and opinions is one of the most precious of the rights of man. Every citizen may, accordingly, speak, write, and print with freedom, but shall be responsible for such abuses of this freedom as shall be defined by law.

12. The security of the rights of man and of the citizen requires public military forces. These forces are, therefore, established for the good of all and not for the personal advantage of those to whom they shall be entrusted.

13. A common contribution is essential for the maintenance of the public forces and for the cost of administration. This should be equitably distributed among all the citizens in proportion to their means.

14. All the citizens have a right to decide, either personally or by their representatives, as to the necessity of the public contribution; to grant this freely; to know to what uses it is put; and to fix the proportion, the mode of assessment and of collection and the duration of the taxes.

15. Society has the right to require of every public agent an account of his administration.

16. A society in which the observance of the law is not assured, nor the separation of powers defined, has no constitution at all.

17. Since property is an inviolable and sacred right, no one shall be deprived thereof except where public necessity, legally determined, shall clearly demand it, and then only on condition that the owner shall have been previously and equitably indemnified.

A Feminist Perspective on the Revolution, 1791

Olympe de Gouges (1745–1793) was the outspoken and unyielding feminist leader of the French Revolution who demanded that the revolutionary liberal reforms be extended to include gender equality in all aspects of public and private life. Born to a modest working-class family in 1745, de Gouges at the age of sixteen married a wealthier older man who died shortly after the birth of their only son. Vowing never to remarry, she moved to Paris in 1788, and with the funds bequeathed to her by her husband, she decided to become a writer. When the revolution broke out the following year, she immediately embraced the ideals and goals of the liberals but was disappointed when the French Assembly failed to expand the new rights and liberties to women. She became a more ardent feminist and a vocal critic of the liberals, but her ideas on gender equality were considered radical and were never fully accepted by any group. When she dared to criticize the centralization of power under the rule of Robespierre and the Jacobins, she was branded a counterrevolutionary and guillotined in 1793.

A prolific writer, de Gouges produced more than thirty political pamphlets during the French Revolution, championing such diverse causes as the abolition of slavery, the creation of a national theater, and the extension of paved roads. But her primary passion was equal rights for women. In the Declaration of the Rights of Women and the Female Citizen (1791), de Gouges provided an interesting view of the role and status of women in France in late-eighteenth-century France. Taking the Declaration of the Rights of Man and Citizen as her inspiration, she wrote a strongly worded counterdeclaration that blamed gender inequality on both male chauvinism and female complicity. Although her efforts to promote women's rights were largely unsuccessful, her admonition to women that "it is in your power to free yourselves" has been heralded as one of the defining moments in feminist history.

QUESTIONS TO CONSIDER

1. Olympe de Gouges asserts that gender inequality is not "natural." What is the basis for her argument? What is the importance of this argument? How does it fit with the philosophy of the Enlightenment?

2. Compare the articles in the Declaration of the Rights of Women with those in the Rights of Man. What are the commonalities? What are the differences? In your view, is de Gouges arguing for equal rights or for special rights for women?

3. Olympe de Gouges claims that the initial stage of the French Revolution produced a "more pronounced scorn, a more marked disdain" for women. Why might this be true?

4. According to de Gouges, women have done "more harm than good" in reinforcing their inferior position. How does she explain this? How do you assess her argument?

5. Using her "Form for a Social Contract between Men and Women" as a guide, how would you infer the status and position of most married women? How does her form attempt to correct these problems? Would you accept this kind of contract in your own marriage relationship?

DECLARATION OF THE RIGHTS OF WOMAN AND THE FEMALE CITIZEN (1791)

Olympe de Gouges

Man, are you capable of being just? It is a woman who poses the question; you will not deprive her of that right at least. Tell me, what gives you sovereign empire to oppress my sex? Your strength? Your talents? Observe the Creator in his wisdom; survey in all her grandeur that nature with whom you seem to want to be in harmony, and give me, if you dare, an example of this tyrannical empire. Go back to animals, consult the elements, study plants, finally glance at all the modifications of organic matter, and surrender to the evidence when I offer you the means; search, probe, and distinguish, if you can, the sexes in the administration of nature. Everywhere you will find them mingled; everywhere they cooperate in harmonious togetherness in this immortal masterpiece.

Man alone has raised his exceptional circumstances to a principle. Bizarre, blind, bloated with science and degenerated—in a century of enlightenment and wisdom—into the crassest ignorance, he wants to command as a despot a sex which is in full possession of its intellectual faculties; he pretends to enjoy the Revolution and to claim his rights to equality in order to say nothing more about it.

Mothers, daughters, sisters [and] representatives of the nation demand to be constituted into a national assembly. Believing that ignorance, omission, or scorn for the rights of woman are the only causes of public misfortunes and of the corruption of

Source: From *Women in Revolutionary Paris 1789–1795: Selected Documents Translated with Notes and Commentary* by Daline Gay Levy, Harriet Branson Applewhite, and Mary Durham Johnson, 87–96. Copyright © 1979 University of Illinois. Reprinted with permission.

governments, [the women] have resolved to set forth in a solemn declaration the natural, inalienable, and sacred rights of woman in order that this declaration, constantly exposed before all the members of the society, will ceaselessly remind them of their rights and duties. . . .

Consequently, the sex that is as superior in beauty as it is in courage during the suffering of maternity recognizes and declares in the presence and under the auspices of the Supreme Being, the following Rights of Woman and of Female Citizens.

1. Woman is born free and lives equal to man in her rights. Social distinctions can be based only on the common utility.

2. The purpose of any political association is the conservation of the natural rights of woman and man; these rights are liberty, property, security, and especially resistance to oppression.

3. The principle of all sovereignty rests essentially with the nation, which is nothing but the union of woman and man; no body and no individual can exercise any authority which does not come expressly from it [the nation].

4. Liberty and justice consist of restoring all that belongs to others; thus, the only limits on the exercise of the natural rights of woman are perpetual male tyranny; these limits are to be reformed by the laws of nature and reason.

. . .

6. The laws must be the expression of the general will; all female and male citizens must contribute either personally or through their representatives to its formation; it must be the same for all: male and female citizens, being equal in the eyes of the law, must be equally admitted to all honors, positions, and public employment according to their capacity and without other distinctions besides those of their virtues and talents.

7. No woman is an exception: she is accused, arrested, and detained in cases determined by law. Women, like men, obey this rigorous law. . . .

. . .

17. Property belongs to both sexes whether united or separate; for each it is an inviolable and sacred right; no one can be deprived of it, since it is the true patrimony of nature, unless the legally determined public need obviously dictates it, and then only with a just and prior indemnity.

Woman, wake up; the tocsin* of reason is being heard throughout the whole universe; discover your rights. The powerful empire of nature is no longer surrounded by prejudice, fanaticism, superstition, and lies. The flame of truth has dispersed all the clouds of folly and usurpation. Enslaved man has multiplied his strength and needs recourse to yours to break his chains. Having become free, he has become unjust to his companion. Oh, women, women! When will you cease to be blind? What advantage have you received from the Revolution? A more pronounced scorn, a more marked disdain. . . . [C]ourageously oppose the force of reason to the empty

---

*An alarm bell; a warning signal.

pretensions of superiority; unite yourselves beneath the standards of philosophy; deploy all the energy of your character, and you will soon see these haughty men, not groveling at your feet as servile adorers, but proud to share with you the treasures of the Supreme Being. Regardless of what barriers confront you, it is in your power to free yourselves; you have only to want to. . . .

Women have done more harm than good. Constraint and dissimulation have been their lot. What force has robbed them of, ruse returned to them; they had recourse to all the resources of their charms, and the most irreproachable persons did not resist them. Poison and the sword were both subject to them . . . anything which characterizes the folly of men, profane and sacred, all have been subject to the cupidity and ambition of this sex, formerly contemptible and respected, and since the revolution, respectable and scorned.

. . . Under the Old Regime, all was vicious, all was guilty. . . . A woman only had to be beautiful or amiable; when she possessed these two advantages, she saw a hundred fortunes at her feet. If she did not profit from them, she had a bizarre character or a rare philosophy which made her scorn wealth; then she was deemed to be like a crazy woman; the most indecent made herself respected with gold. . . . [A]nd at an age when the slave has lost all her charms, what will become of this unfortunate woman? The victim of scorn, even the doors of charity are closed to her; she is poor and old, they say; why did she not know how to make her fortune.

Reason finds other examples that are even more touching. A young, inexperienced woman, seduced by a man whom she loves, will abandon her parents to follow him; the ingrate will leave her after a few years, and the older she has become with him, the more inhuman is his inconstancy; if she has children, he will likewise abandon them. If he is rich, he will consider himself excused from sharing his fortune with his noble victims. . . .

. . . Marriage is the tomb of trust and love. The married woman can with impunity give bastards to her husband, and also give them the wealth which does not belong to them. The woman who is unmarried has only one feeble right; ancient and inhuman laws refuse to her for her children the right to the name and the wealth of their father; no new laws have been made in this matter. . . .

[De Gouges proposes a new marriage contract between man and woman]

We, [name of man] and [name of woman], moved by our own will, unite ourselves for the duration of our lives, and for the duration of our mutual inclinations, under the following conditions: We intend and wish to make our wealth communal, meanwhile reserving to ourselves the right to divide it in favor of our children and of those toward whom we might have a particular inclination, mutually recognizing that our property belongs directly to our children, from whatever bed they come, and that all of them without distinction have the right to bear the name of the fathers and mothers who have acknowledged them, and we are charged to subscribe to the law which punished the renunciation of one's own blood. We likewise obligate ourselves, in case of separation, to divide our wealth and to set aside in advance the portion the law indicates for our children, and in the event of a perfect union, the one who dies will divest himself of half his property in his children's favor, and if one dies childless, the survivor will inherit by right, unless the dying person has disposed of half the common property in favor of one who he judged deserving. That is approximately the formula for the marriage act I propose for execution. . . .

I offer a foolproof way to elevate the soul of women; it is to join them to all the activities of man; if man persists in finding this way impractical, let him share his fortune with woman, not at his caprice, but by the wisdom of laws. Prejudice falls, morals are purified, and nature regains all her rights. Add to this the marriage of priests and the strengthening of the king on his throne, and the French government cannot fail.

Terror in Defense of Liberty

Maximilien Robespierre (1758–1794), known to his contemporaries as "the Incorruptible," remains one of the most controversial figures of the French Revolution. To his enemies, he was viewed as the Devil incarnate; to the Parisian masses of 1793, he was seen as the unwavering champion of freedom and equality. Under his leadership, the French Revolution entered its so-called radical phase (1792–1794), when as many as 40,000 people were guillotined in order to complete what he viewed as "the war of liberty against tyranny."

Robespierre was born to a poor family in the French town of Arras in 1758. With the aid of a scholarship, he studied law in Paris and became enamored with the ideas of Rousseau, especially his concept of the ultimate and infallible "general will" of the people. After practicing law for several years, Robespierre was elected to the Estates General in 1789, where he joined the more radical, prodemocratic Jacobin party. He was an energetic and uncompromising advocate of democratic reforms, and he won the admiration and support of the Parisian working classes as he rose to leadership within the Jacobins. In 1793, he was elected to the twelve-member Committee of Public Safety, where he continued to consolidate his power. Robespierre believed that he understood the needs and aspirations of the people, as well as the cunning treacheries of their enemies, and he was willing to adopt extreme measures in order to protect and preserve his vision of the revolution. In early 1794, he arrested and executed some of his former political allies, but by midyear, his own position was growing precarious within a divided Committee of Public Safety. In July, his enemies issued an arrest warrant and Robespierre was tried and guillotined the following day.

Six months prior to his death, when he was at the height of his power, Robespierre gave a speech on "The Moral and Political Principles of Domestic Policy" (February 1794). By this time, the revolutionary armies of France had succeeded in repelling the foreign invaders, but Robespierre still worried about domestic counterrevolutionaries and spies at home. His speech offers a fascinating insight into Robespierre's vision of the revolution, as well as his justification for the use of terror. It also raises some interesting questions about the meaning of the French Revolution, the use of extremism in defense of liberty, and the relationship between democracy, nationalism, and "virtue."

QUESTIONS TO CONSIDER

1. What kind of society did Robespierre wish to create in France? How did his vision compare with the one implied in the Declaration of the Rights of Man and Citizen? What is significant about the differences?

2. Robespierre claimed that democracy was sustained by "virtue." What does he mean by virtue? Do you agree with his assessment? Why or why not?

3. In order to finish the "war of liberty against tyranny," Robespierre said that one must "lead the people by reason, and the people's enemies by terror." How did he define "terror" and justify its usage? In your view, does the use of terror betray or defend the ideals of the revolution?

4. In the immediate aftermath of the French Revolution, Robespierre was remembered as an evil and radical zealot. From today's perspective, how radical were his ideas and methods? Was he evil?

5. Contrary to Robespierre's assessment, some historians have concluded that the ideals of liberalism/democracy and nationalism are actually in opposition to each other. Using Robespierre's speech and life as evidence, how might you explain the relationship between democracy and nationalism?

"THE MORAL AND POLITICAL PRINCIPLES OF DOMESTIC POLICY" (1794)

Maximilien Robespierre

Some time ago we set forth the principles of our foreign policy; today we come to expound the principles of our internal policy.

After having proceeded haphazardly for a long time, swept along by the movement of opposing factions, the representatives of the French people have finally demonstrated a character and a government. . . . But, up to the very moment when I am speaking, it must be agreed that we have been guided, amid such stormy circumstances, by the love of good and by the awareness of our country's needs rather than by an exact theory and by precise rules of conduct, which we did not have even leisure enough to lay out. . . .

What is the goal toward which we are heading? The peaceful enjoyment of liberty and equality; the reign of that eternal justice whose laws have been inscribed, not in marble and stone, but in the hearts of all men, even in that of the slave who forgets them and in that of the tyrant who denies them.

We seek an order of things in which all the base and cruel passions are enchained, all the beneficent and generous passions are awakened by the laws; where ambition becomes the desire to merit glory and to serve our country; where distinc-

Source: From *The Ninth of Thermidor,* by Richard Bienvenu, 32–49. Copyright © 1970 by Oxford University Press, Inc. Used by permission of Oxford University Press, Inc.

tions are born only of equality itself; where the citizen is subject to the magistrate, the magistrate to the people, and the people to justice; where our country assures the well-being of each individual, and where each individual proudly enjoys our country's prosperity and glory; where every soul grows greater through the continual flow of republican sentiments, and by the need of deserving the esteem of a great people; where the arts are the adornments of the liberty which ennobles them and commerce the source of public wealth rather than solely the monstrous opulence of a few families.

In our land we want to substitute morality for egotism, integrity for formal codes of honor, principles for customs, a sense of duty for one of mere propriety, the rule of reason for the tyranny of fashion, scorn of vice for scorn of the unlucky; self respect for insolence, grandeur of soul for vanity, love of glory for the love of money, good people in place of good society . . . which is to say, all the virtues and all the miracles of the republic in place of all the vices of the monarchy. . . .

What kind of government can realize these wonders? Only a democratic or republican government. . . . Democracy is not a state in which the people, continually meeting, regulate for themselves all public affairs, still less is it a state in which a tiny fraction of the people, acting by isolated, hasty, and contradictory measures, decide the fate of the whole society. . . . Democracy is a state in which the sovereign people, guided by laws which are of their own making, do for themselves all that they can do well, and by their delegates do all that they cannot do for themselves. . . .

But, in order to lay the foundations of democracy among us and to consolidate it, in order to arrive at the peaceful reign of constitutional laws, we must finish the war of liberty against tyranny and safely cross through the storms of the revolution: that is the goal of the revolutionary system which you have put in order. . . .

Now, what is the fundamental principle of popular or democratic government, that is to say, the essential mainspring which sustains it and makes it move? It is virtue. I speak of the public virtue which worked so many wonders in Greece and Rome and which ought to produce even more astonishing things in republican France—that virtue which is nothing other than the love of the nation and its laws. . . .

Since the soul of the Republic is virtue . . . it follows that the first rule of your political conduct ought to be to relate all your efforts to maintaining equality and developing virtue. . . . Thus everything that tends to excite love of country, to purify morals, to elevate souls, to direct the passions of the human heart toward the public interest ought to be adopted or established by you. Everything which tends to concentrate them in the abjection of selfishness, to awaken enjoyment for petty things and scorn for great ones, ought to be rejected or curbed by you. Within the scheme of the French revolution, that which is immoral is impolitic, that which is corrupting is counterrevolutionary. . . .

This great purity of the French Revolution's fundamental elements . . . is precisely what creates our strength and our weakness: our strength, because it gives us the victory of truth over deception and the rights of public interest over private interests; our weakness, because it rallies against us all men who are vicious, all those who in their hearts plan to despoil the people. . . . We must smother the internal and external enemies of the Republic or perish, [and] in these circumstances, the first maxim of our policy ought to be to lead the people by reason and the people's enemies by terror.

If the mainspring of popular government in peacetime is virtue, amid revolution it is at the same time [both] virtue and terror: virtue, without which terror is fatal; terror, without which virtue is impotent. Terror is nothing but prompt, severe, inflexible justice; it is therefore an emanation of virtue. . . . It has been said that terror was the mainspring of despotic government. Does our government, then, resemble a despotism? Yes! . . . Subdue liberty's enemies by terror, and you will be right, as founders of the Republic. The government of the revolution is the despotism of liberty against tyranny. . . .

Some people would like to govern revolutions by the quibbles of the law courts and treat conspiracies against the Republic like legal proceedings against private persons. Tyranny kills; liberty argues. And the code made by the conspirators themselves is the law by which they are judged.

REVOLUTIONS IN THE CARIBBEAN AND LATIN AMERICA
The Haitian Revolution

Toussaint L'Ouverture was the founder of the second independent nation in the New World and the leader of the most successful slave revolt in western history. He was born on a plantation in the French colony of Saint-Domingue (now Haiti) and lived his first thirty-four years as a slave. His experience in bondage was less brutal and more fortunate than that of most slaves in Haiti, and in 1777 he was granted his freedom. When the slave revolt broke out in 1791, Toussaint first helped his former master to escape before he joined the attacks on other plantations. He soon emerged as a principal leader among the former slaves and was determined to preserve their liberty from slavery.

When France and Spain went to war in 1793, Toussaint and his fighters initially sided with the Spaniards of Santo Domingo (now the Dominican Republic), and they scored several victories against their former masters. But a year later, Toussaint shifted his allegiances back to France after the Jacobin-controlled government had abolished slavery. In return for his assistance, the French government named him lieutenant governor of the colony. Toussaint proved himself a skilled diplomat and master politician who eventually dismissed the island's governor and placed himself in command. But when Napoleon seized power in France, the government announced its decision to restore Saint-Domingue as a profitable colony, which also meant a restoration of slavery on the island. In 1802, French forces invaded Haiti, and after first declaring their willingness to negotiate, they secretly arrested Toussaint and sent him to life confinement in France, where he died in 1803. In that same year, after continued bloody resistance, French forces quit Saint-Domingue, and Haiti won its liberty and independence.

The readings from the Haitian Revolution cover a seven-year time span that highlights the tension between Toussaint's idealistic principles and the pragmatic policies he felt compelled to adopt. In the short Proclamation of 29 August 1793, Toussaint makes clear his goals and attempts to encourage others to join him. In his letter to the French Minister of Marine (13 April 1799), Toussaint further explains his goals and actions to the French government now controlled by the more conservative Directory, which viewed Toussaint with suspicion and disfavor. In a similar letter to the Directory (28 October 1797), Toussaint attempted to reaffirm his commitment to the ideals of liberty while also exposing the double standards by which colonial nations have condemned the actions of the colonized. The last document, the Forced Labor Decree of 1800, contains the essence of Toussaint's social and economic policy, which was centered on the militarization of Haitian society. Although Toussaint's forced-labor policy did help restore the economy of the island, it was perceived by many to contradict his stance on liberty, and it significantly weakened his support among the black working classes. Consequently, when French forces invaded in 1802, Toussaint was unable to rally sufficient support, and he was arrested and sent into exile. But although Haitians were unhappy with Toussaint, they were not willing to lose their liberty to the French. Fighting soon resumed, and when the French recognized the futility of their efforts and withdrew their forces, Haiti proclaimed its independence in 1803.

QUESTIONS TO CONSIDER

1. How does Toussaint explain the origins of the slave uprising in the letter to the Minister of Marine? Toussaint further explains his failure to maintain alliance between blacks and "men of color." What caused this failure, and why is it significant? What might it tell us about identities on Haiti?

2. In the letter to the Directory, how does Toussaint refute the charge that the "gross negroes" of Haiti are "incapable of distinguishing between unrestrained license and austere liberty"? Why does he suggest that the French are hypocritical in their assessments? What impact does this have?

3. Why does Toussaint wish to militarize agricultural society? How do his actions and explanations compare with Robespierre's justification for terror?

4. The revolution in Haiti was clearly made more complex because of race perceptions. How does Toussaint see the issue of race? How does he view whites? How does he view blacks?

5. In your assessment, was Toussaint a man guided more by principle or by pragmatic expediency? Be sure to reinforce your conclusions with evidence.

SPEECHES AND LETTERS ON THE HAITIAN REVOLUTION (1793–1800)

Toussaint L'Ouverture

Proclamation of 29 August 1793

Brothers and Friends:

I am Toussaint L'Ouverture. My name is perhaps known to you. I have undertaken to avenge you. I want liberty and equality to reign throughout St. Domingue. I am

Source: George Tyson, ed., *Toussaint L'Ouverture*, 28, 30–31. Copyright © 1973 Prentice-Hall. Reprinted by permission of Pearson Education, Inc., Upper Saddle River, NJ.

working toward that end. Come and join me, brothers, and combat by our side for the same cause.

Letter to the Minister of Marine, 13 April 1799

The first successes obtained in Europe by the partisans of liberty over the agents of despotism were not slow to ignite the sacred fire of patriotism in the souls of all Frenchmen in St. Domingue. At that time, men's hopes turned to France, whose first steps toward her regeneration promised them a happier future. . . . [The whites in St. Domingue] wanted to escape from their arbitrary government, but they did not intend the revolution to destroy either the prejudices that debased the men of color* or the slavery of the blacks, whom they held in dependency by the strongest law. In their opinion, the benefits of the French regeneration were only for them. They proved it by their obstinate refusal to allow the people of color to enjoy their political rights and the slaves to enjoy the liberty that they claimed. Thus, while whites were erecting an-other form of government upon the rubble of despotism, the men of color and the blacks united themselves in order to claim their political existence; the resistance of the former having become stronger, it was necessary for the latter to rise up in order to obtain [political recognition] by force of arms. The whites, fearing that this legiti-mate resistance would bring general liberty to St. Domingue, sought to separate the men of color from the cause of the blacks in accordance with Machiavelli's principle of divide and rule. Renouncing their claims over the men of color, they accepted the April Decree [1792].† As they had anticipated, the men of color, many of whom are slave holders, had only been using the blacks to gain on political commands. Fearing the enfranchisement of the blacks, the men of color deserted their comrades in arms, their companions in misfortune, and aligned themselves with the whites to sub-due them.

Treacherously abandoned, the blacks fought for some time against the reunited whites and the men of color; but, pressed on all sides, losing hope, they accepted the offers of the Spanish king, who, having at that time declared war on France, offered freedom to those blacks of St. Domingue who would join his armies. Indeed, the si-lence of pre-Republican France on the long-standing claims for their natural rights made by the most interested, the noblest, the most useful portion of the population of St. Domingue . . . extinguished all glimmer of hope in the hearts of the black slaves and forced them, in spite of themselves, to throw themselves into the arms of a pro-tective power that offered the only benefit for which they would fight. More unfortu-nate than guilty, they turned their arms against their fatherland. . . .

Such with the crimes of these blacks, which have earned them to this day the in-sulting titles of brigands, insurgents, rebels. . . . At that time, I was one of the leaders of these auxiliary troops, and I can say without fear of contradiction that I owed my

---

*By "men of color" Toussaint refers to the mulattos, or people of mixed racial ancestry. In Haiti, their status and position in society was barely above that of blacks.

†In the April Decree of 1792, the French Assembly, now dominated by liberals from the business and commercial classes, issued a law that gave full citizenship to people of color but not to blacks or slaves. Some historians contend that this measure was intended to weaken Toussaint's forces and allow white plantation owners to retake control of the island.

elevation in these circumstances only to the confidence that I had inspired in my brothers by the virtues for which I am still honored today. . . .

Letter to the Directory, 28 October 1797

Second Assertion [made by a critic in the French Assembly]: "Everyone is agreed in portraying the Colony in the most shocking state of disorder and groaning under the military government. And what a military government! In whose hands is it confined? In that of ignorant and gross negroes, incapable of distinguishing between unrestrained license and austere liberty."

This shocking disorder in which the Commission* found St. Domingue was not the consequence of the liberty given to the blacks, but the result of the uprising of thirty Ventose [mulattos],[†] for prior to this period, order and harmony reigned in all Republican territory as far as the absence of laws would allow. All citizens blindly obeyed the orders of General Laveaux; his will was the national will for them, and they submitted to him as a man invested with the authority emanating from the generous nation that had shattered their chains.

If, upon the arrival of the Commission, St. Domingue groaned under a military government, this power was not in the hands of the blacks; they were subordinate to it, and they only executed the orders of General Laveaux. These were the blacks who, when France was threatened with the loss of this Colony, employed their arms and their weapons to conserve it, to reconquer the greatest part of its territory that treason had handed over to the Spanish and English. . . . These were the blacks who . . . flew to the rescue of General Laveaux . . . and who, by repressing the audacious rebels who wished to destroy the national representation, restored it to its rightful depository.

Such was the conduct of those blacks in whose hands . . . the military government of St. Domingue found itself, such are those negroes accused of being ignorant and gross; undoubtedly they are, because without education there can only be ignorance and grossness. But must one impute to them the crime of this educational deficiency or, more correctly, accuse those who prevented them by the most atrocious punishments from obtaining it? And are only civilized people capable of distinguishing between good and evil, of having notions of charity and justice? The men of St. Domingue have been deprived of an education; but even so, they no longer remain in a state of nature, and because they haven't arrived at the degree of perfection that education bestows, they do not merit being classed apart from the rest of mankind, being confused with animals. . . .

Undoubtedly, one can reproach the inhabitants of St. Domingue, including the blacks, for many faults, even terrible crimes. But even in France, where the limits of sociability are clearly drawn, doesn't one see its inhabitants, in the struggle between

---

*In 1796, a group of civil commissioners arrived from France, instructed by the Directory to ascertain the situation and to begin to reestablish full French authority over the island. By this time, Toussaint had privately come to the conclusion that the liberty of blacks could be guaranteed only under an independent black government.

†Refers to an attempted coup in 1796 by the mulattos against French Governor Laveaux. The plotters were thwarted by Toussaint and his army, and a grateful (and militarily weak) Governor Laveaux rewarded Toussaint by naming him lieutenant governor.

despotism and liberty, going to all the excesses for which the blacks are reproached by their enemies? The fury of the two parties has been equal in St. Domingue; and if the excesses of the blacks in these critical moments haven't exceeded those committed in Europe, must not an impartial judge pronounce in favor of the former? Since it is our enemies themselves who present us as ignorant and gross, aren't we more excusable than those who, unlike us, were not deprived of the advantages of education and civilization?

Forced Labor Decree, 12 October 1800

Citizens,

After putting an end to the war in the South, our first duty has been to return thanks to the Almighty; which we have done with the zeal becoming so great a blessing: Now, Citizens, it is necessary to consecrate all our moments to the prosperity of St. Domingo, to the public tranquility, and consequently, to the welfare of our fellow citizens.

But, to attain this end in an effectual manner, all the civil and military officers must make it their business, everyone in their respective department, to perform the duties of their offices with devotion and attachment to the public welfare.

You will easily conceive, Citizens, that Agriculture is the support of Government; since it is the foundation of Commerce and Wealth, the source of Arts and Industry, it keeps everybody employed, as being the mechanism of all Trades. And, from the moment that every individual becomes useful, it creates public tranquility; disturbances disappear together with idleness, by which they are commonly generated, and everyone peaceably enjoys the fruits of his industry. Officers civil and military, this is what you must aim at; such is the plan to be adopted, which I prescribe to you; and I declare in the most peremptory manner, that it shall be enforced: My country demands this salutary step; I am bound to it by my office, and the security of our liberties demands it imperiously. But in order to secure our liberties, which are indispensable to our happiness, every individual must be usefully employed, so as to contribute to the public good, and the general tranquility.

Considering that the soldier, who has sacred duties to perform, as being the safeguard of the people . . . is strictly subordinate to his superior officers: It is of great importance that overseers, drivers and field-negroes, who in like manner have their superiors, should conduct themselves as officers . . . and soldiers in whatever may concern them.

Considering that when an officer . . . or a soldier deviates from his duty he is delivered over to a court-martial to be tried and punished according to the laws of the Republic, for in military service no rank is to be favoured when guilty: The overseers, drivers and field-negroes, as subject to constant labour, and equally subordinate to their superiors, shall be punished in like manner, in case of failure in their respective duties.

Whereas a soldier cannot leave his company, his battalion, or half-brigade, and enter into another, without the severest punishment, unless provided with a commission in due form from his Chief; field-negroes are forbidden to quit their respective plantations without a lawful permission. This is by no means attended to, since they change their place of labour as they please, go to and fro, and pay not the least attention to agriculture, though the only means of furnishing sustenance to the military, their protectors. They even conceal themselves in towns, in villages, and mountains, where . . . they live by plunder, and in a state of open hostility to society. . . .

The Liberator of South America, 1815

Simón Bolívar (1783–1830), known as "the Liberator"of South America from Spanish colonial rule, hardly fits the stereotypical image of a revolutionary. Born to an aristocratic Venezuelan Creole family that owned plantations worked by slave labor, Bolívar seemed destined for a life of wealth and privilege. But after he was orphaned at the age of nine, he was raised and educated by private tutors who inspired in him an admiration for the ideals of the Enlightenment. After a period of study in Europe during the height of Napoleon's career, he returned to South America at the age of twenty-four committed to the cause of independence. Venezuela was already in ferment, and when the colony declared its independence from Spanish rule in 1811, Bolívar joined the army of the young republic and soon gained command. After several years of inconclusive military victories and defeats in Venezuela and elsewhere, Bolívar launched a brilliant surprise attack across the Andes that defeated the Spanish in Colombia. Thereafter, Bolívar's forces gained unstoppable momentum and successively liberated Venezuela (1821), Ecuador (1822), Peru (1824), and Bolívia (1825), the latter named in his honor. Following the wars of independence, Bolívar played a pivotal role in the forma-tion of new republican governments, and he dreamed of creating a league of His-panic American states that would unite much of South America. But both tasks were undermined by regional disputes and factional infighting, and several new republics fell into civil war. In his effort to maintain the unity of Gran Colombia (comprising the modern nations of Colombia, Venezuela, and Ecuador), Bolívar assumed dictatorial powers in 1828 but was unable to prevent the secession of Venezuela a year later. Feeling embittered and betrayed by self-serving political opportunists posing as liberal reformers, Bolívar retired from public life in 1829, and he died of tuberculosis the following year.

"The Jamaican Letter" (1815) is one of Bolívar's earliest and most important political essays on the course of South American independence. It was written during his self-imposed exile on Jamaica (then a British colony) after a major mili-tary defeat in Venezuela. Historians are uncertain to whom the letter was ad-dressed, but they speculate that the recipient was the English governor of the island. The letter affirms Bolívar's unfailing dedication to the cause of indepen-dence and the ideals of liberty and freedom. But in his ruminations on the future, Bolívar also reveals his antiliberal, authoritarian leanings. Believing that the masses lacked the experience and "virtue" for a democracy, Bolívar advocated an oligarchic government with power concentrated in the hands of a strong, paternal executive and a hereditary legislature. His political philosophy is an interesting mixture of liberal and authoritarian ideas, and it is still frequently reflected in current political debate in much of South America. As you read the following letter, also keep in mind how Bolívar's ideas compare with those of Madison and Robespierre.

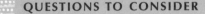

QUESTIONS TO CONSIDER

1. According to Bolívar, what are the unique challenges of ethnicity and identity faced by the leaders of the revolution? How does this affect his political ideas? What role does he envision for indigenous Indians and imported black slaves in the new nations?

2. Bolívar laments the fact that Spanish America was denied "active and effective tyranny." What does he mean by this? Why does he think it is significant?

3. According to Bolívar, what stands in the way of liberal and republican governments? Why can't South America follow the model of the United States? What kind of governmental system does Bolívar favor?

4. Some historians claim that Bolívar's political philosophy was based on liberal principles tempered by a realistic assessment of the current situation. Others claim that his authoritarianism stems from a deep distrust of the masses. In your view, which assessment is more correct?

5. How might future leaders in South America use Bolívar's letter to press for more liberal reforms? How might others use his writing to justify the curtailment of freedoms?

"THE JAMAICAN LETTER" (1815)

Simón Bolívar

Kingston, Jamaica, September 6 1815

My dear Sir . . .

With what a feeling of gratitude I read that passage in your letter in which you say to me: "I hope that the success which then followed Spanish arms may now turn in favor of their adversaries, the badly oppressed people of South America." I take this hope as a prediction, if it is justice that determines man's contests. Success will crown our efforts, because the destiny of America has been irrevocably decided; the tie that bound her to Spain has been severed. . . . At present . . . we are threatened with the fear of death, dishonor, and every harm; there is nothing we have not suffered at the hands of that unnatural stepmother—Spain. The veil has been torn asunder. We have already seen the light, and it is not our desire to be thrust back into darkness. The chains have been broken; we have been freed, and now our enemies seek to enslave us anew. For this reason America fights desperately, and seldom has desperation failed to achieve victory. . . .

Source: Simón Bolívar, "Reply of a South American to a Gentleman of this Island [Jamaica]," in *Selected Writings of Bolívar, Vol. 1 (1810–1822)*, ed. Harold Bierck; compiled by Vincente Lecuna; transl. Lewis Bertrand (New York: Colonial Press, 1951), 103–22.

It is even more difficult to foresee the future fate of the New World, to set down its political principles, or to prophesy what manner of government it will adopt. . . . We are young in the ways of almost all the arts and sciences, although, in a certain manner, we are old in the ways of civilized society. I look upon the present state of America as similar to that of Rome after its fall. Each part of Rome adopted a political system conforming to its interest and situation or was led by the individual ambitions of certain chiefs, dynasties, or associations. But this important difference exists: those dispersed parts later reestablished their ancient nations, subject to the changes imposed by circumstances or events. But we scarcely retain a vestige of what once was; we are, moreover, neither Indian nor European, but a species midway between the legitimate proprietors of this country and the Spanish usurpers. In short, though Americans by birth we derive our rights from Europe, and we have to assert these rights against the rights of the natives, and at the same time we must defend ourselves against the invaders. This places us in a most extraordinary and involved situation. Notwithstanding that it is a type of divination to predict the result of the political course which America is pursuing, I shall venture some conjectures which, of course, are colored by my enthusiasm and dictated by rational desires rather than by reasoned calculations.

The role of the inhabitants of the American hemisphere has for centuries been purely passive. Politically they were nonexistent. We are still in a position lower than slavery, and therefore it is more difficult for us to rise to the enjoyment of freedom. Permit me these transgressions in order to establish the issue. States are slaves because of either the nature or the misuse of their constitutions; a people is therefore enslaved when the government, by its nature or its vices, infringes on and usurps the rights of the citizen or subject. Applying these principles, we find that America was denied not only its freedom but even an active and effective tyranny. . . .

We have been harassed by a conduct which has not only deprived us of our rights but has kept us in a sort of permanent infancy with regard to public affairs. If we could at least have managed our domestic affairs and our internal administration, we could have acquainted ourselves with the processes and mechanics of public affairs. We should also have enjoyed a personal consideration, thereby commanding a certain unconscious respect from the people, which is so necessary to preserve amidst revolutions. That is why I say we have even been deprived of an active tyranny, since we have not been permitted to exercise its functions. . . .

The Americans have risen rapidly without previous knowledge of, and, what is more regrettable, without previous experience in public affairs, to enact upon the world stage the eminent roles of legislator, magistrate, minister of the treasury, diplomat, general, and every position of authority, supreme or subordinate, that comprises the hierarchy of a fully organized state. . . .

. . . Uncertain of our destiny, and facing anarchy for want of a legitimate, just, and liberal government, we threw ourselves headlong into the chaos of revolution. Attention was first given to obtaining domestic security against enemies within our midst, and then it was extended to the procuring of external security. Authorities were set up to replace those we had deposed, empowered to direct the course of our revolution and to take full advantage of the fortunate turn of events; thus we were able to found a constitutional government worthy of our century and adequate to our situation.

The first steps of all the new governments are marked by the establishment of *juntas** of the people. These *juntas* speedily draft rules for the calling of congresses, which produce great changes. Venezuela erected a democratic and federal government, after declaring for the rights of man. A system of checks and balances was established, and general laws were passed granting civil liberties, such as freedom of the press and others. In short, an independent government was created. New Granada uniformly followed the political institutions and reforms introduced by Venezuela, taking as the fundamental basis of her constitution the most elaborate federal system ever to be brought into existence. Recently the powers of the chief executive have been increased, and he has been given all the powers that are properly his. . . .

[However] events in Costa Firme [Venezuela] have proved that institutions which are wholly representative are not suited to our character, customs, and present knowledge. In Caracas [Venezuela], party spirit arose in the societies, assemblies, and popular elections; these parties led us back into slavery.[†] Thus, while Venezuela has been the American republic with the most advanced political institutions, she has also been the clearest example of the inefficacy of the democratic and federal system for our new-born states. In New Granada, the large number of excess powers held by the provincial governments and the lack of centralization in the general government have reduced that fair country to her present state. For this reason her foes, though weak, have been able to hold out against all odds. As long as our countrymen do not acquire the abilities and political virtues that distinguish our brothers of the north [the United States], wholly popular systems, far from working to our advantage, will, I greatly fear, bring about our downfall. Unfortunately, these traits, to the degree in which they are required, do not appear to be within our reach. On the contrary, we are dominated by the vices that one learns under the rule of a nation like Spain, which has only distinguished itself in ferocity, ambition, vindictiveness, and greed.

It is harder, Montesquieu[‡] has written, to release a nation from servitude than to enslave a free nation. This truth is proven by the annals of all times, which reveal that most free nations have been put under the yoke, but very few enslaved nations have recovered their liberty. Despite the convictions of history, South Americans have made efforts to obtain liberal, even perfect, institutions, doubtless out of that instinct to aspire to the greatest possible happiness, which, common to all men, is bound to follow in civil societies founded on the principles of justice, liberty, and equality. But are we capable of maintaining in proper balance the difficult charge of a republic? Is it conceivable that a newly emancipated people can soar to the heights of liberty, and, unlike Icarus, neither have its wings melt nor fall into an abyss? Such a marvel is inconceivable and without precedent. There is no reasonable probability to bolster our hopes. . . .

Among the popular and representative systems, I do not favor the federal system. It is over-perfect, and it demands political virtues and talents far superior to our own. For the same reason I reject a monarchy that is part aristocracy and part democracy, although with such a government England has achieved much fortune and splendor.

---

*A group or committee that takes governmental power, often in the aftermath of a revolution.

†Bolívar refers to an incident in 1811, when treasonable action by a local faction opened the fortress at Caracas to Spanish forces.

‡The baron de Montesquieu (1689–1755) was a prominent political philosopher of the Enlightenment.

Since it is not possible for us to select the most perfect and complete form of government, let us avoid falling into demagogic anarchy or monocratic tyranny. These opposite extremes would only wreck us on similar reefs of misfortune and dishonor; hence, we must seek a mean between them. I say: Do not adopt the best system of government, but the one that is most likely to succeed.

By the nature of their geographic location, wealth, population, and character, I expect that the Mexicans, at the outset, intend to establish a representative republic in which the executive will have great powers. These will be concentrated in one person, who, if he discharges his duties with wisdom and justice, should almost certainly maintain his authority for life. . . .

New Granada will unite with Venezuela, if they can agree to the establishment of a central republic. . . . The Indians living there can be civilized, and our territorial possessions could be increased. . . . This nation should be called Colombia as a just and grateful tribute to the discoverer of our hemisphere. Its government might follow the English pattern, except that in place of a king there will be an executive who will be elected for life, but his office will never be hereditary, if a republic is desired. There will be a hereditary legislative chamber or senate. This body can interpose itself between the violent demands of the people and the great powers of the government during periods of political unrest. . . .

Surely unity is what we need to complete our work of regeneration. The division among us, nevertheless, is nothing extraordinary, for it is characteristic of civil wars to form two parties, conservatives and reformers. The former are commonly the more numerous, because the weight of habit induces obedience to established powers; the latter are always fewer in number although more vocal and learned. Thus, the physical mass of the one is counterbalanced by the moral force of the other; the contest is prolonged, and the results are uncertain. Fortunately, in our case, the mass has followed the learned.

I shall tell you with what we must provide ourselves in order to expel the Spaniards and to found a free government. It is *union,* obviously; but such union will come about through sensible planning and well-directed actions rather than by divine magic. America stands together because it is abandoned by all other nations. It is isolated in the center of the world. It has no diplomatic relations, nor does it receive any military assistance; instead, America is attacked by Spain, which has more military supplies than any we can possibly acquire through furtive means.

When success is not assured, when the state is weak, and when results are distantly seen, all men hesitate; opinion is divided, passions rage, and the enemy fans these passions in order to win an easy victory because of them. As soon as we are strong and under the guidance of a liberal nation which will lend us her protection, we will achieve accord in cultivating the virtues and talents that lead to glory. Then will we march majestically toward that great prosperity for which South America is destined. Then will those sciences and arts which, born in the East, have enlightened Europe, wing their way to a free Colombia, which will cordially bid them welcome.

I am, Sir, etc., etc.

Simón Bolívar

NOTES

1. Liberalism (derived from the Latin *liber,* or "free") has been defined in many different ways, and its meaning has changed over time. In its original, classic definition, it meant a political philosophy that favored the maximum individual freedom possible, the protection of political and civil liberties, and a limited government based on the consent of the people.

2. Historians also attribute the rise of liberal philosophy to changes associated with European economic expansion overseas and the pressures for reform that accompanied the widening of trade and increased prosperity. These changes and their impact are further discussed in chapter 7.

3. *The Federalist Papers* also contain essays written by Madison's key political allies, Alexander Hamilton and John Jay, both of New York. They were published between 1787 and 1788.

4. See chapter 3 for Jefferson's views on slavery.

5. Jefferson's bill provided for complete religious liberty and was one of the first of its kind in America.

6. As expressed in his *Notes on the State of Virginia* (see chapter 3), Jefferson agonized over the morality of slavery but was able to rationalize it on the basis of perceived racial differences. In his original draft of the Declaration of Independence, Jefferson included a clause that criticized Britain for introducing slavery to North America, but this was deleted by the Continental Congress prior to its adoption in 1776.

7. Some scholars contend that Madison and Hamilton employed the pseudonym *Publius* (Latin for "the public") to highlight their admiration for the Roman Republic.

8. When Lincoln was assassinated in 1865, Bancroft was chosen to write and deliver the official eulogy at the funeral.

9. The transcendental movement of the early nineteenth century was part of the larger Romantic movement in the United States, which, in turn, was a reaction against the impersonal and overly rational philosophy of the Enlightenment. As expressed by Emerson, all people could experience a higher morality and closer union with God through the love and contemplation of nature.

10. Douglass was born Frederick Augustus Washington Bailey, but adopted the surname "Douglass" to elude slave hunters.

11. The definition of "middle class" has changed considerably since the French Revolution. At that time, "middle class" generally designated a career choice, either in commercial activities (from banker to shopkeeper) or in professional trades (lawyers, doctors, etc.).

CHAPTER 7

The Industrial Revolution and Its Impact on Work, Wealth, and Power

INTRODUCTION

The Industrial Revolution of the late eighteenth and nineteenth centuries was one of the major transformative moments in world history, an event frequently perceived as a milestone in human progress. The vast expansion of technological innovation and mechanized labor made possible the creation of more goods, services, and wealth than ever before. Machines revolutionized work patterns; factories and new businesses stimulated the growth of cities and towns; and the accumulation of wealth transformed lifestyles, facilitated the spread of capitalism, and led to a growing consumer-oriented society. Moreover, as industrialism spread from Britain to western Europe and the United States, it fundamentally altered the international balance of military and political power, providing new incentives and opportunities for western powers to dominate the lands and resources of the Americas, Africa, and Asia. In the view of many scholars, the Industrial Revolution was the single most dramatic episode in human history since the development of agriculture.

But although few would deny the magnitude of change ushered in by modern industry, there have been profound disagreements over the relative merits of its impact. Whereas many nineteenth-century observers saw industrialism in terms of opportunity and advancement, others viewed it as the beginning of a new age of exploitation, the demise of skilled craftsmanship in favor of cheap mass production, and the chief cause behind a lamentable shift in values that placed profit making above all else. Critics also condemned the rise of economic inequality, charging that industrial capitalism created new forms of class conflict and the exploitation of the so-called Third World by the stronger, industrialized powers of the west.

This chapter examines differing perspectives on the impact of the Industrial Revolution on work, wealth, and power from some of the most famous and influential figures of the late eighteenth and nineteenth centuries, including Adam Smith, Karl Marx, Andrew Carnegie, and Thorstein Veblen. The readings present some of the most historically important ideas on capitalism, socialism, and philan-thropy that continue to shape political debates and national ideologies to this day. They also allow us to examine and appreciate economic models as unique philosophies, for they all encompass fundamental notions about history, ethics, and human nature. By reading the selections in chronological order, we can also trace and assess the changing impact of the Industrial Revolution and altering per-spectives on that impact from the mid-eighteenth century to the turn of the twen-tieth century.

Historians generally link the beginnings of the Industrial Revolution to mid-eighteenth-century England and point to a complex combination of factors to explain its origins. Thanks to a rising domestic population, ample deposits of energy-supplying coal, and a thriving overseas trade, Britain in the mid-1700s possessed the capital, resources, labor, and markets essential to start any modern business. The nation also built on technical achievements begun during the Scien-tific Revolution, and it developed new systems of finance and credit to facilitate trade and business. Equally important, the Industrial Revolution was fueled by the attitudes, ideas, and policies of the European Enlightenment—most specifi-cally, the principles and policies of political liberalism discussed in the preceding chapter. The British government protected private property and allowed the econ-omy to operate fairly freely, which encouraged overseas trade, technological inno-vations, and the expansion of commercial activities.

The man whose work most reflects and explains the character of the early In-dustrial Revolution was Adam Smith (1723–1790), one of the most important and influential economic thinkers in world history. Smith has often been called the father of free-market capitalism and the creator of the "laissez-faire" model of political economy, and his major work, *The Wealth of Nations* (1776), is consid-ered the most comprehensive exposition of economic liberalism[1] ever written. As did other great intellectuals of the European Enlightenment, Smith based his eco-nomic philosophy on his identification of certain universal laws and principles that he believed would naturally provide the best outcome for all if allowed to operate without interference.[2] Yet it is also clear that his ideas were shaped by historical conditions in Britain in the mid-eighteenth century. By advocating a liberal econ-omy based on free trade, open competition, and few governmental controls, he provided an economic and political model consistent with the interests of Britain's growing commercial and industrial classes. Moreover, he was quick to understand the tremendous productive advantages arising from the division of labor,[3] which paralleled England's early innovations in machine technology and factory produc-tion. But although Smith's model was rooted in history, it has also withstood the test of time, and his laws and principles continue to shape modern economic thought and political economies around the world.

By the early nineteenth century, the Industrial Revolution was profoundly transforming Britain's economy and society. James Watt's steam engine (originally patented in 1769) created a new boom in machine labor, as well as the expansion of factories and railroads and a huge rise in productivity and national wealth. By 1815, Britain's export of factory-made cotton textiles accounted for nearly 40 percent of the value of all its domestic exports, and the rapidly expanding industrial economy made the island nation the wealthiest and most powerful in Europe. But there were also negative consequences to these far-reaching changes. Romantic poets, painters, and writers, such as William Wordsworth (1770–1850), John Constable (1776–1837), and Mary Shelley (1797–1851), condemned industry's destruction of nature, beauty, and human spirituality.[4]

Other critics were more concerned with industrialism's social impact, particularly the growing poverty and misery of the working classes. This issue came to a head in England in the 1830s, when Parliament appointed one of its members, Michael Sadler, to chair a committee to investigate the use and treatment of child labor in factories. The Sadler Committee testimony (1832) uncovered such extensive workplace abuses as to promote further governmental inquiries, as well as new legislation that regulated labor practices. Not surprisingly, many liberals and factory owners were outraged at this unwelcome government interference in business and the economy, and they found an articulate spokesman in Andrew Ure (1778–1857). A chemist by training, Ure conducted his own tour of factories and wrote *The Philosophy of Manufactures* (1835) to counter what he saw as the erroneous conclusions and harmful policies that resulted from the Sadler Committee. Taken together, the two documents present very different interpretations of the impact of early industrial capitalism in England, and they reflect the growing ideological and social divisions that were emerging as a result of the Industrial Revolution.

The most profound challenge to liberal capitalism came from Karl Marx (1818–1883). Whereas reformers like Michael Sadler wanted to modify the existing system, Marx wanted to destroy it through a revolution of the working class. As he (and his collaborator Friedrich Engels) explained in *The Communist Manifesto* (1848), economic competition and the pursuit of self-interest created only anguish, inequality, and the exploitation by the "haves" of the "have-nots." Real reform could not be achieved by legislation, Marx argued, for the state was controlled by the capitalist elites, who used their political power to support and protect their economic interests. The only viable solution was revolution, directed toward the elimination of property and class conflict and dedicated to the creation of a more humane world in which "the free development of each is the condition for the free development of all." Although Marx achieved only limited success in the spread of his ideas during his lifetime, his *Communist Manifesto* remains the clearest and most concise critique of capitalism ever produced, and his vision (commonly referred to as *Marxism*) served as the motivation and blueprint for generations of revolutionaries in the twentieth century.

Notwithstanding Marx's criticisms, the Industrial Revolution continued to expand in scope and scale during the second half of the nineteenth century, spreading from Britain across northern Europe and North America, laying the foundations for a new global economic system. Historians frequently call this period the "Second Industrial Revolution" to highlight important changes that occurred in economic production and organization. For example, whereas the early Industrial Revolution was centered on textiles, iron, coal, and steam power, the second revolution was founded on steel and chemicals, electricity and petroleum, and great improvements in communication (telegraph) and transportation (a vast expansion of railways). And as the magnitude of economic production increased, so too did the scale of economic organization. The latter half of the 1800s saw the rise of "big business," the evolution of corporations and cartels, and the creation of an extremely wealthy and powerful industrialist class.

Nowhere were these trends more apparent than in the United States after the Civil War (1860–1865), and nowhere more strikingly than in the person of Andrew Carnegie (1835–1919). A true "rags-to-riches" story, Carnegie was an Irish-born immigrant who rose from a childhood of poverty to become the leader in American steel production, which made him one of the most influential and wealthy businessmen in the United States in the late nineteenth century. His success partly reflects and validates the business opportunities found in America during its "Gilded Age," which produced other wealthy tycoons such as John D. Rockefeller (Standard Oil Company), Cornelius Vanderbilt (New York Central Railroad), and Leland Stanford (Central Pacific Railroad). But although Carnegie was a shrewd businessman and, at times, a ruthless competitor, he also worried about the growing gap between the rich and poor in America, and he valued social welfare as much as he did individual enterprise and initiative. In an essay simply entitled "Wealth" that was published in the *North American Review* in 1889, Carnegie proposed a new social ethic centered on philanthropy,[5] which sought a compromise between the seemingly irreconcilable differences between liberals and radicals.

By the turn of the twentieth century, the social and cultural impact of the Industrial Revolution in the United States was becoming increasingly apparent. The emerging corporate economy spawned a new salaried middle class, the rapid growth of cities, and the rise of a consumer culture. Such dramatic changes were of great interest to Thorstein Veblen (1857–1929), a professor and scholar of economics. Influenced by Darwinian theory,[6] Veblen examined the workings of the economy from an evolutionary perspective. In *The Theory of the Leisure Class* (1899), he concluded that the human drive to become "the fittest" required not only the accumulation of wealth and power but its display as well. The result was "conspicuous consumption," whereby one's wealth, status, and "reputation" were increasingly defined by the quantity and quality of one's material possessions. Veblen's sharp tongue and biting satire of the wealthy classes earned him the label of social gadfly, but his unique evolutionary analysis has shed new light on economic behavior and highlighted the close interrelationship between the economy and cultural values.

The spread of the Industrial Revolution to the world outside the west was delayed by a host of historical and cultural factors. In Russia, the historic dominance of an agrarian-based aristocracy helped to block economic innovations that might have introduced radical ideas and political change. But as a result, Russia fell increasingly behind the industrialized western countries in wealth and power, which was made abundantly clear in its loss to Britain and France in the Crimean War (1854–1856). Following this embarrassment, the tsarist government of Russia led the national campaign to modernize and industrialize the country. A key proponent and leader of this movement was Count Sergei Witte (1849–1915), the determined minister of finance from 1892 to 1903. In a series of reports to Tsar Nikolai II (r. 1894–1917), Witte expressed his belief that Russia's economic backwardness threatened its future power and greatness. In a secret memorandum dated 1899, Witte outlined a detailed program whereby the government would actively foster industrialization by erecting high protective tariffs and soliciting capital investments from foreigners. His memo is fascinating, for its articulated nationalist goals and government-led strategies seem to depart sharply from the "laissez-faire" vision put forth by Adam Smith. Under Witte's guidance, industrial production grew quickly, and by 1900, only the United States, Germany, and Britain were producing more steel than Russia was. But the new wealth and opportunities produced by industry barely trickled down to improve the lives of the Russian factory worker or rural peasant, and ultimately their growing discontent became one of the main causes of the Russian Revolution (1917).

The readings in this section are challenging yet crucial to a better understanding of the economic history and ideas that have shaped the modern world. Each selection can also be assessed as a product of its unique time and place, reflecting the changing nature and impact of the Industrial Revolution over the course of nearly 150 years. But it is equally significant to analyze and compare the differing interpretations in a philosophical manner by examining and assessing the assumptions and implications inherent in each position. As you read the accounts in this chapter, you may wish to keep the following questions in mind.

CHAPTER QUESTIONS

1. Adam Smith and Karl Marx seem to differ sharply on the issue of human competition. Explain how each man might assess the causes and consequences of competition. What significant factors, such as historical events or theoretical assumptions, might account for their differing views?

2. Imagine a debate between Michael Sadler, Andrew Ure, and Sergei Witte on the relative merits of industrialization. What evidence might they use to support their particular positions? What factors might explain their opposing ideas and positions?

3. Andrew Carnegie feared that the rise of industrial wealth in America would lead to a decline in social homogeneity and a potential rise in class conflict. In contrast, Thorstein Veblen believed that the pursuit of wealth promoted social cohesion and common cultural values. Explain how they came to their different conclusions. Which interpretation seems to have more merit in explaining contemporary American society?

4. Several of the readings in this chapter suggest that the operation of a free market does not always lead to socially desirable results. What is your assessment? In your opinion, is there a proper role for government in the operation of the economy?

5. When all of the readings are assessed and considered in their chronological context, what story emerges about the evolving impact and social perceptions of the Industrial Revolution?

THE RATIONALITY AND BENEFITS OF INDUSTRIAL CAPITALISM AND ECONOMIC LIBERALISM

Adam Smith was one of the towering figures of the European Enlightenment and one of the greatest economic thinkers of the modern era. In his effort to examine and understand the universal principles of the marketplace, he discovered what he called "the obvious and simple system of natural liberty," a system that we now commonly refer to as capitalism. Smith was a man who loved ideas, analytical thought, and philosophical debate, but he was also an eccentric and absent-minded individual, a lifelong bachelor who cherished his quiet and private life in the company of his books, his studies, and his elderly mother.

Born in 1723 in Kirkcaddy, Scotland, to a family of modest means, Adam Smith was the son of a customs official. A talented and hard-working student, he studied moral philosophy and classics at Oxford University, which led to a professorship at Glasgow University, where he lectured on ethics and political economy and wrote *The Theory of Moral Sentiments* (1759), a philosophical study of moral decision making. At the age of forty, he resigned his academic position to accept a three-year tenure as a private tutor to the young duke of Buccleuch, the son of Lord Charles Townshend.[7] Smith and his student traveled throughout Europe, and the experience proved highly inspiring and educational for both.[8] Upon completion of his tutoring duties in 1766, Smith returned to Scotland and began work on *An Inquiry into the Nature and Causes of the Wealth of Nations,* which he did not complete until ten years later. His book brought him high praise and immediate fame, and he won election to Britain's prestigious and exclusive Royal Society. Yet Smith preferred to avoid the public spotlight, and he chose to retire to Scotland to continue his writing and to take care of his ailing mother. After a long illness, he died in 1790 at the age of sixty-seven.

Adam Smith's *Wealth of Nations* is considered to be the classic exposition of liberal economic theory, which grants individuals the greatest amount of liberty to pursue and advance their own material well-being without interference or dependence on others. His theories were in stark contrast to prevailing mercantilist policies,[9] and they helped to provide the foundation for the growth of capitalism that has ultimately reshaped economic structures and strategies around the world. Equally important, Smith pioneered economic inquiry as a "social science," for he was one of the first to undertake a systematic, rational, and comprehensive analysis of the organization and operation of the marketplace. In the reading selection that follows, one can trace Smith's analytical approach and his major ideas as he systematically examines and explains work and productivity, wages and prices, labor relations, and the proper role of government in the economy.

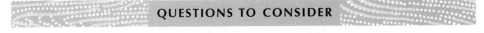

QUESTIONS TO CONSIDER

1. What does Smith mean by "division of labor"? Why does he consider it so beneficial? How are his ideas related to the beginning of the Industrial Revolution?

2. What is the difference between "natural prices" and "market prices"? What is significant about this choice of terms? By what universal laws or principles are prices always moving toward their "natural" level?

3. Smith argues for an economy based on individuals pursuing their own self-interest. Why? According to his argument, how can self-interest also promote the general welfare of society?

4. Some people believe that Adam Smith was a mere apologist for the business interests of the elite classes. Do you agree? Why, or why not?

5. According to Smith, what should be the proper role of government in the economy? To what extent are his views currently followed by the United States government?

WEALTH OF NATIONS (1776)

Adam Smith

Of the Division of Labor

The greatest improvement in the productive powers of labor, and the greater part of the skill, dexterity, and judgment with which it is anywhere directed, or applied, seem to have been the effects of the division of labor. . . . To take an example, the trade of the pin-maker; a workman not educated to this business, nor acquainted with the use of the machinery employed in it, could scarce, perhaps, with his utmost industry, make one pin in a day, and certainly could not make twenty. But in the way in which this business is now carried on, not only the whole work is a peculiar trade, but it is divided into a number of branches, of which the greater part are likewise peculiar trades. One man draws out the wire, another straights it, a third cuts it, a fourth points it, a fifth grinds it at the top for receiving, the head; to make the head requires two or three distinct operations; to put it on is a peculiar business, to whiten the pins is another; it is even a trade by itself to put them into the paper; and the important business of making a pin is, in this manner, divided into about eighteen distinct operations, which, in some factories, are all performed by distinct hands, though in others the same man will sometimes perform two or three of them.

I have seen a small manufactory of this kind where ten men only were employed, and where some of them consequently performed two or three distinct operations. But though they were very poor, and therefore but indifferently accommodated with the necessary machinery, they could, when they exerted themselves, make among them about twelve pounds of pins in a day. There are in a pound upwards of four thousand pins of a middling size. Those ten persons, therefore, could make among them upwards of forty-eight thousand pins in a day. Each person, therefore, making a

Source: Adam Smith, *An Inquiry into the Nature and Causes of the Wealth of Nations,* ed. Edwin Canaan, 6th ed. (London: Methuen & Co. 1950), 7–9, 11, 15, 17–18, 34–35, 62–63, 65, 69–70, 72–73, 75, 475, 477–78.

tenth part of forty-eight thousand pins, might be considered as making four thousand eight hundred pins in a day. But if they had all wrought separately and independently, and without any of them having been educated to this peculiar business, they certainly could not each of them have made twenty, perhaps not one pin in a day; that is, certainly, not the two hundred and fortieth, perhaps not the four thousand eight hundredth part of what they are at present capable of performing, in consequence of a proper division and combination of their different operations. . . .

The division of labor, so far as it can be introduced, occasions, in every art, a proportionable increase of the productive powers of labor. . . . This great increase of the quantity of work which, in consequence of the division of labor, the same number of people are capable of performing, is owing to three different circumstances; first, to the increase of dexterity in every particular workman; secondly, to the saving of the time which is commonly lost in passing from one species of work to another; and lastly, to the invention of a great number of machines which facilitate and abridge labor, and enable one man to do the work of many. . . .

It is the great multiplication of the productions of all the different arts, in consequence of the division of labor, which occasions, in a well-governed society, that universal wealth which extends itself to the lowest ranks of the people. Every workman has a great quantity of his own work to dispose of beyond what he himself has occasion for; and every other workman being exactly in the same situation, he is enabled to exchange a great quantity of his own goods for a great quantity, or, what comes to the same thing, for the price of a great quantity of theirs. He supplies them abundantly with what they have occasion for, and they accommodate him as amply with what he has occasion for, and a general plenty diffuses itself through all the different ranks of the society. . . .

Of the Principle Which Gives Occasion to the Division of Labor

This division of labor, from which so many advantages are derived, is not originally the effect of any human wisdom, which foresees and intends that universal wealth to which it gives occasion. It is the necessary, though very slow and gradual consequence of a certain propensity in human nature . . . the propensity to truck [trade], barter, and exchange one thing for another. . . .

But man has almost constant occasion for the help of his brethren, and it is in vain for him to expect it from their benevolence only. He will be more likely to prevail if he can interest their self-love in his favor, and show them that it is for their own advantage to do for him what he requires of them. Whoever offers to another a bargain of any kind, proposes to do this. Give me that which I want, and you shall have this which you want, is the meaning of every such offer; and it is in this manner that we obtain from one another the far greater art of those good offices which we stand in need of. It is not from the benevolence of the butcher, the brewer, or the baker that we expect our dinner, but from their regard to their own interest. . . .

Of the Real and Nominal Price of Commodities, or Their Price in Labor, and Their Price in Money

Every man is rich or poor according to the degree in which he can afford to enjoy the necessaries, conveniences, and amusements of human life. But after the division of labor has once thoroughly taken place, it is but a very small part of these with which a man's own labor can supply him. The far greater part of them he must derive from the labor of other people, and he must be rich or poor according to the quantity of that labor which he can command, or which he can afford to purchase. The value of any commodity, therefore, to the person who possesses it, and who means not to use or consume it himself, but to exchange it for other commodities, is equal to the quantity of labor which it enables him to purchase or command. Labor, therefore, is the real measure of the exchangeable value of all commodities.

The real price of everything, what everything really costs to the man who wants to acquire it, is the toil and trouble of acquiring it. What everything is really worth to the man who has acquired it, and who wants to dispose of it or exchange it for something else, is the toil and trouble which it can save to himself, and which it can impose upon other people. What is bought with money or with goods is purchased by labor as much as what we acquire by the toil of our own body. That money or those goods indeed save us this toil. . . . Labor was the first price, the original purchase money that was paid for all things. It was not by gold or silver, but by labor, that all the wealth of the world was originally purchased. . . .

Of the Natural and Market Price of Commodities

There is in every society or neighborhood an average rate both of wages and profit in every different employment of labor and [business]. This rate is naturally regulated, partly by the general circumstances of the society, their riches or poverty, their advancing, stationary, or declining condition; and partly by the particular nature of each employment. There is likewise in every society or neighborhood an average rate of rent, which is regulated too. . . . These average rates may be called the natural rates of wages, profit, and rent, at the time and place in which they commonly prevail. When the price of any commodity is neither more nor less than what is sufficient to pay the rent of the land, the wages of the labor, and the profits of the stock employed in raising, preparing, and bringing it to market, according to their natural rates, the commodity is then sold for what may be called its natural price. . . .

The actual price at which any commodity is commonly sold is called its market price. It may either be above, or below, or exactly the same with its natural price. The market price of every particular commodity is regulated by the proportion between the quantity which is actually brought to market, and the demand of those who are willing to pay the natural price of the commodity, or the whole value of the rent, labor, and profit, which must be paid in order to bring it thither. When the quantity of any commodity which is brought to market falls short of the effectual demand, all those who are willing to pay . . . cannot be supplied with the quantity which they want. Rather than lack it altogether, some of them will be willing to [pay] more. A competition will immediately begin among them, and the market price will rise more or less above the natural price, according as either the greatness of the deficiency, or the wealth and wanton luxury of the competitors. . . .

If at any time [quantity] exceeds . . . demand, the price must be paid below their natural rate. If it is rent, the interest of the landlords will immediately prompt them to withdraw a part of their land; and if it is wages, the interest of the laborers . . . will prompt them to [reduce] their labor. . . . The quantity brought to market will soon be no more than sufficient to supply the effectual demand. All the different parts of its price will rise to their natural rate, and the whole price to its natural price. . . .

The natural price, therefore, is the central price to which the prices of commodities are continually moving. Different factors may sometimes keep them suspended a good deal above it, and sometimes force them down even somewhat below it. But whatever may be the obstacles which hinder them from settling on this center, they are constantly tending toward it. . . . A monopoly granted either to an individual or to a trading company has the same effect as a secret in trade or manufactures. The monopolists, by keeping the market constantly understocked, by never fully supplying the effectual demand, sell their commodities much above the natural price, and raise their emoluments, whether they consist in wages or profit, greatly above their natural rate. The price of monopoly is upon every occasion the highest . . . which can be squeezed out of the buyers, or which they will consent to pay. . . .

The exclusive privileges of corporations . . . and all those laws which restrain . . . competition to a smaller number than might otherwise go into them, have the same tendency, though in a less degree. They are a sort of enlarged monopolies, and may frequently, for ages together, and in whole classes of employments, keep up the market price of particular commodities above the natural price, and maintain both the wages of the labor and the profits of the stock employed about them somewhat above their natural rate. Such enhancements of the market price may last as long as the regulations of police which give occasion to them. . . .

Of the Wages of Labor

The produce of labor constitutes the natural recompense or wages of labor. In that original state of things, which precedes both the appropriation of land and the accumulation of stock, the whole produce of labor belongs to the laborer. He has neither landlord nor master to share with him. Had this state continued, the wages of labor would have augmented with all those improvements in its productive powers to which the division of labor gives occasion. All things would gradually have become cheaper. They would have been produced by a smaller quantity of labor; and as the commodities produced by equal quantities of labor would naturally in this state of things be exchanged for one another, they would have been purchased likewise with the produce of a smaller quantity. But this original state of things, in which the laborer enjoyed the whole produce of his own labor, could not last beyond the first introduction of the appropriation of land and the accumulation of stock. It was at an end, therefore, long before the most considerable improvements were made in the productive powers of labor, and it would be to no purpose to trace further what might have been its effects upon the recompense or wages of labor. As soon as land becomes private property, the landlord demands a share of almost all the produce which the laborer can either raise, or collect from it. His rent makes the first deduction from the produce of the labor which is employed upon land. . . .

. . . Masters are always and everywhere in a sort of tacit, but constant and uniform combination, not to raise the wages of labor above their actual rate. To violate this combination is everywhere a most unpopular action, and a sort of reproach to a master among his neighbors and equals. Masters, too, sometimes enter into particular combinations to sink the wages of labor even below this rate. These are always conducted with the utmost silence and secrecy, till the moment of execution, and when the workmen yield, as they sometimes do, without resistance, though severely felt by

them, they are never heard of by other people. Such combinations, however, are frequently resisted by a contrary defensive combination of the workmen; who sometimes too, without any provocation of this kind, combine of their own accord to raise
the price of their labor. . . . A man must always live by his work, and his wages must
at least be sufficient to maintain him. They must even upon most occasions be somewhat more; otherwise it would be impossible for him to bring up a family, and the
race of such workmen could not last beyond the first generation. . . .

Of Restraints upon the Importation from Foreign Countries of Such Goods as Can Be Produced at Home

Every individual is continually exerting himself to find out the most advantageous
employment for whatever capital he can command. It is his own advantage, indeed,
and not that of the society, which he has in view. But the study of his own advantage
naturally, or rather necessarily, leads him to prefer that employment which is most advantageous to the society. . . .

. . . As every individual, therefore, endeavors as much as he can both to employ
his capital in the support of domestic industry, and so to direct that industry that its
produce may be of the greatest value; every individual necessarily labors to render
the annual revenue of the society as great as he can. He generally, indeed, neither intends to promote the public interest, nor knows how much he is promoting it. By pre-
ferring the support of domestic to that of foreign industry, he [seeks] only his own
security; and by directing that industry in such a manner as its produce may be of the
greatest value, he [seeks] only his own gain, and he is in this, as in many other cases,
led by an invisible hand to promote an end which was no part of his intention. Nor is
it always the worse for the society that it was no part of it. By pursuing his own interest he frequently promotes that of the society more effectually than when he really intends to promote it. I have never known much good done by those who affected to
trade for the public good. It is an affectation, indeed, not very common among merchants, and very few words need be employed in dissuading them from it. . . .

. . . Every individual, it is evident, can judge [his self-interest] much better than
any statesman or lawgiver can do for him. The statesman who should attempt to direct
private people in what manner they ought to employ their [investments] would not
only load himself with a most unnecessary attention, but assume an authority which
could safely be trusted by no single person nor council or senate whatever. . . . To give
the monopoly of the home market to the produce of domestic industry, in any particular art or manufacture, is in some measure to direct private people in what manner
they ought to employ their capitals, and must, in almost all cases, be either a useless
or a hurtful regulation. If the produce of domestic can be brought there as cheap as
that of foreign industry, the regulation is evidently useless. If it cannot, it must generally be hurtful. It is the maxim of every prudent master of a family never to attempt to
make at home what it will cost him more to make than to buy. The tailor does not attempt to make his own shoes, but buys them of the shoemaker. The shoemaker does
not attempt to make his own clothes, but employs a tailor. . . . All of them find it for
their interest to employ their whole industry in a way in which they have some advantage over their neighbors, and to purchase with a part of its produce, or what is the
same thing, with the price of a part of it, whatever else they have occasion for.

What is prudence in the conduct of every private family can scarce be folly in that of a great kingdom. If a foreign country can supply us with a commodity cheaper than we ourselves can make it, better buy it of them with some part of the produce of our own industry employed in a way in which we have some advantage. The general industry of the country . . . will not be diminished, no more than that of the above-mentioned [tailor and shoemaker]; but only left to find out the way in which it can be employed with the greatest advantage.

TWO PERSPECTIVES ON THE FACTORY SYSTEM IN ENGLAND

The introduction of machinery and steam power into England's factories dramatically increased the productivity of human labor and introduced a new era of cheap, mass-produced consumer goods. The increased productivity of machinery-based manufacturing lowered the price of many consumer goods, such as textiles, tools, and household products, making them affordable to many more people. It also allowed relatively unskilled women and children, who had previously been denied apprenticeships, to now find wage labor in the factories. But the new factories also caused hardship and dislocation. Skilled and experienced craftsmen such as hand-loom weavers were increasingly replaced by mechanization and unskilled child labor. The factory system also created severe problems in working and living conditions, which attracted the attention of critics and would-be reformers. The result was a series of government investigations and labor laws that are known collectively as the "Factory Acts," and one of the earliest and most important of these was the Sadler Committee Testimony and Report of 1832.

Michael Sadler (1780–1835) was raised in an affluent and prominent English family, and after a brief stint in the family import-export business (for which he had no liking), he was elected to Parliament in 1829 as a member of the Tory party. Although the Tories generally advocated the interests of the landed aristocracy in England, they also showed a paternalistic concern for the welfare of the lower working classes. Sadler persuaded Parliament to appoint a select committee to investigate the problem of child labor in textile factories, and as chairman of the committee, he collected testimony from eighty-seven witnesses that produced a 682-page report. Critics charged that the committee's leading questions biased the testimony of witnesses such as Matthew Crabtree (in the reading that follows), but Sadler achieved his goals when Parliament accepted the report and passed the Factory Act of 1833, which, for the first time, regulated working conditions for children.[10] From this point on, government implicitly accepted the right and responsibility to monitor and regulate private economic concerns.

Despite the well-publicized and scandalous reports of the reformers, there remained many supporters of unregulated factory labor among British liberals. One of the most influential was Andrew Ure (1778–1857), a Scotsman who taught chemistry at the University of Glasgow and who later conducted scientific research for the government and several private companies. Angered by Sadler's attempt to harness free enterprise, Ure toured the textile factory districts of Britain in 1834, collecting evidence from business owners and factory foremen. The result was *The Philosophy of Manufactures* (1835), which he hoped would provide a more accurate assessment of industrialization and stem Parliament's pursuance of "dangerous ideas." Although Ure did not attain his immediate goals, he did give voice to advocates of "laissez-faire" capitalism whose arguments continue to echo in contemporary political debates.

QUESTIONS TO CONSIDER

1. How does Matthew Crabtree explain the impact of the factory system on workers, especially children? How does Andrew Ure respond to these allegations? How does he justify the use of child labor?
2. Compare and contrast how Crabtree and Ure portray workers' encounters with machinery. According to Ure, what is the ultimate goal of machine labor? How might Crabtree react to Ure's assessments?
3. Ure claims that the "constant aim and effect of scientific improvement in manufactures are philanthropic." How convincing do you find his argument? Explain your reasoning.
4. If the Industrial Revolution did indeed increase productivity and wealth (as Ure argues), how can we explain the conditions described by Crabtree? Does this suggest some fatal flaw in Adam Smith's theory?
5. The Sadler Report was written on evidence collected from workers such as Matthew Crabtree, whereas Ure's account came from his personal discussions with factory owners. In your opinion, do the two different accounts reflect irreconcilable class conflict? To what degree and in what way are these differing views and attitudes reflected in modern America?

TESTIMONY OF MATTHEW CRABTREE FROM THE SADLER COMMITTEE REPORT (1832)

[The Committee members' questions to the witness, Mr. Matthew Crabtree, have been italicized]

What age are you? Twenty-two. *What is your occupation?* A blanket manufacturer.

Source: "The Sadler Committee Testimony and Report," in Charles Wing, *Evils of the Factory System, Demonstrated by Parliamentary Evidence* (London: Saunders and Otley, 1837), 28–30.

Have you ever been employed in a factory? Yes. *At what age did you first go to work in one?* Eight. *How long did you continue in that occupation?* Four years.

Will you state the hours of labor, at the period when you first went to the factory in ordinary times? From six in the morning to eight at night.

With what intervals for refreshment and rest? An hour at noon. *When trade was brisk, what were your hours?* From five in the morning to nine in the evening. . . .

Will you state the effect that those long hours had upon the state of your health and feelings? I was, when working those long hours, commonly very much fatigued at night when I left my work; so much so, that I sometimes should have slept as I walked, if I had not stumbled and started awake again; and so sick that I could not eat, and what I did eat I vomited.

State the condition of the children towards the latter part of the day, who have thus to keep up with the machinery. It is as much as they can do, when they are not very much fatigued, to keep up with their work, and towards the close of the day, when they come to be more fatigued, they cannot keep up with it very well; and the consequence is, that they are beaten to spur them on. . . .

Were you beaten under those circumstances? Yes. *Frequently?* Very frequently. . . .

And is it your belief that if you had not been so beaten, you should not have got through the work? I should not if I had not been kept up to it by some means. . . .

Do you think that if the overlooker were naturally a humane person it would be still found necessary for him to beat the children, in order to keep up their attention and vigilance at the termination of those extraordinary days of labor? Yes; the machine turns off a regular quantity of cardings,* and of course they must keep as regularly to their work the whole of the day; they must keep with the machine; and therefore, however humane the slubber† may be, as he must keep up with the machine or be found fault with, he spurs the children to keep up also, by various means; but that which be commonly resorts to, is to strap them when they become drowsy. . . .

Then it is your impression from what you have seen, and from your own experience, that those long hours of labor have the effect of rendering young persons who are subject to them exceedingly unhappy? Yes.

You have already said it had a considerable effect on your health? Yes.

Do you conceive that it diminished your growth? I did not pay much attention to that; but I have been examined by some persons who said they thought I was rather stunted, and that I should have been taller if I had not worked at the mill. . . .

Is the work done as well when you are so many hours engaged in it, as it would be if you were at it less time? I believe it is not done so well in those long

---

*Cardings were bundles of wool [or cotton] processed by a machine to get all the fibers running in the same direction in preparation for spinning.

†A slubber was a person in charge of preparing the raw wool (or cotton) for spinning. It normally required an experienced worker, for if the work was done poorly, the wool or cotton would be ruined.

hours, toward the latter end of the day the children become completely bewildered, and know not what they are doing, so that they spoil their work
without knowing.
*Then you do not think that masters gain much by the continuance of the work to
so great a length of time?* I believe not.

THE PHILOSOPHY OF MANUFACTURES (1835)

Andrew Ure

This island [Britain] is pre-eminent among civilized nations for the prodigious development of its factory wealth, and has been therefore long viewed with a jealous admiration by foreign powers. This very pre-eminence, however, has been contemplated
in a very different light by many influential members of our own community, and has
been even denounced by them as the certain origin of innumerable evils to the
people, and of revolutionary convulsions to the state. If the affairs of the kingdom
be wisely administered, I believe such allegations and fears will prove to be ground-
less. . . .

In recent discussions concerning our factories, no circumstance is so deserving
of remark, as the gross ignorance evinced by our leading legislators and economists—
gentlemen well informed in other respects—relative to the nature of those stupen-
dous manufactures which have long provided the rulers of the kingdom with the
resources of war, and a great body of the people with subsistence; which have, in
fact, made this island the arbiter of many nations and the benefactor of the globe itself. Until this ignorance be dispelled, no sound legislation need be expected on manufacturing subjects. . . .

The blessings which mechanical science has bestowed on society, and the means
it has still in store for ameliorating* the lot of mankind, have been too little dwelt
upon; [instead] it has been accused of lending itself to the rich capitalists as an instrument for harassing the poor, and of exacting from the operative an accelerated rate of
work. It has been said, for example, that the steam-engine now drives the power-
looms with such velocity as to urge on their attendant weavers at the same rapid pace;
but that the hand-weaver, not being subjected to this restless agent, can throw his
shuttle and move his treddles† at his convenience. There is, however, this difference
in the two cases, that in the factory, every member of the loom is so adjusted, that the
driving force leaves the attendant nearly nothing at all to do, certainly no muscular
fatigue to sustain, while it procures for him good, unfailing wages, besides a healthy

---

Source: Andrew Ure, *The Philosophy of Manufactures, or An Exposition of the Scientific, Moral, and Commercial Economy of the Factory System of Great Britain* (London: Chas. Knight, 1835), 5–8, 13–15, 17–19, 29–30.

*To make better or more tolerable.

†Treddles (or treadles) are the foot pedals on a weaving loom.

workshop *gratis**: whereas the non-factory weaver, having everything to execute by muscular exertion, finds the labor irksome, makes in consequence innumerable short pauses, separately of little account, but great when added together; earns therefore proportionally low wages, while he loses his health by poor diet and the dampness of his hovel. . . .

The constant aim and effect of scientific improvement in manufactures are philanthropic, as they tend to relieve the workmen either from niceties of adjustment which exhaust his mind and fatigue his eyes, or from painful repetition of efforts which distort or wear out his frame. At every step of each manufacturing process described in this volume the humanity of science will be manifest. . . .

. . . In my recent tour . . . through the manufacturing districts [of England], I have seen tens of thousands of old, young, and middle-aged of both sexes, many of them too feeble to get their daily bread by any of the former modes of industry, earning abundant food, raiment, and domestic accommodation, without perspiring at a single pore, screened meanwhile from the summer's sun and the winter's frost, in apartments more airy and salubrious than those of the metropolis in which our legislative and fashionable aristocracies assemble.

In those spacious halls the benignant power of steam summons around him his myriads of willing menials, and assigns to each the regulated task, substituting for painful muscular effort on their part, the energies of his own gigantic arm, and demanding in return only attention and dexterity to correct such little aberrations as casually occur in his workmanship. The gentle docility of this moving force qualifies it for impelling the tiny bobbins of the lace-machine with a precision and speed inimitable by the most dexterous hands, directed by the sharpest eyes. Hence, under its auspices . . . magnificent edifices,† surpassing in number, value, usefulness, and the boasted monuments of Asiatic, Egyptian, and Roman despotism, have, within the short period of fifty years, risen up in this kingdom, to show to what extent capital, industry, and science may augment the resources of a state, while they ameliorate the condition of its citizens. Such is the factory system, replete with [innovations] in mechanics and political economy, which promises in its future growth to become the great minister of civilization to the [world], enabling this country, as its heart, to diffuse along with its commerce the life-blood of science and religion to myriads of people still lying "in the region and shadow of death."

When Adam Smith wrote his immortal elements of economics,‡ automatic machinery being hardly known he was properly led to regard the division of labor as the grand principle of manufacturing improvement; and he showed, in the example of pin-making, how each handicrafts-man, being thereby enabled to perfect himself by practice in one point, became a quicker and cheaper workman. In each branch of manufacture he saw that some parts were, on that principle, of easy execution, like the cutting of pin wires into uniform lengths, and some were comparatively difficult, like the formation and fixation of their heads; and therefore he concluded that to each a workman of appropriate value and cost was naturally assigned. . . . In fact, the divi-

---

*Without cost; for free.

†Large and important structures.

‡Referring to Adam Smith's *Wealth of Nations* (1776).

sion, or rather adaptation of labor to the different talents of men, is little thought of in factory employment. . . .

The principle of the factory system is to substitute mechanical science for hand skill, and the partition of a process into its essential constituents, for the division or graduation of labor among artisans. On the handicraft plan, labor more or less skilled was usually the most expensive element of production . . . but on the automatic plan, skilled labor gets progressively superseded, and will, eventually, be replaced by mere overlookers of machines.

By the infirmity of human nature it happens, that the more skillful the workman, the more self-willed and intractable he is apt to become, and, of course, the less fit a component of a mechanical system. . . . The grand object therefore of the modern manufacturer is, through the union of capital and science, to reduce the task of his work-people to the exercise of vigilance and dexterity—[skills which are] speedily brought to perfection in the young. . . .

It is, in fact, the constant aim and tendency of every improvement in machinery to supersede human labor altogether, or to diminish its cost, by substituting the industry of women and children for that of men; or that of ordinary laborers for trained artisans. In most cotton-mills, the spinning is entirely managed by females of sixteen years and upwards. The effect of substituting the self-acting [machine] mule* for the common [human labor] mule, is to discharge the greater part of the men spinners, and to retain adolescents and children. The proprietor of a factory states, in evidence to the commissioners, that, by such substitution, he would save £50 a week in wages in consequence of dispensing with nearly forty male spinners. . . . This tendency to employ children with watchful eyes and nimble fingers, instead of journeymen of long experience, shows how the scholastic dogma of the division of labor into degrees of skill has been exploded by our enlightened manufactures.

The constant aim and effect of scientific improvement in manufactures are philanthropic, as they tend to relieve the workman either from the niceties of adjustment which exhaust his mind and fatigue his eyes, or from painful repetition of effort which distort or wear out his frame. At every step of each manufacturing process described in this volume, the humanity of science will be manifest. . . .

THE MARXIST CRITIQUE OF CAPITALISM AND THE COMMUNIST ALTERNATIVE

Karl Marx (1818–1883) is one of the most reviled and feared men in history and also one of the least understood. His philosophy, commonly known as Marxism, is frequently associated with the creation of a harsh totalitarian state and a rigidly organized society, where people toil like robots without personal incentives, wealth, or freedom. But although Marx called for a revolutionary overthrow of

---

*A machine for simultaneously pulling and twisting fibers into yarn or thread and winding it onto spindles.

the capitalist system described and advocated by Adam Smith, his vision was more utopian than draconian. Marx envisioned a better world, where work, wealth, and power would be returned to the people, where individuals would be able to find true happiness and fulfillment, and where workers would toil not merely for self-interest and individual profit but for the welfare of all, guided by the simple maxim, "From each according to his ability; to each according to his need."

There is little in Karl Marx's early life to forecast his lifelong dedication to revolution. Born in 1818 in the German city of Trier to a middle-class family, Marx initially pursued a law degree like his father, but ultimately switched fields and earned a Ph.D. in philosophy from the University of Jena. He then turned to journalism, and for a while he was a newspaper editor until his criticisms of German absolutism resulted in his dismissal. In the autumn of 1843, Marx went to Paris, where he met his lifelong friend and associate Friedrich Engels.[11] Marx and Engels both became active in various revolutionary groups and together they worked out the theory and tactics of "revolutionary proletarian socialism," which was first published as *The Communist Manifesto* (1848).

Due to his revolutionary views and activities, Marx was banished from France, Belgium, and Germany before finally ending up in England in 1849. He spent the bulk of his time in London conducting research, writing essays on politics and economics, and creating organizations to facilitate the spread of socialism. Marx helped to create the International Working Men's Association in London in 1864 and aided associates in Germany in founding the Social Democratic Labor Party (1869). The first volume of his great work, *Das Kapital,* was completed in 1867. It describes in much greater detail the argument and vision first put forth in *The Communist Manifesto.* When Marx died suddenly in 1883, the remaining two volumes were completed and published by Engels from the notes that Marx left behind.

The Communist Manifesto was originally written to express the views of and generate support for the "Communist League," a small organization of discontented workers and intellectuals. It contains three basic parts: first, Marx's critique of the flaws and injustices of capitalism, focusing on the struggle between the bourgeoisie (middle class) and proletariat (working class)[12]; second, his alternative Communist vision for human society; and lastly, his views on the misleading doctrines of competing socialist ideologies. Marx's theory is ultimately imbedded in a theory of history known as dialectical materialism,[13] which asserts that economic inequality and class conflict have been the prime engines of historical change. Like Adam Smith before him, Marx believed that history and human society were governed by certain immutable laws that must be rationally examined in order to comprehend the past and to predict and shape the future. It is for these reasons that Marxism is often called "scientific socialism," for it is based on a systematic study of economic relations and the forces of production. Yet Marx's model is also based on certain key assumptions about human nature and the most appropriate definitions and strategies for human progress, fulfillment, and happiness. Although he did not live long enough to witness the implementation of his vision, his ideas have inspired millions of followers in the twentieth century and have provided the single most powerful challenge to the philosophy of capitalism advanced by Adam Smith. Indeed, as you read the edited selections from *The*

Communist Manifesto that follow, it is useful to compare and contrast the theories and assumptions of Marx and Smith on such pivotal issues as competition, property, wealth, and power.

QUESTIONS TO CONSIDER

1. As was true of Adam Smith, Karl Marx's theory is partly based on a particular interpretation of human history. What is Marx's perspective? In his view, what role did the Industrial Revolution and overseas expansion play in history?

2. Who is the bourgeoisie and who is the proletariat? What impact has the bourgeoisie had on reshaping social structures and cultural values? How have conditions of the proletariat changed in industrialized, bourgeois society?

3. What are Marx's reasons for abolishing bourgeois property? How do his views on property compare with the ideas of Smith and Locke? How radical do you find his ten proposals for a communist society?

4. According to Marx, what role has the State played in the history of class conflict? What role does he suggest it might play in the implementation of his communist vision? Why does he conclude that, ultimately, the State will be replaced by a "vast association" of the whole nation?

5. In Marx's plan, communism will introduce a new societal ethic in which "the free development of each is condition for the free development of all." What might be the implications of this vision in the restructuring of society? What assumptions about human nature does this vision suggest?

THE COMMUNIST MANIFESTO (1848)

Karl Marx and Friedrich Engels

Prologue

A specter is haunting Europe—the specter of Communism. All the Powers of old Europe have entered into a holy alliance to exorcize this specter: Pope and Czar, Metternich and Guizot,* French Radicals and German police-spies.

Where is the party in opposition that has not been decried as Communistic by its opponents in power? Where the Opposition that has not hurled back the branding

Source: Karl Marx and Friedrich Engels, "Manifesto of the Communist Party," in *Birth of the Communist Manifesto*, ed. Dirk Struik, 87, 89–92, 96–97, 103–04, 106–07, 109, 110–12. Copyright © 1971 International Publishers. Reprinted with permission.

*Prince Metternich of Austria (1773–1859) and French Premier Francois Guizot (1787–1874) were two of the most prominent conservative leaders of Europe who undertook strong measures to repress both liberal ideas and revolutionary movements.

reproach of Communism, against the more advanced opposition parties, as well as against its reactionary adversaries?

Two things result from this fact:

I. Communism is already acknowledged by all European Powers to be itself a Power.
II. It is high time that Communists should openly, in the face of the whole world, publish their views, their aims, their tendencies, and meet this nursery tale of the Specter of Communism with a Manifesto of the party itself.

Bourgeois and Proletarians

The history of all hitherto existing society is the history of class struggles.

Freeman and slave, patrician and plebeian, lord and serf, guild-master and journeyman, in a word, oppressor and oppressed, stood in constant opposition to one another, carried on an uninterrupted, now hidden, now open fight, a fight that each time ended, either in a revolutionary re-constitution of society at large, or in the common ruin of the contending classes.

In the earlier epochs of history, we find almost everywhere a complicated arrangement of society into various orders, a manifold gradation of social rank. In ancient Rome we have patricians, knights, plebeians, slaves; in the Middle Ages, feudal lords, vassals, guild-masters, journeymen, apprentices, serfs; in almost all of these classes, again, subordinate gradations.

The modern bourgeois society that has sprouted from the ruins of feudal society has not done away with class antagonisms. It has but established new classes, new conditions of oppression, new forms of struggle in place of the old ones.

Our epoch, the epoch of the bourgeoisie, possesses, however, this distinctive feature: it has simplified the class antagonisms. Society as a whole is more and more splitting up into two great hostile camps, into two great classes directly facing each other: Bourgeoisie and Proletariat.

Modern industry has established the world market, for which the discovery of America paved the way. This market has given an immense development to commerce, to navigation, to communication by land. This development has, in its turn, reacted on the extension of industry; and in proportion as industry, commerce, navigation, railways extended, in the same proportion the bourgeoisie developed, increased its capital, and pushed into the background every class handed down from the Middle Ages.

We see, therefore, how the modern bourgeoisie is itself the product of a long course of development, of a series of revolutions in the modes of production and of exchange.

Each step in the development of the bourgeoisie was accompanied by a corresponding political advance of that class. An oppressed class under the sway of the feudal nobility, an armed and self-governing association in the medieval commune; here independent urban republic (as in Italy and Germany), there taxable "third estate" of the monarchy (as in France), afterwards, in the period of manufacture proper, serving either the semi-feudal or the absolute monarchy as a counterpoise against the nobility, and, in fact, cornerstone of the great monarchies in general, the bourgeoisie has at last, since the establishment of Modern Industry and of the world market, conquered for itself, in the modern representative State, exclusive political sway. The executive of the modern State is but a committee for managing the common affairs of the whole bourgeoisie.

The bourgeoisie, historically, has played a most revolutionary part.

The bourgeoisie, wherever it has got the upper hand, has put an end to all feudal, patriarchal, idyllic relations. It has pitilessly torn asunder the motley feudal ties that bound man to his "natural superiors" and has left remaining no other nexus between man and man than naked self-interest, than callous "cash payment." It has drowned the most heavenly ecstasies of religious fervor, of chivalrous enthusiasm, of philistine sentimentalism, in the icy water of egotistical calculation. It has resolved personal worth into exchange value, and in place of the numberless indefeasible chartered freedoms, has set up that single, unconscionable freedom—Free Trade. In one word, for exploitation, veiled by religious and political illusions, it has substituted naked, shameless, direct, brutal exploitation. . . .

In proportion as the bourgeoisie, *i.e.,* capital, is developed, in the same proportion is the proletariat, the modern working class, developed—a class of laborers, who live only so long as they find work, and who find work only so long as their labor increases capital. These laborers, who must sell themselves piecemeal, are a commodity, like every other article of commerce, and are consequently exposed to all the vicissitudes of competition to all the fluctuations of the market.

Owing to the extensive use of machinery and to division of labor, the work of the proletarians has lost all individual character, and, consequently, all charm for the workman. He becomes an appendage of the machine, and it is only the most simple, most monotonous, and most easily acquired knack, that is required of him. Hence, the cost of production of a workman is restricted, almost entirely, to the means of subsistence that he requires for his maintenance, and for the propagation of his race. But the price of a commodity, and therefore also of labor, is equal to its cost of production. In proportion, therefore, as the repulsiveness of the work increases, the wage decreases. Nay more, in proportion as the use of machinery and division of labor increases, in the same proportion the burden of toil also increases, whether by prolongation of the working hours, by increase of the work exacted in a given time or by increased speed of the machinery, etc.

Modern industry has converted the little workshop of the patriarchal master into the great factory of the industrial capitalist. Masses of laborers, crowded into the factory, are organized like soldiers. As privates of the industrial army they are placed under the command of a perfect hierarchy of officers and sergeants. Not only are they slaves of the bourgeois class, and of the bourgeois State; they are daily and hourly enslaved by the machine, by the overlooker, and, above all, by the individual bourgeois manufacturer himself. The more openly this despotism proclaims gain to be its end and aim, the more petty, the more hateful and the more embittering it is. . . .

Proletarians and Communists

The immediate aim of the Communists is the same as that of all the other proletarian parties: formation of the proletariat into a class, overthrow of the bourgeois supremacy, conquest of political power by the proletariat. . . .

The distinguishing feature of Communism is not the abolition of property generally, but the abolition of bourgeois property.* But modern bourgeois private property is the final and most complete expression of the system of producing and appropriating products, that is based on class antagonisms, on the exploitation of the many by the few.

In this sense, the theory of the Communists may he summed up in the single sentence: Abolition of private property.

We Communists have been reproached with the desire of abolishing the right of personally acquiring property as the fruit of a man's own labor, which property is alleged to be the groundwork of all personal freedom, activity and independence.

Hard-won, self-acquired, self-earned property! Do you mean the property of the petty artisan and of the small peasant, a form of property that preceded the bourgeois form? There is no need to abolish that; the development of industry has to a great extent already destroyed it, and is still destroying it daily. . . .

You are horrified at our intending to do away with private property. But in your existing society, private property is already done away with for nine-tenths of the population; its existence for the few is solely due to its non-existence in the hands of those nine-tenths. You reproach us, therefore, with intending to do away with a form of property, the necessary condition for whose existence is the non-existence of any property for the immense majority of society.

In one word, you reproach us with intending to do away with your property. Precisely so; that is just what we intend. . . .

Communism deprives no man of the power to appropriate the products of society; all that it does is to deprive him of the power to subjugate the labor of others by means of such appropriation.

It has been objected that upon the abolition of private property all work will cease, and universal laziness will overtake us.

According to this, bourgeois society ought long ago to have gone to the dogs through sheer idleness; for those of its members who work, acquire nothing, and those who acquire anything, do not work. . . .

But don't wrangle with us so long as you apply, to our intended abolition of bourgeois property, the standard of your bourgeois notions of freedom, culture, law, etc. Your very ideas are but the outgrowth of the conditions of your bourgeois production and bourgeois property, just as your jurisprudence[†] is but the will of your class made into a law for all, a will, whose essential character and direction are determined by the economical conditions of existence of your class. . . .

In proportion as the exploitation of one individual by another is put an end to, the exploitation of one nation by another will also be put an end to. In proportion as the antagonism between classes within the nation vanishes, the hostility of one nation to another will come to an end. . . .

---

*Marx defined bourgeoisie property as the wealth and goods appropriated unfairly by the middle class from the exploited labor of the working classes.

†A body or collection of laws.

. . . The history of all past society has consisted in the development of class antagonisms, antagonisms that assumed different forms at different epochs.

But whatever form they may have taken, one fact is common to all past ages: the exploitation of one part of society by the other. No wonder, then, that the social consciousness of past ages, despite all the multiplicity and variety it displays, moves within certain common forms, or general ideas, which cannot completely vanish except with the total disappearance of class antagonisms.

The Communist revolution is the most radical rupture with traditional property relations; no wonder that its development involves the most radical rupture with traditional ideas. . . .

These measures will of course be different in different countries. Nevertheless in the most advanced countries, the following will be pretty generally applicable:

1. Abolition of property in land and application of all rents of land to public purposes.
2. A heavy progressive or graduated income tax.
3. Abolition of all right of inheritance.
4. Confiscation of the property of all emigrants and rebels.
5. Centralization of credit in the hands of the State, by means of a national bank with State capital and an exclusive monopoly.
6. Centralization of the means of communication and transport in the hands of the State.
7. Extension of factories and instruments of production owned by the State; the bringing into cultivation of waste-lands, and the improvement of the soil generally in accordance with a common plan.
8. Equal liability of all to labor. Establishment of industrial armies, especially for agriculture.
9. Combination of agriculture with manufacturing industries; gradual abolition of the distinction between town and country, by a more equable distribution of the population over the country.
10. Free education for all children in public schools. Abolition of children's factory labor in its present form. Combination of education with industrial production, and so forth.

When, in the course of development, class distinctions have disappeared, and all production has been concentrated in the hands of a vast association of the whole nation, the public power will lose its political character. Political power, properly so called, is merely the organized power of one class for oppressing another. If the proletariat during its contest with the bourgeoisie is compelled, by the force of circumstances, to organize itself as a class, if, by means of a revolution, it makes itself the ruling class, and, as such, sweeps away by force the old conditions of production, then it will, along with these conditions, have swept away the conditions for the existence of class antagonisms and of classes generally, and will thereby have abolished its own supremacy as a class.

In place of the old bourgeois society, with its classes and class antagonisms, we shall have an association, in which the free development of each is the condition for the free development of all.

ANDREW CARNEGIE'S GOSPEL OF WEALTH

From the end of the Civil War in 1865 to the turn of the century, the Industrial Revolution transformed life in the United States. A nation of rural farmers and skilled craftsmen was being replaced by businessmen, factory workers, and industrialists. Across the country, the tremendous expansion of new railroads, corporations, and cities was a clear sign of America's new economic orientation. The gross national product (GNP), or the overall value of goods and services produced by the nation, increased sixfold during this time period, and America surpassed Britain as the leading industrial power in the world. But although the new industrial economy produced unprecedented levels of wealth in what historians have dubbed the Gilded Age, it also created new tensions and greater divisions between the lower and upper classes that threatened the stability and cohesion of the country.

One of the great leaders of America's industrial success was Andrew Carnegie (1835–1919), who rose from poverty to become one of the wealthiest and most powerful men in the United States. Carnegie was born to a working-class family in Scotland that emigrated to Pennsylvania in 1848 when his father, a skilled weaver, lost his job with the advent of mechanized looms. With little formal education, Carnegie went to work at the age of twelve as a bobbin boy[14] in a textile factory, but with hard work and determination, he became an expert telegraph operator and was hired by the Pennsylvania Railroad. He ultimately was promoted to the rank of superintendent, but he left the railroad in 1865 when he correctly foresaw America's future need for iron and steel. After touring factories in England, Carnegie founded his own company near Pittsburgh, and his mill soon became a model for the modern steel industry. Carnegie produced high-quality steel by investing in the most advanced equipment of the day, and he cut costs by gaining control of the raw materials and transportation required to make steel—a process known as "vertical integration"[15]—which foreshadowed future trends in American manufacturing.

Carnegie was also a tough competitor. He took advantage of boom-and-bust business cycles to undersell his competitors, and when they floundered, he purchased them at reduced prices and added them to his growing empire. In 1900, the profits of Carnegie Steel Corporation were approximately $40 million, of which Carnegie's personal share was $25 million. In the following year, he sold his company to J. P. Morgan's newly created United States Steel Corporation for $250 million, and he retired as one of the wealthiest men in the country.

One might imagine that a self-made multimillionaire such as Andrew Carnegie would fully embrace the values of free enterprise capitalism, and indeed he was a staunch defender of individual initiative and the survival of the fittest.[16] But Carnegie was also concerned about what he called "the proper administration of wealth" and the creation of an American corporate aristocracy. He frequently wrote about these problems, and he proposed a specific solution in an essay entitled "Wealth" that was published in the *North American Review* in 1889. Concluding that "a man who dies rich dies disgraced," Carnegie proposed a new "gospel of wealth" that would provide tangible benefits for all without infringing upon individual liberty. Backing up his words with action, Carnegie became one of the greatest philanthropists of his era, providing funds for parks, concert halls, universities, and hospitals. Such gifts continued after his death in 1919, for he created perpetual trusts for the support of education, scientific research, and international peace.[17]

QUESTIONS TO CONSIDER

1. According to Carnegie, what were the successes of the American economic system? What were the problems?

2. How did Carnegie view human competition? How did his views compare with those of Smith and Marx? Do his opinions justify inequality?

3. Why did Carnegie support the estate tax? Is this consistent with his views on free enterprise? Is this a justifiable violation of "laissez-faire" principles?

4. The English playwright and Socialist critic George Bernard Shaw implicitly criticized Carnegie's plan by stating, "We often give to public objects money that we should devote to raising the wages" of the working classes. Do you agree? Why did Carnegie believe that the wealthy are better suited to assist the poor than the poor are themselves? Is this a realistic or paternalistic view?

5. Some historians contend that Carnegie's goal was to find a compromise between economic liberalism and Marxist socialism. Do you believe that his proposals achieve this middle ground? Is philanthropy the solution to narrowing the gap between the wealthy and the poor in order to bring "peace on earth, among men good-will"?

"WEALTH" (1889)

Andrew Carnegie

The problem of our age is the administration of wealth, so that the ties of brotherhood may still bind together the rich and poor in harmonious relationship. The conditions of human life have not only been changed, but revolutionized, within the past few hundred years. In former days there was little difference between the dwelling, dress, food, and environment of the chief and those of his retainers. The Indians are today

Source: Andrew Carnegie, "Wealth," *North American Review* 148, no. 391 (June 1889): 653, 657–62.

where civilized man then was. When visiting the Sioux, I was led to the wigwam of the chief. It was just like others in appearance, and even inside, the difference was trifling between it and those of the poorest of his braves. The contrast between the palace of the millionaire and the cottage of the laborer with us today measures the change which has come with civilization.

This change, however, is not to be deplored, but welcomed as highly beneficial. It is well, nay, essential for the progress of the race, that the houses of some should be homes for all that is highest and best in literature and the arts, and for all the refinements of civilization, rather than that none should be so. Much better this great irregularity than universal squalor. . . . The "good old times" were not good old times. Neither master nor servant was as well situated then as today. A relapse to old conditions would be disastrous to both—not the least so to him who serves—and would sweep away civilization with it. . . .

. . . Today the world obtains commodities of excellent quality at prices which even the generation preceding this would have deemed incredible. In the commercial world similar causes have produced similar results, and the race is benefitted thereby. The poor enjoy what the rich could not before afford. What were the luxuries have become the necessaries of life. The laborer has now more comforts than the farmer had a few generations ago. The farmer has more luxuries than the landlord had, and is more richly clad and better housed. The landlord has books and pictures rarer, and appointments more artistic, than the King could then obtain.

The price we pay for this salutary change is, no doubt, great. We assemble thousands of operatives in the factory, in the mine, and in the counting-house, of whom the employer can know little or nothing, and to whom the employer is little better than a myth. All intercourse between them is at an end, Rigid Castes are formed, and, as usual, mutual ignorance breeds mutual distrust. Each Caste is without sympathy for the other, and ready to credit anything disparaging in regard to it. Under the law of competition, the employer of thousands is forced into the strictest economies, among which the rates paid to labor figure prominently, and often there is friction between the employer and the employed, between capital and labor, between rich and poor. Human society loses homogeneity.

The price which society pays for the law of competition, like the price it pays for cheap comforts and luxuries, is also great; but the advantages of this law are also greater still, for it is to this law that we owe our wonderful material development, which brings improved conditions in its train. But, whether the law be benign or not, we must say of it, as we say of the change in the conditions of men to which we have referred: It is here; we cannot evade it; no substitutes for it have been found; and while the law may be sometimes hard for the individual, it is best for the race, because it insures the survival of the fittest in every department. We accept and welcome, therefore, as conditions to which we must accommodate ourselves, great inequality of environment, the concentration of business, industrial and commercial, in the hands of a few, and the law of competition between these, as being not only beneficial, but essential for the future progress of the race. . . . It is a law, as certain as any of the others named, that men possessed of this peculiar talent for affairs, under the free play of economic forces, must, of necessity, soon be in receipt of more revenue than can be judiciously expended upon themselves; and this law is as beneficial for the race as others.

We start, then, with a condition of affairs under which the best interests of the race are promoted, but which inevitably gives wealth to the few. Thus far, accepting conditions as they exist, the situation can be surveyed and pronounced good. The question then arises. . . . What is the proper mode of administering wealth after the laws upon which civilization is founded have thrown it into the hands of the few? And it is of this great question that I believe I offer the true solution. . . .

There are but three modes in which surplus wealth can be disposed of. It can be left to the families of the decedent; or it can be bequeathed for public purposes; or, finally, it can be administered during their lives by its possessors. . . . The first is the most injudicious. In monarchical countries, the estates and the greatest portion of the wealth are left to the first son, that the vanity of the parent may be gratified by the thought that his name and title are to descend to succeeding generations unimpaired. The condition of this class in Europe today teaches the futility of such hopes or ambitions. The successors have become impoverished through their follies or from the fall in the value of land. . . . Beyond providing for the wife and daughters moderate sources of income, and very moderate allowances indeed, if any, for the sons, men may well hesitate, for it is no longer questionable that great sums bequeathed oftener work more for the injury than for the good of the recipients. . . .

As to the second mode, that of leaving wealth at death for public uses, it may be said that this is only a means for the disposal of wealth, provided a man is content to wait until he is dead before it becomes of much good in the world. . . . The cases are not few in which the real object sought by the testator is not attained, nor are they few in which his real wishes are thwarted. In many cases, the bequests are so used as to become only monuments of his folly. . . .

The growing disposition to tax more and more heavily large estates left at death is a cheering indication of the growth of a salutary change in public opinion. The State of Pennsylvania now takes—subject to some exceptions—one-tenth of the property left by its citizens. . . . Of all forms of taxation, this seems the wisest. . . . By taxing estates heavily at death the state marks its condemnation of the selfish millionaire's unworthy life. . . .

There remains, then, only one mode of using great fortunes; but in this we have the true antidote for the temporary unequal distribution of wealth, the reconciliation of the rich and the poor—a reign of harmony—another ideal, differing, indeed, from that of the Communist in requiring only the further evolution of existing conditions, not the total overthrow of our civilization. It is founded upon the present most intense individualism, and the race is prepared to put it in practice by degrees whenever it pleases. Under its sway we shall have an ideal state, in which the surplus wealth of the few will become, in the best sense, the property of the many, because administered for the common good, and this wealth, passing through the hands of the few, can be made a much more potent force for the elevation of our race than if it had been distributed in small sums to the people themselves. Even the poorest can be made to see this, and to agree that great sums gathered by some of their fellow-citizens and spent for public purposes, from which the masses reap the principal benefit, are more valuable to them than if scattered among them through the course of many years in trifling amounts. . . .

This, then, is held to be the duty of the man of Wealth: First, to set an example of modest, unostentatious living, shunning display or extravagance; to provide moderately for the legitimate wants of those dependent upon him; and after doing so to consider all surplus revenues which come to him simply as trust funds, which he is called upon to administer, and strictly bound as a matter of duty to administer in the manner which, in his judgment, is best calculated to produce the most beneficial results for the community—the man of wealth thus becoming the mere agent and trustee for his poorer brethren, bringing to their service his superior wisdom, experience, and ability to administer, doing better than they would or could do for themselves. . . .

Thus is the problem of Rich and Poor to be solved. The laws of accumulation are left free; the laws of distribution free. Individualism will continue, but the millionaire will be but a trustee for the poor; intrusted for a season with a part of the increased wealth of the community, but administering it for the community far better than it could or would have done for itself. . . .

Such, in my opinion, is the true Gospel concerning Wealth, obedience to which is destined to some day solve the problem of the Rich and the Poor, and to bring "Peace on earth, among men of Good-Will."

WEALTH, POWER, AND CONSPICUOUS CONSUMPTION IN AMERICA

During America's Gilded Age (1865–1900), individuals and families who achieved great wealth celebrated it as never before. Elegant city townhouses, huge country manors, lavish parties, and an extensive set of leisure activities were pursued by the wealthy elite, while the rising middle class emulated their "superiors" in fashion, food, and dress. The result was a period of unprecedented material accumulation in American history, a new emphasis on reputation and respectability, and the rise of "conspicuous consumption"[18]—a term coined by economist Thorstein Veblen to describe one of the major cultural impacts of the Industrial Revolution.

Thorstein Veblen (1857–1929) grew up on a farm in Minnesota, the son of a first-generation Norwegian family. He graduated from Carleton College (Minnesota) and earned a Ph.D. in philosophy from Yale in 1884, but he returned in frustration to the family farm when he was unable to secure an academic position in philosophy. Seven years later, he reentered graduate school at Cornell to study economics, and he ultimately won a teaching position at the University of Chicago in 1896. Three years later, Veblen wrote *The Theory of the Leisure Class* (1899), which was later followed by *The Theory of Business Enterprise* (1904) and *An Inquiry into the Nature of Peace and the Terms of Its Perpetuation* (1917). Although Veblen's writings earned him fame, his academic career was far less successful, and his personal life was often in turmoil. He acquired a reputation for being a remote and careless lecturer, and he appalled his colleagues by his philandering and extra-marital affairs, which destroyed his first marriage. Unable to avoid scandals at several universities, Veblen left academia to work as editor for a literary and political magazine in New York, and he briefly served in the Food Administration during World War I. In 1926, he retired to California, where he lived with a stepdaughter in a remote cabin in the mountains overlooking the sea until his death three years later.

Although Veblen has earned the reputation as a skilled satirist and harsh critic of the lifestyles of the rich and famous during America's Gilded Age, his *Theory of the Leisure Class* (1899) also provides a deeper understanding of the intimate relationship between the economy and society, and between wealth and cultural values. Veblen's most unique contribution was to examine the workings of the economy through the lens of evolutionary theory. The business world, he claimed, was dominated by men such as Andrew Carnegie: highly competitive, aggressive, and desiring of power and profits. Their outlook and values, he reasoned, were essentially "survivalist," a legacy of a predatory, primitive past. In modern times, individual prowess was also sought and openly displayed in the pastimes, fashions, and shopping habits of the ruling classes, leading to a new cultural pattern of "conspicuous consumption." Consequently, whereas Adam Smith saw economic behavior in terms of the rational pursuit of self-interest, Veblen argued that it arose from the irrational human desire to dominate and control for greater status and prestige. His theories on economic behavior, patterns of consumption, and business excess are worthy of careful consideration, for they continue to have meaning in the corporate and consumer-oriented society of the United States a hundred years later.

QUESTIONS TO CONSIDER

1. What does Veblen mean by "conspicuous consumption"? How is it related to "survival of the fittest"? How does it also reflect the transient nature of modern society?

2. Veblen argues that the wealthy elite—a small minority of the total population—have nonetheless set the standards for cultural tastes and values. How did this happen? Do you find his reasoning persuasive?

3. According to Veblen, what motives and concerns shape the lifestyles of many middle-class housewives? Why does he consider most of their actions "a wasteful expenditure of time and substance"?

4. In contrast to Marx, Veblen suggests that the emulation of the rich by the not-so-rich provides a form of social cohesion. In your estimation, might this help explain the lack of radical political tradition in the United States?

5. Veblen concludes that in order for consumption to be "reputable," it must be wasteful. How does he come to this conclusion? Is his argument convincing? If so, what does this say about the rationality of Americans' economic behavior?

THE THEORY OF THE LEISURE CLASS (1899)

Thorstein Veblen

During the earlier stages of economic development, consumption of goods without stint, especially consumption of the better grades of goods,—ideally all consumption in excess of the subsistence minimum,—pertains normally to the leisure class. This restriction tends to disappear, at least formally, after the later peaceable stage has been reached, with private ownership of goods and an industrial system based on wage labor or on the petty household economy. But during the earlier quasi-peaceable stage, when so many of the traditions through which the institution of a leisure class has affected the economic life of later times were taking form and consistency, this principle has had the force of a conventional law. It has served as the norm to which consumption has tended to conform, and any appreciable departure from it is to be regarded as an aberrant form, sure to be eliminated sooner or later in the further course of development.

The quasi-peaceable gentleman of leisure, then, not only consumes of the staff of life beyond the minimum required for subsistence and physical efficiency, but his consumption also undergoes a specialization as regards the quality of the goods consumed. He consumes freely and of the best, in food, drink, narcotics, shelter, services, ornaments, apparel, weapons and accouterments, amusements, amulets, and idols or divinities. . . . Since the consumption of these more excellent goods is an evidence of wealth, it becomes honorific; and conversely, the failure to consume in due quantity and quality becomes a mark of inferiority and demerit.

This growth of punctilious* discrimination as to qualitative excellence in eating, drinking, etc. presently affects not only the manner of life, but also the training and intellectual activity of the gentleman of leisure. He is no longer simply the successful, aggressive male,—the man of strength, resource, and intrepidity. In order to avoid stultification[†] he must also cultivate his tastes, for it now becomes incumbent on him to discriminate with some nicety between the noble and the ignoble in consumable goods. . . . Closely related to the requirement that the gentleman must consume freely and of the right kind of goods, there is the requirement that he must know how to consume them in a seemly manner. His life of leisure must be conducted in due form. Hence arise good manners. . . . High-bred manners and ways of living are items of conformity to the norm of conspicuous leisure and conspicuous consumption.

As wealth accumulates, the leisure class develops further in function and structure, and there arises a differentiation within the class. There is a more or less elaborate system of rank and grades. This differentiation is furthered by the inheritance of wealth and the consequent inheritance of gentility. . . . Those who stand near the

---

Source: Thorstein Veblen, *The Theory of the Leisure Class; an Economic Study of Institutions* (New York: Macmillan, 1902), 68–101.

*Marked by extreme care and attention to detail, convention, and fashion.

[†]To look foolish or stupid.

higher and the highest grades of the wealthy leisure class, in point of birth, or in point of wealth, or both, outrank the remoter-born and the pecuniarily weaker. . . .

And here occurs a curious inversion. It is a fact of common observance that in [the] lower middle class there is no pretense of leisure on the part of the head of the household. Through force of circumstances it has fallen into disuse. But the middle-class wife still carries on the business of vicarious* leisure, for the good name of the household and its master. . . . The head of the middle-class household has been reduced by economic circumstances to turn his hand to gaining a livelihood by occupations which often partake largely of the character of industry, as in the case of the ordinary business man of today. But the derivative fact—the vicarious leisure and consumption rendered by the wife, and the auxiliary vicarious performance of leisure by menials—remains in vogue as a conventionality which the demands of reputability will not suffer to be slighted. It is by no means an uncommon spectacle to find a man applying himself to work with the utmost diligence, in order that his wife may in due form render for him that degree of vicarious leisure which the common sense of the time demands.

The leisure rendered by the wife in such cases is, of course, not a simple manifestation of idleness or indolence. It almost invariably occurs disguised under some form of work or household duties or social amenities, which prove on analysis to serve little or no ulterior end beyond showing that she does not occupy herself with anything that is gainful or that is of substantial use. As has already been noticed under the head of manners, the greater part of the customary round of domestic cares to which the middle-class housewife gives her time and effort is of this character. Not that the results of her attention to household matters, of a decorative nature, are not pleasing to the sense of men trained in middle-class proprieties; but the taste to which these effects of household adornment and tidiness appeal is a taste which has been formed under the selective guidance of a canon of propriety that demands just these evidences of wasted effort. The effects are pleasing to us chiefly because we have been taught to find them pleasing. There goes into these domestic duties much care for a proper combination of form and color, and for other ends that are to be classed as aesthetic in the proper sense of the term; and it is not denied that effects having some substantial aesthetic value are sometimes attained. Pretty much all that is here insisted on is that, as regards these amenities of life, the housewife's efforts are under the guidance of traditions that have been shaped by the law of conspicuously wasteful expenditure of time and substance. If beauty or comfort is achieved—and it is a more or less fortuitous circumstance if they are—they must be achieved by means and methods that commend themselves to the great economic law of wasted effort. The more reputable, "presentable" portion of middle-class household paraphernalia are, on the one hand, items of conspicuous consumption, and on the other hand, apparatus for putting in evidence the vicarious leisure rendered by the housewife. . . .

This vicarious consumption practiced by the household of the middle and lower classes can not be counted as a direct expression of the leisure-class scheme of life, since the household of this pecuniary grade does not belong within the leisure class.

---

*To experience through one's imagination, or by a sympathetic participation in the experiences of others.

It is rather that the leisure-class scheme of life here comes to an expression at the second remove. The leisure class stands at the head of the social structure in point of reputability; and its manner of life and its standards of worth therefore afford the norm of reputability for the community. The observance of these standards, in some degree of approximation, becomes incumbent upon all classes lower in the scale. In modern civilized communities the lines of demarcation between social classes have grown vague and transient, and wherever this happens the norm of reputability imposed by the upper class extends its coercive influence with but slight hindrance down through the social structure to the lowest strata. The result is that the members of each stratum accept as their ideal of decency the scheme of life in vogue in the next higher stratum, and bend their energies to live up to that ideal. On pain of forfeiting their good name and their self-respect in case of failure, they must conform to the accepted code, at least in appearance. . . .

. . . No class of society, not even the most abjectly poor, forgoes all customary conspicuous consumption. The last items of this category of consumption are not given up except under stress of the direst necessity. Very much of squalor and discomfort will be endured before the last trinket or the last pretense of pecuniary* decency is put away. There is no class and no country that has yielded so completely before the pressure of physical want as to deny themselves all gratification of this higher or spiritual need.

From the foregoing survey of the growth of conspicuous leisure and consumption, it appears that the utility of both alike for the purposes of reputability lies in the element of waste that is common to both. In the one case it is a waste of time and effort, in the other it is a waste of goods. Both are methods of demonstrating the possession of wealth, and the two are conventionally accepted as equivalents. . . .

The modern organization of industry works in the same direction also by another line. The exigencies† of the modern industrial system frequently place individuals and households in juxtaposition between whom there is little contact in any other sense than that of juxtaposition. One's neighbors, mechanically speaking, often are socially not one's neighbors, or even acquaintances; and still their transient good opinion has a high degree of utility. The only practicable means of impressing one's pecuniary ability on these unsympathetic observers of one's everyday life is an unremitting demonstration of ability to pay. In the modern community there is also a more frequent attendance at large gatherings of people to whom one's everyday life is unknown; in such places as churches, theaters, ballrooms, hotels, parks, shops, and the like. In order to impress these transient observers, and to retain one's self-complacency under their observation, the signature of one's pecuniary strength should be written in characters which he who runs may read. It is evident, therefore, that the present trend of the development is in the direction of heightening the utility of conspicuous consumption as compared with leisure. . . .

Throughout the entire evolution of conspicuous expenditure, whether of goods or of services or human life, runs the obvious implication that in order to effectually

---

*Relating to money or finances.

†Demands, requirements, or necessities.

mend the consumer's good fame it must be an expenditure of superfluities. In order to be reputable it must be wasteful. No merit would accrue from the consumption of the bare necessaries of life, except by comparison with the abjectly poor who fall short even of the subsistence minimum; and no standard of expenditure could result from such a comparison, except the most prosaic* and unattractive level of decency. . . .

INDUSTRIALIZATION IN IMPERIAL RUSSIA

Russia in the mid-nineteenth century was politically conservative, economically backward, and falling increasingly behind the industrialized nations of western Europe and the United States. Russia's tsars and the aristocratic elite, fearful of the liberal revolutions that rocked Europe in the 1830s and 1840s, used various forms of repression and censorship to resist change and radical ideas in order to retain their historical tradition of power and privilege. But the Russian emphasis on stability and the status quo meant that the economy remained overwhelmingly agrarian and dependent upon the labor of indentured serfs. Although some Russian aristocrats took advantage of expanding global commerce to increase grain exports to western markets, they did so by increasing the work demands on serfs instead of by introducing more efficient technological and productive innovations. Despite its vast natural resources and economic potential, preindustrial Russia was an economic backwater.

The impetus for change came with Russia's shocking defeat in the Crimean War (1854–1856) and the accession of Tsar Aleksandr II (ruled 1855–1881) to the throne.[19] The military debacle in the Crimea was largely attributed to the superior weaponry and transport capabilities of the industrialized western powers, which convinced the tsar that wide-scale reforms were urgently needed if Russia were not to be further humiliated in the future. Consequently, in the 1860s and 1870s, Tsar Aleksandr II initiated his "Great Reforms," the most radical Russian program for change since Tsar Peter the Great. In successive order, Tsar Aleksandr II abolished serfdom, liberalized the judicial system, sought to modernize military training, and temporarily allowed greater political freedoms and some forms of local government.

But it was industrialization that emerged most clearly as the centerpiece of this wider process of change. Under the sponsorship of Tsar Aleksandr II and (after his assassination in 1881) Aleksandr III (r. 1881–1894), then Nikolai II (r. 1894–1917), the Russian government used its powers to promote rapid economic change. A national railroad system was begun in the 1870s, which culminated with the completion of the 5,400-mile Trans-Siberian Railway in 1903. The

---

*Dull, unimaginative.

railroads opened up Siberia and other vast regions to new development and helped to consolidate Russian power in the far Asian regions of the empire. The railroads also helped to stimulate subsidiary industries in iron, coal, and steel and facilitated the export of grain to western markets.

The prime architect of Russia's railroad and industrial expansion was Sergei Witte (1849–1915). Witte traced his ancestry on his father's side to Dutch immigrants, but the family had worked its way up in Russian society. Sergei's father held the rank of a midlevel bureaucrat in Russia and had married into a noble and well-connected Russian family. Sergei earned a degree from Novorossiiskii University and wanted to pursue a career in mathematics, but he lacked the resources to do so. Oddly, for someone with his family connections, he took a job as a cashier at a ticket window, but by dint of work and a genius for detail, he worked his way up to head the Department of Railways in 1889. His adept handling of the railroad, along with his proven managerial skills, ultimately led to his appointment as minister of communications (1892) and minister of finance (1892–1903).

In 1899, Minister of Finance Witte wrote a "secret memorandum" on economic strategy to Tsar Nikolas II, outlining his program of industrialization. The reading that follows comprises excerpts from this official memo to the tsar. This memo is particularly revealing and interesting because the goals and methods proposed for industrialization are so clearly contrary to the philosophy set forth by Adam Smith. Sergei Witte's interest in economic productivity was much more connected with national power than with individual prosperity and freedom. In order to achieve industrialization, he also advocated governmental planning, protective tariffs, and reliance on foreign creditors and loans. Some scholars have suggested that his policy was merely a new expression of state power and centralization in Imperial Russia; others have contended that Witte's proposals foreshadowed the development of the massive "five-year plans" devised in later years by the Soviets.

Witte's program had decidedly mixed results. The value of textiles, metal goods, and chemicals more than tripled between 1877 and 1897. By 1900, Russia was fourth in the world in steel production and second (to the United States) in the newer area of petroleum production and refining. Railroads continued to expand, and by the turn of the century, Russia had more track than any other nation but the United States. Overall, the pace of Russia's industrialization made it the most rapidly industrializing nation in the world in the 1890s. But beneath these glowing statistics, Russia still lagged far behind. Despite its dramatic increase in industrial exports, these were still less than one-third those of the United States or Germany and less than one-fifth those of Great Britain. Russia's factories were among the world's largest, but they were hampered by inferior machinery, horrid working conditions, and poorly skilled labor. The reliance on foreign capital enlarged the Russian national debt, and by 1900, nearly half of Russia's industries were foreign owned. And while industrialization grew, the agricultural sector of the economy remained primitive, and the vast majority of Russians continued to live at bare subsistence levels in rural villages.

Such profound economic transformations also caused considerable social up-heaval, dislocation, and dissatisfaction, which found expression in new forms of political discord that were to have dramatic consequences in future years. The direct involvement of the Russian government in economic planning allied Russian industrialists and capitalists to imperial policy and consequently caused them to support imperial autocracy. In contrast, the "Populists"—a loosely knit youth group from the small middle class—supported modernization, but not on a western model. Instead, they wanted to construct a new society on the foundation of the traditional village commune, which was to serve as the basis for a socialist society. Other dissident groups included the Socialist Revolutionaries, who advocated radical agrarian reform, and the Social Democrats, who, under the leadership of a young Vladimir Ilich Ulyanov (more commonly known as Lenin), proposed Marxist models for widespread social change.

Sergei Witte found himself in the middle of these conflicting movements. He was dismissed as minister of finance in 1903, which most historians attribute to his opposition of the aggressive policy of Tsar Nikolai II in the Far East. However, he was recalled in 1905 at the close of the Russo-Japanese War (1904–1905) to negotiate peace with Japan, and he was rewarded with the title of count after winning unexpectedly favorable terms for Russia in the Treaty of Portsmouth. Returning to Russia during the Revolution of 1905, he was called on by the tsar to draw up the October Manifesto of 1905, in which Nikolai II promised more liberal government under a *duma*, or national assembly. However, Witte was unable to mobilize liberal support for the tsar against the challenges and opposition posed by the Social Democrats, and he was dismissed by the tsar in the following year.

QUESTIONS TO CONSIDER

1. According to Witte, what are the problems with Russia's economy? Why does he equate Russia with one of Europe's colonial territories? Based on his perception of the problems, what are his solutions?

2. Witte begins with a strong argument on behalf of protectionism. What is protectionism? According to Witte, what are the benefits of such a policy? What might also be some of the detriments?

3. Witte's memorandum has been called a prime example of economic nationalism. How are his economic plans consistent with national policies? How are they consistent with governmental power?

4. By 1900, nearly half of all Russian industries were foreign owned. Is this fact a repudiation of Witte's reliance on foreign capital? To what degree do you think governments should restrict foreign investment in domestic economies?

5. How would Adam Smith criticize Witte's economic policy? How would Karl Marx respond?

SECRET MEMORANDUM ON INDUSTRIALIZATION (1899)

Sergei Witte

The measures taken by the government for the promotion of a national trade and industry have at present a far deeper and broader significance than they had at any time before. Indeed, the entire economic structure of the empire has been transformed in the course of the second half of the current century, so that now the market and its price structure represent the collective interest of all private enterprises which constitute our national economy. Buying and selling and wage labor penetrate now into much deeper layers of our national existence than was the case at the time of serf economy, when the landlord in his village constituted a self-sufficient economic little world, leading an independent life, almost without relation to the market. The division of labor; the specialization of skills; the increased exchange of goods among a population increasingly divided among towns, villages, factories, and mines; the greater complexity of the demands of the population—all these processes rapidly developed in our fatherland under the influence of the emancipation of the serfs, the construction of a railroad network, the development of credit, and the extraordinary growth of foreign trade. Now all organs and branches of our national economy are drawn into a common economic life, and all its individual units have become far more sensitive and responsive to the economic activities of the government. Because of the extremely interlaced network of contemporary economic relationships, any change in the conditions of one or the other industry, of one or the other branch of trade, credit, or communications, touches and influences, often in hidden ways, the fate of a considerable majority of our enterprises. . . .

In view of these facts, the minister of finance concludes that the country, which in one way or the other is nurtured by the commercial and industrial policy of the government, requires above all that this policy be carried out according to a definite plan, with strict system and continuity. . . . A government with an unsteady commercial and industrial policy is like a businessman who constantly reorganizes his production without producing anything. No matter how great the technical perfection of such a business, it always ends in ruins. . . .

Now, as the attacks on the existing commercial and industrial policy continue and even increase in bitterness, I consider it my duty to review once more its chief foundations and to submit them to Your Imperial Highness. . . .

In Russia at the present moment the protectionist system is in force. . . . What are the tasks of the protectionist system?

Source: Sergei Witte, Report of The Minister of Finance to His Majesty on The Necessity of Formulating And Thereafter Steadfastly Adhering to a Definite Program of a Commercial And Industrial Policy of The Empire (Extremely Secret). In T. H. Von Laue, "A Secret Memorandum of Sergei Witte on the Industrialization of Imperial Russia," *Journal of Modern History,* 26, no. 1 (March 1954): 60–74.

Russia remains even at the present essentially an agricultural country. It pays for all its obligations to foreigners by exporting raw materials, chiefly of an agricultural nature, principally grain. It meets its demand for finished goods by imports from abroad. The economic relations of Russia with western Europe are fully comparable to the relations of colonial countries with their metropolises. The latter consider their colonies as advantageous markets in which they can freely sell the products of their labor and their industry and from which they can draw with a powerful hand the raw materials necessary for them. This is the basis of the economic power of the governments of western Europe, and chiefly for that end do they guard their existing colonies or acquire new ones. Russia was, and to a considerable extent still is, such a hospitable colony for all industrially developed states, generously providing them with the cheap products of her soil and buying dearly the products of their labor.

But there is a radical difference between Russia and a colony: Russia is an independent and strong power. She has the right and the strength not to want to be the eternal handmaiden of states which are more developed economically. She should know the price of her raw materials and the natural riches hidden in the womb of her abundant territories, and she is conscious of the great, not yet fully displayed, capacity for work among her people. She is proud of her great might, by which she jealously guards not only the political but also the economic independence of her empire. She wants to be a metropolis herself. On the basis of the people's labor, liberated from the bonds of serfdom, there began to grow our own national economy, which bids fair to become a reliable counterweight to the domination of foreign industry. . . .

A new industry cannot arise on short order. Protective duties must, therefore, be continued for decades in order to lead to positive results. Meanwhile, in the course of the long preparation, the population will need the products of industry. And as domestic production cannot yet satisfy the domestic demand, the consumers are forced to buy foreign goods at increased prices because of the customs duties; and they have to pay almost as much for the goods of domestic origins. So, for instance, an Englishman pays for a pood of pig iron 26 kopecks, an American 32 kopecks, but a Russian up to 90 kopecks. . . . These imposts are a heavy sacrifice made by the entire population, and not from surplus but out of current necessities. Naturally, the question is asked: Are there no ways to avoid or to reduce those sacrifices which have such an enervating effect on our economy?

It must be stated first of all that the system, because it is coherently carried out, is already beginning to show results. Industry numbers now more than 30,000 factories and mills, with an annual production surpassing 2,000,000,000 rubles. That by itself is a big figure. A widespread and tight net of economic interests is linked to the welfare of that industry. To upset it by a shift to free trade would undermine one of the most reliable foundations of our national well-being. . . .

In this way the sacrifices of the population are not borne in vain. Industry has grown very considerably . . . [and] Russian enterprise has found new outlets; internal trade has developed. But much remains still to be done before we can say that the building is finished. . . .

. . . In Russia this growth is yet too slow, because there is yet too little industry, capital, and spirit of enterprise. But we cannot be content with the continuation of such slow growth. No matter how great the results attained by the present protectionist system, to accomplish what is still ahead and what the entire country so impatiently waits for is by all accounts the most difficult matter. We have to develop mass-production industries, widely dispersed and variegated, in which not custom duties but the more powerful and beneficial laws of competition play the dominant role. We must give the country such industrial perfection as has been reached by the United States of America, which firmly rests its prosperity on two pillars: agriculture and industry. In order to reach these ultimate goals, we must still pass through the most difficult stretch of the road we have chosen. We have not only to direct the flow of capital into this or that field or to find new spheres for its investment, but we have to have above all a great abundance of capital, so that by its natural competition it undermines its own present monopoly position. But not even the most powerful government can create capital.

What, then, must we do? . . .

The influx of foreign capital is . . . the sole means by which our industry can speedily furnish our country with abundant and cheap goods. . . . Replenishing the poor store of popular savings by foreign capital makes it possible for all capital in the country to flow more freely over a broader field and to work up not only the fat but also the leaner sources of profit. Hence the natural riches of the Russian land and the productive energies of its population will be utilized to a considerable extent. . . .

But in recent times objections have been raised against the influx of foreign capital. It has said that this influx is detrimental to basic national interests, that it tries to siphon off all profits from our growing Russian industries, that it will lead to the sale of our rich productive forces to foreigners. [But] it is no secret . . . that the influx of foreign capital is disadvantageous primarily to entrepreneurs, who are harmed by any kind of competition. Not only our own [entrepreneurs], but also foreign capitalists who have already obtained an advantageous place in Russian industry join these heart-rending complaints and thus try to guard their own monopolistic profits. . . .

. . . We have at our disposal cheap labor, tremendous natural riches, and only the high price of capital now stands in the way of getting cheap goods. So why not let foreign capital help us obtain still more cheaply that productive force of which alone we are destitute? Then we will be able to raise our industry to such a high level that it can provide us with cheap goods in sufficient quantity not only for domestic consumption, but also for export. Even at present, we are getting closer to that goal. By bringing the transformation which is occurring under our eyes to its natural conclusion, we will eventually be able to pay the interest charges for capital received from Europe out of the profits of our Asiatic trade. . . .

In submitting this program to favorable consideration by Your Imperial Highness, I respectfully ask that it may please you, my sovereign, to make certain that it may not be endangered henceforth by waverings and changes, because our industries, and our national economy in general, require a firm and consistent system carried to its conclusion. If this program does not find the support of Your Imperial Highness, then, pray, tell me which economic policy I am to pursue.

State Secretary S. IU. Witte

NOTES

1. Economic liberalism is a system of economic thought that advocates individual initiative in the marketplace, free and open competition, and minimal restrictions or restraints imposed by government.

2. Other Enlightenment intellectuals to discover universal laws include Isaac Newton (1642–1727), whose law of gravity helped to explain the operation of the universe, and John Locke (1632–1704), whose analysis of the "laws of nature" led him to identify mankind's natural rights of life, liberty, and property.

3. The division of labor refers to a productive process whereby each worker is given a small and repetitive task to complete over and over, rather than allowing each worker to handcraft a product from start to finish.

4. As expressed by Wordsworth in "The Excursion" (1814):
   . . . I grieve, when on the darker side
   Of this great change [industrialism] I look; and there behold
   Such an outrage done to nature as compels
   The indignant power to justify herself;
   Yea, to avenge her violated rights
   For England's bane.

5. Philanthropy is the practice of making benevolent or charitable contributions (often in the form of financial donations) to serve or assist others in need.

6. As discussed in his work *Origin of Species* (1859), Darwin's theory of evolution was based on two basic concepts. First, there is random variation of traits within all species—some are taller, bigger, keener sighted, etc., than others. Second, nature "selects" those traits best fit for survival, and these are then passed on to the next generation.

7. Lord Charles Townshend's name may be familiar to students of American history, for he was to become the Royal Exchequer responsible for introducing new taxes (Townshend Act) that provoked the American Revolution.

8. In Paris, Smith's curiosity and creativity were sparked by his debates with the French intellectual elite, especially with the economic thinker Francois Quesnay (1694–1774), the leading spokesmen of the "physiocrats" who believed that land was the single most important source of value and wealth.

9. Mercantilism called for government regulation of economic activity through trade restrictions, tariffs, and the creation of state-controlled enterprises, such as charter companies. It was based on the assumption that there was a finite amount of wealth (measured primarily in precious metals) in the world, and in order to remain wealthy, governments had to erect policies to maintain a favorable balance of trade (via tariffs and other restrictions). Smith saw it differently: "It was not by gold or silver, but by labor that all the wealth of the world was produced." This labor theory of value was a revolutionary concept in economic thought and was embraced by future thinkers, including Karl Marx.

10. The Factory Act of 1833 specifically prohibited the employment of children under age nine in textile mills, limited the workday to twelve hours for workers under the age of eighteen, and provided for inspectors to ensure that the required reforms were actually carried out.

11. Friedrich Engels (1820–1895) was brought up in an affluent German family that owned a factory in England. While training for a position in the family firm, Engels collected evidence for *The Condition of the Working Class of England* (1845), which described the misery of the industrialized working class. Although Engels collaborated with Marx in the formulation of ideas and strategies, Marx is generally credited as the dominant partner.

12. For Marx, social classes were defined in terms of relations of production. The bourgeoisie (or middle class) owned and controlled the means of production (businesses, trading companies, etc.), and they derived their wealth from the management of such affairs, and not from land (the aristocracy) or labor (the working classes). In contrast, the proletariat (the working class) derived their income from wages obtained by working for others.

13. Marx's theory of dialectical materialism was deeply influenced by his studies of the German philosopher Georg Hegel (1770–1831). Hegel had proposed that each stage of history was defined by dominant and opposing ideas and that their ultimate clash (the dialectic) yielded a synthesis that served to advance human progress and a new stage in history. Marx borrowed Hegel's concept of the dialectic but asserted that class conflict, borne of economic inequality (materialism), provided the clash of opposing forces and the prime force of historical change.

14. A bobbin boy was responsible for maintaining and replacing the bobbins of thread or yarn on a weaving machine.

15. Vertical integration is a system by which a single firm or business attempts to own or control the most important elements in the production and distribution of its product or service in order to increase its efficiency and power in the marketplace.

16. Carnegie was a great admirer of Herbert Spencer (1820–1903), an English advocate of "social Darwinism," or the belief that competition and "survival of the fittest" were natural laws of nature and human society.

17. Some of the most significant trusts include the Carnegie Institute of Pittsburgh (for the improvement of the city's cultural and educational institutions), the Carnegie Endowment for International Peace (to fund research and conferences), and the Carnegie Corporation of New York (which bestows grants to educational facilities, libraries, research centers, and public television).

18. Conspicuous consumption is the overt pursuit of goods and a lifestyle intended to make a favorable impression on others.

19. Russia's loss to France and Britain in the Crimean War was a great jolt to the ruling elite, for it came less than fifty years after the Russian Imperial Army had thwarted the full might of Napoleon's invasion of the fatherland.

CHAPTER 8

The Frontier Experience
and Cultural Self-Images

INTRODUCTION

Frontier experiences are as old and as enduring as human history itself. Because a frontier is by definition a zone of encounter between different cultures, few human societies have not had some sort of frontier experience. In the nineteenth century, however, owing to revolutionary technological changes and the power of related economic forces, the nature and extent of frontier interactions was fundamentally transformed. Because of the unprecedented change in the scope and scale of human migration, the extent of frontier zones was greatly expanded, and the character of frontier interactions underwent an extraordinary transformation. Although these changes were initiated by Europeans and European-derived societies, such as that of the United States, they ultimately encompassed peoples of many different cultures and ethnicities on the way to the creation of our contemporary "global village." Some peoples conceive of frontiers as areas of mutual, two-way interaction. For others, the frontier is thought of as the zone of contact between civilization and the "uncivilized," whether that "uncivilized" realm involves another human culture or nature itself. However frontiers are conceived, the frontier experience and how it was interpreted by different cultures became a central component of many modern identities.

Because frontiers are extremely fertile zones for the shaping of identities, the study of frontier experiences and how they are understood in different cultures can be a very revealing undertaking. On the one hand, frontiers are areas of intersection, cooperation, and contest. As a result, they involve issues of cultural communication and cross-fertilization. It is frequently the case that much of what defines and enriches a given civilization was absorbed selectively from another culture (for example, the adaptation of Chinese noodles into modern Italian cuisine as pasta). Often, the frontier is the semipermeable membrane through which these influences are absorbed and screened. On the other hand, because frontiers involve contact with different peoples, they also serve to heighten self-awareness

237

and to shape self-definitions. That is, it is often along the frontier that civilizations define both themselves and the cultures they come into contact with. Hence, the self-understanding of a civilization can be assessed by examining the differences that it perceives between itself and the other culture. In fact, the image of the other culture often says more about the culture that produced the image than it does about the culture it is supposed to describe. These issues of cultural identity—based on images of self and other resulting from frontier experiences—are the main themes of this chapter.

It is not surprising that frontiers would be particularly rich regions, in which the process of identification and articulation of a society's distinguishing values occurs. Especially in the case of the United States, the frontier has been invested with an extraordinary amount of meaning. For most Americans, the frontier experience remains the subject of myth and romance. The idea of independent homesteaders carving farms out of the pristine wilderness and in the process demonstrating an inherently American self-reliance, "rugged individualism," and adventurous spirit is deeply imbedded in our culture. Layered on top of this idea are romantic images of daring defenders of justice and order, with only their trusty six-shooter or repeating rifle by their side, standing up to the forces of lawlessness and violence, whether in the form of white outlaws or Native American braves "on the warpath." It is not accidental that car manufacturers choose such names for their sport utility vehicles as Expedition, Cherokee, Blazer, Explorer, Yukon, Tahoe, and so on. Their advertising aims at that mythic spot in the American soul, our reassuring belief that at any moment we might pack everything up, shake off the dust of the city, and go stake out our piece of the frontier.

The American use of the word *frontier* reflects the dominant understanding in the United States that the frontier is the zone of interaction between civilization and wilderness. Americans tend to think of the frontier in "either-or" ways. One side is thought of as settled and civilized; the other is considered not settled—even if it has inhabitants—because it is "uncivilized." The encounter experience plays a similar role in the self-definitions of all frontier cultures. Representations of frontier experiences function as a window through which we can see and assess a culture's self-image. Furthermore, the way that each society "sees" the culture across the border of the frontier reflects, mirrorlike, its own values and self-construction. The selections included here were chosen because of the clarity with which they present this process of cultural formation and self-definition. They also reveal the endurance of the frontier images and the way that they are reconfigured in a continuous process of cultural redefinition over time.

The first set of readings comes from American history. The first document is one of the most important articles in American history. Frederick Jackson Turner's "The Significance of the Frontier in American History" was presented at a meeting of the fledgling American Historical Association in Chicago on July 12, 1893. In this article, he defined the frontier as the defining factor behind the development of the American national character. It became the dominant paradigm in the study of the American West for half a century, and its influence can still be felt in the way that the history of the West is understood. More significantly still, it percolated into popular culture, reinforcing the predominant picture of America as, in Ronald Reagan's formulation, "hopeful, bighearted, idealistic—daring, decent and fair." Finally, Turner's thesis regarding the frontier in American history inspired the study of the frontier experience in a wide variety of other historical contexts. It is hard to overstate its impact.

Following the Turner text is a reproduction of a nineteenth-century painting by an otherwise unremarkable Brooklyn artist named John Gast. The painting is titled *American Progress,* and it was commissioned as part of a promotion for a travel guide. It was reproduced in both color and black and white as a lithograph, so it had a wider audience than a painting alone would have had. It captures the dominant American attitude in the nineteenth century toward the West and toward Native Americans.

Next comes a set of documents that respond to Turner and to Americans' conception of their past as the heroic and happy westward march of European civilization, reformed in a uniquely democratic American mode on the frontier. They were composed by Chief Joseph, an extraordinary character in American history. Chief Joseph was a leader of the Native American people known to us as the Nez Percé. The documents reproduced here contain items from Chief Joseph's dealings with the federal government, his surrender speech, and his request to the federal government to be allowed to leave the restrictive and destructive circumstances of the Oklahoma Indian territory and to return to his native lands. They contain his side of the story of U.S.–Nez Percé relations. It is also significant that he bases his request both on the beliefs and values of his people and on the practices, freedoms, and frontier values that America claimed to stand for.

The third text is excerpted from Owen Wister's famous novel of the Old West, *The Virginian* (1902). Wister (1860–1938) was a member of the east coast elite, who came of age at a time when America was experiencing rapid urban growth because of industrialization and new waves of immigration. He feared, as did Theodore Roosevelt, that America would lose its virility and its leadership in the mass cities of the Gilded Age. Having lived in the West for a while and visited it over several summers, Wister saw the Western frontier as a forge for exceptional characters and as an antidote for the problems he saw facing America. His novel helped create a "literary West," in which the American self-identity of rugged individualism was constantly reaffirmed and reinforced.

Following this, there is the text of a speech by President Ronald Reagan on space and the frontier. It is notable that this speech was part of the celebration of American Independence Day on July 4, 1982. In it, Reagan highlighted explicitly the connections between America's character as a frontier nation and its role in the exploration and conquest of space. This speech indicates the ongoing significance of the frontier in Americans' self-image, because they continue to see themselves as rugged explorers and space as "the final frontier."

From America, we turn to southern Africa and to a different frontier environment. In southern Africa, European expansion and British imperial encroachment gave rise to two distinctive national identities: the Zulu and the Afrikaner. Each of these cultures was framed in the context of a frontier experience. The first set of southern African documents relates to the great leader Shaka (1787–1828) and the way that he helped forge a Zulu identity via frontier conquest and cultural absorption. The first document is an oral history record of Shaka's great battle against Zwide and his methods of empire building. It was narrated by Jantshi ka Nongila, who learned about Zulu history from his father, a former lieutenant in Shaka's army. Nongila's testimony presents a vivid Zulu interpretation and memory of the way that Shaka forged a Zulu identity via frontier conquest and cultural absorption.

The second text is a Zulu *izibongo*. An *izibongo*, or "praise poem," primarily served to portray the character of a chief and his rule, but it also expressed popular attitudes about a chief's rule. Although the *izibongo* reproduced here was not written down until the latter part of the nineteenth century, scholars believe that it most likely embodies images of Shaka from an earlier era. The praise poem emphasizes Shaka's greatness, but there is also a sense of the cost that Shaka's restless energy and imperial expansion along a constantly moving frontier imposed on southern Africa.

The final Zulu document is a modern *izibongo* published in 1979 by Mazisi Kunene (1930–), a well-known Zulu poet and political leader. At the time this was written, South Africa was ruled by a white government based on a policy of severe racial segregation and discrimination, known as *apartheid*. Although Kunene was well versed in Zulu poetry and knew the traditional *izibongo* about Shaka well, he wrote his *izibongo* with an eye to the problems and challenges that faced the Zulu in apartheid-dominated South Africa. In this text, Shaka's role as a leader and the process of imperial expansion through frontier war and absorption are reconfigured once again, partially in response to the realities of life under the apartheid system.

Interestingly enough, the white Afrikaners[1] who established the apartheid system in South Africa had their own frontier myths, which comprise the final set of readings in this chapter. The first document is Piet Retief's "Manifesto of the Emigrant Farmers," written in 1837. Retief (1780–1838) was one of the leaders of the "Great Trek," a name given to the expansion of Afrikaner presence and power into the interior regions of southern Africa in the 1830s and 1840s. His "Manifesto" is an assertion of the goals and beliefs behind the exodus, as well as a statement of Afrikaner grievances against the British who then ruled the Cape Colony.

The second text in this section is a recollection of the events surrounding the Battle of Blood River (1848) by Sarel Cilliers (1801–1871), one of the key participants. This battle between the Afrikaners and the Zulu was a decisive victory for the Afrikaners and allowed them to proceed with their plan to settle in the interior. Cilliers was a man who inspired the Afrikaners with his vision of the religious rightness of their cause. In his interpretation, the *voortrekker* [pioneers] frontier wars with the Zulu expressed the working out of a divinely ordained Afrikaner destiny and identity.

The final document is the text of a speech by Daniel Malan, the Afrikaner political leader and prime minister (1848–1954) who helped establish apartheid. The speech was given on the 1938 anniversary of the Great Trek. Titled "The Second Great Trek," the speech was a call for a reestablishment of Afrikaner separateness, and it was a reaffirmation of the frontier identity justified by Retief and made sacred by Cilliers. The speech demonstrates again the amazing durability of the frontier myth, and it mirrors the way that the Zulu and American political leaders, Kunene and Reagan, continued to connect the collective identities of their people with frontier experiences and identities.

In their various ways, the texts reproduced here demonstrate the significance of frontier experiences in modern history and the centrality of frontier ideals to the self-conceptions of many peoples. Perhaps more so even than in earlier times, frontier contacts in modern times produced conflict. This conflict contributed to radically different views of the nature of the encounter between cultures and, in fact, to very distinct understandings of the frontier itself. It is those different views and the way that they both reflected and shaped the self-image of the various cultures involved in these frontier encounters that are the subject of this chapter.

CHAPTER QUESTIONS

1. How are frontiers defined in the documents included in this chapter? Identify specific words that point to different understandings of frontier.
2. How do frontiers shape the identity of self? How do they inform a culture's images of other peoples and cultures?
3. How is the frontier identity related to power? In your opinion, is supremacy crucial to forming a positive frontier identity?
4. How do myths and images of the frontier shape national identity? Why do they continue to shape the way that peoples and their leaders look at the world?
5. Do any frontiers exist in our contemporary world? If so, how does the operation and impact of any current frontier compare with the pictures presented in this chapter?

THE FRONTIER IN AMERICAN HISTORY
The Frontier and American Identity

Frederick Jackson Turner's "Frontier Thesis" is one of the most significant paradigms in American historical writing. Turner (1861–1932) was born in Portage, Wisconsin, a region that had been part of the frontier itself not long before his birth. Drawing an interest in history from his father, Turner earned a Ph.D. in American history from Johns Hopkins University in 1890. He taught at both the University of Wisconsin and at Harvard University until 1924. He first presented these ideas in a talk delivered at the American Historical Association Convention in Chicago in 1893. It was written in the wake of an 1890 Census Bureau report that proclaimed the disappearance of the frontier in America.

In this piece, Turner presents the frontier experience as a process that reproduced itself in the march westward of American civilization. As such, it was a common process, mixing migrants from different eastern states and European nations into a new amalgam and allowing Americans from different regions to identify with each other's experiences. Moreover, the transplanting of European values and customs to the uncivilized and untamed borderlands of the American frontier transformed the values and customs and created a new set of distinctive cultural norms that became the common property of the new men and women the experience produced. Turner was in a sense answering the question posed by the French-American Hector St. John de Crèvecoeur in 1782, "What then is the American, this new man?" He is, Turner would have it, what the frontier made him. Here was the crucible in which was forged American character and American exceptionalism.

Following the selection by Turner is a reproduction of an 1872 painting by John Gast, titled *American Progress*. Gast's contribution to this painting was largely that of carrying out the instructions and giving form to the ideas of the publisher George Crofutt. It was Crofutt who conceived of the picture as a beautiful, white woman, floating with the "Star of Empire" on her brow, a schoolbook under her arm, and a coil of telegraph wire in her hand, unwinding as she moved westward away from the cities of the east and the Mississippi River. Although all of the elements of the painting seem to have been Crofutt's, who had lithographs of the painting produced to help promote his travel guides, the painting can be taken to be a physical representation of the idea of "manifest destiny," according to which the United States was destined by God to control the land "from sea to shining sea." It constitutes a romanticized, highly symbolic, yet rich presentation of the frontier and what it entailed for both whites and Native Americans.[2]

The documents chosen to respond to Turner and Gast provide a quite different view of the frontier experience. They were composed by a remarkable individual known to us as Chief Joseph (1840–1904), the leader of the Nez Percé, known in his people's language as *Hin-mah-too-yah-lat-keht*, or "Thunder Rolling Down the Mountain." As he indicates, his people assisted Meriwether Lewis and William Clark on their historic journey (1803–1806), and without Nez Percé aid they probably would have died. These friendly relations were repaid by conquest. White settlers took most of their land, and when the U.S. government tried to force them onto a small reservation in 1877, the Nez Percé tried to flee to Canada. Their experience presents a startling example of a people trying to escape from America and to flee from the onrushing path of Manifest Destiny. They managed to evade pursuing U.S. Army forces for seventy-five days and over thirteen hundred miles before Chief Joseph and the six hundred men, women, and children of his tribe were captured. Their tactics on this march are still studied, and they almost succeeded in reaching Canada. After their surrender, they were forcibly shipped to the Indian Country of Oklahoma, where disease and hardship wreaked further havoc among the survivors. The documents reproduced here contain items from Chief Joseph's dealings with the federal government, his surrender speech, and his request to the federal government to be allowed to leave the restrictive and destructive circumstances of the Oklahoma Indian Territory and to return to his native lands. They present a very different view of the frontier and of its effects on some Americans (the Nez Percé). In addition, in his request for release from the Indian Territory, he presents a picture of the kind of life Native Americans ought to be allowed to live on the frontier that compares favorably with the one presented by Turner.

1. According to Turner, how did the frontier "Americanize" new settlers? Conversely, what impact did "civilization" have on Native American societies and ways of life? What specific words and phrases did Turner use to describe the America of the Native Americans?

2. List the different aspects of American life that have been influenced by the frontier. What specific words and phrases did Turner use to describe the America of the Native Americans? How does John Gast's 1872 painting *American Progress* (Figure 8.1, p. 249) compare with Turner's thesis? Would the artist agree with Turner? How does Gast's painting capture American attitudes and perceptions about the West and about Native Americans?

3. What role has the frontier played in shaping American character, according to Turner? How does this distinguish us from other peoples? Was Turner correct to make it the central experience of American history, at least up to his day?

4. How did the image of the frontier change when it was viewed from the Native American perspective? What does it say about American policy that U.S. soldiers were used to prevent a people from leaving American territory?

5. Turner asserted that the frontier experience gave Americans a common, practical, and democratic approach to things. Examine the advice that Chief Joseph gave on how to treat the Indians. How does his description of proper policy compare with the frontier ideal presented by Turner?

"THE SIGNIFICANCE OF THE FRONTIER IN AMERICAN HISTORY" (1893)

Frederick Jackson Turner

In a recent bulletin of the Superintendent of the Census for 1890 appear these significant words: "Up to and including 1880 the country had a frontier of settlement, but at present the unsettled area has been so broken into by isolated bodies of settlement that there can hardly be said to be a frontier line. In the discussion of its extent, its westward movement, etc., it can not, therefore, any longer have a place in the census reports." This brief official statement marks the closing of a great historic movement. Up to our own day American history has been in a large degree the history of the

Source: Frederick Jackson Turner, *The Frontier in American History* (New York: H. Holt and Company, 1920), 1–3, 4, 6, 7, 9–15, 22–24, 27–33, 35, 37–38.

colonization of the Great West. The existence of an area of free land, its continuous recession, and the advance of American settlement westward, explain American development.

Behind institutions, behind constitutional forms and modifications, lie the vital forces that call these organs into life and shape them to meet changing conditions. The peculiarity of American institutions is the fact that they have been compelled to adapt themselves to the changes of an expanding people—to the changes involved in crossing a continent, in winning a wilderness, and in developing at each area of this progress out of the primitive economic and political conditions of the frontier into the complexity of city life. Said Calhoun* in 1817, "We are great, and rapidly—I was about to say fearfully—growing!" So saying, he touched the distinguishing feature of American life. All peoples show development. . . . In the case of most nations, however, the development has occurred in a limited area; and if the nation has expanded, it has met other growing peoples whom it has conquered. But in the case of the United States we have a different phenomenon. Limiting our attention to the Atlantic coast, we have the familiar phenomenon of the evolution of institutions in a limited area, such as the rise of representative government; into complex organs; the progress from primitive industrial society, without division of labor, up to manufacturing civilization. But we have in addition to this a recurrence of the process of evolution in each western area reached in the process of expansion. Thus American development has exhibited not merely advance along a single line, but a return to primitive conditions on a continually advancing frontier line, and a new development for that area. American social development has been continually beginning over again on the frontier. This perennial rebirth, this fluidity of American life, this expansion westward with its new opportunities, its continuous touch with the simplicity of primitive society, furnish the forces dominating American character. The true point of view in the history of this nation is not the Atlantic coast, it is the Great West. . . .

In this advance, the frontier is the outer edge of the wave—the meeting point between savagery and civilization. . . .

The American frontier is sharply distinguished from the European frontier—a fortified boundary line running through dense populations. The most significant thing about the American frontier is, that it lies at the hither edge of free land. . . .

In the settlement of America we have to observe how European life entered the continent, and how America modified and developed that life and reacted on Europe. . . . The frontier is the line of most rapid and effective Americanization. The wilderness masters the colonist. It finds him a European in dress, industries, tools, modes of travel, and thought. It takes him from the railroad car and puts him in the birch canoe. It strips off the garments of civilization and arrays him in the hunting shirt and the moccasin. It puts him in the log cabin of the Cherokee and Iroquois and runs an Indian palisade around him. Before long he has gone to planting Indian corn and plowing with a sharp stick, he shouts the war cry and takes the scalp in orthodox Indian fashion. In short, at the frontier the environment is at first too strong for the man. He must accept the conditions which it furnishes, or perish, and so he fits himself into

---

*South Carolina Senator John C. Calhoun.

the Indian clearings and follows the Indian trails. Little by little he transforms the wilderness, but the outcome is not the old Europe. . . . The fact is, that here is a new product that is American. At first, the frontier was the Atlantic coast. It was the frontier of Europe in a very real sense. Moving westward, the frontier became more and more American. . . . Thus the advance of the frontier has meant a steady movement away from the influence of Europe, a steady growth of independence on American lines. And to study this advance, the men who grew up under these conditions, and the po-litical, economic, and social results of it, is to study the really American part of our history. . . .

The "West," as a self-conscious section, began to evolve. . . . Grund,* writing in 1836, declares: "It appears then that the universal disposition of Americans to emi-grate to the western wilderness, in order to enlarge their dominion over inanimate na-ture, is the actual result of an expansive power which is inherent in them, and which by continually agitating all classes of society is constantly throwing a large portion of the whole population on the extreme confines of the State, in order to gain space for its development. . . ."

In these successive frontiers we find natural boundary lines which have served to mark and to affect the characteristics of the frontiers. . . . Each was won by a series of Indian wars.

At the Atlantic frontier one can study the germs of processes repeated at each successive frontier. We have the complex European life sharply precipitated by the wilderness into the simplicity of primitive conditions. The first frontier had to meet its Indian question, its question of the disposition of the public domain, of the means of intercourse with older settlements, of the extension of political organization, of reli-gious and educational activity. And the settlement of these and similar questions for one frontier served as a guide for the next. . . . Each tier of new States has found in the older ones material for its constitutions. Each frontier has made similar contribu-tions to American character. . . .

Loria,† the Italian economist, . . . [says,] "America has the key to the historical enigma which Europe has sought for centuries in vain, and the land which has no his-tory reveals luminously the course of universal history." There is much truth in this. The United States lies like a huge page in the history of society. Line by line as we read this continental page from West to East we find the record of social evolution. It begins with the Indian and the hunter; it goes on to tell of the disintegration of sav-agery by the entrance of the trader, the pathfinder of civilization; we read the annals of the pastoral stage in ranch life; the exploitation of the soil by the raising of unro-tated crops of corn and wheat in sparsely settled farming communities; the intensive culture of the denser farm settlement; and finally the manufacturing organization with city and factory system.

Why was it that the Indian trader passed so rapidly across the continent? . . . The explanation of the rapidity of this advance is connected with the effects of the trader

---

*Francis Joseph Grund (1805–1863) was an Austrian-born American journalist, who wrote *The Amer-icans in Their Moral, Social and Political Relations*.

†Achille Loria, author of *Analisi della proprieta capitalista* (Turin, 1889).

on the Indian. The trading post left the unarmed tribes at the mercy of those that had purchased fire-arms—a truth which the Iroquois Indians wrote in blood, and so the remote and unvisited tribes gave eager welcome to the trader. "The savages," wrote La Salle, "take better care of us French than of their own children; from us only can they get guns and goods." This accounts for the trader's power and the rapidity of his advance. Thus the disintegrating forces of civilization entered the wilderness. Every river valley and Indian trail became a fissure in Indian society, and so that society became honeycombed. Long before the pioneer farmer appeared on the scene, primitive Indian life had passed away. . . . [T]he Indian trade pioneered the way for civilization. The buffalo trail became the Indian trail, and this became the trader's "trace"; the trails widened into roads, and the roads into turnpikes, and these in turn were transformed into railroads. . . . The trading posts reached by these trails were on the sites of Indian villages which had been placed in positions suggested by nature; and these trading posts, situated so as to command the water systems of the country, have grown into such cities as Albany, Pittsburgh, Detroit, Chicago, St. Louis, Council Bluffs, and Kansas City. Thus civilization in America has followed the arteries made by geology, pouring an ever richer tide through them, until at last the slender paths of aboriginal intercourse have been broadened and interwoven into the complex mazes of modern commercial lines; the wilderness has been interpenetrated by lines of civilization growing ever more numerous. It is like the steady growth of a complex nervous system for the originally simple, inert continent. . . .

The effect of the Indian frontier as a consolidating agent in our history is important. From the close of the seventeenth century various intercolonial congresses have been called to treat with Indians and establish common measures of defense. Particularism was strongest in colonies with no Indian frontier. This frontier stretched along the western border like a cord of union. The Indian was a common danger, demanding united action. . . . It is evident that the unifying tendencies of the Revolutionary period were facilitated by the previous cooperation in the regulation of the frontier. In this connection may be mentioned the importance of the frontier, from that day to this, as a military training school, keeping alive the power of resistance to aggression, and developing the stalwart and rugged qualities of the frontiersman. . . .

First, we note that the frontier promoted the formation of a composite nationality for the American people. The coast was preponderantly English, but the later tides of continental immigration flowed across to the free lands. . . . Very generally these . . . were of non-English stock. In the crucible of the frontier the immigrants were Americanized, liberated, and fused into a mixed race, English in neither nationality nor characteristics. The process has gone on from the early days to our own. . . .

The legislation which most developed the powers of the national government, and played the largest part in its activity, was conditioned on the frontier. Writers have discussed the subjects of tariff, land, and internal improvement, as subsidiary to the slavery question. But when American history comes to be rightly viewed it will be seen that the slavery question is an incident. . . . The growth of nationalism and the evolution of American political institutions were dependent on the advance of the frontier. . . .

But it was not merely in legislative action that the frontier worked against the sectionalism of the coast. The economic and social characteristics of the frontier worked against sectionalism. The men of the frontier had closer resemblances to the Middle region than to either of the other sections. . . . The Middle region, entered by New York harbor, was an open door to all Europe. The tide-water part of the South represented typical Englishmen, modified by a warm climate and servile labor, and living in baronial fashion on great plantations; New England stood for a special English movement—Puritanism. The Middle region was less English than the other sections. It had a wide mixture of nationalities, a varied society, the mixed town and county system of local government, a varied economic life, many religious sects. In short, it was a region mediating between New England and the South, and the East and the West. It represented that composite. . . . It was democratic and nonsectional, if not national; "easy, tolerant, and contented"; rooted strongly in material prosperity. It was typical of the modern United States. It was least sectional. . . . Thus it became the typically American region. . . .

It was this nationalizing tendency of the West that transformed the democracy of Jefferson into the national republicanism of Monroe and the democracy of Andrew Jackson.* The West . . . had a solidarity of its own with national tendencies. On the tide of the Father of Waters,† North and South met and mingled into a nation. Interstate migration went steadily on—a process of cross-fertilization of ideas and institutions. The fierce struggle of the sections over slavery on the western frontier does not diminish the truth of this statement; it proves the truth of it. Slavery was a sectional trait that would not down, but in the West it could not remain sectional. It was the greatest of frontiersmen‡ who declared: "I believe this Government can not endure permanently half slave and half free. It will become all of one thing or all of the other." Nothing works for nationalism like intercourse within the nation. Mobility of population is death to localism, and the western frontier worked irresistibly in unsettling population. The effect reached back from the frontier and affected profoundly the Atlantic coast and even the Old World.

But the most important effect of the frontier has been in the promotion of democracy here and in Europe. As has been indicated, the frontier is productive of individualism. Complex society is precipitated by the wilderness into a kind of primitive organization based on the family. . . . The frontier individualism has from the beginning promoted democracy. The frontier States that came into the Union in the first quarter of a century of its existence came in with democratic suffrage provisions, and had reactive effects of the highest importance upon the older States whose peoples were being attracted there. An extension of the franchise became essential. . . . The rise of democracy as an effective force in the nation came in with western preponderance under Jackson and William Henry Harrison,§ and it meant the triumph of the frontier—with all of its good and with all of its evil elements. An interesting illustration of the tone of frontier democracy in 1830 comes from the same debates in

---

*Thomas Jefferson (1743–1826) was the third president, James Monroe (1758–1831) was the fifth president, and Andrew Jackson (1767–1845) was the seventh president of the United States.
†The Mississippi River.
‡The reference is to Abraham Lincoln (1809–1865), the sixteenth president of the United States.
§William Henry Harrison (1773–1841) was the ninth president of the United States.

the Virginia convention already referred to. A representative from western Virginia declared:

> But, sir, it is not the increase of population in the West which this gentleman ought to fear. It is the energy which the mountain breeze and western habits impart to those emigrants. They are regenerated, politically I mean, sir. They soon become working politicians, and the difference, sir, between a talking and a working politician is immense. The Old Dominion has long been celebrated for producing great orators; the ablest metaphysicians in policy; men that can split hairs in all abstruse questions of political economy. But at home, or when they return from Congress, they have negroes to fan them asleep. But a Pennsylvania, a New York, an Ohio, or a western Virginia statesman, though far inferior in logic, metaphysics, and rhetoric to an old Virginia statesman, has this advantage, that when he returns home he takes off his coat and takes hold of the plow. This gives him bone and muscle, sir, and preserves his republican principles pure and uncontaminated.

So long as free land exists, the opportunity for a competency exists, and economic power secures political power. . . . Steadily the frontier of settlement advanced and carried with it individualism, democracy, and nationalism, and powerfully affected the East and the Old World. . . .

From the conditions of frontier life came intellectual traits of profound importance. The works of travelers along each frontier from colonial days onward describe certain common traits, and these traits have, while softening down, still persisted as survivals in the place of their origin, even when a higher social organization succeeded. The result is that to the frontier the American intellect owes its striking characteristics. That coarseness and strength combined with acuteness and inquisitiveness; that practical, inventive turn of mind, quick to find expedients; that masterful grasp of material things, lacking in the artistic but powerful to effect great ends; that restless, nervous energy; that dominant individualism, working for good and for evil, and withal that buoyancy and exuberance which comes with freedom—these are traits of the frontier, or traits called out elsewhere because of the existence of the frontier. Since the days when the fleet of Columbus sailed into the waters of the New World, America has been another name for opportunity, and the people of the United States have taken their tone from the incessant expansion which has not only been open but has even been forced upon them. . . . [E]ach frontier did indeed furnish a new field of opportunity, a gate of escape from the bondage of the past; and freshness, and confidence, and scorn of older society, impatience of its restraints and its ideas, and indifference to its lessons, have accompanied the frontier. What the Mediterranean Sea was to the Greeks, breaking the bond of custom, offering new experiences, calling out new institutions and activities, that, and more, the ever retreating frontier has been to the United States directly, and to the nations of Europe more remotely. And now, four centuries from the discovery of America, at the end of a hundred years of life under the Constitution, the frontier has gone, and with its going has closed the first period of American history.

Figure 8.1 John Gast, *American Progress* (1872)

SELECTED STATEMENTS, SPEECHES, AND LETTERS (1877–1879)

Chief Joseph of Nez Percé

The Nez Percé Pentalogue, or "Five Rules," Passed from Father to Son as Related by Chief Joseph

It is a disgrace to tell a lie. Speak only the truth.

Treat all men as they treat you.

Never be the first to break a bargain.

It is a shame for one man to take another man's property or his wife. . . .

The Great Spirit sees and hears everything. He never forgets. Hereafter He will give each man a spirit home according to his merits; if he has been good he will have a good home, if he has been a bad man he will have a bad home.

Source: Chester Anders Fee, *Chief Joseph: The Biography of a Great Indian* (New York: Wilson-Erickson, 1936), 4, 26, 78–79, 262–63, 281–82.

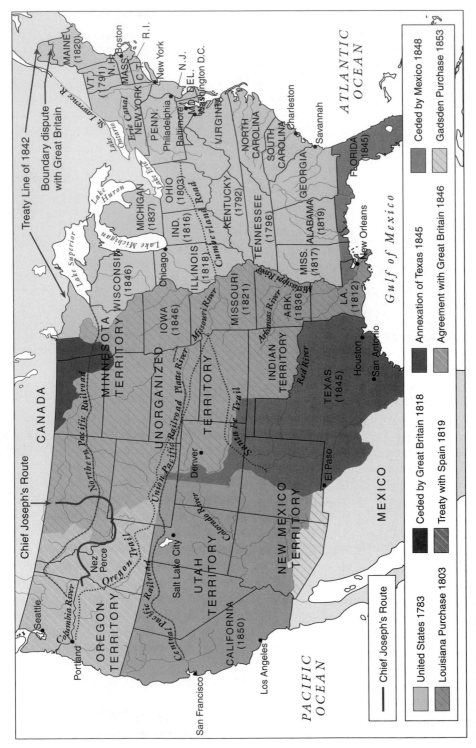

Map 8.1 Chief Joseph's Route

Chief Joseph Describes the Relations between the Whites and the Nez Percé

The first white men of your people who came to our country were named Lewis and Clark. They brought many things which our people had never seen. They talked straight and our people gave them a great feast as proof that their hearts were friendly. They made presents to our chiefs and our people made presents to them. We had a great many horses of which we gave them what they needed, and they gave us guns and tobacco in return. All the Nez Percé made friends with Lewis and Clark and agreed to let them pass through their country and never to make war on white men. This promise the Nez Percé have never broken.

For a short time we lived quietly. But this could not last. White men had found gold in the mountains around the land of the Winding Water. They stole a great many horses from us and we could not get them back because we were Indians. The white men told lies for each other. They drove off a great many of our cattle. Some white men branded our young cattle so they could claim them. We had no friends who would plead our cause before the law councils. It seemed to me that some of the white men in Wallowa were doing these things on purpose to get up a war. They knew we were not strong enough to fight them. I labored hard to avoid trouble and bloodshed. We gave up some of our country to the white men, thinking that then we could have peace. We were mistaken. The white men would not let us alone. We could have avenged our wrongs many times, but we did not. Whenever the Government has asked for help against other Indians we have never refused. When the white men were few and we were strong we could have killed them off, but the Nez Percé wishes to live at peace.

On account of the treaty made by the other bands of the Nez Percé the white man claimed my lands. We were troubled with white men crowding over the line. Some of them were good men, and we lived on peaceful terms with them, but they were not all good. Nearly every year the agent came over from Lapwai and ordered us to the reservation. We always replied that we were satisfied to live in Wallowa. We were careful to refuse the presents or annuities which he offered.

Through all the years since the white man came to Wallowa we have been threatened and taunted by them and the treaty Nez Percé. They have given us no rest. We have had a few good friends among the white men, and they have always advised my people to bear these taunts without fighting. Our young men are quick tempered and I have had great trouble in keeping them from doing rash things. I have carried a heavy load on my back ever since I was a boy. I learned then that we were but few while the white men were many, and that we could not hold our own with them. We were like deer. They were like grizzly bears. We had a small country. Their country was large. We were contented to let things remain as the Great Spirit Chief made them. They were not; and would change the mountains and rivers if they did not suit them.

Chief Joseph's Speech at His Surrender in the Bear Paw Mountains, 1877

Tell General Howard that I know his heart. What he told me before I have in my heart. I am tired of fighting. Our chiefs are killed. Looking Glass is dead, *Tu-hul-hil-sote* is dead. The old men are all dead. It is the young men who now say yes or no.

He who led the young men is dead.* It is cold and we have no blankets. The little children are freezing to death. My people—some of them have run away to the hills and have no blankets and no food. No one knows where they are—perhaps freezing to death. I want to have time to look for my children and see how many of them I can find. Maybe I shall find them among the dead. Hear me, my chiefs, my heart is sick and sad. From where the sun now stands I will fight no more against the white man.

A Letter Written by Chief Joseph after a Visit to Washington, D.C., 1879

At last I was granted permission to come to Washington and bring my friend Yellow Bull and our interpreter with me. I am glad I came. I have shaken hands with a good many friends, but there are some things I want to know which no one seems able to explain. I cannot understand how the Government sends a man out to fight us, as it did General Miles, and then breaks his word.† Such a government has something wrong about it. I cannot understand why so many chiefs are allowed to talk so many different ways, and promise so many different things. I have seen the Great Father Chief [President Hayes]; the Next Great Chief [Secretary of the Interior]; the Commissioner Chief; the Law Chief; and many other law chiefs [Congressmen] and they all say they are my friends, and that I shall have justice, but while all their mouths talk right I do not understand why nothing is done for my people. I have heard talk and talk but nothing is done. Good words do not last long unless they amount to something. Words do not pay for my dead people. They do not pay for my country now overrun by white men. They do not protect my father's grave. They do not pay for my horses and cattle. Good words do not give me back my children. Good words will not make good the promise of your war chief, General Miles. Good words will not give my people good health and stop them from dying. Good words will not give my people a home where they can live in peace and take care of themselves. I am tired of talk that comes to nothing. It makes my heart sick when I remember all the good words and all the broken promises. There has been too much talking by men who had no right to talk. Too many misinterpretations have been made; too many misunderstandings have come up between the white men and the Indians. If the white man wants to live in peace with the Indian he can live in peace. There need be no trouble. Treat all men alike. Give them the same laws. Give them all an even chance to live and grow. All men were made by the same Great Spirit Chief. They are all brothers. The earth is the mother of all people, and all people should have equal rights upon it. You might as well expect all rivers to run backward as that any man who was born a free man should be contented penned up and denied liberty to go where he pleases. If you tie a horse to a stake, do you expect he will grow fat? If you pen an Indian up on a small spot of earth and compel him to stay there, he will not be contented nor will he grow and prosper. I have asked some of the Great White Chiefs where they get their authority to say to the Indian that he shall stay in one place, while he sees white men going where they please. They cannot tell me.

---

*Joseph's brother, Alikut.

†The Nez Percé understood that they would be allowed to return to their own territories, but they were taken to the Indian Territory in Oklahoma, whose climate and environment did not suit them.

I only ask of the Government to be treated as all other men are treated. If I cannot go to my own home, let me have a home in a country where my people will not die so fast. I would like to go to Bitter Root Valley. There my people would be happy; where they are now they are dying. Three have died since I left my camp to come to Washington.

When I think of our condition, my heart is heavy. I see men of my own race treated as outlaws and driven from country to country, or shot down like animals.

I know that my race must change. We cannot hold our own with the white men as we are. We only ask an even chance to live as other men live. We ask to be recognized as men. We ask that the same law shall work alike on all men. If an Indian breaks the law, punish him by the law. If a white man breaks the law, punish him also.

Let me be a free man, free to travel, free to stop, free to work, free to trade where I choose, free to choose my own teachers, free to follow the religion of my fathers, free to talk, think and act for myself—and I will obey every law or submit to the penalty.

Whenever the white man treats the Indian as they treat each other then we shall have no more wars. We shall be all alike—brothers of one father and mother, with one sky above us and one country around us and one government for all. Then the Great Spirit Chief who rules above will smile upon this land and send rain to wash out the bloody spots made by brothers' hands upon the face of the earth. For this time the Indian race is waiting and praying. I hope no more groans of wounded men and women will ever go to the ear of the Great Spirit Chief above, and that all people may be one people. *Hin-mah-too-yah-lat-kekht** has spoken for his people.

Myths of the American West

From real-life figures such as Daniel Boone to fictional characters such as James Fenimore Cooper's Natty Bumppo the frontier hero was a well-established character in American culture by the beginning of the twentieth century. In addition, the "cowboy" West had been the subject of thousands of mass-marketed "dime novels" in the decades between the Civil War and the turn of the century, and Buffalo Bill Cody had enjoyed great commercial success with his Wild West Show. It might seem odd that an archetypal text could appear so late in the development of this cultural tradition, but that is exactly what happened when Owen Wister published his enormously successful novel in 1902. Although the writing can seem stodgy and old-fashioned to us today, Wister's work was much more sophisticated than that of the dime novels. Because of his writing style and because he established so clearly and powerfully certain core themes, Wister produced a foundational text for the American frontier myth. Its cultural resonance was all the more widespread because the 1929 movie version of *The Virginian,* starring Gary Cooper, helped to establish the new "talkies" (movies with sound).

---

*Chief Joseph's name in his native language.

Wister wrote at a time of great changes for the country. The industrialization, urbanization, and immigration of the 1880s and 1890s had fundamentally transformed the nation. From an agrarian, small-town America whose white population overwhelmingly comprised people of British, Irish, and German stock, it had become a nation with large metropolises filled with new immigrants from southern and eastern Europe. This demographic change was accompanied by a shift of power and wealth to the new manufacturing elite—the so-called Robber Barons. Wister shared many similar experiences with Frederick Remington (1861–1909), the famous artist of the West, and with Theodore Roosevelt (1858–1919). All three came from prominent east coast families, had gone to Harvard (Wister and Roosevelt were classmates), and went through a formative life experience in the West. All three were very concerned about these transformations and about what they considered the loss of American virility. It is not surprising, then, that Roosevelt wrote approvingly of Wister's novel. It might also be worthy of note that these men and Frederick Jackson Turner, all of whom were so important to the formulation of the frontier myth, were born within three years of each other.

Wister had gone west in his twenties and had run a large cattle ranch. Although he returned to the East, he frequently revisited the West during the summer. He drew from these experiences hope that the rough-and-tumble frontier environment of the West could select out a new aristocracy of merit. He believed that the equality promised by the Declaration of Independence was an equality of opportunity, and that it would result in inequality, because some people are naturally better than others. This natural and desirable process of social layering was being retarded and subverted in the urbanized East, but it worked as it ought to in the West, and he set out to show this in his novel. The title character had left a decent but monotonous life in Virginia, and it was in the West that his real gifts became obvious. The harsh and unforgiving, yet rich and beautiful, natural environment showed the true character of people, summoning forth and validating innate leadership ability. Lack of refined and "citified" culture did not equate with lack of manners. Rather, true politeness—like true character—emerged in the unrefined, but not uncivilized, environment of the West. The frontier operates like a forge on a blade of steel, burning away impurities and leaving behind a keener, more enduring edge.

QUESTIONS TO CONSIDER

1. Describe the author's view of the frontier on the basis of these passages. Compare his views with those of Frederick Jackson Turner.
2. List the attributes of the Virginian as an ideal cowboy. How is Trampas the antithesis of this ideal type?
3. The Virginian says that out West whatever you do "you've got to do it WELL." What does this statement say about the nature of the frontier and its relationship to the American ideal of self-reliance?

4. Summarize what the judge says to Miss Wood. How does Judge Henry's justification of vigilante justice compare with Turner's interpretation of the frontier?

5. What do you think of the justification of vigilante law? Is this attitude still current in America today? Should it be?

THE VIRGINIAN: A HORSEMAN OF THE PLAINS (1902)

Owen Wister

[The book opens with Wister's note to the reader.]

Certain of the newspapers, when this book was first announced, made a mistake most natural upon seeing the sub-title as it then stood, A TALE OF SUNDRY ADVENTURES. "This sounds like a historical novel," said one of them, meaning (I take it) a colonial romance. As it now stands, the title will scarce lead to such interpretation; yet none the less is this book historical—quite as much so as any colonial romance. Indeed, when you look at the root of the matter, it is a colonial romance. For Wyoming between 1874 and 1890 was a colony as wild as was Virginia one hundred years earlier. As wild, with a scantier population, and the same primitive joys and dangers. There were, to be sure, not so many Chippendale settees.

We know quite well the common understanding of the term "historical novel." . . . Any narrative which presents faithfully a day and a generation is of necessity historical; and this one presents Wyoming between 1874 and 1890. Had you left New York or San Francisco at ten o'clock this morning, by noon the day after to-morrow you could step out at Cheyenne. There you would stand at the heart of the world that is the subject of my picture, yet you would look around you in vain for the reality. It is a vanished world. No journeys, save those which memory can take, will bring you to it now. The mountains are there, far and shining, and the sunlight, and the infinite earth, and the air that seems forever the true fountain of youth, but where is the buffalo, and the wild antelope, and where the horseman with his pasturing thousands? So like its old self does the sage-brush seem when revisited, that you wait for the horseman to appear.

But he will never come again. He rides in his historic yesterday. You will no more see him gallop out of the unchanging silence than you will see Columbus on the unchanging sea come sailing from Palos with his caravels. . . .

What is become of the horseman, the cowpuncher, the last romantic figure upon our soil? For he was romantic. Whatever he did, he did with his might. The bread that he earned was earned hard, the wages that he squandered were squandered hard,—half

Source: Owen Wister, *The Virginian: A Horseman of the Plains* (New York: Macmillan, 1929), ix, x, xi, 1–4, 11–12, 27–30, 401–02, 435–39.

a year's pay sometimes gone in a night,—"blown in," as he expressed it, or "blowed in," to be perfectly accurate. Well, he will be here among us always, invisible, waiting his chance to live and play as he would like. His wild kind has been among us always, since the beginning: a young man with his temptations, a hero without wings.

The cow-puncher's ungoverned hours did not unman him. If he gave his word, he kept it; Wall Street would have found him behind the times. Nor did he talk lewdly to women; Newport [Rhode Island] would have thought him old-fashioned. He and his brief epoch make a complete picture, for in themselves they were as complete as the pioneers of the land or the explorers of the sea.

[The story begins. The narrator is an easterner who has come West to visit his friend, Judge Henry, a wealthy and powerful Wyoming ranch owner, who is the Virginian's employer. The narrator first encounters the Virginian at the train station; he has been sent to escort the judge's friend (the narrator) to the ranch. Wister provides the fullest description of the Virginian in these introductory scenes.]

Some notable sight was drawing the passengers, both men and women, to the window; and therefore I rose and crossed the [train]car to see what it was. I saw near the track an enclosure, and round it some laughing men, and inside it some whirling dust, and amid the dust some horses, plunging, huddling, and dodging. They were cow ponies in a corral, and one of them would not be caught, no matter who threw the rope. We had plenty of time to watch this sport, for our train had stopped that the engine might take water at the tank before it pulled us up beside the station platform of Medicine Bow. We were also six hours late, and starving for entertainment. The pony in the corral was wise, and rapid of limb. Have you seen a skilful boxer watch his antagonist with a quiet, incessant eye? Such an eye as this did the pony keep upon whatever man took the rope. The man might pretend to look at the weather, which was fine; or he might affect earnest conversation with a bystander: it was bootless. The pony saw through it. No feint hoodwinked him. This animal was thoroughly a man of the world. His undistracted eye stayed fixed upon the dissembling foe, and the gravity of his horse-expression made the matter one of high comedy. Then the rope would sail out at him, but he was already elsewhere. . . . Through the window-glass of our Pullman the thud of their mischievous hoofs reached us, and the strong, humorous curses of the cow-boys. Then for the first time I noticed a man who sat on the high gate of the corral, looking on. For he now climbed down with the undulations of a tiger, smooth and easy, as if his muscles flowed beneath his skin. The others had all visibly whirled the rope, some of them even shoulder high. I did not see his arm lift or move. He appeared to hold the rope down low, by his leg. But like a sudden snake I saw the noose go out its length and fall true; and the thing was done. As the captured pony walked in with a sweet, church-door expression, our train moved slowly on to the station, and a passenger remarked, "That man knows his business." . . .

[The visitor disembarks from the train and meets the Virginian.]

Lounging there at ease against the wall was a slim young giant, more beautiful than pictures. His broad, soft hat was pushed back; a loose-knotted, dull-scarlet handkerchief sagged from his throat; and one casual thumb was hooked in the cartridge-belt that slanted across his hips. He had plainly come many miles from somewhere across the vast horizon, as the dust upon him showed. His boots were white with it. His overalls were gray with it. The weather-beaten bloom of his face shone through it duskily, as the ripe peaches look upon their trees in a dry season. But no dinginess of travel or shabbiness of attire could tarnish the splendor that radiated from his youth and strength. . . . He walked toward me, and I saw that in inches he was not a giant. He was not more than six feet. . . . But in his eye, in his face, in his step, in the whole man, there dominated a something potent to be felt, I should think, by man or woman. . . . Here in flesh and blood was a truth which I had long believed in words, but never met before. The creature we call a GENTLEMAN lies deep in the hearts of thousands that are born without chance to master the outward graces of the type.

[They spend that evening in town. The Virginian runs into an old friend, Steve, who affectionately calls the Virginian a "son-of-a—" without any objection being raised by the Virginian. A little bit later, the Virginian gets involved in a card game with the man who becomes his arch-enemy, Trampas, who tries to use the same term and gets a much different response.]

Five or six players sat over in the corner at a round table where counters were piled. Their eyes were close upon their cards, and one seemed to be dealing a card at a time to each, with pauses and betting between. Steve was there and the Virginian; the others were new faces.

"No place for amatures," repeated the voice; and now I saw that it was the dealer's. There was in his countenance the same ugliness that his words conveyed.

"Who's that talkin'?" said one of the men near me, in a low voice.

"Trampas."

"What's he?"

"Cow-puncher, bronco-buster, tin-horn, most anything."

"Who's he talkin' at?"

"Think it's the black-headed guy [the Virginian] he's talking at."

"That ain't supposed to be safe, is it?"

"Guess we're all goin' to find out in a few minutes."

"Been trouble between 'em?"

"They've not met before. Trampas don't enjoy losin' to a stranger." . . .

There had been silence over in the corner; but now the man Trampas spoke again. "AND ten," said he, sliding out some chips from before him. Very strange it was to hear him, how he contrived to make those words a personal taunt. The Virginian was looking at his cards. He might have been deaf.

"AND twenty," said the next player, easily.

The next threw his cards down.

It was now the Virginian's turn to bet, or leave the game, and he did not speak at once. Therefore Trampas spoke. "Your bet, you son-of-a—."

The Virginian's pistol came out, and his hand lay on the table, holding it unaimed. And with a voice as gentle as ever, the voice that sounded almost like a caress, but drawling a very little more than usual, so that there was almost a space between each word, he issued his orders to the man Trampas: "When you call me that, SMILE." And he looked at Trampas across the table.

Yes, the voice was gentle. But in my ears it seemed as if somewhere the bell of death was ringing; and silence, like a stroke, fell on the large room. All men present, as if by some magnetic current, had become aware of this crisis. In my ignorance, and the total stoppage of my thoughts, I stood stock-still, and noticed various people crouching, or shifting their positions.

"Sit quiet," said the dealer, scornfully to the man near me. "Can't you see he don't want to push trouble? He has handed Trampas the choice to back down or draw his steel."

Then, with equal suddenness and ease, the room came out of its strangeness. Voices and cards, the click of chips, the puff of tobacco, glasses lifted to drink,—this level of smooth relaxation hinted no more plainly of what lay beneath than does the surface tell the depth of the sea.

For Trampas had made his choice. And that choice was not to "draw his steel." If it was knowledge that he sought, he had found it, and no mistake! We heard no further reference to what he had been pleased to style "amatures." In no company would the black-headed man who had visited Arizona be rated a novice at the cool art of self-preservation.

One doubt remained: what kind of a man was Trampas? A public back-down is an unfinished thing,—for some natures at least. I looked at his face, and thought it sullen, but tricky rather than courageous.

Something had been added to my knowledge also. Once again I had heard applied to the Virginian that epithet which Steve so freely used. The same words, identical to the letter. But this time they had produced a pistol. "When you call me that, SMILE!" So I perceived a new example of the old truth, that the letter means nothing until the spirit gives it life.

[Toward the end of the novel, the Virginian leads a vigilante group that captures and hangs two cattle thieves. One of them is his old friend, Steve. Trampas escapes after killing the remaining member of the gang, an unlucky character known as Shorty. When the narrator and the Virginian find Shorty's body, the Virginian comments on him and on the Wyoming frontier.]

Now back East you can be middling and get along. But if you go to try a thing on in this Western country, you've got to do it WELL. You've got to deal cyards WELL; you've got to steal WELL; and if you claim to be quick with your gun, you must be quick, for you're a public temptation, and some man will not resist trying to prove he is the quicker. You must break all the Commandments WELL in this Western country. . . . This hyeh country is no country for Shorty, for he will be a conspicuous novice all his days.*

[The Virginian doggedly pursues a young woman, Molly Wood, who has come to Wyoming from Vermont to be the schoolteacher. When she discovers that the Virginian has been part of a vigilante group that hung two men, she is horrified, even though they were clearly guilty. Judge Henry, who sent the Virginian on the manhunt, feels

*This passage was in italics in the original to distinguish it as dialogue.

he must try to make her see that his actions were not only not wrong, they were in full right and just. He relates frontier justice to the American constitutional system.]

But when school was out, . . . he [Judge Henry] knocked at her door, ready, as he had put it, to sacrifice his character in the cause of true love.

"Well," he said, coming straight to the point, "some dark things have happened." And when she made no answer to this, he continued: "But you must not misunderstand us. We're too fond of you for that."

"Judge Henry," said Molly Wood, also coming straight to the point, "have you come to tell me that you think well of lynching*?"

He met her. "Of burning Southern negroes in public, no. Of hanging Wyoming cattle thieves in private, yes. You perceive there's a difference, don't you?" . . .

"What is the difference in principle?" she demanded.

"Well," said the Judge, easy and thoughtful, "what do you mean by principle?"

"I didn't think you'd quibble," flashed Molly. "I'm not a lawyer myself."

A man less wise than Judge Henry would have smiled at this, and then war would have exploded hopelessly between them, and harm been added to what was going wrong already. But the Judge knew that he must give to every word that the girl said now his perfect consideration.

"I don't mean to quibble," he assured her. "I know the trick of escaping from one question by asking another. But I don't want to escape from anything you hold me to answer. If you can show me that I am wrong, I want you to do so. But," and here the Judge smiled, "I want you to play fair, too."

"And how am I not?"

"I want you to be just as willing to be put right by me as I am to be put right by you. And so when you use such a word as principle, you must help me to answer by saying what principle you mean. For in all sincerity I see no likeness in principle whatever between burning Southern negroes in public and hanging Wyoming horse-thieves in private. I consider the burning a proof that the South is semi-barbarous, and the hanging a proof that Wyoming is determined to become civilized. We do not torture our criminals when we lynch them. We do not invite spectators to enjoy their death agony. We put no such hideous disgrace upon the United States. We execute our criminals by the swiftest means, and in the quietest way. Do you think the principle is the same?"

Molly had listened to him with attention. "The way is different," she admitted.

"Only the way?"

"So it seems to me. Both defy law and order.

"Ah, but do they both? Now we're getting near the principle."

"Why, yes. Ordinary citizens take the law in their own hands."

"The principle at last!" exclaimed the Judge. "Now tell me some more things. Out of whose hands do they take the law?"

"The court's."

"What made the courts?"

---

*The verb "to lynch" means to hang someone without having had a trial. It is derived from the name of Charles Lynch, an eighteenth-century Virginia planter and justice of the peace.

"I don't understand."

"How did there come to be any courts?"

"The Constitution."

"How did there come to be any Constitution? Who made it?"

"The delegates, I suppose."

"Who made the delegates?"

"I suppose they were elected, or appointed, or something."

"And who elected them?"

"Of course the people elected them."

"Call them the ordinary citizens," said the Judge. "I like your term. They are where the law comes from, you see. For they chose the delegates who made the Constitution that provided for the courts. There's your machinery. These are the hands into which ordinary citizens have put the law. So you see, at best, when they lynch they only take back what they once gave. Now we'll take your two cases that you say are the same in principle. I think that they are not. For in the South they take a negro from jail where he was waiting to be duly hung. The South has never claimed that the law would let him go. But in Wyoming the law has been letting our cattle-thieves go for two years. We are in a very bad way, and we are trying to make that way a little better until civilization can reach us. At present we lie beyond its pale. The courts, or rather the juries, into whose hands we have put the law, are not dealing the law. They are withered hands, or rather they are imitation hands made for show, with no life in them, no grip. They cannot hold a cattle-thief. And so when your ordinary citizen sees this, and sees that he has placed justice in a dead hand, he must take justice back into his own hands where it was once at the beginning of all things. Call this primitive, if you will. But so far from being a DEFIANCE of the law, it is an ASSERTION of it—the fundamental assertion of selfgoverning men, upon whom our whole social fabric is based. There is your principle, Miss Wood, as I see it. Now can you help me to see anything different?"

She could not.

"But perhaps you are of the same opinion still?" the Judge inquired.

"It is all terrible to me," she said.

"Yes; and so is capital punishment terrible. And so is war. And perhaps some day we shall do without them. But they are none of them so terrible as unchecked theft and murder would be."

The Frontier Remembered

Ronald Reagan (1911–2004) was the fortieth president of the United States, serving from 1981 to 1989. Although he had been born in Illinois, he moved to California when he was twenty-six. From then on, he identified strongly with the West, ultimately buying his own ranch and enjoying horseback riding as a leisure activity. Born to an unsuccessful, alcoholic shoe salesman, Reagan valued the opportunities for wealth and success that America had presented him. He identified his life history with the pioneer spirit and frontier experiences of earlier generations of

Americans, so it is not surprising that he would emphasize pioneer themes in an address on America's space program.

The Space Age began with the launching of the first Sputnik satellite by the Soviet Union in 1957. Although the United States had its own space program under development, the fact that the Soviets were the first in space caused a public uproar in the United States, and in those cold war days was perceived to be a definite setback for the United States. The United States launched its first successful satellite in 1958. Over the next few years, other launches followed. A dramatic acceleration of the space effort occurred in May 1961, when President John F. Kennedy committed the United States to putting a man on the moon by the end of the decade, which was achieved when Neil Armstrong and "Buzz" Aldrin stepped onto the lunar surface July 20, 1969.

After the moon landing, unmanned spacecraft were sent out on scientific missions, a giant "skylab" was planned, and other manned space efforts were undertaken, but starting in 1981 the main focus of U.S. space activity became the space shuttle. The shuttles, which unlike earlier spacecraft were reusable, landed in California when the weather in Florida, where the launches took place, did not allow them to land there. The speech presented here was given by President Reagan in the second year of the shuttle program, after the fourth and final orbital test flight. The fact that this landing occurred on Independence Day gave Reagan, who had become known as "the Great Communicator," owing to his effectiveness as a public speaker and the human touch in his speeches, the opportunity to develop certain of his central ideas.

From the very outset, American involvement in space has been conceptualized in terms of the frontier myth. In a speech in September 1962, President Kennedy had presented the effort to put a man on the moon as a continuation of and variation on the familiar American pattern of conquering new frontiers. He asserted that "this country of the United States was not built by those who waited and rested and wished to look behind them. This country was conquered by those who moved forward—and so will space." This was not a new theme for Kennedy, who had made the slogan the "New Frontier" the rallying cry and organizing idea of his successful 1960 presidential campaign. Presidents and presidential candidates strive to strike a mythic resonance between the challenges and policies of the day and the dominant national self-image. Hence we once again encounter the frontier theme and the continuing significance of the frontier in Americans' self-conception.

QUESTIONS TO CONSIDER

1. Identify the specific comparisons that Reagan made between the shuttle program and previous voyagers and explorers in American history. What images did he elicit by means of these references?

2. According to Reagan, why did Americans in the past conquer new frontiers? How does his portrayal of America's movement along frontiers compare with

that in Gast's *American Progress*? How does it compare with the experience of the Nez Percé presented by Chief Joseph?

3. What has the frontier revealed about or developed in American character, according to Reagan? How do his ideas about the frontier compare with those in Wister's *Virginian*? From what you know of Reagan's personal history, do you think he would identify with the Virginian?

4. Aside from the practical military, economic, and scientific benefits, what positive functions does the shuttle program perform for Americans in Reagan's presentation?

5. Can you think of any events in your own life or in your family history that indicate a "frontier spirit" or that fit the idea that the frontier experience is a fundamental formative influence on American character and history?

REMARKS AT THE COMPLETION OF THE FOURTH MISSION OF THE SPACE SHUTTLE *COLUMBIA* (1982)

Ronald Reagan

T.K. and Hank*—as you can see, we've gotten well acquainted already—you've just given the American people a Fourth of July present to remember. I think all of us, all of us who've just witnessed the magnificent sight of the *Columbia* touching down in the California desert, feel a real swelling of pride in our chests.

In the early days of our Republic, Americans watched Yankee Clippers glide across the many oceans of the world, manned by proud and energetic individuals breaking records for time and distance, showing our flag, and opening up new vistas of commerce and communications. Well, today, I think you have helped recreate the anticipation and excitement felt in those homeports as those gallant ships were spotted on the horizon heading in after a long voyage.

Today we celebrate the 206th anniversary of our independence. Through our history, we've never shrunk before a challenge. The conquest of new frontiers for the betterment of our homes and families is a crucial part of our national character, something which you so ably represent today. The space program in general and the shuttle program in particular have gone a long way to help our country recapture its spirit of vitality and confidence. The pioneer spirit still flourishes in America. In the future, as in the past, our freedom, independence, and national well-being will be tied to new achievements, new discoveries, and pushing back new frontiers.

Source: [U.S. President], *Public Papers of the Presidents of the United States. Ronald Reagan, 1982,* Book Two (Washington, DC: U.S. Government Printing Office, 1983): 892–93.
*Shuttle captain Thomas K. Mattingly II ("T.K.") and crewman Henry W. Hartsfield, Jr. ("Hank").

The fourth landing of the *Columbia* is the historical equivalent to the driving of the golden spike which completed the first transcontinental railroad. It marks our entrance into a new era. The test flights are over. The groundwork has been laid. And now we will move forward to capitalize on the tremendous potential offered by the ultimate frontier of space. Beginning with the next flight, the *Columbia* and her sister ships will be fully operational, ready to provide economical and routine access to space for scientific exploration, commercial ventures, and for tasks related to the national security.

Simultaneously, we must look aggressively to the future by demonstrating the potential of the shuttle and establishing a more permanent presence in space. . . .

There are those who thought the closing of the western frontier marked an end to America's greatest period of vitality. Yet we're crossing new frontiers every day. The high technology now being developed, much of it a byproduct of the space effort, offers us and future generations of Americans opportunities never dreamed of a few years ago. Today we celebrate American independence confident that the limits of our freedom and prosperity have again been expanded by meeting the challenge of the frontier.

We also honor two pathfinders. They reaffirm to all of us that as long as there are frontiers to be explored and conquered, Americans will lead the way. They and the other astronauts have shown the world that Americans still have the know-how and Americans still have the true grit that tackled a savage wilderness.

Charles Lindbergh once said that "Short-term survival may depend on the knowledge of nuclear physicists and the performance of supersonic aircraft, but long-term survival depends alone on the character of man." That, too, is our challenge.

Hank and T.K., we're proud of you. We need not fear for the future of our nation as long as we've got men like you to serve as our inspiration. Thank you both, and God bless you for what you're doing.

THE FRONTIER IN SOUTH AFRICAN HISTORY
Frontier Wars and the Rise of the Zulu

The study of frontiers in African history is a relatively new endeavor. In the past, historians and ethnographers alike assumed that African tribes existed in a state of primitive immobility and timelessness and that their history lacked the dynamic events and dramatic population movements to inspire the kind of ongoing social evolution and change that characterized western history. That perspective is now being challenged by examining Africa's "internal frontiers," those geographic and cultural areas located at the fringes and periphery of established political entities.[3] These frontiers were dynamic areas for many forms of social interaction. It was here where African immigrants met established residents, where rival clans fought over land and resources, where bachelors frequently met their wives, and where new forms of social identity arose. As was the case in the United States, the African frontier was both a region and a force for dramatic social and cultural transformation.

One of the best-documented examples of African frontier history is connected with the rise of the Zulu nation in the Natal region of South Africa during the late eighteenth and early nineteenth centuries. Natal is a fertile but rugged territory of hills and valleys, forests and grasslands, bordered by the steep escarpments of the Drakensberg mountains to the west and the Indian Ocean to the east (see Map 8.2). This area was populated by the Nguni peoples,[4] who were organized into numerous small-scale autonomous clan communities that grew grain and herded cattle for their sustenance. But by the end of the eighteenth century, population growth and a long period of drought increased clan competition over land and water resources, which inspired groups to form confederations to increase their relative military might and protect their lands and peoples from rivals. The two most important confederations at the end of the century were the Mthethwa, ruled by Dingiswayo, and the Ndwandwe, led by Zwide. But the ultimate resolution of this power struggle was not determined by either of these two leaders but rather by Shaka, a young prince of the minor Zulu clan.

Shaka was born in 1787, the illegitimate son of Senzangakhona, chief of the Zulu. Treated as an unwelcome outcast by his father and his kin, he sought refuge among several neighboring groups before distinguishing himself as a skilled and innovative soldier in the Mthethwa army. King Dingiswayo of the Mthethwa was so impressed with Shaka that he helped him seize the Zulu chieftainship after the death of Senzangakhona in 1816. When Dingiswayo was killed by his archenemy Zwide, Shaka avenged the death of his friend and mentor by destroying Zwide's regiments in 1818. Shaka used this occasion to submit the large Mthethwa confederation to his personal rule, and the Zulu emerged as the dominant military and political power in the region. During the 1820s, Shaka continued to expand and consolidate the Zulu empire. Through a series of wars that became known as the *mfecane* ("the time of sorrows"), widespread areas of southern Africa were devastated by warfare, famine, and social dislocation as residents tried to resist or escape from the Zulu regiments.[5] At the height of his power in the mid-1820s, Shaka was visited by British traders, who were duly impressed with the size and power of the Zulu kingdom. Although Shaka was wary of the English, he did initiate commercial and diplomatic relations, and he sent personal emissaries to meet with the British king. But in 1828, Shaka was assassinated and succeeded by Dingane, his half-brother. Dingane ruled in much the same manner as Shaka until his power was broken by an armed force of white settlers at the Battle of Blood River in 1836.

Shaka reorganized Zulu society to meet the needs of warfare on the frontier.[6] Under his leadership, nearly everything was put on a military basis, with Shaka as supreme commander and chief. All men between the ages of fifteen and thirty-five were conscripted into regiments according to their age, creating a standing army of forty thousand warriors. These regiments not only served militarily but also were responsible for protecting the royal cattle herds and performing other public duties and obligations. While in service, men were forbidden to marry and instead resided with their regiments in large military *kraals* (enclosures). Women were also incorporated into their own regiments to provide food, clothing, and other needs to the male regiments. Once individuals completed their regimental service (usually for men in their late thirties and women in their late twenties), they were allowed to marry and establish their own family residences. The mass mobilization of Zulu society, together with Shaka's innovations in weaponry and strategy,[7] allowed the Zulu to create an empire of unprecedented size and strength.

Historians also credit Shaka with fostering a new national identity. The epitome of Zulu manliness that Shaka epitomized—physically strong, courageous, ambitious, and devoted to battle—emerged directly from Zulu wartime experiences on the frontier. Shaka also enlarged ethnic identity by stressing the Zuluness of the state. All subjects of the state became Zulu and owed the king their personal allegiance. Men and women of other clans not killed in battle were assimilated into Zulu regiments, and their children were raised with the traditions and customs of the Zulu. As a result, Shaka cultivated a new and expanded sense of Zulu identity that transcended the original clan and cultural identities of the peoples he conquered.

The two readings in this section derive from Zulu oral histories of Shaka and his campaigns on the frontier.[8] The first selection is from Jantshi ka Nongila, the son of one of Shaka's military intelligence officers. In 1902, when Jantshi was around 55 years old, he recounted his tales to James Stuart, an English colonial civil servant who had a keen interest in recording and preserving the language and history of the Zulu people.[9] The edited selection of his testimony highlights Shaka's frontier battle with Zwide, and it illuminates the traits and behaviors that made the Zulu king a great and feared leader.

The second selection is a Zulu *izibongo* (praise poem) that celebrates the might and power of Shaka. Praise poems played an important function in Zulu society, and they are valuable as historical sources, for they expressed the sentiments and attitudes of people at the time. The official praiser (the *imbongi*) often acted as an intermediary between the chief and the people, and his songs of praise, performed during important meetings and festivals, highlighted the admirable traits and accomplishments of the leader. But at the same time, praise poems represented the opinions of the people to the chief, and they might include criticism of unpopular actions. The poems are therefore not meant to be "factual" histories but rather representations of popular attitudes, values, and beliefs. The *izibongo* chosen for this reading is of undetermined date and origin. It was originally recorded in Zulu by James Stuart sometime in the latter half of the nineteenth century.[10]

QUESTIONS TO CONSIDER

1. How is Shaka portrayed in these Zulu oral histories? What attributes are praised, and how do they relate to the frontier experience?

2. In the Zulu account of history, wars were not fought over competition for resources but rather stem from the ambitions of a forceful leader. Why might the Zulu recount their history in this manner? What purposes might it serve?

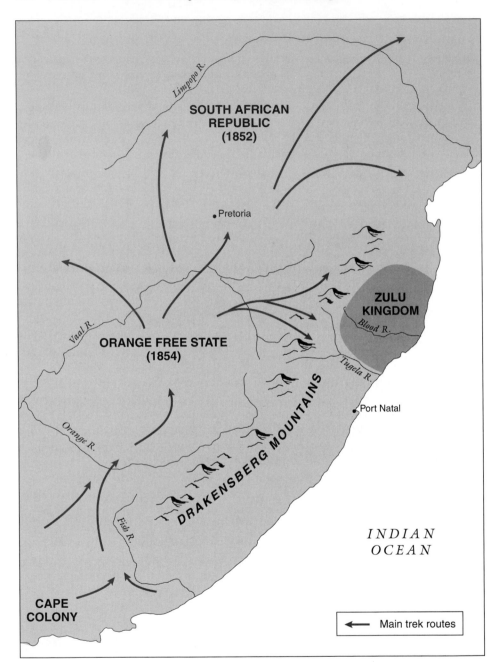

Map 8.2 The South African Frontier

3. What kind of society did the Zulu impose on the frontiers they conquered? How did Shaka's empire change the history of the frontier in South Africa?

4. In your assessment, was Shaka a great leader? What evidence would you select to support your position? How is your assessment shaped by your own value system?

5. How do Shaka's traits and his treatment of rivals compare with the frontier traits of American pioneers and their treatment of native Americans?

THE HISTORY OF SHAKA (recorded 1903)

Jantshi ka Nongila

[Jantshi speaks]: I was born at Nyezane in Zululand. . . . My father's name was Nongila; he was a spy under [the Zulu kings] Senzangakhona, Shaka, and Dingane. . . . Part of the *izibongo* [praise poem] that I will presently recite I learnt from him, as well as other historical facts.

[Jantshi ka Nongila describes Shaka's battle with Zwide, which he interpreted as a major moment in Zulu history. He begins with an account of Zwide's surprise night-time attack on the Zulu.]

. . . Zwide's *impi* [regiments] came in sight at the full of the moon. . . . Shaka sent out many messengers to call his forces together and they assembled at once as he directed. . . . Shaka positioned his regiments inside the cattle pens. As Zwide's army approached, it divided itself into two large bodies with the evident intention of surrounding the cattle pen. Shaka directed his men to allow Zwide's soldiers to come up close for, he exclaimed, "Today I am Zwide's chosen one!" When Zwide's [men] had come close, Shaka unleashed his forces. . . . A fight ensued. Zwide's men retreated and returned several times until all Zwide's sons . . . had been slain.

As the enemy fled, Shaka directed his warriors to follow and continue stabbing them until they were driven from their home. This was done and Shaka's regiments passed on and headed for the place of Zwide's people. . . . When Shaka's forces came in sight [of Zwide's villages], the women all came out to meet them, believing them to be their own people. The women discovered only when the [Zulu] army was at close quarters that it was not theirs. . . . They then turned and ran. Zwide saw what happened and ran off to a hill. Shaka's regiments thereupon stabbed all the women and children they came across and seized large numbers of cattle. . . . The victors then returned to Shaka with their booty. Zwide was not killed, for he ran away in a northerly direction with numbers of his followers. . . .

Source: James Stuart interview with Jantshi ka Nongila, February 9–19, 1903, in *The James Stuart Archive of Recorded Oral Evidence Relating to the History of the Zulu and Neighboring Peoples, Vol. I,* C. de B. Webb and J. B. Wright, eds. and transl., 174, 185–87, 189, 195, 198, 201–02. Copyright © 1979 University of Natal Press. Reprinted with permission. Some of the passages have been reordered from original text for greater clarity.

Apart from the above battles and conquests, Shaka attacked many other so-called kings. . . . I recollect that another was Duzi, chief of the Makanga. Shaka did not kill Duzi; [instead] he made him a [commander in the Zulu army]. . . . Shaka did not put to death the kings he defeated if, when he proceeded against them, they [submitted] and did not show fight. He made them *izinduna* [a term used to designate both chiefs and military officers in Zulu society]. . . .

Shaka was a man of dark color, not yellowish. He was tall, not very tall. . . . His buttocks were broad, so that one could see that he was a chief. . . . His strength was remarkable, for he could, when examining a cow, lift up its leg by one arm and stoop to look under it. . . .

Very frequently did Shaka cause people to be put to death. . . . Amongst Shaka's extraordinary acts was his causing a pregnant woman to be cut open in order to see what position the child took up in its mother's womb. He did this more than once. He would also cut off a man's ears, giving his reason for doing so that "they do not hear." He would say, "The vultures are hungry; they have come to attend the assembly," when he saw vultures hovering about, and then give orders for them to be fed with human corpses.* He would direct people to be killed to satisfy [the vultures'] appetite. . . . Shaka said cowards must be picked out from the regiments. . . . If Shaka saw wounds on the backside, the man was killed because Shaka said he must have been running away. . . . My father said Shaka was a great king, and very clever, because he defeated all the chiefs in every direction. He was very resourceful in his plans for overcoming his rivals. . . . [Subsequent Zulu kings] Dingane and Mpande came on the scene after Shaka had subdued the whole country, and therefore my father did not have very much to say about them. . . .

IZIBONGO: A SHAKA PRAISE POEM (n.d.)

He who beats but is not beaten, unlike water,†
[The] axe that surpasses other axes in sharpness;
Shaka, I fear to say he is Shaka,
Shaka, he is the chief of the Mashobas.‡
He of the shrill whistle, the lion;
He who armed in the forest, who is like a madman,

---

*The recorder of this tale, James Stuart, noted here, "No, this was done by Dingane," referring to Shaka's half-brother and successor to the Zulu throne.

Source: Trevor Cope, ed., *Izibongo: Zulu Praise Poems,* collected by James Stuart and translated by Daniel Malcom, 88, 96, 106–08, 116. Copyright © 1968 Oxford University Press, Inc. Used by permission of Oxford University Press, Inc.

†Water can be beaten, but to no effect; Shaka cannot be beaten at all.

‡*Mthethwa:* One of the Mthethwa military kraals where Shaka first gained prominence.

The madman who is in full view of the men.
He who trudged wearily the [African] plain . . .
The voracious [son] of Senzangakhona,
Spear that is [bloody] red even on the handle . . .

He attacked Phungashe of the Buthelezi clan,
He attacked Sondaba of Mthanda as he sat in council,
He attacked Macingwane at Ngonyameni,
He attacked Dladlama of the Majolas,
He attacked Nxaba son of Mbhekane,
He attacked Gambushe in Pondoland,
He attacked Faku in Pondoland.*
     The young viper grows as it sits,
Always in great rage,
With a shield on its knees.†

     He who while devouring some devoured others,
And as he devoured others he devoured some more;
He who while devouring some devoured others,
And as he devoured others he devoured some more;
He who while devouring some devoured others,
And as he devoured others he devoured some more;
He who while devouring some devoured others,
And as he devoured others he devoured some more . . .
     Painful stabber, they will exhort one another,
Those who are with the enemy and those who are at home.
He who is dark as the bile of a goat. . . .

He who is as big as mountains . . .
He is as rough as the ear of an elephant,
Like gruel made of inedible millet,
Like a pot of millipedes.
     You are a wild animal! A leopard! A lion!
You are a horned viper! An elephant! . . .
You grew while others loitered.
     Snatcher of a staff!‡
He attacks, he rages,
He puts a shield on his knees. . . .

He has not let them settle down, he keeps them in a state of excitement,
     Mighty Power! . . .

---

*Names of chiefs in southern Africa.
†Meaning Shaka is always ready for a fight.
‡Probably referring to Shaka's seizure of the Zulu throne.

Pursuer of a person and he pursues him persistently. . . .
Little leopard that goes about preventing other little leopards at the fords.*
Finisher off! Black finisher off!

Shaka Remembered: A Different Story

The final reading in this section is a modern *izibongo,* written in 1979 by the Zulu poet and political activist Mazisi Kunene (1930–). Born in Durban (South Africa) and educated at the University of Natal, Kunene has taught courses on African literature and languages at colleges and universities in Africa and the United States. In the 1960s, he joined the African National Congress and became its chief representative in Europe and the United States. He is a world-renowned poet whose numerous works—including *Zulu Poems* (1970), *Anthem of the Decades* (1981), and *The Ancestors and the Sacred Mountain* (1982)—share a common commitment to the history and culture of the Zulu. His most famous work, however, is the epic poem *Emperor Shaka the Great* (1979), a portion of which is included in this selection. Kunene's *Emperor Shaka* draws upon the style and themes of the traditional *izibongo,* but it was written under very different circumstances.

By the end of the nineteenth century, most Africans in South Africa, including the Zulu, had been conquered by whites, who proceeded to erect their own governments and economies. The Zulu were allowed to maintain their monarchy and a portion of their kingdom, but all real power belonged to white administrators. In addition, the Zulu were increasingly coerced into the white-dominated economy. The discovery of gold and diamonds created a vast demand for labor, which was supplied by low-cost African migrant workers. To maintain their positions of power and privilege, the white minority imposed a widespread system of segregation and discrimination which found its full fruition in the establishment of apartheid ("apartness") as the official policy of the state in 1948. To protest these policies, Africans founded political organizations such as the African National Congress (ANC), but the peaceful protests of Africans were met with violence and mass arrests. When Mazisi Kunene wrote *Emperor Shaka the Great* in 1979, Nelson Mandela (leader of the ANC and future president of South Africa) was serving a life term in prison for treason; political activity was banned; and poverty, violence, and despair stalked the black townships and tribal reserves. In such conditions, many Africans had lost hope for a better future.

Kunene's *izibongo* must be understood within this context. As a student of Zulu history and cultural traditions, Kunene studied many of the original praise poems collected by James Stuart in the previous century, and one can find certain similarities between his epic poem and those of earlier times. Yet Kunene was also writing for a modern audience with different needs and concerns, which are equally reflected in his tale. In maintaining the role of the traditional *imbongi* (praise singer), Kunene is acting as a kind of arbitrator between the opinions and

---

*Meaning Shaka is in full control of the country.

beliefs of the people (his audience) and the system that oppresses them. As you read this modern version of Shaka, it is interesting to compare and contrast the themes of the "traditional" and modern *izibongo* and to try to assess how variations might be attributable to changing historical conditions.

QUESTIONS TO CONSIDER

1. How is Shaka portrayed in Kunene's account? Identify his most distinguishing traits. How does this modern depiction compare with the earlier accounts?

2. What historical factors might account for the changes in interpretation? Why? Explain your answers fully.

3. Can you identify other historical figures who have been similarly redefined over time? In these instances, what conditions might have caused the changes? Are they similar to the South African situation?

4. Mazisi Kunene received a western-style education and has written numerous works. Why do you think he chose to retell the story of Shaka in the traditional style of the *izibongo*? How does his tale and use of metaphors compare with the older account?

5. Traditional African history was oral history, passed down from one generation to another. What are the implications of this kind of history? What advantages and drawbacks are found in this kind of history?

EMPEROR SHAKA THE GREAT (1979)

Mazisi Kunene

[This selection begins with the aftermath of one of Shaka's early victories, his conquest of Chief Phungashe.]

Shaka was elated with the performance of his new army.
He distributed the fat cows of Phungashe,
Saying, "people must eat what is theirs.
    Through many years Phungashe has robbed and pillaged many homes."
On this great day Shaka addressed the excited gathering:
    "I confer all honor on the [Zulu] regiments.
    They are honored by the living and the dead.
    On them the whole great nation confers the poems of heroes.
    The power of Phungashe has been broken forever!
    His voice of terror has been silenced. . . .

Source: Mazisi Kunene, *Emperor Shaka the Great: A Zulu Epic,* 98–99, 185–87. Copyright © 1979 Heinemann Publishers. Reprinted with permission.

He said, continuing: "The nation of the Zulus embodies all peoples. . . .
  All must abide by the laws of one nation.
  Their share in peace-time and in danger is equal.
  Whoever shall show hostility against them
  Shall have committed a heinous crime against us.
  He shall have challenged the living and the dead."
His words alarmed those of the older generation,
Who thought victory meant the mockery of the defeated enemies.
But they were now accustomed to these startling announcements.

Shaka said, continuing: "I forgive those [former enemies and adversaries]
  Who shall accept the full authority of the Zulu nation;
  Nor shall I confiscate their possessions.
  But the stubborn ones shall get the punishment they deserve."
Even [Shaka's] councillors who had accepted the need for diplomacy
Began to protest; their faces were twisted with doubt.
These men had hoped to amass the wealth from confiscated cattle.
But Shaka took only those that had belonged to Phungashe:
  "I take these cattle for those who were robbed by him.
  Let other little kings and upstarts learn their lesson:
  It is unwise to walk the land triumphantly like a bull elephant.
  People must choose their regions of destruction
  And skirt away from the sacred graves of our Forefathers.
  Our weapons are ever sharp and ready against such wild men. . . ."

Everywhere were feats and festivals in Zululand.
Listen to the words of the great poet who was there,
Who saw with his own eyes the celebration of the new year:
  "You rushed to conquer in distant places.
  You attacked King Phungashe of the Buthelezi nation;
  You attacked Sondaba of Mthandeni royal city as he sat in council;
  You attacked Mangcengcera of the Mbatha clan;
  You attacked Dladlama of the Majola clan;
  You conquered Nxaba the son of Mbhekane.
  Wild one, who, as he sits brooding, swells like a mountain—
  He has his weapons ready on his knees. . . ."

It was these crowds that saw Prince Zihlandlo arrive;
With his many followers he entered the royal city.
He proceeded to ask the Great Ruler of Bulawayo [Shaka] for a place to live. . . .
Prince Zihlandlo said: "King of kings, ruler of many lands,
  You whose shadow overwhelms those of the mountains! . . .
  I have come to you to drink from your wisdom.
  I am by breeding and training a warrior,
  Yet I hate to fight continuous and fruitless wars.
  I have heard with envy the stories of the armies you command;

How by their skill they have crushed even superior enemies.
Throughout Nguniland and beyond your voice is heard.
You speak of the [African] race that must be one.
I have come to ask to serve towards that goal. . . .
To this end I am prepared to die.
All nations must find a home in our land."

For the first time Shaka heard someone
Who spoke and saw clearly as his own vision. . . .
Shaka responded warmly to him,
Causing everyone to stare in consternation.
He said: "Son of Gubhela, I thank you for these great words.
        They fill me with deep satisfaction by their wisdom and meaning.
        Of all the many great people I have met
        I yet have to encounter one whose vision is as close to mine. . . .
        Your thoughts thrust beyond the terror of the battlefield.
        One day nations will no longer fight each other
        But share a common brotherhood.
        I present you to the [Zulu] Assembly;
        At all times you shall be my brother."

The Frontier and the Afrikaner "Great Trek"

In 1652, the Dutch East Indies Company established a small settlement at the Cape of Good Hope in South Africa to serve as a refueling station for its fleet of ships engaged in the Asian spice trade. The settlement was originally intended to be of limited size and duration, but Dutch emigration steadily increased through-out the eighteenth century, reaching an estimated population of more than four-teen thousand by 1793. As the pioneer settlements grew, so too did their conflicts with the local Khoisan people, seminomadic cattle herders who resented the for-eign intrusion on their pastures. With superior weaponry, Dutch settlers defeated Khoisan resistance, seized their cattle, and forced many Khoisan to leave the re-gion or remain as servile herders for the whites. At the same time, the Dutch East Indies Company began to import black slaves from west Africa to perform other forms of manual labor. Thus from the very beginning, the success of whites on the African frontier was dependent on African land and labor.

In the midst of the Napoleonic Wars, Britain seized the Cape from the Dutch in 1814 to prevent its possible capture by the French. Following the war, the British officials and settlers began to consolidate their rule at their new "Cape Colony," establishing their own laws, language, and customs to replace those of the Dutch, who now called themselves *Afrikaners* ("Africans").[11] Afrikaner dis-affection with British rule reached a peak in the 1830s, when large numbers of Afrikaners decided to leave the Cape Colony in an event that has become known as the Great Trek. In a scene reminiscent of American history, Afrikaner farmers and their families packed their belongings, hitched up their oxen-led covered wagons, and set out to find a new life beyond the known and established frontier. One of the leaders of the wagon trains was Piet Retief (1780–1838), a well-respected leader of the *voortrekkers* [pioneers]. Eager to present his reasons for leaving the Cape, Retief explained his motives in a brief letter titled "Manifesto of the Emigrant Farmers," published in a colonial newspaper in 1837. In the reading selection that follows, Retief's specific grievances and intentions reflect his attitudes toward the British and the Africans, as well as his own sense of Afrikaner identity.

Between 1837 and 1845, more than five thousand settlers moved into the South African interior, followed by even larger numbers after 1845. Their timing was opportune, for they crossed the frontier in the immediate aftermath of Shaka's wars (the *mfecane*), which had so depopulated and destabilized the region that the Afrikaners encountered minimal initial resistance. The majority of *voortrekker* wagon trains headed due north, across the Orange and Vaal rivers, to establish new farms, communities, and ultimately two independent Afrikaner states[12] (see Map 8.2). But one wagon train, led by Piet Retief in 1837, split off from the others and headed eastward toward the coast, where there was better rainfall and access to the sea. Their route, however, took them right to the frontiers of the mightly Zulu empire, which was now ruled by Shaka's half-brother, Dingane. Retief and a party of seventy men visited Dingane in early 1838 to seek his permission to settle in his kingdom, but the Zulu leader saw the arrival of whites as a serious threat, and he decided to launch a preemptive strike. Retief and his party were initially welcomed at the Zulu capital, but at Dingane's command, they were all slaughtered. Dingane then sent his regiments to attack the wagon train, killing an additional 250 *voortrekkers*.

Temporarily defeated but not deterred, the Afrikaners decided to send a punitive expedition against the Zulu later that year. Led by Andries Pretorious, the Afrikaners assembled a force of five hundred well-armed male volunteers, two cannon, and fifty-seven wagons to confront a massive Zulu army that may have been as large as ten thousand. At the Battle of Blood River on December 16, 1848, the Afrikaners dealt the Zulu a stunning defeat in one of the most decisive military encounters in the history of colonial Africa. Lashing their wagons together in a defensive *laager* ("a mobile fortress of wagons"), the Afrikaners turned back successive assaults by Zulu regiments before launching a counterattack. When the battle subsided, more than three thousand Zulu lay dead on the battlefield—but not a single Afrikaner had been killed. One of the participants in this campaign was Sarel Cilliers (1801–1871), who led the men in daily prayers and Sunday worship. Cillier's account of the battle[13] highlighted the ferocity of the struggle, as well as the religious fervor that inspired the Afrikaner combatants. In later years, Cilliers became famous and revered as the "Father of the Covenant," the holy promise that the Afrikaners made to God prior to their great battle with the Zulu.

Taken together, the readings in this section from Piet Retief and Sarel Cilliers shed light on the early frontier experience of the Afrikaners. They highlight some of the most important motives, ideas, and events of the Great Trek, which is considered one of the most important events in South African history. Moreover, they illustrate how the frontier experience shaped—and was shaped by—patterns of identity and attitudes about others. And finally, the frontier history of South Africa bears many striking similarities to the American experience, providing an interesting perspective through which to reexamine and assess the history of the frontier in the United States.

QUESTIONS TO CONSIDER

1. According to Piet Retief, what were the primary motives behind the Great Trek? What important beliefs and attitudes underlay these motives?

2. Retief expressed the *voortrekker* desire "to live in peace and friendly discourse" with Africans. Given the ideas and attitudes expressed in Retief's manifesto and Cilliers's account of Blood River, how realistic were his expressed intentions?

3. According to Cilliers, why did the Afrikaners prevail over the Zulu at Blood River? What other explanations might historians add to explain the victory? In your estimation, why might Cilliers's account prevail over other explanations?

4. In what ways might the experience of the Great Trek and the Battle of Blood River have imparted a sense of special identity for the Afrikaners? What might have been some important implications and consequences of this identity?

5. How did Afrikaner attitudes concerning the frontier in the nineteenth century compare with those of Americans in the same century? What might explain the similarities and differences?

"MANIFESTO OF THE EMIGRANT FARMERS" (1837)

Piet Retief

Numerous reports having been circulated throughout the colony, evidently with the intention of exciting in the minds of our countrymen of prejudice against those who have resolved to emigrate from a colony where they have experienced, for so many years past, a series of the most vexatious and severe losses; and, as we desire to stand high in the estimation of our brethren, and are anxious that they and the world at large should believe us incapable of severing that sacred tie which binds a Christian to his native soil, without the most sufficient reasons, we are induced to record the following summary of our motives for taking so important a step, and also our

Source: Piet Retief, "Manifesto of the Emigrant Farmers," *Grahamstown Journal* (February 2, 1837), in G. W. Eybers, ed., *Select Constitutional Documents Illustrating South African History, 1795–1910* (New York: Negro Universities Press, 1918), 143–45.

intentions respecting our proceedings toward the native tribes which we may meet with beyond the boundary:

1. We despair of saving the colony from those evils which threaten it by the turbulent and dishonest conduct of vagrants, who are allowed to infest the country in every part. . . .

2. We complain of the severe losses which we have been forced to sustain by the emancipation of our slaves, and the vexatious laws which have been enacted respecting them.*

3. We complain of the continual system of plunder which we have ever endured from the Caffres [Kaffirs]† and other coloured classes . . . which has desolated the frontier districts and ruined most of the inhabitants. . . .

. . .

5. We are resolved, wherever we go, that we will uphold the just principles of liberty; but, whilst we will take care that no one shall be held in a state of slavery, it is our determination to maintain . . . and preserve proper relations between master and servant.

6. We solemnly declare that we quit this colony with a desire to lead a more quiet life than we have heretofore done. We will not molest any people, nor deprive them of the smallest property; but, if attacked, we shall consider ourselves fully justified in defending our persons and effects, to the utmost of our ability, against every enemy.

. . .

8. We propose, in the course of our journey, and on arriving at the country in which we shall permanently reside, to make known to the native tribes our intentions, and our desire to live in peace and friendly intercourse with them.

9. We quit this colony under the full assurance that the English Government has nothing more to require of us, and will allow us to govern ourselves without its interference in future.

10. We are now quitting the fruitful land of our birth, in which we have suffered enormous losses and continual vexation, and are entering a wild and dangerous territory; but we go with a firm reliance on an all-seeing, just, and merciful Being, whom it will be our endeavour to fear and humbly to obey.

By authority of the farmers who have quitted the Colony.

(signed) P. Retief

---

*In 1833, the British Parliament called for the emancipation of all slaves in the British Empire; the law took effect in South Africa in 1838.

†A derogatory term for Africans.

THE BATTLE OF BLOOD RIVER (1871)

Sarel Cilliers

It is my desire that by a higher Hand I may be placed in the position to write the truth, for our God loves the truth. . . . I shall therefore give a brief account of the encounters that we, emigrants, had with our great enemies, the Kaffirs. . . .

. . . With [a force of about 400 men] we went forth, under the great disadvantage of so small a number against the powerful [Zulu] nation under Dingane. We saw this, and that if the good God was not with us, there was little hope of victory. I saw . . . that we must become suppliants to the Lord to entreat that He would be with us at our standard, as He was with Moses and Joshua. . . .

It was on the 7th of December. . . . I took my place on a gun-carriage. The 407 men of the force were assembled round me. I made the promise in a simple manner, as solemnly as the Lord enabled me to do. As nearly as I can remember, my words were these: "My brethren and fellow-countrymen, at this moment we stand before the holy God of heaven and earth, to make a promise, if He will be with us and pro-tect us, and deliver the enemy into our hands so that we may triumph over him, that we shall observe the day and the date as an anniversary in each year, and a day of thanksgiving like the Sabbath, in His honor; and that we shall enjoin our children that they must take part with us in this, for a remembrance even for our posterity. . . . And I raised my hands towards the heavens in the name of us all. We confirmed this in our prayers each evening, as well as on the next Sabbath. . . . The Lord was with us.

I cannot omit to bring to the notice of all how the Lord in His Holy Providence had appointed a place for us, in which He had determined that the fight should occur. On the west there is a ravine which discharged itself into Blood River, and the bank . . . could not be scaled. Then there was the Blood River . . . on the eastern side. . . . So that the camp, by God's mercy, was protected on two sides. On other sides the en-campment was on open ground. I think, then, that had God not forbidden it, it might have been taken by the Kaffirs, for their power was great, and the Kaffirs are brave. They had, however, open ground on two sides, on which they could make a rush and storm the camp. It pleased God that we "should see the sights of our guns."*

On the 16th they came down on the camp with great courage, and, if I am not mistaken, endeavored four times to take it by storm. Each time they were driven back. We could both hear and see their commander, who wished to repeat the attack, but the men refused to do so. . . .

The [Afrikaner] general then ordered the gates to be opened. Every horse had al-ready been saddled [and] we sallied from the camp. Then the word of our Lord was fulfilled: "By one way shall your enemies come, but by the blessing of the Lord they shall fly before your fire." There was a dense mass of Kaffirs, I think the half of their

Source: Charl Celliers [Sarel Cilliers], "The Journal of the Late Charl Celliers"(1871), in John Bird, ed., *The Annals of Natal, Vol. I: 1495–1845* (Cape Town: C. Struik, 1965), 238, 243–47.
*Could aim well and shoot straight.

whole number, who had not fought. The general directed that they should be fired on by the artillery. When this was done, they came forward, as if to reinforce the assailants and renew the attack on the camp. About 150 of our men rode towards this force in two divisions, and then a number, estimated by me at 2,000, separated themselves from the rest. Against this section of the enemy I was engaged. We were in an open country. They now offered no further resistance. We were on their right and left, and they were huddled together. We were animated by great courage, and when we had got in front of them, the Kaffirs lay on the ground like pumpkins on a rich soil that had borne a large crop. When they saw that there would be no escape, as we were driving them towards the river, they jumped into the water and were among the rashes at the river's edge. I believe that all were killed, that not one escaped. I was witness to the fact that the water looked like a pool of blood, whence came the name of Blood River. . . . It is calculated that not fewer than 3,000 of the enemy perished on that day.

Will not every one who reads this be deeply affected, and convinced that our great God gives ear to prayer? Shall we not redeem the promise made to God? That evening, we had a thanksgiving for the great help and deliverance granted to us. But now, my mind was again greatly disturbed, for their self-laudation amongst many, and such boasting as caused me great fear. I upbraided them with this, and said that I feared more now than when we committed our concerns to the Lord, under the promise made in our prayer. The Lord bade said to us: "Call on Me in the time of anxiety, and I shall help you." Let us not say that our hands and our courage have secured the victory.

The Trek Remembered

The Battle of Blood River foreshadowed the end of African independence in South Africa. Although the Zulu remained a formidable force for several more decades, the military superiority of the whites guaranteed the ultimate conquest and subjugation of all African groups by the end of the nineteenth century. By that time, the Afrikaners were once again in conflict with the British. The discovery of diamonds (1867) and gold (1886) in the independent Afrikaner republics of the Transvaal and the Orange Free State renewed the white power struggle over the future of South Africa and led to the Anglo-Boer war of 1899–1902, a brutal conflict that saw thousands of Afrikaner men, women, and children perish in British prison camps. After the war, the victorious British attempted to reconcile the separate white populations in the new "Union of South Africa," but many Afrikaners remained resentful and angry. In the 1930s and 1940s, the Afrikaners found a spokesman and leader in Daniel Malan (1874–1959), a former minister in the Dutch Reformed Church.

Daniel Malan was educated in South Africa and Holland, earning a doctorate in divinity at the University of Utrecht in 1905. Upon his return to South Africa, he served as a pastor before leaving the church to become an editor of an Afrikaner nationalist newspaper.[14] His outspoken views and personal ambitions propelled him into politics, and he served as a member of parliament and cabinet minister before forming the Purified Nationalist Party in 1934, a militant political organization dedicated to preserving and protecting Afrikaner interests. Campaigning on a platform of racial segregation, the Nationalist Party won the 1948 national (whites-only) elections, and Daniel Malan became prime minister of South Africa. As the country's leader, Malan began to implement his nationalist and racist vision in a policy that became known as apartheid. South Africa became a nation strictly divided by race: Different racial categories determined one's residence, marriage, education, employment, and so on. Racial divisions also paralleled and reinforced economic and social distinctions. Under apartheid, whites monopolized positions of wealth and status, while blacks were denied citizenship, political voice, and equal economic opportunities. Despite African resistance and international protests, the Nationalist Party and its policy of apartheid ruled South Africa until the election of Nelson Mandela in 1991.

The reading selection that follows is a portion of a speech given by Daniel Malan during the centennial commemoration of the Great Trek in 1938. This was a period of crisis for the Afrikaner community. The Great Depression had put thousands out of work and driven many into dire poverty. In their view, it was particularly wrong that many white mineowners, manufacturers, and businessmen (mostly of British ancestry) were replacing white Afrikaner workers with lower-cost black workers. Sympathetic to their plight and perceived injustices, Malan saw an opportunity in this crisis. The commemoration of the Great Trek, one of the most revered moments in Afrikaner history, could be an opportunity to unify the population and mobilize them to political action.[15] In his speech on "The Second Great Trek," Malan made an emotional and powerful appeal using the frontier experience as a means to unify and energize public sentiment in support of Afrikaner nationalism.

QUESTIONS TO CONSIDER

1. According to Malan, what did the Great Trek represent? How does his portrayal compare with that of Piet Retief?

2. When Retief wrote his Manifesto in 1837, his primary grievances were with the British. One hundred years later, what seemed to be Malan's primary concerns? Why did he assert that "your Blood River lies in the city"?

3. What role did religious ideas and beliefs play in Malan's appeal and vision? How are they related to Cilliers's account of Blood River?

4. In what ways did Malan's speech foreshadow the implementation of apartheid in South Africa? From Malan's perspective, was apartheid based on economic concerns, religious views, or nationalist identity?

5. Political leaders frequently manipulate history to serve the needs of the present. Using these readings as evidence, how did Malan seem to manipulate Afrikaner history? Can you find any parallels in American history?

"THE SECOND GREAT TREK" (1938)

Daniel Malan

Here at Blood River you stand on holy ground. Here was made the great decision about the future of South Africa, about Christian civilization in our land, and about the continued existence and responsibility of the white race. . . . [But also] you stand here upon the boundary of two centuries. Behind you, you rest your eyes upon the year 1838 as upon a high, outstanding mountain-top, dominating everything in the blue distance. Before you, upon the yet untrodden Path of South Africa, lies the year 2038, equally far off and hazy. Behind you lie the tracks of the Voortrekker wagons, deeply and ineradicably etched upon the wide, outstretched plains and across the grinning dragon-tooth mountain ranges of our country's history. . . .

The Trekkers heard the voice of South Africa. They received their task from God's hand. They gave their answer. They made their sacrifices. There is still a white race. There is a new People. There is a unique language. There is an imperishable drive to freedom. There is an irrecusable ethnic destiny. . . . Their task is completed. . . . The struggle with weapons has passed. . . . Your Blood River is not here. Your Blood River lies in the city.

I scarcely need tell you that Afrikanerdom is on trek again. . . . It is not a trek away from the centers of civilization, as it was one hundred years ago, but a trek back: back from the country to the city. . . . In that new Blood River, black and white meet together in much closer contact and a much more binding struggle than when one hundred years ago the circle of white tented wagons protected the *laager,* and muzzle-loader clashed with *assegai.* Today black and white jostle together in the same labor market.

So the struggle rages on mercilessly, day after day and year after year, still growing in extent and deadliness. Where he too must stand in the breach for his People, the Afrikaner of the new Great Trek meets the non-white beside his Blood River, partly or completely unarmed, without the defenses of river bank or entrenchment, defenseless upon the open plain of economic equalization. . . .

The groaning of the ox wagon evokes clearly again the stars which held your forefathers on course through the darkest night. Their star of freedom shines brighter on your path as well. But you know now that freedom meant more for them than simply the freedom to rule themselves and to live out their nationhood fully. Their freedom was also, and above all, the freedom to preserve themselves as a white race. As you could never otherwise have realized, you realize today their task to make South Africa a white man's land is ten times more your task. . . .

This centenary year has awakened the People from its sleep of death. Over South Africa's plains, Danskraal* and Blood River again trumpet their message that to win

Source: Daniel Malan, "The Second Great Trek," in T. Dunbar Moodie, *The Rise of Afrikanerdom: Power, Apartheid, and the Afrikaner Civil Religion,* 198–201, University of California Press, 1975.

*Reportedly the spot where the Afrikaners made their oath to God.

you must above all look up and that with the resurrection of Afrikanerdom's old idealism will also arise new hope, new love of fatherland, new will power and new unity.

You want that new unity, and God be praised that you still want it. But have you ever asked yourself seriously: For what? Do you want unity merely to saunter forward aimlessly hand in hand, or do you want it in order purposefully and determinedly to solve great and pressing problems of your People along the Path of South Africa?

There is a power which is strong enough to lead us to our destination along that path of South Africa—the power Above, which creates nations and fixes their lot. . . . [This is also] the power which can go out, and was intended to go out from that sixty percent of South Africa's white population who are flesh and blood of the exhausted trekker struggling in the city. Unite that power purposefully in a mighty salvation-deed [*reddingsdaad*] and then the future of Afrikanerdom will be assured and the white civilization will be saved.

NOTES

1. Afrikaners are descendants of the original Dutch colonists who settled in southern Africa beginning in the mid-seventeenth century.

2. See William H. Truettner, ed., *The West as America* (Washington, DC: Smithsonian Institution Press, 1991), 134–136, 354.

3. See Igor Kopytoff, ed., *The African Frontier: The Reproduction of Traditional African Societies* (Bloomington: Indiana University Press, 1987).

4. The historical understanding of "Nguni," like many other African ethnic identities, is problematic, as it is defined primarily on the basis of common language, culture, and ways of life. However, such terms frequently do not accurately reflect the way traditional Africans identified themselves or others. In the eighteenth century, most Nguni saw themselves as belonging to smaller-scale family clans that traced their common kinship through their descent from common ancestors.

5. The vast displacement of peoples over thousands of miles generated additional frontier conflicts and the rise of new societies. Some of the new states, like the Ndebele and the Sotho, adopted Zulu military methods and incorporated conquered groups as their subordinates.

6. In earlier times, clashes between groups were frequent but of limited ferocity. There were no standing armies, few casualties, and little social disruption.

7. The most important innovation was a new weapon called the *assegai*, a short-stabbing spear that gave Shaka's regiments a decisive advantage in close-combat engagements against others armed with the traditional long-throwing spear.

8. There are also historical accounts from eyewitness European travelers and traders who visited the Zulu kingdom between 1824 and 1840. Although these records are of great value to the historian, they are sometimes problematic in their tendency to sensationalize the "savagery" of the Zulu and their leaders. As one eyewitness source wrote to another, ". . . I mean to show their chiefs, both Chaka [Shaka] and Dingarns [Dingane] treacherous and intrigues. . . . Make them out as bloodthirsty as

you can . . . it all tends to swell up the work and makes it interesting." (Letter from Nathaniel Isaacs to Henry Fynn (1832), cited in David Robinson and Douglas Smith, *Sources of the African Past: Case Studies of Five Nineteenth-Century African Societies* (New York: Africana Publishing Company, 1979), 5.

9. Although some historians assert that Stuart's transcriptions and histories may contain errors, most agree that they are an extremely important historical source that has shaped the understanding of South African history for blacks and whites alike.

10. Stuart collected more than 250 *izibongo* during his lifetime, and scholars credit his work for saving a crucial part of Zulu historical tradition. The edited selection that follows was translated, edited, and annotated by Trevor Cope and published in 1968.

11. The name *Afrikaner* partly reflects a new sense of pioneer identity born out of their history in Africa. The English, however, commonly used the more pejorative term *Boer* (country hick) for the Dutch descendants.

12. The Orange Free State (1854) and the South African Republic (1852, commonly known as the Transvaal).

13. Sarel Cilliers's journal account of the battle was reportedly composed on his death-bed in 1871. It was first published in H. J. Hofstede's *Geschiedenis van den Oranje-Vrijstaat [History of the Orange Free State]* in 1876, and in the opinion of scholars, it became the primary source for the Afrikaner belief in the "covenant."

14. In editorials, Malan expressed his opposition to fighting on the side of Britain during World War I, which gained him an immediate following among militant Afrikaners.

15. In addition to festivals and historical reenactments, the centennial was marked by the erection of a huge granite *voortrekker* monument, which celebrated the heroes of the trek in large marble friezes.

CHAPTER 9

The World Encounters
the West

INTRODUCTION

In his monumental study *Democracy in America,* published first in 1835, Alexis de Tocqueville (1805–1859) made an astonishing prediction. Within a century, he asserted, two great nations would be in a position to "sway the destinies" of the globe. These two countries were Russia and the United States of America. Tocqueville's prediction rested on his perception that the societies lying on either end of the zone of western civilization were both engaged in a process of continental expansionism that was opening vast adjacent landmasses to settlement by Europeans. In America, he recognized the new settlers' Manifest Destiny as a part of what historians would call "western imperialism" and pondered what this historic development meant for displaced natives, increasingly deprived of their ancient lands and confronted with the "magistrates, the customs, and the laws" of an alien culture. In the case of the American Indians, Tocqueville believed the encounters were ending tragically: "As his neighbors grew in numbers, his power diminished more and more; and now, of so many powerful tribes which once covered the surface of what you call the United States, there barely remain a few that the universal disaster has spared. The tribes of the North, so renowned in the past among us for their power, have already almost disappeared. Such has been the destiny of the red man in America."[1] (See chapter 8 for more on the frontier in American history.)

Tocqueville's discussion of the Native Americans' plight reveals some of the harshest consequences of western contact with cultures that lacked equivalent social organization and technology. But people did not have to be nomadic herders, hunter-gatherers, or subsistence agriculturalists to feel the turbulent effects of encounters with the west. The intellectual and technological changes unleashed by the scientific revolution in Europe gradually rendered the west the dominant area in global economic and military power. Europe itself was transformed by these forces during the "age of revolutions." Individualism, capitalist values and institutions, and the nation-state replaced the corporative restrictions, privileged estates, and localized identities of earlier societies. Across Europe and parts of America, governments promoted national identities—while other identities diminished or disappeared—by means of uniform legal, educational, military, and police systems. Western scientific knowledge, capitalist business practices, and powerful centralized governments on the nation-state model made up an enormously dynamic concoction that produced a global trading system and threatened to overwhelm all but the strongest forces of resistance. While the United States and Russia brought these changes to sparsely populated adjacent lands, the European nation-states carried them across the seas to areas densely settled by other peoples.

In most of Africa, Asia, and the Middle East, the period of European direct political control was relatively short. Yet it was a transforming experience in global history, and one whose consequences are still a part of our daily news. Would other societies, proud of their ancient traditions, adopt the challenging new technologies, social forms, and values of the increasingly powerful west? Even if rulers and educated elites wished to undertake reform, could they do so effectively? How did the experience of western domination interfere with "natural" developments that might otherwise have occurred? Did the flow of information, invention, and power go in one direction only, or were western peoples also transformed by "colonial encounters"? These questions had different answers in the many locations where imperialism occurred. At their heart lies the dilemma that our global society still faces: In order to be "modern," is it also essential to be "western"? If so, what are the implications for people who do not come from this tradition themselves?

Western hegemony emerged over the course of many decades. The letters of the Qianlong emperor (1793), in which the ruler of China responded to petitions of a British diplomatic delegation led by Lord Macartney, show how difficult it would be for leaders of long established and successful civilizations to evaluate the changes that even westerners viewed with incomprehension. The Qing empire at the time of Macartney's mission in 1793 was the largest and wealthiest state in the world. There was little reason to predict that Great Britain, a small island nation to the far west, would pose a significant threat within a single generation. Yet Britain's victories over Napoleonic France, combined with such extraordinary Industrial Revolution achievements as steamboats, railroads, and telegraphs, placed her in a position to humiliate the ancient empire, with a population many times her own, in the Opium War of 1839–1842.

As the nineteenth century advanced, the expansionist trade policies, new technologies, and revolutionary political ideas of the west sparked ferment across the great land mass from Asia Minor to Japan. In the Middle Eastern domains of the Ottomans, Sultan Malmud II (ruled 1808–1839) and reformers of the Tanzimat movement (1839–1876) redesigned the army along European principles, improved tax collection, centralized government administration, and promoted educational and legal changes modeled on Enlightenment ideals. Far to the east, Japan's encounters with the west culminated in a show of force by U.S. Navy Commodore Matthew Perry in 1853. This humiliation brought the collapse of the Tokugawa dynasty (1600–1867) and the beginning of the self-directed Meiji modernization era. The peoples of the Indian subcontinent faced the winds of change earlier and longer than most. Ram Mohan Roy's letter to Lord Amherst (1823), which argued for promoting a western curriculum in Indian schools, shows the optimism that some forward-looking intellectuals initially felt as they pondered how the new ideas and knowledge of the west might benefit their own societies.

Especially in the first half of the nineteenth century, Chinese and Indian peoples were apt to encounter traders, soldiers, and administrators as examples of the dynamically transforming west. In the Pacific islands and much of sub-Saharan Africa, where opportunities for trade or white settlement were less favorable, contacts were more likely to be with Christian missionaries. The Catholic Church had long sent priests abroad, especially to East Asia and South America. But starting in the 1790s, the Protestant churches of western Europe and America began an outpouring of activity designed to bring their faith to souls "lost in darkness." In Africa, this fervor was both sparked and aided by the west's long complicity in the Atlantic slave trade (see chapter 3). In 1807 most of the countries involved agreed to end the shipments of Africans to the western hemisphere. France and then Britain abolished slavery in their colonies. Guilt and opportunity mingled to send western missionaries among the sub-Saharan Africans who had suffered so long from the slave trade. One of these missionaries was Samuel Crowther (1806–1891), an African who had converted to Christianity following his rescue from a slave ship. In his letter to Rev. H. Venn (1854), Crowther reported on a successful missionary trip that he helped to organize in the region of the southern Niger River. In his enthusiastic endorsement of Christianity, Crowther seemed to be representative of a new age in European-African relations in the nineteenth century, one in which the barbarities of the slave trade were replaced by a new partnership of respect and cultural exchange.

But the faith that commerce, Christianity, and efficient government would lead shortly to a world of peaceful trade and continuing enlightenment did not last long. For the British, the horrifying Indian Mutiny (1857–1858)[2] is usually seen as the turning point toward a harsher view of prospects for cross-cultural harmony. But the accelerating changes of the second Industrial Revolution meant that an emerging western global hegemony transcended the localized experiences of Britain. In an era of "New Imperialism" that began after 1870, other players appeared on the scene: Germany, Belgium, Japan, and the United States joined the older imperial nations of Britain, France, the Netherlands, Spain, and Portugal in seeking overseas possessions. Most of the globe's remaining "unclaimed" territory, particularly enormous tracts in Africa, was taken over. National rivalry and perceived needs for raw materials or strategic naval bases drove the conquerors. They were aided by technologies of conquest such as automatic weapons, quinine prophylaxis, and diesel engines. And many were propelled by a new "scientific" vision of inevitable conflict between the world's different races and cultures. The philosophy of Social Darwinism at its simplest implied that a nation's success in projecting power was evidence enough of the right and duty to rule others. In a series of cynical treaties and agreements, the western powers worked out their claims to other lands and set about establishing ways in which their hopes could be realized.

The impact on many of the world's people in the generation before World War I was catastrophic as western military interventions became more violent and more frequent. In the brief seven years between 1895 and 1902, for example, the British invaded the Sudan, the Boer republics in South Africa, and Tibet; the Americans fought in Cuba and the Philippines; and the Germans ruthlessly repressed revolt in Tanganyika, as did the Portuguese in neighboring Mozambique. Recent scholarship has shown that the accelerated pace of confrontation was not happenstance. In the 1890s, global "El Niño"[3] weather patterns caused crop failures from Brazil to east and south Africa, India, and north China. As global markets and foreign incursions prevented traditional forms of famine relief, perhaps 30 million people died of starvation and disease worldwide.[4] The European powers, the United States, and Japan took advantage of the social disruption to engage in a final burst of empire building. In places where European contact was most recent and disruptive, native millenarian movements[5] arose prophesying the destruction of foreigners and the restoration of favor in the eyes of the gods. The Boxers United in Righteousness, whose Proclamation (1900) is printed below, were the indigenous Chinese example of separate popular movements that included those of Antonio Conselheiro in Brazil, Dionisio Sigobela in the Philippines, the Shona and Ndebele of Zimbabwe, and the Cambuemba in Mozambique. In India, where the British had regulated the economy for close to a century, nationalist leaders such as Ramesh Dutt (1848–1909) used the statistical data and economic theory they had learned from the west to argue that foreign rulers impoverished those they were supposed to benefit and exacerbated the effects of natural disaster.

The horrors of the years of conquest were largely over before the European powers turned on each other in 1914. For many people, the full impact of encounters with the west did not develop until after conquest was complete. Then, as "At the Feet of the Village Elders" (1957) by Oginga Odinga (1911–1994) shows, villagers from the Pacific to Africa first experienced the taxes, laws, schools, medicine, property regulations, engineering projects, and work patterns that Europeans had adjusted to decades before. The reactions of nonwesterners were varied and complex. Some took advantage of new opportunities to develop power or skills they would never have had otherwise. Many saw their living standards decline as traditional patterns of agriculture and village life were destroyed. Others resisted, either directly by promoting "nationalist" causes or indirectly by subverting the control of local authorities. "Shooting an Elephant" (1936) by George Orwell (1903–1950) provides a rare glimpse into encounters between imperialists and subjects at the local level. Orwell, a raw young policeman in Burma in the 1920s, saw better than many at the time that western rule of non western people was not a one-directional assertion of control. On the ground, where cross-cultural encounters actually took place, power, collaboration, contest, and subversion played out in a variety of ways.

The readings in this chapter are organized geographically and chronologically, which allows them to be used in two ways. Those wishing to concentrate on China, India, or Africa will find readings that reflect the changing experiences of these regions from the early to late nineteenth century. Alternately, students may wish to read the first selection from each group to study the early part of the century and the latter selections to reflect upon the "New Imperialism." In either case, the collection of documents reveal the wide range of peoples' reactions to western imperialism. Some saw potential opportunities in their encounters with westerners, whereas others resisted the perceived threat to their culture and autonomy. Yet they all show that, despite the overwhelming military power of the European colonizers, nonwestern peoples in Asia and Africa were neither passive nor helpless in their reactions to western rule.

CHAPTER QUESTIONS

1. When the readings are considered collectively, how would you identify and classify the range of responses to western imperialism? Do you note any particular trends according to time period or region?

2. What types of problems seem most persistent when different cultures encounter each other, especially if the power differential is great? How do you assess the cause of the problems? Communication gaps? Cultural distinctions? Incompatible goals?

3. What social groups in colonial societies would be most likely to adopt western ideas and behaviors? What groups are most likely to resist?

4. The selections by Ram Mohun Roy and Oginga Odinga both discuss the place of education in the imperial project. What were the perceived advantages of western education? Why might subject peoples be ambivalent about their children being educated by westerners?

5. Compare the accounts of village life in a British colony provided by Oginga Odinga and by George Orwell. One is set in Africa and the other in Burma. What similarities can you find in the attitudes of villagers toward the foreign authorities?

CHINESE RESPONSES TO IMPERIALISM
An Imperial Response to the British King, 1793

In 1793 the Earl of Macartney arrived in Beijing with a retinue of assistants and a baggage train of gifts carefully selected to impress the Qianlong emperor (1735–1795) with the ingenuity, utility, and scientific sophistication of British manufactures. Macartney was on a mission from King George III of Great Britain. His goals were to establish diplomatic relations between the two great sovereign powers for the first time and to negotiate agreements that would allow British traders access to coastal ports other than the established center at Canton, as well as relief from various fees, bribes, and fines that the Celestial Emperor's officials imposed. The following document shows the emperor's response. The British delegation was unsuccessful, and diplomatic relations were rebuffed. Half a century would pass before the irritating trade restrictions were repealed at gunpoint in the aftermath of the First Opium War (1839–1842).

For most of the past century western scholars interpreted the emperor's refusal as evidence of the traditionalism and cultural arrogance that prevented China from adopting modernizing reforms until forced to do so by internal strife and the threat of external domination. Recent scholarship modifies this view.[6] China's Manchu rulers (the Qing dynasty was founded by conquest in 1644) presided over a vigorous, even expansionist multiethnic empire whose guiding assumption held that the world's numerous "lesser lords" could be induced to acknowledge the emperor as overlord by a combination of impressive ritual, just treatment, and privileges granted in return for submission and respect.[7] Among the privileges most frequently sought by "men from afar" was opportunity for trade. Chinese merchant monopolies called *hongs* handled contacts with men from "West Ocean Kingdoms" whose rulers had not performed the proper submissions at the imperial court. Hence, in a system well developed by the late eighteenth century, European merchants found their activities confined to a waterfront compound in Canton. From this restricted area all negotiations with Chinese traders and officials were conducted. For the Chinese, the activity of trading implied a suppliant's position and deserved to be carefully controlled because of its propensity to foster conflict and personal greed. The privilege was granted by the emperor and subject to the restrictions he or his representatives imposed.

It would have been difficult for Chinese officials to understand why this system was so irritating to the British. One reason was economic. By the 1790s, Britain, under the auspices of its own trade monopolists in the East India Company, was rapidly replacing its lost colonies in North America with a new "jewel in the crown" in India. In the early stages of mechanized manufacturing, British factories produced textiles in the interests of overseas markets, and the country's consumers had come to crave such imports as tea and sugar. A quite significant imbalance of trade was emerging in which Britain imported quantities of China tea but had nothing that Chinese merchants wanted in return beyond highly precious silver bullion. Raw cotton, and increasingly opium, from British-controlled India made up some of the deficit, but British officials were anxious to expand direct contacts along the China coast without the fees, impositions, and regulations of official intermediaries.

Equally important in British eyes, however, was acknowledgment of their king's sovereign equality with the Qing court through the establishment of permanent diplomatic exchange. An international system of theoretically equal states, regulated by treaty and law, was a relatively recent development within Europe itself. Its rationale and benefits were by no means obvious to the officials of a vast, successful political entity like Qing China, who interpreted Macartney's insistence as a disguised appeal for help in Britain's wars with revolutionary France. A real conflict of interests and assumptions is apparent in the Qianlong emperor's carefully reasoned response to the British.

1. How does the Qianlong emperor view the British petitioners in this selection? What does he think they have to offer China, and what do they have a right to expect from China?

2. How does the emperor regard the inventions and devices Lord Macartney brought on his mission? Was this the response the British intended?

3. What does the emperor's letter teach about international relations, the different ways that political states can relate to each other? What are ambassadors and what are their rights and privileges?

4. How does the emperor view his responsibilities to other countries? What is China's "global" position?

5. Do the emperor's arguments make sense to you? Does he make a good case for rejecting the British request for a different kind of relationship between the two countries?

LETTERS TO GEORGE III (1793)

The Qianlong Emperor

You, O King [George III], live beyond the confines of many seas, nevertheless, impelled by your humble desire to partake of the benefits of our civilization, you have dispatched a mission respectfully bearing your memorial. Your Envoy has crossed the seas and paid his respect at my Court on the anniversary of my birthday. To show your devotion, you have also sent offerings of your country's produce.

I have perused your memorial: the earnest terms in which it is couched reveal a respectful humility on your part, which is highly praiseworthy. In consideration of the fact that your Ambassador and his deputy have come a long way with your memorial and tribute, I have shown them high favour and have allowed them to be introduced into my presence. To manifest my indulgence, I have entertained them at a banquet and made them numerous gifts. I have also caused presents to be forwarded to the Naval Commander and six hundred of his officers and men, although they did not come to Peking [Beijing], so that they too may share in my all-embracing kindness.

As to your entreaty to send one of your nationals to be accredited to my Celestial Court and to be in control of your country's trade with China, this request is contrary to all usage of my dynasty and cannot possibly be entertained. It is true that Europeans, in the service of the dynasty, have been permitted to live at Peking, but they are compelled to adopt Chinese dress, they are strictly confined to their own precincts and are never permitted to return home. You are presumably familiar with our dynastic regulations.

Source: E. Backhouse and J. O. P. Bland, *Annals and Memoirs of the Court of Peking* (Boston: Houghton Mifflin, 1914), 322–24, 326, 330–31.

Your proposed Envoy to my Court could not be placed in a position similar to that of European officials in Peking who are forbidden to leave China, nor could he, on the other hand, be allowed liberty of movement and the privilege of corresponding with his own country; so that you would gain nothing by his residence in our midst.

Moreover, our Celestial dynasty possesses vast territories, and tribute missions from the dependencies are provided for by the Department for Tributary States, which ministers to their wants and exercises strict control over their movements. It would be quite impossible to leave them to their own devices. Supposing that your Envoy should come to our Court, his language and national dress differ from that of our people, and there would be no place in which to bestow him. It may be suggested that he might imitate the Europeans permanently resident in Peking and adopt the dress and customs of China, but, it has never been our dynasty's wish to force people to do things unseemly and inconvenient. Besides, supposing I sent an Ambassador to reside in your country, how could you possibly make for him the requisite arrangements? Europe consists of many other nations besides your own: if each and all demanded to be represented at our Court, how could we possibly consent? The thing is utterly impracticable. How can our dynasty alter its whole procedure and system of etiquette, established for more than a century, in order to meet your individual views? . . .

If you assert that your reverence for Our Celestial dynasty fills you with a desire to acquire our civilization, our ceremonies and code of laws differ so completely from your own that, even if your Envoy were able to acquire the rudiments of our civilization, you could not possibly transplant our manners and customs to your alien soil. Therefore, however adept the Envoy might become, nothing would be gained thereby. . . .

Yesterday your Ambassador petitioned my Ministers to memorialize me regarding your trade with China, but his proposal is not consistent with our dynastic usage and cannot be entertained. Hitherto, all European nations, including your own country's barbarian merchants, have carried on their trade with our Celestial Empire at Canton. Such has been the procedure for many years, although our Celestial Empire possesses all things in prolific abundance and lacks no product within its own borders. There was therefore no need to import the manufactures of outside barbarians in exchange for our own produce. But as the tea, silk and porcelain which the Celestial Empire produces, are absolute necessities to European nations and to yourselves, we have permitted, as a signal mark of favour, that foreign *hongs* [commercial companies] should be established at Canton, so that your wants might be supplied and your country thus participate in our beneficence. But your Ambassador has now put forward new requests which completely fail to recognize the Throne's principle to "treat strangers from afar with indulgence," and to exercise a pacifying control over barbarian tribes, the world over. Moreover, our dynasty, swaying the myriad races of the globe, extends the same benevolence towards all. Your England is not the only nation trading at Canton. If other nations, following your bad example, wrongfully importune my ear with further impossible requests, how will it be possible for me to treat them with easy indulgence? Nevertheless, I do not forget the lonely remoteness of your island, cut off from the world by intervening wastes of sea, nor do I overlook your excusable ignorance of the usages of our Celestial Empire. I have consequently commanded my Ministers to enlighten your Ambassador on the subject, and have ordered the departure of the mission. . . .

[The emperor explains his reasons for turning down seven specific requests dealing with opening trade to the British and allowing more access to Christian missionaries.]

It may be, O King, that the above proposals have been wantonly made by your Ambassador on his own responsibility, or peradventure you yourself are ignorant of our dynastic regulations and had no intention of transgressing them when you expressed these wild ideas and hopes. I have ever shown the greatest condescension to the tribute missions of all States which sincerely yearn after the blessings of civilization, so as to manifest my kindly indulgence. I have even gone out of my way to grant any requests which were in any way consistent with Chinese usage. Above all, upon you, who live in a remote and inaccessible region, far across the spaces of ocean, but who have shown your submissive loyalty by sending this tribute mission, I have heaped benefits far in excess of those accorded to other nations. But the demands presented by your Embassy are not only a contravention of dynastic tradition, but would be utterly unproductive of good result to yourself, besides being quite impracticable. I have accordingly stated the facts to you in detail, and it is your bounden duty reverently to appreciate my feelings and to obey these instructions henceforward for all time, so that you may enjoy the blessings of perpetual peace. If, after the receipt of this explicit decree, you lightly give ear to the representations of your subordinates and allow your barbarian merchants to proceed to Chekiang and Tientsin, with the object of landing and trading there, the ordinances of my Celestial Empire are strict in the extreme, and the local officials, both civil and military, are bound reverently to obey the law of the land. Should your vessels touch the shore, your merchants will assuredly never be permitted to land or to reside there, but will be subject to instant expulsion. In that event your barbarian merchants will have had a long journey for nothing. Do not say that you were not warned in due time! Tremblingly obey and show no negligence! A special mandate!

The Antiforeigner Boxer Uprising, 1900

The century after the Macartney mission saw an accumulation of disasters for China. In two Opium Wars in the 1840s and 1850s, British invasion forced the trade concessions demanded earlier. These conflicts helped to prompt the immensely destructive Tai-ping Rebellion (1850–1864). Various official reform movements encountered too many internal obstacles to effect much change. China lost a war to Japan in 1894 and was forced to accept a series of "unequal treaties" and agreements that granted "spheres of influence" to European powers. In 1899 internal disorder escalated. This time a portion of the imperial court headed by the Empress Dowager backed the opponents of western domination. The Boxers, drawing recruits throughout the north China plain, killed western and Chinese Christians and besieged the embassies of foreign powers in Beijing itself.[8] In July 1900 an unprecedented multinational army of British, German, American, Russian, French, Japanese, Austrian, and Italian troops entered Beijing to restore order and rescue the hostages. The International Expeditionary Force smashed the native army, looted Beijing, and, under the watchful eye of the international press, engaged in "punitive picnics" to exterminate opposition in the countryside.

China had a long tradition of secret societies and popular support for "social banditry" to help the poor. The Boxers United in Righteousness, who arose in Shandong province during the famines described earlier, followed ancient forms of aid and famine relief for their recruits. But the Boxers combined their appeals for social justice with calls to "Support the Qing, destroy the Foreign." Like resistance movements in other parts of the world, they saw their country's disasters as caused by its toleration of foreigners, especially the Christian missionaries whose numbers were increasing as western control of China became more pronounced. Recruits to the Boxers undoubtedly believed the terrible rumors of bizarre western religious practices requiring mutilation of women and children. They used magical charms and physical exercise rituals to invite the gods to inhabit their bodies, making them invulnerable to the guns and explosives of western armies. As with other resisters, this faith proved illusory. The Boxers were easily dispatched by the soldiers of the west, as were countless Chinese peasants who were innocent of any role in this conflict between cultures.

QUESTIONS TO CONSIDER

1. Outline the criticisms that the Boxers have of westerners. Why would the items they mention make a powerful appeal to Chinese peasants suffering poverty and dislocation?
2. What role do religious beliefs play in the political actions of the Boxers?
3. The Boxers claim to be "united in righteousness." How would they define this term? Why is it significant in their strategy?
4. Why would the Boxers wish to destroy such benefits of western technology as railroads and telegraphs?
5. The Qianlong emperor and the Boxer poets lived a century apart in time and occupied vastly different positions in Chinese society. Do you find any similarities in their attitudes toward western culture and what it has to offer China?

PROCLAMATION OF THE BOXERS UNITED IN RIGHTEOUSNESS

Divinely aided Boxers,
United-in-righteousness Corps
Arose because the Devils
Messed up the Empire of yore.

Source: Reprinted from Joseph Esherick, *The Origins of the Boxer Uprising*, 299–300. Copyright © 1987 by The Regents of the University of California. By permission of The Regents.

They proselytize their sect,
And believe in only one God,
The spirits and their own ancestors
Are not even given a nod.

Their men are all immoral;
Their women truly vile.
For the Devils it's mother-son sex
That serves as the breeding style.

And If you don't believe me,
Then have a careful view:
You'll see the Devils' eyes
Are all a shining blue.

No rain comes from Heaven.
The earth is parched and dry.
And all because the churches
Have bottled up the sky.

The gods are very angry.
The spirits seek revenge.
En masse they come from Heaven
To teach the way to men.

The Way is not a heresy,
It's not the White Lotus Sect.*
The chants and spells we utter,
Follow mantras, true and correct.

Raise up the yellow charm,
Bow to the incense glow.
Invite the gods and spirits
Down from the mountain grotto.

Spirits emerge from the grottos;
Gods come down from the hills,
Possessing the bodies of men,
Transmitting their boxing skills.

When their martial and magic techniques
Are all learned by each one of you,

---

*White Lotus believers were part of a centuries-old, unauthorized group of sects that combined aspects of Buddhism, Taoism, and other religious faiths. Their "millenarianism" (belief in the coming of an ideal society accompanied by the arrival of a deity) was not shared by the Boxers.

Suppressing the Foreign Devils
Will not be a tough thing to do.

Rip up the railroad tracks!
Pull down the telegraph lines!
Quickly! Hurry up! Smash them—
The boats and the steamship combines.

The mighty nation of France
Quivers in abject fear,
While from England, America, Russia
And from Germany nought do we hear.

When at last all the Foreign Devils
Are expelled to the very last man,
The Great Qing, united, together,
Will bring peace to this our land.

INDIAN RESPONSES TO IMPERIALISM
The View of an Indian Modernizer

By 1818 the British East India Company's initially opportunistic establishment of territorial footholds in India's Bengal and Madras provinces had become a London-sponsored imperial project governing 40 million people and controlling revenues valued at one-third those of the British government at home. Within three more decades, British direct rule would expand into upper Burma, the northwestern provinces of Punjab and Sind, and greater portions of the subcontinent's interior. Some of India's traditional rulers were allowed semiautonomy in "princely states" in return for welcoming British advisers and troops. But it was increasingly clear that possession of India, where British rule was known simply as the *Raj* (rule), was what made tiny Britain the global superpower of the nineteenth century.

Raja Ram Mohun Roy (1772–1833) witnessed this transformation during his lifetime. Born to a Bengalese Brahmin family, he was an extraordinary linguist, scholar, educator, publisher, and civil servant. Roy was especially concerned with the ways that western knowledge could be applied to India's mixed Hindu and Islamic culture. Curious and optimistic, he hoped that British rule might bring a "milder, more enlightened and more liberal" era to the subcontinent. East India Company administrators and British governors shared this hope. As pressures to open India's trade to rival businesses reduced the Company's role in commodity trade, ambitious plans to "westernize" Indian society took the place of the former mercantile activity. Indians such as Roy encouraged the government's efforts to abolish widow burning, female infanticide, and the religious cult of spiritual murderers called Thugs.[9]

In the following selection, Roy explains to the British Governor General Lord Amherst why he opposes the creation of a government-sponsored school for the scholarly study of Sanskrit, the ancient Indo-European language in which Hinduism's sacred literature was written. Roy anticipated what many historians now believe did occur: that by codifying Indian beliefs and social practices, British rulers actually fostered traditionalism, as they declared to be timeless and immutable aspects of belief that had previously been fluid and adaptable. Doing so justified their own role as introducers of "the modern" and made it more difficult for Indians to adopt new technology, law, and social relations in their own way. In the end the Sanskrit school was established next to the Hindu College Roy founded in Calcutta to educate sons of prosperous Bengali families according to a western curriculum. Schools such as the Hindu College represented a double-edged sword for the Raj. On the one hand, the European presence in India in the nineteenth century constituted only about 45,000 people who were in charge of a population of at least 150 million. A new class of Indians educated in English was essential to staff lower levels of the civil service and businesses. At the same time, exposure to Enlightenment ideals of liberty and self-determination could challenge the legitimacy of an alien rule based on force. Roy is considered one of the fathers of modern India for his realization that mastering the tools of the west promised the best way to regain autonomy.

QUESTIONS TO CONSIDER

1. Why does Ram Mohun Roy oppose establishing a school that would study and preserve an important part of his country's heritage, the Sanskrit language and literature?
2. Roy begins his letter with a tone of great deference. Why would he do this? Is this a deferential request?
3. What kind of skills and education would Roy like the British to provide? How would these benefit India?
4. How does Roy evaluate the motives of the British governors of India?
5. What attitudes toward government authority and duties does Roy display? How do these relate to his overall goals?

LETTER TO LORD AMHERST ON EDUCATION (1823)

Ram Mohun Roy

Humbly reluctant as the natives of India are to obtrude upon the notice of government the sentiments they entertain on any public measure, there are circumstances when silence would be carrying this respectful feeling to culpable excess. The present rulers

Source: Rammohun Roy, The English Works of Rammohun Roy (Allahabad: Panini Office, 1906), 471–74.

of India [the British], coming from a distance of many thousand miles to govern a people whose language, literature, manners, customs, and ideas, are almost entirely new and strange to them, cannot easily become so intimately acquainted with their real circumstances as the natives of the country are themselves. We should therefore be guilty of a gross dereliction of duty to ourselves and afford our rulers just grounds of complaint at our apathy did we omit, on occasions of importance like the present, to supply them with such accurate information as might enable them to devise and adopt measures calculated to be beneficial to the country, and thus second by our local knowledge and experience their declared benevolent intentions for its improvement.

The establishment of a new Sanscrit School in Calcutta evinces the laudable desire of government to improve the natives of India by education—a blessing for which they must ever be grateful, and every well-wisher of the human race must be desirous that the efforts made to promote it should be guided by the most enlightened principles, so that the stream of intelligence may flow in the most useful channels.

When this seminary of learning was proposed, we understood that the government of England had ordered a considerable sum of money to be annually devoted to the instruction of its Indian subjects. We were filled with sanguine hopes that this sum would be laid out in employing European men of talent and education to instruct the natives of India in mathematics, natural philosophy, chemistry, anatomy, and other useful sciences, which the natives of Europe have carried to a degree of perfection that has raised them above the inhabitants of other parts of the world.

While we looked forward with pleasing hope to the dawn of knowledge thus promised to the rising generation, our hearts were filled with mingled feelings of delight and gratitude, we already offered up thanks to Providence for inspiring the most generous and enlightened nations of the West with the glorious ambition of planting in Asia the arts and sciences of modern Europe.

We find that the government are establishing a Sanscrit school under Hindu pandits [learned men] to impart such knowledge as is already current in India. This seminary (similar in character to those which existed in Europe before the time of Lord Bacon)* can only be expected to load the minds of youth with grammatical niceties and metaphysical distinctions of little or no practical use to the possessors or to society. The pupils will there acquire what was known two thousand years ago with the addition of vain and empty subtleties since then produced by speculative men such as is already commonly taught in all parts of India.

The Sanscrit language, so difficult that almost a lifetime is necessary for its acquisition, is well known to have been for ages a lamentable check to the diffusion of knowledge, and the learning concealed under this almost impervious veil is far from sufficient to reward the labor of acquiring it. But if it were thought necessary to perpetuate this language for the sake of the portion of valuable information it contains, this might be much more easily accomplished by other means than the establishment of a new Sanscrit College; for there have been always and are now numerous professors of Sanscrit in the different parts of the country engaged in teaching this language, as well as the other branches of literature which are to be the object of the new seminary. Therefore their more diligent cultivation, if desirable, would be effectually pro-

---

*Francis Bacon (1561–1626): English philosopher who attacked the metaphysical speculations of theology, while embracing the experimental methods and discoveries of the emerging scientific revolution.

moted, by holding out premiums and granting certain allowances to their most eminent professors, who have already undertaken on their own account to teach them,
and would by such rewards be stimulated to still greater exertion.

 . . . [N]o improvement can be expected from inducing young men to consume a
dozen years of the most valuable period of their lives in acquiring the niceties of . . .
Sanscrit Grammar . . . neither can much improvement arise from such speculations as
the following which are the themes suggested by the *Vedanta:** In what manner is the
soul absorbed in the Deity? What relation does it bear to the Divine Essence? Nor
will youths be fitted to be better members of society by the Vedantic doctrines which
teach them to believe that all visible things have no real existence, that as father,
brother, etc. have no entity, they consequently deserve no real affection, and therefore the sooner we escape from them and leave the world the better. . . . The student
cannot be said to have improved his mind after he has learned [from the texts] into
how many ideal classes the objects in the universe are divided, and what speculative
relation the soul bears to the body, the body to the soul, the eye to the ear, &c.

 In order to enable your Lordship to appreciate the futility of encouraging such
imaginary learning as above characterized, I beg your Lordship will be pleased to
compare the state of science and literature in Europe before the time of Lord Bacon
with the progress of knowledge made since he wrote.

 If it had been intended to keep the British nation in ignorance of real knowledge,
the Baconian philosophy would not have been allowed to displace the system of the
schoolmen which was the best calculated to perpetuate ignorance. In the same manner the Sanscrit system of education would be the best calculated to keep this country
in darkness, if such had been the policy of the British legislature. But as the improvement of the native population is the object of the government, it will consequently
promote a more liberal and enlightened system of instruction, embracing mathematics, natural philosophy, chemistry, anatomy, with other useful sciences, which may be
accomplished with the sums proposed by employing a few gentlemen of talent and
learning educated in Europe and providing a college furnished with necessary books,
instruments, and other apparatus.

 In presenting this subject to your Lordship, I conceive myself discharging a
solemn duty which I owe to my countrymen, and also to that enlightened sovereign
and legislature which have extended their benevolent care to this distant land, actuated by a desire to improve the inhabitants, and therefore humbly trust you will excuse the liberty I have taken in thus expressing my sentiments to your Lordship.

A Critique of British Exploitation, 1904

Indians and Europeans optimistic about the possibilities of peaceful development
of imperial society had their hopes confounded in the next decades. Continued
territorial expansion, disruption of traditional economic patterns, and the encroachment of western laws, religion, property relations, and ideas provoked wide-

---

*A school of teaching within Hindu tradition that centers on the last and most philosophic of the
sacred texts.

spread rebellion in India in 1857. The Indian Mutiny began with deep discontents among the native, or sepoy, troops who made up 85 percent of the British Army in India. But the conflagration spread. The British lost control of large swaths of north and central India before restoring order through a ruthless campaign of indiscriminate reprisals. Perhaps eleven thousand westerners and hundreds of thousands of Indians lost their lives in a race war that transformed relations between the two groups. Finally abolishing the East India Company, the British crown took over formal rule of the subcontinent, reorganized the army to increase the European component, and concentrated on infrastructure development rather than economic diversification or social reform. British civil servants and businessmen retreated into life within European enclaves and "hill stations." Attitudes about any potential that natives might have for "improvement" hardened. Order, efficiency, and revenue collection became the overriding considerations of successive viceroys to India.

The selection by Ramesh Dutt (1848–1909) provides a window on the world of late Victorian India. His life shares many features with that of Ram Mohun Roy (in fact, Dutt attended the Sanskrit College that Roy had opposed). Dutt was also from the privileged and "westernized" stratum of Bengali society. He was among the small number of Indians educated in London, receiving degrees from University College and the Middle Temple. Like Roy he was a linguist, scholar, and writer on Indian affairs. He served twenty-six years in the Indian Civil Service but retired in 1897 as his views on the need for political and economic reform of the Raj grew stronger.

In 1901 the authoritative British medical journal *Lancet* estimated that 19 million Indians had died of famine and starvation-induced disease in the preceding five years. (This figure was six times as high as the government acknowledged.) Dutt, living in London, provided his explanation for this "late Victorian holocaust."[10] He laid the roots of India's endemic poverty to decades of British policy that had restricted India's manufacturing at key moments in the economy's development, overtaxed a peasant class made increasingly vulnerable by destruction of older land-use patterns, and siphoned off Indian revenues to pay for imperial wars and costs of occupation. Although Dutt's analysis was for years dismissed as special pleading, recent scholarship finds merit in his appraisal. The hard realities of economics—resource use and distribution—configured the Indian peoples' encounters with the British Empire.

QUESTIONS TO CONSIDER

1. According to Dutt, what is exceptional about India's position within the British Empire? Why should British policy makers be concerned about the situation?

2. Examine the statistics that Dutt uses. Do they make sense for framing an indictment of British policy in India? What are the Indian people paying for that Dutt believes to be unjustified? What should Indian taxes be used for?

3. What reforms might Dutt suggest to improve India's economic position, given his criticism of British policy?

4. The selection from Dutt begins and ends with statements of appreciation for the greatness of the British imperial experiment. Why would Dutt include these passages? Is he insincere, or are there aspects of the empire he would value?

5. The selections from Roy and Dutt were written with an educated British audience in mind. Compare how these authors use evidence and construct arguments to appeal to enlightened westerners.

INDIA IN THE VICTORIAN AGE (1904)

Ramesh Dutt

Six years ago [1897], there was a celebration in London which was like a scenic representation of the Unity of the British Empire. Men from all British Colonies and Dependencies came together to take part in the Diamond Jubilee of a Great Queen's reign [the sixtieth anniversary of Queen Victoria's rule]. Indian Princes stood by the side of loyal Canadians and hardy Australians. The demonstration called forth an outburst of enthusiasm seldom witnessed in these islands. And to thoughtful minds it recalled a long history of bold enterprises, arduous struggles, and a wise conciliation, which had cemented a world-wide Empire. Nations, living in different latitudes and under different skies, joined in a celebration worthy of the occasion.

One painful thought, however, disturbed the minds of the people. Amidst signs of progress and prosperity from all parts of the Empire, India alone presented a scene of poverty and distress. A famine, the most intense and the most widely extended yet known, desolated the country in 1897. The most populous portion of the Empire had not shared its prosperity. Increasing wealth, prospering industries, and flourishing agriculture, had not followed the flag of England in her greatest dependency.

The famine was not over till 1898. There was a pause in 1899. A fresh famine broke out in 1900 over a larger area, and continued for a longer period. The terrible calamity lasted for three years, and millions of men perished. Tens of thousands were still in relief camps when the Delhi Darbar [formal reception where Indian princes acknowledged fealty to the British crown] was held in January 1903.

The economic gulf which separates India from other parts of the Empire has widened in the course of recent years. In Canada and other Colonies, the income per head of the population is 48 pounds per year. In Great Britain it is 42 pounds. In India it is officially estimated at 2 pounds. At the last meeting of the British Association, one of the greatest of British Economists, Sir Robert Giffin, pointed out that this was a "permanent and formidable difficulty in the British Empire, to which more thought must be given by our public men, the more the idea of Imperial Unity becomes a

Source: Ramesh Dutt, *India in the Victorian Age* (Boston: Houghton Mifflin, 1904), v–vii, xiii–xix.

working force." Imperial Unity cannot be built on the growing poverty and decadence of five-sixths of the population of the Empire.

For the famines, though terrible in their death-toll, are only an indication of a greater evil—the permanent poverty of the Indian population in ordinary years. The food supply of India, as a whole, has never failed. Enough food was grown in India, even in 1897 and 1900, to feed the entire population. But the people are so resourceless, so absolutely without any savings, that when crops fail within any one area, they are unable to buy food from neighbouring provinces rich in harvests. The failure of rains destroys crops in particular areas; it is the poverty of the people which brings on severe famines. . . .

The sources of a nation's wealth are Agriculture, Commerce and Manufactures, and sound Financial Administration. British rule has given India peace; but British Administration has not promoted or widened these sources of National Wealth in India. . . .

[Dutt explains how the government's tariff policies have crippled manufactures in India and why changes in property laws and taxation have worked to destroy traditional village protections against destitution.]

If we turn from the sources of wealth to its distribution, and to the financial arrangements of India, the same melancholy picture is presented to us. The total revenues of India during the last ten years of the Queen's reign—1891–92 to 1900–01—came to 647 millions sterling. The annual average is thus under 65 millions, including receipts from railways, irrigation works, and all other sources. The expenditure in England during these ten years was 159 millions, giving an annual average of nearly 16 millions sterling. One-fourth, therefore, of all the revenues derived in India, is annually remitted [sent back] to England as Home Charges. And if we add to this the portion of their salaries which European officers employed in India annually remit to England, the total annual drain out of the Indian Revenues to England considerably exceed 20 millions. The richest country on earth stoops to levy this annual contribution from the poorest. Those who earn 42 pounds per head ask for 10 shillings per head from a nation earning 2 pounds per head.* And this 10 shillings per head which the British people draw from India impoverishes Indians, and therefore impoverishes British trade with India. The contribution does not benefit British commerce and trade, while it drains the life-blood of India in a continuous, ceaseless flow.

For when taxes are raised and spent in a country, the money circulates among the people, fructifies trades, industries, and agriculture, and in one shape or another reaches the mass of the people. But when the taxes raised in a country are remitted out of it, the money is lost to the country for ever, it does not stimulate her trades or industries, or reach the people in any form. Over 20 millions sterling are annually drained from the revenues of India; and it would be a miracle if such a process, continued through long decades, did not impoverish even the richest nation upon earth.

The total Land Revenue of India was 17½ millions in 1900–1. The total Home Charges in the same year came to 17 millions. It will be seen, therefore, that an

---

*There were 20 shillings to a pound. Dutt is saying that the poorest Indians paid up to 25 percent of their income in forms of revenue that left India.

amount equivalent to all that is raised from the soil, in all the Provinces of India, is annually remitted out of the country as Home Charges. An additional sum of several millions is sent in the form of private remittances by European officers, drawing their salaries from Indian Revenues; and this remittance increases as the employment of European officers increases in India.

The 17 millions remitted in Home Charges are spent in England (1) as interest payable on the Indian Debt; (2) as interest on railways; and (3) as Civil and Military Charges. A small portion, about a million, covers the cost of military and other stores supplied to India.

A very popular error prevails in this country that the whole Indian Debt represents British capital sunk in the development of India. It is shown in the body of this volume that this is not the genesis of the Public Debt in India. When the East India Company ceased to be rulers of India in 1858 [the British crown took direct control of India after the Mutiny of 1857], they had piled up an Indian Debt of 70 millions. They had in the meantime drawn a tribute from India, financially an unjust tribute, exceeding 150 millions, not calculating interest. They had also charged India with the cost of Afghan wars, Chinese wars, and other wars outside India. Equitably, therefore, India owed nothing at the close of the Company's rule; her Public Debt was a myth; there was a considerable balance of over 100 millions in her favour out of the money that had been drawn from her.

Within the first eighteen years of the Administration of the Crown the Public Debt of India was doubled. It amounted to about 140 millions in 1877, when the Queen became Empress of India. This was largely owing to the cost of the Mutiny wars, over 40 millions sterling, which was thrown on the revenues of India. And India was made to pay a large contribution to the cost of the Abyssinian War of 1867.

Between 1877 and 1900, the Public Debt rose from 139 millions to 224 millions. This was largely due to the construction of railways by Guaranteed Companies or by the State, beyond the pressing needs of India and beyond her resources. It was also largely due to the Afghan Wars of 1878 and 1897. The history of the Indian Debt is a distressing record of financial unwisdom and injustice; and every impartial reader can reckon for himself how much of this Indian Debt is morally due from India.

The last items of the Home Charges are the Civil and Military Charges. This needs a revision. If Great Britain and India are both gainers by the building up of the British Indian Empire, it is not fair or equitable that India alone should pay all the cost of the maintenance of that superb edifice. It is not fair that all the expenses incurred in England, down to the maintenance of the India Office and the wages of the charwoman employed to clean the rooms at Whitehall, should be charged to India. Over forty years ago one of the greatest of Indian administrators suggested an equitable compromise. In a work on *Our Financial Relations with India,* published in 1859, Sir George Wingate suggested that India should pay all the expenses of Civil and Military Administration incurred in India, while Great Britain should meet the expenses incurred in England, as she did for her Colonies. Is it too late to make some such equitable adjustment to-day? India's total Civil and Military Charges, incurred in England, come to 6 millions—a sum which would be considerably reduced if it came from the British taxpayer. Is it too much to expect that Great Britain might share this burden, while India paid all the Civil and Military charges incurred in India?

These are the plain facts of the economic situation in India. Given these conditions, any fertile, industrious, peaceful country in the world would be what India is to-day. If manufactures were crippled, agriculture over-taxed, and a third of the revenue remitted out of the country, any nation on earth would suffer from permanent poverty and recurring famines. Economic laws are the same in Asia as in Europe. If India is poor to-day, it is through the operation of economic causes. If India were prosperous under these circumstances, it would be an economic miracle. Science knows no miracles. Economic laws are constant and unvarying in their operation. . . .

The Indian Empire will be judged by History as the most superb of human institutions in modern times. But it would be a sad story for future historians to tell that the Empire gave the people of India peace but not prosperity; that the manufacturers lost their industries; that the cultivators were ground down by a heavy and variable taxation which precluded any saving; that the revenues of the country were to a large extent, diverted to England; and that recurring and desolating famines swept away millions of the population. On the other hand, it would be a grateful story for Englishmen to tell that England in the twentieth century undid her past mistakes in India as in Ireland; that she lightened land taxes, revived industries, introduced representation, and ruled India for the good of her people; and that the people of India felt in their hearts that they were citizens of a great and United Empire.

AFRICAN RESPONSES TO IMPERIALISM
An African Missionary Promotes Christian Conversion

In 1807 most of the countries enriched by the centuries-long Atlantic slave trade signed an international agreement to abolish the shipments of Africans to the western hemisphere. The British Royal Navy established a west Africa duty station to intercept smugglers of contraband human cargo. Africans freed by the British were returned to Freetown in Sierra Leone. Surrounded by strangers and often far from their native lands, many stayed to be educated at schools set up by the Church of England's Church Missionary Society (CMS). Often they converted to Christianity, and their knowledge of two very different worlds helped European missionaries to reach peoples of the interior.

Perhaps the most famous African to follow the path described above was Samuel Crowther (c. 1806–1891). As a young teenager Crowther was captured and sold to Portuguese slave traders. Leaving the Nigerian port of Lagos, the ship carrying him to South America was spotted by a Royal Navy squadron, which took Crowther and his fellow captives to Freetown. There Crowther was one of the first students at the Church Missionary Society's Fourah Bay College. He became a teacher and evangelical Christian with strong ideas on the value of the Christian message for Africans. In 1841 he joined the First Niger Expedition to explore commercial and missionary opportunities away from the Nigerian coast. The mission is usually considered a failure. As was frequently the case, most Europeans could not survive the diseases they encountered in the African interior, and many of the party died. But Crowther proved himself to the British as a translator and intermediary with the village peoples. In 1842 he was sent to England for training and ordination in the Church of England.

When Crowther returned to Africa, the mission he established among the Yoruba people became a model for others. As much as possible, each mission community became self-sufficient, so that it would not be dependent on the villages around it. The residents grew cash crops[11] that authorities hoped would replace revenues lost with the abolition of slavery, ran schools for the young, wore western clothes, and accepted any tribal peoples who wished to receive education and learn of the Christian religion. Crowther was so successful in managing the Yoruba and Niger missions that he was invited back to England to be consecrated as bishop of the Niger territories, a huge tract reaching from Nupe in the north to the Niger Delta along the coast. He was the first African to reach such a position in the Anglican Church.

By the last decades of Crowther's life, however, the tone of African-European relations was souring. New church leaders in England advocated more direct European control over missions. Many new English missionaries left for Africa with a diminished willingness to work with African clergy, whom they accused of tolerating heathenish tribal customs at the expense of strict Christian practice. In 1887 the new secretary of the Niger Mission, J. S. Robinson, seized control of the Yoruba mission, forcing Crowther to resign his position. Although Crowther's son, also a clergyman, expressed his indignation by removing his churches from CMS control (thus creating one of the first African-run Christian churches), his father died in 1891, a forgotten man. Not until 1952 would an African be appointed successor to Bishop Samuel Crowther.

QUESTIONS TO CONSIDER

1. From the evidence of Samuel Crowther's letter, why were Africans so important to missionary efforts to reach beyond the coast? What skills and special qualities did African converts bring to expeditions among tribal peoples?
2. How does Crowther think that African Christians will bring about conversions among the peoples of the Niger River? What aspects of the Christian life will be most important in influencing the tribes?
3. The natives that Crowther's party encounter seem anxious to meet with the expedition. Why would a local tribal leader want to make contact with Europeans?
4. Why does Crowther himself think it is so important to convert the Niger peoples to Christianity? Do Africans lack their own religion?
5. Compare Crowther's views with those of the Boxer rebels in the earlier selection above. How do religious beliefs affect imperial relationships?

LETTER TO THE REV. H. VENN (1854)

Samuel Crowther

Rev. and Dear Sir,

You will, no doubt be glad to hear that we have returned from the Niger in good health and spirits,—a singular instance, without any death, either among the Europeans, twelve in number, or among the fifty-four Africans, either from sickness or accident. The Expedition was in the river exactly sixteen weeks, the very day it returned to the mouth of the Nun. We commenced our ascent of the Tshadda on the 7th of August, and the last point we were able to reach was Gurowa, above Bomanda, a port of Hamaruwa, about 300 miles from the confluence of the Kowara and Tshadda, on the 22nd of September, when we were completely short of fuel, no wood being obtainable within three or four miles of the banks of the river. This was the only difficulty we met with, and which prevented our reaching the confluence of the Binue and Faro. . . . According to all the accounts we have received, [we] could not have been more than 100 miles from Hamaruwa. It could be reached in five days' journey on foot, traveling by the course of the river, but dangerous on account of unsubdued natives, and ten days' journey by a circuitous route around the Fumbina mountains, which was said to be safer. The reception we met with all along from the kings and chiefs of the countries on the Binue was beyond expectation. We made two visits to Mohamma, the Sultan of Hamaruwa, fourteen miles from the river, in both which we were most respectfully received and entertained by the Sultan [the northern portions of the Niger territory practiced Islam].

We returned to Aboh on the 31st of October, and met Simon Jonas [a member of Crowther's team], whom we had left there, quite well and much respected by all, both chiefs and people. He moved about among them with perfect freedom, and made several visits up the river, to Ossamare, Onitsha, and Asaba markets, and to an interior town called Oko-Ala, on the back of Aboh, of about a day's journey; the chief of which place asked Simon Jonas, why we always stopped at Aboh, and never paid them a visit; to whom Jonas replied, that there will not be left a place unvisited in due time. He was about three days absent from Aboh, when he returned, for fear the steamer might arrive in his absence.

Simon Jonas spoke to them of the folly of their superstitious customs, and he said, the one of chewing stick to clean their teeth early in the morning, and spouting the spittle before their country fashion, invoking his blessing upon those who wish them good, and imprecating his anger upon those who desire their hurt, was given up by some of them at his speaking to them of the folly of so doing. . . .

Having found this favourable state of things in Aboh, I took the step to secure a parcel of ground for a contemplated Mission station, to prevent the spot being spoiled by the people, and gave Aje strict charge to keep the people away from it. My further proceedings in Aboh will be seen more fully in my journal to that place. I have fur-

Source: Samuel Crowther, *Journal of an Expedition up the Niger and Tshadda Rivers* (London: Church Missionary House, 1855), xiii–xviii.

nished the Bishop of Sierra Leone with a copy of my journals to Aboh for his fuller information; and I have suggested to Dr. Baikie [another of the missionaries] the advantage of taking Simon Jonas to Sierra Leone, to give his Lordship verbal information of Aboh country from actual knowledge of three months stay among them. I have taken these steps from the instruction I had received from the Bishop, to ascertain what reception Native Teachers would meet with in Aboh should any be sent there. . . .

I believe the time is fully come when Christianity must be introduced on the banks of the Niger: the people are willing to receive any who may be sent among them. The English are still looked upon as their friends, with whom they themselves desire to have connexion as with the first nation in the world. Could the work have been begun since 1841, how imperfect soever it might have been, yet it would have kept up the thread of connexion with England and the countries of the banks of the Niger. God has provided instruments to begin the work, in the liberated Africans in the Colony of Sierra Leone,* who are the natives of the banks of this river.

If this time is allowed to pass away, the generation of the liberated teachers who are immediately connected with the present generation of the natives of the interior will pass away with it also; many intelligent men who took deep interest in the introduction of trade and Christianity by the Niger, who had been known to the people, have died since; so have many of the chiefs and people in the country, who were no less interested to be brought in connexion with England by seeing their liberated countrymen return. Had not Simon Jonas been with us, who was well known to Obi and his sons, we should have had some difficulty in gaining the confidence of the people at Aboh at our ascent.

It would be of very great advantage if the colony-born young men were introduced by their parents or countrymen to their fatherland; it has many advantages which have not been sufficiently noticed. It cannot be expected that children born in [Sierra Leone] should become acquainted with the countries and characters of the people so soon as their parents and countrymen. Though the parents are illiterate, yet if they are sincere followers of the Lord Jesus Christ, their service will be of much worth in introducing Christianity to their own people. They are brought back to their country as a renewed people, looked upon by their countrymen as superior to themselves, as long as they continue consistent in the Christian walk and conversation, and do not disgrace themselves by following heathenish practices. The language of the people of Abbeokuta will be that of the natives on the banks of the Niger: "Let those who come from the white man's country teach us and condemn our heathenish practices, we shall listen to them." It takes great effect when returning liberated Christians sit down with their heathen countrymen, and speak with contempt of their own former superstitious practices, of whom, perhaps, many now alive would bear testimony as to their former devotedness in their superstitious worship; all which he now can tell them he has found to be foolishness, and the result of ignorance; when he with all earnestness, invites them, as Moses did Hobab, Come with us, for the Lord has promised good to Israel: and all this in his own language, with refined Christian feelings and sympathy, not to be expressed in words, but evidenced by an exemplary

*Slaves liberated by British Royal Navy patrols from the ships taking them to the western hemisphere were freed and returned to Africa at Sierra Leone.

Christian life. The services of such persons will prove most useful in the introduction of the Gospel of Jesus Christ among the heathens. Let such persons be employed as readers or Christian visitors, and thus they will gradually introduce their children into the country, who in course of time will be able to carry on the work more effectually; as pioneers, we must not look for instruments of the keenest edge, anything that will open the path for future improvement will answer as well at the onset.

A View of Village Life in British Kenya, 1920s

The attitudes of firm, aloof paternalism that characterized British authorities by the late Victorian era are apparent in Oginga Odinga's memories of his childhood in a Kenyan village. The British government took over Kenya in 1895 after the privately sponsored East Africa Company failed to keep order or find sufficient revenues to reward investors. Although Kenya became one of the few African colonies to receive a large number of white settlers, Oginga Odinga's village in the remote southwest Nyanza region seldom saw white people. By this time (shortly before World War I) the British had perfected a system of administration that required fewer costly European functionaries and placed responsibility for carrying out government policies in the hands of natives. In this process of "indirect rule" the British appointed headmen or chiefs to serve as intermediaries between villagers and remote district or provincial administrators who were British. Odinga's memoir describes some of the complexity in the roles of these natives who received enhanced opportunities, wealth, and status from the government, but at the risk of being isolated from their own people.

Oginga Odinga estimated that he was born in 1911 or 1912. He was educated at an English school and became a teacher. In the 1940s he emerged as a leader of the Luo people in his native Nyanza district, pressing for economic development and political rights for Africans. He was the first vice president of independent Kenya, but quickly parted from nationalist leader Jomo Kenyatta because of his insistence that Kenya should have a multiparty political system. After his death in 1994 Odinga was honored for a lifetime of involvement in nationalist and democratic politics in Kenya.

QUESTIONS TO CONSIDER

1. In what ways did villagers such as Oginga Odinga encounter Europeans? How would these experiences influence the ways that Africans viewed their government?

2. Odinga describes two kinds of decision making at the village level, one characteristic before British authority arrived and one after. What are the strengths and weaknesses of each process?

3. How would a British authority describe the same activities that Odinga discusses?

4. Crowther and Odinga have different views on what Christianity offers Africans. Why would their attitudes be so far apart?
5. Compare the ideas of the people in Odinga's village with the ideas of the Boxers. Do you find any similarities in their ways of viewing the technologies and activities of the westerners?

"AT THE FEET OF THE VILLAGE ELDERS" (1967)

Oginga Odinga

Among the Luo of Central Nyanza [in Kenya], the forecasters [diviners of the future] had said of the White people "If you touch them the skin will remain in your hand because they are very soft. But they will come with thunderstorms and they will burn the people." Omuodo Alogo was the chief elder of my village and he told me he had seen these people, some of whom were as white as snow, some as red as fire, and that they had an instrument that harboured the thunder, and that hit from afar. When these people first came (the story goes), the elders had warned that we should never, never try to fight them because their weapons were better than ours. They would be intent on devouring our land and our wealth but we should be wary of them. If they asked for cooking flour we should give it; we should give whatever they requested, even animals. But we knew that when we had studied them our children would probably be able to get rid of them.

Not that we saw many Whites. The first White man I saw was the missionary Archdeacon Owen. This was the time of a plague outbreak. The children of our village were taken to be inoculated. We were very frightened, for we thought we might die. We allowed the Archdeacon only to touch us, and then ran home as fast as we could. We were lucky we did not catch the plague, for that year it claimed many of our relatives and neighbours. The villagers were told that to stop the plague we should trap the rats, cut off the tails and send them to the Chief's *baraza* [residence and meeting place]. From there, I learnt later, the rats' tails were bundled in tens and sent to Kisumu headquarters; on the walls of the Commissioners' offices hung charts of the monthly rat returns. It was in these years that the government started to collect taxes from our people: taxes and the orders to produce rats' tails have always been associated together as the arm of government reaching out to our villages. When the time came to take a register of taxpayers, government clerks were sent to the villages. Our mothers had news of the approach of these awesome strangers and they hid the children in the bush and brought us food there. We children were curious and we crept out to gaze secretly at the encroachers. We watched them take a papyrus reed from the roof of each hut and cut it neatly in two. When the reeds were tied in neat bundles they represented the registration of that *boma* [district]. One bundle was given to the elder for him to take to the Chief's *baraza* when he paid in the taxes; the other set

---

Source: Oginga Odinga, *Not Yet Uhuru* (New York: Hill and Wang, 1967), 1–3, 15–16, 20–22.

of bundles was taken away by the clerks as a tally of the taxpayers of the area, a sort of carbon copy of the registration. The clerks who came with the Whites for the tax registration were not people of our tribe; they spoke Swahili and we called them *Okoche.*

We connected Whites and Government with five main things. There were the inoculations against the plague from which the children ran in fear. There were the tax collections. There was the order to the villagers to work on the roads. There were clothes, *kanzu,* the long robes copied from Arab garb at the coast, given free to the chiefs and elders to wear to encourage others in the tribe to clothe themselves in modern dress. There were the schools, which came later, and to which, in the beginning, only orphans, foster children, poor nieces and nephews and never the favourite sons were sent, for the villagers distrusted the pressure on them to send their children out of the home and away from herding the animals; and the more alert objected to the way the Christian missions taught "This custom (yours) is bad, and this (ours) is good," for they could see that the children at the missions would grow up to despise Luo ways. . . .

My first experience of the government of Kenya was in our home when my cousin, Migaya Oburu, the government-appointed headman, came from attending the Chief's *baraza* to tell people the government's orders and requirements for our locality. Omuodo Alogo had himself been asked to act as government headman, but he had refused, saying that he had no wish to be sent about by the Whites as a little child. He deputed his nephew Migaya instead.

The District Commissioner was remote from the people. He lived in Kisumu and we heard about him as the head of all the chiefs, but the people never or rarely saw him. The Provincial Commissioner seemed like a king, so far away and exalted that we doubted his existence. As we heard there was a King and a Governor, so we heard there was a Provincial Commissioner: we knew little about him. The government was feared rather than respected. Agricultural instructors came to inspect our fields for cotton, but they never taught us anything. They only asked questions and if we did not answer quickly or did not give them the answers they wanted, they hit us with a hippo whip. Veterinary inspectors came too, but they wanted to be respected as chiefs, and they accepted as good and loyal only those villagers who gave them beer parties and presents. As a boy I watched from a distance the goings-on at the *barazas.* The Chief was harsh in both his language and his treatment of the people, and did not hesitate to slap an elder if the man did not stand quickly or sit where he was told. Any instructions given to the people were accompanied by beatings. The *askari kanga** was cruel and weighed heavily into the people singled out by the Chief. When the District Commissioner was due at a baraza, the atmosphere was tense and the people frightened. As the Commissioner approached all had to stand and if you were slow to rise to your feet the *askaris* might seize a chair and hit out with it. Sometimes people were beaten to a point of helplessness and near death. The Government, I decided, had come not to help us but to instill fear into us, and, out of fear, obedience. The Commissioner was remote, yet his power was felt. . . .

---

* *Askari:* police, soldiers; *kanga:* cloth; in this case, a lash.

Our Luo system of government was by consent and after consultation between the elders. As I have described, the clan head did not inherit his position but, once he belonged to the right lineage, had to prove his leadership qualities and use them to interpret tribal tradition and weld the agreement of his people. His strength derived from his closeness to the elders and his people. The British changed that. They did not want leaders in whom the people had confidence, but men who could be used for their purposes. When chiefs and headmen came to be selected, men whom the British found in positions of leadership were frequently by-passed, and others installed over them. . . . There was not always a consistent way of appointing chiefs. Sometimes individuals were chosen arbitrarily; in other cases there was some attempt at getting the clan to arrive at a popular choice. In many cases the people were given as chiefs individuals whom they would not have chosen themselves. Above all, the candidates for chieftainship had to be acceptable to the District Commissioner—and District Commissioners often manipulated the Locations* to have their candidates imposed. . . . Chiefs were no longer the custodians of their peoples' tribal law and custom; they were now civil servants, pensionable, but also subject to instant dismissal by the government. They were the expression of the power of the new government in the village. They could use their position to amass and exercise personal power, something which was previously unheard of among the Luo.

A BRITISH VIEW OF THE PARADOXES OF EMPIRE
Confessions of a British Administrator, 1936

George Orwell is the pen name of Eric Blair (1903–1950), one of the most important writers in the English language of the twentieth century. Orwell is famous now for two widely read novels, *Animal Farm* (1946) and *Nineteen Eighty-Four* (1949), in which he pilloried modern totalitarian governments whose suave claims to act in the name of "the people" could not disguise their unprecedented intrusion into the private lives of citizens. But Orwell deserves to be well known for his investigative reporting and prose essays of the interwar period as well. After World War I he worked as a police officer in Burma (modern Myanmar), lived the life of homeless and subsistence workers in Paris and London, explored the hardships of Welsh coal miners, and fought against fascism in the Spanish Civil War (1936–1938). His writing about these experiences, along with criticism and political commentary, is distinctive for its clarity and vivid detail and for the unsentimental decency with which he addressed the realities of life for ordinary people.

Orwell was educated, not very happily, at boarding schools in England. Rather than go to university he joined the Indian Imperial Police in Burma for five years in the 1920s. The experience produced his novel *Burmese Days* (1934) and the essay reprinted here. Britain fought three wars in the Victorian era (1824–1826, 1852, 1885) to bring the ancient Burmese kingdoms under its control. Even after

---

*In colonial Kenya, tribal lands under British rule were known as "Locations."

annexation to the Raj, village resistance and jungle insurgency taxed the authorities' ability to police the countryside. Very few Europeans wished to settle in Burma for long. Those who did tended to be employees of distant firms attempting to establish rubber plantations in the drier zones of upper Burma. As *Burmese Days* reveals, British soldiers, police, minor civil servants, and businessmen, with a handful of family members, secluded themselves as much as possible from native life. Those any distance from the cultural life of the capital city experienced long periods of discomfort, tedium, and frustration, unalleviated by much sense that they were bringing progress or prosperity to those they ruled.

Orwell returned from his years of service an anti-imperialist. As such he joined an articulate group of participants and firsthand observers of the British Empire who concluded that rulers were affected as profoundly as subject peoples by imperial encounters. Even before Orwell, British writers J. A. Hobson (1858–1940) and Leonard Woolf (1880–1969) described the need for those who dealt with native peoples on a daily basis to assume a mask of command, of confident and unquestioning control. The expectations of subjects as to how an authority would behave "created" the ruler whether he wished it or not. Orwell describes this situation in "Shooting an Elephant."

QUESTIONS TO CONSIDER

1. Why does Orwell shoot the elephant? Did he have a choice? Can the elephant be seen as a metaphor for Orwell's ideas about empire?
2. How does Orwell present his fellow imperialists and their attitudes toward the Burmese?
3. How do the Burmese villagers view the British official? Would they behave differently with a native policeman?
4. Why is it so important to Orwell not to be laughed at? Why is laughter a particular threat?
5. What is the "dirty side" of empire? Is Orwell being too hard on the local authorities trying to do their jobs? Why would lower-level police and magistrates be ambivalent about their role in the empire?

"SHOOTING AN ELEPHANT" (1936)

George Orwell

In Moulmein, in lower Burma, I was hated by large numbers of people—the only time in my life that I have been important enough for this to happen to me. I was subdivisional police officer of the town, and in an aimless, petty kind of way anti-

Source: George Orwell, *Shooting an Elephant and Other Essays,* 3–12. Copyright © 1950 by Harcourt, Inc. Reprinted by permission of the publisher.

European feeling was very bitter. No one had the guts to raise a riot, but if a European woman went through the bazaars alone somebody would probably spit betel juice over her dress. As a police officer I was an obvious target and was baited whenever it seemed safe to do so. When a nimble Burman tripped me up on the football field and the referee (another Burman) looked the other way, the crowd yelled with hideous laughter. This happened more than once. In the end the sneering yellow faces of young men that met me everywhere, the insults hooted after me when I was at a safe distance, got badly on my nerves. The young Buddhist priests were the worst of all. There were several thousands of them in the town and none of them seemed to have anything to do except stand on street corners and jeer at Europeans.

All this was perplexing and upsetting. For at that time I had already made up my mind that imperialism was an evil thing and the sooner I chucked up my job and got out of it the better. Theoretically—and secretly, of course—I was all for the Burmese and all against their oppressors, the British. As for the job I was doing, I hated it more bitterly than I can perhaps make clear. In a job like that you see the dirty work of Empire at close quarters. The wretched prisoners huddling in the stinking cages of the lock-ups, the gray, cowed faces of the long-term convicts, the scarred buttocks of the men who had been flogged with bamboos—all these oppressed me with an intolerable sense of guilt. But I could get nothing into perspective. I was young and ill educated and I had had to think out my problems in the utter silence that is imposed on every Englishman in the East. I did not even know that the British Empire is dying, still less did I know that it is a great deal better than the younger empires that are going to supplant it. All I knew was that I was stuck between my hatred of the empire I served and my rage against the evil-spirited little beasts who tried to make my job impossible. With one part of my mind I thought of the British Raj as an unbreakable tyranny, as something clamped down . . . upon the will of prostrate peoples; with another part I thought that the greatest joy in the world would be to drive a bayonet into a Buddhist priest's guts. Feelings like these are the normal by-products of imperialism; ask any Anglo-Indian official, if you can catch him off duty.

One day something happened which in a roundabout way was enlightening. It was a tiny incident in itself, but it gave me a better glimpse than I had had before of the real nature of imperialism—the real motives for which despotic governments act. Early one morning the sub-inspector at a police station the other end of the town rang me up on the 'phone and said that an elephant was ravaging the bazaar. Would I please come and do something about it? I did not know what I could do, but I wanted to see what was happening and I got on to a pony and started out. I took my rifle, an old .44 Winchester and much too small to kill an elephant, but I thought the noise might be useful *in terrorem* [to frighten the elephant]. Various Burmans stopped me on the way and told me about the elephant's doings. It was not, of course, a wild elephant, but a tame one which had gone "must."* It had been chained up, as tame elephants always are when their attack of "must" is due, but on the previous night it had broken its chain and escaped. Its *mahout* [trained keeper of elephants], the only person who could manage it when it was in that state, had set out in pursuit, but had

---

*A variation of "musth": the male elephant's annual period of sexual activity, often accompanied by heightened aggressiveness.

taken the wrong direction and was now twelve hours' journey away, and in the morning the elephant had suddenly reappeared in the town. The Burmese population had no weapons and were quite helpless against it. It had already destroyed somebody's bamboo hut, killed a cow and raided some fruit-stalls and devoured the stock; also it had met the municipal rubbish van and, when the driver jumped out and took to his heels, had turned the van over and inflicted violences upon it.

The Burmese sub-inspector and some Indian constables were waiting for me in the quarter [neighborhood] where the elephant had been seen. It was a very poor quarter, a labyrinth of squalid bamboo huts, thatched with palm-leaf, winding all over a steep hillside. I remember that it was a cloudy, stuffy morning at the beginning of the rains. We began questioning the people as to where the elephant had gone and, as usual, failed to get any definite information. That is invariably the case in the East; a story always sounds clear enough at a distance, but the nearer you get to the scene of events the vaguer it becomes. Some of the people said that the elephant had gone in one direction, some said that he had gone in another, some professed not even to have heard of any elephant. I had almost made up my mind that the whole story was a pack of lies, when we heard yells a little distance away. There was a loud, scandalized cry of "Go away, child! Go away this instant!" and an old woman with a switch in her hand came round the corner of a hut, violently shooing away a crowd of naked children. Some more women followed, clicking their tongues and exclaiming; evidently there was something that the children ought not to have seen. I rounded the hut and saw a man's dead body sprawling in the mud. He was an Indian . . . almost naked, and he could not have been dead many minutes. The people said that the elephant had come suddenly upon him round the corner of the hut, caught him with its trunk, put its foot on his back and ground him into the earth. This was the rainy season and the ground was soft, and his face had scored a trench a foot deep and a couple of yards long. He was lying on his belly with arms crucified and head sharply twisted to one side. His face was coated with mud, the eyes wide open, the teeth bared and grinning with an expression of unendurable agony. (Never tell me, by the way, that the dead look peaceful. Most of the corpses I have seen looked devilish.) The friction of the great beast's foot had stripped the skin from his back as neatly as one skins a rabbit. As soon as I saw the dead man I sent an orderly to a friend's house nearby to borrow an elephant rifle. I had already sent back the pony, not wanting it to go mad with fright and throw me if it smelt the elephant.

The orderly came back in a few minutes with a rifle and five cartridges, and meanwhile some Burmans had arrived and told us that the elephant was in the paddy fields below, only a few hundred yards away. As I started forward practically the whole population of the quarter flocked out of the houses and followed me. They had seen the rifle and were all shouting excitedly that I was going to shoot the elephant. They had not shown much interest in the elephant when he was merely ravaging their homes, but it was different now that he was going to be shot. It was a bit of fun to them, as it would be to an English crowd; besides they wanted the meat. It made me vaguely uneasy. I had no intention of shooting the elephant—I merely sent for the rifle defend myself if necessary—and it is always unnerving to have a crowd following you. I marched down the hill, looking and feeling a fool, with the rifle over my shoulder and an ever-growing army of people jostling at my heels. At the bottom, when you got away from the huts, there was a metalled road and beyond that a miry waste of paddy fields a thousand yards across, not yet ploughed but soggy from the first rains and dotted with coarse grass. The elephant was standing eight yards from the road, his left side toward us. He took not the slightest notice of the crowd's approach. He was tearing up bunches of grass, beating them against his knees to clean them, and stuffing them into his mouth.

I had halted on the road. As soon as I saw the elephant I knew with perfect certainty that I ought not to shoot him. It is a serious matter to shoot a working elephant—it is comparable to destroying a huge and costly piece of machinery—and obviously one ought not to do it if it can possibly be avoided. And at that distance, peacefully eating, the elephant looked no more dangerous than a cow. I thought then and I think now that his attack of "must" was already passing off; in which case he would merely wander harmlessly about until the *mahout* came back and caught him. Moreover, I did not in the least want to shoot him. I decided that I would watch him for a little while to make sure that he did not turn savage again, and then go home.

But at that moment I glanced round at the crowd that had followed me. It was an immense crowd, two thousand at the least and growing every minute. It blocked the road for a long distance on either side. I looked at the sea of yellow faces above the garish clothes—faces all happy and excited over this bit of fun, all certain that the elephant was going to be shot. They were watching me as they would watch a conjurer about to perform a trick. They did not like me, but with the magical rifle in my hands I was momentarily worth watching. And suddenly I realized that I should have to shoot the elephant after all. The people expected it of me and I had got to do it; I could feel their two thousand wills pressing me forward, irresistibly. And it was at this moment, as I stood there with the rifle in my hands, that I first grasped the hollowness, the futility of the white man's dominion in the East. Here was I, the white man with his gun, standing in front of the unarmed native crowd—seemingly the leading actor of the piece; but in reality I was only an absurd puppet pushed to and fro by the will of those yellow faces behind. I perceived in this moment that when the white man turns tyrant it is his own freedom that he destroys. He becomes a sort of hollow, posing dummy, the conventionalized figure of a *sahib* [master]. For it is the condition of his rule that he shall spend his life in trying to impress the "natives," and so in every crisis he has got to do what the "natives" expect of him. He wears a mask, and his face grows to fit it. I had got to shoot the elephant. I had committed myself to doing it when I sent for the rifle. A *sahib* has got to act like a *sahib;* he has got to appear resolute, to know his own mind and do definite things. To come all that way, rifle in hand, with two thousand people marching at my heels, and then to trail feebly away, having done nothing—no, that was impossible. The crowd would laugh at me. And my whole life, every white man's life in the East, was one long struggle not to be laughed at.

But I did not want to shoot the elephant. I watched him beating his bunch of grass against his knees with that preoccupied grandmotherly air that elephants have. It seemed to me that it would be murder to shoot him. At that age I was not squeamish about killing animals, but I had never shot an elephant and never wanted to. (Somehow it always seems worse to kill a *large* animal.) Besides, there was the beast's owner to be considered. Alive, the elephant was worth at least a hundred pounds; dead, he would only be worth the value of his tusks, five pounds, possibly. But I had got to act quickly. I turned to some experienced-looking Burmans who had been there when we arrived, and asked them how the elephant had been behaving. They all said the same thing: he took no notice of you if you left him alone, but he might charge if you went too close to him.

It was perfectly clear to me what I ought to do. I ought to walk up to within, say, twenty-five yards of the elephant and test his behavior. If he charged, I could shoot; if he took no notice of me, it would be safe to leave him until the *mahout* came back. But also I knew that I was going to do no such thing. I was a poor shot with a rifle and the ground was soft mud into which one would sink at every step. If the elephant charged and I missed him, I should have about as much chance as a toad under a steam-roller. But even then I was not thinking particularly of my own skin, only of the watchful yellow faces behind. For at that moment, with the crowd watching me, I was not afraid in the ordinary sense, as I would have been if I had been alone. A white man mustn't be frightened in front of "natives"; and so, in general, he isn't frightened. The sole thought in my mind was that if anything went wrong those two thousand Burmans would see me pursued, caught, trampled on, and reduced to a grinning corpse like that Indian up the hill. And if that happened it was quite probable that some of them would laugh. That would never do. There was only one alternative. I shoved the cartridges into the magazine and lay down on the road to get a better aim.

The crowd grew very still, and a deep, low, happy sigh, as of people who see the theater curtain go up at last, breathed from innumerable throats. They were going to have their bit of fun after all. The rifle was a beautiful German thing with cross-hair sights. I did not then know that in shooting an elephant one would shoot to cut an imaginary bar running from ear-hole to ear-hole. I ought, therefore, as the elephant was sideways on, to have aimed straight at his ear-hole; actually I aimed several inches in front of this, thinking the brain would be further forward.

When I pulled the trigger I did not hear the bang or feel the kick—one never does when a shot goes home—but I heard the devilish roar of glee that went up from the crowd. In that instant, in too short a time, one would have thought, even for the bullet to get there, a mysterious, terrible change had come over the elephant. He neither stirred nor fell, but every line of his body had altered. He looked suddenly stricken, shrunken, immensely old, as though the frightful impact of the bullet had paralyzed him without knocking him down. At last, after what seemed a long time—it might have been five seconds, I dare say—he sagged flabbily to his knees. His mouth slobbered. An enormous senility seemed to have settled upon him. One could have imagined him thousands of years old. I fired again into the same spot. At the second shot he did not collapse but climbed with desperate slowness to his feet and stood weakly upright, with legs sagging and head drooping. I fired a third time. That was the shot that did for him. You could see the agony of it jolt his whole body and knock the last remnant of strength from his legs. But in falling he seemed for a moment to rise, for as his hind legs collapsed beneath him he seemed to tower upward like a huge rock toppling, his trunk reaching skyward like a tree. He trumpeted, for the first and only time. And then down he came, his belly toward me, with a crash that seemed to shake the ground even where I lay.

I got up. The Burmans were already racing past me across the mud. It was obvious that the elephant would never rise again, but he was not dead. He was breathing very rhythmically with long rattling gasps, his great mound of a side painfully rising and falling. His mouth was wide open—I could see far down into caverns of pale pink throat. I waited a long time for him to die, but his breathing did not weaken. Finally I fired my two remaining shots into the spot where I thought his heart must be. The thick blood welled out of him like red velvet, but still he did not die. His body did not even jerk when the shots hit him, the tortured breathing continued without a pause. He was dying, very slowly and in great agony, but In some world remote from me where not even a bullet could damage him further. I felt that I had got to put an end to that dreadful noise. It seemed dreadful to see the great beast lying there, powerless to move and yet powerless to die, and not even to be able to finish him. I sent back for my small rifle and poured shot after shot into his heart and down his throat. They seemed to make no impression. The tortured gasps continued as steadily as the ticking of a clock.

In the end I could not stand it any longer and went away. I heard later that it took him half an hour to die. Burmans were bringing . . . baskets even before I left, and I was told they had stripped his body almost to the bones by the afternoon.

Afterward, of course, there were endless discussions about the shooting of the elephant. The owner was furious, but he was only an Indian and could do nothing. Besides, legally I had done the right thing, for a mad elephant has to be killed, like a mad dog, if its owner fails to control it. Among the Europeans opinion was divided. The older men said I was right, the younger men said it was a damn shame to shoot an elephant for killing a coolie, because an elephant was worth more than any damn Coringhee coolie. And afterwards I was very glad that the coolie had been killed; it put me legally in the right and it gave me a sufficient pretext for shooting the elephant. I often wondered whether any of the others grasped that I had done it solely to avoid looking a fool.

NOTES

1. Alexis de Tocqueville, *Democracy in America*, trans. George Lawrence (Garden City, NY: Anchor Doubleday, 1969), 338.

2. Called the "epic of the Race" at the time, the Indian Mutiny was perceived by many Britons as a battle of enlightened civilization against savage barbarism. The bloody war dragged on for nearly two years before British forces were able to reassert their authority in India.

3. "El Niño" is a disturbance of normal ocean-atmospheric systems in the tropical Pacific Ocean, which affects weather patterns around the world.

4. Mike Davis, *Late Victorian Holocausts: El Niño Famines and the Making of the Third World* (London: Verso, 2002).

5. Millenarian movements are often religiously inspired programs whose adherents believe in the coming of a new age of peace and prosperity.

6. James L. Hevia, *Cherishing Men From Afar: Qing Guest Ritual and the Macartney Embassy of 1793* (Durham, NC: Duke University Press, 1995).

7. Submission was demonstrated in part by kowtowing in the imperial presence. Lord Macartney refused to do this, though Dutch officials performed the ritual numerous times in the same era.

8. The name of this popular, antiforeign movement has caused much confusion. The Boxers did not practice organized fistfighting as the west understands it, but rather a variety of physical rituals designed to protect them from their enemies. Current translations stress that the word *righteousness* is the most important part of the name.

9. *Thuggee* was a hereditary secret society whose members strangled travelers as sacrifice to the goddess Kali.

10. Mike Davis, *Late Victorian Holocausts: El Niño Famines and the Making of the Third World* (London: Verso, 2002).

11. Foodstuffs and materials grown and produced for the marketplace rather than for personal consumption.

CHAPTER 10

Nationalism and Nation Building in the Nineteenth Century

INTRODUCTION

Nation-states and nationalism are such fundamental components of the contemporary world that we sometimes take their existence for granted and think of them as "natural" parts of the human order. In fact, though, both nation-states and the sense of identity that comes with them (nationalism) are very recent historical developments that have reshaped the world in revolutionary ways. During the nineteenth century, nationalist developments contributed to the emergence of powerful new nation-states, such as Germany, and to the further strengthening of integrative nationalism (the predominance of a national over regional, religious, and other identities) in existing nations, such as the United States. The continued emergence of new nation-states across the globe can be seen in the fact that fifty nations participated in the conference in 1945 that founded the United Nations and that the UN now has nearly two hundred members. Clearly, the development of nation-states and nationalism is one of the most significant and dynamic global developments of the past two hundred years.

For a variety of reasons, by the eighteenth century in western Europe natural-rights theory and the concept of the social contract served as the legitimating myth of social order and government. But, although social contract theory provided an intellectual legitimation of state power, it had little emotional appeal for masses of people. Nationalism filled this void, as was dramatically demonstrated in September 1792, when the French revolutionary armies of the *patrie*, or fatherland, defeated the armies of the crowned kings of Europe. The victory inspired the great German poet Johann Wolfgang von Goethe to utter, "From this place and from this day forth commences a new era in the world's history. . . ." That era was the era of nationalism, which carried the day in the nineteenth century.

But the seeming inevitability of this phenomenon should not blind us to the fact that the development of nationalism has been contested and even opposed at almost every stage of its history. Nor should we ignore the fact that different definitions of nationalism have emerged out of different cultural traditions and diverse historical circumstances. There is a French saying that "a language is a dialect that won, and a dialect is a language that lost." This idea reminds us that every increase in the political power of unitary national governments and every incremental growth in popular identification with those governments had to come at the expense of previously existing political structures and identities. These momentous issues were worked out in the course of the nineteenth century, often as a result of war and other conflicts. It was a violent, messy, and very dramatic process.

The very power of nationalism threw into disarray existing cultural and political systems. What would happen, for example, to political structures that did not coincide with "national" boundaries? The myth of "the people" seemed to imply that political power should reside with them (popular sovereignty). How would this affect the power of existing elites and how would it be reconciled with traditional cultural systems? What would happen to "subidentities," such as regional, religious, and class identities, and how would they be integrated into the new national identity? Moreover, who exactly constituted "the people," especially the so-called political nation, that is, those with a vote or a voice in the political structure? Thus the emergence of nationalism produced extremely significant encounters between different ideas, identities, and interests, whose impact is still felt up to the present day.

The hurly-burly history of the development of modern nationalism in the nineteenth century allows us to explore a number of crucial issues and themes. It provides an opportunity to analyze a significant historical process in terms of the social and political elements that favored it, those who resisted or rejected the new phenomenon of nation building and nationalism, and the rationale on which each side based its case. This process throws into stark relief the struggle between tradition and change that occurs when new cultural and political entities (in this case, nation-states) are elaborated. Along with identity, nation building and nationalism were preeminently issues of power, involving in especially vivid ways the role of the state. Finally, the study of nationalism enables us to investigate the way that these different components—social forces, political ideologies, and new forms of power relations—were molded into dominant, but also contested, visions of the proper form and direction that national governments and cultures ought to take. Hence, the key themes and issues of this chapter can be seen as two distinct encounters: (1) the encounter between particular cultural traditions and the changes required by nation building and nationalism, and (2) the encounter within different societies over the question of how the new nation was going to be constructed and defined.

These issues are approached in this chapter by means of case studies of the transformation or formation in the nineteenth century of what would become three of the most important nation-states of the twentieth century: the United States, Japan, and Germany. By the end of the nineteenth century, the United States, Japan, and Germany were the most powerful nations in the Americas, Asia, and Europe, respectively, and by 1941 they would be locked in the first truly global war. Although they had arrived at similar dominant positions, the process of nation building and the formation of national identity took different paths in each of these countries. Geography, culture, and historical experience combined to forge quite different nation-states and national identities in these three cases.

We turn first to the United States, in part because it took the form of a modern nation-state before the other two and in part because its example was a significant factor behind the national revolutions that swept across Europe and ultimately Asia, as well. Moreover, the questions of who constituted the nation and how power ought to be arranged were dramatically and tragically contested in the American Civil War of 1861–1865, the bloodiest war in the nation's history. Central to that war were two issues: (1) states' rights versus federal power and (2) the status of the black minority, especially the "peculiar institution" of African slavery in the American South. Our first reading is from an 1833 Senate speech, On Nullification and the Force Bill, in which John C. Calhoun (1782–1850) of South Carolina defended states' rights. In the second reading, the argument for federal power is excerpted from the First Inaugural Address of Abraham Lincoln (1809–1865), words which were spoken as the first steps toward the Civil War were under way.

By the 1890s, the most troubling questions about American national identity no longer revolved around slavery and the status of African Americans, which had been resolved, at least for white America, by the abolition of slavery and the establishment of racial segregation. The most prominent issue of national identity at the end of the nineteenth century was immigration and the influx of people from southern and eastern Europe. Our next reading is a selection from a work by the prominent Congregational minister Josiah Strong (1847–1916), *Our Country: Its Possible Future and Its Present Crisis,* in which he argued that immigration was a peril that must be addressed. Our final selection on the United States is the article "What 'Americanism' Means" by Theodore Roosevelt (1858–1919), in which he defined an alternative national identity that was much broader and more inclusive than Strong's narrow Anglo-Saxon Protestant model.

We turn next to Japan, whose nation building took place in the context of aggressive foreign demands that it change radically and rapidly its traditional policies. Forced in the mid-nineteenth century by the armed demands of western powers to end its centuries-old policy of seclusion, Japan faced in extreme form two severe tests of its national order and self-definition. Those tests were a profound national conflict between the forces of tradition and change and the unavoidable need to respond to western imperialism. Our first source on Japanese nationalism, an excerpt from Tokugawa Nariaki's 1853 "Memorandum to the Bakufu" (Shogunate) urges a xenophobic and isolationist response to the west. Our next source for Meiji Japan comes from the reminiscences of the principal author of the Japanese constitution, Ito Hirobumi (1841–1901), in which he argues that Japan drew on western models for its new constitution but did so in a manner they considered consistent with Japanese traditions, culture, and governmental principles. The third Japanese document is excerpted from the Preamble to the Constitution of Japan (1889), which demonstrates the way that Ito's constitution-writing principles for situating the new political order relative to traditional Japanese political beliefs and culture were translated into practice. The final text from Meiji Japan, "Good-bye Asia" (1885), was written by the intellectual Fukuzawa Yukichi, and in it he advocated a movement by Japan away from traditional eastern practices and an embracing of western ways, even to the extent of absorbing the spirit of western imperialism.

Last, we present sources relating to German nation building and nationalism in the nineteenth century. Although Germans were among the first to react to the emergence of French nationalism, a unified German nation was the last of these three countries to come into existence. Even then, a significant German-speaking population existed outside the boundaries of the new German *Reich,* or empire. German nationalism evolved from cultural nationalism in the eighteenth century to political and finally militarized nationalism in the nineteenth. Our first document is from Johann Gottlieb Fichte's *Addresses to the German Nation* (1807–1808), a work that summoned the German people to the cause of a vitalized, liberal German nationalism after the crushing defeat of the Prussian armies by Napoleon. The next document—a selection from the *Memoirs* of Otto von Bismarck (1815–1898), the man who founded the German empire—articulates a radically different form of German national identity from Fichte's, one that placed dynastic identity at the forefront of German consciousness. The final source on German nationalism included here, by the eminent German historian Heinrich Treitschke (1834–1896), presents an aggressive nationalism of the late nineteenth century that glorified war and aspired to German dominion over Europe and a global German empire, as well.

The United States, Japan, and Germany represented three distinctive traditions. The United States was the first broadly democratic nation, and its revolution marked the beginning of the process of formation of new nation-states. Unique among these three nations, because of its racial and slavery issues, and owing to its peculiar nature as a nation of immigrants, the United States had to resolve these issues in the process of defining itself as a nation in the nineteenth century. Japan, on the other hand, had a very sharply etched national identity in terms of political culture, ethnicity, and geography. The challenges Japan encountered revolved around the question of how to preserve Japan's distinctive identity and culture while still adapting and responding to the threat and challenge presented by the west. For the Germans, finally, foreign domination inspired an effort to define a successful path to cultural self-expression and political independence. There, the tension was between a cultural definition of Germanness, which encompassed all German speakers and thus would be very difficult to unite in one political body, and a monarchical definition of German nationalism, which would be politically effective, but which would exclude many people of German language and culture.

Ultimately, each of these case studies involved an "encounter" between aspects of historically evolved political and cultural circumstances, on the one hand, and the new forces of nation building and national self-definition on the other—a complex instance of the tension between tradition and change. They allow us to examine the intricate phenomenon of historical change and to explore the process of elaboration of political positions and the implications of those political stances—who favored the new national identity, who opposed it and why. Finally, they present one of the most enduring aspects of modern life, the human encounter with self-identity in the form of conflicting visions of nation and community. In all of these ways, nationalism represents one of the most profoundly emotional and enduring encounters of the modern age.

CHAPTER QUESTIONS

1. What is nationalism? What historical forces promoted the development of nationalism and nation building in each of the three case studies?
2. Who promoted nationalism and how was it justified or explained? Who opposed it? What tensions arose from the encounter between tradition and change?
3. What was the relationship between the state and nationalism? Did nationalism create the state, or did the state create nationalism?
4. What "vision" of nationalism arose in each case study? How was it a reflection of specific cultural traditions and historical events? To what degree was history or culture "reinvented" to meet the needs of nationalists? Are there any commonalities between the three cultures?
5. What implications do these case studies and the issues they involve have for the present-day world? To what extent and in what ways might similar processes be under way in the contemporary world?

AMERICAN NATIONALISM IN THE NINETEENTH CENTURY
States' Rights Versus the Union

In the first half of the nineteenth century, the primary exponent of states' rights and of the idea that ultimate sovereignty lay in the states and not with the federal government was John C. Calhoun of South Carolina. He was not born to the planter elite, but he made his way to the top by dint of his powerful intellect. Self-educated to that point, he went to Yale University in 1801, graduating with honors. He earned a law degree and practiced law in South Carolina before beginning his political career. Calhoun distinguished himself by the tight, forceful logic of his political and legal argumentation. He died in March of 1850 with an impressive record of governmental service to his credit, having served as a congressman, secretary of war, vice president, secretary of state, and senator. An ardent nationalist early on, he became a states' rights spokesman and bitter political enemy of President Andrew Jackson. The defining contest between Jackson and Calhoun was the battle over the limits of the power of the federal government, which came to be known as the Nullification Controversy.[1]

The Nullification Controversy arose after the passage of 1832 tariff legislation that benefited northern manufacturers while harming the economic interests of southern farmers, especially the cotton-exporting, slave-owning elite. Operating from a states' rights position, South Carolina actually called a state convention in 1832, which voided the tariff and then made moves to oppose its implementation in the state. President Jackson responded with a Force Bill, authorizing the use of force in imposing the law. Eventually, a compromise was arrived at, but not before Calhoun had elaborated in the speech excerpted here an argument that ultimate sovereignty lay in the individual states, not in the federal government. Underlying the constitutional dispute were two rival visions of the nation: one of the nation as a union of citizens, not states, and the other of national identity as secondary to regional and state loyalty.

The ultimate extension of the idea of states' rights was their ability to withdraw from the Union. This is the step that the seven states of the Deep South had taken by the time Lincoln made his First Inaugural Address. Significant developments had raised the slavery issue to a position of the gravest importance to the young American system of government. By 1860, slavery had become an exclusively southern institution, attacked by abolitionists and viewed as a threat by white northern workers. Moreover, the South had become a minority region within the rapidly growing country. Also by the 1850s, the slavery issue and nativism [2] had destroyed the Whig party and replaced it with the Republicans, for whom slavery was one of the most significant issues. National parties with bases of support in different regions of the country had given way to sectional parties in the North and South. The issues of slavery and states' rights were back on the front burner of American politics.

In 1860, Abraham Lincoln, the Republican party candidate from Illinois, won the presidential election without carrying a single southern state. Although he had worked his way up from humble beginnings to a comfortable law practice and even one term in the House of Representatives, before 1858 Lincoln had not earned the political prominence that he burned to achieve. In that year, in a series of debates as part of a campaign for a seat in the U.S. Senate, Lincoln established a national reputation. Although he lost the battle for the Senate, he won the much more important war for national political power. It is important to note that Lincoln had established a much stronger antislavery position than he would present in his First Inaugural Address, as his famous assertion that "a house divided against itself cannot stand" demonstrates. He maintained at that point that America would be all slave or all free. By March 1861, with southern states openly seceding, Lincoln espoused the position of limiting slavery to its existing locales, but not interfering with it there. Although he was willing to compromise on this issue, he would not, as his subsequent actions so forcefully prove, allow the southern states to secede from the Union. In his view, the Union was perpetual, unless dissolved by the citizens of the whole nation. Unlike Calhoun, who ardently advocated "states' rights," Lincoln argued that the Constitution and the sovereignty of the people demanded that he preserve and defend the Union. In his First Inaugural Address, excerpted here, he presented his modified position on slavery but also his own interpretation of the American nation and of the nature of the Union.

QUESTIONS TO CONSIDER

1. Identify the main arguments of both Calhoun and Lincoln. They stated opposing positions, but are there any common elements in their different arguments?

2. Calhoun and Lincoln each based his understanding of American nationalism in history. What historical precedents or developments did each cite to buttress his argument?

3. What vision of America as a nation did each man develop? Does it seem to you that either or both were "inventing" or creating, as opposed to merely expressing, a vision of the United States?

4. Whose interests were Calhoun and Lincoln, respectively, promoting with their different views of American nationalism? Whose argument is most compelling, in your opinion? In the nineteenth century it was considered grammatically correct to say "the United States are," whereas we now say "United States is." Does the former usage support either side's argument? If so, whose and why?

5. What is the relationship between the government (either federal or state) and nationalism in this encounter? How are the different conceptions of nationalism put forward by Calhoun and Lincoln connected with issues of power and progress?

ON NULLIFICATION AND THE FORCE BILL (1833)

John C. Calhoun

The people of Carolina believe that the Union is a union of States, and not of individuals; that it was formed by the States, and that the citizens of the several States were bound to it through the acts of their several States; that each State ratified the Constitution for itself, and that it was only by such ratification of a State that any obligation was imposed upon its citizens. Thus believing, it is the opinion of the people of Carolina that it belongs to the State which has imposed the obligation to declare, in the last resort, the extent of this obligation, as far as her citizens are concerned; and this upon the plain principles which exist in all analogous cases of compact between sovereign bodies. On this principle the people of the State, acting in their sovereign capacity in convention, precisely as they did in the adoption of their own and the Federal Constitution, have declared . . . the acts of Congress therefore null and void. The ordinance thus enacted by the people of the State themselves, acting as a sovereign community, is as obligatory on the citizens of the State as any portion of the

Source: *Register of Debates in Congress,* vol. IX (Washington, DC: Gales and Seaton, 1833), 532, 534, 535, 537–40.

Constitution. In prescribing, then, the oath to obey the ordinance, no more was done than to prescribe an oath to obey the Constitution. It is, in fact, but a particular oath of allegiance, and in every respect similar to that which is prescribed, under the Constitution of the United States, to be administered to all the officers of the State and Federal governments. . . . It ought to be borne in mind that, according to the opinion which prevails in Carolina, the right of resistance to the unconstitutional acts of Congress belongs to the State, and not to her individual citizens; and that, though the latter may . . . resist through the courts an unconstitutional encroachment upon their rights, yet the final stand against usurpation rests not with them, but with the State of which they are members; and such act of resistance by a State binds the conscience and allegiance of the citizen. . . .

It is next objected that the enforcing acts have legislated the United States out of South Carolina. . . . [T]hey have been legislated out only to the extent that they had no right to enter. The Constitution has admitted the jurisdiction of the United States within the limits of the several States only so far as the delegated powers authorize; beyond that they are intruders, and may rightfully be expelled; and that they have been efficiently expelled by the legislation of the State through her civil process . . . is only a confirmation of the truth of the doctrine for which the majority in Carolina have contended.

The very point at issue between the two parties there is, whether nullification is a peaceful and an efficient remedy against an unconstitutional act of the general government, and may be asserted, as such, through the State tribunals. . . . Sir, I consider . . . that nullification is peaceful and efficient, and so deeply intrenched in the principles of our system, that it cannot be assailed but by prostrating the Constitution, and substituting the supremacy of military force in lieu of the supremacy of the laws. . . . That, in a contest between the State and the general government, if the resistance be limited on both sides to the civil process, the State, by its inherent sovereignty, standing upon its reserved powers, will prove too powerful in such a controversy, and must triumph over the Federal government, sustained by its delegated and limited authority; and in this answer we have an acknowledgment of the truth of those great principles for which the State has so firmly and nobly contended. . . .

Is this a Federal Union? a union of States, as distinct from that of individuals? Is the sovereignty in the several States, or in the American people in the aggregate? The very language which we . . . use . . . affords proof conclusive as to its real character. The terms union, federal, united, all imply a combination of sovereignties, a confederation of States. They never apply to an association of individuals. Who ever heard of the United State of New York, of Massachusetts, or of Virginia? Who ever heard the term federal or union applied to the aggregation of individuals into one community? Nor is the other point less clear—that the sovereignty is in the several States, and that our system is a union of twenty-four sovereign powers, under a constitutional compact, and not of a divided sovereignty between the States severally and the United States? In spite of all that has been said, I maintain that sovereignty is in its nature indivisible. It is the supreme power in a State. . . . But if the Senator [opposing Calhoun in this debate] . . . means to assert that the twenty-four States form but one community, with a single sovereign power as to the objects of the Union, it will be but the revival of the old question, of whether the Union is a union between States, as distinct communities, or a mere aggregate of the American people, as a mass of individuals. . . .

Disguise it as you may, the controversy is one between power and liberty; and I tell the gentlemen who are opposed to me, that, as strong as may be the love of power on their side, the love of liberty is still stronger on ours. History furnishes many instances of similar struggles, where the love of liberty has prevailed against power under every disadvantage, and among them few more striking than that of our own Revolution; where, as strong as was the parent country, and feeble as were the Colonies, yet, under the impulse of liberty, and the blessing of God, they gloriously triumphed in the contest. There are, indeed, many striking analogies between that and the present controversy. They both originated substantially in the same cause. . . . The very arguments resorted to at the commencement of the American Revolution, and the measures adopted, and the motives assigned [by Great Britain] to bring on that contest (to enforce the law), are almost identically the same.

But to return . . . to the consideration of the bill. Whatever difference of opinion may exist upon other points, there is one on which I should suppose there can be none; that this bill rests upon principles which, if carried out, will ride over State sovereignties, and that it will be idle for any advocates hereafter to talk of State rights. . . . I am compelled to say, that "in cases of deliberate and dangerous infractions of the Constitution, the States, as parties to the compact, have the right, and are in duty bound, to interpose to arrest the progress of the evil, and to maintain within their respective limits the authorities, rights, and liberties appertaining to them." . . .*

FIRST INAUGURAL ADDRESS (1861)

Abraham Lincoln

[Lincoln began his speech by addressing the south's fear of his new Republican administration. He promised not to "interfere with the institution of slavery in the States where it exists." Lincoln then made the case that the Constitution is "perpetual" unless changed by the people.]

I hold that . . . the Union of these States is perpetual. . . . If the United States be not a government proper, but an association of States in the nature of contract merely, can it, as a contract, be peaceably unmade by less than all the parties who made it? One party to a contract may violate it—break it, so to speak—but does it not require all to lawfully rescind it?

[T]he proposition that . . . the Union is perpetual [is] confirmed by the history of the Union itself. The Union is much older than the Constitution. It was formed, in fact, by the Articles of Association in 1774. It was matured and continued by the Declaration of Independence in 1776. It was further matured, and the faith of all the then thirteen States expressly plighted and engaged that it should be perpetual, by the

---

*Calhoun is quoting from "The Virginia and Kentucky Resolution."

Source: Abraham Lincoln, *Abraham Lincoln: Complete Works,* ed. John G. Nicolay and John Hay (New York: The Century Co., 1894), 2: 1–7.

Articles of Confederation in 1778. And finally, in 1787, one of the declared objects for ordaining and establishing the Constitution was "to form a more perfect Union."

But if destruction of the Union by one or by a part only of the States be lawfully possible, the Union is less perfect than before the Constitution, having lost the vital element of perpetuity.

It follows from these views that no State upon its own mere motion can lawfully get out of the Union; that resolves and ordinances to that effect are legally void, and that acts of violence within any State or States against the authority of the United States are insurrectionary or revolutionary, according to circumstances.

I therefore consider that . . . the Constitution and . . . the Union is unbroken, and to the extent of my ability, I shall take care, as the Constitution itself expressly enjoins upon me, that the laws of the Union be faithfully executed in all the States. Doing this I deem to be only a simple duty on my part, and I shall perform it so far as practicable unless my rightful masters, the American people, shall . . . in some authoritative manner direct the contrary. I trust this will not be regarded as a menace, but only as the declared purpose of the Union that it will constitutionally defend and maintain itself. . . .

All profess to be content in the Union if all constitutional rights can be maintained. . . . [A]ll the vital rights of minorities and of individuals are so plainly assured to them . . . in the Constitution that controversies never arise concerning them. But no organic law can ever be framed with a provision specifically applicable to every question which may occur in practical administration. . . . May Congress prohibit slavery in the Territories? The Constitution does not expressly say. Must Congress protect slavery in the Territories? The Constitution does not expressly say.

From questions of this class spring all our constitutional controversies, and we divide upon them into majorities and minorities. If the minority will not acquiesce, the majority must, or the Government must cease. There is no other alternative. . . .

Plainly the central idea of secession is the essence of anarchy. A majority held in restraint by constitutional checks and limitations, and always changing easily with deliberate changes of popular opinions and sentiments, is the only true sovereign of a free people. Whoever rejects it does of necessity fly to anarchy or to despotism. Unanimity is impossible. The rule of a minority, as a permanent arrangement, is wholly inadmissible; so that, rejecting the majority principle, anarchy or despotism in some form is all that is left. . . .

One section of our country believes slavery is right and ought to be extended, while the other believes it is wrong and ought not to be extended. This is the only substantial dispute. . . .

This country, with its institutions, belongs to the people who inhabit it. Whenever they shall grow weary of the existing Government, they can exercise their constitutional right of amending it or their revolutionary right to dismember or overthrow it. . . . I fully recognize the rightful authority of the people over the whole subject, to be exercised in either of the modes prescribed in the instrument itself*. . . .

---

*Lincoln is referring to Article V of the Constitution, which establishes that Congress shall either propose amendments or call a convention for proposing amendments on the votes of two-thirds of both Houses of Congress or the votes of the legislatures of two-thirds of the states.

Why should there not be a patient confidence in the ultimate justice of the people? Is there any better or equal hope in the world? In our present differences, is either party without faith of being in the right? If the Almighty Ruler of Nations, with His eternal truth and justice, be on your side of the North, or on yours of the South, that truth and that justice will surely prevail by the judgment of this great tribunal of the American people. . . .

I am loath to close. We are not enemies, but friends. We must not be enemies. Though passion may have strained it must not break our bonds of affection. The mystic chords of memory, stretching from every battlefield and patriot grave to every living heart and hearthstone all over this broad land, will yet swell the chorus of the Union, when again touched, as surely they will be, by the better angels of our nature.

The Question of Immigration and "Americanization" in the 1890s

By the 1890s, the United States had reestablished an equilibrium based on southern acceptance of northern dominance of the country in return for white predominance over blacks in the South itself. Although slavery had been abolished, by means of the so-called Jim Crow laws, a system of racial segregation and inequality was created that was to last into the 1960s. Yet, as the country neared the end of the century, significant questions of national identity continued to trouble America. This occurred because large-scale immigration, along with rapid industrialization and urbanization, was changing the very face of the country. The new wealth and political power of the cities, as well as the decline in status and control of rural America, which was also suffering through a long agricultural depression, contributed to the sense on the part of many Americans that immigrants threatened to swamp the nation and destroy it. Members of the white working class sometimes supported nativist movements because they believed that immigrants would work for almost nothing, and hence they undercut wages and put jobs in jeopardy.

Already before the Civil War, the influx of large numbers of Catholic Germans and Irish had led to ethnic conflict and to nativist reactions among native-born white Americans, who were largely of Protestant British descent. Nativism essentially argues that the country should belong to those who were born here, or sometimes even to those whose parents were born here. It usually arises at a time of high immigration accompanied by heightened social and economic tensions. Like the 1850s, the 1880s and 1890s witnessed large-scale immigration, this time of Roman Catholics, Orthodox Catholics, and Jews from southern and eastern Europe. Nativist discontent rose again.

Added to the equation by 1890 were social Darwinist ideas. Social Darwinism essentially applies Charles Darwin's biological theories to human social life. Darwin argued that all life forms are the product of evolution, that occurs as a result of a struggle for existence that is based on "survival of the fittest." Different species compete for limited resources, and those that cannot successfully compete become extinct. One of the applications of Darwinian theory to human life was the common practice in late-nineteenth-century European writing of referring to ethnic groups and nations as "races." This fed a growing sense of competition among nations, an emphasis on military might as necessary for survival, and an imperialist drive to divide up the globe so that the "race" would have sufficient resources and room. In terms of debates over American national identity and the issue of immigration, social Darwinist thought contributed to a concern that the "Anglo-Saxon race" (essentially, Protestants of British descent) not be swamped by the tide of non-Anglo-Saxon immigrants.

So once more America had encountered the question of what the true and legitimate nature of the country was, and the question of who constitutes a good American had reached a level of prominence and volume in the national dialogue. This issue is examined through texts written by two prominent leaders of white traditional America: Reverend Josiah Strong and Theodore Roosevelt. The two men shared many common assumptions. For example, they each held social Darwinist and imperialist convictions. Each believed that immigrants should be assimilated, but they differed fundamentally on what that assimilation process should include. As a result, they elaborated distinct visions of what a "true American," to paraphrase Roosevelt's title, should do and be.

Josiah Strong (1847–1916) was an eminent Congregationalist minister, head of the influential American Evangelical Alliance, and a leading spokesman of a movement for social activism among white Protestant Christians known as the Social Gospel. In essence, Strong believed that a Protestant America was destined to lead the world to an earthly Christian Kingdom of faith, prosperity, and social justice. He held that American superiority was based on its Anglo-Saxon "race," its pure, spiritual Protestant Christianity, its love of civil liberty, and its material abundance. Hence he supported a specific ethnic and cultural view of who constitutes a good American, and he combined this with a social Darwinist and imperialist view of America's racial and cultural superiority and its world mission. The work excerpted here, *Our Country,* was published in 1885, republished more than once, and translated into numerous languages. It is filled with dire discussions of dangers, such as the "perils" of immigration, Romanism,[3] religion and the public schools, Mormonism, intemperance,[4] socialism, wealth, and the city. Fundamentally, then, Strong opposed the new America that was coming into existence as a result of industrialization, urbanization, and immigration, yet his vision of America's world leadership was based on market forces as a means of "civilizing" the world. Thus his work was not without its contradictory elements, but it was extraordinarily influential in its day.

Paired with the selection from Strong's work, we include a passage from a work by his contemporary and friend, Theodore Roosevelt (1858–1919). The Roosevelts were an old established New York clan of mixed Dutch and English ancestry, and his mother came from a well-to-do Georgia plantation family. Despite this impressive pedigree, Roosevelt came to embrace a form of social Darwinism according to which the privilege of leadership derived from individual merit and not birthright. TR, as he would later be called, graduated Phi Beta Kappa from Harvard in 1880, and he moved in and out of politics for the next decade and a half, establishing a reputation as a reformer. Along the way, he developed an ideal of the "strenuous life," based in part on his own struggle with poor health as a child and a two-year interval he spent on a cattle ranch in the West. He organized the "Rough Riders" when war broke out with Spain in 1898 and fought in Cuba. Within three years, he would become the youngest president in U.S. history. Although he also embraced imperialism and the special role the Anglo-Saxon "race" should occupy in the world, he articulated a definition of "Americanism" that was not as religiously and culturally exclusive as Strong's.

Together, the two readings illustrate how nationalist issues and views evolved from the Civil War era to the end of the century. Immigrants had become the new "threat," despite their contributions to the industrialization of the country. In defining the immigrant as "the other," both Strong and Roosevelt expressed a vision of "Americanism" that continues to have meaning today.

QUESTIONS TO CONSIDER

1. What were the evil influences of immigration, according to Strong, and what could be done about them? What stereotypes helped shape his views? Did Roosevelt share any of these concerns?

2. Considering the evils that Strong associated with immigrants, what traits would Strong identify with a good American? What would he have had America look like? List the three main features of "true Americanism," according to Roosevelt. What vision of America and Americans emerges from his essay?

3. What did Roosevelt mean when he discussed "Americanizing" immigrants? How would Strong "Americanize" immigrants? What is different about their two views of America?

4. How had the definition of America changed in the half century since slavery and states' rights were the main issues of American national identity? How were issues of progress and power connected to the changing definition of American national identity?

5. How does the current American debate on immigration compare with the views and ideas of Strong and Roosevelt? What do their similarities or differences tell you?

OUR COUNTRY (1891)

Josiah Strong

The Time Factor in the Problem

There are certain great focal points of history toward which the lines of past progress have converged, and from which have radiated the molding influences of the future. Such was the Incarnation, such was the German Reformation of the sixteenth century,

Source: Josiah Strong, *Our Country: Its Possible Future and Its Present Crisis,* rev. ed. (New York: American Home Missionary Society, 1891), 15, 20, 44–45, 54–61.

and such are the *closing years of the nineteenth century,* second in importance to . . . only . . . the birth of Christ.

Many are not aware that we are living in extraordinary times. Few suppose that these years of peaceful prosperity, in which we are quietly developing a continent, are the pivot on which is turning the nation's future. And fewer still imagine that the destinies of mankind, for centuries to come, can be seriously affected, much less determined, by the men of this generation in the United States. . . . Several years ago Professor Austin Phelps said: "Five hundred years of time in the process of the world's salvation may depend on the next twenty years of United States history.". . .

Perils—Immigration

Political optimism is one of the vices of the American people. There is a popular faith that "God takes care of children, fools, and the United States." We deem ourselves a chosen people, and incline to the belief that the Almighty stands pledged to our prosperity. . . . Such optimism is as senseless as pessimism is faithless. The one is as foolish as the other is wicked.

Thoughtful men see perils on our national horizon. . . . America, as the land of promise to all the world, is the destination of the most remarkable migration of which we have any record. During the last ten years we have suffered a peaceful invasion by an army more than four times as vast as the estimated number of Goths and Vandals that . . . overwhelmed Rome. During the past hundred years fifteen million foreigners have made their homes in the United States, and three-quarters of them have come since 1850*. . . .

In view of the fact that Europe is able to send us six times as many immigrants during the next thirty years as during the thirty years past . . . , is it not reasonable to expect a rising tide of immigration unless Congress takes effective measures to check it? . . .

So immense a foreign element must have a profound influence on our national life and character. Immigration brings unquestioned benefits, but. . . [i]t . . . furnishes the soil which feeds the life of several of the most noxious growths of our civilization. . . .

Consider briefly the moral and political influence of immigration. . . . The typical immigrant is a European peasant, whose horizon has been narrow, whose moral and religious training has been meager or false, and whose ideas of life are low. Not a few belong to the pauper and criminal classes. . . . Moreover, immigration is demoralizing. . . . We have a good deal of piety in our churches that will not bear transportation. . . . American travelers in Europe often grant themselves license, on which, if at home, they would frown. Very many church-members, when they go west, seem to think . . . that the Ten Commandments are not binding west of the Missouri. Is it strange, then, that those who come from other lands, whose old associations are all broken and whose reputations are left behind, should sink to a lower moral level? . . .

Moreover, immigration not only furnishes the greater portion of our criminals, it is also seriously affecting the morals of the native population. It is disease and not health which is contagious. Most foreigners bring with them continental ideas of the Sabbath, and the result is sadly manifest in all our cities, where it is being transformed

---

*The numbers that are generally accepted for immigration are 20 million immigrants from 1820 to 1900, with more than half of them arriving in the period after 1865 (5 million in the 1880s alone).

from a holy day into a holiday. But by far the most effective instrumentality for debauching popular morals is the liquor traffic, and this is chiefly carried on by foreigners. . . .

We can only glance at the political aspects of immigration. As we have already seen, it is immigration which has fed fat the liquor power; and there is a liquor vote. Immigration furnishes most of the victims of Mormonism; and there is a Mormon vote. Immigration is the strength of the Catholic church; and there is a Catholic vote. Immigration is the mother and nurse of American socialism; and there is to be a socialist vote. Immigration tends strongly to the cities, and gives to them their political complexion. And there is no more serious menace to our civilization than our rabble-ruled cities. . . . Immigration has created the "German vote" and the "Irish vote." . . . A mass of men but little acquainted with our institutions, who will act in concert and who are controlled largely by their appetites and prejudices, constitute a very paradise for demagogues.

[I]mmigration . . . has a [detrimental] . . . influence upon popular intelligence, for the percentage of illiteracy among the foreign-born population is thirty-eight per cent greater than among the native-born whites. Thus immigration complicates our moral and political problems by swelling our dangerous classes. . . . It goes without saying, that there is a dead-line of ignorance and vice in every republic, and when it is touched by the average citizen, free institutions perish. . . .

Our safety demands the assimilation of these strange populations, and the process of assimilation will become slower and more difficult as the proportion of foreigners increases. . . .

Foreigners are not coming to the United States in answer to any appetite of ours, controlled by an unfailing moral or political instinct. They naturally consult their own interests in coming, not ours. . . .

"WHAT 'AMERICANISM' MEANS" (1894)

Theodore Roosevelt

We shall never be successful over the dangers that confront us; we shall never achieve true greatness, nor reach the lofty ideal which the founders and preservers of our mighty Federal Republic have set before us, unless we are Americans in heart and soul, in spirit and purpose, keenly alive to the responsibility implied in the very name of American, and proud beyond measure of the glorious privilege of bearing it.

There are two or three sides to the question of Americanism, and two or three senses in which the word "Americanism" can be used to express the antithesis of what is unwholesome and undesirable. In the first place we wish to be broadly American and national, as opposed to being local or sectional. We do not wish, in politics, in literature, or in art, to develop that unwholesome parochial spirit, that over-exaltation of

Source: Theodore Roosevelt, "What 'Americanism' Means," *Forum*, vol. XVIII (April 1894): 196–205.

the little community at the expense of the great nation, which produces what has been described as the patriotism of the village, the patriotism of the belfry*. . . . However, politically this question of American nationality has been settled once for all[†]. . . .

There is a second side of this question of a broad Americanism, however. The patriotism of the village or the belfry is bad, but the lack of all patriotism is even worse. . . . The man who becomes Europeanized, who loses his power of doing good work on this side of the water, and who loses his love for his native land, is . . . as emphatically a noxious element in our body politic as is the man who comes here from abroad and remains a foreigner.

It is not only necessary to Americanize the immigrants of foreign birth who settle among us, but it is even more necessary for those among us who are by birth and descent already Americans not to throw away our birthright. . . . [T]o be a first-class American is fifty-fold better than to be a second-class imitation of a Frenchman or Englishman. . . .

We believe in waging relentless war on rank-growing evils of all kinds, and it makes no difference to us if they happen to be of purely native growth. We grasp at any good, no matter whence it comes. . . . But it remains true that, in spite of all our faults and short-comings, no other land offers such glorious possibilities to the man able to take advantage of them, as does ours; it remains true that no one of our people can do any work really worth doing unless he does it primarily as an American. It is because certain classes of our people still retain their spirit of colonial dependence on, and exaggerated deference to, European opinion, that they fail to accomplish what they ought to. It is precisely along the lines where we have worked most independently that we have accomplished the greatest results; and it is in those professions where there has been no servility to, but merely a wise profiting by foreign experience, that we have produced our greatest men. Our soldiers and statesmen and orators; our explorers, our wilderness-winners, and commonwealth-builders, . . . and the other men whose energy and ingenuity have created our marvelous material prosperity . . . have drawn wisdom from the experience of every age and nation, but . . . have nevertheless thought, and worked, and conquered, and lived, and died, purely as Americans; and on the whole they have done better work than has been done in any other country during the short period of our national life. . . .

The third sense in which the word "Americanism" may be employed is with reference to the Americanizing of the newcomers to our shores. We must Americanize them in every way, in speech, in political ideas and principles. . . . We welcome the German or the Irishman who becomes an American. We have no use for the German or Irishman who remains such. We do not wish German-Americans and Irish-Americans, . . . we want only Americans, and, provided they are such, we do not care whether they are of native or of Irish or of German ancestry. We have no room in any healthy American community for a German-American vote or an Irish-American vote. . . . We have no room for any people who do not act and vote simply as Americans, and as nothing else. Moreover, we have as little use for people who carry religious prejudices into our politics as for those who carry prejudices of caste or

---

*Loyalty that extends only as far as the sound of the town's bells can be heard.

[†]By the victory of the North in the Civil War.

nationality. We stand unalterably in favor of the public school system in its entirety. We believe that English, and no other language, is that in which all the school exercises should be conducted. . . . But we are equally opposed to any discrimination against or for a man because of his creed. We demand that all citizens, Protestant and Catholic, Jew and Gentile, shall have fair treatment in every way; that all alike shall have their rights guaranteed them. We maintain that it is an outrage, in voting for a man for any position, whether State or national, to take into account his religious faith, provided only he is a good American. When a secret society does what in some places the American Protective Association* seems to have done, and tries to proscribe Catholics both politically and socially, the members of such society show that they themselves are as utterly un-American, as alien to our school of political thought, as the worst immigrants who land on our shores . . . ; they should receive the hearty condemnation of all Americans who are truly patriotic.

The mighty tide of immigration to our shores has brought in its train much of good and much of evil; and whether the good or the evil shall predominate depends mainly on whether these newcomers do or do not throw themselves heartily into our national life, cease to be Europeans, and become Americans like the rest of us. More than a third of the people of the Northern States are of foreign birth or parentage. An immense number of them have become completely Americanized, and these stand on exactly the same plane as the descendants of any Puritan, Cavalier, or Knickerbocker among us,† and do their full and honorable share of the nation's work. . . . It is an immense benefit to the European immigrant to change him into an American citizen. To bear the name of American is to bear the most honorable titles. . . .

We freely extend the hand of welcome and of good-fellowship to every man, no matter what his creed or birthplace, who comes here honestly intent on becoming a good United States citizen like the rest of us; but we have a right, and it is our duty to demand that he . . . must take pride in the things which we can all take pride in. He must revere only our flag. . . . He must learn to celebrate Washington's birthday rather than that of the Queen or Kaiser, and the Fourth of July instead of St. Patrick's Day. . . . Above all, the immigrant must learn to talk and think and *be* United States.

JAPANESE NATIONALISM IN THE NINETEENTH CENTURY
Initial Responses to the West

The period in Japanese history from 1600 to 1867 is known as the era of the Tokugawa Shogunate. Although there continued to be emperors throughout this era, power was held and exercised by the great lords of the Tokugawa family, who were known by the title of *shogun*. The emperors were kept from real decision-making power, their incomes were limited, and their activities were largely

---

*An anti-Catholic nativist group started in Iowa in 1887. Its membership peaked in the early 1890s.
†Original immigrants to Massachusetts, Virginia, and New York.

ceremonial. Although the shoguns exercised effective political power, they were not strong enough to do away with the imperial office entirely.

One of the main policies established and enforced by the shoguns in this era was the policy of "seclusion." Worried about the political and cultural implications of the spread of Christianity through the Japanese islands and about the "divide and conquer" policies foreign powers might try to play in Japan's decentralized feudal system, the government of the shogunate, known as the *bakufu,* issued a series of decrees that restricted European presence to a tiny Dutch trading post and that forbade Japanese from leaving and returning to the islands. This last provision carried with it the death penalty. Trade and cultural contact with China continued, and some information about and influence of Western civilization reached Japanese scholars and leaders, but widespread contact and interaction was avoided.

But by the first half of the nineteenth century, Japan was experiencing widespread social difficulties and pressure from the western powers. A major source of concern for the *bakufu* was unrest among the samurai. Samurai were hereditary nobles (some 5–7 percent of the population), an elite class that still lived according to the *Bushido* code, or the Way of the Warrior. By the nineteenth century, this group became a force for instability. They were horribly underemployed and financially strapped, violating both their financial well-being and their ethos of service. Prosperous merchants and farmers frequently lived better than samurai, but they had their own grievances, because the trade and social policies of the shogunate hindered their economic expansion. All classes suffered, because the shogunate had increased its fiscal demands on the population to meet rising governmental expenses.

So there was general unhappiness with the *bakufu* government, and even before the humiliation of Commodore Matthew Perry's demarche, there was a growing feeling that the emperor ought to be restored. The power of the shogunate had always been complicated by the unique role of the emperor in Japanese political history. In Japan—"the land of the rising sun"—the emperor was held to be a direct descendant of the sun in an uninterrupted line. No matter how powerful the shogunate became, the emperor could not be fully replaced, because he was viewed not as a representative of the gods but as a god himself. Political theory viewed the shoguns as stewards or agents of the emperor. Hence, when discontent with the shogunate became a significant force, restoration of the emperor suggested itself as both traditional and legitimate.

Finally, they also learned of developments in China and Chinese-Western relations via their semipermeable exclusion institutions. Particularly worrisome to informed Japanese of the ruling class was the fate of China as a result of the Opium War. The so-called "treaty ports" established by the Treaty of Nanking in 1842 forced China to open up to foreign trade and to accept unequal status in the world of international affairs. If that could be done to China, what would prevent it from happening to Japan?

The coming of Commodore Perry's "black ships" confirmed the worst fears of Japanese leaders. The west had come to make the same demands of Japan that it had successfully imposed on China. What was going to be Japan's response?

With the advantage of historical hindsight, we know that a remarkable group of young samurai became the leadership of the movement to end the shogunate and "restore" the emperor in a political movement known as the Meiji Restoration of 1867. We know as well that the leaders of the Meiji movement pushed through a thorough reform of Japan's social system, ending the feudal legislation that had divided the population into different estates and even abolishing the samurai. They supported industrialization, and they studied the constitutional systems in the west and devised a conservative constitution for the new Japan. They did all this with the view of bringing Japan up to par with the western powers so that they could undo the unequal treaties that acceptance of American demands had imposed on Japan.

That events occurred this way can obscure the fact that at the time a much wider range of responses were discussed and promoted. Some were put forward as being more consistent with Japan's historical and cultural traditions, and others were thought to be more in keeping with the way Japanese national identity ought to be defined in the contemporary world. Taken as a whole, the selections presented here were chosen to reveal the range of the most significant responses generated in Japan by the need to clarify Japanese national identity in the face of the humiliating western demands.

The first document is a set of recommendations made by Tokugawa Nariaki (1800–1860), one of the leading Japanese political and military leaders of the nineteenth century. As possessor of the Mito territories, he was one of the most powerful and influential *daimyo,* or feudal lords, and a member of a collateral branch of the Tokugawa family. Nariaki was a very forceful and polarizing personality. Although a confirmed believer in the superiority of the Japanese way of life and of the imperial tradition, he was not an unreflective or "knee-jerk" conservative. Already in 1841 he had established an academy in his feudal domain for the study of useful western knowledge, and it was there that the phrase "revere the emperor, expel the barbarians" was first used publicly. He was an adviser on maritime defense, and, when Commodore Perry and the Americans demanded change, he penned an aggressive and sharply defined response, which urged resistance.

QUESTIONS TO CONSIDER

1. What are Nariaki's main recommendations? What kinds of arguments does he use to support his recommendations?

2. What understanding of Japanese national identity does Nariaki provide here? What are the main bases of national identity implied or stated in Nariaki's argument?

3. What is the relationship between the state and nationalism in Nariaki's presentation? Does it surprise you that Nariaki favored ending the *bakufu* and restoring the emperor?

4. How do issues of power figure in Nariaki's calculations? What role does Nariaki think Christianity plays in western diplomacy?
5. In your opinion, could Japan have successfully defied the western powers had
   it followed Nariaki's recommendations? Why or why not?

"MEMORANDUM TO THE BAKUFU" (1853)

Tokugawa Nariaki

It is my belief that the first and most urgent of our tasks is for the *Bakufu* to make its
choice between peace and war, and having determined its policy to pursue it un-
waveringly thereafter. When we consider the respective advantages and disadvan-
tages of war and peace, we find that if we put our trust in war the whole country's
morale will be increased and even if we sustain an initial defeat we will in the end
expel the foreigner; while if we put our trust in peace, even though things may seem
tranquil for a time, the morale of the country will be greatly lowered and we will
come in the end to complete collapse. This has been amply demonstrated in the history of China. . . . [I]n my view we must never choose the policy of peace.

Although our country's territory is not extensive, foreigners both fear and respect
us. . . . Despite this, the Americans who arrived recently, though fully aware of the
Bakufu's prohibition, . . . insisted on presenting their written requests. Moreover they
entered Edo Bay,* fired heavy guns in salute and even went so far as to conduct sur-
veys without permission. They were arrogant and discourteous, their actions an outrage. Indeed, this was the greatest disgrace we have suffered since the dawn of our
history. . . . [S]hould it happen that the *Bakufu* fails to expel them but also that it concludes an agreement in accordance with their requests, then I fear it would be impossible to maintain our national prestige. . . .

The prohibition of Christianity is the first rule of the Tokugawa house. . . . The
Bakufu can never ignore or overlook the evils of Christianity. Yet if the Americans are
allowed to come again this religion will inevitably raise its head once more, however
strict the prohibition; and this, I fear, is something we could never justify to the spirits
of our ancestors. . . .

To exchange our valuable articles like gold, silver, copper, and iron for useless
foreign goods like woollens and satin is to incur great loss while acquiring not the
smallest benefit. The best course of all would be for the *Bakufu* to put a stop to
the trade with Holland. By contrast, to open such valueless trade with others besides
the Dutch would . . . inflict the greatest possible harm on our country. . . .

For some years Russia, England, and others have sought trade with us, but the
Bakufu has not permitted it. Should permission be granted to the Americans, on what
grounds would it be possible to refuse if Russia and the others [again] request it? . . .

Source: G. Beasley, trans. and ed., *Select Documents on Japanese Foreign Policy, 1853–1868* (London:
Oxford University Press, 1960), 102–06.

*Uraga harbor near Yokohama. The Japanese wanted negotiations to take place there, not in Edo
(Tokyo).

It is widely stated that [apart from trade] the foreigners have no other evil designs and that if only the *Bakufu* will permit trade there will be no further difficulty. However, it is their practice first to seek a foothold by means of trade and then go on to propagate Christianity and make other unreasonable demands. . . . Thus we would be repeating the blunders of others, seen . . . recently in the Opium War in China. . . .

Though the *Rangakusha** group may argue secretly that world conditions are much changed from what they were, . . . seclusion in isolation amidst the seas . . . is a constant source of danger to us and that our best course would therefore be to communicate with foreign countries and open an extensive trade; yet, to my mind, if the people of Japan stand firmly united, if we complete our military preparations and return to the state of society that existed before the middle ages, then we will even be able to go out against foreign countries and spread abroad our fame and prestige. But if we open trade at the demand of the foreigners, for no better reason than that . . . men have shown fear merely at the coming of a handful of foreign warships, then it would truly be a vain illusion to think of evolving any long-range plan for going out against foreign countries. . . .

I hear that all, even though they be commoners, who have witnessed the recent actions of the foreigners, think them abominable; and if the *Bakufu* does not expel these insolent foreigners root and branch there may be some who will complain in secret, asking to what purpose have been all the preparations of gun-emplacements. It is inevitable that men should think in this way when they have seen how arrogantly the foreigners acted at Uraga. That, I believe, is because even the humblest are conscious of the debt they owe their country, and it is indeed a promising sign. Since even ignorant commoners are talking in this way, I fear that if the *Bakufu* does not decide to carry out expulsion, . . . then the lower orders may fail to understand its ideas and hence opposition might arise from evil men who had lost their respect for *Bakufu* authority. It might even be that *Bakufu* control . . . would itself be endangered. . . .

[It is argued], the *Bakufu* should show itself compliant at this time and should placate the foreigners, meanwhile exerting all its efforts in military preparations, so that when these preparations have been completed it can more strictly enforce the ancient laws. However, . . . there is not the slightest chance that the feudal lords will complete military preparations . . . unless they are set an example in military matters by the *Bakufu*. . . . I therefore believe that if there be any sign of the *Bakufu* pursuing a policy of peace, morale will never rise. . . . But if the *Bakufu* . . . shows itself resolute for expulsion, the immediate effect will be to increase ten-fold the morale of the country. . . . Hesitant as I am to say so, only by so doing will the Shogun be able to fulfill his "barbarian-expelling" duty. . . .

Japanese National Identity and the Meiji Restoration

The fifteen years between Perry's visit and the overthrow of the shogunate were filled with violence and unrest. Assassinations, violent popular uprisings, shelling by western navies (in retaliation for the murder of a British merchant), and

---

*Rangaku or "Dutch knowledge"; *Rangakusha* are the scholars of western knowledge.

increasing pressure from the emperor overwhelmed the shogunate and led in 1868 to the end of that governmental system. A new imperial system was established. It was effective in meeting the challenges facing Japan for two reasons. First of all, the support of Emperor Meiji provided a legitimizing force, given Japanese beliefs about the divine origins of the emperor. The second vital factor was the talent of the group of mostly young samurai who led the Meiji Restoration. They were energetic, flexible, and unified.

Still, there remained profound disagreements about what form the Japanese nation should take and what the new definition of Japanese nationalism should be. Some of these questions were resolved in April 1868, when the Emperor Meiji issued a declaration known as the Charter Oath. In essence, the Charter Oath declared the end of the feudal system in the social, economic, and governmental realms and committed Japan to adapting its system based on current practices in the west. Although this still did not determine with full finality all questions about the new system, it did mark a fundamental break with both the feudal past and the policy of seclusion.

The leaders of the Meiji Restoration sought to align Japan with "civilization and enlightenment," which to them meant the nationalist structures of the western world. However, because there were deep disagreements in the west over definitions of nationalism, the Japanese would have to work out their own definition of "civilization and enlightenment."

The following two documents address that debate in terms of the shape that the new government would take. The first document is a reminiscence about the principles that guided the Japanese leaders in establishing their new system by Ito Hirobumi (1841–1909), the man who more than any other decided the shape that the new Japanese government would take. Ito's background captures some of the forces for change at work in Japan in the mid-nineteenth century. Son of a wealthy farmer, he was adopted by a samurai and educated at a leading school for study of western military techniques. The school's founder had coined the phrase "western knowledge, eastern ethics." Because of his western training and his ability, Ito was one of the leading figures on a mission that spent eighteen months traveling through America, Europe, and Asia studying foreign systems. He then became the main author of the new Meiji constitution, later serving as prime minister. He based the constitution heavily on the Prussian model, because it was more conservative and accorded much wider powers to the emperor than did the British system. Shortly before his death, he reflected on the drafting of the new constitution and the principles that governed his choices as he constructed the document, and those reflections are excerpted here.

The Meiji Constitution was promulgated in 1889 on the national holiday associated with the mythological founding of the country in the seventh century BCE. Elaborate ceremonies were devised for the emperor to perform, including traditional Shinto religious rituals to the imperial ancestors and a public ceremony, with the emperor garbed in western clothing. Here we excerpt brief passages from the Preamble to the Constitution to provide an understanding of how the new political order was tied to traditional Japanese understanding of the place of the emperor in their system.

Taken together, these two documents demonstrate the role of tradition in the significant changes Japan underwent in this time period. While adjusting to western patterns of "civilization and enlightenment," the Meiji leadership paid close attention to the unique political culture of Japan, providing us with a vivid example of the forces of continuity and change that swirled around the issue of nationalism and nation building in the nineteenth century.

QUESTIONS TO CONSIDER

1. How are "civilization and enlightenment" understood in these two documents? Are there any common elements across the two texts?

2. Identify the specifically Japanese components put forward in these texts and distinguish them from aspects that are similar to western constitutional systems. Which is more prominent, the uniquely Japanese elements or the features in common with western systems? What role does tradition play?

3. What vision of the nation and of national identity emerges from these two texts? Are there any differences between the understanding of nation that each text presents? How are Japan's relations with the outside world addressed in these sources? How do relations with other nations affect the definition of Japan and national identity?

4. How is the relationship between the state and the nation defined in these texts? Is the nation defined independently of the state in either of the texts? What role do the people play?

5. The phrase "civilization and enlightenment" sounds as if the main concern is culture and education. Do these texts seem concerned with those issues? What part does concern with power and progress seem to play in the political positions defined by these texts?

REMINISCENCES ON THE DRAFTING OF THE NEW CONSTITUTION

Ito Hirobumi

The advent of Commodore Perry . . . roughly awakened us to the consciousness of mighty forces at work to change the face of the outside world. We were ill-prepared to bear the brunt of these forces, but once awakened to the need, were not slow to grapple with them. So, first of all, the whole fabric of the feudal system . . . had to be uprooted and destroyed. The annihilation of [the] centrifugal forces . . . of autocratic feudal provinces was a necessary step to . . . a strong central government, without

Source: From Shigenobu Okuma, comp., *Fifty Years of New Japan*, 2nd ed. (London: Smith, Elder, and Co., 1910), 1: 122–26, 128–30.

which we would not have been able to offer a united front to the outside forces or stand up as a united whole to maintain the country's very existence.

. . . [H]owever, . . . there . . . is this false impression . . . that our civilization . . . is nothing but a hastily donned, superficial veneer. On the contrary, I am not exaggerating when I say that, for generations and centuries, we have been enjoying a moral education of the highest type. The great ideals . . . developed and sanctified by the continual usage of centuries under the comprehensive name of *bushido*, offered us splendid standards of morality, rigorously enforced in the everyday life of the educated classes. The result, as everyone who is acquainted with Old Japan knows, was an education which aspired to the attainment of Stoic heroism, a rustic simplicity and a self-sacrificing spirit unsurpassed in Sparta, and the aesthetic culture and intellectual refinement of Athens. Art, delicacy of sentiment, higher ideals of morality and of philosophy, as well as the highest types of valor and chivalry all these we have tried to combine in the man as he ought to be. We laid great stress on the harmonious combination of all the known accomplishments of a developed human being, and it is only since the introduction of modern technical sciences that we have been obliged to pay more attention to specialized technical attainments than to the harmonious development of the whole. . . .

Thus it will be seen that what was lacking in our countrymen of the feudal era was not mental or moral fiber, but the scientific, technical, and materialistic side of modern civilization. Our present condition is not the result of the ingrafting of a civilization entirely different from our own, as foreign observers are apt to believe, but simply a different training and nursing of a strongly vital character already existent. The mass of the rural population, i.e., of common folk, did not fail to be influenced by the ideals prevailing amongst the higher and educated classes. They too were honest, industrious, ready to sacrifice. . . . Here was a splendid material with which to build up a strong nation, if only it could be properly guided and educated so as to be able to meet the demands of modern, materialistic life. The Government was not slow in its endeavour to complement the incomplete side of our ancient education, and to equip the rising generation with the intellectual arms required for the modern struggle for existence and supremacy. . . .

It . . . has been the unswerving policy of our Sovereign (1) to educate the people to the requirements of a constitutional state, (2) to fortify the nation with the best results and resources of modern civilisation, and (3) thus to secure for the country prosperity, strength, and culture, and the consequent recognized status of membership upon an equal footing in the family of the most powerful and civilized nations of the world, . . . [as] has been vividly illustrated very recently by the way in which the whole country stood up to the Titanic struggle in defence of its honour and interests against the nation hitherto considered as almost the most powerful in the world.* Even the simplest soldier was fully conscious . . . of and intensely interested in the national mission and the national destiny. It was not the defence of his hearth and of his nearest kin, as in older times, . . . but conscientious fulfillment of a duty—nay, he even considered it as an honour and as a privilege towards the body politic of which he felt himself an organic and living unit. . . .

---

*He refers to the Russo-Japanese War of 1904–1905, won by the Japanese, the first major victory of a non-European power over a European nation in centuries.

Peculiar Features of the National Life

It was evident from the outset that mere imitation of foreign models would not suffice, for there were historical peculiarities of our country which had to be taken into consideration. For example, the Crown was, with us, an institution far more deeply rooted in the national sentiment and in our history than in other countries . . . , so that . . . we had to take care . . . not to let the institution degenerate into an ornamental crowning piece of the edifice. At the same time, it was also evident that any form of constitutional regime was impossible without full and extended protection of honor, liberty, property, and personal security of citizens, entailing necessarily many important restrictions on the powers of the Crown.

Emotional Elements in Social Life of People

On the other hand, there was one peculiarity of our social conditions that is without parallel in any other civilized country. Homogeneous in race, language, religion, and sentiments, so long secluded from the outside world, with the centuries-long traditions and inertia of the feudal system, in which the family and quasi-family ties permeated and formed the essence of every social organization, and moreover with such moral and religious tenets as laid undue stress on duties of fraternal aid and mutual succor, we had during the course of our seclusion unconsciously become a vast village community where cold intellect and calculation of public events were always restrained and even often hindered by warm emotions between man and man. . . . There still survives the bond of patron and *protégé* between them and the capitalist employers. . . . The good side of this social peculiarity had to be retained as much as possible, while its baneful influences had to be safeguarded. These and many other peculiarities had to be taken into account in order to have a constitution adapted to the actual condition of the country.

"IMPERIAL PROCLAMATION ON THE CONSTITUTION OF THE EMPIRE OF JAPAN" (1889)

Having, by virtue of the glories of Our Ancestors, ascended the throne of a lineal succession unbroken for ages eternal; desiring to promote the welfare of, and to give development to the moral and intellectual faculties of Our beloved subjects, . . . and hoping to maintain the prosperity of the State, in concert with Our people and with their support, We hereby promulgate, in pursuance of Our Imperial Rescript . . . , a fundamental law of the State, to exhibit the principles, by which We are guided in Our conduct, and to point out to what Our descendants and Our subjects and their descendants are forever to conform.

Source: "Imperial Proclamation on the Constitution of the Empire of Japan, February 11, 1889," in *The Meiji Japan Through Contemporary Sources,* Vol. 1 (Tokyo: Centre for East Asian Cultural Studies, 1969), 93–94.

The right of sovereignty of the State, We have inherited from Our Ancestors, and We shall bequeath them to Our descendants. Neither We nor they shall in the future fail to wield them, in accordance with the provisions of the Constitution hereby granted.

We now declare to respect and protect the security of the rights and of the property of Our people, and to secure to them the complete enjoyment of the same, within the extent of the provisions of the present Constitution and of the law. . . .

When in the future it may become necessary to amend any of the provisions of the present Constitution, We or Our successors shall assume the initiative right, and . . . [t]he Imperial Diet shall pass its vote upon it, . . . and in no otherwise shall Our descendants or Our subjects be permitted to attempt any alteration thereof. . . .

Our present and future subjects shall forever assume the duty of allegiance to the present Constitution.

Japanese Nationalism and Imperialism

One of the most interesting figures of Meiji Japan was Fukuzawa Yukichi (1835–1901). Trained in western languages, Fukuzawa served as interpreter on missions taken by Meiji leaders to study the wider world, especially the United States and Europe. Fukuzawa concentrated on the study of western societies and became the leader in introducing the Japanese people to western ways in a wide range of books he wrote, through a newspaper he published, and via the academy he established, which became the first private university in Japan. Characterized by a broad curiosity, great energy, and a rare independence of mind, Fukuzawa was the leading intellectual of Meiji Japan.

Although Fukuzawa consistently refused government offices and pursued his own maverick path, he shared with many other prominent Japanese a concern with the international standing and national self-assertion of Japan. By means of a Perry-esque naval expedition in 1876, Japan imposed its own unequal treaty on Korea. This force projection would continue. In 1894–1895, Japan fought a successful war against China, followed a decade later by victory over Russia, which led to a protectorate over Korea, establishing Japan as the dominant power in the region. In this manner, the Japanese imitated the western powers, who were establishing and extending their own colonial domains. In the text excerpted here, Fukuzawa reveals his exposure to reigning social Darwinist ideas and the extent to which he had assimilated western ways of viewing the world.

QUESTIONS TO CONSIDER

1. What analogy did Fukuzawa use to describe the movement of civilization? Based on this analogy, how should Japan have reacted to Western civilization, according to Fukuzawa?

2. How did China and Korea compare with Japan, in Fukuzawa's presentation? What should Japan have done about these two neighbors and why?

3. Compare Fukuzawa's views with those expressed in the other Japanese documents presented here. What similarities are there and what differences?

4. How are power and progress linked in Fukuzawa's understanding? What would Josiah Strong think about Fukuzawa's argument?

5. How did Fukuzawa define "civilization and enlightenment"? Had he correctly understood and absorbed the "civilization and enlightenment" of western nationalism? Based on the American and Japanese cases, was imperialism an inherent part of nineteenth-century nationalism?

"GOOD-BYE ASIA" (1885)

Fukuzawa Yukichi

[O]nce the wind of Western civilization blows to the East, every blade of grass and every tree in the East follow what the Western wind brings. Ancient Westerners and present-day Westerners are from the same stock and are not much different from one another. The ancient ones moved slowly, but their contemporary counterparts move vivaciously at a fast pace. . . . For those of us who live in the Orient, unless we want to prevent the coming of Western civilization with a firm resolve, it is best that we cast our lot with them. If one observes carefully what is going on in today's world, one knows the futility of trying to prevent the onslaught of Western civilization. Why not float with them in the same ocean of civilization, sail the same waves, and enjoy the fruits and endeavors of civilization?

The movement of a civilization is like the spread of measles. Measles in Tokyo start in Nagasaki and come eastward with the spring thaw. We may hate the spread of this communicable disease, but is there any effective way of preventing it? I can prove that it is not possible. In a communicable disease, people receive only damages. In a civilization, damages may accompany benefits, but benefits always far outweigh them, and their force cannot be stopped. This being the case, there is no point in trying to prevent their spread. A wise man encourages the spread and allows our people to get used to its ways.

The Opening to the modern Civilization of the West began in the reign of [emperor] Kaei (1848–58). Our people began to discover its utility and gradually and yet actively moved toward its acceptance. . . . We could have prevented the entry of this civilization, but it would have meant loss of our national independence. The struggles taking place in the world civilization were such that they would not allow an Eastern island nation to slumber in isolation. At that point, . . . public and the private sectors alike, everyone in our country accepted the modern Western civilization. Not only were we able to cast aside Japan's old conventions, but we also succeeded in creating a new axle toward progress in Asia. Our basic assumptions could be summarized in two words: "Good-bye Asia (Datsu-a)."

Source: David Lu, ed., *Japan: A Documentary History* (Armonk, NY: M. E. Sharpe, 1997), 351–53.

Japan is located in the eastern extremities of Asia, but the spirit of her people ha[s] already moved away from the old conventions of Asia to the Western civilization. Unfortunately for Japan, there are two neighboring countries. One is called China and another Korea. These two peoples, like the Japanese people, have been nurtured by Asiatic political thoughts and mores. It may be that we are different races of people, or it may be due to the differences in our heredity or education; significant differences mark the three peoples. The Chinese and Koreans are more like each other and together they do not show as much similarity to the Japanese. These two peoples do not know how to progress either personally or as a nation. In this day and age with transportation becoming so convenient, they cannot be blind to the manifestations of Western civilization. But they say that what is seen or heard cannot influence the disposition of their minds. Their love affairs with ancient ways and old customs remain as strong as they were centuries ago. In this new and vibrant theater of civilization when we speak of education, they only refer back to Confucianism. As for school education, they can only cite [Chinese philosopher Mencius's] precepts of humanity, righteousness, decorum, and knowledge. . . . As for their morality, one only has to observe their unspeakable acts of cruelty and shamelessness. Yet they remain arrogant and show no sign of self-examination.

In my view, these two countries cannot survive as independent nations with the onslaught of Western civilization to the East . . . and within a few short years they will be wiped out from the world with their lands divided among the civilized nations. Why is this so? Simply at a time when the spread of civilization and enlightenment (*bummei kaika*) has a force akin to that of measles, China and Korea violate the natural law of its spread. They forcibly try to avoid it by shutting off air from their rooms. Without air, they suffocate to death. It is said that neighbors must extend helping hands to one another because their relations are inseparable. Today's China and Korea have not done a thing for Japan. From the perspectives of civilized Westerners, they may see what is happening in China and Korea and judge Japan accordingly, because of the three countries' geographical proximity. The governments of China and Korea still retain their autocratic manners and do not abide by the rule of law. Westerners may consider Japan likewise a lawless society. Natives of China and Korea are deep in their hocus pocus of nonscientific behavior. Western scholars may think that Japan still remains a country dedicated to the yin and yang and five elements. Chinese are mean-spirited and shameless, and the chivalry of the Japanese people is lost to the Westerners. Koreans punish their convicts in an atrocious manner, and that is imputed to the Japanese as heartless people. There are many more examples I can cite. It is not different from the case of a righteous man living in a [bad] neighborhood. . . . His action is so rare that it is always buried under the ugliness of his neighbors' activities. . . . How unfortunate it is for Japan.

What must we do today? We do not have time to wait for the enlightenment of our neighbors so that we can work together toward the development of Asia. It is better for us to leave the ranks of Asian nations and cast our lot with civilized nations of the West. As for the way of dealing with China and Korea, no special treatment is necessary just because they happen to be our neighbors. We simply follow the manner of the Westerners in knowing how to treat them. Any person who cherishes a bad friend cannot escape his bad notoriety. We simply erase from our minds our bad friends in Asia.

GERMAN NATIONALISM IN THE NINETEENTH CENTURY

A Call for German Unity

The situation faced by the German-speaking population of Europe as regards issues of national identity and nation building was different from that of either the Americans or the Japanese. Situated in the heart of Europe, the Germans had never been united under the same government, and in fact there were scores of German states, ranging in size from a free city to Prussia. During the Middle Ages and into the early modern period, much of the German-speaking territory had been nominally grouped under the Holy Roman Empire, but it provided only a weak unity at best, and it was not exclusively German. In fact, the leading "German" power in the nineteenth century up until unification occurred was the Austrian Empire, which was dominated by a German-speaking minority but which was predominantly a non-German state. Ethnically, German peoples encountered the issue of national identity and nation building in a unique context.

The beginnings of German national identity, then, were not political but, rather, cultural. Already in the eighteenth century, Germans had begun to react against the intellectual domination of the French Enlightenment and against the idea of a purely rational and universal definition of human nature. Instead, German thinkers began to develop the idea that humanity consists of different peoples (in German, *Volk,* people or folk) who share a common language, culture, and history. This idea was picked up on and carried forward by the Romantic movement, which emphasized emotion and particularity as opposed to the reason and universality of the Enlightenment. An example of German Romantic identification with the *Volk* is the well-known collection of fairy (or folk) tales, gathered by the brothers Grimm in the German countryside, inspired in part by a fear that these manifestations of true German culture were in danger of disappearing forever.

Against this backdrop of growing German cultural self-identity, the military and political humiliation of the crushing Prussian defeat at Jena by Napoleon in 1806 flashed like a bolt of lightning. Prussia was forced to surrender all of its territory west of the Elbe River, and Napoleon even occupied Berlin. This defeat led to reforms of the feudal system in Prussia in 1807, not wholly unlike the changes in Japan after the Meiji Restoration. It also inspired one of the most important statements of German nationalism, a series of lectures delivered in Berlin in 1807–1808 by the most important German philosopher of the time, Johann Gottlieb Fichte (1762–1814).

As was true of Ito Hirobumi in Japan, Fichte's parents were commoners, and he was adopted and educated by a nobleman who had noted his ability. He became the leading German philosopher of his day, taught in a number of universities, and distinguished himself by both his moral fervor and his oratorical ability. Despite his success as an academic philosopher, Fichte's best-known work derived from a series of lectures inspired by the nationalist awakening he experienced as a result of Napoleon's defeat and occupation of Prussia, the leading German state. He gave the lectures, entitled *Addresses to the German Nation* (1807), to raise morale and inspire patriotism among Germans. In essence, they represent the encounter between German national consciousness and the reality of French political and cultural dominance. Fichte's vision was significant because it encompassed all Germans, regardless of which of the many German states they lived in. He also looked beyond the confessional differences that divided Catholic Germans of the south and west from the Protestant Germans of the north and east. Finally, these addresses are excerpted here, because this was a statement of German nationalism on which all German nationalist thinkers through World War I were raised.

QUESTIONS TO CONSIDER

1. How did Fichte define the German nation? What was the source of national feeling, according to Fichte?
2. What forces were behind the development of German national identity and nation building, in Fichte's presentation? Did those forces favor a cultural development of German nationalism or a state-oriented nationalism? Why?
3. How did Fichte use history to explain German nationalism? How did he use it to motivate Germans of his day to rally around the German nation, as he defined it?
4. In your opinion, does Fichte's view of German nationalism have more in common with the nationalism advocated by Calhoun, by Lincoln, by Strong, or by Roosevelt? Why?
5. How was German nationalism as presented by Fichte connected with issues of power? In your opinion, could Germany have been unified on the basis of his liberal, cultural nationalism?

ADDRESSES TO THE GERMAN NATION
(1807–1808)

Johann Gottlieb Fichte

[I]t is only by means of the common characteristic of being German that we can avert the downfall of our nation. . . . I perceive that organic unity in which no member regards the fate of another as the fate of a stranger. . . .

[T]o a nation which has lost her independence* . . . the means of salvation . . . consists in the fashioning of an entirely new self . . . and in the education of the

---

Source: Johann Gottlieb Fichte, *Addresses to the German Nation* (1807–1808), trans. R. F. Jones and G. H. Turnbull (Westport, CT: Greenwood Press, 1979), 3–4, 12–13, 15, 131, 132, 135–36, 138, 143–44, 145, 146–47, 151, 153, 223–24, 264, 266, 268.

*He is referring to the defeat and occupation by Napoleon.

nation . . . to a completely new life. . . . By means of the new education we want to mold the Germans into a corporate body. . . .

The natural impulse of man, which should be abandoned only in case of real necessity, is to find heaven on this earth, and to endow his daily work on earth with permanence and eternity; to plant and to cultivate the eternal in the temporal. . . .

Hence, the noble-minded man will . . . sacrifice himself for his people. . . . [P]ermanence is promised to him only by the continuous and independent existence of his nation. In order to save his nation he must be ready even to die that it may live. . . .

[O]ur earliest common forefathers . . . bravely resisted the on-coming world-dominion of the Romans. . . . Had they no appreciation of the advantages of Roman civilization . . . ? They cannot be charged with ignorance . . . of these things. . . . Freedom to them meant . . . remaining Germans and continuing to settle their own affairs independently and in . . . the original spirit of their race. . . . They assumed as a matter of course that . . . a true German could only want to . . . be . . . just a German and to bring up his children as Germans.

It is neither the strong right arm nor the efficient weapon that wins victories, but only the power of the soul. . . . From all this it follows that the State, merely as the government of human life . . . is not something which is primary and which exists for its own sake, but is merely the means to the higher purpose of the eternal, regular, and continuous development of what is purely human in this nation. . . .

These addresses . . . propose that you establish deeply and indelibly in the hearts of all . . . the true and all-powerful love of fatherland, the conception of our people as an eternal people and as the security for our own eternity.

A particular German State could, at most, have aimed at uniting the whole German nation under its sway, and at introducing autocracy in place of the established republic of peoples. . . . Then, if the unity of government which we are presupposing had itself borne, not the republican, but the monarchical form, . . . it would certainly have been a great disaster for the cause of German love of fatherland, . . . and every man of noble mind throughout the whole length and breadth of the common soil would have been bound to resist it. Yet, even in this most unfortunate event, it would always have been Germans who ruled over Germans. . . . [T]he essential point in our calculation is always that German national love itself either is at the helm of the German State or can reach it with its influence. . . .

[T]he first, original, and truly natural boundaries of states are beyond doubt their internal boundaries. Those who speak the same language are joined to each other by a multitude of invisible bonds by nature herself . . . ; they understand each other and . . . they belong together and are by nature one and an inseparable whole. Such a whole, if it wishes to absorb and mingle with itself any other people of different descent and language, cannot do so without . . . violently disturbing the even progress of its culture. From this internal boundary, . . . the marking of the external boundary . . . results . . . ; and . . . it is not because men dwell between certain mountains and rivers that they are a people, but, on the contrary, men dwell together . . . because they were a people already by a law of nature which is much higher. . . . Thus was the German nation placed . . . in the middle of Europe. . . .

Your forefathers unite themselves with these addresses, and make a solemn appeal to you. Think that in my voice there are mingled the voices of your ancestors of the hoary past, who with their own bodies stemmed the onrush of Roman world-dominion, who with their blood won the independence of those mountains, plains and rivers which under you have fallen prey to the foreigner. . . . There comes a solemn appeal to you from your descendants not yet born. ". . . Take care that the chain does not break off with you; see to it that we, too, may boast of you and use you as an unsullied link to connect ourselves with the same illustrious line." . . . If there is truth in . . . these addresses, then are you of all modern peoples the one in whom the seed of human perfection most unmistakably lies, and to whom the lead in its development is committed!

Unification Through "Blood and Iron"

After the fall of Napoleon in 1815, Germany was still divided into thirty-eight German states, the most important of which were Austria and Prussia. Until mid-century, memories of the French Revolution and Napoleonic wars would make the rulers of German states more concerned with preventing revolution than with achieving unity. In 1848, though, revolution again swept Europe, representatives from German states met in the Frankfurt Parliament, and hope was once more kindled that Germany could be united from below by the people, as Fichte had claimed. The powers of the old states had only been temporarily eclipsed, however, and eventually they reasserted themselves and the dreams of German unity via the Frankfurt Parliament evaporated.

With this new setback, nationalists increasingly came to embrace what was called the *Kleindeutsch* (or small German) solution, deciding that, if they waited to unify all Germans, German national unification would never occur. Hence, they were willing to accept a less-than-total unification led by Prussia, the largest essentially German state.[5] Prussian leadership posed a problem for liberal German nationalists, because it was a conservative, militaristic state. In addition, Prussia was largely Lutheran, which disturbed Roman Catholic Germans of the south and west.

Yet it was Prussia, under the leadership of the brilliant but domineering Otto von Bismarck (1815–1898), which would succeed in unifying Germany. Bismarck was the prime minister of Prussia from 1862 to 1871 and then of the united Germany until 1890. He engineered the unification of non-Austrian Germans in the German Reich (or empire) by 1871, but he did so at the expense of many of the liberal hopes of German nationalists. Bismarck was a Prussian *Junker,* or landed aristocrat. The *Junker* class was known to be conservative and authoritarian and in Bismarck's case not overly wealthy. He studied law at the University of Göttingen and entered the Prussian civil service. Although he rose to be Prussian ambassador to Russia, it was still a surprise when, as a result of a conflict between the Prussian king and the liberal *Landtag,* or Prussian parliament, Bismarck was named prime minister of Prussia. By extremely adroit maneuvering and a willingness to use force, he involved Prussia in three wars (with Denmark, Austria, and France) that resulted in German unification under the Prussian king, who was crowned the German *Kaiser,* or emperor, in the Hall of Mirrors at the Palace of Versailles outside Paris in 1871.

Bismarck's approach to government and diplomacy is usually described as *Realpolitik*, or the politics of realism, because he did not deal with the abstractions and ideals of Fichte and the Frankfurt Parliament. In a famous and oft-quoted phrase, he stated that "Germany doesn't look to Prussia's liberalism, but to its power: . . . [N]ot by means of speeches and majority verdicts will the great decisions of the time be made—that was the great mistake of 1848 and 1849— but by blood and iron. . . ."[6] In the passage excerpted here from his 1899 *Memoirs*, Bismarck presents a dynastic understanding of German identity that required unification from above. Bismarck defined the issue as an encounter between German subnational identities and the task of German state building.

QUESTIONS TO CONSIDER

1. Compare Fichte's representation of German nationalism with that of Bismarck. Why couldn't the Germans have united without leadership from a monarchy, according to Bismarck? What caused this situation, in Bismarck's view?

2. Bismarck served the king of Prussia and made him into the emperor of Germany. In your opinion, based on this text, was Bismarck a Prussian loyalist or a German nationalist?

3. Fichte asserted that German unity achieved under a monarchy would not be desirable. In your opinion, would the cultural-liberal Fichte have embraced the conservative German empire created by Bismarck? In other words, which do you think was a more powerful force in nineteenth-century Germany, political liberalism or political nationalism?

4. What was the role of the state in German nationalism, according to Bismarck? How does it compare with the role of the state in the cases of American and Japanese nation building?

5. How did Bismarck use history to justify his view of German nationalism? How does his view of German history differ from that of Fichte?

MEMOIRS (1899)

Otto von Bismarck

Never, not even at Frankfort, did I doubt that the key to German politics was to be found in princes and dynasties, not in publicists, whether in parliament and the press, or on the barricades.* The opinion of the cultivated public as uttered in parliament

---

Source: Otto von Bismarck, *Bismarck: The Man and the Statesman*, 2 vols., trans. A. J. Butler (New York and London: Harper and Brothers, 1899), 1:318–25.
*Bismarck is referring to revolution.

and the press might promote and sustain the determination of the dynasties, but perhaps provoked their resistance more frequently than it urged them forward in the direction of national unity. . . . The Prussian dynasty might anticipate that the hegemony
in the future German Empire would eventually fall to it, with an increase of consideration and power. It could foresee its own advantage, so far as it were not absorbed by
a national parliament, in the lowering of status so much dreaded by the other dynasties. . . . I acquired the conviction that . . . it would not be possible even to recover
for Prussia that position which she had held . . . before the events of March,* to say
nothing of such a reform . . . as might have afforded the German people a prospect of
the realization of their pretension to a position recognized by international law as
one of the great European nations. . . .

. . . The Gordian knot of German circumstances was not to be untied by the gentle
methods . . . [and] could only be cut by the sword; it came to this, that the King of
Prussia, conscious or unconscious, and with him the Prussian army, must be gained
for the national cause. . . . So much was clear to me, and I hinted at it when . . .
I made the much misrepresented deliverance concerning iron and blood. . . .

Prussia was nominally a Great Power, at any rate the fifth. The transcendent
genius of Frederick the Great[†] had given her this position, and it had been reestablished by the mighty achievements of the people in 1813[‡]. . . . Prussia's material
weight did not then correspond to her moral significance and her achievement in the
war of liberation.

In order that German patriotism should be active and effective, it needs as a rule
to hang on the peg of dependence upon a dynasty; independent of dynasty it rarely
comes to the rising point. . . . [I]n practice the German needs either attachment to a
dynasty or the goad of anger, hurrying him into action; the latter phenomenon, however, by its own nature is not permanent. It is as a Prussian, a Hanoverian, a Wurtem-
berger, a Bavarian or a Hessian, rather than as a German, that he is disposed to give
unequivocal proof of patriotism; and in the lower orders and the parliamentary groups
it will be long before it is otherwise. We cannot say that the Hanoverian, Hessian,
and other dynasties were at any special pains to win the affections of their subjects;
but nevertheless the German patriotism of their subjects is essentially conditioned by
their attachment to the dynasty after which they call themselves. It is not differences
of stock, but dynastic relations upon which in their origin the centrifugal elements repose. It is not attachment to Swabian, Lower Saxon, Thuringian,[§] or other particular
stock that counts for most, but the dynastic incorporation with the people of some
severed portion of a ruling princely family, as in the instances of Brunswick, Brabant,
and Wittelsbach** dynasties. . . . The German's love of Fatherland has need of a prince
on whom it can concentrate its attachment. Suppose that all the German dynasties

---

*The Revolution of 1848.

†Frederick the Great (1740–1786) raised Prussia to the ranks of the great powers.

‡Prussian national uprising that drove out Napoleon and the French.

§These are regional identities within the territory we know as Germany.

**Some of the ruling families of German dynastic states.

were suddenly deposed; there would then be no likelihood that German national sentiment would suffice to hold all Germans together from the point of view of international law amid the friction of European politics. . . . The Germans would fall a prey to more closely welded nations if they once lost the tie which resides in the princes' sense of community of rank. . . .

The other nations of Europe have need of no such go-between for their patriotism and national sentiment. Poles, Hungarians, Italians, Spaniards, Frenchmen would under any or without any dynasty preserve their homogeneous national unity. . . . The preponderance of dynastic attachment, and the use of a dynasty as the indispensable cement to hold together a definite portion of the nation calling itself by the name of a dynasty is a specific peculiarity of the German Empire.

Whatever may be the origin of this factitious union of Particularist elements, its result is that the individual German readily obeys the command of a dynasty to harry with fire and sword, and with his own hands to slaughter his German neighbors and kinsfolk as a result of quarrels unintelligible to himself. To examine whether this characteristic be capable of rational justification is not the problem of a German statesman, so long as it is strongly enough pronounced for him to reckon upon it. The difficulty of either abolishing or ignoring it, or making any advance in theory towards unity without regard to this practical limitation, has often proved fatal to the champions of unity; conspicuously so in the advantage taken of the favorable circumstances in the national movements of 1848–50. . . .

In the German national sentiment I see the preponderant force always elicited by the struggle with particularism; for particularism—Prussian particularism too—came into being only by resistance to the collective German community, to Emperor and Empire, in revolt from both, leaning . . . in all cases on foreign support, all alike damaging and dangerous to the German community. . . .

So far, however, as dynastic interests threaten us once more with national disintegration and impotence, they must be reduced to their proper measure.

The German people and its national life cannot be portioned out in private possessions of princely houses.

A German "Place in the Sun"

One might expect German nationalism after unification had been achieved to become more mellow. Indeed, Bismarck declared Germany a satisfied power. As the end of the century approached, however, German nationalism became much more virulent and overheated. Many Germans began to think that the eighteenth century had been France's century of greatness, the nineteenth century the era of the British empire, and that the twentieth century would belong to Germany. Across Europe, more aggressive social Darwinist and antirational movements were developing. This was the great age of European imperialism, when European nations scrambled to divide up Africa and southeast Asia, and the United States acquired imperial possessions from the Caribbean to the Philippines. So the Germans were not alone in this movement toward a militaristic nationalism. On the whole, however, nationalism took a more virulent form in Germany than it did in France and Britain.

A good expression of this exaggerated, aggressive, and state-centered nationalism occurs in the writings of Heinrich Treitschke, a widely read historian of late-nineteenth-century Germany. In fact, Treitschke faithfully traces out the trajectory of German national feeling in the second half of the nineteenth century. He moved from a youthful fling with liberalism to Bismarckian nationalism and then on to imperialist nationalism. Perhaps because his father was a general it was easier for him to embrace the new militaristic nationalism. For him and for other German nationalists of the late nineteenth century, the ideal changed from being a *Grossmacht* (Great Power) to being a *Weltmacht,* or World Power. Treitschke and his fellow nationalists wanted Germany to rise to greatness as an imperial power, even if this meant conflict with existing imperial powers, such as Britain. For Treitschke, the situation involved nothing less than the encounter between the legitimate and historically determined ascent to domination of Germany and those powers and peoples who would deny Germany her "place in the sun."

The sources cited here come from his very popular *German History in the Nineteenth Century* and from a collection of his historical and political writings. His interpretations carried with them a specific definition of German nationalism and national identity. His writing represents a kind of closing of the circle from the time that Fichte appealed to Germans to awake to their national identity and to resist French domination.

QUESTIONS TO CONSIDER

1. What is the relationship between the state and German nationalism in Treitschke's writings? How did this relationship as he described it compare with the way it was presented in the pieces by Fichte and Bismarck? Who was Treitschke closer to, Fichte or Bismarck?

2. What social Darwinist elements—for example, ideas such as struggle for existence, survival of the fittest, applied to human life—can you identify in Treitschke? How are they related to his political ideas?

3. How does German nationalism relate to power in Treitschke's writing? How does the relationship between power and nationalism in Treitschke's excerpts compare with their relationship in the understandings of Fichte and Bismarck?

4. How did Treitschke define German national character? How did it contrast with British national character, as he presents it?

5. Based on the writings of these three Germans, how does the German encounter with national identity and nation building compare with that in the United States and Japan? What common elements can you identify across these case studies? What conclusions can you draw about nationalism and tradition from these examples?

GERMAN HISTORY IN THE NINETEENTH CENTURY (1915–1919)

Heinrich Treitschke

On the State

The state is a moral community, which is called upon to educate the human race by positive achievement. Its ultimate object is that a nation should develop in it, a nation distinguished by a real national character. To achieve this state is the highest moral duty for nation and individual alike. All private quarrels must be forgotten when the state is in danger.

At the moment when the state cries out that its very life is at stake, social selfishness must cease and party hatred be hushed. The individual must forget his egoism, and feel that he is a member of the whole body.

The most important possession of a state, its be-all and end-all, is power. He who is not man enough to look this truth in the face should not meddle in politics. The state is not physical power as an end in itself, it is power to protect and promote the higher interests. Power must justify itself by being applied for the greatest good of mankind. It is the highest moral duty of the state to increase its power.

The true greatness of the state is that it links the past with the present and future; consequently, the individual has no right to regard the state as a means for attaining his own ambitions in life. Every extension of the activities of the state is beneficial and wise if it arouses, promotes, and purifies the independence of free and reasoning men; it is evil when it kills and stunts the independence of free men. It is men who make history.

The state does not stand for the whole life of the nation. Its function is essentially protective and administrative. The state does not swallow up everything; it can only influence by external compulsion. It represents the nation from the point of view of power. For in the state it is not only the great primitive forces of human nature that come into play; the state is the basis of all national life. Briefly, it may be affirmed that a state which is not capable of forming and maintaining an external organization of its civilizing activities deserves to perish.

Only the truly great and powerful states ought to exist. Small states are unable to protect their subjects against external enemies; moreover, they are incapable of producing genuine patriotism or national pride and are sometimes incapable of *Kultur** in great dimensions. Weimar[†] produced a Goethe and a Schiller;[‡] still these poets would have been greater had they been citizens of a German national state.

Source: Heinrich Treitschke, *German History in the Nineteenth Century* [*Deutsche Geschichte im neunzehnten Jahrhundert*], 7 vols. (1915–1919). In Louis L. Snyder, ed., *Documents of German History*, 259–62. Copyright © 1975 Greenwood Press. Reproduced by permission of Greenwood Publishing Group, Inc., Westport, CT.

*Culture.

[†]A small German principality noted as a cultural center.

[‡]Two great German writers of the eighteenth century.

On Monarchy

The will of the state is, in a monarchy, the expression of the will of one man who wears the crown by virtue of the historic right of a certain family; with him the final authority rests. Nothing in a monarchy can be done contrary to the will of the monarch. In a democracy, plurality, the will of the people, expresses the will of the state. A monarchy excels any other form of government, including the democratic, in achieving unity and power in a nation. It is for this reason that monarchy seems so natural, and that it makes such an appeal to the popular understanding. We Germans had an experience of this in the first years of our new empire. How wonderfully the idea of a united Fatherland was embodied for us in the person of the venerable Emperor! How much it meant to us that we could feel once more: "That man is Germany; there is no gainsaying it!"

On War

The idea of perpetual peace is an illusion supported only by those of weak character. It has always been the weary, spiritless, and exhausted ages which have played with the dream of perpetual peace. A thousand touching portraits testify to the sacred power of the love which a righteous war awakes in noble nations. It is altogether impossible that peace be maintained in a world bristling with arms, and even God will see to it that war always recurs as a drastic medicine for the human race. Among great states the greatest political sin and the most contemptible is feebleness. It is the political sin against the Holy Ghost.

War is elevating because the individual disappears before the great conception of the state. The devotion of the members of a community to each other is nowhere so splendidly conspicuous as in war. Modern wars are not waged for the sake of goods and chattels. What is at stake is the sublime moral good of national honor, which has something in the nature of unconditional sanctity, and compels the individual to sacrifice himself for it.

On the English

The hypocritical Englishman, with the Bible in one hand and a pipe of opium in the other, possesses no redeeming qualities. The nation was an ancient robber-knight, in full armor, lance in hand, on every one of the world's trade routes.

The English possess a commercial spirit, a love of money which has killed every sentiment of honor and every distinction of right and wrong. English cowardice and sensuality are hidden behind unctuous, theological fine talk which is to us free-thinking German heretics among all the sins of English nature the most repugnant. In England all notions of honor and class prejudices vanish before the power of money, whereas the German nobility has remained poor but chivalrous. That last indispensable bulwark against the brutalization of society—the duel—has gone out of fashion in England and soon disappeared, to be supplanted by the riding whip. This was a triumph of vulgarity. The newspapers, in their accounts of aristocratic weddings, record in exact detail how much each wedding guest has contributed in the form of presents or in cash; even the youth of the nation have turned their sports into a business, and contend for valuable prizes, whereas the German students wrought havoc on their countenances for the sake of a real or imaginary honor.*

NOTES

1. The issue of states' rights versus federal power first arose over the Alien and Sedition Acts, passed by the Adams administration as a result of a conflict with revolutionary France. The acts, which empowered the federal government to deport any "dangerous" aliens (noncitizen residents) and to arrest citizens who criticized the government, were disputed in the Kentucky and Virginia Resolutions, written by Thomas Jefferson and James Madison, respectively.

2. An anti-immigration movement whose main platform was basically "America for Americans."

3. Roman Catholicism.

4. Excessive use of alcohol.

5. Prussia had significant territories that were ethnically Polish, but it was primarily a German state, whereas in Austria the dominant German population was a minority.

6. Bismarck's speech in the Prussian Landtag, September 29, 1862, in D. G. Williamson, *Bismarck and Germany 1862–1890*, 2nd ed. (London: Longman, 1998), 97.

---

*German students often got scars on their cheeks from dueling with sabres.

PART THREE

THE TWENTIETH-CENTURY WORLD AND FUTURE PROSPECTS

Collectivist Ideologies
in the Twentieth Century

INTRODUCTION

In the roughly one hundred years from the defeat of Napoleon at Waterloo in 1815 to the outbreak of World War I in 1914, the ascendant political philosophy in Europe and America was liberalism. The philosophical foundation of liberalism, as its name indicates, is that human society ought to be based on individual liberty and driven by individual initiative (see chapter 6). From these philosophical assumptions stemmed the liberal political and economic ideals of representative democracy and laissez-faire capitalism. During the nineteenth century, pure liberalism was modified by the introduction of government regulations in areas such as factory and mine working conditions, child labor, public health, and housing (see chapter 7). In the decades before the outbreak of World War I, additional new political, intellectual, and cultural currents, such as Marxism, social Darwinism, and modernism, called into question the assumptions and viability of the liberal system. Nonetheless, liberalism remained the dominant philosophy in Europe until it was buried along with millions of soldiers in the trenches of World War I.[1]

The theme of this chapter is collectivism, defined broadly as a wide range of antiliberal ideas and values that emphasize the role and welfare of the group over the liberty and self-interest of the individual. As a historical phenomenon, collectivist ideas arose in the twentieth century as a reaction to the traumatic social crises generated by world wars, the economic collapse of the Great Depression, and the poverty and underdevelopment of the so-called "Third World."[2] As an ideological phenomenom,[3] collectivism challenged the basic precepts of liberalism and offered an alternative vision and interpretation of human society and social progress. Taken together, an analysis of some of the most significant collectivist movements in the last century from Europe, America, and Africa provides us with a unique perspective for understanding the past and an alternative framework through which to view and assess the foundations of our own ideological positions.

The first and most influential collectivist movement of the twentieth century occurred as a consequence of the successful Bolshevik Revolution in Russia in 1917. Vladimir Lenin had successfully overthrown a tsarist monarchy weakened by military defeats during World War I, severe economic crises, and widespread popular discontent. But were the Russian masses ready for the collectivist reorganization of society advocated by Marx and Lenin? Our first reading comes from a "popular" book on Marxism, written in the first years of the Soviet regime to present the Communist point of view to a wider audience. *The ABC of Communism* was written by Nikolai Bukharin and Evgeny Preobrazhensky, two true believers, who saw in Marxist socialism and the proletariat (working class) a solution to the hardship and inequity of human life. The authors had two audiences in mind when they wrote this elementary guidebook to Marxism. First, because the Bolsheviks had taken power in the most unevenly developed of the European Great Powers, they felt the need to educate their own population about Marxist "scientific" socialism.[4] Second, Bukharin and Preobrazhensky assumed that World War I represented the death throes of capitalism and that the successful revolution in Russia would spark uprisings in the economically more advanced countries of western Europe. Therefore, their work was also intended for the working-class populations of western Europe. Because most Marxist writings were difficult political and ideological tracts laden with philosophical and economic theory, Bukharin and Preobrazhensky believed that "an elementary textbook of communist knowledge"[5] was required in order to educate and persuade a larger domestic and international audience. For the historian, their work remains one of the clearest expressions of Marxist collectivist philosophy and its condemnation of liberal capitalism.

The second selection comes from Adolf Hitler, the German Führer [leader] who established fascism as the reigning political philosophy in Germany in the 1930s to mid-1940s. Fascism is most frequently characterized as a totalitarian political philosophy that stands in extreme opposition to the political philosophies of socialism and communism. But although important differences do exist, fascism may also be viewed as a collectivist movement that sought to protect and promote the interests of the German people. As described in his *Mein Kampf* [*My Struggle*], written in 1923, Hitler hated liberalism's emphasis on individualism, economic competition, and self-interest. Appealing to a German citizenry disillusioned by wartime defeat, weak liberal leaders, and economic hardship, Hitler promised a brighter future for Germany, reunited and protected by his National Socialist German Workers' Party (commonly called the Nazi Party) and rededicated to the collective welfare of the *Volk*, or "the people." Herein lies an important distinction: Whereas Marxists advocated a collectivist society based on economic equality and the elimination of class conflict, fascism envisioned a collectivist society based on blood, or common nationality and kinship. From Hitler's perspective, a primary obstacle to this collective unity was the Jews, who sought to manipulate both liberalism and Marxism to undermine the natural unity and ambitions of the German people. Although fascism officially ended in Germany at the conclusion of World War II, the selections from Hitler's *Mein Kampf* may help explain why so many Germans were enthralled with his vision, and why fascism, in its different guises, remains an attractive and persuasive ideology in many pockets of the world community today.

In the United States, the liberal ideals of representative democracy and free-market capitalism remained unchallenged in the nineteenth century. As we have seen, even such critics as Andrew Carnegie and Thorstein Veblen (see chapter 7) sought moderate reforms, not radical change. But the Great Depression of the 1930s transformed the American political and economic landscape so deeply that it challenged and changed American society forever. The two historical documents in this section provide a brief yet instructive perspective on the transformations that occurred as a result of the century's greatest economic crisis. The first selection comes from a 1928 presidential campaign speech by Herbert Hoover, who became the thirty-first President of the United States (1928–1932). At that time, Hoover was a confident and successful man, and America was experiencing an economic boom known as the "Roaring Twenties." In his campaign speech, he laid out his view that individualism had made America great, and he contrasted the successful American reliance on the individual with the failure of Europe's excessive orientation toward governmental solutions to social and economic problems. Hoover's 1928 speech is a clear endorsement of liberalism, and it reflects the popular mood and governing philosophy of the United States at the time.

Approximately one year later, America's boom turned to bust with the infamous stock market crash of 1929, which heralded the long economic decline known as the Great Depression. In the presidential election of 1932, Hoover was defeated in a landslide by Franklin Delano Roosevelt, former governor of New York and secretary of the navy. By then, the Great Depression had left millions of Americans bankrupt, unemployed, and disillusioned with laissez-faire capitalism. Whereas Hoover claimed that the market would eventually correct itself according to the principles of Adam Smith (see chapter 7), Roosevelt put forward a different vision of America in his First Inaugural Address of 1933, one in which public and collective responses were needed to overcome problems too enormous and systemic to be solved solely by the individual effort so prized by liberalism. Although the following excerpts from Roosevelt's 1933 address include few policy details, they do express key collectivist themes and principles that continue to be meaningful in American politics today.

The final case study of collectivist ideology comes from the very different political and cultural tradition of east Africa and was written by the first president of postcolonial Tanzania, Julius Nyerere. Following World War II, many leaders of the newly independent colonies in Africa and Asia turned to collectivist models of economic and social development. Some leaders were consciously rejecting western liberal models that were associated with colonial exploitation; others were undoubtedly motivated by their desire to obtain economic and military assistance from socialist countries during the height of the Cold War (see chapter 13), President Nyerere added his own justifications. As he explained in his book, *Freedom and Socialism* (1968), he believed that a collectivist approach to economic and social development would alleviate poverty, reduce tribalism, and build upon traditional African values and customs of sharing and cooperation. He termed his plan

Ujamaa ("familyhood") and sought to create a self-reliant, egalitarian Tanzanian society based on collectivized villages and communal farming. Although *Ujamaa* failed to generate the economic prosperity envisioned by Nyerere, it served as a role model for other developing nations and called into question the appropriateness of western political and economic models for the nonwestern world.

The readings in this chapter illustrate how various crises of the twentieth century challenged the basic assumptions that underlay the philosophy of liberalism—that the individual should and must handle his or her own problems, lest individual freedom and initiative be eroded. From a historical perspective, such fears must have seemed trivial to the millions of Russians seeking a better life after the turmoils of World War I and the civil war, or to the millions of Germans and Americans thrown into poverty by the Great Depression, or to the newly liberated citizens of Tanzania, who struggled to overcome the legacies of colonial exploitation. In the midst of crisis and uncertainty, millions of people in the twentieth century turned to antiliberal intellectual and social philosophies that promised a better future. The shape that collectivism took differed from society to society, conforming both to historically developed cultural traditions and to the immediate circumstances and crises of the day. Leaders in each country strove to frame the problems, devise solutions, and formulate policies consistent with and acceptable to a proportion of the population sufficient to carry the political day. To do so, they had to answer within a collectivist, antiliberal framework certain substantive questions about human nature and human society.

CHAPTER QUESTIONS

1. On the basis of these readings, provide your own definition of collectivism. How does it differ from liberalism in political, economic, and social terms?

2. Marxism, fascism, and the American "New Deal" are most commonly depicted as quite different. Clearly, there are important differences. But what basic commonalities can be identified?

3. What is the role of the state in the promotion of collectivism? In your assessment, do collectivist solutions solve problems that liberalism cannot?

4. As a general philosophy, collectivism is based on a set of certain assumptions about human nature and human society. What assumptions do you find in these case studies? Why and how do proponents of collectivism believe that their models of social organization will provide mankind with the greatest amount of freedom?

5. As you think about the problems that face America and the world today, are we headed toward greater collectivism or greater individualism? Is it possible that we are becoming more collectivist in some ways and more individualist in others? If so, compile a list of collectivist and individualist areas of contemporary life.

SOVIET MARXISM

Our first selection was written as a guidebook to the new Soviet system that was emerging in the former Russian empire, the first political casualty of World War I. The tsarist empire was a singularly troubled Great Power on the eve of the war. Defeat in the Crimean War in the 1850s had demonstrated that a basically agrarian society could not compete with the armed might of newly industrialized states. Beginning in 1861, the tsarist government sought to catch up with the west by means of a series of domestic reforms centered on the abolition of serfdom. The reforms accomplished a great deal, but left Russia with a hybrid, semiwestern system, containing an archconservative government, a westernized elite, and a backward peasantry that was separate from and opposed to both the government and the elite. Despite rapid economic growth, the empire grew weaker, not stronger. The social developments that accompanied industrialization—urbanization, literacy, nationalism, and emergence of the working class—all went against the political and cultural conservatism of the Russian ruling elite in a multinational empire. Moreover, industrial development concentrated radical and violent workers in the cities, a volatile and dangerous supplement to the seething peasant masses in the countryside.

Tragically, Emperor Nicholas II was a deeply flawed leader. Defeat and military incompetence in the Russo-Japanese War sparked the Revolution of 1905, which ended only when the tsar conceded the need for a national parliament and brought the troops home to put down the peasant revolt. Despite this clear lesson, Nicholas stifled reform and made only grudging concessions, relying on his romantic and grossly outdated idea of the mystical bond between the tsar and the Russian peasantry. The result was an uneasy domestic peace between 1905 and 1917. World War I led once again to military defeats and greater economic hardship, making the country ripe for revolution. It came suddenly in March of 1917, when the tsarist autocracy was replaced by a republic, the liberal Provisional Government. The Provisional Government, however, proved extremely unstable. There were enormous problems facing any government in Russia in 1917, but the fundamental weakness of the Provisional Government was the fact that the majority of Russian peasants and workers rejected completely the liberal economic order of 1861–1917 and the liberal political principles of the Provisional Government. This left the door open for the most radical, most authoritarian, and most antiliberal of the left-wing parties, Lenin's Communists, to seize power in November 1917.[6]

Lenin was able to seize power because he had a clear political vision, a relatively unified party, and the will to make common cause with anyone who favored a radical revolution. He was able to hold power during the Civil War (1917–1920) because the Communist Party operated more like a military organization than a traditional political party and because Communist policies appealed to the people marginally more than those of the conservative "White" forces. They also enjoyed the benefit of superior leadership, interior lines of communication, and the ability to claim the mantle of "legitimate" authority.[7]

It defied all of Marx's supposedly scientific predictive powers that one of the most backward and agrarian countries of Europe should be the site of the first socialist revolution. Yet the Bolsheviks believed that their revolution was the spark that would set off a worldwide conflagration, that would mark "the resurrection day of mankind."[8] They envisioned nothing less than the complete transformation of society, starting with the abolition of private property and the nationalization of land and industry. This was to lead to a society without classes and to the end of "exploitation of man by man." Over the short term, however, the former exploiting capitalist classes could be expected to resist; hence, a temporary "dictatorship of the proletariat" would be required to win and hold power. Once the remnants of the old order had been removed and the failings of capitalism overcome, there would be enough for everyone, socialism would be achieved, and mankind could escape from the realm of "necessity to freedom."

With such an ambitious agenda, it is hardly surprising that they should turn immediately to the task of educating the masses about Marxism. The two authors of *The ABC of Communism* were independent-minded men, who both were ultimately victims of Stalinism. Nikolai Bukharin (1888–1938) was the more important and better known of the two. He had joined the Communists in 1906 and was arrested and exiled under the tsars. Later, as editor of the Communist Party newspaper *Pravda,* he had risen to become one of the most important leaders in the 1920s. Stalin allied himself with Bukharin briefly and then turned on him. Bukharin was the key figure in one of the most important "show trials" of the 1930s and was executed.[9] Evgeny Preobrazhensky (1886–1937) was also an important figure in the Communist Party in the 1920s. Preobrazhensky was associated with Lev Trotsky and favored more rapid industrialization. The fact that his proposals were similar in many ways to the policies Stalin later set in motion did not spare Preobrazhensky. He was arrested and died in the prison camp system.

At the time of the first publication of *The ABC* in 1919, the Communist "Reds" were locked in a bloody civil war with the so-called "Whites," a loose alliance of monarchists, liberals, and nationalists who received military and financial assistance from western powers. Russia approached total collapse, with cities evaporating, famine stalking the land, and chaos the only constant. It is a testament to the faith and optimism of the authors of *The ABC* that they would write a popular presentation of the principles of communism in these circumstances. It remains to this day the best single introduction to Communist theory written by one of its adherents and has been translated into many languages. Ironically, it was not available in the Soviet Union from the 1930s until the collapse of the Communist system in 1991.[10]

QUESTIONS TO CONSIDER

1. The authors of *The ABC* claimed that capitalism was a "badly constructed machine." What flaws did they find in capitalism? What were their views on property?
2. Why were the authors also critical of liberal democracy and nationalism? How could communism provide a better alternative? In your assessment, how persuasive is their argument?

3. According to the authors, what role would the state play in implementing collectivism? Why did they believe that the state would eventually cease to exist? How would society organize itself without state apparatus?

4. What assumptions did the authors make about human nature? What were their views on history and progress? How do these views compare and contrast with those inherent in liberal philosophy?

5. Describe what the ideal life for the average individual would be like in a communist society as described in *The ABC*. How would this life promote greater freedom than that experienced in a capitalist society?

THE ABC OF COMMUNISM (1919)

Nikolai Bukharin and Evgeny Preobrazhensky

Characteristics of the Communist System

[T]he destruction of the capitalist system was inevitable. It is now perishing under our very eyes . . . because it is affected by two fundamental contradictions: on the one hand, anarchy of production, leading to competition, crises, and wars; on the other hand, the class character of society, owing to which one part of society inevitably finds itself in mortal enmity with the other part (class war). Capitalist society is like a badly constructed machine, in which one part is continually interfering with the movements of another. . . . That is why it was inevitable that this machine would break down sooner or later.

It is evident that the new society must be much more solidly constructed than capitalism . . . , upon the ruins of that system there must arise a new society which will be free from the contradictions of the old. That is to say, the communist method of production must . . . be an *organized* society; it must be free from anarchy of production, from competition between individual entrepreneurs, from wars and crises. . . . [I]t must be a *classless* society, not a society in which the two halves are at eternal enmity one with the other; it must not be a society in which one class exploits the other. Now a society in which there are no classes, and in which production is organized, can only be *a society of comrades, a communist society based upon labor.* . . .

The basis of communist society must be the social ownership of the means of production and exchange. Machinery, locomotives, steamships, factory buildings, warehouses, grain elevators, mines, telegraphs and telephones, the land, sheep, horses, and cattle, must all be . . . under the control of society as a whole, and not as at present under the control of individual capitalists or capitalist combines. . . . [O]wnership and control is not the privilege of a class but of all the persons who make up society. In these circumstances society will be transformed into a huge working organization for cooperative production. There will then be neither disintegration of

Source: N. Bukharin and E. Preobrazhensky, *The ABC of Communism: A Popular Explanation of the Program of the Communist Party of Russia*, 69–75, 77, 168–71, 177–79, 192–94. Copyright © 1988 University of Michigan Press. Reprinted with permission.

production nor anarchy of production. . . . No longer will one enterprise compete with another; the factories, workshops, mines, and other productive institutions will all be subdivisions, as it were, of one vast people's workshop. . . . [S]o comprehensive an organization presupposes a general plan of production [and] everything must be precisely calculated. We must know in advance how much labor to assign to the various branches of industry; what products are required and how much of each it is necessary to produce; how and where machines must be provided. This is how the organization of communist production will be effected. . . .

Mere organization does not, however, suffice. The essence of the matter lies in . . . the . . . cooperative organization of *all* the members of society. The communist system, in addition to affecting organization, is further distinguished by the fact that *it puts an end to exploitation,* that *it abolishes the division of society into classes.* We might conceive the organization of production as being effected in the following manner: a small group of capitalists, a capitalist combine, controls everything; production has been organized so that capitalist no longer competes with capitalist; conjointly they extract surplus value from the workers, who have been practically reduced to slavery. Here we have organization, but we also have the exploitation of one class by another. Here there is a joint ownership of the means of production, but it is joint ownership by one class, an exploiting class. . . . Such an organization of society would have removed only one of the fundamental contradictions, the anarchy of production. But it would have strengthened the other fundamental contradiction of capitalism, the division of society into two warring halves; the class war would be intensified. . . . Communist society does not merely organize production; in addition, it frees people from oppression by others.

The cooperative character of communist production is likewise displayed in every detail of organization. Under communism, for example, there will not be permanent managers of factories, nor will there be persons who do one and the same kind of work throughout their lives. . . . Under communism people receive a many-sided culture, and find themselves at home in various branches of production: today I work in an administrative capacity, I reckon up how many felt boots or how many French rolls must be produced during the following month; tomorrow I shall be working in a soap factory, next month perhaps in a steam laundry, and the month after in an electric power station. This will be possible when all the members of society have been suitably educated.

The communist method of production presupposes in addition that production is not for the market, but for use. . . . [P]roducts . . . are simply stored in the communal warehouses, and are subsequently delivered to those who need them. In such conditions, money will no longer be required. "How can that be?" some of you will ask. "In that case one person will get too much and another too little." . . . At first, doubtless, and perhaps for twenty or thirty years, it will be necessary to have various regulations. Maybe certain products will only be supplied to those persons who have a special entry in their workbook or on their work card. Subsequently, when communist society has been consolidated and fully developed, no such regulations will be needed. There will be an ample quantity of all products, our present wounds will long since have been healed, and everyone will be able to get just as much as he needs. "But will not people find it to their interest to take more than they need?" Certainly not. Today, for example, no one thinks it worth while when he wants one seat in a tram, to take three tickets and keep two places empty. It will be just the same in the case of all products. A person will take from the communal storehouse precisely as much as he needs, no more. . . .

In a communist society there will be no classes. But if there will be no classes, this implies that *in communist society there will likewise be no State*. . . . [T]he State is a class organization of the rulers. The State is always directed by one class against the other. . . . In the communist social order there are neither landlords, nor capitalists, nor wage workers; there are simply people—comrades. If there are no classes, then there is no class war, and there are no class organizations. Consequently the State has ceased to exist. . . . There is no one to be held in restraint, and there is no one to impose restraint.

But how, they will ask us, can this vast organization be set in motion without any administration? . . . In a word, who is going to supervise the whole affair? It is not difficult to answer these questions. The main direction will be entrusted to various kinds of bookkeeping offices or statistical bureaus. There, from day to day, account will be kept of production and all its needs; there also it will be decided whither workers must be sent, whence they must be taken, and how much work there is to be done. And inasmuch as, from childhood onwards, all will have been accustomed to social labor, and since all will understand that this work is necessary and that life goes easier when everything is done according to a prearranged plan and when the social order is like a well-oiled machine, all will work in accordance with the indications of these statistical bureaus. There will be no need for special ministers of State, for police and prisons, for laws and decrees—nothing of the sort. Just as in an orchestra all the performers watch the conductor's baton and act accordingly, so here all will consult the statistical reports and will direct their work accordingly. . . . [I]n these statistical bureaus one person will work today, another tomorrow. The bureaucracy, the permanent officialdom, will disappear. . . .

Manifestly this will only happen in the fully developed and strongly established communist system, after the complete and definitive victory of the proletariat. . . . For a long time yet, the working class will have to fight against all its enemies, and in especial against the relics of the past, such as sloth, slackness, criminality, pride. All these will have to be stamped out. Two or three generations of persons will have to grow up under the new conditions before the need will pass for laws and punishments and for the use of repressive measures by the workers' State. Not until then will all the vestiges of the capitalist past disappear. Though in the intervening period the existence of the workers' State is indispensable, subsequently, in the fully developed communist system, when the vestiges of capitalism are extinct, the proletarian State authority will also pass away. The proletariat itself will become mingled with all the other strata of the population, for everyone will by degrees come to participate in the common labor. Within a few decades there will be quite a new world, with new people and new customs. . . .

The communist method of production will signify an enormous development of productive forces. As a result, no worker in communist society will have to do as much work as of old. The working day will grow continually shorter, and people will be to an increasing extent freed from the chains imposed on them by nature. As soon as man is enabled to spend less time upon feeding and clothing himself, he will be able to devote more time to the work of mental development. Human culture will climb to heights never attained before. It will no longer be a class culture, but will become a genuinely human culture. Concurrently with the disappearance of man's tyranny over man, the tyranny of nature over man will likewise vanish. Men and women will for the first time be able to lead a life worthy of thinking beings instead of a life worthy of brute beasts.

Proletarian Democracy and Bourgeois Democracy

A bourgeois democratic republic is based upon universal suffrage and upon the so-called "will of the people," the "will of the whole nation," the "united will of all classes." The advocates of a bourgeois democratic republic, of a Constituent Assembly, etc., tell us that we are doing violence to the united will of the nation. . . . Peace between the classes is as impossible as peace between wolves and sheep. Between them there is war to the knife. How can they possibly have a common will, a bourgeois-proletarian will? Obviously there is no more possibility of bourgeois-proletarian desires and aspirations than of wolf-sheep desires and aspirations. . . . [T]he very phrase about a will common to the whole nation is humbug, . . . [b]ut this fraud is necessary to the bourgeoisie, necessary for the maintenance of capitalist rule. The capitalists are in the minority. They cannot venture to say openly that this small minority rules. This is why the bourgeoisie has to cheat, declaring that it rules in the name of "the whole people," "all classes," "the entire nation," and so on. . . .

The Soviet Power realizes a new, a much more perfect type of democracy—*proletarian democracy.* The essence of this proletarian democracy consists in this, that it *is based upon the transference of the means of production into the hands of the workers.* . . . [T]hose who formerly constituted the oppressed masses and their organizations have become the instruments of rule. The mass organizations of the workers, the semi-proletarian peasants, etc. (soviets, trade unions, factory committees, etc.), have become the actual foundations of the proletarian State authority. . . .

Soviet democracy does not merely not exclude the workers' organizations from government, but it actually makes of them the instruments of government. . . . Soviet Power entrusts with new functions innumerable masses of persons who were formerly oppressed and degraded. To an ever greater extent the masses of the people, the workers and the poor peasants, come to participate in the joint labors of the soviets, the trade unions, and the factory committees. . . . [P]eople who never did anything of the kind before are now actively participating in the work of administration and in the building of a new life. In this way the Soviet Power secures the widest self-government . . . and . . . summons the broad masses . . . to participate in . . . government. . . .

The Equality of the Workers, Irrespective of Sex

Bourgeois democracy proclaims in words a whole series of freedoms, but from the oppressed these freedoms are safeguarded by five locks and seven seals. Among other things, bourgeois democracy has often declared that people are equal irrespective of sex, creed, race, and nationality. Proudly has the pledge been given that under the bourgeois democratic system all are equals: women and men; whites, yellows, and blacks; Europeans and Asians; Buddhists, Christians, and Jews. In reality . . . during the imperialist epoch, there has been all over the world a terrible increase in racial and national oppression. . . . [And] woman has remained a being without rights, a domestic animal, part of the furniture of the marital couch.

The working woman in capitalist society . . . is peculiarly oppressed, peculiarly deprived of rights. In all matters she . . . has even less than the beggarly rights which the bourgeoisie grants to the working man. . . . In family life she is always subject to her husband, and everything that goes wrong is considered to be her fault. In a word, bourgeois democracy everywhere exhibits as regards women laws and customs which strongly remind us of the customs of savages, who exchange, buy, punish, or steal women just as if they were chattels, dolls, or beasts of burden. Our Russian proverb runs, "A hen is not a bird, and a woman is not a person"; here we have the valuation of a slave society. . . . There are more women than men among the workers. It is obvious that the struggle of the proletariat must be greatly hindered by the lack of equality between the two halves of which it is composed. Without the aid of the women of the proletariat, it is idle to dream of a general victory, it is idle to dream of the "freeing of labor." . . . [T]here should be complete fighting comradeship between the female and the male portions of the proletariat . . . strengthened by equality. The Soviet Power is the first to have realized such equality in all departments of life: in marriage, in the family, in political affairs, etc., . . . women are the equals of men. . . .

But . . . [h]ow can a working woman effectively realize her rights when she has to devote so much time to housekeeping, must go to the market and wait her turn there, must do the family washing, must look after her children, must bear the heavy burden of all this domestic drudgery? [Our] . . . aim . . . must be to deliver working women from such slavery. . . . The organization of house communes . . . with central wash-houses; the organization of communal kitchens; the organization of communal nurseries, kindergartens, playgrounds, summer colonies for children, schools with communal dining rooms, etc., . . . will enfranchise woman, and will make it possible for her to interest herself in all those matters which now interest the proletarian man.

Communism and the Problem of Nationality

One of the forms of the oppression of man by man is the oppression of subject nationalities. Among the barriers by which human beings are separated, we have, in addition to the barriers of class, those of national disunity, of national enmity and hatred.

National enmity and ill-feeling are among the means by which the proletariat is stupefied and by which its class consciousness is dulled. The bourgeoisie knows how to cultivate these sentiments skillfully in order to promote its own interests. . . .

Should the Russian worker and the Russian peasant look upon the Germans, the French, the British, the Jews, the Chinese, or the Tartars, as enemies, irrespective of the class to which these belong . . . , for the sole reason that these latter speak a different tongue, that their skins are black or yellow, that they have different customs and laws? Obviously, this would be quite wrong. [They] are just as much proletarians as the Russians are [and] . . . the essential feature of their condition lies in this, that they are all exploited by capital, that they are all comrades, that they all alike suffer from poverty, oppression, and injustice.

Is the Russian worker to love the Russian capitalist because his fellow-countryman abuses him in the familiar Russian terms, because his employer cuffs him with a Russian fist, or lashes him with a Russian whip? Of course not. . . . The workers of all lands are brothers of one class, and they are the enemies of the capitalists of all lands. . . . Brothers in oppression and slavery must be brothers in one world-wide league for the struggle with the capitalists. Forgetting all the national differences that tend to hinder union, they must unite in one great army to carry on a joint war against capitalism. Only by closing their ranks in such an international alliance, can they hope to conquer world capitalism. This is why, more than seventy years ago, the founders of communism, Marx and Engels, in their famous *Communist Manifesto,* fulminated the splendid slogan: "Proletarians of all lands, unite!"

GERMAN FASCISM

The rise and popularity of fascism in Germany must be understood within its historical context. Like Soviet communism, German fascism grew in an age of anger, uncertainty, and insecurity. Germany was the great loser of World War I. The peace established by the Treaty of Versailles in 1919 placed sole responsibility for the war on Germany, saddled it with crippling reparation payments, stripped it of its overseas colonies, and shackled its military forces with significant restrictions. All of this was made even more unacceptable to many Germans because they had believed the war ended in a stalemate marked by the signing of an armistice. Consequently, the Versailles Treaty was to most Germans a "*diktat*," an unfair, punitive peace imposed by the Allies and foolishly accepted by the postwar liberal government.

The situation in Germany was made worse by political weakness and economic instability. Like the Romanov dynasty in Russia, the autocratic government of Kaiser Wilhelm was destroyed by the war and was replaced by the Weimar Republic, a feeble, liberal parliamentary system that lacked the popular support and political power to address Germany's enormous problems. Certainly, one of the greatest problems facing the government was the war reparations. Unable to meet its payments, the government simply printed more money, causing the value of the German mark to fall dramatically. The result was hyperinflation. At the end of the war in 1918, one U.S. dollar equaled eight German marks; by 1923, one dollar was equivalent to 4.5 million marks. The currency fell so much in value that people had to carry their money in wheelbarrows, and life savings were wiped out in a matter of weeks. The middle class was especially hard hit, and they became more receptive to radical movements that sought to topple the liberal government.

The economy began to recover in the latter half of the 1920s, only to collapse once again as the Great Depression spread to Europe. By the early 1930s, nearly 40 percent of the German workforce was unemployed, angry, and confused about their future opportunities.

These were the conditions that helped to propel Adolf Hitler (1889–1945) into power. He was born in a small town in Austria, the son of a government civil servant. He quit high school before graduating and lived a drifter's life for some time, living off of his orphan's pension (both parents had died by his nineteenth birthday) and occasional odd jobs. His one ambition at this time seems to have been art, for he twice applied to the Vienna Academy of Arts—and was rejected both times. Biographers assert that Hitler lived a lonely and brooding life during this time and created a list of enemies who were, in his perception, responsible for his problems and failures.

World War I offered a new opportunity for Hitler. He volunteered for the German army at the age of twenty-five, fought at the front, and received two Iron Crosses. Disillusioned by the terms of the Versailles Treaty at the end of the war, Hitler turned to politics, joining the German Workers' Party in 1919. Discovering his talents as a manager and orator, he quickly became its leader and instilled a military discipline and radical agenda to the party, which he renamed the National Socialist German Workers' Party, or the Nazi Party.

In November of 1923, Adolf Hitler staged the failed "Beer-Hall Putsch," an armed attempt to seize power in Munich. The Nazis failed, and Hitler was arrested and tried for treason; he received a very mild sentence. It was while in prison that he composed his famous *Mein Kampf* (*My Struggle*), a philosophical tract that many historians claim was the blueprint for Hitler's future actions and policies. Released after nine months, Hitler rejoined the Nazis and worked on mobilizing popular support. Blaming a host of others for Germany's woes and promising a return to German greatness, Hitler's party gained political strength during the Depression of the 1930s, until it gained a plurality of votes in the election of 1932. Hitler became Chancellor of Germany.

Once in power, Hitler shrewdly dismantled the constitutional limitations on his power and ruled as the unlimited *Führer*. Political opposition was banned, personal freedoms were curtailed, and anti-Semitic legislation threatened the well-being of Germany's Jewish population. But Hitler also pursued policies designed to win public support. He put thousands of unemployed laborers back to work on government-funded projects, promoted German festivals and traditional culture, and vowed vengeance on all those who had thwarted the natural ambitions and greatness of the German people. By 1939, he had rearmed the nation and had even annexed Austria and Czechoslovakia as part of Germany, which was now once again the greatest power in Europe. In September 1939, Hitler demanded new territorial concessions from Poland, pushing the British and French too far. Just twenty-five years after the start of World War I, Europe found itself once again at war.

Hitler's worldview, and his ambitions for the German people, are explicitly expressed in the pages of *Mein Kampf*, although few took him seriously when he wrote the tract in 1923. The main themes developed in *Mein Kampf* are based on a biological model of society, which asserts that humans naturally belong to different "races" characterized by their different levels of ability. Hitler's race theories were extreme variants of social Darwinism, a crude application of Charles Darwin's theories of biological evolution, natural selection, and survival of the fittest to human society (see chapter 10). His assumptions colored his vision of the world. In *Mein Kampf*, Hitler condemned what he considered weak, decadent, and inferior: liberalism, Marxism, and the Jews. But he spent equal time discussing what he thought was strong and superior: the German race and its elevated culture. The duty of the government, he added, was to do whatever was necessary in order to protect and promote the collective interests of German *Volk* [people], the "fittest" of all the races. Hitler's philosophy has been termed "volkish philosophy," and it embodied important variants of collectivist ideology that shaped his policies once he attained power. Hitler's autocratic political control over Germany, his use of propaganda and terror, his promotion of traditional German culture and racial purity, as well as his persecution of communists, homosexuals, and Jews, were all extensions of his volkish philosophy. For millions of Germans disoriented and disillusioned by wartime defeat, hyperinflation, and unemployment, Hitler's message of hope, his identification of enemies to blame, his call for self-sacrifice and patriotism, and his vision of a greater future for a reunited German people had a tremendous emotional appeal and helps to explain his popularity.

QUESTIONS TO CONSIDER

1. What did Hitler see as the main problems of liberal individualism and democracy? What are the assumptions about human nature on which he based his criticism of liberalism?

2. What collectivist solutions did he suggest? What is the connection between Hitler's collectivist ideas and his later military aggression and death camps?

3. How, in Hitler's explanation, was it possible for the Jews to be responsible both for capitalist exploitation and for the Marxist movement that aimed to overthrow capitalism? If the Jews were so inferior to Aryans, why were they such a threat to Germany? In your opinion, were Hitler's ideas about Jews consistent?

4. Hitler was not alone in identifying selfish individualism with both capitalism and democracy. What collectivist solutions are put forward today to counterbalance excessive materialism and individualism? How do their principles differ from those of Hitler's militant racism?

5. How would you assess Hitler's appeal? In your opinion, would it be possible for a leader to make similar successful appeals in this day and age?

MEIN KAMPF (1923)

Adolf Hitler

After the turn of the century, . . . in Vienna I saw that only a twofold road could lead to the goal of improving these conditions: *The deepest sense of social responsibility*

Source: Adolf Hitler, *Mein Kampf,* transl. Ralph Manheim (Boston: Houghton Mifflin Co., 1943), 23–24, 29–30, 50–51, 60, 64–65, 284–88, 290, 300, 305–06, 314–16, 318–20, 324–25, 391, 393–94, 401–04, 623, 642–43, 645–46, 653–54. All italics in the original. Some sections have been rearranged for conciseness.

for the creation of better foundations for our development, coupled with brutal deter-mination in breaking down incurable tumors.

Just as Nature does not concentrate her greatest attention in preserving what ex-ists, but in breeding offspring to carry on the species, likewise, in human life, it is less important artificially to alleviate existing evil, which, in view of human nature, is ninety-nine per cent impossible, than to ensure from the start healthier channels for a future development.

During my struggle for existence in Vienna, it had become clear to me that *Social activity must never and on no account be directed toward philanthropic flim-flam, but rather toward the elimination of the basic deficiencies in the organization of our economic and cultural life that must—or at all events can—lead to the degeneration of the individual. . . .*

Only when an epoch ceases to be haunted by the shadow of its own conscious-ness of guilt will it achieve the inner calm and outward strength brutally and ruth-lessly to prune off the wild shoots and tear out the weeds.

Nation and Race

There are some truths which are so obvious that for this very reason they are not seen or at least not recognized by ordinary people. . . . Thus men without exception wander about in the garden of Nature; they imagine that they know practically everything and yet with few exceptions pass blindly by one of the most patent principles of Nature's rule: the inner segregation of the species of all living beings on this earth. . . . Every an-imal mates only with a member of the same species. . . . This is only too natural.

Any crossing of two beings not at exactly the same level produces a medium be-tween the level of the two parents . . . : the offspring will probably stand higher than the racially lower parent, but not as high as the higher one. . . . Such mating is con-trary to the will of Nature for a higher breeding of all life. . . . Nature looks on calmly, with satisfaction, in fact. In the struggle for daily bread all those who are weak and sickly or less determined succumb, while the struggle of the males for the female grants the right or opportunity to propagate only to the healthiest. And struggle is al-ways a means for improving a species' health and power of resistance and, therefore, a cause of its higher development. . . . No more than Nature desires the mating of weaker with stronger individuals, even less does she desire the blending of a higher with a lower race. . . .

The result of all racial crossing is therefore in brief always the following:
(a) Lowering of the level of the higher race;
(b) Physical and intellectual regression and hence the beginning of a slowly but surely progressing sickness.

To bring about such a development is, then, nothing else but to sin against the will of the eternal creator. And as a sin this act is rewarded. When man attempts to rebel against the iron logic of Nature, he comes into struggle with the principles to which he himself owes his existence as a man. And this attack must lead to his own doom. . . .

Everything we admire on this earth today—science and art, technology and in-ventions—is only the creative product of a few peoples and originally perhaps of one race. On them depends the existence of this whole culture. . . . All the human culture, all the results of art, science, and technology that we see before us today, are almost exclusively the creative product of the Aryan.*

. . . [H]e alone was the founder of all higher humanity, therefore representing the prototype of all that we understand by the word "man." He is the Prometheus of mankind. . . .

Aryan races—often absurdly small numerically—subject foreign peoples, and then, stimulated by the special living conditions of the new territory (fertility, climatic conditions, etc.) and assisted by the multitude of lower-type beings standing at their disposal as helpers, develop the intellectual and organizational capacities dormant within them. . . . In the end, however, the conquerors transgress against the principle of blood purity, to which they had first adhered; they begin to mix with the subjugated inhabitants and thus end their own existence. . . . True genius is always inborn and never cultivated, let alone learned. . . . Blood mixture and the resultant drop in the racial level is the sole cause of the dying out of old cultures. . . .

The . . . inner causes of the Aryan's importance . . . are to be sought less in a natural instinct of self-preservation than in the special type of its expression. The will to live, subjectively viewed, is everywhere equal and different only in the form of its actual expression. In the most primitive living creatures the instinct of self-preservation does not go beyond concern for their own ego. . . . [T]he animal lives only for himself, seeks food only for his present hunger, and fights only for his own life. . . . [E]very basis is lacking for the formation of a group, even the most primitive form of family. . . .

The greater the readiness to subordinate purely personal interests, the higher rises the ability to establish comprehensive communities. This self-sacrificing will to give one's personal labor and if necessary one's own life for others is most strongly developed in the Aryan. The Aryan is not greatest in his mental qualities as such, but in the extent of his willingness to put all his abilities in the service of the community. In him the instinct of self-preservation has reached the noblest form, since he willingly subordinates his own ego to the life of the community and, if the hour demands, even sacrifices it. . . .

This state of mind, which subordinates the interests of the ego to the conservation of the community, is really the first premise for every truly human culture. From it alone can arise all the great works of mankind. . . . What applies to work as the foundation of human sustenance and all human progress is true to an even greater degree for the defense of man and his culture. In giving one's own life for the existence of the community lies the crown of all sense of sacrifice. Our own German language possesses a word which magnificently designates this kind of activity: *Pflichterfuellung* (fulfillment of duty); it means not to be self-sufficient but to serve the community. The basic attitude from which such activity arises, we call—to distinguish it from egoism

---

*Aryan is a pseudo-racial distinction that arose out of a combination of social Darwinism and nationalism. In essence, national or ethnic characteristics were taken to be signs of racial distinctiveness, and then competition between these "races" was interpreted as identical to competition and "survival of the fittest," which the Darwinian theory of evolution sees at work in nature. Aryan is a slippery category, sometimes designating whites as opposed to nonwhites. At other times, only German-speaking peoples, or "Nordic" peoples or northern Europeans, could be included. In Hitler's time, it especially distinguished "normal" Europeans from Jews.

and selfishness—idealism. By this we understand only the individual's capacity to make sacrifices for the community, for his fellow men. . . . It is to this inner attitude that the Aryan owes his position in this world, and to it the world owes man; for it alone formed from pure spirit the creative force which, by a unique pairing of the brutal fist and the intellectual genius, created the monuments of human culture.

Marxism (Social Democracy)

. . . I saw before me a doctrine, comprised of egotism and hate, which can lead to victory pursuant to mathematical laws, but in so doing must put an end to humanity. Meanwhile, I had learned to understand the connection between this doctrine of destruction and the nature of a people of which, up to that time, I had known next to nothing. Only a knowledge of the Jews provides the key with which to comprehend the inner, and consequently real, aims of Social Democracy. . . . When I recognized the Jew as the leader of the Social Democracy, the scales dropped from my eyes. A long soul struggle had reached its conclusion. . . . For me this was the time of the greatest spiritual upheaval I have ever had to go through. I had ceased to be a weak-kneed cosmopolitan and become an anti-Semite. . . .

The Jewish doctrine of Marxism rejects the aristocratic principle of Nature and replaces the eternal privilege of power and strength by the mass of numbers and their dead weight. Thus it denies the value of personality in man, contests the significance of nationality and race, and thereby withdraws from humanity the premise of its existence and its culture. . . . If, with the help of his Marxist creed, the Jew is victorious over the other peoples of the world, his crown will be the funeral wreath of humanity. . . .

Eternal Nature inexorably avenges the infringement of her commands. Hence today I believe that I am acting in accordance with the will of the Almighty Creator: by defending my self against the Jew, I am fighting for the work of the Lord. . . .

Jews

The mightiest counterpart to the Aryan is . . . the Jew. . . . [T]he Jew of all times has lived in the states of other peoples, and there formed his own state . . . under the disguise of "religious community" . . . . The Jew's life as a parasite in the body of other nations and states explains a characteristic which once caused Schopenhauer*. . . to call him the "great master in lying." Existence impels the Jew to lie, and to lie perpetually. . . . His life within other peoples can only endure for any length of time if he succeeds in arousing the opinion that he is not a people but a "religious community," though of a special sort. And this is the first great lie. . . .

The Jew has always been a people with definite racial characteristics and never a religion. . . . [W]hat would have been more expedient and at the same time more innocent than the "embezzled" concept of a religious community? For here, too, everything is borrowed or rather stolen. Due to his own original special nature, the Jew cannot possess a religious institution, if for no other reason because he lacks idealism in any form, and hence belief in a hereafter is absolutely foreign to him. And a religion

---

*Arthur Schopenhauer (1788–1860). A German philosopher and chief expounder of pessimism.

in the Aryan sense cannot be imagined which lacks the conviction of survival after death in some form. . . .

The Jew also becomes liberal and . . . makes himself the spokesman of a new era. . . . By way of stock shares he pushes his way into the circuit of national production . . . , thus robbing the enterprises of the foundations of a personal ownership. Between employer and employee there arises that inner estrangement which later leads to political class division. Finally, the Jewish influence on economic affairs grows with terrifying speed through the stock exchange. He becomes the owner, or at least the controller, of the national labor force.

To strengthen his political position he tries to tear down the racial and civil barriers which for a time continue to restrain him at every step. To this end he fights with all the tenacity innate in him for religious tolerance. . . . His ultimate goal . . . is the victory of "democracy," or . . . parliamentarianism. It is most compatible with his requirements; for it excludes the personality and puts in its place the majority characterized by stupidity, incompetence, and last but not least, cowardice. . . .

[W]hile on the one hand he organizes capitalist methods of human exploitation to their ultimate consequence, [the Jew] approaches the very victims of his spirit and his activity and in a short time becomes the leader of their struggle against himself. "Against himself" is only figuratively speaking; for the great master of lies understands as always how to make himself appear to be the pure one and to heap the blame on others. . . . Scarcely has the new class [the proletariat] grown out of the general economic shift than the Jew, clearly and distinctly, realizes that it can open the way for his own further advancement. First, he used the bourgeoisie as a battering-ram against the feudal world, then the worker against the bourgeois world. If formerly he knew how to swindle his way to civil rights in the shadow of the bourgeoisie, now he hopes to find the road to his own domination in the worker's struggle for existence. . . . Thus there arises a pure movement entirely of manual workers under Jewish leadership, apparently aiming to improve the situation of the worker, but in truth planning the enslavement and with it the destruction of all non-Jewish peoples. . . .

[The Jew] stops at nothing, and in his vileness he becomes so gigantic that no one need be surprised if among our people the personification of the devil as the symbol of all evil assumes the living shape of the Jew. . . . With satanic joy in his face, the black-haired Jewish youth lurks in wait for the unsuspecting girl whom he defiles with his blood, thus stealing her from her people. With every means he tries to destroy the racial foundations of the people he has set out to subjugate. Just as he himself systematically ruins women and girls, he does not shrink back from pulling down the blood barriers for others, even on a large scale. It was and it is Jews who bring the Negroes into the Rhineland,* always with the same secret thought and clear aim of ruining the hated white race by the necessarily resulting bastardization, throwing it down from its cultural and political height, and himself rising to be its master. For a racially pure people which is conscious of its blood can never be enslaved by the Jew. In this world he will forever be master over bastards and bastards alone.

---

*Like other European powers, the French recruited soldiers from their colonies in Africa, especially during World War I. Some of these were part of the postwar occupation force in the Rhineland.

And so he tries systematically to lower the racial level by a continuous poisoning of individuals.

Now begins the great last revolution. . . . In a few years he tries to exterminate the national intelligentsia and by robbing the peoples of their natural intellectual leadership makes them ripe for the slave's lot of permanent subjugation. The most frightful example of this kind is offered by Russia, where he killed or starved about thirty million people with positively fanatical savagery, in part amid inhuman tortures, in order to give a gang of Jewish journalists and stock exchange bandits domination over a great people. . . .

The Jewish train of thought in all this is clear. The Bolshevization of Germany— that is, the extermination of the national folkish . . . intelligentsia to make possible the sweating of the German working class under the yoke of Jewish world finance—is conceived only as a preliminary to the further extension of this Jewish tendency of world conquest. As often in history, Germany is the great pivot in the mighty struggle. If our people and our state become the victim of these blood-thirsty and avaricious Jewish tyrants of nations, the whole earth will sink into the snares of this octopus; if Germany frees herself from this embrace, this greatest of dangers to nations may be regarded as broken for the whole world. . . . In Russian Bolshevism we must see the attempt undertaken by the Jews in the twentieth century to achieve world domination. . . .

Thus, the highest purpose of a folkish state is concern for the preservation of those original racial elements which bestow culture and create the beauty and dignity of a higher mankind. We, as Aryans, can conceive of the state only as the living organism of a nationality which not only assures the preservation of this nationality, but by the development of its spiritual and ideal abilities leads it to the highest freedom. . . . [T]here is only one holiest human right, and this right is at the same time the holiest obligation, to wit: to see to it that the blood is preserved pure and, by preserving the best humanity, to create the possibility of a nobler development of these beings.

A folkish state must therefore begin by raising marriage from the level of a continuous defilement of the race, and give it the consecration of an institution which is called upon to produce images of the Lord and not monstrosities halfway between man and ape. . . .

In this present-day state of law and order . . . the prevention of the procreative faculty in sufferers from syphilis, tuberculosis, hereditary diseases, cripples, and cretins is a crime, while the actual suppression of the procreative faculty in millions of the very best people is not regarded as anything bad and does not offend against the morals of this hypocritical society. . . . People no longer bother to breed the best for posterity, but let things slide along as best they can. . . . The folkish state must . . . *set race in the center of all life. It must take care to keep it pure. It must declare the child to be the most precious treasure of the people. It must see to it that only the healthy beget children; that there is only one disgrace: despite one's own sickness and deficiencies, to bring children into the world, and one highest honor: to renounce doing so. And conversely it must be considered reprehensible: to withhold healthy children from the nation. Here the state must act as the guardian of a millennial culture in the face of which the wishes and the selfishness of the individual must appear as nothing and submit. It must put the most modern medical means in the service of this knowledge. It must declare unfit for propagation all who are in any way visibly sick or who have inherited a disease and can therefore pass it on, and put this into actual practice. Conversely, it must take care that the fertility of the healthy woman is not limited by the financial irresponsibility of a state regime which turns the blessing of children into a curse for the parents. . . .*

Foreign Policy and War

The foreign policy of the folkish state must safeguard the existence on this planet of the race embodied in the state, by creating a healthy, viable natural relation between the nation's population and growth on the one hand and the quantity and quality of its soil on the other hand. . . . Only an adequately large space on this earth assures a nation of freedom of existence.

[T]he German nation can defend its future only as a world power. . . . *If the National Socialist movement really wants to be consecrated by history with a great mission for our nation, it must . . . find the courage to gather our people and their strength for an advance along the road that will lead this people from its present restricted living space to new land and soil, and hence also free it from the danger of vanishing from the earth or of serving others as a slave nation. The National Socialist Movement must strive to eliminate the disproportion between our population and our area— viewing this latter as a source of food as well as a basis for power politics. . . .*

State boundaries are made by man and changed by man. . . . But we National Socialists must go further. *The right to possess soil can become a duty if without extension of its soil a great nation seems doomed to destruction.* And most especially when not some little nigger nation or other is involved, but the Germanic mother of life, which has given the present-day world its cultural picture. *Germany will either be a world power or there will be no Germany.* And for world power she needs that magnitude which will give her the position she needs in the present period, and life to her citizens.

DEBATES ON COLLECTIVISM IN AMERICA

In the United States, the stock market crash of October 1929 began an economic collapse from which the country would not fully recover until the mobilization for World War II. The American economic disaster resulted from a number of factors. The farm economy had struggled for over a decade. Underregulated banking and stock-market sectors were subject to excesses of investment and even to fraud. There was a serious problem of income distribution both within the United States and between the United States and its trading partners. Domestically, the income and wages of farmers and workers declined during the 1920s, while the percentage of national income in the hands of the wealthiest Americans grew. This mirrored the international trading situation, in which the United States ran large positive trade balances with many debtor nations. As a result, when overexpansion and excess productive capacity became a problem in the late 1920s, neither the American consumer nor the international economy could absorb what the United States businesses produced. The European economy had been propped up by

American loans in the mid-1920s, but they dried up after the market crashed. All countries maintained high tariffs that choked off international trade. Finally, the stock market bubble of the late 1920s primed the market for a devastating collapse. It came on October 29, 1929.

The man in the White House when the "Crash" occurred should have been an ideal choice to address the problems. Herbert Clark Hoover (1874–1964) was born into a poor farm family in Iowa. Orphaned at the age of nine, Hoover went on to work his way through Stanford University, finishing as the top student in its first graduating class. He went on to make millions as a mining engineer—including work in China at the time of the Boxer Rebellion—and by the age of forty he had retired from business to a life of public service. He was revered in Europe for his work as head of the American Relief Administration, providing desperately needed aid to a devastated continent in the aftermath of World War I. A devout Quaker and an activist Republican of the Theodore Roosevelt stripe, as secretary of commerce under Harding he had encouraged businesses to extend benefits to their workers. In sum, his career was that of an able and compassionate man, with a background in crisis relief.

Hoover's response to the catastrophe was active but limited. Traditional economic theory at the time dictated that during economic downturns governments had to cut expenditures and raise taxes in order to avoid running a deficit. Hoover reacted differently, cutting taxes and increasing the federal government's expenditures on public works. As the downturn deepened, he laid out programs to aid businesses, help farmers facing foreclosure, reform the banking system, and provide relief to the unemployed. Through it all, though, he maintained that relief for the poor was not a federal responsibility and that it should be taken care of by local government and private charities.

As the economy continued to spiral downward, America was in no mood for Hoover's fine distinctions about federal and local responsibilities or for his concerns about excessive government. They faulted Hoover for not doing more to address a national disaster, and he suffered a landslide defeat in the 1932 election. Out of office, Hoover devoted himself to writing, and after World War II he served on commissions to reform and streamline the federal government. He died at the age of ninety.

QUESTIONS TO CONSIDER

1. Identify the distinguishing features of what Hoover called the "American system." How did it differ, according to Hoover, from the European system of government? What view of human nature is implicit in his argument?
2. Why did centralization and bureaucracy threaten both individual freedom and economic prosperity, in Hoover's opinion?
3. Hoover rejected absolute *laissez-faire* in the name of the public interest in economic, political, and social justice. In your opinion, is it possible to achieve that justice with the type of limited government that Hoover advocated?

4. How does Hoover's view of the benefits of "ordered liberty" compare with the interpretation of capitalism presented in *The ABC of Communism?*

5. At the end of his speech, Hoover presented his ideal vision of America. How did he argue that a free economic system benefits the American family? In your view, are there instances in which government action is required to strengthen the home and family?

PRESIDENTIAL CAMPAIGN SPEECH (1928)

Herbert Hoover

. . . Tonight, I will not deal with the multitude of issues which have been already well canvassed [in the campaign], I intend rather to discuss some of those more fundamental principles and ideals upon which I believe the Government of the United States should be conducted. . . .

The Republican Party has ever been a party of progress. . . . It has reflected the spirit of the American people. . . . But in addition to this great record of contributions of the Republican Party to progress, there has been a further fundamental contribution—a contribution underlying and sustaining all the others—and that is the resistance of the Republican Party to every attempt to inject the government into business in competition with its citizens. . . .

During one hundred and fifty years we have builded up a form of self-government and a social system which is peculiarly our own. It differs essentially from all others in the world. It is the American system. It is just as definite and positive a political and social system as has ever been developed on earth. It is founded upon . . . the conception that only through ordered liberty, freedom and equal opportunity to the individual will his initiative and enterprise spur the march of progress. And in our insistence upon equality of opportunity has our system advanced beyond all the world.

During the war we necessarily turned to the Government to solve every difficult economic problem. The Government having absorbed every energy of our people to war there was no other solution. . . . [T]he Federal Government became a centralized despotism which undertook responsibilities, assumed autocratic powers, and took over the business of citizens. To a large degree we regimented our whole people temporarily into a socialistic state. However justified in time of war, if continued in peacetime it would destroy not only our American system but with it our progress and freedom as well.

When the war closed . . . , [w]e were challenged with a peace-time choice between the American system of rugged individualism and a European philosophy of diametrically opposed doctrines—doctrines of paternalism and state socialism. The acceptance of these ideas would have meant the destruction of self-government through centralization of government. It would have meant the undermining of the

Source: Herbert Hoover, *The New Day: Campaign Speeches of Herbert Hoover 1928,* 2nd ed. (Stanford, CA: Stanford University Press, 1929), 149–50, 152–59, 162–65, 167–68, 175–76.

individual initiative and enterprise upon which our people have grown to unparalleled greatness. . . .

If anyone will study the causes of retarded recuperation in Europe, he will find much of it due to the stifling of private initiative on one hand, and overloading of the Government with business on the other. . . . I should like to state to you the effect that this projection of government in business would have upon our system of self-government and our economic system. . . . Commercial business requires a concentration of responsibility. Self-government requires decentralization and many checks and balances to safeguard liberty. Our government to succeed in business would need become in effect a despotism. There at once begins the destruction of self-government. . . .

The first problem of the government about to adventure in commercial business is to determine a method of administration. It must secure leadership and direction. . . . The hard practical fact is that leadership in business must come through the sheer rise in ability and character. That rise can only take place in the free atmosphere of competition. Competition is closed by bureaucracy. Political agencies are feeble channels through which to select able leaders to conduct commercial business. . . .

Moreover, our legislative bodies cannot in fact delegate their full responsibility to commissions or to individuals for the conduct of matters vital to the American people. . . . Thus, every time the Federal Government goes into a commercial business five hundred and thirty-one Senators and Congressmen become the Board of Directors of that business. . . . Even if they were supermen and if there were no politics in the United States, no body of such numbers could competently direct commercial activities. . . .

The effect upon our economic progress would be even worse. Business progressiveness is dependent on competition. New methods and new ideas are the outgrowth of the spirit of adventure, of individual initiative and of individual enterprise. Without adventure there is no progress. No government administration can rightly take risks with taxpayers' money. . . .

Bureaucracy does not tolerate the spirit of independence; it spreads the spirit of submission into our daily life, penetrates the temper of our people not with the habit of powerful resistance to wrong but with the habit of timid acceptance of the irresistible might. . . . Bureaucracy is ever desirous of spreading its influence and its power. You cannot extend the mastery of the government over the daily working life of a people without at the same time making it the master of the peoples' souls and thoughts. . . . It is false liberalism that interprets itself into the government operation of business. Every step of bureaucratizing of the business of our country poisons the very roots of liberalism—that is, political equality, free speech, free assembly, free press, and equality of opportunity. It is the road not to more liberty, but to less liberty. Liberalism should not be found striving to spread bureaucracy but striving to set bounds to it. True liberalism seeks all legitimate freedom first in the confident belief that without such freedom the pursuit of all other blessings and benefits is vain. That belief is the foundation of all American progress, political as well as economic. . . .

I do not wish to be misunderstood in this statement. I am defining a general policy. It does not mean that our government is to part with one iota of its national resources without complete protection to the public interest. I have already stated that where the government is engaged in public works for purposes of flood control, of navigation, of irrigation, of scientific research or national defense, or in pioneering a new art, that it will at times necessarily produce power or commodities as a by-product. But they must be by-products, not the major purpose itself.

Nor do I wish to be misinterpreted as believing that the United States is free-for-all and the devil-take-the-hindmost. The very essence of equality of opportunity and of American individualism is that there shall be no domination by any group or trust or combination in this republic, whether it be business or political. On the contrary, it demands economic justice as well as political and social justice. It is no system of laissez faire.

I feel deeply on this subject because during the war I had some practical experience with governmental operation and control. I have witnessed not only at home but abroad the many failures of government in business. I have seen its tyrannies, its injustices, its destructions of self-government, its undermining of the very instincts which carry our people forward to progress. I have witnessed the lack of advance, the lowered standards of living, the depressed spirits of people working under such a system. My objection is based not upon theory or upon a failure to recognize wrong or abuse, but I know the adoption of such methods would strike at the very roots of American life and would destroy the very basis of American progress.

Our people have the right to know whether we can continue to solve our great problems without abandonment of our American system. I know we can. We have demonstrated that our system is responsive enough to meet any . . . economic problem and still maintain our democracy as master in its own house, and that we can at the same time preserve equality of opportunity and individual freedom. . . .

The wisdom of our forefathers in their conception that progress can only be attained as the sum of the accomplishment of free individuals has been reenforced by all of the great leaders of the country since that day. Jackson, Lincoln, Cleveland, McKinley, Roosevelt, Wilson, and Coolidge have stood unalterably for these principles.

And what have been the results of our American system? Our country has become the land of opportunity to those born without inheritance, not merely because of the wealth of its resources and industry but because of this freedom of initiative and enterprise. Russia has natural resources equal to ours. Her people are equally industrious, but she has not had the blessings of one hundred and fifty years of our form of government and of our social system.

By adherence to the principles of decentralized self-government, ordered liberty, and opportunity and freedom to the individual, our American experiment in human welfare has yielded a degree of well-being unparalleled in all the world. It has come nearer to the abolition of poverty, to the abolition of fear of want, than humanity has ever reached before. . . .

I have endeavored to present to you that the greatness of America has grown out of a political and social system and a method of [non-governmental] control of economic forces distinctly its own—our American system—which has carried this great experiment in human welfare farther than ever before in history. . . . And I again repeat that the departure from our American system . . . will jeopardize the very liberty and freedom of our people, will destroy equality of opportunity not only to ourselves, but to our children. . . .

To me the foundation of American life rests upon the home and the family. I read into these great economic forces, these intricate and delicate relations of the government with business and with our political and social life, but one supreme end—that we reinforce the ties that bind together the millions of our families, that we strengthen the security, the happiness, and the independence of every home.

My conception of America is a land where men and women may walk in ordered freedom in the independent conduct of their occupations; where they may enjoy the advantages of wealth, not concentrated in the hands of the few but spread through the lives of all; where they build and safeguard their homes, and give to their children the fullest advantages and opportunities of American life; where every man shall be respected in the faith that his conscience and his heart direct him to follow; where a contented and happy people, secure in their liberties, free from poverty and fear, shall have the leisure and impulse to seek a fuller life.

Some may ask where all this may lead beyond mere material progress. It leads to a release of the energies of men and women from the dull drudgery of life to a wider vision and a higher hope. It leads to the opportunity for greater and greater service, not alone from man to man in our own land, but from our country to the whole world. It leads to an America, healthy in body, healthy in spirit, unfettered, youthful, eager— with a vision searching beyond the farthest horizons, with an open mind, sympathetic and generous. It is to these higher ideals and for these purposes that I pledge myself and the Republican Party.

THE GREAT DEPRESSION AND ROOSEVELT'S CALL TO ACTION

By 1932, Herbert Hoover's liberal principles had proven unequal to the task of dealing with the national economic and social crisis. Economic statistics vividly demonstrate the extent of the disaster that had overwhelmed the U.S. economy. Unemployment that had averaged 5 percent in the 1920s soared to 33 percent by 1932. Overall production fell by 50 percent between 1929 and 1932. Over the same time span, agricultural income was even harder hit, plummeting to one-third of its 1929 level. The Dow Jones average fell from 364 in 1929 to just 62 in 1932. The Depression hit every economic sector, every social class, every ethnic group (though some harder than others), and every region in America.

As the economy continued to crater, radical political solutions began to get a sympathetic hearing in distressed America. Huey P. Long ("the Kingfish"), the flamboyant populist governor of Louisiana at the time of Hoover's administration, put forward a program known as Share Our Wealth, which would guarantee every family a minimum income by confiscating and limiting the property of the very wealthy. A Roman Catholic priest, Father Charles E. Coughlin, used his national radio show to attack unbridled capitalism and to call for "social justice."

It is more than a bit ironic that Herbert Hoover, a man who was born in straitened circumstances, orphaned young, and forced to make his own way in life, should have been unable to address the national economic crisis in a way acceptable to his suffering fellow citizens. And it is even more ironic that Franklin Roosevelt, born into privilege and power, was the man whose leadership and policies during America's darkest times would earn him an unequaled four terms in office.

Franklin Delano Roosevelt (1882–1945), or FDR as he came to be known, was born on an estate in Hyde Park, New York. An only child, he knew private tutors and elite prep schools; he went to Harvard for his undergraduate degree and Columbia University for his law degree. Imbued with the sense that he was destined for great things, he entered politics out of a sense of obligation to serve the common man. He was also strongly influenced by the image and reputation of a famous distant cousin, Theodore Roosevelt. One can scarcely imagine a more privileged path to the corridors of power than that experienced by FDR.

His early activities in politics bore all the hallmarks of this privileged birth. His first elected office was to the New York Senate in 1910. He was chosen to serve as secretary of the navy (1913–1920) through both Wilson administrations, in part because sailing on his family's yachts was his favorite pastime. Despite this rather shallow political background, he was named vice-presidential candidate on Al Smith's Democratic ticket in 1920. Defeat in that election probably did him more good than harm by giving him national political exposure and name recognition (already achieved, of course, because of Theodore Roosevelt). He succeeded Al Smith as governor of New York, the nation's most populous state, where he established a mildly progressive political reputation. In 1921, though, he contracted polio. Although he recovered enough to continue his political life, he was crippled from the waist down. This experience toughened and deepened Roosevelt.

FDR won the party's presidential nomination in 1932, and his selection virtually guaranteed his election, given Hoover's unpopularity. By then, Hoover's name was attached by the American public to the makeshift shanty towns that sprang up around the country (Hoovervilles) and to newspapers used as blankets by the homeless and unemployed masses (Hoover blankets). Along with the presidency, the Democrats also won decisive majorities in the House and the Senate.

Many of the policies that FDR would pursue had antecedents in the Hoover administration, but FDR was willing to go much further than Hoover. He projected an active and energetic optimism, reaching out to Americans by radio via his "fireside chats." FDR also took significant symbolic steps, such as declaring a bank holiday to stem the flood of bank failures. Finally, when the economy still had not rebounded, he tried more radical measures, such as price fixing, and more extensive programs (for example, the famous "alphabet soup" agencies, such as the WPA [Works Progress Administration], CCC [Civilian Conservation Corps], NLRB [National Labor Relations Board], and Social Security). Despite all of these efforts, the economic recovery was incomplete and uncertain before the full production of World War II propelled America completely out of the Depression. Nonetheless, Roosevelt's four terms marked a turning point in American history, establishing the principle of federal government responsibility for public welfare and creating the federal governmental system that continues to the present day. It also established Keynesian economics (named after the British economist John Maynard Keynes), which calls for greater governmental expenditures in times of economic recession to compensate for lower spending by the private sector. FDR would go on to be reelected three times. He led America through most of World War II but died in office in April 1945, just three months before the end of the war.

In the selection that follows, he lays out the general lines of his vision for America. Roosevelt had broken with tradition to fly to Chicago to accept his party's nomination. This act shows us that Roosevelt understood the importance of projecting a positive image to counter the nation's dark mood. Some of that attitude comes across in his acceptance speech, as well. In terms of the theme of this chapter, the speech is less significant for the specific proposals it outlines than it is for the general atmosphere it seeks to establish and for the broad contours of the relationship between individual and collective that it lays out.

QUESTIONS TO CONSIDER

1. According to Roosevelt, what had gone wrong and put America in such an awful situation? Who was to blame for the nation's problems?
2. Compare FDR's description of wealthy capitalists with what Herbert Hoover had to say about businessmen in his speech. What implications did each man's view of capitalist businessmen have for the types of policies and responses each recommended?
3. What were Roosevelt's views concerning materialism (concern with material wealth)? How do his views of materialism compare with those expressed in *The ABC of Communism* and *Mein Kampf*?
4. FDR compared the national crisis to a war. How is the balance between individual rights and collective rights affected by war? In your opinion, was he right to treat the Great Depression as a wartime crisis?
5. What are the implications for individual freedom of the changed role of the federal government that began under FDR? Has the balance between individual and collective in America changed radically as a result of Roosevelt's New Deal policies? If so, is that change a good thing or a bad thing, in your opinion?

FIRST INAUGURAL ADDRESS (1933)

Franklin Delano Roosevelt

I am certain that my fellow Americans expect that on my induction into the Presidency I will address them with a candor and a decision which the present situation of our Nation impels. This is preeminently the time to speak the truth, the whole truth, frankly and boldly. Nor need we shrink from honestly facing conditions in our country today. This great Nation will endure as it has endured, will revive and will prosper. So, first of all, let me assert my firm belief that the only thing we have to fear is fear

Source: Franklin Delano Roosevelt, *The Public Papers and Addresses of Franklin D. Roosevelt*, Vol. 2 (New York: Randon House, 1938), 11–16.

itself—nameless, unreasoning, unjustified terror which paralyzes needed efforts to convert retreat into advance. In every dark hour of our national life a leadership of frankness and vigor has met with that understanding and support of the people themselves which is essential to victory. I am convinced that you will again give that support to leadership in these critical days.

In such a spirit on my part and on yours we face our common difficulties. They concern, thank God, only material things. Values have shrunken to fantastic levels; taxes have risen; our ability to pay has fallen; government of all kinds is faced by serious curtailment of income; the means of exchange are frozen in the currents of trade; the withered leaves of industrial enterprise lie on every side; farmers find no markets for their produce; the savings of many years in thousands of families are gone.

More important, a host of unemployed citizens face the grim problem of existence, and an equally great number toil with little return. Only a foolish optimist can deny the dark realities of the moment.

Yet our distress comes from no failure of substance. We are stricken by no plague of locusts. Compared with the perils which our forefathers conquered because they believed and were not afraid, we have still much to be thankful for. Nature still offers her bounty and human efforts have multiplied it. Plenty is at our doorstep, but a generous use of it languishes in the very sight of the supply. Primarily this is because the rulers of the exchange of mankind's goods have failed, through their own stubbornness and their own incompetence, have admitted their failure, and abdicated. Practices of the unscrupulous money changers stand indicted in the court of public opinion, rejected by the hearts and minds of men.

True they have tried, but their efforts have been cast in the pattern of an outworn tradition. Faced by failure of credit they have proposed only the lending of more money. Stripped of the lure of profit by which to induce our people to follow their false leadership, they have resorted to exhortations, pleading tearfully for restored confidence. They know only the rules of a generation of self-seekers. They have no vision, and when there is no vision the people perish.

The money changers have fled from their high seats in the temple of our civilization. We may now restore that temple to the ancient truths. The measure of the restoration lies in the extent to which we apply social values more noble than mere monetary profit.

Happiness lies not in the mere possession of money; it lies in the joy of achievement, in the thrill of creative effort. The joy and moral stimulation of work no longer must be forgotten in the mad chase of evanescent profits. These dark days will be worth all they cost us if they teach us that our true destiny is not to be ministered unto but to minister to ourselves and to our fellow men. Recognition of the falsity of material wealth as the standard of success goes hand in hand with the abandonment of the false belief that public office and high political position are to be valued only by the standards of pride of place and personal profit; and there must be an end to a conduct in banking and in business which too often has given to a sacred trust the likeness of callous and selfish wrongdoing. Small wonder that confidence languishes, for it thrives only on honesty, on honor, on the sacredness of obligations, on faithful protection, on unselfish performance; without them it cannot live.

Restoration calls, however, not for changes in ethics alone. This Nation asks for action, and action now.

Our greatest primary task is to put people to work. This is no unsolvable problem if we face it wisely and courageously. It can be accomplished in part by direct recruiting by the Government itself, treating the task as we would treat the emergency of a war, but at the same time, through this employment, accomplishing greatly needed projects to stimulate and reorganize the use of our natural resources.

Hand in hand with this we must frankly recognize the overbalance of population in our industrial centers and, by engaging on a national scale in a redistribution, endeavor to provide a better use of the land for those best fitted for the land. The task can be helped by definite efforts to raise the values of agricultural products and with this the power to purchase the output of our cities. It can be helped by preventing realistically the tragedy of the growing loss through foreclosure of our small homes and our farms. It can be helped by insistence that the Federal, State, and local governments act forthwith on the demand that their cost be drastically reduced. It can be helped by the unifying of relief activities which today are often scattered, uneconomical, and unequal. It can be helped by national planning for and supervision of all forms of transportation and of communications and other utilities which have a definitely public character. There are many ways in which it can be helped, but it can never be helped merely by talking about it. We must act and act quickly.

Finally, in our progress toward a resumption of work we require two safeguards against a return of the evils of the old order; there must be a strict supervision of all banking and credits and investments; there must be an end to speculation with other people's money, and there must be provision for an adequate but sound currency.

There are the lines of attack. I shall presently urge upon a new Congress in special session detailed measures for their fulfillment, and I shall seek the immediate assistance of the several States.

Through this program of action we address ourselves to putting our own national house in order and making income balance outgo. Our international trade relations, though vastly important, are in point of time and necessity secondary to the establishment of a sound national economy. I favor as a practical policy the putting of first things first. I shall spare no effort to restore world trade by international economic readjustment, but the emergency at home cannot wait on that accomplishment.

The basic thought that guides these specific means of national recovery is not narrowly nationalistic. It is the insistence, as a first consideration, upon the interdependence of the various elements in all parts of the United States—a recognition of the old and permanently important manifestation of the American spirit of the pioneer. It is the way to recovery. It is the immediate way. It is the strongest assurance that the recovery will endure.

In the field of world policy I would dedicate this Nation to the policy of the good neighbor—the neighbor who resolutely respects himself and, because he does so, respects the rights of others—the neighbor who respects his obligations and respects the sanctity of his agreements in and with a world of neighbors.

If I read the temper of our people correctly, we now realize as we have never realized before our interdependence on each other; that we can not merely take but we must give as well; that if we are to go forward, we must move as a trained and loyal army willing to sacrifice for the good of a common discipline, because without such discipline no progress is made, no leadership becomes effective. We are, I know, ready and willing to submit our lives and property to such discipline, because it makes possible a leadership which aims at a larger good. This I propose to offer, pledging that the larger purposes will bind upon us all as a sacred obligation with a unity of duty hitherto evoked only in time of armed strife.

With this pledge taken, I assume unhesitatingly the leadership of this great army of our people dedicated to a disciplined attack upon our common problems.

Action in this image and to this end is feasible under the form of government which we have inherited from our ancestors. Our Constitution is so simple and practical that it is possible always to meet extraordinary needs by changes in emphasis and arrangement without loss of essential form. That is why our constitutional system has proved itself the most superbly enduring political mechanism the modern world has produced. It has met every stress of vast expansion of territory, of foreign wars, of bitter internal strife, of world relations.

It is to be hoped that the normal balance of executive and legislative authority may be wholly adequate to meet the unprecedented task before us. But it may be that an unprecedented demand and need for undelayed action may call for temporary departure from that normal balance of public procedure.

I am prepared under my constitutional duty to recommend the measures that a stricken nation in the midst of a stricken world may require. These measures, or such other measures as the Congress may build out of its experience and wisdom, I shall seek, within my constitutional authority, to bring to speedy adoption.

But in the event that the Congress shall fail to take one of these two courses, and in the event that the national emergency is still critical, I shall not evade the clear course of duty that will then confront me. I shall ask the Congress for the one remaining instrument to meet the crisis—broad Executive power to wage a war against the emergency, as great as the power that would be given to me if we were in fact invaded by a foreign foe. For the trust reposed in me I will return the courage and the devotion that befit the time. I can do no less.

We face the arduous days that lie before us in the warm courage of the national unity; with the clear consciousness of seeking old and precious moral values; with the clean satisfaction that comes from the stern performance of duty by old and young alike. We aim at the assurance of a rounded and permanent national life.

We do not distrust the future of essential democracy. The people of the United States have not failed. In their need they have registered a mandate that they want direct, vigorous action. They have asked for discipline and direction under leadership. They have made me the present instrument of their wishes. In the spirit of the gift I take it.

In this dedication of a Nation we humbly ask the blessing of God. May He protect each and every one of us. May He guide me in the days to come.

COLLECTIVISM AND DEVELOPMENT IN TANZANIA

The colonial history of Tanzania (then known as Tanganyika) bears many similarities to the experiences of other African colonies. The primary intention of both the German and British colonizers[11] was the extraction of raw materials to be processed and sold in Europe. But although the production of such cash crops[12] as cotton, coffee, sisal, and peanuts was ultimately dependent upon low-cost African labor, there was very little reciprocal European investment in local food production, education, or public health. Overall, the colonial economy in Tanzania (as in most other African colonies) was created by Europeans to serve their interests and their profits, and for many decades Tanzania was a net exporter of goods and wealth to Europe.

When Tanzanians began to demand self-rule in the 1950s, they found a ready leader and eloquent spokesman in Julius Nyerere, known fondly as *mwalimu,* or "teacher" in the national language of Kiswahili. Nyerere was born in a small rural village in colonial Tanzania in 1922, and as a young boy, he is reputed to have walked twenty-six miles to attend one of the few primary schools established by British missionaries. His superior academic performance and hard work led to a scholarship to study at Makerere University in neighboring Uganda, and later he became the first Tanzanian to study at a British University (the University of Edinburgh). Graduating with an M.A. in history and economics, Nyerere left Britain and returned to Tanzania in 1952, where he taught for several years.

In the 1950s, Nyerere became increasing involved in the national struggle for Tanzanian independence. In 1954, he founded the Tanganyika Africa National Union (TANU), a broad-based political party that advocated self-rule through national unity and nonviolent protest. After a period of difficult and protracted negotiations, Britain agreed to grant Tanzania complete independence in 1961, and Nyerere was duly elected president in the nation's first democratic elections. Serving four successive terms from 1961 to 1985, Nyerere emerged as one of Africa's most popular, respected, and idealistic leaders. He was one of the founders of the Organization of African Unity, a leader of the international "nonaligned movement" during the Cold War, and an active opponent of racism and apartheid in colonial Zimbabwe (Rhodesia) and South Africa. Nyerere was also a prominent writer and political thinker, whose works include *Freedom and Unity* (1966), *Freedom and Socialism* (1968), *Freedom and Development* (1973), and *Ujamaa* (1968). In addition, he also translated Shakespeare's *Julius Caesar* and *The Merchant of Venice* into Kiswahili. At the end of his final term in office, Nyerere continued to serve as an elder statesman and public servant until his death in 1999.

In 1967, President Nyerere announced the Arusha Declaration, a new political and economic charter for Tanzania that sought to end the exploitive legacies of colonialism and transform the nation into a self-reliant, collectivist, and egalitarian society. As he explained in his speech "Socialism and Rural Development" (1967), his plan would provide a new path for economic development that would build upon traditional African values of hard work, sharing, and cooperation. To achieve these goals, Nyerere proposed the policy of *ujamaa* ["familyhood" in Kiswahili], which centered on the restructuring of society around cooperative farming communes. Nyerere believed that *ujamaa* agriculture would increase farming productivity, promote tribal harmony, and facilitate the development of a classless society.[13]

Nyerere's lofty plans for Tanzania had decidedly mixed results. Great improvements were made in education and public health, and levels of inequality, corruption, and political oppression were much lower than in neighboring African nations. But *ujamaa* failed as the engine of economic development, and the country remained poor, underdeveloped, and heavily dependent on foreign assistance. Moreover, the government frequently had to resort to coercive and sometimes violent measures to relocate farmers from their traditional lands to the new communal villages. Additional economic strains caused by droughts, rising debt, and a dramatic drop in commodity prices[14] forced the government to reassess its development policies. Since the mid-1980s, Tanzania has largely abandoned *ujamaa* and, like the rest of Africa, has adopted more capitalist-oriented economic policies recommended and favored by such powerful institutions as the World Bank and International Monetary Fund (IMF). But if African nations fail to achieve economic or social progress with western models, it is likely that future leaders may be willing to experiment with variations of Nyerere's collectivist vision.

QUESTIONS TO CONSIDER

1. Nyerere begins by stating that his policy is based on three basic assumptions. What are these assumptions, and how crucial are they to the creation of a collectivist society?

2. What arguments does Nyerere make in support of *ujamaa* agriculture? How would you assess the strength and weaknesses of his argument?

3. How does Nyerere envision the role of government in implementing and fostering collectivist goals? In what ways might the government become oppressive? How do Nyerere's ideas on the role of the state compare with the other readings in this chapter?

4. Nyerere wrote, "It is not long before an individual, working alone, reaches the limit of his powers. Only by working together can men overcome that limitation. The truth is that when human beings want to make great progress they have no alternative but to combine their efforts." How do you assess this view? Does it support the creation of a collectivist society?

5. In your opinion, is Nyerere's philosophy irrational? Is it antiwestern? Is it antimodern? Be sure to carefully define your terms in your responses.

"SOCIALISM AND RURAL DEVELOPMENT" (1967)

Julius Nyerere

The traditional African family lived according to the basic principles of *ujamaa*. Its members did this unconsciously, and without any conception of what they were doing

Source: Julius Nyerere, "Socialism and Rural Development," in *Freedom and Socialism: A Selection from Writings and Speeches 1965–1967*, 337–39, 340, 345–48, 351–52, 364–66. Copyright © 1968 Oxford University Press, Inc. Used by permission of Oxford University Press, Inc.

in political terms. They lived together and worked together because that was how they understood life, and how they reinforced each other against the difficulties they had to contend with—the uncertainties of weather and sickness, the depredations of wild animals (and sometimes human enemies), and the cycle of life and death. The results of their joint effort were divided unequally between them, but according to well-understood customs. And the division was always on the basis of the fact that every member of the family had to have enough to eat, some simple covering, and a place to sleep, before any of them (even the head of the family) had anything extra. The family members thought of themselves as one, and all their language and behavior emphasized their unity. The basic goods of life were "our food," "our land," "our cattle." And identity was established in terms of relationships; mother and father of so-and-so; daughter of so-and-so; wife of such-and-such a person. They lived together and they worked together; and the result of their joint labor was the property of the family as a whole.

The Assumptions of Traditional Ujamaa Living

This pattern of living was made possible because of three basic assumptions of traditional life. . . . The first of these assumptions, or principles of life, I have sometimes described as "love," but that word is so often used to imply a deep personal affection that it can give a false impression. A better word is perhaps "respect," for it was—and is—really a recognition of mutual involvement in one another, and may or may not involve any affection deeper than that of familiarity. Each member of the family recognized the place and the rights of the other members, and although the rights varied according to sex, age, and even ability and character, there was a minimum below which no one could exist without disgrace to the whole family.

While the first principle of the *ujamaa* unit related to persons, the second related to property. It was that all the basic goods were held in common, and shared among all members of the unit. There was an acceptance that whatever one person had in the way of basic necessities, they all had; no one could go hungry while others hoarded food and no one could be denied shelter if others had space to spare. Within the extended family, and even within the tribe, the economic level of one person could never get too far out of proportion to the economic level of others. . . . Inequalities existed, but they were tempered by comparable family or social responsibilities, and they could never become gross and offensive to the social equality which was at the basis of the communal life.

Finally, and as a necessary third principle, was the fact that everyone had an obligation to work. The work done by different people was different, but no one was exempt. Every member of the family, and every guest who shared in the right to eat and have shelter, took it for granted that he had to join in whatever work had to be done. Only by the universal acceptance of this principle was the continuation of the other two made possible. . . .

The Objective

This is the objective of socialism in Tanzania. To build a society in which all members have equal rights and equal opportunities; in which all can live at peace with their neighbors without suffering or imposing injustice, being exploited, or exploiting; and in which all have a gradually increasing basic level of material welfare before any individual lives in luxury.

To create this kind of nation we must build on the firm foundations of the three principles of the *ujamaa* family. But we must add to these principles the knowledge and the instruments necessary for the defeat of poverty which existed in traditional African society. In other words, we must add those elements which allow for increased output per worker, and which make a man's efforts yield more satisfactions to him. We must take our traditional system, correct its shortcomings, and adapt to its service the things we can learn from the technologically developed societies on other continents. . . .

Summarizing the Present Position

At this point let us try to sum up the present position in Tanzania in a few words. We have the vast majority of our people living in the rural areas, most of them working on their own as farmers who do not employ any labor, but produce their own food and some additional crops which they sell. Many of them try to adopt modern methods, each on his own particular farm and while working in isolation. This is like every worker trying to have his own factory! . . .

Thus we still have in this country a predominantly peasant society in which farmers work for themselves and their families, and are helped and protected from exploitation by co-operative marketing arrangements. Yet the present trend is away from the extended family production and social unity, and towards the development of a class system in the rural areas. It is this kind of development which would be inconsistent with the growth of a socialist Tanzania in which all citizens could be assured of human dignity and equality, and in which all were able to have a decent and constantly improving life for themselves and their children. . . .

If we are to succeed in this, certain things are essential. The first of these is hard work by our people. There is no substitute for this, especially as we do not have large accumulations of capital which can be invested in agricultural labor-saving devices or in increased productivity. We have to increase the amount we produce from our land, and we shall have to do it "by the use of our own hands and our own brains." No organization of society can do away with this; whether we are capitalist, socialist, communist, fascist, or anything else, only an increase in output can provide the extra goods needed for our people to have the opportunity for a good life. . . .

Not only this, there must also be an efficient and democratic system of local government, so that our people make their own decisions on the things which affect them directly, and so that they are able to recognize their own control over community decisions and their own responsibility for carrying them out. Yet this local control has to be organized in such a manner that the nation is united and working together for common needs and for the maximum development of our whole society.

And finally, the whole rural society must be built on the basis of the equality of all Tanzanian citizens and their common obligations and common rights. There must be no masters and servants, but just people working together for the good of all and thus their own good. We shall be unable to fulfill these objectives if we continue to produce as individuals for individual profit. Certainly a man who is working for himself and for his own profit will not suffer from exploitation in this employment. But neither will he make much progress. It is not long before an individual, working alone, reaches the limit of his powers. Only by working together can men overcome that limitation. The truth is that when human beings want to make great progress they have no alternative but to combine their efforts.

And there are only two methods by which this can be done; people can be made to work together, or they can work together. We can be made to work together by, and for the benefit of, a slave owner, or by, and for the profit, of, a capitalist; alternatively we can work together voluntarily, for our own benefit. We shall achieve the goals we in this country have set ourselves If the basis of Tanzanian life consists of rural economic and social communities where people live together and work together for the good of all, and which are interlocked so that all of the different communities also work together in co-operation for the common good of the nation as a whole. The principles upon which the traditional extended family was based must be reactivated. We can start with extended family villages, but . . . the basis of rural life in Tanzania must be the practice of co-operation in its widest sense—in living, in working, and in distribution, and all with an acceptance of the absolute equality of all men and women. . . .

Ujamaa Agriculture

In a socialist Tanzania then our agricultural organization would be predominantly that of co-operative living and working for the good of all. This means that most of our farming would be done by groups of people who live as a community and work as a community.

They would live together in a village; they would farm together; market together; and undertake the provision of local services and small local requirements as a community. Their community would be the traditional family group, or any other group of people living according to *ujamaa* principles, large enough to take account of modern methods and the twentieth century needs of man. The land this community farmed would be called "our land" by all the members; the crops they produced on that land would be "our crops"; it would be "our shop" which provided individual members with the day-to-day necessities from outside; "our workshop" which made the bricks from which houses and other buildings were constructed, and so on. . . .

The return from the produce of the farm, and from all other activities of the community, would be shared according to the work done and to the needs of the members, with a small amount being paid in taxes and another amount (which is determined by the members themselves) invested in their own future. There would be no need to exclude private property in houses or even in cattle; some energetic members may wish to have their own gardens as well as share in the community farm. . . .

Such living and working in communities could transform our lives in Tanzania. We would not automatically become wealthy, although we could all become a little richer than we are now. But most important of all, any increase in the amount of wealth we produce under this system would be "ours"; it would not belong just to one or two individuals, but to all those whose work had produced it. At the same time we should have strengthened our traditional equality and our traditional security. For in a village community a man who is genuinely sick during the harvest would not be left to starve for the rest of the year, nor would the man whose wife is ill find the children uncared for—as he might do if he farms on his own. Traditional African socialism always made such questions as these irrelevant, and our modern socialism, by resting on the same foundations, will also make them irrelevant. . . .

The Role of Government

Ujamaa villages will have to be established, and will grow through the self-reliant activities of our people. They will be created by the village people themselves, and maintained by them. It must be done from their own resources.

The Government's role is to help people to make a success of their work and their decisions. Further, where a village community has been established, the Ministry of Agriculture and Co-operatives should ensure that the necessary agricultural advice . . . is available to the villagers. . . .

The Ministry of Local Government and Rural Development, too, must be active in these villages; their field workers should be available to help the people to organize themselves, to advise them on how they can become eligible for advances in seed, or for small loans for farm equipment. It would be this Ministry, too, which should draw up a model constitution for the villages at different stages, although it must be stressed that no one model should be imposed on any village. Any model which is drawn up should just be a guide which draws the attention of people to the decisions which have to be made by them; each village community must be able to make its own decisions. . . . But the most important thing is not that the Government should do this or that for all villages, but that within its resources it should give priority to requests from villages where the people are living together and working together for the good of all.

Conclusion

What is here being proposed is that we in Tanzania should move from being a nation of individual peasant producers who are gradually adopting the incentives and the ethics of the capitalist system. Instead we should gradually become a nation of *ujamaa* villages where the people co-operate directly in small groups and where these small groups co-operate together for joint enterprises. This can be done. We already have groups of people who are trying to operate this system in many parts of our country. We must encourage them and encourage others to adopt this way of life too. It is not a question of forcing our people to change their habits. It is a question of . . . all of us together making a reality of the principles of equality and freedom which are enshrined in our policy of Tanzanian socialism.

NOTES

1. Many historians contend that the shock of World War I—a seemingly irrational conflict with few victories and huge casualties—caused such widespread disillusionment and despair that many people began to question their long-standing faith in their social institutions and values.

2. This is not to suggest that collectivist thought was solely a product of the twentieth century. One can find features of collectivist thought in Plato's *Republic* and many additional examples since then. Indeed, some scholars claim that the teachings of Jesus were essentially collectivist in orientation.

3. Meaning the analysis and understanding of collectivism as a set of assumptions, ideas, and strategies.

4. Marxism is frequently called "scientific socialism" because of Marx's belief that human society could be studied scientifically and that society could be refashioned according to the scientific laws of social development.

5. N. Bukharin and E. Preobrazhensky, *The ABC of Communism: A Popular Explanation of the Program of the Communist Party of Russia*, Preface and Introduction by Sidney Heitman (Ann Arbor: University of Michigan Press, 1988), 15.

6. The Bolshevik Party was renamed the Communist Party in March of 1918. We will use the name Communist throughout to avoid confusion. The dates of the March and November Revolutions are according to the new-style calendar that was also adopted in 1918.

7. In addition to these factors, many scholars also highlight the Communists' ruthless willingness to use any means necessary to achieve victory.

8. N. Bukharin and E. Preobrazhensky, *The ABC of Communism: A Popular Explanation of the Program of the Communist Party of Russia*, Preface and Introduction by Sidney Heitman (Ann Arbor: University of Michigan Press, 1988), 5.

9. "Show trials" were publicly staged trials of supposed traitors or "wreckers" who were branded enemies of the people. They were used to destroy Stalin's opponents, to create paranoia, and to justify terror.

10. It was banned because it depicted an open, democratic socialist society that conflicted with Stalinist Communism.

11. From 1886 to 1918, Tanganyika was a German colony. Following World War I, Germany lost her overseas colonial possessions, and the League of Nations mandated Tanganyika to the British.

12. *Cash crop* is a term used to designate a commodity produced for the market, rather than for local consumption.

13. To expedite his plan, Nyerere also called for the creation of a unified, one-party TANU government and state control over the primary means of production in the country.

14. The great rise in oil prices following the Arab-Israeli Yom Kippur War in 1973 encouraged inflation and a rapid rise in the price of industrial goods, which was not matched by a similar rise in prices in raw commodities. Consequently, the cost of imports to Tanzania (and other developing nations) greatly outpaced the value of its exports, which increased the need for borrowing and the incurrence of a massive national debt.

CHAPTER 12

Confronting Human Aggression in the Twentieth Century

INTRODUCTION

During the 1950s, British scholar and linguist J. R. R. Tolkien published his three-volume epic narrative *The Lord of the Rings*. In the story, a great conflict is waged for control of Middle Earth. The opposing sides fight battles of unimaginable scale, individuals perform deeds of solitary heroism, and whole peoples face annihilation. Many readers found the saga to be a reimagination of the colossal conflagration that was World War II, with the evil lord Sauron representing Hitler and the dwarves, elves, humans, hobbits, and wizards who opposed him reflecting the great alliance of nations that triumphed in 1945. Others argued that Tolkien's vision was shaped as much by his own experiences of combat in the Great War of 1914–1918. In either case, the enormity of the sacrifices and horrific nature of the menace in *The Lord of the Rings* seemed to capture something profound about the twentieth century's experience of human violence.

For many people, literature, poetry, art, and film provide the only way to understand the depths of human sadness and wrongdoing that have filled the recent past. Others have searched for more systematic, even scientific, ways to explain and hopefully prevent the tendency of humans to carry out organized, violent attacks upon each other. Some found the answers deep within individual human psychology. Others blamed the ways that modern societies have been organized, with expropriating classes of elites manipulating governments and common citizens for selfish material interests. The tendency of nations and religions to create community among people who are strangers by defining "others" as hostile aliens provides another way to understand conflict. This chapter explores some of the most significant approaches that artists, social scientists, and political actors have used to address human aggression and warfare. All convey the urgency of the inquiry, for the technological innovations that have improved life for so many in the past century have given humans the ability to destroy our species as well.

Warfare had been endemic throughout the nineteenth century as the western nations expanded overseas and brought Asians and Africans into their colonial empires. For the peoples of the west, these conflicts were remote and undemanding, however. On very few occasions after the Napoleonic wars ended in 1815 did citizens of the "advanced" nations encounter large-scale conflict;[1] in none were the total resources of millions of common citizens called upon. Although historians note that optimism about humanity's potential to outgrow large-scale conflict was waning at the end of the Victorian century, nonetheless there were still many educated westerners who believed that prosperity, open economic exchange, and democratic governments were so transforming human society that warfare between developed nations was literally unthinkable, a "great illusion," as the English writer Norman Angell put it in 1910.

World War I shattered any such optimism. The losses to all sides were so catastrophic that no rational policy outcomes seemed to justify them. Not only was the scale of the slaughter shocking, but also the mechanistic "assembly line" nature of death overturned all images of soldierly heroism. Many died simply from the daily attrition of sitting in mud-filled trenches exposed to random artillery and sniper fire. Millions more walked slowly across barren moonscapes into entrenched machine-gun fire. Chemical weapons, aircraft bombing, and submarine attacks brought death from directions never encountered before. World War I introduced such horrors to the western experience that new vocabularies and uses of language were necessary to describe them. The first readings in this chapter are two powerful and contrasting poems by Herbert Asquith and Wilfred Owen, British soldiers who experienced firsthand the terror and ugliness of war. Implicit in the realism of these poems was the idea that such atrocities could be avoided only if people everywhere would use language that looked clearly at the realities of violence and inhumanity. This hope that confronting the actual effects of war would help to reduce it has grounded the work of combat photographers and journalists in the expanding media coverage of wars to the present day.

The idea that knowledge and accurate information would help to contain violence by mobilizing the humanitarian sentiments of voters and the weight of world opinion provided some consolation in the face of the enormous dislocations of the first half of the century. In the immediate aftermath of World War I, others were not so sanguine. The selection in this chapter by the founder of modern psychology, Sigmund Freud (1856–1939), represents the wide array of arguments that found violent behavior to be innate to humans and hence largely unavoidable. In creating his theories of personality, Freud believed that he was scientifically mapping the inner terrain of the human psyche. There, embedded in the nature of individual existence, he found endemic conflict between different aspects of the self. The unconscious *id* of instinctual impulses toward self-gratification and aggrandizement was held only partially in check by an embattled conscious *ego* that relied on reasoned calculation and society's various punishments and rewards to guide individual action. Freud's review of both ancient and recent history indicated how weak the controls of civilized conduct were, in part because adhering to them caused so much repression of inner, personal desires. From the psychoanalytic perspective, the requirements of living in large-scale, complex communities were so great that the periodic unleashing of collective violence was only to be expected.

Another group of twentieth-century thinkers argued that humanity's bad behavior resulted from faulty social institutions rather than innate biological drives. Marxists and socialists, represented here by the Chinese Communist leader Mao Zedong (1893–1976), found the enormous inequalities in rights and access to resources that were embedded in capitalistic systems of private property to be the prime cause of social conflict. In a future socialist world in which each individual could rely on others to live by the guideline "from each according to his ability; to each according to his need," there would be no "spoils" to fight over. In this interpretation, the wars of the twentieth century were all related in some way to capitalist imperialism. Capitalist nations fought among themselves for dominance, whereas oppressed peoples fought wars of revolution and liberation against native "class" oppressors and foreign exploiters. With the soon-to-be accomplished creation of socialist societies, the Marxists foresaw a "new" humanity that was both free and cooperative, resulting in "perpetual peace" for mankind.

Both explanations for violence, the biological and the social, can be found in the writings of feminists such as the English novelist and essayist Virginia Woolf (1882–1941). It did not escape the notice of women that the decisions to go to war were made exclusively by men. And although men bore the brunt of combat horrors, the expansion of modern warfare to include civilian targets in bombings, blockades, ethnic cleansing, and guerrilla warfare meant that women and children who had no say in government policies could suffer as severely as military actors. Women writers were divided on whether this largely male aggression was the result of instinctual drives or socially created lusts for power and identification with a dominant group. They could agree at least on the indisputable outcomes: ever more horrific "body counts," high expenditures on military armaments to the detriment of social programs, and the too-often-overlooked plight of people victimized by hostilities they were powerless to influence or prevent.

The overwhelming sense of foreboding contained in the writings of authors from the 1930s was amply born out by events of the next decade. World War II dwarfed its predecessor in almost every way. There were active military theaters in eastern, western, and southern Europe, in north Africa, southeast Asia, China, and the islands of the Pacific. In the utterly savage engagements between Nazi Germany and the Soviet Union, the siege of Leningrad cost more Russian lives than the United States and Britain lost in the entire war; the same was true for the Soviets in the Battle of Stalingrad, in the campaign at Kursk, and in the assault on Berlin. Moreover, unlike World War I, civilian populations suffered as much as or more than armies, as they were targeted in bombing campaigns and such atrocities of occupation as the notorious Rape of Nanjing.[2] Historians estimate that more than fifty million people died worldwide, at least half of them noncombatants. It was perhaps fitting that the violence ended in the explosion of atom bombs. With the arrival of nuclear weapons, an extraordinary new technology designed to end a specific war created the means to annihilate human civilization itself.

No feature of the convulsive, yet systematic, mayhem of the 1930s and 1940s was more confounding than the Holocaust orchestrated by Nazi Germany against the Jewish people and other marginalized groups in Europe. These deaths were not the result of battlefield frenzies or "collateral damage" but rather were controlled administrative murders that brought the full resources of the state to exterminate whole categories of people. The success of such policies relied on routine work undertaken by thousands of ordinary citizens who served in roundups, deportations, transport, and provisioning of other citizens marked for the death camps. In *Eichmann in Jerusalem,* scholar and political theorist Hannah Arendt (1906–1975) explored the personality of one such functionary brought to trial for his participation in the Holocaust. She described the way that the specialization of jobs in modern bureaucracies allowed each actor to escape feeling personally responsible for what the organization was actually doing and noted the troubling moral collapse of peoples in the west who seemed reluctant to believe that individuals could act on their own conscience-driven judgments of right and wrong when confronted with the powers of modern states and mass society.

To the surprise of many, the nuclear weapons of mass destruction possessed by the United States and Soviet Union brought a respite in "hot wars" for the peoples of Europe and North America after 1945. Violence shifted to the nationalist movements and civil conflicts that accompanied the breakup of the European and Soviet empires. Until late in the century, it seemed that these might remain localized, and familiar, forms of conflict in "new" states attempting to establish governing institutions and sort out power relationships among different social groups. But as the fortunes of international communism collapsed after the demise of the Soviet system in the 1990s, another transnational social movement in opposition to the west seemed to take its place. This was the force of revolutionary Islam, represented here by the message of Iranian Imam Ruhollah Khomeini (1900–1989). In attempting to preserve centuries-old traditions of spirituality and social organization, revolutionary Islam threatened to reintroduce wide-scale conflict based on differing visions of God's will for man.

Taken together, the readings in this chapter offer a wide range of perspectives on war and aggression. Some thinkers have emphasized humankind's biological condition and our innate competitive instincts. Others have focused on social conditions and cultural conflicts. Yet it might be noted that nearly all the selections presented here outline some vision of a human future free of organized violence and inhumanity.

CHAPTER QUESTIONS

1. Compare what the sections by the Great War poets and Hannah Arendt have to say about the relationship between clichéd language and violence. Is man's inhumanity to man the result of being unable to convey convincingly in words or images that all members of the species share in a common humanity? Are

there other explanations for people being able to inflict pain and death on others? What does Freud say?

2. Many of the selections deal with violence as an age-old human tendency. Does that mean that the technologies, bureaucracies, and mass societies of the twentieth century added nothing new to the historical record? In your opinion, in what ways has conflict evolved?

3. Perhaps the most radical voice in this chapter is Virginia Woolf's, because her solution to violence seems to involve eliminating hierarchies, competition, and "false loyalties" from every facet of society, including the most deeply ingrained, the hierarchy between men and women. How might a feminist evaluate the statements of Freud, Mao Zedong, and Imam Khomeini?

4. In the past, people explained great misfortunes as the malice or punishment of supernatural beings (the gods or God). Many people in the past century, and not just those of the west, replaced religious metaphors with those of abstract historical forces: capitalism, imperialism, nationalism, racism, elite self-interest, and mass gullibility. What are the implications for human action if the forces propelling aggression are themselves human creations, rather than divine interventions?

5. Beginning with the Enlightenment, many theorists have predicted that a world of high global productivity, able to provide for the basic human needs of all people and dependent on specialization and cooperative exchange to get things done, would dramatically reduce the causes of violent encounters. How would the various authors in this chapter evaluate this view? Is there any evidence in the history of the past century to suggest that it might be right?

TWO SOLDIERS VIEW THE GREAT WAR

In a pathbreaking book written in 1975, literary scholar Paul Fussell described how the completely unanticipated nature of conflict on the western front in World War I forced a change in language, and hence in mentality, among soldiers from Great Britain.[3] The transition is reflected in the two poems here, but its implications went far beyond the lives of those who experienced combat directly. Previously unfamiliar military terms came into common usage among civilians: *barrage, sector, home front, bombard, lousy,* and *trench coat* are all words from this era. They are still part of our everyday vocabulary, along with imagery of irreconcilable enemies and battlefields that have become generalized to all sorts of nonmilitary activities, as in our "war on drugs." World War I began a century in which the threat of catastrophic war became taken for granted, even in periods of peace and rising prosperity, a situation that has not changed to this day.

Herbert Asquith (1881–1947) was the son of prime minister Herbert Henry Asquith, leader of Britain's government during the first three years of World War I. Well educated and well connected (in 1910 he married the daughter of an earl), the younger Asquith volunteered for service when the conflict broke out. He saw some of the war's fiercest engagements on the western front, was wounded on several occasions, and suffered debilitating shell shock. His older brother Raymond became a casualty at the Battle of the Somme (1916), and another sibling lost his foot when he was shot by a sniper during a dawn patrol. In 1915, before his family experienced its worst casualties, he published *The Volunteer and Other Poems.* Herbert Asquith survived the war and became a minor novelist and memoirist in the interwar period. In the eyes of his family, he never fully recovered from the horrors he had witnessed on the western front.

Wilfred Owen (1893–1918) was the son of middle-class parents whose financial fortunes declined when he was a child. He received an education from a local clergyman but never attended university and was teaching English in France when World War I broke out. Owen volunteered for service in 1915. He was able to attend a school for officers before joining the Second Manchesters near the Somme in January 1916, six months before the great battle in that area began. Owen saw heavy combat and received several minor wounds before succumbing to shell shock in May 1917. He was sent to the famous hospital for shell-shock victims at Craiglockhart near Edinburgh. There he worked on a series of poems describing soldiers' experiences that he had witnessed. He was helped by an older and more established poet, Siegfried Sassoon, who shared Owen's view that the usual language and metaphors of poetry were unable to convey the realities of twentieth-century war. Now considered the best of the new generation of war poets, Owen returned to combat in September 1918 and received the Military Cross for taking an entrenched machine-gun position. He was killed leading an attack across the Oise-Sambre Canal on November 4, 1918, one week before the armistice came into effect.

QUESTIONS TO CONSIDER

1. There are many parallels in the imagery of the two poems. Both speak of dreams, for example, of the carts that bear dead soldiers, and of heroic fighters of the past. How do the authors use similar images to create different emotions and ideas?

2. Why has the young "white-collar" worker in Asquith's poem volunteered for service? What does Owen come to think about this motivation?

3. Why does Owen insist on presenting such graphic details of a gas attack and of death caused by inhaling poison gas? What is he trying to convey to readers who have not seen the war front?

4. How can the reader tell from these poems that World War I is a new and modern war? How is it a different conflict from those of the past?

5. How might the trench warfare and mechanized killing of World War I change a society's understanding of what constitutes heroism? Is the twentieth-century vision of a hero different from what Asquith's "volunteer" envisions?

"THE VOLUNTEER" (1915)

Herbert Asquith

Here lies a clerk who half his life had spent
Toiling at ledgers in a city grey,
Thinking that so his days would drift away
With no lance broken in life's tournament.
Yet ever 'twixt the books and his bright eyes
The gleaming eagles of the legions came,
And horsemen, charging under phantom skies,
Went thundering past beneath the oriflamme.*

And now those waiting dreams are satisfied;
From twilight to the halls of dawn he went;
His lance is broken; but he lies content
With that high hour, in which he lived and died.
And falling thus he wants no recompense,
Who found his battle in the last resort;
Nor need he any hearse to bear him hence,
Who goes to join the men of Agincourt.†

"DULCE ET DECORUM EST" (1917)

Wilfred Owen

Bent double, like old beggars under sacks,
Knock-kneed, coughing like hags, we cursed through
    sludge,
Till on the haunting flares we turned our backs
And towards our distant rest began to trudge.
Men marched asleep. Many had lost their boots
But limped on, blood-shod. All went lame; all blind;
Drunk with fatigue; deaf even to the hoots
Of tired, outstripped Five-Nines that dropped behind.

Source: Herbert Asquith, "The Volunteer," in *The Volunteer and Other Poems* (London: Sidgwick & Jackson, 1915), 1.

*A banner or flag that serves as a symbol and rallying standard.

†The great victory of English knights over French armies in the Hundred Years' War.

Source: Wilfred Owen, "Dulce et Decorum Est" in *The Collected Poems of Wilfred Owen*, ed. C. Day Lewis (London: Chatto and Windus, 1963), 55. Reprinted with permission of New Directions Publishing Corporation.

Gas! Gas! Quick, boys!—An ecstacy of fumbling,
Fitting the clumsy helmets just in time;
But someone still was yelling out and stumbling
And flound'ring like a man in fire or lime. . . .
Dim, through the misty panes and thick green light,
As under a green sea, I saw him drowning.

In all my dreams, before my helpless sight,
He plunges at me, guttering, choking, drowning.

If in some smothering dreams you too could pace
Behind the wagon that we flung him in,
And watch the white eyes writhing in his face,
His hanging face, like a devil's sick of sin;
If you could hear, at every jolt, the blood
Come gargling from the froth-corrupted lungs,
Obscene as cancer, bitter as the cud
Of vile, incurable sores on innocent tongues,—
My friend, you would not tell with such high zest
To children ardent for some desperate glory,
The old Lie: Dulce et decorum est
Pro patria mori.*

PSYCHOLOGY AND THE INSTINCT FOR DESTRUCTION

Sigmund Freud (1856–1939) was born in the Austro-Hungarian empire and lived in Vienna nearly all his life. (He fled to London in 1938, when Nazi Germany invaded Austria.) As a young man, Freud began a medical career specializing in neurology and nervous disorders. He became interested in the problems of hysterics, individuals suffering from debilitating symptoms or behaviors for which there was no obvious physiological cause. Trying first hypnosis and then the "talking cure," Freud developed his theories that traumatic events repressed from conscious memory nevertheless profoundly affected an individual's emotions and daily behaviors. *The Interpretation of Dreams* (1900) and *The Psychopathology of Everyday Life* (1901) introduced his ideas about the powers of the unconscious mind. Dreams, jokes, slips of the tongue, habits, characteristic emotional responses—almost any aspect of a patient's behavior could be used by a skilled interpreter to uncover the past events that caused present suffering.

Freud's first and most controversial explanation for the childhood traumas that affected adult personality involved the sexual drive—a generalized eroticism

*"Sweet and right is it to die for your country."

or urge for pleasure that he detected even in the very young. The various ways that families controlled such drives accounted for the neuroses so common to adults. But Freud's ideas changed over the decades, partly from work with patients, partly from controversies with such students as Alfred Adler and Carl Jung,[4] and partly from his observations of the disasters overtaking Europe after 1914. As the selection here reveals, by the 1920s he had come to believe that men harbored an instinct for destruction, a "death wish," as much as one for pleasure and love.

Freud's ideas have been attacked on so many fronts, from the realm of theory to that of practical therapy, that many have been tempted to dismiss his importance. Yet his approach was seminal and enormously influential. The idea that humans cannot fully understand their own psyches without confronting the events that shaped them provides the foundation of most therapy, as well as self-help literature, today.

QUESTIONS TO CONSIDER

1. What reasons does Freud give for thinking that aggressiveness is instinctive to mankind? Does he address whether it is instinctive to women?
2. What reasons does Freud give for thinking that the communists' assessment of human nature is wrong?
3. Are the interests of individuals and the interests of social groups at odds, according to Freud? How do societies try to make those interests the same?
4. If, as Freud argues, the tendency to violence is innate to individual humans, does this mean that societies are fated to engage in large-scale conflict with each other? Are there other outlets that can be devised to meet the desires of individuals to achieve or distinguish themselves?
5. What is the "lullaby" that we, according to Freud, are taught in the nursery? What do you think Freud is suggesting by using this image of childhood?

CIVILIZATION AND ITS DISCONTENTS (1931)

Sigmund Freud

. . . [M]en are not gentle creatures who want to be loved, and who at the most can defend themselves if they are attacked; they are, on the contrary, creatures among whose instinctual endowments is to be reckoned a powerful share of aggressiveness. As a result, their neighbour is for them not only a potential helper or sexual object, but also someone who tempts them to satisfy their aggressiveness on him, to exploit his capacity for work without compensation, to use him sexually without his consent, to seize his possessions, to humiliate him, to cause him pain, to torture and to kill him. . . . Who, in the face of all his experience of life and of history, will have the courage to dispute this assertion? As a rule this cruel aggressiveness waits for some provocation or puts itself at the service of some other purpose, whose goal might also have been reached by milder measures. In circumstances that are favourable to it, when the mental counter-forces which ordinarily inhibit it are out of action, it also manifests itself spontaneously and reveals man as a savage beast to whom consideration towards his own kind is something alien. Anyone who calls to mind the atrocities committed during the racial migrations or the invasions of the Huns, or by the people known as Mongols under Jenghiz Khan and Tamerlane, or at the capture of Jerusalem by the pious Crusaders, or even, indeed, the horrors of the recent World War—anyone who calls these things to mind will have to bow humbly before the truth of this view.

The existence of this inclination to aggression, which we can detect in ourselves and justly assume to be present in others, is the factor which disturbs our relations with our neighbour and which forces civilization into such a high expenditure [of energy]. In consequence of this primary mutual hostility of human beings, civilized society is perpetually threatened with disintegration. The interest of work in common would not hold it together; instinctual passions are stronger than reasonable interests. Civilization has to use its utmost efforts in order to set limits to man's aggressive instincts and to hold the manifestations of them in check by psychical reaction-formations. Hence, therefore, the use of methods intended to incite people into identifications and aim-inhibited relationships of love, hence the restriction upon sexual life, and hence too the . . . commandment to love one's neighbour as oneself—a commandment which is really justified by the fact that nothing else runs so strongly counter to the original nature of man. In spite of every effort, these endeavours of civilization have not so far achieved very much. It hopes to prevent the crudest excesses of brutal violence by itself assuming the right to use violence against criminals, but the law is not able to lay hold of the more cautious and refined manifestations of human aggressiveness. The time comes when each one of us has to give up as illusions the expectations which, in his youth, he pinned upon his fellowmen, and when he may learn how much difficulty and pain has been added to his life by their ill-will. At the same time, it would be unfair to reproach civilization with trying to eliminate strife and competition from human activity. These things are undoubtedly indispensable. But opposition is not necessarily enmity*; it is merely misused and made an *occasion* for enmity.

The Communists believe that they have found the path to deliverance from our evils. According to them, man is wholly good and is well-disposed to his neighbour; but the institution of private property has corrupted his nature. The ownership of private wealth gives the individual power, and with it the temptation to ill-treat his neighbour; while the man who is excluded from possession is bound to rebel in hostility against his oppressor. If private property were abolished, all wealth held in common, and everyone allowed to share in the enjoyment of it, ill-will and hostility would disappear among men. Since everyone's needs would be satisfied, no one would have any reason to regard another as his enemy; all would willingly undertake the work

---

*Hostility, animosity, or hatred.

that was necessary. I have no concern with any economic criticisms of the communist system; I cannot enquire into whether the abolition of private property is expedient or advantageous. But I am able to recognize that the psychological premises on which the system is based are an untenable illusion. In abolishing private property we deprive the human love of aggression of one of its instruments, certainly a strong one, though certainly not the strongest; but we have in no way altered the differences in power and influence which are misused by aggressiveness, nor have we altered anything in its nature. Aggressiveness was not created by property. It reigned almost without limit in primitive times, when property was still very scanty, and it already shows itself in the nursery almost before property has given up its primal, anal form; it forms the basis of every relation of affection and love among people (with the single exception, perhaps, of the mother's relation to her male child). If we do away with personal rights over material wealth, there still remains prerogative in the field of sexual relationships, which is bound to become the source of the strongest dislike and the most violent hostility among men who, in other respects, are on an equal footing. If we were to remove this factor, too, by allowing complete freedom of sexual life and thus abolishing the family, the germ-cell of civilization, we cannot, it is true, easily foresee what new paths the development of civilization could take; but one thing we can expect, and that is that this indestructible feature of human nature will follow it there.

It is clearly not easy for men to give up the satisfaction of this inclination to aggression. They do not feel comfortable without it. The advantage which a comparatively small cultural group offers of allowing this instinct an outlet in the form of hostility against intruders is not to be despised. It is always possible to bind together a considerable number of people in love, so long as there are other people left over to receive the manifestations of their aggressiveness. I once discussed the phenomenon that it is precisely communities with adjoining territories, and related to each other in other ways as well, who are engaged in constant feuds and in ridiculing each other— like the Spaniards and Portuguese, for instance, the North Germans and South Germans, the English and Scotch, and so on. I gave this phenomenon the name of "the narcissism of minor difference," a name which does not do much to explain it. We can now see that it is a convenient and relatively harmless satisfaction of the inclination to aggression, by means of which cohesion between the members of the community is made easier. In this respect the Jewish people, scattered everywhere, have rendered most useful services to the civilizations of the countries that have been their hosts; but unfortunately all the massacres of the Jews in the Middle Ages did not suffice to make that period more peaceful and secure for their Christian fellows. When once the Apostle Paul had posited Universal Love between men as the foundation of his Christian community, extreme intolerance on the part of Christendom towards those who remained outside it became the inevitable consequence. . . . Neither was it an unaccountable chance that the dream of a Germanic world-dominion called for anti-Semitism as its complement; and it is intelligible that the attempt to establish a new, communist civilization in Russia should find its psychological support in the persecution of the bourgeois. One only wonders, with concern, what the Soviets will do after they have wiped out their bourgeois. . . .

When we justly find fault with the present state of our civilization for so inadequately fulfilling our demands for a plan of life that shall make us happy, and for allowing the existence of so much suffering which could probably be avoided—when, with unsparing criticism, we try to uncover the roots of its imperfection, we are undoubtedly exercising a proper right and are not showing ourselves enemies of civilization. We may expect gradually to carry through such alterations in our civilization as will better satisfy our needs and will escape our criticisms. But perhaps we may also familiarize ourselves with the idea that there are difficulties attaching to the nature of civilization which will not yield to any attempt at reform. . . .

In all that follows I adopt the standpoint, therefore, that the inclination to aggression is an original, self-subsisting instinctual disposition in man, and I return to my view that it constitutes the greatest impediment to civilization. At one point in the course of this enquiry I was led to the idea that civilization was a special process which mankind undergoes, and I am still under the influence of that idea. I may now add that civilization is a process in the service of Eros,* whose purpose is to combine single human individuals, and after that families, then races, peoples and nations, into one great unity, the unity of mankind. Why this has to happen, we do not know; the work of Eros is precisely this. These collections of men are to be libidinally bound to one another. Necessity alone, the advantages of work in common, will not hold them together. But man's natural aggressive instinct, the hostility of each against all and of all against each, opposes this programme of civilization. This aggressive instinct is the derivative and the main representative of the death instinct which we have found alongside of Eros and which shares world-domination with it. And now, I think, the meaning of the evolution of civilization is no longer obscure to us. It must present the struggle between Eros and Death, between the instinct of life and the instinct of destruction, as it works itself out in the human species. This struggle is what all life essentially consists of, and the evolution of civilization may therefore be simply described as the struggle for life of the human species. And it is this battle of the giants that our nurse-maids try to appease with their lullaby about Heaven.

A COMMUNIST ASSESSMENT

For most people, the greatest conflict of the second half of the twentieth century was one that emerged within and then divided peoples of the western tradition: that is, the rival philosophies of democratic capitalism and communism. Yet one of the most successful practitioners and developers of communist thinking was not western but Asian, the extraordinary Chinese leader Mao Zedong (1893–1976). Mao came from a peasant family from Hunan province. He was a student in 1911 when revolution overturned the Manchu dynasty and established China as a republic for the first time in the country's history. In 1921 he and eleven others established the Chinese Communist Party, but the movement soon ran afoul of the nationalist party of Chiang Kai-shek that was attempting to consolidate its hold

---

*By Eros, Freud means the instinctual desire of people to be loved, accepted, and included in the group. Freud also believed that humans embodied Thanatos, the "death instinct," which was the source of aggression. In his view, the history of civilization was the struggle between Eros and Thanatos.

on power. Chiang's extermination campaigns against the communists led to the Long March beginning in 1934, when Mao led his followers over 6,000 miles to sanctuary in the northwest Shaanxi province. From there he immediately became engaged in resistance to Japanese forces that had invaded China in 1937. Mao was a genius in organizing and articulating the principles of guerrilla warfare. Under his leadership the Chinese Communists, more than any other group, became identified with resistance to the Japanese invaders. This contributed to the Communist Party's defeat of the Nationalists in the civil war that ended in 1949 with Chiang Kai-shek's flight to the offshore island of Taiwan.

Mao's attempts to establish a pure, yet technologically advanced communist society in China were both transforming and devastating for the Chinese people. Policies such as the Great Leap Forward of the 1950s and the Cultural Revolution of the 1960s resulted in the deaths of millions. As a communist, Mao identified the inequities and exploitations of capitalism as the greatest cause of violence in the world; that did not make him any more friendly with the Soviet Union, however, as the two nations jostled for leadership of the communist movement. Mao's death in 1976 contributed to the country's abandonment of strict communist economic policies and the beginning of its integration into the international community.

The passage that follows was written shortly after the Japanese invasion of China in 1937. In his essay, Mao showed his discernment in recognizing that World War II had already begun, though Europeans would not realize it until 1939. Aside from the Japanese conquests, Italy had invaded Ethiopia (Abyssinia), and Italian and German forces had intervened in the Spanish Civil War (as, indeed, did forces of the Soviet Union). Mao predicted correctly that a war among the western powers would begin shortly, and that it would be followed by "revolutionary" wars of liberation against the western colonial powers. When these were successful, he argued, and socialist governments established around the world, an era of "perpetual peace" would be inaugurated for mankind.

QUESTIONS TO CONSIDER

1. How does Mao's vision make China's war against Japanese aggression part of larger, global developments?

2. Where does Mao find the roots of human aggression? Does he answer Freud's argument that they lie in human nature itself?

3. How does Mao define "just war" and "unjust war"? Are these definitions clear enough to be a guide to action?

4. It is clear now that totalitarian Communist regimes such as those in the Soviet Union and China carried out atrocities on a wide scale against their own and other people. How would Mao Zedong explain such actions?

5. What would Wilfred Owen and Hannah Arendt make of Mao Zedong's use of language when he writes about aggression?

FIGHTING FOR PERPETUAL PEACE (1938)

Mao Zedong

The protracted nature of China's anti-Japanese war is inseparably connected with the fight for perpetual peace in China and the whole world. Never has there been a historical period such as the present in which war is so close to perpetual peace. For several thousand years since the emergence of classes, the life of mankind has been full of wars; each nation has fought countless wars, either internally or with other nations. In the imperialist epoch of capitalist society, wars are waged on a particularly extensive scale and with a peculiar ruthlessness. The first great imperialist war of twenty years ago was the first of its kind in history, but not the last. Only the war which has now begun comes close to being the final war, that is, comes close to the perpetual peace of mankind. By now one-third of the world's population has entered the war. Look! Italy, then Japan; Abyssinia [Ethiopia], then Spain, then China. The population of the countries at war now amounts to almost 600 million, or nearly a third of the total population of the world. The characteristics of the present war are its uninterruptedness and its proximity to perpetual peace. Why is it uninterrupted? After attacking Abyssinia, Italy attacked Spain, and Germany joined in; then Japan attacked China. What will come next? Undoubtedly Hitler will fight the great powers. "Fascism is war"—that is perfectly true. There will be no interruption in the development of the present war into a world war; mankind will not be able to avoid the calamity of war.

Why then do we say the present war is near to perpetual peace? The present war is the result of the development of the general crisis of world capitalism which began with World War I; this general crisis is driving the capitalist countries into a new war and, above all, driving the fascist countries into new war adventures. This war, we can foresee, will not save capitalism, but will hasten its collapse. It will be greater in scale and more ruthless than the war of twenty years ago, all nations will inevitably be drawn in, it will drag on for a very long time, and mankind will suffer greatly. But, owing to the existence of the Soviet Union and the growing political consciousness of the people of the world, great revolutionary wars will undoubtedly emerge from this war to oppose all counter-revolutionary wars, thus giving this war the character of a struggle for perpetual peace. Even if later there should be another period of war, perpetual world peace will not be far off. Once man has eliminated capitalism, he will attain the era of perpetual peace, and there will be no more need for war. Neither armies, nor warships, nor military aircraft, nor poison gas will then be needed. Thereafter and for all time, mankind will never again know war. The revolutionary wars which have already begun are part of the war for perpetual peace. The war between China and Japan, two countries which have a combined population of over 500 million, will take an important place in this war for perpetual peace, and out of it will come the liberation of the Chinese nation. The liberated new China of the future will

Source: Mao Tse-tung [Zedong], "On Protracted War," in *Selected Works of Mao Tse-tung,* Vol. II (Peking: Foreign Languages Press, 1967), 148–50.

be inseparable from the liberated new world of the future. Hence our War of Resistance Against Japan takes on the character of a struggle for perpetual peace.

History shows that wars are divided into two kinds, just and unjust. All wars that are progressive are just, and all wars that impede progress are unjust. We Communists oppose all unjust wars that impede progress, but we do not oppose progressive, just wars. Not only do we Communists not oppose just wars, we actively participate in them. As for unjust wars, World War I is an instance in which both sides fought for imperialist interests; therefore the Communists of the whole world firmly opposed that war. The way to oppose a war of this kind is to do everything possible to prevent it before it breaks out and, once it breaks out, to oppose war with war, to oppose unjust war with just war, whenever possible. Japan's war is an unjust war that impedes progress, and the peoples of the world, including the Japanese people, should oppose it and are opposing it. In our country the people and the government, the Communist Party and the Kuomintang,* have all raised the banner of righteousness in the national revolutionary war against aggression. Our war is sacred and just, it is progressive and its aim is peace. The aim is peace not just in one country but throughout the world, not just temporary but perpetual peace. To achieve this aim we must wage a life-and-death struggle, be prepared for any sacrifice, persevere to the end and never stop short of the goal. However great the sacrifice and however long the time needed to attain it, a new world of perpetual peace and brightness already lies clearly before us. Our faith in waging this war is based upon the new China and the new world of perpetual peace and brightness for which we are striving. Fascism and imperialism wish to perpetuate war, but we wish to put an end to it in the not too distant future. The great majority of mankind should exert their utmost efforts for this purpose. The 450 million people of China constitute one quarter of the world's population, and if by their concerted efforts they overthrow Japanese imperialism and create a new China of freedom and equality, they will most certainly be making a tremendous contribution to the struggle for perpetual world peace. This is no vain hope, for the whole world is approaching this point in the course of its social and economic development, and provided that the majority of mankind work together, our goal will surely be attained in several decades.

A WOMAN WRITER'S PERSPECTIVE

Virginia Stephen was born in London in 1882. Both of her parents came from the small group of families—Darwins, Stracheys, Huxleys, Trevelyans—that constituted England's "intellectual aristocracy." Her mother's aunt was the famous mid-Victorian photographer Julia Cameron. Her father, Sir Leslie Stephen, became the guiding force behind the authoritative *Dictionary of National Biography*. Nonetheless, Virginia and her sister Vanessa received no education beyond that of

---

*The Kuomintang was Chiang Kai-shek's Nationalist party. The Communists were in uneasy alliance with them in opposition to the Japanese at this time.

the governesses normally provided for girls of their social class. Orphaned in their early twenties, the Stephen sisters established a household in the London residential district known as Bloomsbury. They became the center of a famous artistic and intellectual circle that included biographer Lytton Strachey, economist John Maynard Keynes, artist Duncan Grant, critic Clive Bell, and writer-publisher Leonard Woolf, whom Virginia married in 1912.

Virginia Woolf suffered from periods of severe mental illness throughout her life. Nevertheless, she became perhaps the most important "woman of letters" in England of the twentieth century. Her output of letters, essays, reviews, and diaries is enormous. Equally important were pathbreaking novels such as *Mrs. Dalloway, The Waves,* and *To the Lighthouse,* in which Woolf experimented with ways to capture in words the profound yet evanescent musings of an individual's interior life. Her essays, "A Room of One's Own" and "Three Guineas," articulate a feminist position on citizenship, work, family relations, and creative enterprise that grew in influence throughout the century. Woolf committed suicide in 1941, in part in despair at the global fury unleashed by World War II.

"Three Guineas"[5] is an extended essay written, ostensibly, in response to a petition Woolf had received in the mail asking for her contribution (the three guineas of the title) and support in answering the question "How in your opinion can the women of England help to prevent war?" Woolf's cool, deeply ironic reply was scathing. Using statistics and examples from the morning's newspaper, she noted how infrequently women, even those from affluent social classes, received the kind of education that would enable them to address such a problem; how seldom they had opportunities to gain the independence of mind that comes from supporting oneself with paid work; how long and completely their voices had been neglected in making political decisions; how little, in fact, the opinions of women had ever mattered in deciding issues of war and peace. Embedded in her response is the hope, which continues to inspire many feminists, that the admission of women to full equality of rights and status with men would modify the competitions and belligerence that characterized twentieth-century civilization.

QUESTIONS TO CONSIDER

1. Woolf acknowledges that in private life men and women in the same family can form relationships of mutual respect and support. Is there really a difference in the behavior of the two genders in public settings? If so, why?

2. What is patriotism for Woolf? Does she reject it entirely? Can it be reconciled with a common humanity? Why does Woolf expect women to succumb less easily to aggressive nationalism than men do? Do you think she is correct?

3. What kind of new education system does Woolf lay out? In her view, how would it work to foster productive and cooperative people?

4. Woolf implies that the competitions and institutional distinctions built into modern education, professions, and business life themselves give rise to attitudes that lead to war. Do you agree?

5. The opportunities and material status of women in the west have improved considerably in the sixty years since Woolf wrote. Have her predictions on how the inclusion of women in public life, business, and the professions might change society worked as she hoped?

THREE GUINEAS (1938)

Virginia Woolf

[M]any brothers and sisters in private, as individuals . . . respect each other and help each other and have aims in common. Why then, if such can be their private relationship, as biography and poetry prove, should their public relationship, as law and history prove, be so very different? And here, since you are a lawyer, with a lawyer's memory [Woolf is addressing this to the writer of the letter she had received in the mail], it is not necessary to remind you of certain decrees of English law from its first records to the year 1919 by way of proving that the public, the society relationship of brother and sister has been very different from the private. The very word "society" sets tolling in memory the dismal bells of a harsh music: shall not, shall not, shall not. You [women] shall not learn; you shall not earn; you shall not own; you shall not—such was the society relationship of brother to sister for many centuries. And though it is possible, and to the optimistic credible, that in time a new society may ring a carillon of splendid harmony . . . inevitably we ask ourselves, is there not something in the conglomeration of people into societies that releases what is most selfish and violent, least rational and humane in the individuals themselves? Inevitably we look upon society, so kind to you [to men], so harsh to us, as an ill-fitting form that distorts the truth; deforms the mind; fetters the will. Inevitably we look upon societies as conspiracies that sink the private brother, whom many of us have reason to respect, and inflate in his stead a monstrous male, loud of voice, hard of fist, childishly intent upon scoring the floor of the earth with chalk marks, within whose mystic boundaries human beings are penned, rigidly, separately, artificially; where, daubed red and gold, decorated like a savage with feathers he goes through mystic rites and enjoys the dubious pleasures of power and dominion while we, "his" women, are locked in the private house without share in the many societies of which his society is composed. For such reasons compact as they are of many memories and emotions . . . it seems both wrong for us rationally and impossible for us emotionally to join your society. For by so doing we should merge our identity in yours; follow and repeat and score still deeper the old worn ruts in which society, like a gramophone whose needle has stuck, is grinding out with intolerable unanimity "Three hundred millions spent upon arms." . . . [W]e believe that we can help you most effectively by refusing to join your society; by working for our common

Source: Virginia Woolf, *Three Guineas,* 159–66, 43–44, 49–51, 171–73. Copyright © 1938 by Harcourt, Inc. Reprinted by permission of the publisher.

ends—justice and equality and liberty for all men and women—outside your society, not within.

Let us then draw rapidly in outline the kind of society which the daughters of educated men might found and join outside your society but in co-operation with its ends. In the first place, this new society, you will be relieved to learn, would have no honorary treasurer, for it would need no funds. It would have no office, no committee, no secretary; it would call no meetings; it would hold no conferences. If name it must have, it could be called the Outsiders' Society. That is not a resonant name, but it has the advantage that it squares with fact—the facts of history, of law, of biography; even, it may be, with the still hidden facts of our still unknown psychology. It would consist of educated men's daughters working in their own class—how indeed can they work in any other?—and by their own methods for liberty, equality and peace. Their first duty, to which they would bind themselves not by oath, for oaths and ceremonies have no part in a society which must be anonymous and elastic before everything, would be not to fight with arms. This is easy for them to observe, for in fact, as the papers inform us, "the Army Council have no intention of opening recruiting for any women's corps." The country ensures it. Next they would refuse in the event of war to make munitions or nurse the wounded. Since in the last war both these activities were mainly discharged by the daughters of working men, the pressure upon them here too would be slight, though probably disagreeable. On the other hand the next duty to which they would pledge themselves is one of considerable difficulty, and calls not only for courage and initiative, but for the special knowledge of the educated man's daughter. It is, briefly, not to incite their brothers to fight, or to dissuade them, but to maintain an attitude of complete indifference. But the attitude expressed by the word "indifference" is so complex and of such importance that it needs even here further definition. Indifference in the first place must be given a firm footing upon fact. As it is a fact that she cannot understand what instinct compels him, what glory, what interest, what manly satisfaction fighting provides for him—"without war there would be no outlet for the manly qualities which fighting develops"—as fighting thus is a sex characteristic which she cannot share, the counterpart, some claim, of the maternal instinct which he cannot share, so is it an instinct which she cannot judge. The outsider therefore must leave him free to deal with this instinct by himself, because liberty of opinion must be respected, especially when it is based upon an instinct which is as foreign to her as centuries of tradition and education make it.

But the outsider will make it her duty not merely to base her indifference upon instinct, but upon reason. When he says, as history proves that he has said, and may say again, "I am fighting to protect our country" and thus seeks to rouse her patriotic emotion, she will ask herself, "What does 'our country' mean to me an outsider?" To decide this she will analyse the meaning of patriotism in her own case. She will inform herself of the position of her sex and her class in the past. She will inform herself of the amount of land, wealth and property in the possession of her own sex and class in the present—how much of "England" in fact belongs to her. From the same sources she will inform herself of the legal protection which the law has given her in the past and now gives her. And if he adds that he is fighting to protect her body, she will reflect upon the degree of physical protection that she now enjoys when the words "Air

Raid Precaution" are written on blank walls. And if he says that he is fighting to protect England from foreign rule, she will reflect that for her there are no "foreigners," since by law she becomes a foreigner if she marries a foreigner. . . . All these facts will convince her reason (to put it in a nutshell) that her sex and class has very little to thank England for in the past; not much to thank England for in the present; while the security of her person in the future is highly dubious.

But probably she will have imbibed, even from the governess, some romantic notion that Englishmen, those fathers and grandfathers whom she sees marching in the picture of history, are "superior" to the men of other countries. This she will consider it her duty to check by comparing French historians with English; German with French; the testimony of the ruled—the Indians or the Irish, say—with the claims made by their rulers. Still some "patriotic" emotion, some ingrained belief in the intellectual superiority of her own country over other countries may remain. Then she will compare English painting with French painting; English music with German music; English literature with Greek literature, for translations abound. When all these comparisons have been faithfully made by the use of reason, the outsider will find herself in possession of very good reasons for her indifference. She will find that she has no good reason to ask her brother to fight on her behalf to protect "our" country. "Our country," she will say, "throughout the greater part of its history has treated me as a slave; it has denied me education or any share in its possessions. 'Our' country still ceases to be mine if I marry a foreigner. 'Our' country denies me the means of protecting myself, forces me to pay others a very large sum annually to protect me, and is so little able, even so, to protect me that Air Raid precautions are written on the wall. Therefore if you insist upon fighting to protect me, or 'our' country, let it be understood, soberly and rationally between us, that you are fighting to gratify a sex instinct which I cannot share; to procure benefits which I have not shared and probably will not share; but not to gratify my instincts, or to protect myself or my country." "For," the outsider will say, "in fact, as a woman, I have no country. As a woman I want no country. As a woman my country is the whole world." And if, when reason has said its say, still some obstinate emotion remains, some love of England dropped into a child's ears by the cawing of rooks in an elm tree, by the splash of waves on a beach, or by English voices murmuring nursery rhymes, this drop of pure, if irrational, emotion she will make it serve her to give to England first what she desires of peace and freedom for the whole world. . . .

[In other sections Woolf describes some of the changes that she thinks would "produce the kind of society, the kind of people that will help to prevent war." In one passage she describes a new sort of education, in another the ways that women admitted to the professions and the world of work should behave.]

Need we collect more facts from history and biography to prove our statement that all attempt to influence the young against war through the education they receive at the universities must be abandoned? For do they not prove that education, the finest education in the world, does not teach people to hate force, but to use it? Do they not prove that education, far from teaching generosity and magnanimity, makes them on the contrary so anxious to keep their possessions, that "grandeur and power" of which the poet speaks, in their own hands, that they will use not force but much subtler methods than force when they are asked to share them? And are not force and possessiveness very closely connected with war? Of what use then is a university education in influencing people to prevent war? . . .

Let us then discuss as quickly as we can the sort of education that is needed. Now since history and biography—the only evidence available to an outsider—seem to prove that the old education of the old colleges breeds neither a particular respect for liberty nor a particular hatred of war it is clear that you must rebuild your college differently. It is young and poor; let it therefore take advantage of those qualities and be founded on poverty and youth. . . . What should be taught? Not the arts of dominating other people; not the arts of ruling, of killing, of acquiring land and capital. They require too many overhead expenses; salaries and uniforms and ceremonies. The poor college must teach only the arts that can be taught cheaply and practiced by poor people; such as medicine, mathematics, music, painting and literature. It should teach the arts of human intercourse; the art of understanding other people's lives and minds, and the little arts of talk, of dress, of cookery that are allied with them. The aim of the new college, the cheap college, should be not to segregate and specialize, but to combine. It should explore the ways in which mind and body can be made to co-operate; discover what new combinations make good wholes in human life. The teachers should be drawn from the good livers [those who live good lives] as well as from the good thinkers. There should be no difficulty in attracting them. For there would be none of the barriers of wealth and ceremony, of advertisement and competition which now make the old and rich universities such uneasy dwelling-places—cities of strife, cities where this is locked up and that is chained down; where nobody can walk freely or talk freely for fear of transgressing some chalk mark, of displeasing some dignitary. But if the college were poor it would have nothing to offer; competition would be abolished. Life would be open and easy. People who love learning for itself would gladly come there. Musicians, painters, writers, would teach there, because they would learn. What could be of greater help to a writer than to discuss the art of writing with people who were thinking not of examinations or degrees or of what honour or profit they could make literature give them, but of the art itself?

And so with the other arts and artists. They would come to the poor college and practice their arts there because it would be a place where society was free; not parceled out into the miserable distinctions of rich and poor, of clever and stupid; but where all the different degrees and kinds of mind, body and soul merit cooperated. Let us then found this new college; the poor college; in which learning is sought for itself; where advertisement is abolished; and there are no degrees; and lectures are not given, and sermons are not preached, and the old poisoned vanities and parades which breed competition and jealousy [have no place]. . . .

The outsiders then would bind themselves not only to earn their own livings, but to earn them so expertly that their refusal to earn them would be a matter of concern to the work master. They would bind themselves to obtain full knowledge of professional practices, and to reveal any instance of tyranny or abuse in their professions. And they would bind themselves not to continue to make money in any profession, but to cease all competition and to practice their profession experimentally, in the interests of research and for love of the work itself, when they had earned enough to live upon. Also they would bind themselves to remain outside any profession hostile to freedom, such as the making or the improvement of the weapons of war. And they would bind themselves to refuse to take office or honour from any society which, while professing to respect liberty restricts it. . . . And they would consider it their duty to investigate the claims of all public societies to which, like the Church and the universities, they are forced to contribute as taxpayers. . . . [T]hey would be creative in their activities, not merely critical. By criticizing education they would help to create a civilized society which protects culture and intellectual liberty. By criticizing religion they would attempt to free the religious spirit from its present servitude and could help, if need be, to create a new religion based, it might well be, upon the New Testament, but, it might well be, very different from the religion now erected upon that basis. And in all this, and in much more than we have time to particularize, they would be helped, you will agree, by their position as outsiders, that freedom from unreal loyalties, that freedom from interested motives which are at present assured them by the State.

It would be easy to define in greater number and more exactly the duties of those who belong to the Society of Outsiders, but not profitable . . . [T]he description thus loosely and imperfectly given is enough to show you, Sir, that the Society of Outsiders has the same ends as your society—freedom, equality, peace; but that it seeks to achieve them by the means that a different sex, a different tradition, a different education, and the different values which result from those differences have placed within our reach.

THE BANALITY OF EVIL

In 1960, Israeli security forces kidnapped a Nazi war criminal named Adolph Eichmann (1906–1962) from his exile in Argentina and brought him back to Jerusalem for trial. Eichmann had been a bureaucrat in the Nazi SS (the security force most responsible for carrying out the policies of genocide), a nonideological functionary whose responsibilities included organizing the deportation of Jews across Europe to the death camps located in Germany and Poland. Eichmann's own testimony indicated that he had been aware of what he was doing and of the fate that awaited those he rounded up. He argued that his actions had in fact been "lawful," and he prided himself on being someone who had performed his duty to the best of his ability in difficult circumstances. The Israeli court found Eichmann guilty of crimes against humanity and executed him in 1962.

Hannah Arendt covered Eichmann's trial for *The New Yorker* magazine. Arendt, a Jewish exile from Germany, was an established author and academic; she was the first woman to become a full professor at Princeton University and taught at the University of Chicago, Wesleyan University, and the New School for Social Research. In her youth she had been educated under such noted German philosophers as Martin Heidegger and Karl Jaspers, received a doctorate from the University of Heidelberg, and organized Jewish opposition to Hitler before being forced to leave Germany after escaping from the Gestapo, Hitler's secret police. She fled Europe for America in 1941, escaping a second detention in occupied France. By the time of the Eichmann trial, Arendt had already written several works of political theory and history, most notably *The Origins of Totalitarianism* (1951), in which she brilliantly articulated the similarities between totalitarian regimes of the right (fascism) and the left (communism). Her assessment of the Eichmann trial proved equally profound and upsetting.

Arendt attributed Eichmann's behavior, and by extension the behavior of thousands of others, not to sadism, fanaticism, maniacal evil, or even hatred of the alien Jew, but rather to mediocrity, an inability to think clearly about what one was actually doing. This she called the "banality of evil." Modern governments provided hosts of comforting clichés to persuade people who preferred to not think too deeply to carry out activities that, in culmination, amounted to moral horrors. Equally disturbing to Arendt was a hesitation she saw in her contemporaries to judge such historic actors unless they could be identified as actual monsters. Too many people, she felt, seemed to believe that the forces of both nature and environment were so overwhelming that there was no way to judge individual moral culpability. If individuals did not feel accountable for their own actions, the possibilities of preventing future violence and aggression would indeed seem grim.

QUESTIONS TO CONSIDER

1. What does it mean to think and speak in clichés? Can you find clichés in other places in this chapter? Can we avoid clichés in communicating with each other? Does it matter?

2. As early as the ancient Greeks the philosopher Plato introduced the notion that some people, similar to Eichmann, suffer from "lies of the soul," that is, self-deceptions so profound that individuals are unaware that they are being false to reality and to their own motivations. How might Freud analyze such illusions and self-deceptions?

3. How do modern bureaucratic systems of getting work done make it easier for people to delude themselves about their actions? Do you consider this an expression of "dehumanization"?

4. Compare Arendt's image of Eichmann with the image of a man at war contained in Herbert Asquith's poem, *The Volunteer*. How had individual participation in national conflict changed?

5. Arendt says that, if we are unwilling to make moral judgments about the actions of individuals, there is no place for law courts or for the writing of history. What does she mean? Is explaining behavior the same thing as excusing it, in Arendt's view?

EICHMANN IN JERUSALEM (1963)

Hannah Arendt

The German text of the taped police examinations, conducted from May 29, 1960, to January 17, 1961, each page corrected and approved by Eichmann, constitutes a veritable gold mine for a psychologist—provided he is wise enough to understand that the horrible can be not only ludicrous but outright funny. Some of the comedy cannot be conveyed in English, because it lies in Eichmann's heroic fight with the German language, which invariably defeats him. . . . Dimly aware of a defect that must have plagued him even in school—it amounted to a mild form of aphasia [impairment of the ability to understand language]—he apologized, saying, "Officialese is my only language." But the point here is that officialese became his language because he was genuinely incapable of uttering a single sentence that was not a cliché. . . . [T]he judges were right when they finally told the accused that all he had said was "empty talk"—except that they thought the emptiness was feigned, and that the accused wished to cover up other thoughts which, though hideous, were not empty. This supposition seems refuted by the striking consistency with which Eichmann, despite his rather bad memory, repeated word for word the same stock phrases and self-invented clichés (when he did succeed in constructing a sentence of his own, he repeated it until it became a cliché) each time he referred to an incident or event of importance to him. Whether writing his memoirs in Argentina or in Jerusalem, whether speaking to the police examiner or to the court, what he said was always the same, expressed in the same words. The longer one listened to him, the more obvious it became that his inability to speak was closely connected with an inability to *think,* namely, to think from the standpoint of somebody else. No communication was possible with him, not because he lied but because he was surrounded by the most reliable of all safeguards against the words and the presence of others, and hence against reality as such. . . .

[Was his] a textbook case of bad faith, of lying self-deception combined with outrageous stupidity? . . . Eichmann needed only to recall the past in order to feel assured that he was not lying and that he was not deceiving himself, for he and the world he lived in had once been in perfect harmony. And that German society of eighty million people had been shielded against reality and factuality by exactly the same means, the same self-deception, lies, and stupidity that had now become ingrained in Eichmann's mentality. These lies changed from year to year, and they frequently contradicted each other; moreover, they were not necessarily the same for the various branches of the Party hierarchy or the people at large. But the practice of self-deception had become so common, almost a moral prerequisite for survival, that even now, eighteen years after the collapse of the Nazi regime, when most of the specific content of the lies has been forgotten, it is sometimes difficult not to believe that

Source: Hannah Arendt, *Eichmann in Jerusalem: A Report on the Banality of Evil* (New York: Penguin Books, 1987), 48–52, 276, 289–92, 296–97. Copyright © 1987. Used by permission of Penguin Putnam Group (USA) Inc.

mendacity* has become an integral part of the German national character. During the war, the lie most effective with the whole of the German people was the slogan of "the battle of destiny for the German people," coined either by Hitler or by Goebbels, which made self-deception easier on three counts: it suggested, first, that the war was no war; second, that it was started by destiny and not by Germany; and, third, that it was a matter of life and death for the Germans, who must annihilate their enemies or be annihilated. . . .

For all this, it was essential that one take him seriously, and this was very hard to do, unless one sought the easiest way out of the dilemma between the unspeakable horror of the deeds and the undeniable ludicrousness of the man who perpetrated them, and declared him a clever, calculating liar—which he obviously was not. . . . Despite all the efforts of the prosecution, everybody could see that this man was not a "monster," but it was difficult indeed not to suspect that he was a clown. . . .

[The judges] knew, of course, that it would have been very comforting indeed to believe that Eichmann was a monster. . . . The trouble with Eichmann was precisely that so many were like him, and that the many were neither perverted nor sadistic, that they were, and still are, terribly and terrifyingly normal. From the standpoint of our legal institutions and of our moral standards of judgment, this normality was much more terrifying than all the atrocities put together, for it implied that this new type of criminal commits his crimes under circumstances that make it well-nigh impossible for him to know or to feel that he is doing wrong. . . .

Seemingly more complicated, but in reality far simpler than examining the strange interdependence of thoughtlessness and evil, is the question of what kind of crime is actually involved here—a crime, moreover, which all agree is unprecedented. For the concept of genocide, introduced explicitly to cover a crime unknown before, although applicable up to a point is not fully adequate, for the simple reason that massacres of whole people are not unprecedented. They were the order of the day in antiquity, and the centuries of colonization and imperialism provide plenty of examples of more or less successful attempts of that sort. The expression "administrative massacres" seems better to fill the bill. . . . [I]t is apparent that this sort of killing can be directed against any given group, that is, that the principle of selection is dependent only upon circumstantial factors. It is quite conceivable that in the automated economy of a not-too-distant future men may be tempted to exterminate all those whose intelligence is below a certain level.

In Jerusalem this matter was inadequately discussed because it is actually very difficult to grasp juridically [in the law court]. We hear the protestations of the defense that Eichmann was after all only a "tiny cog" in the machinery of the Final Solution, and of the prosecution, which believed it had discovered in Eichmann the actual motor. I myself attributed no more importance to both theories than did the Jerusalem court, since the whole cog theory is legally pointless and therefore it does not matter at all what order of magnitude is assigned to the "cog" named Eichmann. In its judgment the court naturally conceded that such a crime could be committed only by a giant bureaucracy using the resources of government. But insofar as it remained a crime—and that, of course, is the premise for a trial—all the cogs in the machinery, no matter how

---

*Dishonesty.

insignificant, are in court forthwith transformed back into perpetrators, that is to say, into human beings. If the defendant excuses himself on the ground that he acted not as a man but as a mere functionary whose functions could just as easily have been carried out by anyone else, it is as if a criminal pointed to the statistics on crime—which set forth that so-and-so many crimes per day are committed in such-and-such a place—and declared that he only did what was statistically expected, that it was mere accident that he did it and not somebody else, since after all somebody had to do it.

Of course it is important to the political and social sciences that the essence of totalitarian government, and perhaps the nature of every bureaucracy, is to make functionaries and mere cogs in the administrative machinery out of men, and thus to dehumanize them. And one can debate long and profitably on the rule of Nobody, which is what the political form known as bureaucracy truly is. . . . [W]e have become very much accustomed by modern psychology and sociology, not to speak of modern bureaucracy, to explaining away the responsibility of the doer for his deed in terms of this or that kind of determinism. Whether such seemingly deeper explanations of human actions are right or wrong is debatable. But what is not debatable is that no judicial procedure would be possible on the basis of them. . . . When Hitler said that a day would come in Germany when it would be considered a "disgrace" to be a jurist, he was speaking with utter consistency of his dream of a perfect bureaucracy.

There remains one fundamental problem, which was implicitly present in all these postwar trials and which must be mentioned here because it touches upon one of the central moral questions of all time, namely upon the nature and function of human judgment. What we have demanded in these trials, where the defendants had committed "legal" crimes, is that human beings be capable of telling right from wrong, even when all they have to guide them is their own judgment, which, moreover, happens to be completely at odds with what they must regard as the unanimous opinion of all those around them. . . . How troubled men of our time are by this question of judgment (or, as is often said, by people who dare "sit in judgment") . . . what has come to light is neither nihilism nor cynicism, as one might have expected, but a quite extraordinary confusion over elementary questions of morality—as if instinct in such matters were truly the last thing to be taken for granted in our time. . . . [S]ome American literati [intellectuals and critics] have professed their naïve belief that temptation and coercion are really the same thing, that no one can be asked to resist temptation. (If someone puts a pistol to your heart and orders you to shoot your best friend, then you simply *must* shoot him. Or, as it was argued—some years ago in connection with the quiz program scandal in which a university teacher had hoaxed the public—when so much money is at stake, who could possibly resist?) The argument that we cannot judge if we were not present and involved ourselves seems to convince everyone everywhere, although it seems obvious that if it were true, neither the administration of justice nor the writing of history would ever be possible. In contrast to these confusions, the reproach of self-righteousness raised against those who do judge is age-old; but that does not make it any the more valid. Even the judge who condemns a murderer can still say when he goes home: "And there, but for the grace of God, go I."

Another escape from the area of ascertainable facts and personal responsibility are the countless theories, based on non-specific, abstract, hypothetical assumptions—from the *Zeitgeist* [climate or culture of the times] down to the Oedipus complex [a component of Freud's psychoanalytic model]—which are so general that they explain and justify every event and every deed: no alternative to what actually happened is even considered and no person could have acted differently from the way he did act. . . . Although we can understand the reluctance of those immediately affected by the disaster [of the Holocaust] to examine too closely the conduct of groups and persons that seemed to be or should have been unimpaired by the totality of the moral collapse—that is, the conduct of the Christian churches, the Jewish leadership, the men of the anti-Hitler conspiracy of July 20, 1944—this understandable disinclination is insufficient to explain the reluctance evident everywhere to make judgments in terms of moral responsibility.

AN ISLAMIC VOICE

Ruhollah Musavi Khomeini (1900–1989) was a leader-in-exile of the revolution that overthrew the Shah of Iran (1919–1980) in 1979, but his influence extended far beyond the politics of one Middle Eastern country. The Imam, as he continues to be known to his followers,[6] was one of the century's most important voices articulating the need for an Islamic "worldview" to counter globalizing forces of western economic structures, secular values, and popular culture.

Khomeini's family had a long tradition of religious scholarship, and his early education came from male relatives who took over responsibility for the boy after his father was murdered in 1903. The family had land holdings in Khumayn in Iran that provided material wealth but did not allow them to escape the lawlessness and political instability that characterized Iran in the early part of the century. As a young man Khomeini settled in Qum, one of the centers of instruction in the Shi`a branch of the Islamic faith. Even in his early years, his interests lay in ethics and philosophy, rather than legalistic branches of study. Although not yet challenging the political quietism of an elder generation of spiritual leaders, by the 1930s and 1940s he had begun to articulate the religious grounds for action against the Pahlavi dynasty that ruled Iran with, in his view, too much deference to the interests of colonial powers such as Britain. His opposition burst forth in 1963 when the reigning shah attempted an ambitious reforming program backed by the United States.

Khomeini's success in using mass prayers, lectures, and demonstrations to appeal to ordinary Iranians earned him exile in Najaf for thirteen years from 1965 through 1978. From this center of Shi`a learning in southern Iraq, Khomeini continued to denounce the increasingly repressive regime of the shah. But he transcended the politics of his own country by calling for solidarity and unified action among Muslims across the world, regardless of their ethnic group or adherence to a particular branch of the faith. He identified Israel and the United States as the enemies who sought to create divisions among Muslims and to transform Islamic communities into godless societies devoted to material consumption and corrupting individualism. He maintained contact with numerous religious and political figures in Iran who transmitted his message to citizens increasingly distressed by the shah's regime. Throughout 1978 mass demonstrations convulsed the country, and in January 1979 the shah retreated into exile when the military would no longer support his attempts to quell dissent by force. In March Khomeini was welcomed back by crowds numbering in the millions.

Khomeini prided himself that the new constitution he oversaw allowed for an elected legislature and president. At the same time, an Assembly for Determination of the Interest of the Islamic Order had the final authority to decide whether a law was in accord with religious teachings designed to create a godly society. Throughout the 1980s, a decade that included horrific war with the secular Ba'ath regime of Saddam Hussein in Iraq, Khomeini continued to represent those forces of "revolutionary Islam" that argued that the societies represented by the United States and its western allies were the sources of violence, injustice, and irreligion in the world. The struggles of some followers of traditional Islam to preserve the faith as they understood it introduced the "clash of cultures" as yet another way to understand the continuing violence between human communities.

QUESTIONS TO CONSIDER

1. Did Khomeini and Mao Zedong identify the same enemies to peace? In what ways were their enemies the same, and in what ways were they different?
2. What did Khomeini offer to warriors for Islam that might inspire them as Asquith's "Volunteer" is inspired?
3. Khomeini implied that western powers were trying to divide the different peoples who embraced various versions of the Islamic faith. What would Freud say about the reasons that distinct groups of Muslims, particularly Sunnis and the Shi`is, are unable to pursue united action?
4. What did Khomeini accuse the United States of doing that was harmful? What were America's motives?
5. On the basis of this message to all Muslims, what did Khomeini seem to think was necessary to bring lasting peace to mankind?

"MESSAGE TO THE PILGRIMS" (1980)

Ruhollah Khomeini

Greetings to the visitors to God's Sacred House who have gathered at the focal point of revelation, the place where God's angels alight. Greetings to the believers who have migrated from their own homes to the House of God. Greetings to all Muslims

Source: Imam Khomeini, *Islam and Revolution,* trans. Hamid Algar (Berkeley, CA: Mizan Press, 1981), 300–06. Reprinted with permission. This was a message to the Muslims of all countries making the annual pilgrimage to Mecca that year.

of the world whose prophet is the Most Noble Messenger [Muhammad, founder of the Islamic faith], the Seal of the Prophets, whose book is the Noble Qur'an, and whose *qibla* [the point toward which Muslims turn to pray] is the Exalted Ka'ba [the small building containing a sacred black stone, the objective of pilgrimage to Mecca]. Greetings to those . . . who have freed themselves from the fetters of slavery and obedience to the idols installed in the centers of tyranny, imperialism, and satanic power, who have joined themselves to the absolute power of God and the firm rope of *tauhid* [divine unity]. Greetings to those who have grasped the sense of God Almighty's summons and set out, in response, to His House.

Now it is necessary for me to bring certain matters to your attention, free Muslims who have gathered at the site of revelation in order to fulfill a duty that relates both to worship and politics, so that you may be made aware of what is happening in the Muslim countries; what plans are underway to subjugate, exploit, and dominate the Muslims; and what impure hands are engaged in kindling the fires of division.

1. At a time when all the Muslims in the world are about to join together and achieve mutual understanding between the different schools of thought in Islam, in order to deliver their nations from the foul grasp of the superpowers; at a time when the arms of the Eastern and Western oppressors are about to be foreshortened in Iran, by means of unity of purpose and reliance on God Almighty—precisely at this time, the Great Satan has summoned its agents and instructed them to sow dissension among the Muslims by every imaginable means, giving rise to hostility and dispute among brothers in faith who share the belief in *tauhid,* so that nothing will stand in the way of complete domination and plunder. Fearing that the Islamic Revolution of Iran will spread to other countries, Muslim and non-Muslim alike, and thus compel it to remove its foul hands from the lands it dominates, the Great Satan is resorting to another stratagem now, after the failure of both the economic boycott and the military attack. It is attempting to distort the nature of our Islamic Revolutions in the eyes of Muslims throughout the world in order to set the Muslims at each others' throats while it continues its exploitation and oppression of the Muslim countries. . . .

3. One of the themes that the planners of disunion among the Muslims have put forward, and their agents are engaged in promoting, is that of race and nationalism. For years the government of Iraq has been busy promoting nationalism, and certain other groups have followed the same path, setting the Muslims against each other as enemies. To love one's fatherland and its people and to protect its frontiers are both quite unobjectionable, but nationalism, involving hostility to other Muslim nations, is something quite different. It is contrary to the Noble Qur'an and the orders of the Most Noble Messenger. Nationalism that results in the creation of enmity between Muslims and splits the ranks of the believers is against Islam and the interests of the Muslims. It is a stratagem concocted by the foreigners who are disturbed by the spread of Islam.

5. Part of the extensive propaganda campaign being waged apparently against Iran, but in reality against Islam, is intended to show that the Revolution of Iran cannot administer our country or that the Iranian government is about to fall, since Iran supposedly lacks a healthy economy, proper educational system, disciplined army, and armed forces ready for combat. Propaganda to this effect is put out by all the mass media of America and its allies, giving comfort to the enemies of Iran and Islam.

The propaganda is actually directed against Islam, for they want to pretend that Islam in the present day is incapable of administering a country. The Muslims should study matters carefully, comparing the Iranian Islamic Revolution with non-Islamic revolutions. Our Islamic Revolution inherited a country that was completely dependent upon the outside world that was ruined and backward in every respect. For more than fifty years, the Pahlavi puppet* had dragged our country down, filling the pockets of the foreigners—particularly Britain and America—with the abundant wealth of our land, and awarding what little remained to itself and its agents and hangers-on. In short, it left us many problems to face. But by the blessing of Islam and our Muslim people, in the space of less than two years, we have voted on, approved, and put into practice all the measures necessary for the administration of the country. Despite all the difficulties that America and its satellites have created for us—economic boycott, military attack, and the planning of extensive coups d'etat—our valiant people have attained self-sufficiency in foodstuffs. Soon we will transform the imperialist-inspired education system that existed under the previous regime into an independent and Islamic education system. The armed forces, the Revolutionary Guards, the gendarmerie [soldiers who have police authority over civilians], and the police stand ready to defend the country and uphold order, and they are prepared to offer their lives in *jihad* [divinely authorized struggle] for the sake of Islam. In addition, a general mobilization of the entire nation is under way, with the nation equipping itself to fight for the sake of Islam and the country. Let our enemies know that no revolution in the world was followed by less bloodshed or brought greater achievements than our Islamic Revolution, and that this is due entirely to the blessing of Islam. Do our enemies know what they are saying? Is Islam supposed to be incapable of administering countries, the same Islam that for several centuries ruled over more than half the populated areas of the globe, and that overthrew the governments of unbelief and oppression in less than half a century? . . . [T]he true nature of Islamic rule has been abandoned and obscured. It must now be presented to the world anew through the efforts of all Muslims, particularly the scholars and thinkers, so that the bright visage of Islam will shine over the world like the sun.

Muslims the world over who believe in the truth of Islam, arise and gather beneath the banner of *tauhid* and the teachings of Islam! Repel the treacherous superpowers from your countries and your abundant resources. Restore the glory of Islam, and abandon your selfish disputes and differences, for you possess everything! Rely on the culture of Islam, resist Western imitation, and stand on your own feet. Attack those intellectuals who are infatuated with the West and the East, and recover your true identity. Realize that intellectuals in the pay of foreigners have inflicted disaster upon their people and countries. As long as you remain disunited and fail to place your reliance in true Islam, you will continue to suffer what you have suffered already. We are now in an age when the masses act as the guides to the intellectuals and are rescuing them from abasement* and humiliation by the East and the West. For today is the day that the masses of the people are on the move; they are the guides to those who previously sought to be the guides themselves.

---

*Pahlavi was the name of the dynasty of the deposed Shah.

Know that your moral power will overcome all other powers. With a population of almost one billion and with infinite sources of wealth, you can defeat all the powers. Aid God's cause so that he may aid you. Great ocean of Muslims, arise and defeat the enemies of humanity. If you turn to God and follow the heavenly teachings, God Almighty and His vast hosts will be with you.

6. The most important and painful problem confronting the subjugated nations of the world, both Muslim and non-Muslim, is the problem of America. In order to swallow up the material resources of the countries it has succeeded in dominating, America, the most powerful country in the world, will spare no effort.

America is the number-one enemy of the deprived and oppressed people of the world. There is no crime America will not commit in order to maintain its political, economic, cultural, and military domination of those parts of the world where it predominates. It exploits the oppressed people of the world by means of the large-scale propaganda campaigns that are coordinated for it by international Zionism. By means of its hidden and treacherous agents, it sucks the blood of the defenseless people as if it alone, together with its satellites, had the right to live in this world.

Iran has tried to sever all its relations with this Great Satan and it is for this reason that it now finds wars imposed upon it. America has urged Iraq to spill the blood of our young men, and it has compelled the countries that are subject to its influence to boycott us economically in the hope of defeating us. Unfortunately, most Asian countries are also hostile to us. Let the Muslim nations be aware that Iran is a country effectively at war with America, and that our martyrs—the brave young men of our army and the Revolutionary Guard—are defending Iran and the Islam we hold dear against America. Thus, it is necessary to point out, the clashes now occurring in the west of our beloved country are caused by America; every day we are forced to confront various godless and treacherous groups there. This is a result of the Islamic content of our Revolution, which has been established on the basis of true independence. Were we to compromise with America and the other superpowers, we would not suffer these misfortunes. But our nation is no longer ready to submit to humiliation and abjection; it prefers a bloody death to a life of shame. We are ready to be killed and we have made a covenant with God to follow the path of our leader, the Lord of the Martyrs.

Muslims who are now sitting next to the House of God, engaged in prayer! Pray for those who are resisting America and the other superpowers, and understand that we are not fighting against Iraq. The people of Iraq support our Islamic Revolution; our quarrel is with America, and it is America whose hand can be seen emerging from the sleeve of the Iraqi government. God willing, our struggle will continue until we have achieved real independence, for, as I have said repeatedly, we are warriors, and for Muslims surrender has no meaning.

NOTES

1. The Crimean War of 1854 and the "nation-building" wars of the 1860s and 1870s were notable exceptions.

2. In December 1937 Japanese soldiers in occupied Nanjing engaged in a frenzy of destruction and atrocities authorized by their superiors. At least 400,000 Chinese were tortured, raped, and machine-gunned over two months of looting and murder.

3. Paul Fussell, *The Great War and Modern Memory* (New York: Oxford University Press, 1975).

4. Alfred Adler (1870–1937) is commonly credited as the founder of "individual psychology," whereas Carl Jung (1875–1961), a Swiss psychiatrist, is best known for postulating the "collective unconscious," or those thought processes and behaviors shared universally by all human beings.

5. A guinea is a British coin, originally gold, worth slightly over one pound.

6. Khomeini is frequently referred to as Ayatollah. Devoted followers also consider him Imam, one in a very small series of divinely inspired religious leaders of the Shi`i.

CHAPTER 13

Perspectives on the Cold War, Decolonization, and the Vietnam War

INTRODUCTION

World War II was a watershed event in world history, for it dramatically altered power relationships and spawned new conflicts that were to dominate world events in the second half of the twentieth century. First, the war destroyed much of the power and prestige of Europe and enabled two new "superpowers"—the United States and the Soviet Union—to take the place of Europe in the center of world affairs. Former allies in the fight against the Axis powers of Germany, Italy, and Japan, the United States and the Soviet Union (USSR) entered the postwar era as adversaries, and their competition for global supremacy produced what has been called the "Cold War" (1945–1989). World War II also helped to accelerate the pace of nationalism in the former colonies of Europe. Between 1945 and 1985, more than ninety countries, representing approximately one-third of the world's population, won their independence from colonial rule. As decolonization coincided with the Cold War, the two global phenomena had a close and interrelated history, with each influencing the context and character of the other.

This chapter utilizes a variety of historical documents to explore the perceptions, ideas, and strategies that shaped the course of the Cold War and decolonization. Three major themes and issues deserve special attention. First, how were the Cold War and decolonization defined and portrayed at the time? How did leaders of various nations view the origins and nature of conflicts, and how were those sentiments expressed and formulated into policies? Second, in what ways did the Cold War and decolonization interact with each other? Using Vietnam as a case study, how did Cold War attitudes and policies shape the character and direction of Vietnamese nationalism and American military intervention? And finally, what basic cross-cultural assumptions and ideological biases shaped the history of this era? To what degree were actions and ideas fashioned more by fears and emotions than by objective rational thought? Taken together, the readings allow us to pursue an attitudinal survey of the Cold War and decolonization and to examine and assess the molding of paradigms and perceptions that forged specific policies and actions. It is difficult to date the exact beginnings of the Cold War. Despite their wartime cooperation, the leadership of the United States and the Soviet Union harbored deep suspicions of each other based on antagonistic national ideologies and past historical events. From the Soviet perspective, the United States was the leading capitalist power, and it had intervened briefly against the Bolsheviks during the Russian Civil War.[1] For their part, most Americans were repulsed by the socialist and atheist system of Communist Russia, and believed Stalin to be a brutal dictator who could not be trusted. Tensions between the new superpowers began almost immediately following the surrender of Nazi Germany in 1945. In eastern Europe, the USSR installed Communist governments friendly to the Kremlin and used the Red Army to ensure their loyalty. In western Europe, the United States' Marshall Plan[2] helped to restore capitalism, democracy, and pro-American allies. Although Europe became an armed camp, divided between the pro-American forces of the North Atlantic Treaty Organization (NATO) and the pro-Soviet Warsaw pact[3], neither the United States nor the USSR sought a direct military confrontation, owing to the assured mutual destruction that would have resulted from their arsenals of thermonuclear weapons. Still, what resulted was a decades-long tense and guarded peace.[4]

In both rhetoric and sentiment, the Cold War was frequently portrayed and perceived as a "moral crusade," or a protracted struggle between right and wrong. Each side viewed itself as the exclusive and superior model for the rest of the world, and each sought to use this perception as a justification for its actions. That an air of a crusade hung over the Cold War can be seen from the language each used to characterize the other. To the Soviets, Americans were "capitalist imperialists," "exploiters," "warmongers," and "aggressors." From the American point of view, Communists were "fanatics," "expansionists," "dishonorable," and "deceitful." Hence, the Cold War became something far more than just a geopolitical struggle for advantage and for spheres of influence; it was also a contest between good and evil, morality and immorality.

The readings in this chapter on the Cold War highlight the intensely moral component of superpower competition and illustrate the crucial importance of paradigms and perceptions in the molding of world events. The first set of texts consists of two documents that represent the Soviet point of view. The first is the text of a February 1931 speech by Soviet leader Josef Stalin, explaining why the rapid pace of industrialization in the USSR could not be moderated. In his justifications, Stalin presents his view of Russian history and explains why the nation had to become a great power. Stalin's speech is followed by excerpts from a telegram sent by Nikolai Novikov, the Soviet ambassador to the United States, to the Kremlin in 1946. Novikov provides a detailed analysis of the postwar world and lays out for the Soviet side his perspectives on American foreign policy goals and strategies.

After the Soviet documents come three texts prepared by leading U.S. government officials. The first reading is derived from a highly influential article titled "The Sources of Soviet Conduct," anonymously written by George Kennan in 1947. As an official in the American Embassy in Moscow, Kennan wrote an account of Soviet goals and strategies that provides an interesting counterpoint to the Soviet perspective. The next reading comes from President Harry S. Truman's speech to a joint session of Congress in March 1947. In this address, Truman outlined a set of principles and objectives that have become known as the Truman Doctrine and that have shaped American foreign policy ever since. Finally, we present the text of an important speech by J. Edgar Hoover, the director of the FBI and one of the leading figures in the domestic hunt for Communists and Communist sympathizers.

The Cold War served as the backdrop for the decolonization of much of Africa and Asia. Although resistance against European colonialism began much earlier[5], the independence movement gained momentum after World War II when European powers began to lose their ability and will to maintain their overseas possessions. Led by a determined and educated elite, nationalist organizations in Africa and Asia mobilized their populations to oppose colonial authority and to support full independence. In some colonies, the creation of political parties and the use of mass strikes and civil disobedience compelled the colonizers to grant independence in a relatively orderly and peaceful process. But in other colonies, such as British Kenya, French Algeria, Portuguese Angola, and French Indochina, the colonizing powers stubbornly tried to hang on to power, which led to the creation of liberation movements and armed struggles. It was in these former colonies that the struggle for independence became most intertwined with the Cold War. The superpowers battled for global power, prestige, and influence by providing arms and assistance to rival political factions, while at the same time, opportunistic leaders in Africa and Asia sought beneficial alliances with either the United States or the Soviet Union in order to further their own ambitions and objectives.

One of the most tragic examples of Cold War decolonization occurred in Vietnam, a country most Americans would have been hard pressed to locate on a map before the 1960s. Located at the extreme corner of southeast Asia, Vietnam was a largely agrarian land of small peasant farmers. Beginning in the mid-nineteenth century, the French began to occupy and control the country, attracted by its natural resources and economic potential. Eventually, the French created the colony of Indochina, which comprised the present-day nations of Vietnam, Laos, and Cambodia. But French rule, particularly their labor policies, was widely unpopular and led to the formation of resistance movements even before World War II. The most successful movement was the Vietminh, led by Ho Chi Minh, a self-identified Communist and ardent nationalist. Ho Chi Minh organized military resistance first against the French and then against the Japanese after their invasion of the colony during World War II. With the defeat and retreat of the Japanese, an enfeebled French control was reestablished, but it took only nine years—till the disastrous military defeat at Dien Bien Phu—for the French to admit that they could no longer control their colony. This was formally recognized at the Geneva Conference in 1954, which set up two separate, independent zones in the north and south of Vietnam and which called for national elections to decide the fate of the newly independent territories. Before that could happen, the United States had moved in to replace the French in supporting the anti-Communist forces in the south. Fearing that the Communists would win a nationwide referendum, the

United States supported the South Vietnamese government in its refusal to let elections take place. The United States also rapidly expanded its economic aid and sent in military advisors, as well.

The ensuing Vietnam War was a disaster for both the United States and Vietnam. Over a twenty-five-year period, it is estimated that over 2.5 million people on all sides were killed. In America, the war became the most divisive issue since the Civil War. Widespread domestic protests against the war destroyed the presidency of Lyndon Johnson, pitted war "hawks" against "doves," and undermined public faith in government. For Vietnam, the war was a costly success. Despite massive American bombings of cities and countryside, the Vietnamese Communists refused to capitulate. In 1975, North Vietnam ignored a negotiated settlement made earlier with the United States and took advantage of the withdrawal of U.S. troops to launch an invasion of the south. On April 30, 1975, the long Vietnamese struggle was over, and the country was reunified under Communist control.

The documents on Vietnam present a variety of views and perspectives. The first is the Vietnamese Declaration of Independence, written by the nationalist leader Ho Chi Minh in 1945. This is followed by two Vietnamese documents relating to the war itself. The first is by General Vo Nguyen Giap, the great North Vietnamese military leader and architect of the decisive military victory over both the French and the Americans, who explains the North Vietnamese tactics and why they succeeded. Next, there is the statement of a common Vietnamese fighter, which provides a view "from below" as to why someone would join the Communist side. These are followed by two American texts. The first of these is President Lyndon Johnson's 1965 speech to the American people, explaining the reasons for America's involvement in Vietnam. The second text comes from John Kerry, a Vietnam veteran who explained his opposition to the war in testimony before the U.S. Senate Armed Services Committee.

Taken together, the readings in this chapter provide important insights into two of the most important historical events of the twentieth century. They impart information about the origins and character of the cold war and decolonization, particularly the way they were perceived and justified at the time. They also highlight the interconnectedness of both events, showing how seemingly unrelated episodes are commonly intertwined in history. And last, the readings allow us to investigate and assess the important roles played by cross-cultural assumptions and ideological paradigms that shape our views and policies toward others.

CHAPTER QUESTIONS

1. Cold War policies were frequently based on certain assumptions about the character and mentality of "the enemy." What were the Soviet views of America and Americans? How did Americans typically view the Soviets and their ambitions? When the differing perspectives are compared, what insights and general conclusions can be gained?

2. Many observers believe that the American policy of "containment" succeeded in limiting the spread of Communism after World War II. Other critics, however, contend that "containment" actually helped to create adversarial opponents in the Soviet Union and North Vietnam. Using the documents presented here, what tentative conclusions do you reach?

3. It has been said that the Cold War embodied a "crusading spirit" on the part of both major adversaries. What evidence is there to support this? What are the implications of infusing political rivalries with a strong moral component?

4. How would you characterize the differing American views on the Vietnam War? What factors account for the contrasting views between Johnson and Kerry? Which explanation do you find the most persuasive, and why?

5. What does the history of the Cold War and Vietnam teach us about the way that paradigms are generated, adapted, and applied? Do the assumptions or their application change over time? What lessons can be applied to our foreign relations today?

SOVIET VIEWS OF THE UNITED STATES AND THE COLD WAR

As leader of the Soviet Union for over two decades, including during the formative early years of the Cold War, Josef Vissarionovich Stalin (1879–1953) was one of the most important figures of the twentieth century. A professional revolutionary from 1900 on, Stalin joined V. I. Lenin (1870–1924) and the Bolshevik (Communist) Party and became one of Lenin's closest collaborators, especially during the desperate and bloody days of the Civil War (1918–1920). Having cautiously consolidated his political position by 1929, Stalin oversaw a series of radical economic, social, and political initiatives that laid the industrial foundation of the USSR, broke the political resistance of the peasantry, and created a terror apparatus that made Stalin the uncontested dictator of the country. In August 1939, Stalin entered into a nonaggression pact with Hitler that kept the USSR out of World War II until the German invasion of Russia in June 1941. Ultimately, at the cost of 25 million deaths and untold destruction, the Soviets drove the Nazi forces out of their country, contributing the lion's share to the Allied victory over Hitler. The experiences of World War II did nothing to soften Stalin's ways, and he was a tough negotiator during the wartime conferences. After the war, Stalin established a zone of Soviet occupation and domination in eastern Europe that lasted until 1989.

In 1931, Stalin gave a speech titled "On the Tasks of Workers in the Economy" to a nationwide workers' conference in the Soviet Union. In this speech, Stalin explained and justified the quick pace of Russian industrialization and the extraordinary demands that it imposed on the Russian people. The address is noteworthy, for it provides a concise yet compelling view into Stalin's political philosophy, particularly regarding Russia's relations with its neighbors. Although the speech was given eight years prior to the start of World War II, it captures the Soviet leader's understanding of Russian history and Marxist ideology and their implications for Soviet domestic and foreign policy.

The Soviet view of the Cold War world is available to us in Ambassador Nikolai Novikov's extended 1946 analysis of the postwar global situation and of U.S. policies and goals. Novikov's assessment is significant, both because he was based in Washington, D.C., and because his assessment was produced almost exactly one year after the surrender of Japan had ended World War II.[6] In a lengthy telegram to Moscow, Novikov surveyed American involvement in the main global arenas, assessed U.S. goals, and analyzed the roots of anti-Soviet sentiments in America. He concluded that America was an aggressive power that was actively preparing for a future war with Russia in order to achieve complete "world domination." Given Novikov's rank and responsibilities as ambassador to the United States, most scholars conclude that his opinions and assessments were generally consistent with the views of the upper leadership of the Soviet Union.[7]

QUESTIONS TO CONSIDER

1. What reasons did Stalin provide for refusing to slow the pace of industrialization? What part of his explanation rested on the centuries-long experience of the Russians, and what was based on Marxist ideology? Given Stalin's views and the Russian experience during World War II, what foreign policy goals and objectives might have been expected after the war?

2. According to Ambassador Novikov, what were American objectives in the postwar world? How did these objectives compare with American policy and leadership during the war?

3. Novikov asserted that America was an aggressive power that sought world domination. To what degree was his argument based on Marxist ideology? To what degree was it based on a rational assessment of events? What evidence did he include to support his case? Is it reliable?

4. In his analysis of anti-Soviet sentiment among Americans, Ambassador Novikov believed that the U.S. government manipulated the American media in order to create "an atmosphere of war psychosis." What did he mean by this? Why did he include this in his telegram? How do you assess his argument on this point?

5. In your assessment, what were the most significant misconceptions that the Soviets had of American policy and goals after World War II? What factors most contributed to these misconceptions?

"ON THE TASKS OF WORKERS IN THE ECONOMY" (1931)

Josef V. Stalin

It is sometimes asked whether it is not possible to slow down the tempo [of industrialization] somewhat, to put a check on the movement. No, comrades, it is not possible! The tempo must not be reduced! On the contrary, we must increase it as much as is within our powers and possibilities. This is dictated to us by our obligations to the workers and peasants of the USSR. This is dictated to us by our obligations to the working class of the whole world.

To slacken the tempo would mean falling behind. And those who fall behind get beaten. But we do not want to be beaten. No, we refuse to be beaten! One feature of the history of old Russia was the continual beatings she suffered because of her backwardness. She was beaten by the Mongol khans. She was beaten by the Turkish beys. She was beaten by the Swedish feudal lords. She was beaten by the Polish and Lithuanian gentry. She was beaten by the British and French capitalists. She was beaten by the Japanese barons.* All beat her—because of her backwardness, because of her military backwardness, cultural backwardness, political backwardness, industrial backwardness, agricultural backwardness. They beat her because to do so was profitable and could be done with impunity. You remember the words of the revolutionary poet: "You are poor and abundant, mighty and impotent, Mother Russia." Those gentlemen were quite familiar with the verses of the old poet. They beat her, saying, "You are abundant," so one can enrich oneself at your expense. They beat her, saying, "You are poor and impotent," so you can be beaten and plundered with impunity. Such is the law of the exploiters—to beat the backward and the weak. It is the jungle law of capitalism. You are backward, you are weak—therefore you are wrong; hence you can be beaten and enslaved. You are mighty—therefore you are right; hence we must be wary of you. That is why we must no longer lag behind.

In the past we had no Fatherland, nor could we have had one. But now that we have overthrown capitalism and power is in our hands, in the hands of the people, we have a Fatherland, and we will uphold its independence. Do you want our socialist fatherland to be beaten and to lose its independence? If you do not want this, you must put an end to its backwardness in the shortest possible time and develop a genuine Bolshevik tempo in building up its socialist economy. There is no other way. That is why Lenin said on the eve of the October Revolution: "Either perish, or overtake and outstrip the advanced capitalist countries."

Source: Josef V. Stalin, "On the Tasks of Workers in the Economy," in *Works*, Vol. XIII (Moscow: Foreign Language Publishing House, 1955), 40–41. The speech to the First All-Union Conference of Workers of Socialist Industry was originally printed the next day in the official state-run newspaper *Pravda*, No. 35, February 5, 1931.

*These are all powers that had inflicted military defeats on Russia in its history.

We are fifty or a hundred years behind the advanced countries. We must make good this distance in ten years. Either we do it, or we shall go under. . . .

"TELEGRAM TO MOSCOW" (1946)

Nikolai Novikov

The foreign policy of the US, which reflects the imperialist tendencies of American monopolistic capital, is characterized in the postwar period by a striving for world supremacy. This is the real meaning of the many statements by President Truman and other representatives of American ruling circles: that the US has the right to lead the world. All the forces of American diplomacy—the army, the air force, the navy, industry, and science—are enlisted in the service of this foreign policy. For this purpose broad plans for expansion have been developed and are being implemented through diplomacy and the establishment of a system of naval and air bases stretching far beyond the boundaries of the US, through the arms race, and through the creation of ever newer types of weapons.

The foreign policy of the US is conducted now in a situation that differs greatly from the one that existed in the prewar period. This situation does not fully conform to the calculations of those reactionary circles [in the American government] which hoped that during the Second World War they [the United States] would succeed in avoiding . . . the main battles in the war, [and] would enter it only at the last minute, when it could easily affect the outcome of the war, completely ensuring its interests.

In this regard, [the Americans] thought that the main competitors of the US would be crushed or greatly weakened in the war, and the US by virtue of this circumstance would assume the role of the most powerful factor in resolving the fundamental questions of the postwar world. These calculations were also based on the assumption . . . that the USSR . . . would also be exhausted or even completely destroyed as a result of the war.

Reality did not bear out the calculations of the American imperialists.

The two main aggressive powers, fascist Germany and militarist Japan, which were at the same time the main competitors of the US in both the economic and foreign policy fields, were thoroughly defeated. The third great power Great Britain . . . now faces enormous economic and political difficulties. . . . Europe has come out of the war with a completely dislocated economy, and the economic devastation that occurred in the course of the war cannot be overcome in a short time. All of the countries of Europe and Asia are experiencing a colossal need for consumer goods, industrial and transportation equipment, etc. Such a situation provides American monopolistic capital with prospects for . . . it to infiltrate their national economies. Such

---

Source: Nikolai Novikov, "Telegram to Moscow" (27 September 1946), in *Origins of the Cold War,* ed. Kenneth M. Jensen (Washington, DC: United States Institute of Peace, 1991), 3–10, 12–16. The editors have modified the original text by using the abbreviations "US," "USSR," and "UN."

a development would mean a serious strengthening of the economic position of the US in the whole world and would be a stage on the road to world domination by the US.

On the other hand, we have seen a failure of calculations . . . that the USSR would be destroyed in the war or . . . weakened. . . . Had that happened, they would have been able to dictate conditions . . . without hindrance from the USSR. In actuality, despite all of the economic difficulties of the postwar period connected with the enormous losses inflicted by the war and the German fascist occupation, the USSR continues to remain economically Independent of the outside world and is rebuilding its national economy with its own forces.

At the same time the USSR's international position is currently stronger than it was in the prewar period. Thanks to the historic victories of Soviet weapons, the Soviet armed forces are located on the territory of Germany and other formerly hostile countries, thus guaranteeing that these countries will not be used again for an attack on the USSR. . . . [D]emocratic* reconstruction [in Eastern and Southeastern Europe] has established regimes . . . friendly . . . with the USSR. . . . The enormous relative weight of the USSR in international affairs in general and in the European countries in particular, the independence of its foreign policy, and the economic and political assistance that it provides to neighboring countries . . . cannot help but be regarded by the American imperialists as an obstacle in the path of the expansionist policy of the US.

The foreign policy of the US is not determined at present by the circles in the Democratic party that (as during Roosevelt's lifetime) strive to strengthen the cooperation of the three great powers† that constituted the basis of the anti-Hitler coalition during the war. The ascendance to power of President Truman, a politically unstable person but with certain conservative tendencies . . . meant a strengthening of the influence on US foreign policy of the most reactionary circles. . . . This is the source of . . . "bi-partisan" foreign policy. At the same time, there has been a decline in the influence on foreign policy of those who follow Roosevelt's course for cooperation among peace-loving countries. . . .

Obvious indications of the US effort to establish world dominance are also to be found in the increase in military potential in peacetime and in the establishment of a large number of naval and air bases both in the US and beyond its borders. In 1946, for the first time in the history of the country, Congress passed a law on the establishment of a peacetime army, not on a volunteer basis but on the basis of universal military service. The size of the army . . . about one million . . . was also increased significantly. . . . At the present time, the American navy occupies first place in the world, leaving far behind [the navies] of other countries. Expenditures on the army and navy have risen colossally, amounting to . . . about 40 percent of the total budget. . . . This is more than ten times greater than corresponding expenditures in the budget for 1938. . . . [A] very extensive system of naval and air bases in the Atlantic and Pacific oceans . . . clearly indicates the offensive nature of the strategic concepts of the commands of the US army and navy.

---

*"Democratic" here refers to socialist governments, organized along lines dictated by the Soviets.
†Great Britain, the USSR, and the United States.

The US at the present time is in control of China* and Japan. . . . The American policy in China is striving for the complete economic and political submission of China to the control of American monopolistic capital. Following this policy . . . there are more than 50,000 American soldiers. . . . China is gradually being transformed into a bridgehead for the American armed forces. . . . In Japan, despite the small contingent of American troops . . . control is in the hands of the Americans. . . .

The US [is also interested in] its own more thorough penetration of the Mediterranean basin and Near East, to which the US is attracted by the area's natural resources, primarily oil. In recent years American capital has penetrated very intensively into the economy of the Near Eastern countries [and] American capital . . . now controls about 42 percent of all proven reserves in the Near East, excluding Iran. . . . In expanding in the Near East, American capital has English capital as its greatest and most stubborn competitor. The fierce competition between them is the chief factor preventing England and the US from reaching an understanding on the division of spheres of influence in the Near East, a division that can occur only at the expense of direct British interests in this region. . . .

. . . The ruling circles of the US obviously have a sympathetic attitude toward the idea of a military alliance with England, but at the present time the matter has not yet culminated in an official alliance. Churchill's speech in Fulton† calling for the conclusion of an Anglo-American military alliance for the purpose of establishing joint domination over the world was therefore not supported officially by Truman . . . although Truman by his presence [during the speech] did indirectly sanction Churchill's appeal. Even if the US does not go so far as to conclude a military alliance with England just now, in practice they still maintain very close contact on military questions. . . .

The "hard-line" policy with regard to the USSR . . . of the reactionary Democrats with the Republicans is at present the main obstacle on the road to cooperation of the Great Powers. The present policy of the American government with regard to the USSR is also directed at limiting or dislodging the influence of the USSR from neighboring countries. . . . [T]he US attempts . . . to support reactionary forces with the purpose of creating obstacles to the process of democratization of these countries. In so doing, it also attempts to secure positions for the penetration of American capital into their economies. . . .

One of the most important elements in the general policy of the US, which is directed toward limiting the international role of the USSR in the post war world, is the policy with regard to Germany. . . . The American occupation policy does not have the objective of eliminating the remnants of German Fascism and rebuilding German political life on a democratic basis, so that Germany might cease to exist as an aggressive force. . . . Instead, the US is considering the possibility of terminating the Allied occupation of German territory before [achieving] the main tasks of the occu-

---

*At that time, there was a civil war in China between the so-called Nationalist forces of Chiang Kai-shek and the Communists led by Mao Zedong. In 1949, the Communists defeated the Nationalists, who then fled to the island of Taiwan (see chapter 12).

†Former British Prime Minister Winston Churchill gave a speech at Westminster College in Fulton, Missouri, on March 5, 1946, in which he coined the phrase "iron curtain" to describe Soviet control of Eastern Europe. Whatever his intention, he did not directly call for joint Anglo-American domination of the world.

pation—the demilitarization and democratization of Germany. . . . One cannot help seeing that such a policy has a clearly outlined anti-Soviet edge and constitutes a serious danger to the cause of peace.

The numerous and extremely hostile statements by American government, political, and military figures with regard to the USSR and its foreign policy are very characteristic of the current relationship between the ruling circles of the US and the USSR. These statements are echoed in an even more unrestrained tone by the overwhelming majority of the American press organs.

Talk about a "third war," meaning a war against the USSR, even a direct call for this war—with the threat of using the atomic bomb—such is the content of the statements on relations with the USSR. . . . [P]reaching war against the USSR is not a monopoly of the far-right, yellow American press. . . . This anti-Soviet campaign also has been joined by the "reputable" and "respectable" organs of the conservative press, such as the *New York Times*. . . .

The basic goal of this anti-Soviet campaign of American "public opinion" is to exert political pressure on the USSR and compel it to make concessions. Another, no less important goal of the campaign is the attempt to create an atmosphere of war psychosis among the masses, who are weary of war, thus making it easier for the US government to carry out measures for the maintenance of high military potential. It was in this very atmosphere that the law on universal military service in peacetime was passed by Congress, that the huge military budget was adopted, and that plans are being worked out for the construction of an extensive system of naval and air bases.

Of course, all of these measures . . . are only intended to prepare the conditions for winning world supremacy in a new war . . . which is contemplated by the most bellicose circles of American imperialism.

Careful note should be taken of the fact that the preparation by the US for a future war is being conducted with the prospect of war against the USSR, which in the eyes of the American imperialists is the main obstacle in the path of the US to world domination. This is indicated by facts such as the tactical training of the American army for war with the USSR as the future opponent, the siting of American strategic bases in regions from which it is possible to launch strikes on Soviet territory, intensified training and strengthening of Arctic regions as close approaches to the USSR, and attempts to prepare Germany and Japan to use those countries in a war against the USSR.

AMERICAN VIEWS OF THE SOVIET UNION AND THE COLD WAR

George Kennan (1904–2005) was one of the most distinguished American diplomats of the twentieth century, and his article "The Sources of Soviet Conduct" (1947) is one of the most influential documents in American diplomatic history. As chargé d'affaires in the American embassy in Moscow, he was singularly well placed to observe and assess the Soviet leadership, particularly because he had served in a variety of foreign service positions in Europe since 1927. From 1947 to 1950, he worked in the State Department in high-level planning and advisory roles. He was ambassador to Moscow briefly in 1952. It is hard to overestimate his impact on American Cold War foreign policy. Possessed of a unique combination of knowledge of Russian history, the ability to synthesize and communicate insights based on that knowledge, and the authority within the foreign policy community of the United States to ensure that his opinions would be heard and heeded, Kennan left a deep imprint on America's view of the Soviet Union, both through his government service and especially through the document excerpted here.[8] In 1989, Kennan was awarded the Medal of Freedom by President Bush in honor of his many years in government and lifetime of scholarly writings.

In "The Sources of Soviet Conduct," Kennan elaborated on the ideas that he had addressed in his famous "long telegram" of February 1946. This had come just six months after the surrender of Japan had marked the effective end of World War II. The main purpose of both of Kennan's documents was to present the essential elements of the Russo-Soviet historical experience, worldview, and political system in order that the United States could formulate effective, well-grounded policies consistent with its own traditions, experiences, and values. His conclusions provided the framework for a set of policies that have become known as "containment," which shaped American cold war strategy for at least four decades and articulated America's self-perception in its struggle against the forces of Communism.

If the idea of containment was Kennan's brainchild, it was left to the presidency of Harry S. Truman (1945–1953) to give it shape in actual policies. Harry Truman (1884–1972) was a man of modest background who achieved the nation's highest office by dint of ability, effort, honesty, and straightforwardness. Although his early political success owed a great deal to the support of the corrupt Kansas City political machine of Democrat Thomas Pendergast, Truman established a reputation of honesty and trust among the voters that earned him two terms as a U.S. Senator from Missouri. Selected by Roosevelt to be his vice-presidential running mate in the 1944 elections, Truman succeeded to the presidency less than three months after the inauguration, when Roosevelt died unexpectedly. Possessing little of Roosevelt's flair and popular appeal, Truman was nonetheless a capable administrator and a no-nonsense leader. This style was evident in his dealings with Stalin, and it is best remembered in his come-from-behind 1948 re-election campaign, during which he condemned the "do-nothing, good-for-nothing Republican Congress." Voters responded by urging him to "Give 'em hell, Harry!" and elected him to another term as president.

Truman's presidency coincided with the early and uncertain days of the Cold War. During his administration (1945–1952), Soviet victories in World War II had placed the Red Army in control of Poland, Romania, Bulgaria, Hungary, Czechoslovakia, eastern Germany, and part of Austria. In devastated western Europe, Communist Party members were also gaining power and influence. It did not take Truman long to respond to this perceived threat. In March 1946, he traveled from Washington to Fulton, Missouri, to be present at the speech by Winston Churchill, in which the former British prime minister said that "an iron curtain has descended across Europe." Churchill also called on the United States to assume global leadership and to constrain Soviet aggression by means of a strong defense and an active cooperation with England. Exactly one year and one week later, Truman addressed Congress in joint session in the speech in which he laid out his broad foreign policy objectives to contain the Communist menace.[9] The Truman Doctrine provided a coherent strategy for American foreign policy in the Cold War and justified America's intervention in the Korean War (1950–1953). In 1952, Truman declined to run for reelection and retired to his home in Missouri, where he died twenty years later at the age of 88.

Although American efforts to contain Communism in Europe were largely effective, the results were less successful elsewhere, particularly in Asia. In 1948, the Communist armies of Mao Zedong succeeded in gaining control of mainland China, pushing the American-backed forces of Chiang Kai-shek and the Chinese Nationalists to seek refuge on the island of Taiwan. Then, from 1950 to 1953, the United States was embroiled in the Korean War, which also involved combat against Chinese Communist forces. Because the Soviet Union had successfully developed a nuclear weapon by 1949, because the Communists controlled the most populous country in the world (China), and because the United States could not even unseat the Communist government in North Korea, it seemed to many Americans that the United States was losing the Cold War.

In America, fear of further Communist advances and frustration that the "superior" American system was losing ground to Communism led to the search for someone to blame. These problems bred accusations that President Truman was "soft" on Communism. The discovery of a limited number of Communists working for the federal government and the conviction in 1951 and execution in 1953 of Julius and Ethel Rosenberg, who stole nuclear secrets for the Soviets, further aggravated the siege mentality of the country.[10] In the context of the Cold War and the Korean War, a spasm of paranoia and defensiveness rippled across America that has become known as the Red Scare. Unsupported accusations were made that ruined both careers and lives, and suspected Communist supporters were "blacklisted" (banned from employment).

One of the leading figures of the domestic anti-Communism movement was J. Edgar Hoover (1895–1972), the long-time director of the Federal Bureau of Investigation (FBI). Under Hoover's direction, the FBI took the lead in the hunt for suspected Communists and Communist sympathizers. Hoover had participated in the roundup of suspected radicals during the first Red Scare in the 1920s, and he had developed a close relationship with other fervent anti-Communists, including former FBI subordinates who were highly placed in the American Legion. In later years, Hoover's staunch views compelled him to amass secret files on liberal politicians and to order the FBI to conduct surveillance on Dr. Martin Luther King, Jr., and the civil rights movement.

An important statement of Hoover's anti-Communism was his September 1946 speech to the annual convention of the American Legion in San Francisco. It contains in succinct form his ideas about the insidious nature of the threat posed by Communism to the United States and what must be done to combat that threat.

Taken together, George Kennan's article, President Truman's speech to Congress, and Hoover's address to the American Legion set the tone for American understanding of the nature of Communism and of the Soviet Union in the postwar period and what America's relationship to them ought to be. They formed the frame of the window through which most Americans viewed the Cold War in the 1950s and early 1960s

QUESTIONS TO CONSIDER

1. How, according to Kennan, did "ideology and circumstances" combine to produce the "political personality" of the Soviet Union? Was the Soviet worldview based on rational or irrational principles?

2. As outlined by Kennan, what were Soviet foreign policy goals after World War II? What evidence did he include to support his case? Is it reliable?

3. According to President Truman, what should be the primary policy objective of the United States? How does The Truman Doctrine symbolize American self-identity during the Cold War? In your estimation, to what degree does this policy and manner of self-identification continue at present?

4. How did J. Edgar Hoover characterize American Communists, and why did he consider them a threat? As FBI director, what policies might he propose to deal with the threats? In your opinion, were his views consistent with or antithetical to the values of American freedom?

5. In your assessment, what were the most significant misconceptions that the Americans had of Soviet policy and goals after World War II? What factors most contributed to these misconceptions?

"THE SOURCES OF SOVIET CONDUCT"
(1947)

X [George F. Kennan]

The political personality of Soviet power as we know it today is the product of ideology and circumstances: ideology inherited by the present Soviet leaders from the movement in which they had their political origin, and circumstances of the power which they now have exercised for nearly three decades in Russia. There can be few tasks of psychological analysis more difficult than to try to trace the interaction of these two forces and the relative role of each in the determination of official Soviet conduct. Yet the attempt must be made if that conduct is to be understood and effectively countered. . . .

Source: X [George F. Kennan], "The Sources of Soviet Conduct," Foreign Affairs 25 (July 1947): 566–78, 580–82. Reprinted with permission.

The outstanding features of Communist thought . . . may perhaps be summarized as follows: (a) that the central factor in the life of man . . . is the system by which material goods are produced and exchanged; (b) that the capitalist system of production is a nefarious one which inevitably leads to the exploitation of the working class by the capital-owning class . . . ; (c) that capitalism contains the seeds of its own destruction and must . . . result eventually and inescapably in a revolutionary transfer of power to the working class; and (d) that imperialism, the final phase of capitalism, leads directly to war and revolution. . . . It must be noted that there was no assumption that capitalism would perish without proletarian revolution. . . .

[T]his pattern of thought had exercised great fascination for the members of the Russian revolutionary movement. Frustrated, discontented, hopeless of finding self-expression . . . , yet lacking wide popular support for their choice of bloody revolution as a means of social betterment, these revolutionists found in Marxist theory a highly convenient rationalization for their own instinctive desires . . . , pseudo-scientific justification for their . . . yearning for power and revenge. . . . It is therefore no wonder that they had come to believe implicitly in the truth and soundness of the Marxist-Leninist teachings. . . .

Stalin, and those whom he led in the struggle for succession to Lenin's position of leadership, were not the men to tolerate rival political forces. . . . Their sense of insecurity was too great. Their particular brand of fanaticism, unmodified by any of the Anglo-Saxon traditions of compromise, was too fierce and too jealous to envisage any permanent sharing of power. From the Russian-Asiatic world out of which they had emerged they carried with them a skepticism as to the possibilities of permanent and peaceful coexistence of rival forces. Easily persuaded of their own doctrinaire "rightness," they insisted on the submission or destruction of all competing power. . . .

Now it lies in the nature of the mental world of the Soviet leaders, as well as in the character of their ideology, to justify the retention of the dictatorship by stressing the menace of capitalism abroad. . . . By the same token, tremendous emphasis has been placed on the original Communist thesis of a basic antagonism between the capitalist and Socialist worlds. It is clear, from many indications, that this emphasis is not founded in . . . the realities of foreign antagonism but in the necessity of explaining away the maintenance of dictatorial authority at home. . . .

So much for the historical background. What does it spell in terms of the political personality of Soviet power as we know it today?

The first of these [Soviet guiding] concepts is that of the innate antagonism between capitalism and Socialism. . . . It has profound implications for Russia's conduct as a member of international society. . . . If the Soviet government occasionally sets its signature to [diplomatic] documents . . . , this is to be regarded as a tactical maneuver permissible in dealing with the enemy (who is without honor). . . . Basically, the antagonism remains. . . . And from it flow[s] the Kremlin's conduct of foreign policy: the secretiveness, the lack of frankness, the duplicity, the wary suspiciousness, and the basic unfriendliness of purpose. These phenomena are there to stay. . . . These characteristics of Soviet policy . . . are basic to the internal nature of Soviet power, and will be with us until the internal nature of Soviet power is changed. . . .

What is vital [to them] is that the "Socialist fatherland" . . . should be cherished and defended by all good Communists at home and abroad. . . . The cause of Socialism is the support and promotion of Soviet power, as defined in Moscow.

This brings us to the second of the concepts important to contemporary Soviet outlook. That is the infallibility of the Kremlin. The Soviet concept of power . . . requires that the Party leadership remain in theory the sole repository of truth. . . . The leadership of the Communist Party is therefore always right. . . .

On the principle of infallibility there rests the iron discipline of the Communist Party. In fact, the two concepts are mutually self-supporting. . . . But their effect cannot be understood unless a third factor be taken into account: namely, the fact that the leadership is at liberty to put forward for tactical purposes any particular thesis which it finds useful . . . and to require the faithful and unquestioning acceptance of that thesis by the members of the movement as a whole. This means that truth is not a constant but is actually created, for all intents and purposes, by the Soviet leaders themselves. . . . It is nothing absolute and immutable—nothing which flows from objective reality. . . . Thus those at the top, who are capable of changing the party line [cannot be] . . . swayed by any normal logic. . . . For this reason, facts speak louder than words to the ears of the Kremlin. . . .

The very teachings of Lenin himself require great caution and flexibility in the pursuit of Communist purposes. Again, these precepts are fortified by the lessons of Russian history: of centuries of obscure battles between nomadic forces over the stretches of a vast unfortified plain. Here caution, circumspection, flexibility and deception are the valuable qualities; and their value finds a natural appreciation in the Russian or the oriental mind. Thus the Kremlin has no compunction about retreating in the face of superior forces. . . . Its political action is a fluid stream which moves constantly, wherever it is permitted to move, toward a given goal. . . . But if it finds unassailable barriers in its path, it accepts these philosophically and accommodates itself to them. The main thing is that there should always be pressure, unceasing constant pressure, toward the desired goal. . . .

And the patient persistence by which it is animated means that it can be effectively countered not by sporadic acts . . . but only by intelligent long-range policies on the part of Russia's adversaries—policies no less steady in their purpose, and no less variegated and resourceful in their application, than those of the Soviet Union itself.

In these circumstances it is clear that the main element of any United States policy toward the Soviet Union must be that of long-term, patient but firm and vigilant containment of Russian expansive tendencies. . . . For these reasons it is a sine qua non of successful dealing with Russia that the foreign government in question should remain at all times cool and collected. . . .

In the light of the above, it will be clearly seen that the Soviet pressure against the free institutions of the western world is something that can be contained by the adroit and vigilant application of counter-force at a series of constantly shifting geographical and political points, corresponding to the shifts and maneuvers of Soviet policy, but which cannot be charmed or talked out of existence. The Russians look forward to a duel of infinite duration. . . .

Let us suppose that the western world finds the strength and resourcefulness to contain Soviet power over a period of ten to fifteen years. What does that spell for Russia itself? . . . The Kremlin accomplish[ed] its purpose of building up Russia . . . at a terrible cost in human life and in human hopes and energies. . . . It has involved the neglect or abuse of other phases of Soviet economic life. . . . To all that, the war [World War II] has added its tremendous toll of destruction, death and human exhaustion. . . .

It is difficult to see how these deficiencies can be corrected at an early date by a tired and dispirited population working largely under the shadow of fear and compulsion. And as long as they are not overcome, Russia will remain economically as vulnerable, and in a certain sense an impotent, nation, capable of exporting its enthusiasms and of radiating the strange charm of its primitive political vitality but unable to back up those articles of export by the real evidences of material power and prosperity. . . .

Thus the future of Soviet power may not be by any means as secure as Russian capacity for self-delusion would make it appear to the men of the Kremlin. . . . [T]he possibility remains (and in the opinion of this writer it is a strong one) that Soviet power . . . bears within it the seeds of its own decay, and that the sprouting of these seeds is well advanced.

It is clear that the United States . . . must continue to regard the Soviet Union as a rival, not a partner, in the political arena. It must continue to expect that Soviet policies will reflect . . . no real faith in the possibility of a permanent happy coexistence of the Socialist and capitalist worlds, but rather a cautious, persistent pressure toward the disruption and weakening of all rival influence and rival power.

Balanced against this are the facts that Russia . . . is still by far the weaker party, that Soviet policy is highly flexible, and that Soviet society may well contain deficiencies which will eventually weaken its own total potential. This would of itself warrant the United States entering with reasonable confidence upon a policy of firm containment, designed to confront the Russians with unalterable counter-force at every point where they show signs of encroaching upon the interests of a peaceful and stable world.

But in actuality the possibilities for American policy are by no means limited to holding the line and hoping for the best. It is entirely possible for the United States to influence by its [ability to] create among the peoples of the world generally the impression of a country which knows what it wants, which is coping successfully with the problem of its internal life and with the responsibilities of a World Power, and which has a spiritual vitality capable of holding its own among the major ideological currents of the time. To the extent that such an impression can be created and maintained, the aims of Russian Communism must appear sterile and quixotic, the hopes and enthusiasm of Moscow's supporters must wane, and added strain must be imposed on the Kremlin's foreign policies. . . .

It would be an exaggeration to say that American behavior unassisted and alone could exercise a power of life and death over the Communist movement and bring about the early fall of Soviet power in Russia. But the United States has it in its power to increase enormously the strains under which Soviet policy must operate, to force upon the Kremlin a far greater degree of moderation and circumspection than it has had to observe in recent years, and in this way to promote tendencies which must eventually find their outlet in either the breakup or the gradual mellowing of Soviet power. For no mystical, Messianic movement—and particularly not that of the Kremlin—can face frustration indefinitely without eventually adjusting itself in one way or another to the logic of that state of affairs. . . .

The issue of Soviet-American relations is in essence a test of the overall worth of the United States as a nation among nations. To avoid destruction the United States need only measure up to its own best traditions and prove itself worthy of preservation as a great nation.

Surely, there was never a fairer test of national quality than this. In the light of these circumstances, the thoughtful observer of Russian-American relations will find no cause for complaint in the Kremlin's challenge to American society. He will rather experience a certain gratitude to a Providence which, by providing the American people with this implacable challenge, has made their entire security as a nation dependent on their pulling themselves together and accepting the responsibilities of moral and political leadership that history plainly intended them to bear.

THE TRUMAN DOCTRINE (1947)

Harry S. Truman

Mr. President [of the Senate], Mr. Speaker, Members of the Congress of the United States:

The gravity of the situation which confronts the world today necessitates my appearance before a joint session of the Congress. The foreign policy and the national security of this country are involved. . . .

One of the primary objectives of the foreign policy of the United States is the creation of conditions in which we and other nations will be able to work out a way of life free from coercion. This was a fundamental issue in the war with Germany and Japan. Our victory was won over countries which sought to impose their will, and their way of life, upon other nations.

To ensure the peaceful development of nations, free from coercion, the United States has taken a leading part in establishing the United Nations. The United Nations is designed to make possible lasting freedom and independence for all its members. We shall not realize our objectives, however, unless we are willing to help free peoples to maintain their free institutions and their national integrity against aggressive movements that seek to impose upon them totalitarian regimes.

This is no more than a frank recognition that totalitarian regimes imposed on free peoples, by direct or indirect aggression, undermine the foundations of international peace and hence the security of the United States.

The peoples of a number of countries of the world have recently had totalitarian regimes forced upon them against their will. The Government of the United States has made frequent protests against coercion and intimidation, in violation of the Yalta agreement*. . . .

Source: Harry S. Truman, Message to Congress (March 12, 1947); Document 171; 80th Cong. 1st sess., *Records of the United States House of Representatives;* Record Group 233; National Archives.

*The Yalta Conference in February 1945 was one of the wartime meetings between Stalin, Roosevelt, and Prime Minister Winston Churchill of Great Britain. The agreement, which became very controversial, called for the creation of the United Nations, yielded concessions to the Soviets in the Far East in return for a promise to help the U.S. in the war against Japan, and granted the USSR territorial gains in Europe. It also called for "free and unfettered elections," which were never allowed by the Soviets.

At the present moment in world history nearly every nation must choose between alternative ways of life. The choice is too often not a free one. One way of life is based upon the will of the majority, and is distinguished by free institutions, representative government, free elections, guarantees of individual liberty, freedom of speech and religion, and freedom from political oppression. The second way of life is based upon the will of a minority forcibly imposed upon the majority. It relies upon terror and oppression, a controlled press and radio; fixed elections, and the suppression of personal freedoms. I believe that it must be the policy of the United States to support free peoples who are resisting attempted subjugation by armed minorities or by outside pressures. I believe that we must assist free peoples to work out their own destinies in their own way. I believe that our help should be primarily through economic and financial aid which is essential to economic stability and orderly political processes. . . .

The seeds of totalitarian regimes are nurtured by misery and want. They spread and grow in the evil soil of poverty and strife. They reach their full growth when the hope of a people for a better life has died. We must keep that hope alive.

The free peoples of the world look to us for support in maintaining their freedoms. If we falter in our leadership, we may endanger the peace of the world—and we shall surely endanger the welfare of our own nation. Great responsibilities have been placed upon us by the swift movement of events. I am confident that the Congress will face these responsibilities squarely.

"THE THREAT OF COMMUNISM" (1946)

J. Edgar Hoover

I accept the Distinguished Service Medal of the American Legion on behalf of my associates in the Federal Bureau of Investigation who have made its achievements possible. Bulwarking the men and women of the FBI are the high hopes and expectations of the loyal Americans whom we serve. The American Legion is a great force for good in this nation. It exemplifies the traditions of our country and is living testimony to the spirit of America. . . .

The record of your achievements is now history. Today, there is a greater need than ever before for the American Legion and its stabilizing force. We of the FBI need your help now even more than during the war years if the battle for a safe and secure America is to be won. Our enemies are massing their forces . . . and we have a formidable foe. I refer to the growing menace of Communism in the United States.

During the past five years, American Communists have made their deepest inroads upon our national life. In our vaunted tolerance for all peoples the Communist

Source: J. Edgar Hoover's speech at the annual convention of the American Legion, San Francisco, CA, September 30, 1946, is cited in full in House Report No. 2742, "Investigation of Un-American Activities and Propaganda," Report of the Committee on Un-American Activities, 79th Cong., 2d sess., Reel 17.

has found our "Achilles' heel." The American Legion represents a force which holds within its power the ability to expose the hypocrisy and ruthlessness of this foreign "ism" which has crept into our national life—an "ism" built and supported by dishonor, deceit, tyranny and a deliberate policy of falsehood.

It is a matter of self-preservation. The veteran who fought for America will be among the first to suffer if the Communists succeed in carrying out their diabolical plots to wreck the American way of life. The "divide and conquer" tactics did not die with Hitler—they are being employed with greater skill today by American Communists with their "boring from within" strategy. Their propaganda, skillfully designed and adroitly executed, has been projected into practically every phase of our national life. The fact that the Communist Party in the United States claims some 100,000 members* has lulled many Americans into feelings of false complacency. I would not be concerned if we were dealing with only 100,000 Communists. The Communists themselves boast that for every Party member there are ten others ready to do the Party's work. These include their satellites, their fellow-travelers and their so-called progressive and phony liberal allies. They have maneuvered themselves into positions where a few Communists control the destinies of hundreds who are either willing to be led or have been duped into obeying the dictates of others.

The average American working man is loyal, patriotic and law-abiding. He wants security for his family and himself. But in some unions the rank and file find themselves between a Communist pincers, manipulated by a few leaders who have hoodwinked and browbeaten them into a state of submission. . . .

The Communist influence has projected itself into some newspapers, magazines, books, radio and the screen. Some churches, schools, colleges and even fraternal orders have been penetrated, not with the approval of the rank and file but in spite of them. I have been pleased to observe that the Communist attempts to penetrate the American Legion have met with failure. Eternal vigilance will continue to keep your ranks free of shifty, double-crossing Communist destructionists.

We are rapidly reaching the time when loyal Americans must be willing to stand up and be counted. The American Communist Party, despite its claims, is not truly a political party. The Communist Party in this country is not working for the general welfare of all our people—it is working against our people. It is not interested in providing for the common defense. It has for its purpose the shackling of America and its conversion to the Godless, Communist way of life. If it were a political party its adherents could be appealed to by reason. Instead, it is a system of intrigue, actuated by fanaticism. It knows no rules of decency. Its unprincipled converts would sell America short if it would help their cause of furthering an alien way of life conceived in darkness and motivated by greed for power whose ultimate aim is the destruction of our cherished freedom. Let us no longer be misled by their sly propaganda and false preachments on civil liberty. They want civil license to do as they please and, if they get control, liberty for Americans will be but a haunted memory. For those who seek to provoke prejudice and stir up the public mind to angry resentment against our form of government are a menace to the very powers of law and order which guarantee and safeguard popular rights.

---

*This is a very high estimate.

We, of this generation, have faced two great menaces in America—Fascism and Communism. Both are materialistic; both are totalitarian; both are anti-religious; both are degrading and inhuman. In fact, they differ little except in name. Communism has bred Fascism and Fascism spawns Communism. Both are the antithesis of American belief in liberty and freedom. If the peoples of other countries want Communism, let them have it, but it has no place in America. [German and Japanese] brands of Fascism were met and defeated on the battlefield. All those who stand for the American way of life must arise and defeat Red Fascism in America by focusing upon it the spotlight of public opinion and by building up barriers of common decency through which it cannot penetrate.

Such a crusade cannot be spearheaded by any force more potent than the American Legion, composed as it is of America's heroes who have proved their mettle in battle.

The men and women who defeated the Nazi brand of Fascism with bullets can defeat the Red brand of Fascism by raising their voices in behalf of Democracy and by exposure and denunciation of every force which weakens America.

The American Legion, ordained to bring together the veterans of World War I to perpetuate the associations made on foreign soil, is being expanded by the influx of veterans of World War II, who likewise fought that America might live. To allow America to become infected with the malignant growth of Communism or to be infested by crime is a breach of our trust to those who gave their lives for American principles.

Let us gird ourselves with the determination that those basic freedoms and spiritual ideals for which so many have sacrificed so much shall not be destroyed from within.

Let us be steadfast for America, work and live for America, and eternally be on guard to defend our Constitution and our way of life against the virulent poison of Communistic ideology.

VIETNAMESE VIEWS ON DECOLONIZATION AND THE VIETNAM WAR

In September 1945, the same month that World War II officially ended, Ho Chi Minh (1890–1969) declared both Vietnamese independence and the establishment of the Democratic Republic of Vietnam. Ho, the head of the Vietminh (the League for the Independence of Vietnam), was both a Communist and the main leader of the Vietnamese nationalist, anticolonial movement. Ho had been raised in a proindependence family, and he actually tried to present a petition for Vietnamese independence to President Woodrow Wilson in Paris in 1919. Rebuffed by the west, Ho turned to Communism and the Soviet Union, where he trained as a revolutionary in the 1920s. Having worked in the 1920s and 1930s as a revolutionary organizer in China and Moscow, Ho returned to Vietnam with the outbreak of World War II. There he established the Vietminh and cooperated, especially with American intelligence agents, in the war against the Japanese. The Japanese had ruled Indochina through the remaining French colonial authorities up to the very end of the war, when they set up direct Japanese rule. Thus, when the Japanese forces withdrew, there was no established government in Vietnam. Ho took advantage of this vacuum to proclaim the Vietnamese Declaration of Independence (1945), hoping that the United States would support his cause.[11]

Although Ho Chi Minh was the main political leader of the Vietminh, the dominant military figure was Vo Nguyen Giap (1912–). Like Ho, Giap was a long-time revolutionary and nationalist. He studied guerrilla warfare with the Chinese Communist leader, Mao Zedong, and he devised the successful strategy for defeating first the French and then the Americans. When Ho proclaimed the Democratic Republic of Vietnam, Giap was both minister of defense and commander-in-chief of the army. He was the mastermind behind both the decisive Vietnamese victory over the French at Dien Bien Phu in 1954 and the politically decisive Tet Offensive against the United States and South Vietnamese in 1968. In his essay, "The People's War" (1961), he explains the general strategic conceptions that governed Vietnamese military tactics throughout the struggle for Vietnamese independence.

A final Vietnamese perspective is offered by Nguyen Tan Thanh, a common soldier from the Communist Vietcong forces. He explains his social and economic experiences before joining the military and how these affected his worldview. His perspective supplements the grand political and military visions of Ho and Giap and allows us a glimpse of the way the average Vietnamese received and responded to the Communist interpretation of the struggle against the South Vietnamese and the Americans.

QUESTIONS TO CONSIDER

1. What are the ideas and values expressed in the Vietnamese Declaration of Independence? How does it reflect Ho Chi Minh's view of Vietnamese history and decolonization? To what degree is the Declaration shaped by Ho Chi Minh's Marxist ideology?

2. Identify the main elements of the grand strategy mapped out by General Giap in "The People's War." Why is guerrilla warfare necessary—does it reflect an attempt by a minority to impose its will on the majority?

3. What assumptions did General Giap make about the duration of the conflict and the Vietnamese people's commitment to it? In your estimation, would a long stuggle have undermined or strengthened the people's commitment to decolonization? How might it have affected the values expressed in the Vietnamese Declaration of Independence?

4. What was the perspective of the Vietcong recruit, Nguyen Tan Thanh, on the struggle against the South Vietnamese government and the Americans? How does it compare with the views of Ho and Giap?

5. How were these Vietnamese views shaped by Communist ideology and by anticolonial sentiments? Could the United States have supported the anticolonialism and not the Communism? How do the values revealed in the Vietnamese documents compare with Kennan's view of Russian Communism?

THE VIETNAMESE DECLARATION
OF INDEPENDENCE (1945)

Ho Chi Minh

All men are created equal; they are endowed by their Creator with certain unalienable Rights; among these are Life, Liberty, and the pursuit of Happiness

This immortal statement was made in the Declaration of Independence of the United States of America in 1776. In a broader sense, this means: All the peoples on the earth are equal from birth, all the peoples have a right to live, to be happy and free.

The Declaration of the French Revolution made in 1791 on the Rights of Man and the Citizen also states: "All men are born free and with equal rights, and must always remain free and have equal rights." Those are undeniable truths.

Nevertheless, for more than eighty years, the French imperialists, abusing the standard of Liberty, Equality, and Fraternity,* have violated our Fatherland and oppressed our fellow citizens. They have acted contrary to the ideals of humanity and justice.

In the field of politics, they have deprived our people of every democratic liberty.

They have enforced inhuman laws; they have . . . prevent[ed] our people from being united.

They have built more prisons than schools. They have mercilessly slain our patriots; they have drowned our uprisings in rivers of blood. . . .

In the field of economics, they have fleeced us to the backbone, impoverished our people and devastated our land. . . .

[W]hen the Japanese fascists violated Indochina's territory to establish new bases in their fight against the Allies, the French imperialists went down on their bended knees and handed over our country to them.

Thus, from that date, our people were subjected to the double yoke of the French and the Japanese [and] more than two million of our fellow citizens died from starvation. . . . The French colonialists either fled or surrendered. . . .

The Viet Minh League urged the French to ally themselves with it against the Japanese. Instead . . . before fleeing they massacred a great number of our political prisoners. . . . From the autumn of 1940, our country had in fact ceased to be a French colony and had become a Japanese possession.

After the Japanese had surrendered to the Allies, our whole people rose to regain our national sovereignty and to found the Democratic Republic of Viet-Nam. . . . The French have fled, the Japanese have capitulated, Emperor Bao Dai† has abdicated. Our people have broken the chains which . . . have fettered them and have won independence for the Fatherland. . . .

Source: Ho Chi Minh, Declaration of Independence of the Democratic Republic of Vietnam, in *On Revolution*, ed. Bernard B. Fall, 143–45. Copyright © 1967 by Praeger Publishers. Reproduced by permission of Greenwood Publishing Group, Inc., Westport, CT.

*The rallying cry of the French Revolution.

†The last Vietnamese emperor, he was little more than a figurehead under the French colonial administration. He abdicated in 1945.

We are convinced that the Allied nations, which at Teheran and San Francisco* have acknowledged the principles of self-determination and equality of nations, will not refuse to acknowledge the independence of Viet-Nam.

A people who have courageously opposed French domination for more than eighty years, a people who have fought side by side with the Allies against the fascists during these last years, such a people must be free and independent.

For these reasons, we, members of the Provisional Government of the Democratic Republic of Viet-Nam, solemnly declare to the world that Viet-Nam has the right to be a free and independent country—and in fact it is so already. The entire Vietnamese people are determined to mobilize all their physical and mental strength, to sacrifice their lives and property in order to safeguard their independence and liberty.

"THE PEOPLE'S WAR" (1961)

Vo Nguyen Giap

The Vietnamese people's war of liberation was a just war, aiming to win back the independence and unity of the country, to bring land to our peasants and guarantee them the right to it, and to defend the achievements of the August Revolution. That is why it was first and foremost a people's war. To educate, mobilise, organise and arm the whole people in order that they might take part in the Resistance was a crucial question.

The enemy of the Vietnamese nation was aggressive imperialism, which had to be overthrown. But the latter having long since joined up with the feudal landlords, the anti-imperialist struggle could definitely not be separated from anti-feudal action. On the other hand, in a backward colonial country such as ours where the peasants make up the majority of the population, *a people's war is essentially a peasant's war under the leadership of the working class.* Owing to this fact, a general mobilisation of the whole people is neither more nor less than the mobilisation of the rural masses. The problem of land is of decisive importance. From an exhaustive analysis, the Vietnamese people's war of liberation was essentially a people's national democratic revolution carried out under armed form and had a twofold fundamental task: the overthrowing of imperialism and the defeat of the feudal landlord class, the anti-imperialist struggle being the primary task.

A backward colonial country which had only just risen up to proclaim its independence and install people's power, Viet Nam only recently possessed armed forces,

---

*The conference in 1943 at Teheran in modern-day Iran issued a joint declaration by Stalin, Churchill, and Roosevelt calling for the establishment on democratic principles of a United Nations, and the conference in San Francisco in 1945 laid the foundation for the United Nations.

Source: General Vo Nguyen Giap, *People's War, People's Army*, 27–30. Copyright © 1967 by Praeger Publishers. Reproduced by permission of Greenwood Publishing Group, Inc., Westport, CT. All italics in the original.

equipped with still very mediocre arms and having no combat experience. Her enemy, on the other hand, was an imperialist power [France] which has retained a fairly considerable economic and military potentiality despite the recent German occupation [during World War II] and benefitted, furthermore, from the active support of the United States. The balance of forces decidedly showed up our weaknesses against the enemy's power. The Vietnamese people's war of liberation had, therefore, to be a hard and long-lasting war in order to succeed in creating conditions for victory. All the conceptions born of impatience and aimed at obtaining speedy victory could only be gross errors. It was necessary to firmly grasp the strategy of a long-term resistance, and to exalt the will to be self-supporting in order to maintain and gradually augment our forces, while nibbling at and progressively destroying those of the enemy; it was necessary to accumulate thousands of small victories to turn them into a great success, thus gradually altering the balance of forces, in transforming our weakness into power and carrying off final victory.

At an early stage, our Party was able to discern the characteristics of this war: a people's war and a long-lasting war, and it was by proceeding from these premises that, during the whole of hostilities and in particularly difficult conditions, the Party solved all the problems of the Resistance. This judicious leadership by the Party led us to victory.

From the point of view of directing operations, *our strategy and tactics had to be those of a people's war and of a long-term resistance.*

Our strategy was, as we have stressed, to wage a long-lasting battle. A war of this nature in general entails several phases; in principle, starting from a stage of contention, it goes through a period of equilibrium before arriving at a general counteroffensive. In effect, the way in which it is carried on can be more subtle and more complex, depending on the particular conditions obtaining on both sides during the course of operations. Only a long-term war could enable us to utilise to the maximum our political trump cards, to overcome our material handicap and to transform our weakness into strength. To maintain and increase our forces, was the principle to which we adhered, contenting ourselves with attacking when success was certain, refusing to give battle likely to incur losses to us or to engage in hazardous actions. We had to apply the slogan: to build up our strength during the actual course of fighting.

The forms of fighting had to be completely adapted . . . to raise the fighting spirit to the maximum and rely on the heroism of our troops to overcome the enemy's material superiority. In the main, especially at the outset of the war, we had recourse to guerrilla fighting. In the Vietnamese theatre of operations, this method carried off great victories: it could be used in the mountains as well as in the delta, it could be waged with good or mediocre material and even without arms, and was to enable us eventually to equip ourselves at the cost of the enemy. Wherever the Expeditionary Corps came, the entire population took part in the fighting; every commune had its fortified village, every district had its regional troops fighting under the command of the local branches of the Party and the people's administration, in liaison with the regular forces in order to wear down and annihilate the enemy forces.

Thereafter, with the development of our forces, guerrilla warfare changed into a mobile warfare—a form of mobile warfare still strongly marked by guerrilla warfare—which would afterwards become the essential form of operations on the main front, the northern front. In this process of development of guerrilla warfare and of accentuation of the mobile warfare, our people's army constantly grew and passed from the stage of combats involving a section or company, to fairly large-scale campaigns bringing into action several divisions. Gradually, its equipment improved, mainly by the seizure of arms from the enemy—the material of the French and American imperialists.

From the military point of view, *the Vietnamese people's war of liberation proved that an insufficiently equipped people's army, but an army fighting for a just cause, can, with appropriate strategy and tactics, combine the conditions needed to conquer a modern army of aggressive imperialism.*

"WHY I JOINED THE VIETCONG" (1961)

Nguyen Tan Thanh

I joined the VC [Vietcong] when I was thirty-five years old. I was married and had four children. I was leasing farmland—one hectare [about 2.5 acres]—that was very poor in quality, almost sterile. That was why the owner rented it out to us. Despite working hard all year round, we got only about 100 *gia* of rice out of it. Of this amount, 40 *gia* went to the landlord. We borrowed money to buy ducks and geese. We lived a very hard life. But I cultivated the land carefully, and in time it became fertile. When it did, the owner took it back; my livelihood was gone. I had to go back to my parents, to raise ducks for my father.

I was poor. I had lost my land and I didn't have enough money to take care of my children. In 1961 propaganda cadres of the Front [National Liberation Front] contacted me. These guys had joined the resistance against the French, and after Geneva* they had stayed underground in the South. They came to all the poor farmers and made an analysis of the poor and rich classes. They said that the rich people had always served the French and had used the authority of the French to oppress the poor. The majority of the people were poor, not because they wasted their money but because they had been exploited by the landlords who had worked with the French. In the past, the ancestors of the poor had broken ground for tillage. Then powerful people had seized their land. Without any other means to live, the poor had become slaves of the landlords. The cadres told us that if the poor people don't stand up to the rich people, we would be dominated by them forever. The only way to ensure freedom and a sufficient life was to overthrow them.

When I heard the cadres, I thought that what they said was correct. In my village there were about forty-three hundred people. Of these, maybe ten were landlords.

Source: Nguyen Tan Thanh, "Why I Joined the Vietcong," in *Portrait of the Enemy,* eds. D. Chanoff and Doan Van Roai, 42–43. Copyright © 1967 Random House. Used by permission of Random House, Inc.

*The 1954 Geneva Accords that provided for French withdrawal and the division of the country into north and south, pending nationwide elections in 1956.

The richest owned five hundred hectares [1,236 acres], and the others had at least twenty hectares [49 acres] apiece. The rest of the people were tenants or honest poor farmers. I knew that the rich oppressed the poor. The poor had nothing to eat, and they also had no freedom. We had to get rid of the regime that allowed a few people to use their money and authority to oppress the others.

So I joined the Liberation Front. I followed the VC to fight for freedom and prosperity for the country. I felt that this was right.

AMERICAN VIEWS ON DECOLONIZATION AND THE VIETNAM WAR

American involvement in Vietnam began even before the French withdrawal. In fact, the United States provided significant funding to assist the French effort to reestablish colonial control after World War II. From the outset, counsels in the American government were divided. The main issues were whether the anti-Communist movement was strong enough to succeed with U.S. assistance and whether the Vietminh were primarily anticolonial nationalists or representatives of "monolithic" Communism. Despite the policy reservations, American diplomatic, military, and economic investment continued to creep upward. From the mid-1950s to the early 1960s, after the French withdrawal and the division of the country into North and South Vietnam, the Communists tried to destabilize the government in the South by means of guerrilla forces, who came to be known as the Vietcong. When that effort proved insufficient, regular North Vietnamese army units began semiclandestine operations in the South, too. By the mid-1960s, American involvement had escalated dramatically, and by the end of 1965 almost 200,000 American troops were serving in Vietnam.

The man most associated with this buildup was President Lyndon B. Johnson. Johnson was strongly motivated to enact a progressive legislative agenda that included signature "Great Society" programs, such as civil rights legislation and the "War on Poverty." He feared that a withdrawal from Vietnam would be compared by his Republican opponents to the "loss" of China and that this would lead to the defeat of his ambitious domestic agenda. Moreover, both he and American military leaders had been strongly influenced by their cold war experiences. Ironically, Johnson's domestic programs became law, but the financial cost of the Vietnam involvement drastically reduced the funding available for them. In his speech, "Why Americans Fight in Vietnam" (1965), he attempted to explain to the American people why the United States needed to undertake a difficult, dangerous, and expensive endeavor. But three years later, with his popularity at its lowest point, President Johnson announced that he would not seek a second term as president, and he retired to his Texas ranch in 1969.

Although Johnson provided an elevated and noble rationale for American involvement in Vietnam, the reality on the ground was brutal and ugly. Vietnam was nothing like World War II or the Korean War. It was not a theater of fixed fronts, along which regular armies fought for territory. Rather, it was a guerrilla war, characterized more by ambush and booby traps than by the open clash of regular military forces. Typically, American forces would move through an area, searching for Communist troops and sympathizers, which meant that the Communists could choose the time and place for battle. In addition, the population of South Vietnam was not reliable from the point of view of the American soldier. One never knew if a seemingly friendly Vietnamese was a secret supporter of the Communists. For these reasons, and because of the long, nasty history of combat in the region dating back to before the Japanese occupation, it was an exceptionally "dirty" war.

The reality of this ugly warfare and the cost it imposed on the young Americans who served there (not to mention on the Vietnamese themselves) was the focus of John Kerry's testimony before the U.S. Senate, which is excerpted here. John Kerry (1943–) was a highly decorated (Silver Star, Bronze Star, and three Purple Hearts) Vietnam veteran who cofounded and became the leading spokesman for the Vietnam Veterans Against the War. Born in Massachusetts and graduating from Yale University, Kerry enlisted in the navy and served two tours of duty in Vietnam leading gunboat patrols in the Mekong Delta. Upon his return, he became a leading critic of the war and its "hypocrisy." After completing law school, Kerry entered Massachusetts politics in 1976 and later was elected to three terms as U.S. Senator from Massachusetts before running for U.S. President in 2004. The speech presented here was his introductory statement made to the Senate Foreign Relations Committee in April 1971. In explaining his opposition to the Vietnam War, Kerry provides a view on the Vietnam conflict that stands in stark contrast to the ideas of Lyndon Johnson, and it highlights the divisive bitterness that the war created in America. Equally important, the Johnson-Kerry split also shows the range of public and political opinion regarding decolonization and its relationship to the cold war.

QUESTIONS TO CONSIDER

1. List the reasons provided by Lyndon Johnson that the United States must fight in Vietnam. What parts of his argument can be traced to Cold War considerations and to the general views behind containment? What other factors seem to shape his views?

2. Johnson concluded, "The central issue of our time is that the appetite of aggression is never satisfied. To withdraw from one battlefield means only to prepare for the next." Using the insights gained from prior readings, how might Stalin or Novikov respond to this assumption? Would they agree? If so, what might that suggest about the origins of the Cold War?

3. What are the reasons John Kerry opposed the Vietnam War? Why did he accuse the American government of "criminal hypocrisy"?

4. In contrast to Johnson, how did Kerry characterize the conflict in Vietnam? What policies might he have suggested in Vietnam? Why did he seem so little concerned about Communism?

5. What had happened to the idea of "containment" from the time of Kennan's article (1947) to John Kerry's testimony before the Senate Foreign Relations Committee (1971)? If you think that the idea of containment was rational at the outset, was it still rational by the time of the Vietnam War, or had emotion clouded American decision making? Or was "containment" a flawed concept and policy right from the start?

"WHY AMERICANS FIGHT IN VIETNAM" (1965)

Lyndon B. Johnson

Why must this nation hazard its ease, its interest, and its power for the sake of a people so far away?

We fight because we must fight if we are to live in a world where every country can shape its own destiny, and only in such a world will our own freedom be finally secure. This kind of world will never be built by bombs or bullets. Yet the infirmities of man are such that force must often precede reason and the waste of war, the works of peace. We wish that this were not so. But we must deal with the world as it is, if it is ever to be as we wish.

The world as it is in Asia is not a serene or peaceful place. The first reality is that North Viet-Nam has attacked the independent nation of South Viet-Nam. Its object is total conquest. . . . And it is a war of unparalleled brutality. Simple farmers are the targets of assassination and kidnapping. Women and children are strangled in the night because their men are loyal to their government. And helpless villages are ravaged by sneak attacks. Large-scale raids are conducted on towns, and terror strikes in the heart of cities.

The confused nature of this conflict cannot mask the fact that it is the new face of an old enemy. Over this war—and all Asia—is another reality: the deepening shadow of Communist China. The rulers in Hanoi are urged on by Peking. This is a regime . . . which is helping the forces of violence in almost every continent. The contest in Viet-Nam is part of a wider pattern of aggressive purposes.

Why are these realities our concern? Why are we in South Viet-Nam?

We are there because we have a promise to keep. Since 1954 every American President has offered support to the people of South Viet-Nam. We have . . . made a national pledge to help South Viet-Nam defend its independence. And I intend to keep that promise.

We are there also to strengthen world order. Around the globe from Berlin to Thailand are people whose well being rests in part on the belief that they can count

Source: Lyndon B. Johnson, "Why Americans Fight in Vietnam," in *The Public Papers of the Presidents of the United States: Lyndon B. Johnson, 1965,* volume 1, 172 (Washington, DC: Government Printing Office, 1966), 394–99.

on us if they are attacked. To leave Viet-Nam to its fate would shake the confidence of all these people in the value of an American commitment and in the value of America's word. The result would be increased instability, and even wider war.

We are also there because there are great stakes in the balance. Let no one think for a moment that retreat from Viet-Nam would bring an end to conflict. The battle would be renewed in one country and then another. The central lesson of our time is that the appetite of aggression is never satisfied. To withdraw from one battlefield means only to prepare for the next. We must say in Southeast Asia—as we did in Europe—in the words of the Bible: "Hitherto shalt thou come, but no further." . . .

There are those who wonder why we have a responsibility there. Well, we have it there for the same reason that we have a responsibility for the defense of Europe. World War II was fought in both Europe and Asia and when it ended we found ourselves with continued responsibility for the defense of freedom.

Our objective is the independence of South Viet-Nam and its freedom from attack. We want nothing for ourselves—only that the people of South Viet-Nam be allowed to guide their own country in their own way.

We will do everything necessary to reach that objective and we will do only what is absolutely necessary. . . . We will not be defeated. We will not grow tired. We will not withdraw, either openly or under the cloak of a meaningless agreement. . . . We hope that peace will come swiftly. But that is in the hands of others besides ourselves. And we must be prepared for a long continued conflict. It will require patience as well as bravery—the will to endure as well as the will to resist.

I wish it were possible to convince others with words of what we now find it necessary to say with guns and planes: armed hostility is futile. Our resources are equal to any challenge because we fight for values and we fight for principle, rather than territory or colonies, our patience and our determination are unending.

"WHY I OPPOSE THE VIETNAM WAR" (1971)

John Kerry

Thank you very much, Senator[s]. . . . I would like to say for the record, and also for the men behind me who are also wearing the uniform and their medals, that my sitting here is really symbolic. I am not here as John Kerry. I am here as one member of the group of 1,000 which is a small representation of a very much larger group of veterans in this country, and were it possible for all of them to sit at this table they would be here and have the same kind of testimony. . . .

Source: John Kerry, "Why I Oppose the Vietnam War," in *Legislative Proposals Relating to the War in Southeast Asia, Hearings before the Committee on Foreign Relations, United States Senate,* 92d Congress, 1st sess., April–May 1971 (Washington, DC: Government Printing Office, 1971), 180–83, 185.

[I]n Detroit we had an investigation at which over 150 honorably discharged, and many very highly decorated, veterans testified to war crimes committed in Southeast Asia. These were not isolated incidents but crimes committed on a day to day basis with the full awareness of officers at all levels of command.

It is impossible to describe to you exactly what did happen in Detroit—the emotions in the room and the feelings of the men who . . . relived the absolute horror of what this country, in a sense, made them do.

They told stories that at times they had personally raped, cut off ears, cut off heads, taped wires from portable telephones to human genitals and turned up the power, cut off limbs, blown up bodies, randomly shot at civilians, razed villages in a fashion reminiscent of Genghis Khan, shot cattle and dogs for fun, poisoned food stocks, and generally ravaged the countryside of South Vietnam. . . .

We . . . have come here because we feel we have to. . . . We could come back to this country, we could be quiet, we could hold our silence, we could not tell what went on in Vietnam, but we feel because of what threatens this country, not the reds, but the crimes which we are committing that threaten it, that we have to speak out. . . .

The country doesn't know it yet but it has created a monster, a monster in the form of millions of men who have been taught to deal and to trade in violence and who are given the chance to die for the biggest nothing in history; men who have returned with a sense of anger and a sense of betrayal which no one has yet grasped. . . .

In 1970 at West Point Vice President Agnew said "some glamorize the criminal misfits of society while our best men die in Asian rice paddies to preserve the freedom which most of those misfits abuse," and this was used as a rallying point for our effort in Vietnam.

But for us, as boys in Asia whom the country was supposed to support, his statement is a terrible distortion . . . because . . . we cannot consider ourselves America's best men when we are ashamed of and hated for what we were called on to do in Southeast Asia.

In our opinion, and from our experience, there is nothing in South Vietnam which could happen that realistically threatens the United States of America. And to attempt to justify the loss of one American life in Vietnam . . . by linking such loss to the preservation of freedom . . . , is to us the height of criminal hypocrisy, and it is that kind of hypocrisy which we feel has torn this country apart.

We are probably . . . angriest about all that we were told about Vietnam and about the mystical war against communism.

We found that not only was it a civil war, an effort by a people who had for years been seeking their liberation from any colonial influence whatsoever, but also we found that the Vietnamese whom we had enthusiastically molded after our own image were hard put to take up the fight against the threat we were supposedly saving them from.

We found most people didn't even know the difference between communism and democracy. They only wanted to work in rice paddies without helicopters strafing them and bombs with napalm burning their villages and tearing their country apart. They wanted everything to do with the war, particularly with this foreign presence of the United States of America, to leave them alone in peace. . . .

We rationalized destroying villages in order to save them. We saw America lose her sense of morality as she accepted very coolly a My Lai* and refused to give up the image of American soldiers who hand out chocolate bars and chewing gum. . . .

We watched pride allow the most unimportant battles to be blown into extravaganzas, because we couldn't lose, and we couldn't retreat, and because it didn't matter how many American bodies were lost to prove that point . . . .

Each day to facilitate the process by which the United States washes her hands of Vietnam someone has to give up his life so that the United States doesn't have to admit something that the entire world already knows, so that we can't say that we have made a mistake. Someone has to die so that President Nixon won't be, and these are his words, "the first President to lose a war." How do you ask a man to be the last man to die for a mistake? But . . . if you read carefully the President's last speech to the people of this country, . . . he says, and says clearly, "but the issue, gentlemen, is communism, and the question is whether or not we will leave that country to the communists or whether or not we will try to give it hope to be a free people." But the point is they are not a free people now under us. They are not a free people, and we cannot fight communism all over the world. I think we should have learned that lesson by now. . . .

We wish that a merciful God could wipe away our own memories of that service as easily as this administration has wiped away their memories of us. But all that they have done and all that they can do by this denial is to make more clear than ever our own determination to undertake one last mission—to search out and destroy the last vestige of this barbaric war, to pacify our own hearts, to conquer the hate and the fear that have driven this country these last ten years and more, so when 30 years from now our brothers go down the street without a leg, without an arm, or a face, and small boys ask why, we will be able to say "Vietnam" and not mean a desert, not a filthy obscene memory, but mean instead the place where America finally turned and where soldiers like us helped it in the turning.

Thank you.

NOTES

1. The United States took a small role in the international force that intervened in the Russian civil war. The stated goal of the intervention was to ensure that Russian arms did not fall into German hands and to provide the means for trapped Allied troops to escape. The American forces were withdrawn in 1920.

2. The Truman Administration (1945–1952) determined that the vast physical destruction of Europe provided a fertile ground for revolutionary Communism. In response, the American secretary of state, George C. Marshall, pledged $13 billion to aid European recovery and to prevent the spread of Communism.

---

*In March 1968, a company of American soldiers, inflamed by recent guerrilla attacks in the area that had led to many casualties, massacred over three hundred unarmed civilians, mainly women and children, in the village of My Lai. The officer in charge, Lt. William Calley, was found guilty of murder. He received a sentence of life in prison, but was released in 1974.

3. In 1949, the United States, Canada, and their western European allies formed the North Atlantic Treaty Organization (NATO), a military alliance intended to contain the perceived expansionist tendencies of the Soviet Union. In response, the USSR and its eastern European allies formed the Warsaw Pact in 1955.

4. Tensions sometimes nearly boiled over into conflict, such as the crisis which resulted from the building of the Berlin Wall in 1961.

5. Although many Africans and Asians lost their independence to the European colonizers, resistance to foreign rule was never totally quelled. However, prior to World War II, resistance was generally small scale and of limited success.

6. Novikov's telegram also happened to come about half a year after George Kennan's "long telegram" had analyzed the motivations and paradigms of the Soviet leadership and of the Communist/Russian worldview as Kennan understood them but about half a year before his anonymous article would appear in *Foreign Affairs*.

7. Some historians also note that the oppressive nature of Stalin's regime would have made it unlikely that Novikov would have knowingly put forward views that were radically different from those of his superiors.

8. Although Kennan's article was published under a pseudonym ("X"), it was fairly common knowledge who the author was.

9. Although the Soviets and Communism were not named specifically, there could be no doubt that Truman had them in mind.

10. The Rosenbergs' controversial conviction in 1951 helped to fuel Senator Joseph McCarthy's anti-Communist crusade against "anti-American activities" by U.S. citizens. Although their devotion to the Communist cause was well documented, the Rosenbergs denied the spying charges even as they faced the electric chair. Their defenders said they never had an opportunity for a fair trial given the anti-Communist Red Scare that permeated the United States in the 1950s.

11. Ho Chi Minh's hope for American support was based largely on the Viet Minh's wartime cooperation with America and the western allies. There were American officers from the OSS (the Office of Strategic Services, the predecessor the Central Intelligence Agency) present in the audience when Ho announced Vietnamese independence, and he consulted with them in writing the Vietnamese Declaration of Independence.

CHAPTER 14

Shifting Identities of Ethnicity, Race, Gender, and Sexuality

INTRODUCTION

Meeting in secrecy aboard a battle cruiser in the north Atlantic in August 1941, British Prime Minister Winston Churchill and American President Franklin Delano Roosevelt issued what has become known as the "Atlantic Charter," a joint declaration of common principles upon which they planned "a better future for the world." The charter is quite short and contains only eight principles, but it gave the World War II Allies a mission statement and moral cause that mobilized public support and justified military actions against the Axis powers. Chief among the principles noted in the charter were the rights of self-determination and self-government, equal economic opportunity, and the ability "to live in freedom from fear and want."

Neither Churchill nor Roosevelt foresaw how prescient the Atlantic Charter was to be, for in the three decades following the conclusion of the war, an unprecedented number and variety of people came forward to demand the rights, privileges, and principles that the great nations of Europe and America claimed to support. The developing world would demand its independence from western imperial control, people of color would claim their full civil rights and mutual human inheritance alongside whites, gays would challenge prevailing social values, and women would force a reconsideration of their roles onto the agendas of nations, employers—and their husbands. But in order for this process to take shape, gain momentum, and ultimately succeed, the first battle that had to be fought was intellectual and ideological: It was the battle over identity and self-definition. Drawing inspiration and ideas from each other, the various groups began to challenge established authority over how they should be defined and what changes ought to ensue as a result of the new self-definitions they crafted. Although colonial resistance, women's liberation, and the civil rights movements varied considerably in specific goals and strategies, they all began with and were founded on fundamentally new conceptions of self.

460

This chapter examines shifting patterns of social and personal identity in the twentieth century, focusing on the anticolonial, women's liberation, civil rights, and gay rights movements. Our readings come from some of the most significant leaders of these movements—Mohandas Gandhi, Simone de Beauvoir, Malcolm X, and others—who rose to the top of their respective movements because they were able to articulate essential problems and propose alternative solutions to their predicament. They also offer a unique and revealing glimpse into the experiences, ideas, and perspectives of people who have been marginalized by mainstream society. In doing so, they each provide us a view of the world that may be very different from our own.

Although World War II did not initiate the search and shift in identities, it clearly invigorated and reshaped the process, particularly in the colonies of Asia and Africa. The war served to strengthen the resolve and determination of colonized people who had fought at the front and worked at home to provide crucial raw materials for the Allied cause. They believed in the promise of the Atlantic Charter—especially in the principles of self-determination and self-government—which they considered to be their reward for their wartime sacrifices. At the same time, the war diminished the power of the colonizers. Not only did many European nations lack the will and the means to hold on to their empires, but the war had also weakened their prior aura of invincibility. Led by the example of Mohandas Gandhi, who led India to independence in 1947, nationalist leaders in Africa and Asia formed mass political parties and demanded independence.[1]

The first selection is from Gandhi (1869–1948), who truly pioneered what some call the "Third World" movement of the twentieth century. For our purposes, what is most interesting about Gandhi and the Indian independence movement is the way that Indian self-definition and identity was wrenched out of British imperial hands and recrafted to align with Indian cultural and historical traditions. As Gandhi explains, this action provided him the means and ability to implement *satyagraha*, a form of civil disobedience that allowed the powerless to triumph over the powerful.

The women's liberation movement also received new impetus and a change in direction following the war. The vastly increased demands for labor caused by wartime factory production, coupled with the loss of male laborers drafted into the armed forces, had opened up many new jobs and opportunities for women in America and Europe that had heretofore been denied them because of their gender. In the 1950s, expanded educational opportunities for women and the desire of many families to adopt the consumer-oriented "suburban lifestyle" swelled the number of women seeking wage labor. According to census figures, the percentage of married women in the workplace doubled between 1940 (15 percent) and 1960 (30 percent). But many working women experienced limits to their advancement and outright hostility to their ambitions, for they were criticized by some men and women for undermining traditional family values and notions about femininity. It was out of these conditions that the modern feminist movement arose and spread to nearly all nations and cultures. One of the most important early leaders was the French writer Simone de Beauvoir (1908–1986), who challenged both male authority and female passivity in her book *The Second Sex* (1949). By placing women within the category of "the other," she argues that societal-imposed concepts of "femininity" both reflected and reinforced the inferior status of women in western society.

The movements of people of color to demand their equal rights also grew steadily in the postwar years. In the United States and South Africa, countries that shared a troubled history of racism and discrimination, blacks renewed with greater intensity their long-standing civil rights movements. They were inspired in great part by the success of decolonization, in which they had strongly identified with the cause of liberation. They were equally motivated by conditions at home. Although whites in both America and South Africa enjoyed unprecedented prosperity in the 1950s and 1960s, wealth hardly trickled down to blacks, who were stuck in the lowest socioeconomic class in each country. Borrowing the tactics of nonviolent protest from Mohandas Gandhi, Martin Luther King, Jr., and Nelson Mandela mobilized mass, multiracial support for reform. But the imprisonment of Mandela and the assassination of King, along with a limited record of success, was more than enough proof to some that the process, strategies, and sometimes even the goals of the civil rights movement needed drastic reforming. Beginning with the premise that racial identities, especially the white/superior versus black/inferior dichotomy, played a key role in promoting subjugation, new leaders also understood that reborn identities were the key to liberation. In both South Africa and America, new spokesmen created new organizations that proposed a new identity for blacks, one rooted in a new sense of "black consciousness" and dedicated to securing their full rights and freedoms. In the United States, Malcolm X became a hero to many because of his uncompromising sense of self, as well as his uncompromising stance on racism in America. In South Africa, a young medical student named Steve Biko forever changed the nature of the anti-apartheid struggle by advocating a new philosophy called "Black Consciousness." Together, they both argued for a new sense of black identity, one much more empowered to demand their rights.

The gay rights movement of the 1960s and 1970s was the last to join the other movements in demanding their full legal rights and equality of opportunity. Prior to the 1960s, most gay men and women around the world lived invisible lives due to widespread societal disapproval of their sexual orientation. Homosexuality was commonly viewed as an aberration and immoral, and people who were identified as "queer" were frequently ostracized, ridiculed, and targeted for abuse. But unlike people of color and women, gays could mask their identity and live covert lives. Although this has historically allowed many gays to avoid persecution, it has also deterred activism and the building of a gay community. The impetus for change came in part from the models of success pioneered by the civil rights and women's liberation movements. The successful efforts of feminists and people of color to accept proudly their identity and to challenge societal norms gave inspiration to gay men and women. Using tactics of civil disobedience and street protest borrowed in part from previous movements, the gay rights movement has created an unprecedented sense of community and solidarity, as it has also challenged societal laws and values. The final reading is from the 1970 Manifesto of the London Gay Liberation Front, which explains, from the gay perspective, the forces behind their oppression and their long-term goals.

Although anticolonial campaigns, civil rights, women's liberation, and the gay rights movement naturally differ due to their unique membership, needs, goals, and historical contexts, they all share some important common features that are worthy of further investigation. First, each of the leaders included in this chapter discusses the forms of oppression that their group has experienced. To varying degrees, each group considers itself "marginalized," or somehow locked out of mainstream society. They remain inferior in regard to status, power, and autonomy. Some spokesmen favor integration as a solution, others separation from mainstream society. But no matter what the goal, there is general consensus that the key to overcoming marginalization is through recasting of identities. The process of marginalization, many argue, has helped to create identities of inferiority that have inhibited action. What is needed is the autonomous creation of a newly empowered and assertive identity that will have the pride and courage to fight the forces of marginalization. Using this argument as a starting point, the readings also provide a means to explore the origins and sociological functions of identities. It is particularly useful to draw comparisons between the various movements in order to consider the degree to which identities are self-created or imposed by others and the ways that identities reflect and reinforce patterns of status and power.

CHAPTER QUESTIONS

1. Compare and contrast how marginalization is described and experienced in each of the readings. What factors (people, organizations, ideas) are deemed responsible for this marginalization? What conclusions can be drawn when these explanations are compared?

2. Why is resistance considered so important to the forging of a new identity? What different expressions of resistance are found in the readings? What commonalities can be found?

3. As defined by Simone de Beauvoir, is "otherness" a fundamental category of human thought? Do the other readings support or undermine her assertion? What relationship is there between "otherness" and identity?

4. Steve Biko wrote, "The most powerful weapon in the hands of the oppressor is the mind of the oppressed." To what degree, if any, is this perspective applicable to any of the other movements?

5. Comparing all the readings, what conclusions can be made about the origins and functions of identities? How are they linked to social values? How are they related to patterns of authority and power?

SELF-IDENTITY, SELF-RULE, AND DECOLONIZATION

Mohandas K. Gandhi (1869–1948), also known as the Mahatma ("great soul"), came from an upper-class family in western India. His father was the leading administrator of a small principality in western India under British rule. From his mother he derived his concern with Hindu values, including self-purification, vegetarianism, tolerance, and *ahimsa,* or noninjury to all living things. He initially sought to follow in his father's footsteps in the colonial administration, and this led him to London University and a degree in law. But when he returned home to India in 1891, he was unable to find a job, and so he accepted a contract with an Indian law firm in Natal, South Africa.

It was while he was in Africa that Gandhi began to formulate his nationalist ideas. Inspired by personal mistreatment—he was thrown out of a first-class train car, barred from certain hotel rooms, and beaten, all because of his nonwhite status—Gandhi blossomed almost overnight into a proficient political campaigner and organizer of the Indian expatriate community in Natal. In 1915, Gandhi returned home to India, where he refashioned the 35-year-old Indian National Congress into an effective instrument of Indian nationalism. This was no easy task, given the ethnic, religious, and caste divisions within Indian society, as well as the full opposition of the colonial British government and military. But Gandhi persevered through victories and defeats until Britain formally granted independence to the two new dominions of India and Pakistan in 1947.

Gandhi's great success was in winning the allegiance of the masses to the goal of self-rule and to his methods of achieving self-rule. He did so by combining a redefinition of Indian identity with brilliantly conceived, executed, and publicized political campaigns that both embodied Gandhi's moral philosophy and helped to give it shape and substance for the masses. Gandhi asserted that the Indian cultural and historical experience should be set off completely from Britain's western civilization. In particular, Gandhi rejected modern European secular and materialist culture in favor of what he considered India's superior, spiritually based civilization. This rejection clarified for Gandhi both India's uniqueness and the weapons to be used to achieve independence from colonial domination: *satyagraha* (truth-force) and *ahimsa* (nonviolence). *Satyagraha* describes an awareness of good as opposed to evil and truth as opposed to falsehood and arising from that awareness, the dedication of an individual to follow the truth and to resist evil in a spirit of peace and love. *Ahimsa* is the dedication to nonviolence, and it is crucial to retaining the truth and the correct insight. Gandhi employed both weapons in his campaigns against the British. His program of nonviolent noncooperation with the colonial government included boycotts of goods, schools, and courts. It electrified the country, broke the spell of foreign omnipotence, and led to the arrest of thousands of passive resisters, who defied laws and cheerfully accepted beatings and imprisonment. In protests against the salt tax in 1930, for example, more than 60,000 Indians were arrested for their nonviolent protests. Although the country ultimately gained its independence, Gandhi's personal triumph was short-lived. He adamantly opposed and was disheartened by the division of the subcontinent into Hindu India and Muslim Pakistan, and less than a year later, he was assassinated by a Hindu militant. But his legacy has been great: Indian nationalism is inconceivable without the revaluation of Indian culture and identity that lay at the foundation of Gandhi's politics. Moreover, his successful use of *satyagraha* and *ahimsa* has been an inspiration to many other social protestors from around the world, most notably the American civil rights leader

Martin Luther King, Jr., and South African nationalist and former president Nelson Mandela.

The best and earliest expression of Gandhi's redefined India comes from *Hind Swaraj* (Self-Rule), published in 1909. Here Gandhi employs the form of a dialogue between a fictional Reader (the voice of Gandhi) and an Editor to put forward his ideas. Written while Gandhi was still in South Africa, it anticipates the philosophy and course of action that he was to follow in India. Arguing against those reformers whom he believed had too narrow a definition of self-rule, Gandhi asserted that real *hind swaraj* must include not only political autonomy but also a reassertion of Indian pride and culture and a reborn sense of identity.

QUESTIONS TO CONSIDER

1. According to Gandhi, what was wrong with British/western civilization? Why did he think India was superior? What was the basis for his judgments?
2. What did Gandhi mean by "soul force"? How was it an effective means of resistance? How did it relate to Gandhi's definition of civilization?
3. What did Gandhi want to happen to the British and their rule in India? How was this consistent with his definition of *hind swaraj*?
4. Can a civilization truly embrace "antiprogress" and thrive? Assess the strengths and weaknesses of Gandhi's argument.
5. What was the new identity Gandhi proposed for Indians? List the attributes and explain their significance.

HIND SWARAJ (SELF-RULE) (1909)

Mohandas K. Gandhi

[The following text is in the form of an interview.]

What Is Civilization?

Gandhi: If India copies England, it is my firm conviction that she will be ruined. . . . It is not due to any peculiar fault of the English people, but the condition is due to modern civilization. It is a civilization only in name. . . . Let us first consider what state of things is described by the word "civilization." Its true test lies in the fact that people living in it make bodily welfare the object of life. We will take some examples. The people of Europe today live in better-built houses than they did a hundred years ago. This is considered an emblem of civilization, and this is also a matter to promote bodily happiness. Formerly, they wore skins, and used spears as their weapons. Now,

Source: Mohandas Gandhi, *Hind Swaraj or Indian Home Rule,* ed. Jitendra Desai (Ahmedabad, India: Navajivan Publishing House, 1938), 29–30, 45–47, 55–58, 66–69.

they wear long trousers, and a variety of clothing, and, instead of spears, they carry with them revolvers.

If people of a certain country, who have hitherto not been in the habit of wearing much clothing, boots, etc., adopt European clothing, they are supposed to have become civilized out of savagery. . . . Now, they fly through the air in trains at the rate of four hundred and more miles per day. This is considered the height of civilization. It has been stated that, as men progress, they shall be able to travel in airship and reach any part of the world in a few hours. Men will not need the use of their hands and feet. They will press a button, and they will have their clothing by their side. They will press another button, and they will have their newspaper. A third, and a motor-car will be in waiting for them. . . . Everything will be done by machinery. This is civilization. Formerly, men worked in the open air only as much as they liked. Now thousands work in factories or mines. Their condition is worse than that of beasts. They are obliged to work . . . for the sake of millionaires. Formerly, men were made slaves under physical compulsion. Now they are enslaved by temptation of money and of the luxuries that money can buy. . . . What more need I say? . . . This civilization takes note neither of morality nor of religion. . . . This civilization is irreligion and . . . is such that one has only to be patient and it will be self-destroyed. According to the teaching of Mohammed this would be considered a Satanic Civilization. Hinduism calls it a Black Age. I cannot give you an adequate conception of it. It is eating into the vitals of the English nation. It must be shunned. The English deserve our sympathy. They are . . . not inherently immoral. Neither are they bad at heart. I therefore respect them. Civilization is not an incurable disease, but it should never be forgotten that the English are at present afflicted by it.

Question: What, then, is civilization?
Gandhi: The answer to that question is not difficult. I believe that the civilization India has evolved is not to be beaten in the world. . . . India . . . remains immovable and that is her glory. It is a charge against India that her people are so uncivilized, ignorant and stolid that it is not possible to induce them to adopt any changes. It is a charge really against our merit. What we have tested and found true on the anvil of experience, we dare not change. . . . This is her beauty: it is the sheet-anchor of our hope.

Civilization is that mode of conduct which points out to man the path of duty. Performance of duty and observance of morality are convertible terms. To observe morality is to attain mastery over our mind and our passions. So doing, we know ourselves. . . . [C]ivilization means "good conduct".

If this definition is correct, then India, as so many writers have shown, has nothing to learn from anybody else, and this is as it should be. We notice that the mind is a restless bird; the more it gets the more it wants, and still remains unsatisfied. The more we indulge our passions the more unbridled they become. Our ancestors, therefore, set a limit to our indulgences. They saw that happiness was largely a mental condition. A man is not necessarily happy because he is rich, or unhappy because he is poor. The rich are often seen to be unhappy, the poor to be happy. Millions will always remain poor. Observing all this, our ancestors dissuaded us from luxuries and pleasures. . . . We have had no system of life-corroding competition. . . . It was not that we did not know how to invent machinery, but our forefathers knew that, if we set our hearts after such things, we would become slaves and lose our moral fiber. They therefore after due deliberation decided that . . . our real happiness and health consisted in a proper use of our hands and feet. They further reasoned that large cities were a snare and a useless encumbrance and that people would not be happy in them. . . . They were, therefore, satisfied with small villages. They saw that kings and their swords were inferior to the sword of ethics. . . . Justice was tolerably fair. . . . The common people lived independently and followed their agricultural occupation. They enjoyed true Home Rule. And where this cursed modern civilization has not reached, India remains as it was before. . . .

In no part of the world, and under no civilization, have all men attained perfection. The tendency of the Indian civilization is to elevate the moral being, that of the Western civilization is to propagate immorality. The latter is godless, the former is based on a belief in God. So understanding and so believing, it behooves every lover of India to cling to the Indian civilization even as a child clings to the mother's breast.

The Path to Self-Rule

It is a world-known maxim that the removal of the cause of a disease results in the removal of the disease itself. Similarly if the cause of India's slavery be removed, India can become free.

If we become free, India is free. And in this thought you have a definition of *Swaraj* (self-rule). It is *Swaraj* when we learn to rule ourselves. It is, therefore, in the palm of our hands. . . . But such *Swaraj* has to be experienced, by each one for himself. One drowning man will never save another. Slaves ourselves, it would be a mere pretension to think of freeing others. Now you will have seen that it is not necessary for us to have as our goal the expulsion of the English. If the English become Indianised, we can accommodate them. If they wish to remain in India along with their civilization, there is no room for them. It lies with us to bring about such a state of things.

The poet Tulsidas* has said: "Of religion, pity, or love, is the root, as egotism of the body. Therefore, we should not abandon pity so long as we are alive." This appears to me to be a scientific truth. I believe in it as much as I believe in two and two being four. The force of love is the same as the force of the soul or truth. We have evidence of its working at every step. The universe would disappear without the existence of that force. . . . [If history] . . . means the doings of the kings and emperors, there can be no evidence of soul-force or passive resistance in such history. You cannot expect silver ore in a tin mine. . . . History is really a record of every interruption of the even working of this force of love or of the soul . . . a record of an interruption of the course of nature. Soul-force, being natural, is not noted in history.

Passive resistance is a method of securing rights by personal suffering and it is the reverse of resistance by arms. When I refuse to do a thing that is repugnant to my conscience, I use soul-force. . . . [A man] should not do that which he knows to be wrong and [should] suffer the consequence whatever it may be. This is the key to the use of soul-force.

---

*A sixteenth-century Hindu holy man and author of twelve books. The most famous book is the *Ramayan,* which is still read with great reverence in northern India.

We simply want to find out what is right and to act accordingly. . . . A man who has realized his manhood, who fears only God, will fear no one else. Man-made laws are not necessarily binding on him. . . . If man will only realize that it is unmanly to obey laws that are unjust, no man's tyranny will enslave him. This is the key to self-rule or home-rule.

Passive resistance, that is, soul-force, is matchless. . . . What do you think? Where is courage required in blowing others to pieces from behind a cannon? [Or is it more courageous] to approach a cannon with a smiling face and be blown to pieces? Who is the true warrior—he who keeps death always as a bosom-friend, or he who controls the death of others? Believe me that a man devoid of courage and manhood can never be a passive resister.

That nation is great which rests its head upon death as its pillow. Those who defy death are free from all fear. . . . The fact is that, in India the nation at large has generally used passive resistance in all departments of life. We cease to co-operate with our rulers when they displease us. This is passive resistance. . . . Real home rule is possible only where passive resistance is the guiding force of the people. Any other rule is foreign rule.

Question: What, then, would you say to the English?
Gandhi: To them I would respectfully say: "I admit you are my rulers. It is not necessary to debate the question whether, you hold India by the sword or by my consent. I have no objection to your remaining in my country, but although you are the rulers, you will have to remain as servants of the people. It is not we who have to do as you wish, but it is you who have to do as we wish. You may keep the riches that you have drained away from this land, but you may not drain riches henceforth. Your function will be, if you so wish, to police India; you must abandon the idea of deriving any commercial benefit from us. We hold the civilization that you support to be the reverse of civilization. We consider our civilization to be far superior to yours. . . . We consider your schools and law courts to be useless. We want our own ancient schools and courts to be restored. The common language of India is not English but Hindi. You should, therefore, learn it. We can hold communication with you only in our national language.

"We cannot tolerate the idea of your spending money on railways and the military. We see no occasion for either. . . . We do not need any European cloth. We shall manage with articles produced and manufactured at home. You may not keep one eye on Manchester and the other on India. We can work together only if our interests are identical.

"This has not been said to you in arrogance. You have great military resources. Your naval power is matchless. If we wanted to fight with you on your own ground, we should be unable to do so, but if the above submissions are not acceptable to you, we cease to play the part of the ruled. You may, if you like, cut us to pieces. You may shatter us at the cannon's mouth. If you act contrary to our will, we shall not help you; and without our help, we know that you cannot move one step forward.

"We believe that at heart you belong to a religious nation. We are living in a land which is the source of religions. . . . If you will abandon your so-called civilization and search into your own scriptures, you will find that our demands are just. Only on condition of our demands being fully satisfied may you remain in India. . . ."

Question: What will you say to . . . those of us who are affected by European civilization, and who are eager to have Home Rule?
Gandhi: To these I would say, "It is only those Indians who are imbued with real love
who will be able to speak to the English in the above strain without being frightened,
and only those can be said to be so imbued who conscientiously believe that Indian
civilization is the best and that the European is a nine days' wonder. Such ephemeral
civilizations have often come and gone and will continue to do so. Those only can
be considered to be so imbued who, having experienced the force of the soul within
themselves, will not cower before brute-force, and will not, on any account, desire to
use brute-force. . . ."

Question: This is a large order. When will all carry it out?
Gandhi: You make a mistake. You and I have nothing to do with the others. Let each
do his duty. If I do my duty, that is, serve myself, I shall be able to serve others. Before
I leave you, I will take the liberty of repeating:

1. Real home-rule is self-rule or self-control.
2. The way to it is passive resistance: that is soul-force or love-force.
3. In order to exert this force, *Swadeshi** in every sense is necessary.
4. What we want to do should be done, not because we object to the English or because we want to retaliate but because it is our duty to do so. Thus, supposing that
   the English remove the salt-tax, restore our money, give the highest posts to Indians, withdraw the English troops, we shall certainly not use their machine-made
   goods, nor use the English language, nor many of their industries. It is worth noting that these things are in their nature, harmful; hence we do not want them. I
   bear no enmity towards the English but I do towards their civilization.

In my opinion, we have [too often] used the term *"Swaraj"* without understanding
its real significance. I have endeavored to explain it as I understand it, and my conscience testifies that my life henceforth is dedicated to its attainment.

WOMEN AS "THE OTHER"

The second selection comes from Simone de Beauvoir, a leading European intellectual of the mid-twentieth century, the long-term companion of French existentialist Jean-Paul Sartre, and the most prominent feminist of her era. What is
feminism? Definitions vary considerably, according to differing frames of reference. Some claim that it is a movement dedicated to securing for women equal
rights, status, and freedom in society. Others argue that it is a heretical attempt
to undermine the family and overturn the natural order that God created for
mankind. The lack of a common definition shows that society has yet to reach a
consensus on the movement and that it remains a divisive and contentious issue.

---

*A spirit in us that allows us to focus solely on our immediate surroundings.

The modern drive for female equality dates as far back as the era of the French Revolution and Olympe de Gouge's Declaration of the Rights of Women (1791), in which she boldly challenged the prevailing notion that women existed for the benefit and pleasure of men (see chapter 6). In the course of the nineteenth century, feminism made some progress in women's suffrage, but larger political and social transformations took longer to develop. Indicative of the slow pace of change is the fact that both the national income tax (Sixteenth Amendment, 1913) and prohibition of alcohol (Eighteenth Amendment, 1919) passed as amendments to the U.S. Constitution before women's suffrage was enacted as the Nineteenth Amendment in 1920. Moreover, the guarantee of voting rights did not secure equal status in society, for most women continued to be constrained by societal practices and cultural values that limited women's roles to those of wife, mother, and homemaker.

Inspired in part by the civil rights movement in the United States, feminism experienced a rebirth of energy and influence in the 1960s and 1970s. One of the most influential American organizations has been the National Organization for Women (NOW), founded in 1966 by Betty Friedan. Although NOW was unsuccessful in its efforts to ratify the Equal Rights Amendment (ERA; it passed Congress in 1972 but was unable to secure adequate state passage required for ratification), it did significantly raise public awareness of gender issues, and it helped to secure greater freedom and equality at home and in the workplace. Inspired by the success of activists in the west, feminist organizations have spread to South America, Africa, and Asia, where women of varying cultures and ethnicities have begun to mobilize support and organize against entrenched male power and privilege.

A landmark document in the history and process of women's liberation was the 1949 work *The Second Sex* by Simone de Beauvoir (1908–1986). De Beauvoir was born in Paris and received a Roman Catholic upbringing and education before she enrolled at the Sorbonne. It was here in 1929 that she met the French existentialist philosopher and writer Jean-Paul Sartre. The two formed a lifelong personal and professional association, which included the founding and coediting of a highly influential magazine, *Le temps modernes*. After a stint of teaching, de Beauvoir spent the rest of her career writing essays, philosophical tracts, and novels, all of which reflect her existentialist philosophical belief that life gains meaning when humans actively choose what they are to become.

The Second Sex is Simone de Beauvoir's most famous work, and one that has been lauded as "the century's most complete presentation of feminism." Her desire to overcome what she called the "eternal feminine" was in part rooted in her existential quest to choose one's self. But it was also equally shaped by her conviction that contemporary definitions of "femininity" were created and perpetuated to reflect and reinforce patterns of gender inequality. By introducing the concept of the inferior "other," an identity defined by and in reference to dominant and presumably superior maleness, de Beauvoir succinctly defined the problem that feminists faced, as well as an essential part of the solution: a new identity for women.

QUESTIONS TO CONSIDER

1. According to de Beauvoir, what is the origin of the definitions of "female" and "woman" that have predominated in western history? Who devised the historically dominant definition of women and what function did that definition perform?

2. What did she mean by "the other," and what function does it have in women's identity? How is the issue of women's identity different from that of other "others" (such as blacks and Jews)? How do the differences complicate both the problem of women's identity and the struggle for women's liberation?

3. Why had there not been a greater struggle for women's liberation in the past? How were women, according to de Beauvoir, complicit in their own subordination? What would they have to sacrifice to attain liberation?

4. De Beauvoir argued that men should actually support feminism. Why? Isn't "women's liberation" a threat to their interests? Explain and assess her argument.

5. Describe the new identity that de Beauvoir ideally envisioned for women. How is it to be achieved? In your assessment, are the goals and strategies realistic?

THE SECOND SEX (1949)

Simone de Beauvoir

We must first ask: what is a woman? . . . To state the question is, to me, to suggest, at once, a preliminary answer. The fact that I ask it is in itself significant. A man would never set out to write a book on the peculiar situation of the human male. But if I wish to define myself, I must first of all say: "I am a woman." . . . The terms masculine and feminine are used symmetrically only as a matter of form, as on legal papers. In actuality the relation of the two sexes is not quite like that of two electrical poles, for man represents both the positive and the neutral, as is indicated by the common use of man to designate human beings in general; whereas woman represents only the negative, defined by limiting criteria, without reciprocity. . . . It amounts to this: just as for the ancients there was an absolute vertical with reference to which the oblique was defined, so there is an absolute human type, the masculine. Woman has ovaries, a uterus: these peculiarities imprison her in her subjectivity, circumscribe her within the limits of her own nature. It is often said that she thinks with her glands. Man superbly ignores the fact that his anatomy also includes glands, such as the testicles,

Source: Simone de Beauvoir, *The Second Sex,* transl. and ed. H. M. Parshley (New York: Knopf, 1971), x, xv–xix, xxi–xxiv, 717, 719, 721–26, 728–29, 731–32. Copyright © 1971 Alfred A. Knopf. Used by permission of Alfred A. Knopf, a division of Random House, Inc.

and that they secrete hormones. He thinks of his body as a direct and normal connection with the world, which he believes he apprehends objectively, whereas he regards the body of woman as a hindrance, a prison, weighed down by everything peculiar to it. "The female is a female by virtue of a certain lack of qualities," said Aristotle*; "we should regard the female nature as afflicted with a natural defectiveness." And St. Thomas† for his part pronounced woman to be an "imperfect man," an "incidental" being. This is symbolized in Genesis where Eve is depicted as made from what Bossuet‡ called "a super-numerary bone" of Adam.

Thus humanity is male and man defines woman not in herself but as relative to him; she is not regarded as an autonomous being. . . . She is defined and differentiated with reference to man and not he with reference to her; she is the incidental, the inessential as opposed to the essential. He is the Subject, he is the Absolute—she is the Other.

The category of the Other is as primordial as consciousness itself. In the most primitive societies, in the most ancient mythologies, one finds the expression of a duality—that of the Self and the Other. . . . Otherness is a fundamental category of human thought.

Thus it is that no group ever sets itself up as the One without at once setting up the Other over against itself. . . . To the native of a country all who inhabit other countries are "foreigners"; Jews are "different" for the anti-Semite, Negroes are "inferior" for American racists, aborigines are "natives" for colonists, proletarians are the "lower class" for the privileged. . . .

But the other consciousness, the other ego, sets up a reciprocal claim . . . to deprive the concept Other of its absolute sense and to make manifest its relativity; willy-nilly, individuals and groups are forced to realize the reciprocity of their relations. How is it, then, that . . . women do not dispute male sovereignty? . . . There are, to be sure, other cases in which a certain category has been able to dominate another completely for a time. Very often this privilege depends upon inequality of numbers . . . [b]ut women are not a minority, like the American Negroes or the Jews. . . . Again, the two groups concerned have often been originally independent, . . . [b]ut a historical event has resulted in the subjugation of the weaker by the stronger. The parallel . . . between women and the proletariat is valid in that neither ever formed a minority or a separate collective unit of mankind. . . . But proletarians have not always existed, whereas there have always been women. . . . Throughout history they have always been subordinated to men, and hence their dependency is not the result of a historical event or a social change. . . . The reason why otherness in this case seems to be an absolute is in part that it lacks the contingent or incidental nature of historical facts. A condition brought about at a certain time can be abolished at some other time, . . . but it might seem that natural condition is beyond the possibility of change.

---

*Aristotle (384–322 BCE) was a renowned philosopher of ancient Greece who also wrote on biology, physics, politics, and ethics.

†St. Thomas Aquinas (1225–1274) was a theological scholar in medieval Europe best known for his attempt to unite logic and reason with Christian revelation.

‡Jacques-Benign Bossuet (1627–1704) was a French theologian known for his writings on contemporary society and values.

In truth, however, the nature of things is no more immutably given, once for all, than is historical reality. If woman seems to be the inessential which never becomes the essential, it is because she herself fails to bring about this change. . . . [T]he women's effort has never been anything more than a symbolic agitation. They have gained only what men have been willing to grant; they have taken nothing. . . .

The reason for this is that women lack concrete means for organizing themselves into a unit which can stand face to face with the correlative unit. They have no past, no history, no religion of their own, and they have no such solidarity of work and interest. . . . They live dispersed among the males, attached through residence, house-work, economic condition, and social standing to certain men—fathers or hus-bands—more firmly than they are to other women. If they belong to the bourgeoisie, they feel solidarity with men of that class, not with proletarian women; if they are white, their allegiance is to white men, not to Negro women. . . . The bond that unites her to her oppressors is not comparable to any other. The division of the sexes is a bi-ological fact, not an event in human history. . . . The couple is a fundamental unity with its two halves riveted together. . . . Here is to be found the basic trait of woman: she is the Other in a totality of which the two components are necessary to one an-other. . . .

To decline to be the Other, to refuse to be a party to the deal—this would be for women to renounce all the advantages conferred upon them by their alliance with the superior caste. Man-the-sovereign will provide woman-the-liege with material protection and will undertake the moral justification of her existence; thus she can evade at once both economic risk and the metaphysical risk of a liberty in which ends and aims must be contrived without assistance. Indeed, along with the ethical urge of each individual to affirm his subjective existence, there is also the temptation to forgo liberty and become a thing. This is an inauspicious road, for he who takes it—passive, lost, ruined—becomes henceforth the creature of another's will, frustrated in his tran-scendence and deprived of every value. But it is an easy road; on it one avoids the strain involved in undertaking an authentic existence. . . . Thus, woman may fail to lay claim to the status of subject because she lacks definite resources, because she feels the necessary bond that ties her to man regardless of reciprocity, and because she is often very well pleased with her role as the Other.

But it will be asked at once: how did all this begin? . . . How is it that this world has always belonged to the men and that things have begun to change only re-cently? . . . [T]he very fact that woman is the Other tends to cast suspicion upon all the justifications that men have ever been able to provide for it. These have all too ev-idently been dictated by men's interest. A little-known feminist of the seventeenth century, Poulain de la Barre*, put it this way: "All that has been written about women by men should be suspect, for the men are at once judge and party to the lawsuit." Everywhere, at all times, the males have displayed their satisfaction in feeling that they are the lords of creation. "Blessed be God . . . that He did not make me a woman," say the Jews in their morning prayers, while their wives pray on a note of resignation: "Blessed be the Lord, who created me according to His will." The first among the blessings for which Plato thanked the gods was that he had been created

---

*Poulain de la Barre (1647–1723) was an early advocate of women's rights in early modern France.

free, not enslaved; the second, a man, not a woman. . . . "Being men, those who have made and compiled the laws have favored their own sex, and jurists have elevated these laws into principles," to quote Poulain de la Barre once more.

In proving woman's inferiority, the anti-feminists then began to draw not only upon religion, philosophy, and theology, as before, but also upon science—biology, experimental psychology, etc. At most they were willing to grant "equality in difference" to the other sex. That profitable formula is most significant; it is precisely like the "equal but separate" formula of the Jim Crow laws aimed at the North American Negroes. As is well known, this so-called equalitarian segregation has resulted only in the most extreme discrimination. The similarity just noted is in no way due to chance, for whether it is a race, a caste, a class, or a sex that is reduced to a position of inferiority, the methods of justification are the same. "The eternal feminine" corresponds to "the black soul" and to "the Jewish character". . . . [T]here are deep similarities between the situation of woman and that of the Negro. . . . In both cases the dominant class bases its argument on a state of affairs that it has itself created. . . . The question is: should that state of affairs continue?

Today the combat takes a different shape; instead of wishing to put man in a prison, woman endeavors to escape from one; she no longer seeks to drag him into the realms of immanence but to emerge, herself, into the light of transcendence. . . . It is no longer a question of a war between individuals each shut up in his or her sphere: a caste claiming its rights attacks and is resisted by the privileged caste. Here two transcendences are face to face; instead of displaying mutual recognition, each free being wishes to dominate the other. . . .

The quarrel will go on as long as men and women fail to recognize each other as equals; that is to say, as long as femininity is perpetuated as such. Which sex is the more eager to maintain it? Woman, who is being emancipated from it, wishes none the less to retain its privileges; and man, in that case, wants her to assume its limitations.

It must be admitted that the males find in woman more complicity than the oppressor usually finds in the oppressed. And in bad faith they take authorisation from this to declare that she has desired the destiny they have imposed on her. We have seen that all the main features of her training combine to bar her from the roads of revolt and adventure. Society in general—beginning with her respected parents—lies to her by praising the lofty values of love, devotion, the gift of herself. . . . She cheerfully believes these lies because they invite her to follow the easy slope: in this others commit their worst crime against her; throughout her life from childhood on, they damage and corrupt her by designating as her true vocation this submission, which is the temptation of every existent in the anxiety of liberty. . . . The innumerable conflicts that set men and women against one another come from the fact that neither is prepared to assume all the consequences of this situation which the one has offered and the other accepted. The doubtful concept of "equality in inequality," which the one uses to mask his despotism and the other to mask her cowardice, does not stand the test of experience: in their exchanges, woman appeals to the theoretical equality she has been guaranteed, and man the concrete inequality that exists . . . .

Once again it is useless to apportion blame and excuses: justice can never be done in the midst of injustice. A colonial administrator has no possibility of acting rightly towards the natives, nor a general towards his soldiers; the only solution is to be neither colonist nor military chief; but a man could not prevent himself from being a man. So there he is, culpable in spite of himself and laboring under the effects of a fault he did not himself commit; and here she is, victim and shrew in spite of herself.

A world where men and women would be equal is easy to visualize, for that precisely is what the Soviet Revolution promised: women reared and trained exactly like men were to work under the same conditions (That certain too laborious occupations were to be closed to women is not in contradiction to this project. Even among men there is an increasing effort to obtain adaptation to profession; their varying physical and mental capacities limit their possibilities of choice; what is asked is that, in any case, no line of sex or caste be drawn.) and for the same wages. Erotic liberty was to be recognized by custom, but the sexual act was not to be considered a "service" to be paid for; woman was to be obliged to provide herself with other ways of earning a living; marriage was to be based on a free agreement that the contracting parties could break at will; maternity was to be voluntary, which meant that contraception and abortion were to be authorised and that, on the other hand, all mothers and their children were to have exactly the same rights, in or out of marriage; pregnancy leaves were to be paid for by the State, which would assume charge of the children, signifying not that they would be taken away from their parents, but that they would not be abandoned to them.

But is it enough to change laws, institutions, customs, public opinion, and the whole social context, for men and women to become truly equal? . . . Woman is determined not by her hormones or by mysterious instincts, but by the manner in which her body and her relation to the world are modified through the action of others than herself. The abyss that separates the adolescent boy and girl has been deliberately widened between them since earliest childhood; later on, woman could not be other than what she was made, and that past was bound to shadow her for life. If we appreciate its influence, we see clearly that her destiny is not predetermined for all eternity.

We must not believe, certainly, that a change in woman's economic condition alone is enough to transform her, though this factor has been and remains the basic factor in her evolution; but until it has brought about the moral, social, cultural, and other consequences that it promises and requires, the new woman cannot appear. At this moment they have been realized nowhere, in Russia no more than in France or the United States; and this explains why the woman of today is torn between the past and the future. She appears most often as a "true woman" disguised as a man, and she feels herself as ill at ease in her flesh as in her masculine garb. She must shed her old skin and cut her own new clothes. This she could do only through a social evolution. No single educator could fashion a female human being today who would be the exact homologue of the male human being; if she is brought up like a boy, the young girl feels she is an oddity and thereby she is given a new kind of sex specification. . . .

If the little girl were brought up from the first with the same demands and rewards, the same severity and the same freedom, as her brothers, taking part in the same studies, the same games, promised the same future, surrounded with women and men who seemed to her undoubted equals, the . . . little girl would not seek sterile compensation in narcissism and dreaming, she would not take her fate for granted; she would be interested in what she was doing, she would throw herself without reserve into undertakings. . . .

I shall be told that all this is utopian fancy. . . . Conservatives have never failed in such circumstances to refer to that vicious circle; history, however, does not revolve. If a caste is kept in a state of inferiority, no doubt it remains inferior; but liberty can break the circle. Let the Negroes vote and they become worthy of having the vote; let woman be given responsibilities and she is able to assume them. The fact is that oppressors cannot be expected to make a move of gratuitous generosity; but at one time the revolt of the oppressed, at another time even the very evolution of the privileged caste itself, creates new situations; thus men have been led, in their own interest, to give partial emancipation to women: it remains only for women to continue their ascent, and the successes they are obtaining are an encouragement for them to do so. It seems almost certain that sooner or later they will arrive at complete economic and social equality, which will bring about an inner metamorphosis. . . .

It is nonsense to assert that revelry, vice, ecstasy, passion, would become impossible if man and woman were equal in concrete matters. . . . To emancipate woman is to refuse to confine her to the relations she bears to man, not to deny them to her; let her have her independent existence and she will continue none the less to exist for him also: mutually recognizing each other as subject, each will yet remain for the other an other. The reciprocity of their relations will not do away with the miracles—desire, possession, love, dream, adventure—worked by the division of human beings into two separate categories; and the words that move us—giving, conquering, uniting—will not lose their meaning. On the contrary, when we abolish the slavery of half of humanity, together with the whole system of hypocrisy that it implies, then the "division" of humanity will reveal its genuine significance and the human couple will find its true form. . . . [T]he relation of man to woman is the most natural relation of human being to human being. . . . The case could not be better stated. It is for man to establish the reign of liberty in the midst of the world of the given. To gain the supreme victory, it is necessary, for one thing, that by and through their natural differentiation men and women unequivocally affirm their brotherhood.

CIVIL RIGHTS, RACIAL IDENTITY, AND BLACK NATIONALISM IN AMERICA

In the 1950s, it was not uncommon for African Americans in the southern states of America to be denied the vote, even though many blacks were veterans of a world war that was supposedly committed to the ideals of democracy and equality. Segregation and inequality were the norm in the South: In many cities and towns, it was illegal for whites and blacks to eat in the same restaurant dining rooms, use the same public toilets, or ride in the same taxis. If the seats in the whites-only front half of a bus were filled, African Americans were obliged to give up their seats in the back until every white had a place. In the North, segregation was less acute but still widely practiced. Blacks were kept out of the suburbs, barred from better schools, blacklisted from country clubs, and commonly denied all but the most menial of jobs. In 1950, the average family income for whites was about $20,000, nearly double that of African Americans ($10,500); moreover, whereas an estimated 20 percent of whites lived below the poverty level, the percentage soared to more than half of all African American families (55 percent). Similar inequalities could be found in education, health, and consumer spending. The increasingly obvious gap between American ideals and reality in terms of democracy, equal opportunity, and prosperity was the single most important factor in the evolution of the civil rights movement in the 1950s and 1960s.

Although most African Americans in these decades embraced efforts to address the inequities in American society, there were sharp differences in approaches and ultimate goals. This was not unusual; ever since the mid-nineteenth century two main political and ideological currents have run among American blacks. One branch has sought equality of opportunity within the ethnic mosaic of America, arguing for accommodation and assimilation. Leaders and organizations within this group include Booker T. Washington, influential advocate of integration through hard work, and W. E. B. Du Bois, a more militant activist and founder of the National Association for the Advancement of Colored People (NAACP). But the best known—and perhaps the most successful—was the Reverend Martin Luther King, Jr., and his Southern Christian Leadership Conference (SCLC). Adopting the passive-resistance techniques of Gandhi in the face of police brutality, King seized the moral high ground from the Southern political establishment, and in doing so, he turned the tide of American public opinion that ultimately yielded the comprehensive Civil Rights Act of 1964 that barred racial discrimination. In 1968, just weeks after he told a crowd in a moving speech that he had "been to the mountaintop," Martin Luther King, Jr., was killed by an assassin's bullet.

But not all African Americans were satisfied with the results or the methods of the civil rights movement nor, especially, with Dr. King's nonviolent protests. To many Northern, urban, and young blacks, passive acceptance of police beatings, attack dogs, and drenching fire hoses was too reminiscent of the servility of slavery. Moreover, they believed that the pace of change was too slow and the results too little to improve the lives and opportunities of most blacks. Several organizations arose to embody this more militant approach: Stokely Carmichael's black power movement, the Black Panthers, and the Black Muslims. One of the most electrifying and polarizing spokesmen of the militants was Malcolm Little, better known to history as Malcolm X.

Malcolm X converted to the Black Muslims after having been exposed to its teachings while serving a prison sentence for burglary. His father had been a Baptist preacher and a staunch advocate of Marcus Garvey's Universal Negro Improvement Association (UNIA),[2] the most radical movement of its era that advocated a "Back to Africa" campaign as the only solution to white racism. The fiery proselytizing of the UNIA and its policies by Malcolm X's father inspired white fear and anger. The Ku Klux Klan burned down the family home in Lansing, Michigan, when Malcolm was four (his first vivid memory), and two years later his father was murdered, presumably by white racists. The white authorities failed to act, either to find the arsonists and killers or to honor the father's life insurance policy. The strain of these experiences, coupled with the task of raising eight children alone, led to a psychological breakdown on the part of his mother, who spent almost three decades in a mental institution. Malcolm drifted into petty crime and was ultimately found guilty of burglary. It was at this point that he encountered the teachings of the Black Muslims, and it changed the direction of his life.

The Black Muslims (or the Nation of Islam) were founded by an orthodox Muslim immigrant to America, Wallace Fard Muhammad, in 1931, and made into a powerful movement by Elijah Muhammad. Historically and doctrinally distinct from Islam proper, Black Muslims believed that whites are innately evil and that it was necessary to live apart from them. They also condemned Christianity as a slave religion used to hold blacks in a submissive status and advocated discipline and self-reliance to overcome the demoralizing effect of unemployment, broken families, drug abuse, and white racism. Because of his personal charisma, powerful speaking ability, and organizational talents, Malcolm X rose quickly in the leadership of the Nation of Islam and was appointed to lead the important Harlem mosque in New York City. But following a trip to Mecca in 1964, he broke with the Nation of Islam and modified his views on whites and separatism, stating that he could now envision the possibility of a world brotherhood. While addressing a crowd in a Harlem ballroom in 1964, Malcolm X was assassinated by three Black Muslims who were angered by his defection from the Nation of Islam.

The selection included here comes from one of his 1964 speeches warning America that there will be trouble ahead if race issues are ignored. The historical context of the speech is important: The civil rights movement was approaching a climax and about to reach fruition in Lyndon Johnson's Great Society legislative avalanche. Moreover, the focus of American race relations was shifting from the apartheid-like system of the South to the urban ghettoes of the North, Midwest, and West, where unemployment and alienation were about to erupt in paroxysms of violence and rage in a series of riots known as the "long, hot summers" of 1964 and 1965. It is also important to note that the speech was made after Malcolm had separated from the Nation of Islam, and it explains why he made a distinction between his Islamic faith and his identity as a black nationalist.

QUESTIONS TO CONSIDER

1. Why did Malcolm X suggest that there was about to be a "racial explosion" in America? What connections did he draw between race problems in the United States and the global racial and geopolitical situation?
2. What did Malcolm X mean by "black nationalism"? Who were the black nationalists? What were their goals?
3. What reasons did Malcolm X give for rejection of nonviolent forms of protest? How did he use history to defend his position? Were his arguments valid?

4. What was the form of identity that Malcolm X wanted to see among America's black population? How was this identity linked to his goals?

5. Was Malcolm X's rhetoric too harsh? Was he provoking his enemies or unifying his community? Assess the relative strengths and weaknesses of his rhetoric and style.

ADDRESS TO A MEETING IN NEW YORK (1964)

Malcolm X

Friends and enemies, tonight I hope that we can have a little fireside chat with as few sparks as possible tossed around. Especially because of the very explosive condition that the world is in today. Sometimes, when a person's house is on fire and someone comes yelling fire, instead of the person who is awakened by the yell being thankful, he makes the mistake of charging the one who awakened him with having set the fire. I hope that this little conversation tonight about the black revolution won't cause many of you to accuse us of igniting it when you find it at your doorstep.

I'm still a Muslim, that is, my religion is still Islam. I still believe that there is no god but Allah and that Mohammed is the apostle of Allah. That just happens to be my personal religion. But in the capacity which I am functioning in today, I have no intention of mixing my religion with the problems of 22,000,000 black people in this country. . . . I'm still a Muslim, but I'm also a nationalist, meaning that my political philosophy is black nationalism, my economic philosophy is black nationalism, my social philosophy is black nationalism. And when I say that this philosophy is black nationalism, to me this means that the political philosophy for black nationalism is that which is designed to encourage our people, the black people, to gain complete control over the politics and the politicians of our own people.

Our economic philosophy is that we should gain economic control over the economy of our own community, the businesses and the other things which create employment so that we can provide jobs for our own people instead of having to picket and boycott and beg someone else for a job.

And, in short, our social philosophy means that we feel that it is time to get together among our own kind and eliminate the evils that are destroying the moral fiber of our society, like drug addiction, drunkenness, adultery that leads to an abundance of bastard children, welfare problems. We believe that we should lift the level or the standard of our own society to a higher level wherein we will be satisfied and then not inclined toward pushing ourselves into other societies where we are not wanted. . . .

Just as we can see that all over the world one of the main problems facing the West is race, likewise here in America today, most of your Negro leaders as well as

Source: Malcolm X, Address to a Meeting in New York, in *Two Speeches by Malcolm X*, ed. George Breitman, 7–21. Copyright © 1965 Pathfinder Press. Reprinted with permission.

the whites agree that 1964 itself appears to be one of the most explosive years yet in the history of America on the racial front, on the racial scene. Not only is the racial explosion probably to take place in America, but all of the ingredients for this racial explosion in America to blossom into a world-wide racial explosion present themselves right here in front of us. America's racial powder keg, in short, can actually fuse or ignite a world-wide powder keg.

Any whites in this country who are still complacent when they see the possibilities of racial strife getting out of hand, and you are complacent simply because you think you outnumber the racial minority in this country, what you have to bear in mind is wherein you might outnumber us in this country, you don't outnumber us all over the world.

Any kind of racial explosion that takes place in this country today, in 1964, is not a racial explosion that can be confined to the shores of America. It is a racial explosion that can ignite the racial powder keg that exists all over the planet that we call the earth. Now I think that nobody would disagree that the dark masses of Africa and Asia and Latin America are already seething with bitterness, animosity, hostility, unrest, and impatience with the racial intolerance that they themselves have experienced at the hands of the white West.

And just as they themselves have the ingredients of hostility toward the West in general, here we also have 22,000,000 African Americans, black, brown, red, and yellow people in this country [who] are also seething with bitterness and impatience and hostility and animosity at the racial intolerance not only of the white West but of white America in particular. . . .

1964 will be America's hottest year yet; a year of much racial violence and much racial bloodshed. But it won't be blood that's going to flow only on one side. The new generation of black people that have grown up in this country during recent years are already forming the opinion, and it's a just opinion, that if there is to be bleeding, it should be reciprocal—bleeding on both sides. . . .

So today, when the black man starts reaching out for what America says are his rights, the black man feels that he is within his rights—when he becomes the victim of brutality by those who are depriving him of his rights—to do whatever necessary to protect himself. . . .

There are 22,000,000 African Americans who are ready to fight for independence right here. When I say fight for independence right here, I don't mean any nonviolent fight, or turn-the-other-cheek fight. Those days are gone. Those days are over.

If George Washington didn't get independence for this country non-violently, and if Patrick Henry didn't come up with a non-violent statement, and you taught me to look upon them as patriots and heroes, then it's time for you to realize that I have studied your books well. Again I go back to the people who founded and secured the independence of this country from the colonial power of England. . . . They didn't care about the odds.

Our people are becoming more politically mature. . . . The Negro can see that he holds the balance of power in this country politically. It is he who puts in office the one who gets in office. Yet when the Negro helps that person get in office the Negro gets nothing in return. . . . The present administration, the Democratic administration, has been there for four years. Yet no meaningful legislation has been passed by them that proposes to benefit black people in this country, despite the fact that in the House they have 267 Democrats and only 177 Republicans. . . . In the Senate there are 67 Democrats and only 33 Republicans. The Democrats control two thirds of the government and it is the Negroes who put them in a position to control the government. Yet they give the Negroes nothing in return but a few handouts in the form of appointments that are only used as window-dressing to make it appear that the problem is being solved.

No, something is wrong. And . . . you are going to have revolution. And when I say revolution I don't mean that stuff they were talking about last year about "We Shall Overcome."* . . . And the only way without bloodshed that this [revolution] can be brought about is that the black man has to be given full use of the ballot in every one of the 50 states. But if the black man doesn't get the ballot, then you are going to be faced with another man who forgets the ballot and starts using the bullet. . . .

So you have a people today who not only know what they want, but also know what they are supposed to have. And they themselves are clearing the way for another generation that is coming up that not only will know what it wants and know what it should have, but also will be ready and willing to do whatever is necessary to see what they should have materializes immediately. Thank you.

BLACK CONSCIOUSNESS IN SOUTH AFRICA

In November 1997, South African President Nelson Mandela paid tribute to Steve Biko, a black student activist and founder of the Black Consciousness movement, on the twentieth anniversary of his death. Unveiling a large bronze statue of him in Port Elizabeth, Mandela lauded Biko as "one of the greatest sons of our nation" and highlighted his crucial role in the long struggle against the racist policies known as apartheid. He especially praised Biko's efforts to restore a proud, self-confident, and assertive sense of identity to South Africa's black population. In the eyes of Mandela and much of the nation, Steve Biko should be revered and remembered as one of the greatest martyrs of the anti-apartheid movement.

Born in 1946 in the Eastern Cape, Biko engaged in political activism at a very early age, which ultimately caused his permanent expulsion from public schooling. Fortunately, he was able to enroll and graduate from a private school, from which he entered the University of Natal Medical School to fulfill his life's ambition to become a doctor. But his interest in political reform always remained strong, and in 1967 he joined the National Union of South African Students (NUSAS), a multiracial organization dedicated to African civil rights. Biko soon became disillusioned with the NUSAS, however, when it seemed to him that "whites did all the talking and blacks all the listening." The next year, he founded and organized the all-black South African Students' Organization (SASO). While leading SASO, Biko formulated and spread the philosophy of Black Consciousness. The primary

---

*A reference to a popular song of Martin Luther King's Southern Christian Leadership Conference, frequently sung during nonviolent protests.

goals of Black Consciousness were to forge pride and unity among all black South Africans, to foil the government's strategy of divide and rule, and to restore confidence in the ability of Africans to throw off their oppression. As envisioned by Biko, Black Consciousness was both a mental attitude and a way of life. He argued that true freedom could only be achieved once blacks realized that "the most potent weapon in the hands of the oppressor is the mind of the oppressed." By challenging the premises and forces that created identities of inferiority and helplessness, Biko sought to awaken blacks to the potential power within each individual.

The Black Consciousness movement came into its own at an opportune moment in the mid-1970s, for the struggle against apartheid had stalled and lacked energy. For much of the twentieth century, the most prominent African civil rights movement had been the African National Congress (ANC). Under the leadership of Nelson Mandela, the ANC attempted to pursue its goal of racial equality and integration through the creation of a mass multiracial party and the adoption of Gandhi's nonviolent protest. But in the 1950s and 1960s, such tactics found little success in South Africa. On the contrary, apartheid became more extensive and more brutal. New legislation was passed that extended and solidified white minority control over the best land, the best jobs and salaries, the best education, and control over government. Moreover, nonviolent protests were increasingly met with severe violence. At Sharpeville in 1960, sixty-nine unarmed men, women, and children protesting the pass laws[3] were shot and killed by police.

After the massacre at Sharpeville, Mandela announced that the ANC would abandon its long-term commitment to Gandhian principles of nonviolence and form a military wing, known as *Umkonto we Sizwe,* or "Spear of the Nation." The government responded harshly: The ANC was banned, Mandela was tried for treason and sentenced to a life term in prison, and other leaders and activists were either jailed or in exile. Fear of police violence and long prison sentences deterred political activism, and for a time, the struggle against apartheid was suppressed. Thus the emergence of Steve Biko and his new philosophy came at just the right moment to reenergize the struggle and to give it new direction. Inspired by his words and personal charisma, a new generation of activists was born, and their ranks grew steadily in the 1970s as Black Consciousness spread from the universities to secondary schools to urban townships.

The apartheid government first restricted Biko's activities, then banned all speeches and texts containing any reference to his person or his ideas. For a time, Biko cleverly avoided arrest, and Black Consciousness continued to gain momentum, resulting ultimately in the 1976 "Soweto uprising," in which student protests against inferior education served as the spark for a massive, violent confrontation between African residents of townships and government security forces. In August 1977, Biko was finally caught at a roadblock, arrested, and severely beaten and tortured in jail over a period of several days. Bloodied, naked, and unconscious, he was then tossed into the back of truck and driven over 700 miles to Pretoria, where he was pronounced dead at the age of twenty-nine. As was common in those days, an official government inquest after his death absolved the police of any wrongdoing.

The murder of Biko created a national martyr that only intensified the anti-apartheid campaign. Despite a declaration of martial law and military occupation of the townships, the government was unable to quell the unrest that continued into the 1980s. Faced by the prospect of continuing social instability, economic decline, and international isolation, the South African government, now led by Prime Minister F. W. de Klerk, finally decided that apartheid had outlived its utility and must change. In 1991, Nelson Mandela was released from prison to an international hero's welcome, and three years later, he led the ANC to victory in the nation's first democratic elections.

The following text, "Black Consciousness and the Quest for a True Humanity," was written by Biko in 1973 for inclusion in a book on black theology in South Africa.[4] In this essay, Biko discusses the origins and expressions of racism and highlights their effect on people's attitudes and lives. He also provides a clear definition and explanation of Black Consciousness and offers it as a solution to remedy dependency on whites and passivity in blacks. In doing so, he envisions a new identity for South African blacks that will empower individuals and give them the strength and determination to take charge of their own future.

QUESTIONS TO CONSIDER

1. According to Biko, how did the myth of African inferiority get started? What effect has it had on perceptions of identity?
2. Identify and discuss the goals of Black Consciousness. Why would Biko reject the assistance of white liberals in the fight against apartheid?
3. What role did missionaries play in the shaping of South African identity? How might a missionary defend his or her actions against Biko's accusations?
4. What was the identity that Biko ideally would have liked to see created among South African blacks? List the attributes and explain their significance.
5. In your assessment, is Black Consciousness a racist ideology? Explain your response fully.

"BLACK CONSCIOUSNESS AND THE QUEST FOR A TRUE HUMANITY" (1973)

Steve Biko

It is perhaps fitting to start by examining why it is necessary for us to think collectively about a problem we never created. In doing so, I do not wish to concern myself unnecessarily with the white people of South Africa, but to get to the right answers, we must ask the right questions; we have to find out what went wrong—where and when;

Source: Steve Biko, "Black Consciousness and the Quest for a True Humanity," in *I Write What I Like: Selected Writings*, ed. Aelred Stubbs. Copyright © 1979 Harper & Row. Reprinted by permission of HarperCollins Publishers, Inc. This is a collection of Biko's lectures, articles, letters, and trial testimonies that were gathered and smuggled out of South Africa after his death in 1977.

and we have to find out whether our position is a deliberate creation of God or, an artificial fabrication of the truth by power-hungry people whose motive is authority, security, wealth and comfort. In other words, the "Black Consciousness" approach would be irrelevant in a colorless and non-exploitative egalitarian society. It is relevant here because we believe that an anomalous situation is a deliberate creation of man.

There is no doubt that the color question in South African politics was originally introduced for economic reasons. The leaders of the white community had to create some kind of barrier between blacks and whites so that whites could enjoy privileges at the expense of blacks and still feel free to give a moral justification for the obvious exploitation that pricked even the hardest of white consciences. However, tradition has it that whenever a group of people has tasted the lovely fruits of wealth, security and prestige it begins to find it more comfortable to believe in the obvious lie and to accept it as normal that it alone is entitled to privilege. In order to believe this seriously, it needs to convince itself of all the arguments that support the lie. It is not surprising, therefore, that in South Africa, after generations of exploitation, white people on the whole have come to believe in the inferiority of the black man, so much so that while the race problem started as an offshoot of the economic greed exhibited by white people, it has now become a serious problem on its own. White people now despise black people, not because they need to reinforce their attitude and to justify their position of privilege but simply because they actually believe that black is inferior and bad. This is the basis upon which whites are working in South Africa, and it is what makes South African society racist.

The racism we meet does not exist only on an individual basis; it is also institutionalized to make it look like the South African way of life. Although of late there has been a feeble attempt to gloss over the racist elements in the system, it is still true that the system derives its nourishment from the existence of anti-black attitudes in society. To make the lie live even longer, blacks have to be denied any chance of accidentally proving their equality with white men. For this reason there is job reservation, lack of training in skilled work, and a tight orbit around professional possibilities for blacks. Stupidly enough, the system turns back to say that blacks are inferior because they have no economists, no engineers, etc., although it is made impossible for blacks to acquire these skills. . . .

It is not enough for whites to be on the offensive. So immersed are they in prejudice that they do not believe that blacks can formulate their thoughts without white guidance and trusteeship. Thus, even those whites who see much wrong with the system make it their business to control the response of the blacks to the provocation. No one is suggesting that it is not the business of liberal whites to oppose what is wrong. However, it appears to us as too much of a coincidence that liberals—few as they are—should not only be determining the *modus operandi* of those blacks who oppose the system, but also leading it, in spite of their involvement in the system. To us it seems that their role spells out the totality of the white power structure—the fact that though whites are our problem, it is still other whites who want to tell us how to deal with that problem. . . .

It is much more important for blacks to see this difference than it is for whites. We must learn to accept that no group, however benevolent, can ever hand power to the vanquished on a plate. We must accept that the limits of tyrants are prescribed by the endurance of those whom they oppress. As long as we go to Whitey begging cap in hand for our own emancipation, we are giving him further sanction to continue with his racist and oppressive system. We must realize that our situation is not a mistake on the part of whites but a deliberate act, and that no amount of moral lecturing will persuade the white man to "correct" the situation. The system concedes nothing without demand, for it formulates its very method of operation on the basis that the ignorant will learn to know, the child will grow into an adult and therefore demands will begin to be made. It gears itself to resist demands in whatever way it sees fit. When you refuse to make these demands and choose to come to a round table to beg for your deliverance, you are asking for the contempt of those who have power over you. This is why we must reject the beggar tactics that are being forced on us by those who wish to appease our cruel masters. This is where the SASO message and cry *"Black man, you are on your own!"* becomes relevant.

The concept of integration, whose virtues are often extolled in white liberal circles, is full of unquestioned assumptions that embrace white values. It is a concept long defined by whites and never examined by blacks. It is based on the assumption that all is well with the system apart from some degree of mismanagement by irrational conservatives at the top. Even the people who argue for integration often forget to veil it in its supposedly beautiful covering. They tell each other that, were it not for job reservation, there would be a beautiful market to exploit. They forget they are talking about people. They see blacks as additional levers to some complicated industrial machines. This is white man's integration—an integration based on exploitative values. It is an integration in which black will compete with black, using each other as rungs up a step ladder leading them to white values. It is an integration in which the black man will have to prove himself in terms of these values before meriting acceptance and ultimate assimilation, and in which the poor will grow poorer and the rich richer in a country where the poor have always been black. We do not want to be reminded that it is we, the indigenous people, who are poor and exploited in the land of our birth. These are concepts which the Black Consciousness approach wishes to eradicate from the black man's mind before our society is driven to chaos by irresponsible people from Coca-cola and hamburger cultural backgrounds.

Black Consciousness is an attitude of mind and a way of life, the most positive call to emanate from the black world for a long time. Its essence is the realization by the black man of the need to rally together with his brothers around the cause of their oppression—the blackness of their skin—and to operate as a group to rid themselves of the shackles that bind them to perpetual servitude. It is based on a self-examination which has ultimately led them to believe that by seeking to run away from themselves and emulate the white man, they are insulting the intelligence of whoever created them black. The philosophy of Black Consciousness therefore expresses group pride and the determination of the black to rise and attain the envisaged self. Freedom is the ability to define oneself with one's possibilities held back not by the power of other people over one but only by one's relationship to God and to natural surroundings. On his own, therefore, the black man wishes to explore his surroundings and test his possibilities—in other words to make his freedom real by whatever means he deems fit. At the heart of this kind of thinking is the realization by blacks that the most potent weapon in the hands of the oppressor is the mind of the oppressed. If one is free at heart, no man-made chains can bind one to servitude, but if one's mind is so manipulated and controlled by the oppressor as to make the oppressed believe that he is a liability to the white man, then there will be nothing the oppressed can do to scare his powerful masters. Hence thinking along lines of Black Consciousness makes the black man see himself as a being complete in himself. It makes him less dependent and more free to express his manhood. At the end of it all he cannot tolerate attempts by anybody to dwarf the significance of his manhood. . . .

In all aspects of the black-white relationship, now and in the past, we see a constant tendency by whites to depict blacks as of an inferior status. Our culture, our history and indeed all aspects of the black man's life have been battered nearly out of shape in the great collision between the indigenous values and the Anglo-Boer culture.

The first people to come and relate to blacks in a human way in South Africa were the missionaries. They were in the vanguard of the colonization movement to "civilize and educate" the savages and introduce the Christian message to them. The religion they brought was quite foreign to the black indigenous people. African religion in its essence was not radically different from Christianity. We also believed in one God, we had our own community of saints through whom we related to our God, and we did not find it compatible with our way of life to worship God in isolation from the various aspects of our lives. Hence worship was not a specialized function that found expression once a week in a secluded building, but rather it featured in our wars, our beer-drinking, our dances and our customs in general. Whenever Africans drank they would first relate to God by giving a portion of their beer away as a token of thanks. When anything went wrong at home they would offer sacrifice to God to appease him and atone for their sins. There was no hell in our religion. We believed in the inherent goodness of man—hence we took it for granted that all people at death joined the community of saints and therefore merited our respect.

It was the missionaries who confused the people with their new religion. They scared our people with stories of hell. They painted their God as a demanding God who wanted worship "or else." People had to discard their clothes and their customs in order to be accepted in this new religion. Knowing how religious the African people were, the missionaries stepped up their terror campaign on the emotions of the people with their detailed accounts of eternal burning, tearing of hair and gnashing of teeth. By some strange and twisted logic, they argued that theirs was a scientific religion and ours a superstition—all this in spite of the biological discrepancy which is at the base of their religion. This cold and cruel religion was strange to the indigenous people and caused frequent strife between the converted and the "pagans," for the former, having imbibed the false values from white society, were taught to ridicule and despise those who defended the truth of their indigenous religion. With the ultimate acceptance of the western religion down went our cultural values!

While I do not wish to question the basic truth at the heart of the Christian message, there is a strong case for a re-examination of Christianity. It has proved a very adaptable religion which does not seek to supplement existing orders but—like any universal truth—to find application within a particular situation. More than anyone else, the missionaries knew that not all they did was essential to the spread of the message. But the basic intention went much further than merely spreading the word.

Their arrogance and their monopoly on truth, beauty and moral judgment taught them to despise native customs and traditions and to seek to infuse their own new values into these societies.

Here then we have the case for Black Theology. While not wishing to discuss Black Theology at length, let it suffice to say that it seeks to relate God and Christ once more to the black man and his daily problems. It wants to describe Christ as a fighting God, not a passive God who allows a lie to rest unchallenged. It grapples with existential problems and does not claim to be a theology of absolutes. It seeks to bring back God to the black man and to the truth and reality of his situation. This is an important aspect of Black Consciousness, for quite a large proportion of black people in South Africa are Christians still swimming in a mire of confusion—the aftermath of the missionary approach. It is the duty therefore of all black priests and ministers of religion to save Christianity by adopting Black Theology's approach and thereby once more uniting the black man with his God.

A long look should also be taken at the educational system for blacks. The same tense situation was found as long ago as the arrival of the missionaries. Children were taught, under the pretext of hygiene, good manners and other such vague concepts, to despise their mode of upbringing at home and to question the values and customs of their society. The result was the expected one—children and parents saw life differently and the former lost respect for the latter. Now in African society it is a cardinal sin for a child to lose respect for his parent. Yet how can one prevent the loss of respect between child and parent when the child is taught by his know-all white tutors to disregard his family teachings? Who can resist losing respect for his tradition when in school his whole cultural background is summed up in one word—barbarism.

Thus we can immediately see the logic of placing the missionaries in the forefront of the colonization process. A man who succeeds in making a group of people accept a foreign concept in which he is expert makes them perpetual students whose progress in the particular field can only be evaluated by him; the student must constantly turn to him for guidance and promotion. In being forced to accept the Anglo-Boer culture, the blacks have allowed themselves to be at the mercy of the white man and to have him as their eternal supervisor. Only he can tell us how good our performance is and instinctively each of us is at pains to please this powerful, all-knowing master. This is what Black Consciousness seeks to eradicate.

Being part of an exploitative society in which we are often the direct objects of exploitation, we need to evolve a strategy towards our economic situation. We are aware that the blacks are still colonized even within the borders of South Africa. Their cheap labor has helped to make South Africa what it is today. Our money from the townships takes a one-way journey to white shops and white banks, and all we do in our lives is pay the white man either with labor or in coin. Capitalistic exploitative tendencies, coupled with the overt arrogance of white racism, have conspired against us. Thus in South Africa now it is very expensive to be poor. It is the poor people who stay furthest from town and therefore have to spend more money on transport to come and work for white people; it is the poor people who use uneconomic and inconvenient fuel like paraffin and coal because of the refusal of the white man to install electricity in black areas; it is the poor people who are governed by many ill-defined restrictive laws and therefore have to spend money on fines for "technical" offences; it is the poor people who have no hospitals and are therefore exposed to exorbitant charges by private doctors; it is the poor people who use untarred roads, have to walk long distances, and therefore experience the greatest wear and tear on commodities like shoes; it is the poor people who have to pay for their children's books while whites get them free. It does not need to be said that it is the black people who are poor.

We therefore need to take another look at how best to use our economic power, little as it may seem to be. We must seriously examine the possibilities of establishing business co-operatives whose interests will be ploughed back into community development programs. We should think along such lines as the "buy black" campaign once suggested in Johannesburg and establish our own banks for the benefit of the community. Organizational development amongst blacks has only been low because we have allowed it to be. Now that we know we are on our own, it is an absolute duty for us to fulfil these needs. . . .

Some will charge that we are racist but these people are using exactly the values we reject. We do not have the power to subjugate anyone. We are merely responding to provocation in the most realistic possible way. Racism does not only imply exclusion of one race by another—it always presupposes that the exclusion is for the purposes of subjugation. Blacks have had enough experience as objects of racism not to wish to turn the tables. While it may be relevant now to talk about black in relation to white, we must not make this our preoccupation, for it can be a negative exercise. As we proceed further towards the achievement of our goals let us talk more about ourselves and our struggle and less about whites.

We have set out on a quest for true humanity, and somewhere on the distant horizon we can see the glittering prize. Let us march forth with courage and determination, drawing strength from our common plight and our brotherhood. In time we shall be in a position to bestow upon South Africa the greatest gift possible—a more human face.

SEXUAL IDENTITY, SELF-OPPRESSION, AND GAY RIGHTS

The gay rights movement in the United States and Europe owes much to the social protest movements discussed earlier in this chapter. The women's movement helped to pave the way, as social discussion concerning gender very easily led into discussions of sexuality. Moreover, feminists and gays shared many of the same goals (equal status and opportunity) and faced many of the same obstacles (discrimination and deeply seated cultural values), so it was natural that the two movements would reinforce each other indirectly, if not always directly. The civil rights movement also shaped the gay rights movement, showing the need to be more assertive in action and bolder in words. And most important, both feminists and advocates of black power highlighted the need and importance of a positive, empowered, self-created identity. The substitution of "gay" for "homosexual" in the 1970s was one of the earliest expressions of a newly created identity that freed gays from automatic reference to the presumably normal, straight "heterosexual." More recently, some gays have seized for themselves the formerly derogatory word "queer," an action that both mocks and rejects identity labels imposed by others. But up until the mid-1960s, the visibility and self-confidence of gays was much reduced because of societal disapproval. To be considered "queer"—or even to acknowledge it as a part of oneself—was fraught with risks. To be "outed" back then could mean the loss of job, friends, and family. Laws criminalized most homosexual behavior, and society generally turned a blind eye to hate crimes. Homosexuals were expected to remain deep in the closet, out of sight and out of mind.

Two pivotal events helped to transform the way gays viewed themselves, as well as how they were perceived by others. The first was a riot at a popular gay bar in New York's Greenwich Village during the summer of 1969. A routine police raid on the bar met with untypical results: the patrons fought back. As the fight moved back out into the street, a full-fledged riot ensued that continued for two nights. Although order was eventually restored, the riot at the Stonewall Bar marked the beginning of the modern gay rights movement and a new combative spirit. As one activist has put it, "The patrons at Stonewall refused to be treated as second class citizens. We said 'no' to intolerance and 'yes' to empowerment."

The second major event was the formation of the Gay Liberation Front in London and the publication of the Front's Manifesto in 1971. The Gay Liberation Front (GLF) was made up of an international collection of gay men living in London who were frustrated at what they saw as society's constant efforts to humiliate and discriminate against them. Their strategy bears a striking similarity to the one pioneered by Gandhi and Steve Biko: to demonstrate to society and to oneself that the problem was not being gay; the problem was society's homophobia. Or, in the words of one GLF activist, "Instead of us having to justify our existence, we forced the gay-haters to justify their bigotry." The GLF used a variety of strategies and tactics to build a new sense of identity while challenging societal attitudes and norms. Civil disobedience and boycotts were combined with humorous street performances and gay-pride parades. A sense of community was reinforced by the GLF sponsorship of a gay newspaper and counseling center. Most of all, the GLF practiced visibility: a most defiant action made by a group that was supposed to remain invisible.

In more recent years, the identities of gays have been transformed by the HIV/AIDS epidemic, which was first diagnosed among gay men living in America and Europe. Initially, the epidemic had a negative impact on societal perceptions of gays, for the disease was first attributed to a promiscuous, immoral lifestyle. But over time, media attention to the epidemic provided the public with unprecedented exposure to gays and the gay community that has had the effect of challenging or undermining traditional assumptions and attitudes. In addition, gay rights organizations have spread around the world. But as the recent furor over "gay marriage" in the United States suggests, societal definitions of and attitudes about homosexuality are far from fixed.

QUESTIONS TO CONSIDER

1. According to the GLF's Manifesto, what are the institutions that oppress gay men and women? What is the basis for this oppression? Are there similarities between the perceived oppression of gays and women?
2. In addition to institutional oppression, the GLF also discusses "self-oppression." What do they mean by this? Why is it significant? What can be done about it?
3. The Manifesto seems to make the claim that psychiatry is not an objective science. Why? How do you assess their argument?
4. Does the GLF believe that gay people are most likely products of their upbringing? Or products of genetics? Does it make any difference?
5. What is the ideal sense of identity that the GLF would like to see in all gay people? What important attributes would they favor, and why? In what ways—if any—does the ideal gay identity compare with the other identities discussed in this chapter?

"MANIFESTO" (1970)

The London Gay Liberation Front

Introduction

Throughout recorded history, oppressed groups have organised to claim their rights and obtain their needs. Homosexuals, who have been oppressed by physical violence and by ideological and psychological attacks at every level of social interaction, are at last becoming angry.

To you, our gay sisters and brothers, we say that you are oppressed; we intend to show you examples of the hatred and fear with which straight society relegates us to the position and treatment of sub-humans, and to explain their basis. We will show you how we can use our righteous anger to uproot the present oppressive system with its decaying and constricting ideology, and how we, together with other oppressed groups, can start to form a new order, and a liberated lifestyle, from the alternatives which we offer.

How We Are Oppressed

The oppression of gay people starts in the most basic unit of society, the family, consisting of the man in charge, a slave as his wife, and their children on whom

Source: Manifesto Group of the GLF, "Manifesto" (originally printed by Russell Press/Nottingham, 1971 and reprinted by Gay Liberation Information Service/London, 1979). In Lisa Power, No Bath but Plenty of Bubbles: An Oral History of the Gay Liberation Front, 314–20. Copyright © 1995 Cassell Academic Books. Used by permission of The Orion Publishing Group Ltd.

they force themselves as the ideal models. The very form of the family works against homosexuality.

At some point nearly all gay people have found it difficult to cope with having the restricting images of man or woman pushed on them by their parents. It may have been from very early on, when the pressures to play with the "right" toys, and thus prove boyishness or girlishness, drove against the child's inclinations. But for all of us this is certainly a problem by the time of adolescence, when we are expected to prove ourselves socially to our parents as members of the right sex (to bring home a boy/girl friend) and to start being a "real" (oppressive) young man or a "real" (oppressed) young woman. The tensions can be very destructive.

The fact that gay people notice they are different from other men and women in the family situation, causes them to feel ashamed, guilty and failures. How many of us have really dared be honest with our parents? How many of us have been thrown out of home? How many of us have been pressured into marriage, sent to psychiatrists, frightened into sexual inertia, ostracised, banned, emotionally destroyed—all by our parents?

Family experiences may differ widely, but in their education all children confront a common situation. Schools reflect the values of society in their formal academic curriculum, and reinforce them in their morality and discipline. Boys learn competitive ego-building sports, and have more opportunity in science, whereas girls are given emphasis on domestic subjects, needlework, etc. Again, we gays were all forced into a rigid sex role which we did not want or need. It is quite common to discipline children for behaving in any way like the opposite sex; degrading titles like "sissy" and "tomboy" are widely used. . . .

Formal religious education is still part of everyone's schooling, and our whole legal structure is supposedly based on Christianity whose archaic and irrational teachings support the family and marriage as the only permitted condition for sex. Gay people have been attacked as abominable and sinful since the beginning of both Judaism and Christianity, and even if today the Church is playing down these strictures on homosexuality, its new ideology is that gay people are pathetic objects for sympathy. . . .

Anti-homosexual morality and ideology, at every level of society, manifest themselves in a special vocabulary for denigrating gay people. There is abuse like "pansy", "fairy", "lesbo" to hurl at men and women who can't or won't fit stereotyped preconceptions. There are words like "sick", "bent" and "neurotic" for destroying the credence of gay people. But there are no positive words. The ideological intent of our language makes it very clear that the generation of words and meanings is, at the moment, in the hands of the enemy. And that so many gay people pretend to be straight, and call each other "butch dykes" or "screaming queens" only makes that fact the more real. The verbal attack on men and women who do not behave as they are supposed to, reflects the ideology of masculine superiority. A man who behaves like a woman is seen as losing something, and a woman who behaves like a man is put down for threatening men's environment or their privileges. . . .

One way of oppressing people and preventing them getting too angry about it, is to convince them, and everyone else, that they are sick. There has hence arisen a body of psychiatric "theory" and "therapy" to deal with the "problems" and "treatment" of homosexuality. Bearing in mind what we have so far described, it is quite understandable that gay people get depressed and paranoid; but it is also, of course, part of the scheme that gay people should retreat to psychiatrists in times of troubles.

Operating as they do on the basis of social convention and prejudice, NOT scientific truth, mainstream psychiatrists accept society's prevailing view that the male and female sex roles are "good" and "normal", and try to adjust people to them. If that fails, patients are told to "accept themselves" as "deviant". For the psychiatrist to state that homosexuality was perfectly valid and satisfying, and that the hang-up was society's inability to accept that fact, would result in the loss of a large proportion of his patients. Psychiatric "treatment" can take the form either of mind-bending "psychotherapy", or of aversion therapy which operates on the crude conditioning theory that if you hit a person hard enough, he'll do what you want. Another form of "therapy" is chemically induced castration, and there is a further form of "treatment" which consists in erasing part of the brain, with the intent (usually successful) of making the subject an asexual vegetable.

This "therapy" is not the source of the psychiatrist's power, however. Their social power stems from the facile and dangerous arguments by which they contrive to justify the prejudice that homosexuality is bad or unfortunate, and to mount this fundamental attack upon our right to do as we think best. In this respect, there is little difference between the psychiatrist who says: "From statistics we can show that homosexuality is connected with madness", and the one who says: "Homosexuality is unfortunate because it is socially rejected". The former is a dangerous idiot—he cannot see that it is society which drives gay people mad. The second is a pig because he does see this, but sides consciously with the oppressors. . . .

The ultimate success of all forms of oppression is our self-oppression. Self-oppression is achieved when the gay person has adopted and internalized straight people's definition of what is good and bad. Self-oppression is saying: "When you come down to it, we *are* abnormal". Or doing what you most need and want to do, but with a sense of shame and loathing, or in a state of disassociation, pretending it isn't happening; cruising or cottaging not because you enjoy it, but because you're afraid of anything less anonymous. Self-oppression is saying: "I accept what I am", and meaning: "I accept that what I am is second-best and rather pathetic". Self-oppression is any other kind of apology: "We've been living together for ten years and all our married friends know about us and think we're just the same as them". Why? You're not.

Self-oppression is the dolly lesbian who says: "I can't stand those butch types who look like truck drivers"; the virile gay man who shakes his head at the thought of "those pathetic queens". This is self-oppression because it's just another way of saying: "I'm a nice normal gay. Just like an attractive heterosexual".

The ultimate in self-oppression is to avoid confronting straight society, and thereby provoking further hostility: Self-oppression is saying, and believing: "I am not oppressed". . . .

The Way Forward

The long-term goal of Gay Liberation, which inevitably brings us into conflict with the institutionalized sexism of this society, is to rid society of the gender-role system which is at the root of our oppression. This can only be achieved by eliminating the social pressures on men and women to conform to narrowly defined gender roles. It is particularly important that children and young people be encouraged to develop their own talents and interests and to express their own individuality rather than act out stereotyped parts alien to their nature.

As we cannot carry out this revolutionary change alone, and as the abolition of gender roles is also a necessary condition of women's liberation, we will work to form a strategic alliance with the women's liberation movement, aiming to develop our ideas and our practice in close inter-relation. In order to build this alliance, the brothers in gay liberation will have to be prepared to sacrifice that degree of male chauvinism and male privilege that they still all possess.

To achieve our long term goal will take many years, perhaps decades. But attitudes to the appropriate place of men and women in our society are changing rapidly, particularly the belief in the subordinate place for women. Modern conditions are placing increasing strain on the small nuclear family containing one adult male and one adult female with narrowly defined roles and bound together for life.

The starting point of our liberation must be to rid ourselves of the oppression which lies in the head of every one of us. This means freeing our heads from self-oppression and male chauvinism, and no longer organizing our lives according to the patterns with which we are indoctrinated by straight society. It means that we must root out the idea that homosexuality is bad, sick or immoral, and develop a gay pride. In order to survive, most of us have either knuckled under or pretended that no oppression exists, and the result of this has been further to distort our heads. Within gay liberation, a number of consciousness-raising groups have already developed, in which we try to understand our oppression and learn new ways of thinking and behaving. The aim is to step outside the experience permitted by straight society, and to learn to love and trust one another. This is the precondition for acting and struggling together.

By freeing our heads we get the confidence to come out publicly and proudly as gay people, and to win over our gay brothers and sisters to the ideas of gay liberation. . . .

We do not intend to ask for anything. We intend to stand firm and assert our basic rights. If this involves violence, it will not be we who initiate this, but those who attempt to stand in our way to freedom.

NOTES

1. The actual process of decolonization varied considerably. In some colonies, the transition of power was fairly smooth and peaceful, but in others, it involved a long and violent liberation struggle.

2. Marcus Garvey (1887–1940) was a Jamaican-born black who, through his travels in the United States and the Caribbean, concluded that white racism was so firmly entrenched that the only hope for blacks was to emigrate back to Africa. Although his efforts to create a mass exodus failed, he did succeed in raising a new sense of pan-Africanist identity among blacks in the Americas.

3. During the era of apartheid, pass laws segregated the races and ensured white-minority domination. For example, if Africans wished to leave their impoverished tribal reservations to seek opportunities elsewhere, they first required a "pass" granted by the white-controlled government. Pass laws were deeply resented by Africans because the passes represented their oppressed and inferior status in South Africa. They were repealed in 1986.

4. Written for *Black Theology: The South African Voice,* ed. Basil Moore (London: C. Hurst & Co., 1973).

CHAPTER 15

Perspectives on Globalization

INTRODUCTION

A Chinese factory worker in Shanghai produces Mickey Mouse toys to be sold at Disneyland to millions of American and overseas tourists who visit the park every year. A famous South American soccer star plays for a French club team but endorses athletic apparel licensed in Italy and manufactured in Asia. A British rock band performs reggae music at sold-out concerts in the United States to raise money for AIDS programs in Africa. And a North Carolina textile worker loses her job when her factory moves its operations to take advantage of cheaper labor overseas.

These are just a few of the many manifestations of globalization, one of the most hotly debated and discussed topics of the early twenty-first century. Hardly a day passes when one does not hear references to global markets, global warming, global communications, or global security. Broadly defined, globalization is a process of change that is leading to an increasingly interconnected and interdependent world, encompassing all aspects of economic, political, and social life. But beyond this simplistic definition, conceptions and assessments vary widely. For some, globalization represents a process of "internationalization," marked by new forms of global cooperation and a vastly accelerated exchange of people, goods, and ideas around the world. For others, globalization represents modernization—the expansion of free trade, the spread of modern technology, and the broadening of democratic institutions and governments. But many other people see globalization as a dire threat, a thinly disguised form of western or American imperialism that exploits the poor, pollutes the environment, and erodes cultural identities and traditions. With such divergent conceptions, it is easy to understand why globalization has become such a controversial and uneasy process.

This chapter focuses on three crucial issues frequently at the heart of contemporary debates about globalization: the state of the world's environment, the international human rights movement, and the spread of "global culture." Each issue is introduced by a short reading, which provides an overview on the subject, as well as some of the differing perspectives and disputes. The readings are paired with relevant data tables, graphs, and images—contemporary artifacts of our modern age. Our primary goal is to better understand differing perspectives on each of these issues and how they illuminate aspects of globalization. A second goal is to consider the historical forces that have shaped modern globalization and to use the data to make projections about the future. But be forewarned: There are no prescriptive answers or solutions found in the readings or data that follow. Instead, you must employ your own powers of analysis and judgment to make meaningful assessments about the meaning and implications of globalization.

In a historical perspective, globalization is not a new phenomenon. As previous chapters in this volume have shown, cross-cultural encounters that have resulted in a more interdependent and interconnected world are as old as human history. The real uniqueness of our modern age is the unprecedented scope, scale, and pace of globalization, which now reaches into nearly every corner of the world. Fueled by an ever-expanding global system of production and trade, and facilitated by such technological innovations as jet aircraft, televisions, and the personal computer, encounters between the earth's six billion residents have become much more frequent, intense, and multilayered than ever before.

Such fast change has had a dramatic impact, particularly on the planet's natural environment. According to John McNeill, an environmental historian, future history may indeed rank environmental change as the most crucial event of the twentieth century, more important than the two world wars or the spread of democracy. In the reading that follows, taken from *Something New Under the Sun* (2000), McNeill further asserts that any meaningful discussion of environmental health must include an often-neglected historical perspective in order to make sense of present-day statistics. Following this reading is a series of charts and graphs that allow you to make initial assessments about the relationships between human enterprise and environmental change in the past century—and what that might foretell about the future.

The human rights movement is another major and controversial issue intertwined with globalization. In the aftermath of World War II and the Holocaust, human rights became a global issue, defined and monitored by the most global of political institutions, the United Nations. But as our reading "Righting Wrongs" argues, global definitions of universal rights—and the obligation to guarantee them to all peoples—remain open to debate. This is especially true for economic and social human rights, which some believe do not carry the same compelling "moral imperative" as basic civil and political rights. The accompanying Human Development Balance Sheet 2002 from the United Nations Development Program provides data relevant to the reading, and especially related to the issue of economic and social rights.

The last section is on "global culture." This may be the most familiar topic, because we encounter it nearly every day, in the music we listen to, the foods we eat, the movies we watch, and the places we visit. But as the world becomes increasingly interconnected, and as goods and ideas are increasingly exchanged and assimilated, what is happening to regional distinctiveness, national identities, and local culture? These were some of the main issues discussed in the radio talk show *Globally Speaking*, produced by Radio Australia in 2002. The commentators, representing experts from western and nonwestern backgrounds, shared perspectives on the complexities and implications of cross-cultural encounters in an increasingly globalized world. This reading is followed by a picture gallery, a series of photographs that illuminate different dimensions and impacts of modern cross-cultural exchanges.

These three case studies clearly do not represent all aspects and dimensions of globalization, so we must be careful with our generalizations and conclusions. But each case is also certain to remain an important issue in the making of the twenty-first century. Furthermore, when viewed together, they help to illuminate the complexities and character of globalization and the differing perspectives and interpretations that shape contemporary reports and debates. Using the accompanying data tables, balance sheets, and pictures, you can begin to make better assessments about the costs and benefits of an increasingly interrelated and interdependent world.

CHAPTER QUESTIONS

1. What was the single most important or surprising fact that you discovered in the readings or accompanying data tables? Why did you find this so significant or surprising?
2. When the three case studies are compared, are there any common themes or issues that emerge? Is it possible to make any conclusions about the character of globalization from these examples?
3. Where is resistance to globalization strongest? Where is globalization most apparent or advocated? Do these trends tell us anything more about this process of change?
4. How is globalization related to past trends in human history? How might the histories of different regions and countries affect their responses to globalization? To what degree is current change unique and to what degree is it a continuation of older trends?
5. Is globalization an inevitable and uncontrollable feature of human history, or can its structure and impact be realistically controlled? Will the world become more or less interconnected in your lifetime?

THE GLOBAL ENVIRONMENT

How healthy is planet Earth, and what is its prognosis for future human development? Put this question to a dozen scientists and experts and you'll likely get a dozen different interpretations. Optimists claim that the environment is in much better shape than most people have been led to believe and that new technologies will continue to improve the purity of air, water, and soils in future decades.

Pessimists point to increases in global warming, deforestation, and species extinction as causes for great alarm and immediate action. These controversies about the state of the global environment are partly the result of limited evidence, which forces scientists to extrapolate evidence from imprecise mathematical models. They are also generated by basic differences in perspectives—optimists and pessimists may start out with fundamentally different sets of assumptions and values, which may shape their conclusions about the current state of the environment.

Yet another perspective problem concerns time—in this case, trying to understand environmental health solely from a "presentist" perspective. This is the prime complaint of J. R. McNeill, an environmental historian at Georgetown University. In *Something New Under the Sun* (2000), McNeill provides a broad and comprehensive history of environmental change in the twentieth century, which he claims was the most intense period of environmental change in world history, change that was overwhelmingly the result of human action. In the excerpt that follows, McNeill explains why the twentieth century was so peculiar and why a historical understanding is both desirable and crucial for a more complete appreciation of environmental conditions as we enter the new millennium. The reading is followed by a short series of statistical tables and graphs that highlight important issues associated with environmental change in the past century.

QUESTIONS TO CONSIDER

1. According to McNeill, why was the twentieth century so peculiar in terms of environmental history? What factors does he suggest were primarily responsible for environmental change in the past century? Are these ideas consistent with the data provided?

2. McNeill claims that natural systems have crucial "thresholds" that affect their proper functioning. What does he mean by "thresholds"? Give some examples and explain why they are important.

3. Modern science and technology appear to many as double-edged swords—they have improved humankind's mastery over the environment, but sometimes at great cost to nature. What examples emerged from the reading and data tables? In your estimation, will science and technology be the ultimate bane or the savior of the global environment?

4. McNeill summarizes capitalist values as ". . . we can all consume more than we used to, and expect to consume still more in the years to come. . . . [We expect] continuous growth. . . ." Given your understanding of capitalism, do you think this is an accurate representation? Why or why not? In your assessment, is capitalism consistent with environmental health? Explain your answer fully.

5. After examining the data and considering the text, do you believe planet Earth could support a global population living the life of an average American today? What does your response say about the future of humankind?

"PECULIARITIES OF A PRODIGAL CENTURY" (2000)

J. R. McNeill

The disadvantage of men not knowing the past is that they do not know the present.
—G. K. Chesterton (1933)

Environmental change on earth is as old as the planet itself, about 4 billion years. Our genus, *Homo,* has altered earthly environments throughout our career, about 4 million years. But there has never been anything like the twentieth century.

Asteroids and volcanoes, among other astronomical and geological forces, have probably produced more radical environmental changes than we have yet witnessed in our time. But humanity has not. This is the first time in human history that we have altered ecosystems with such intensity, on such scale and with such speed. It is one of the few times in the earth's history to see changes of this scope and pace. Albert Einstein famously refused to "believe that God plays dice with the world." But in the twentieth century, humankind has begun to play dice with the planet, without knowing all the rules of the game.

The human race, without intending anything of the sort, has undertaken a gigantic uncontrolled experiment on the earth. In time, I think, this will appear as the most important aspect of the twentieth-century history, more so than World War II, the communist enterprise, the rise of mass literacy, the spread of democracy, or the growing emancipation of women. To see just how prodigal and peculiar this century was, it helps to adopt long perspectives of the deeper past.

In environmental history, the twentieth century qualifies as a peculiar century because of the screeching acceleration of so many processes that bring ecological change. Most of these processes are not new: we have cut timber, mined ores, generated wastes, grown crops, and hunted animals for a long time. In modern times we have generally done more of these things than ever before, and since 1945, in most cases, far more. Although there are a few kinds of environmental change that are genuinely new in the twentieth century, such as human-induced thinning of the ozone layer, for the most part the ecological peculiarity of the twentieth century is a matter of scale and intensity.

Sometimes differences in quantity can become differences in quality. So it was with twentieth-century environmental change. The scale and intensity of changes were so great that matters that for millennia were local concerns became global. One example is air pollution. Since people first harnessed fire half a million years ago, they have polluted air locally. Mediterranean lead smelting in Roman times even polluted air in the Arctic. But lately, air pollution has grown so comprehensive and large

Source: From J. R. McNeill, *Something New Under the Sun: An Environmental History of the Twentieth Century World,* 3–5, 16–17. Copyright © 2000 by W. W. Norton & Company, Inc. Used by permission of W. W. Norton & Company.

scale that it affects the fundamentals of global atmospheric chemistry. So changes in scale can lead to changes in condition.

Beyond that, in natural systems as in human affairs, there are thresholds and so-called nonlinear effects. In the 1930s, Adolf Hitler's Germany acquired Austria, the Sudetenland, and the rest of Czechoslovakia without provoking much practical response. When in September 1939 Hitler tried to add Poland, he got a six-year war that ruined him, his movement, and (temporarily) Germany. Unknowingly—although he was aware of the risk—he crossed a threshold and provoked a nonlinear effect. Similarly, water temperature in the tropical Atlantic can grow warmer and warmer without generating any hurricanes. But once that water passes 26 degrees Celsius, it begins to promote hurricanes: a threshold passed, a switch thrown, simply by an incremental increase. The environmental history of the twentieth century is different from that of time past not merely because ecological changes were greater and faster, but also because increased intensities threw some switches. For example, incremental increases in fishing effort brought total collapse in some oceanic fisheries. The cumulation of many increased intensities may throw some grand switches, producing very basic changes on the earth. No one knows, and no one will know until it starts to happen—if then. . . .

The human species has shattered the constraints and rough stability of the old economic, demographic, and energy regimes. This is what makes our times so peculiar. In the nineteenth century the world began a long economic boom, which climaxed in the twentieth century, when the world economy grew 14-fold. . . . Energy use embarked on a boom which began with a fivefold growth in the nineteenth century. That boom climaxed (to date) in the twentieth century with a further 16-fold expansion.

Why has all this happened now? The main answer is human ingenuity. Part of the answer is luck. First the luck: in the eighteenth century a large part of the disease load that checked our numbers, and our productivity too, was lifted. Initially this had little to do with medicine or public health measures, but reflected a gradual adjustment between human hosts and some of our pathogens and parasites. We domesticated or marginalized some of our killer diseases, quite unintentionally. This was luck. So was the ending of the Little Ice Age (c. 1550–1850), which may also have had a minor role in permitting the great modern expansions.

Most of the explosive growth of modern times derives from human ingenuity. From the 1760s forward we have continually devised clusters of new technologies, giving access to new forms of energy and enhancing labor productivity. At the same time we have designed new forms of social and business organization that have helped ratchet up the pace of economic activity. Both machines and organization—hardware and software—lie behind the breakthrough of modern times. The great modern expansion, while liberating in a fundamental sense, brought disruption with it. The surges in population, production, and energy use affected different regions, nations, classes, and social groups quite unevenly, favoring some and hurting others. Many inequalities widened, and perhaps more wrenching, fortune and misfortune often were reshuffled. Intellectually, politically, and in every other way, adjusting to a world of rapid growth and shifting status was hard to do. Turmoil of every sort abounded. The preferred policy solution after 1950 was yet faster economic growth and rising living standards: if we can all consume more than we used to, and expect to consume still more in the years to come, it is far easier to accept the anxieties of constant change and the inequalities of the moment. Indeed, we erected new politics, new ideologies, and new institutions predicated on continuous growth. Should this age of exuberance end, or even taper off, we will face another set of wrenching adjustments. . . .

DATA ON ENVIRONMENTAL AND SOCIAL CHANGE

In assessing environmental change, researchers examine data that range widely from global temperature change to the amount of municipal waste produced by humans. In the following section, we have included a range of factors that have been commonly identified as important for understanding the impact of global change. Obviously, the data provided here are far too limited to make definitive assessments and pronouncements, but together, they do show how demographic trends, technological innovations, and lifestyle choices are interrelated on various levels and how they frequently combine to have a potentially huge impact on world environmental conditions. Moreover, by better understanding past trends and current conditions, we might begin to make tentative projections about future problems and potential policies.

QUESTIONS TO CONSIDER

1. What factors might explain the rapid population growth in the past three centuries?
2. Why might the populations of nonindustrialized nations be increasing faster than those of industrialized nations? What are some possible implications for future impact on the environment?
3. What historical forces help explain the growth of world GDP?
4. Using the data from the tables and charts, explain why energy use and production are such important measures for environmental change.
5. What factors might explain the dramatic increase in U.S. farm productivity? What effects might these factors have on the environment?

Demographic Data

Population growth is an indication of man's survivability, ingenuity, and good fortune on planet Earth. According to most researchers, human population growth received its first stimulus from the agricultural revolution (8000 BCE), but

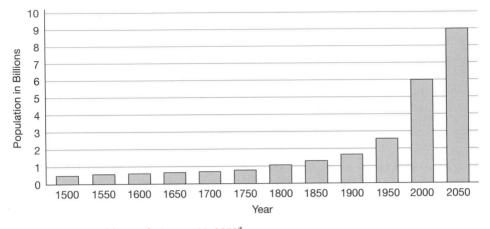

Figure 15.1 World Population, 1500–2050[1]

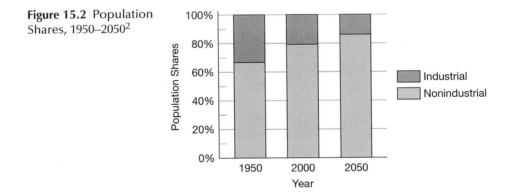

Figure 15.2 Population Shares, 1950–2050[2]

the growth rate remained modest until the past three hundred years. The global growth rate peaked in the 1960s at 2 percent a year, but it has since fallen to 1.26 percent in 2000, and some experts believe it may drop as low as 0.46 percent by 2050.

Technology and Lifestyle

Human lifestyle choices and technological innovations have had the most dramatic impact on global environmental change. A standard means to measure human economic activity is the global gross domestic product (GDP), which equals the total value of goods and services in the marketplace. The other charts and tables illustrate additional important features of human activity and ingenuity that have had significant global impact.

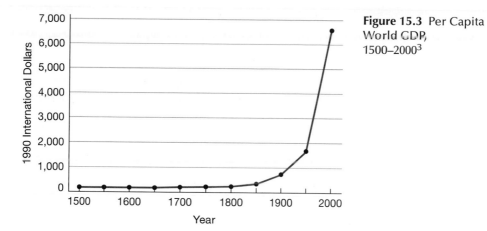

Figure 15.3 Per Capita World GDP, 1500–2000[3]

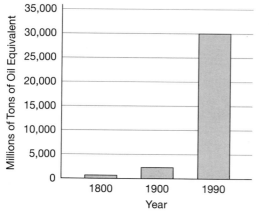

Figure 15.4 World Energy Use, 1800–1990[4]

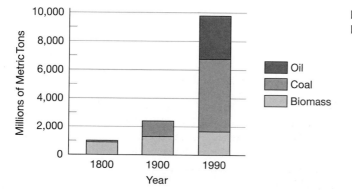

Figure 15.5 World Fuel Production, 1800–1990[5]

Figure 15.6 Number of Motor Vehicles, 1960–2020[6]

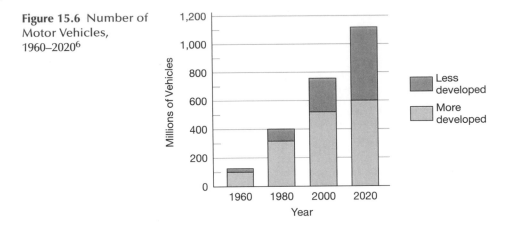

U.S. Agricultural Productivity
(inputs required to produce 100 bushels of corn)

Date	Labor Hours	Acreage of Land	Fertilizer Use (in millions of tons[2])
1850	75–90	2.5	N/A
1890	35–40	2.5	N/A
1930	15–20	2.5	6.6
1945	10–14	2.0	13.5
1975	3.3	1.2	N/A
1987	2.7	1.2	N/A

Figure 15.7 U.S. Agricultural Productivity, 1850–1987[7]

Figure 15.8 Global Marine Fish Catch, 1800–1996[8]

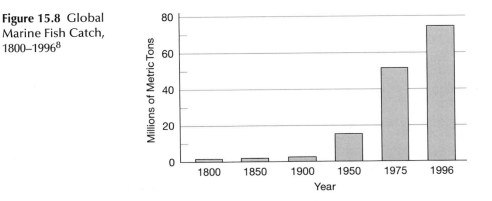

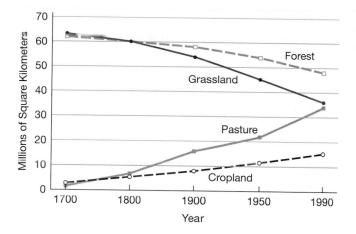

Figure 15.9 Global Vegetation Cover, 1700–1990[9]

Pollutant	Place	Increase Factor
Ozone	Europe	5
Sulfur Dioxide	USA	2.2
Sulfur Dioxide	World	5
Nitrogen Oxides	World	14
Lead	World	7
Methane	World	3.5

Figure 15.10 Increases in Air Pollution Emission Rates, 1900–1990[10]

Taxa	Approximate Number of Species	Total Extinctions
Vertebrates	47,000	321
Mammals	4,500	110
Birds	9,500	103
Reptiles	6,300	21
Amphibians	4,200	5
Fish	24,000	82
Mollusks and crustaceans	104,000	244
Insects	>1,000,000	98
Vascular plants	250,000	396
Total	**Approx. 1,600,000**	**1,033**

Figure 15.11 Number of Species and Documented Extinctions, 1600 to present[11]

HUMAN RIGHTS

On December 10, 1948, the General Assembly of the United Nations adopted and proclaimed the Universal Declaration of Human Rights (UDHR), which declared in its preamble that all human beings "shall enjoy freedom of speech and belief, and freedom from fear and want." Since then, the thirty articles of the UDHR have provided the blueprint for international human rights laws and have obliged governments to work progressively toward their full implementation. In addition, the postwar world witnessed the creation of human rights organizations, such as Amnesty International and Human Rights Watch, to advocate, monitor, and report on the condition of human rights around the world. But the transformation of theoretical ideals and goals into reality has been exceedingly difficult to achieve. Although the end of the cold war may have increased political liberties around the world, global economic and social inequalities have actually increased in the past few decades.

In the view of some researchers, the association of global inequality with human rights crystallized with the spread of the AIDS pandemic in the 1990s. Although no region, population, or culture has been spared from this epidemic, the more affluent nations of the world have been able to afford much more extensive prevention programs and lifesaving medical therapies than poorer countries. But do such disparities of income and health care represent a violation of human rights? This is obviously a controversial issue and was the prime topic of an article titled "Righting Wrongs" (2001), excerpted from the British news journal *The Economist*. The article briefly traces the evolution of human rights organizations since 1950 and the potential benefits and pitfalls inherent in the effort to extend economic and social human rights with equal vigor.

This essay is followed by a summary balance sheet report by the United Nations Development Program (UNDP) on the global state of human rights in 2002, which provides additional data to assess recent progress and problems in the world.

QUESTIONS TO CONSIDER

1. Until recently, western advocates for human rights focused primarily on civil and political rights of people around the world. According to the author, why is this so? What factors might have renewed western interest in universal economic and social rights?

2. Some critics argue that the promotion and attainment of economic and social rights is far more difficult than achieving civil and political rights. What reasons are given in the reading? How do you assess these reasons?

3. The United Nations' report uses the terms "progress" and "fragmentation" in its assessments. How do the data listed under each category reflect upon the philosophy of the United Nations? In their view, what is the ideal world?

4. What are the most important elements of progress? What are the most important signs of fragmentation? What do the data about the HIV/AIDS epidemic tell us? Is it relevant to the issue of human rights?

5. In your assessment, are people around the world equally entitled, as human beings, to a universal standard of rights? Are they entitled to a minimum standard of living and health care? Explain your answer fully.

"RIGHTING WRONGS" (2001)

In [George Bernard] Shaw's "Pygmalion", Colonel Pickering asks Alfred Doolittle whether he has no morals. "Can't afford them, governor," the philanderer replies; "Neither could you if you was as poor as me." Morals are costly to maintain. So are rights, especially the kind of "universal human rights" that become enshrined in United Nations' declarations.

International support for a core group of human rights, mainly civil and political, has been enshrined for more than half a century in the Universal Declaration of Human Rights, ratified by the United Nations in the aftermath of the Second World War and the Holocaust. The declaration proved compelling as a statement of principles, but too general and vague to be useful as a legal instrument. So, during the 1960s, two more covenants were thrashed out in an effort to give the declaration some substance: the International Covenant on Civil and Political Rights and the International Covenant on Economic, Social and Cultural Rights.

During the Cold War, enthusiasm for these covenants split along the obvious divide: capitalists were keen on civil and political rights, Communists on social and economic rights. When Western lobbyists accused the Soviet Union of violating its citizens' civil rights, the Soviet government replied that the economic and social rights of its people were more important. The division survives: today the Chinese make much the same argument.

In terms of publicity and promotion, the rights set out in the first covenant [Civil and Political Rights] have had the benefit of human-rights advocates such as Amnesty International and Human Rights Watch (HRW). They have publicized the plight of prisoners of conscience and victims of torture. As a result, regimes that torture, unjustly imprison or disenfranchise their citizens have sometimes been pushed or shamed into changing their behavior.

Until now, the second covenant [Economic, Social and Cultural Rights] has been used less widely to promote the rights that it enshrines—mainly to economic benefits such as housing, food, health care and fair wages. Now, though, Western human-rights groups, which have traditionally focused only on civil and political violations, are looking again at economic rights, and hope eventually to persuade governments to place the right to a house or a meal on an equal footing with the right to vote. . . .

Source: "Righting Wrongs," in *The Economist* (August 16, 2001), http://www.economist.com. Reprinted with permission.

Over the past four years, Amnesty's main policy committee, the Standing Committee on the Mandate, has been developing a set of resolutions that would explicitly incorporate economic and social rights into Amnesty's mandate. . . . Amnesty may be the most prominent human-rights group debating a shift of focus, but it is by no means alone. Since 1993, the charter of the Centre for Economic and Social Rights in Brooklyn, New York, has demanded that it "challenge economic injustice as a violation of international human rights law." In its strategic plan for the next three years, Oxfam, Britain's leading overseas-development charity, lays out its belief in "rights to a sustainable livelihood, and the rights and capacities to participate in societies and make positive changes to people's lives." The Ford Foundation's program for human rights recently decided to finance a project to create a global network on the Internet that will provide an international directory of non-governmental organizations (NGOs) interested in economic, social and cultural rights, with a view to encouraging them to collaborate.

United Nations' bodies are also keen to extend the concept. Since 1998, the World Health Organization has been asking the international community to recognize health as a human right. In "A Human Rights Approach to TB," a document issued in March, the WHO inelegantly points out the obligation of states to "provide some sort of redress that people know about and can access if they feel that their health-related rights have been impinged on." And the UN Human Rights Commission recently stated that international trade law ought to be harmonized with international human-rights law.

Why, though, are human-rights bodies so keen to broaden their [focus] in this way? The short answer is that they have begun to wonder whether civil and political rights are not a bit beside the point in many of the world's poorest countries. In particular, the AIDS pandemic in Africa is driving the movement to demand that economic and social goods be treated as entitlements. Michael Ignatieff, the director of the Carr Centre of Human Rights Policy at Harvard University's Kennedy School of Government, insists that the ambit of human-rights organizations must expand: "Look at Botswana," he says. "All the gains in civil and political rights that have been made there will be wiped out by the catastrophic losses in economic and social rights. At this level of incidence of AIDS, the virus destroys the infrastructure of a society. It cuts into the defenses that make civil and political rights possible. . . ."

In addition, human-rights groups worry that the governments of the rich world are not responding to this catastrophe with enough vigor, and that using "rights talk" may shake them out of their torpor. "Doing something about AIDS in Africa is not about charity or public-health prevention. It is a matter of obligation," says Mr Ignatieff. "The rights argument is a way to leverage money to fulfil this obligation." Whereas calls for generosity can only pluck weakly at the sleeves of rich governments, perhaps unsubtle claims of legal obligation will twist their arms.

However, the strategy is a perilous one. Even if economic and social rights appear to have the same status on paper as civil and political rights, their philosophical grounding is often questioned. Designating a good as a universal human right means that reasonable people believe that under no jurisdiction, and under no circumstances, may that good be justly denied to anybody. Although freedom from torture certainly now falls into this category—arguably due to the efforts of groups like Amnesty—goods such as food and a decent home do not. Governments may intentionally torture their citizens; they do not usually intentionally inflict on them poverty and ill health. The moral imperative to stop poverty or disease is therefore not as convincing as the moral imperative to stop torture. . . .

Critics of an expanded set of human rights point to another difference between the old sort and the new. To guarantee civil and political rights is relatively cheap, whereas to guarantee economic and social rights is potentially enormously costly. The cost of ensuring the right to vote, for example, is well-defined: the nature of universal franchise is set out in a century of case law and statute, and the costs of staffing and equipping the ballot are easy to assess. Even when an election turns out to require independent observers, extended court sessions and a lot of recounting, as in Florida last November and December, it is still relatively easy for a democratic government to protect its citizens' right to vote.[12] Endorsing a universal right to health care, by contrast, seems a sure start to an expensive ride down a slippery slope. Who is to say when a person has had enough money spent on keeping him fit? . . .

In the case of AIDS, the main question is what pharmaceutical companies should do about drug prices. Mr Roth maintains that a government cannot be said to be upholding the right to health "when it defends excessive corporate profits over the right of access to essential, life-saving medicines in cheap or generic form." Human Rights Watch is currently working out the details of its position on drugs, and is hunting for a role where its investigative capabilities would be useful. But dealing with the complexities of appropriate drug policies in poor countries requires quite different skills from fighting on the simpler issues raised by torture or unjust incarceration.

If human-rights campaigners succeed in deploying their campaigning skills to improve health and reduce poverty, that will be a considerable gain. However, they risk alienating Western countries that have hitherto usually been their allies.

Unsurprisingly, America is at the top of that list. America has not yet ratified the International Covenant on Economic, Social and Cultural Rights. George Moose, the American ambassador to the UN Human Rights Commission (UNHRC), explained in April that his country was "concerned" about changes in international law that would "lead in the direction of the creation of legal, enforceable entitlements to economic, social, and cultural rights". Why? Because "that would mean citizens could sue their governments for enforcement of rights." At a meeting in Geneva in January to prepare for the UN summit on AIDS, the American delegation explicitly rejected a rights-based approach to stopping the disease, which it prefers to consider as a health-policy problem or, when pressed, as one of national security.

However, badgering the United States to change its attitude may be little use. After all, human-rights groups have long tried unsuccessfully to persuade America to abolish the death penalty. If such groups start offering their views on a slew of other issues, Americans may simply stop paying attention to them. Mr Ignatieff admits that human-rights groups risk becoming marginalized. Nevertheless, he argues that "the risk of not going this route is equally great: you become focused on yesterday's challenge and you miss tomorrow's challenge. . . ."

UNDP, Human Development Balance Sheet

The United Nations Development Program (UNDP) is one of the principal international organizations devoted to the implementation of the Universal Declaration of Human Rights. The program helps to set up and monitor international human rights policies, and it has representatives in over 160 countries to offer guidance and assistance. Each year, the UNDP produces its Human Development Reports, containing substantive data on most development indicators. The reports rank every country each year in areas such as per capita income, literacy, life expectancy, and respect for women's rights, with the goal of "putting people back at the centre of the development process." In addition to the full report, the UNDP produces an annual Balance Sheet, which is excerpted here.

THE HUMAN DEVELOPMENT BALANCE SHEET (2002)

I. Democracy and Participation

Global Progress

- Since 1980, 81 countries have taken significant steps toward democracy, with 33 military regimes replaced by civilian governments.
- 140 of the world's nearly 200 countries now hold multiparty elections, more than any time in history.

- 125 countries, with 62% of the total world population, have a free or partly free press.

- The number of countries ratifying the six main human rights conventions has increased dramatically since 1990. Ratifications of the International Covenant on Economic, Social and Cultural Rights (ICESCR) and the International Covenant on Civil and Political Rights (ICCPR) grew from around 90 to 150.

Global Fragmentation

- Of the 81 new democracies, only 47 are fully democratic. Many others do not seem to be in transition to democracy or have lapsed back into authoritarianism or conflict.
- Only 82 countries, with 57% of the world's people, are fully democratic.

- 61 countries, with 38% of the world's population, still do not have a free press.

- 106 countries still restrict important civil and political freedoms.
- 38 countries have not ratified or signed the ICCPR, and 41 have not ratified or signed the ICESCR [including the United States].

Source: United Nations Development Program, "The Human Development Balance Sheet," from *The Human Development Report 2002.* Text slightly edited. Available online at http://www.undp.org/ hdr2002/presskit/HDR%20PR_balance.pdf. The section on HIV/AIDS was added separately, and the data were obtained primarily from UNAIDS, *AIDS Epidemic Update: June 2003,* http:// www.unaids.org.

- In 10 countries more than 30% of parliamentarians are women.

- Only 6 vetoes were cast in the UN Security Council between 1996 and 2001—compared with 243 between 1946 and 1995, an average of 50 a decade.

- Worldwide, only 14% of parliamentarians are women—and in 10 countries none are women.

- The World Trade Organization operates on a one-country, one-vote basis, but most key decisions are made by the leading economic powers in "green room" meetings.
- The executive directors representing France, Germany, Japan, the Russian Federation, Saudi Arabia, the United Kingdom, and the United States account for 46% of the voting rights in the World Bank and 48% in the International Monetary Fund.

II. Economic Justice, Health, and Education

Global Progress

- The proportion of world's people living in extreme poverty fell from 29% in 1990 to 23% in 1999.
- During the 1990s extreme poverty was halved in East Asia and the Pacific and fell 7 percent in South Asia.

- 57 countries, with half of the world's people, have halved hunger or are on track to do so by 2015.

- Worldwide, primary school enrollments rose from 80% in 1990 to 84% in 1998.
- 51 countries, with more than 60% of the world's people, have achieved or are on track to achieve gender equality in primary education by 2015—and more than 80 in secondary education.

Global Fragmentation

- The richest 10% of the U.S. population has a total income equal to that of the poorest 43% of the world.
During the 1990s, the number of people in extreme poverty in sub-Saharan Africa rose from 242 million to 300 million. More than half of the region's people are poorer now than in 1990.

- At the current rate it would take more than 130 years to rid the world of hunger.

- 113 million school-age children are not in school—97% of them in developing countries.
- 93 countries, with 39% of the world's people, do not have data on trends in primary enrollment.
- Of the world's estimated 854 million illiterate adults, 544 million are women.

III. The AIDS Pandemic

Global Progress

- In the 1990s, HIV infection rates moderated or declined in several countries, including much of the developed world.
- In China, home to over a billion people, there were only an estimated 850,000 people living with HIV/AIDS in 2001.
- The estimated annual number of AIDS-related deaths in the United States fell approximately 14% from 1998 to 2002, from 19,005 deaths in 1998 to 16,371 deaths in 2002.

Global Fragmentation

- Worldwide, HIV infection rates continue to rise, especially in low- and middle-income countries, which now represent 95% of all new infections. There were an estimated 34–46 million people living with HIV/AIDS at the end of 2003.
- The rate of new HIV infections in China rose more than 67% in 2001.
- Worldwide, an estimated 30 million people have died due to HIV/AIDS, and more than 15 million children have been orphaned. Low-income countries, especially in Africa, have suffered the highest rate of AIDS-related mortality.

- Modern anti-retroviral AIDS drugs have significantly prolonged the health and lives of people living with HIV/AIDS.
- The price of AIDS drugs has dropped about 50% from 2000. The least expensive generic combination recommended by the World Health Organization is about $300 per person per year.

- Only a fraction received treatment: about 800,000 people worldwide, 500,000 of whom live in high-income countries. In sub-Saharan Africa, where 2.4 million people died of AIDS in 2002, only 50,000 people received treatment.
- In many low-income countries, per capita income is equal to or less than $300 per year. In southern Africa, high rates of AIDS-related sickness and death have significantly reduced family incomes and national wealth.

- Funding for global HIV/AIDS education and prevention programs has shown a steady increase.
- The United States has spent more on global HIV/AIDS programs than any other nation. Since the mid-1980s, the U.S. has spent approximately $1.5 billion.

- UNAIDS estimates that the epidemic is spreading five times faster than the pace of international donations.
- U.S. spending on global HIV/AIDS in 2001 accounted for only $235 million, or about 0.002% of its GDP (estimated at $10 trillion). In 2001, the United States ranked ninth in terms of funding generosity.

TOWARD A GLOBAL CULTURE?

Twentieth-century innovations in technology, commercial production, and media communications have revolutionized cross-cultural encounters. With just a couple of clicks of a mouse, for example, an Internet surfer in Boston can gain instant access to chat rooms in Bombay, to businesses in Birmingham, or to tourist destinations in Brazil. Modern methods of production and exchange allow consumers around the world a greater choice of international foods and goods than ever before. And thanks to television, more than 500 million viewers from around the world simultaneously watched Senegal defeat France in the first round of the 2002 World Cup games, reinforcing soccer's unofficial designation as the foremost global sport.

But what impact are global media and communications having on world cultures? Some critics fear that globalization is a threat to local cultures by creating a single, homogenized world culture. Others disagree, arguing that globalization is actually leading to a rich, new hybridization of cultures. Is the proliferation of McDonald's "golden arches" around the world a sign of American cultural imperialism? Or are local cultures more robust and adaptive than the rhetoric of globalization would have us believe? These issues and others were the subjects of a lively roundtable discussion on global culture hosted by and heard on Radio Australia in 2002. The panelists in this discussion represent a variety of cultures and backgrounds, and their perspectives reflect differing interpretations regarding the impact of globalization on world cultures. This reading is followed by a photo gallery offering examples of the nature and impact of cross-cultural encounters.

QUESTIONS TO CONSIDER

1. Why do some critics view the information revolution as a threat that breeds discontent? How might this perspective be conditioned by historical experiences? How have some groups responded to this perceived threat?
2. According to some observers, cultural flows between nations involve "interpenetrations at different levels." What does this mean? What examples can you supply that support this perspective? What is meant by "Americanization is happening to Americans, too"?
3. How has the global media affected world immigration? How have immigrants contributed to global culture? What is significant about these relationships?
4. How do the images present evidence of cultural assimilation, adaptation, fusion, and/or rejection? How can you begin to explain why some cultural elements are easily assimilated, whereas others are not?
5. In your understanding of past cross-cultural encounters in human history, do you think the world is moving toward a homogenized common global culture? Why or why not? What evidence would you select to reinforce your view?

GLOBALLY SPEAKING: GLOBAL CULTURE

Rena Sarumpaet [Program host]

The word "globalization" can mean many things. But it usually refers to the growing inter-dependence between the nations of the world as they are drawn into a global economy. The main agents of this are transnational corporations. But as well as those with well known brand names like Coca-Cola and McDonald's, many of these corporations are in media, communications and information technologies. For this reason globalization has also come to mean, for some, the threat of cultural homogenization.

R. Ramakrishna [Heads the economic study group of India's ruling party— the Bharatiya Janata Party, or BJP]

The information revolution and particularly the electronic media—these are now slowly and steadily creating a lot of discontent. People are looking to the TV and there is a composite pop culture, pop music culture, there are discotheques all over the towns, now this sort of aping, this sort of trying to come out of your cultural mold and getting into some other mold it is certainly there. It does not have much of a deleterious effect on the urban households, but the rural households in which even necessities of life are being denied, where you see a very artificial life in the media, that breeds discontent. Discontent brings about breakdown of law and order, mafia groups and gun toting—all these things are the products of these things. And we see a lot more of unrest particularly in the youth. I don't know what type of society we will be developing over time.

Rena Sarumpaet [Program host]

The question then is whether regional, national and local cultures are strong enough to resist the forces that appear to be moving us towards a global culture. Professor Tony Milner, Dean of the Faculty of Asian Studies at the Australian National University, believes it is necessary to take an historical perspective in order to understand these fears about cultural homogenization.

Professor Tony Milner [Dean of the Faculty of Asian Studies at the Australian National University]

One must see globalization in a longer historical phase and [as] a continuation of an earlier colonial process. Therefore the response to globalization today links up a bit with the response to colonialism in the past, and that is one reason why we have to take seriously these Asian values and attitudes because they do have a link to the anti-colonial movements. There is a perception in many parts of the region that globalization is fairly close to westernization and therefore it does bring back memories, community memories of the colonial period, a nervousness about being brought into a global situation and sacrificing values which are local.

Source: Radio Australia and Victoria University in Melbourne. *Globally Speaking: The Politics of Globalization. Program 3: Global Culture.* Produced by Sue Slamen and Barry Clarke. Copyright: Australian Broadcasting Corporation. http://www.abc.net.au/global/radio/radio03.htm. Transcript edited and modified.

Professor Wang Gungwu [Director of the East Asian Institute of the National University of Singapore]

Asians, having been weak and humiliated and defeated for several centuries, [are] regaining some confidence in themselves by having acquired many of the institutions from military to legal to commercial to political institutions that have made the nation states of the West so strong. And now that different Asian nations are acquiring them, they are beginning to recover the confidence in their own values, and [they] particularly want to see their values preserved, not to see them all eroded away by the very aggressive modern values of the West which are infecting the young people in Asia. And therefore there is this tendency among the political elites in Asia to say we now have the confidence to restate our own cultural positions if we still believe them, we should affirm them, and not bow our heads in shame because all these have failed in the contest with the West, and to accept just simply defeat and simply bow down to all the new values that are coming from the modern West.

Professor Tony Milner [Dean of the Faculty of Asian Studies at the Australian National University]

There are indications that young people in Asian societies right across the Asian region have been concerned about globalization and concerned to assert or to discover to some extent and then assert their own identity in that. And from what I understand of developments in China we'd be making a great mistake if we assumed that young Chinese were galloping toward a liberal democratic view of the world. I watched in a seminar quite recently, very successful middle-class young Chinese people being lectured about China's human rights and labor relations problems and they were very angry, they were very nationalistic, seemingly speaking in a way one might have thought their grandparents would speak. But they were not going to put up with that sort of western criticism of China and spelt out that China had very great achievements historically and continued to do so. So you sense there very much even among this very commercially minded group a negative response to a globalization if it wasn't a globalization that had great respect for Chinese uniqueness or the Chinese local in the process.

Rena Sarumpaet [Program host]

For all the evidence of cultural resistance there are many contradictions. In the 1960's and seventies the spread of US-based media, advertising and consumer goods around the world, provoked protests against cultural imperialism and Americanization. However, Professor John Sinclair from Victoria University believes cultural flows are never just a one way process—they involve interpenetration at different levels between nations.

Professor John Sinclair [Victoria University]

It occurs to me that Americanization is something that happens to Americans too. So in other words what we're witnessing is not the imposition of one national culture, the American upon all the other national cultures of the world. That was how it was seen in the seventies and that was what cultural imperialism meant. But I think that one of the really useful things about the idea of globalization in fact is that it enables us to get away from that, but what it facilitates is thinking of cultural influence as being a manifold sort of phenomenon which operates at lots of different sorts of levels and operates sort of across nations and across a different strata within nations, from one nation to the next, even from the point of view of the United States that they much to their displeasure in the 1980's discovered that they were caught up in this too when Sony came in and started buying into their media industries.

Chandra Muzzafar [Malaysian commentator]

It would be wrong to equate globalization today with neo-colonialism. It is not. For two reasons—one, if you look at the way in which ideas and values are flowing across borders, it's not just from the dominant to the dominated, sometimes it's from the dominated to the dominant. How else do you explain the popularity of Indian cuisine in London? How do you explain the popularity of certain marshal art forms from Sino civilization, because it's a dominated civilization and yet you find that people in the West are lapping it up you know things of this sort. So there is another flow that is taking place and one must also appreciate the fact that it is not just Western dominance. After all, Japan is a very important actor in the present globalization process, especially when it comes to economics. So it is a very complex process—that's one aspect of globalization. There's another aspect of globalization which makes it very challenging. I think globalization has the potential in spite of everything of empowering the individual, and that empowerment of the individual in this particular form through a certain technological device is something which hasn't happened on such a vast scale at any time in the past.

Rena Sarumpaet [Program host]

Global culture is not just about flows of media and brand names but also about the movement of people. When people move around the world they take their cultures with them. Of course they are influenced by the cultures of the host nations which they move through, but in turn, they exert their own influences on those cultures.

Felipe Fernandez-Armesto [Oxford historian, currently teaching in the Netherlands]

Does the culture of the indigenous peoples change the metropolis? Of course it does [but] it is difficult to generalize about the ways in which it tends to because they're so diverse, and the actual manifestations of this influence tend to be very different according to the environment, according to the political relationships, and according to the period of history one's talking about. But very obviously subject peoples have an effect on the metropolis in challenging the in-comers' ideas about politics and about human nature because they're always going to be surprising things that they encounter in the cultures in which they're guests, visitors or rulers. . . .

Dipesh Chakrabarty [Indian-born academic who lived and worked in Australia for 20 years and now teaches at the University of Chicago]

. . . We used to think that in order to find Indian culture you had to go to India, in order to find Filipino culture you had to go to the Philippines. And now increasingly you [find] Indian culture or Filipino culture is both inside and outside [of traditional regions] as people have become diasporic* as cultures cease to be rooted in particular places. That actually gives rise to the very interesting possibility of "cosmopolitanism". . . . of people enriching themselves by inhabiting consciously more than one culture, and by not having to think or imagine that they belong necessarily and primarily to one culture alone. And that I think is a very exciting possibility.

Rena Sarumpaet [Program host]

As we've heard, globalization involves the accelerated movement of capital, people, products and images aided by new technologies. Media and advertising are opening up a new world of possibilities which encourage people to experience different cultures.

Dipesh Chakrabarty [Indian-born academic who lived and worked in Australia for 20 years and now teaches at the University of Chicago]

Two interesting experiences I had in the United States back in Chicago, one was with an undergraduate student and one was with a graduate student of mine, both from India who are now studying in the States and I asked them what had initially made them think of going to the States. One of them . . . said to me [that] it was his exposure to Nike shoes and sporting gear on sporting grounds, so he was exposed to objects that were being imported into India which still had a protected home market. So it was the extra finesse of objects produced in properly capitalist countries that appealed to his imagination. The younger person talked about American soap operas and he had visions of being in a convertible car with . . . a blonde woman, hair sort of flying in the air, driving along some beautiful highway, and he said [he] was really struck by these images and wanted to be in that place called America. And I said to him, "So how do you find it now?" He said, "Well, the [vision] wasn't unreal, it is possible."

Rena Sarumpaet [Program host]

Although historically, global media flows have been dominated by American movies and TV programs, and indeed for the most part still are today, certain regions of the world have their own vibrant cultural industries. India, for example, has become famous for "Bollywood"—its film industry based in what used to be called "Bombay". Bollywood actually produces more films each year than Hollywood. And the case of Indian TV is remarkable in the way that globalization has actually stimulated local cultural production.

Mahdav Prasad [Indian cultural studies expert on Indian film and television]

Certainly in the beginning you saw a spate of *Dynasty* or *Dallas* clones, and some of that goes on even now. And there is a lot of imitation of programs, and it's also partly because certain people have rights to foreign programs and then they try to reproduce that model. So you have things like the *Price Is Right,* that sort of program and its indigenous versions. Then you have some people who simply imitate *Mind Your*

---

*From *diaspora:* the scattering of people outside of their traditional regions.

Language, Hindi version and that kind of thing. There's a lot of that. [But] there are also interesting programs on Tamil channels* which try to reproduce the atmosphere of a *panchayat,* a [traditional] village council where issues are debated and judgements are given by a council of people. So there is an attempt to reproduce that kind of atmosphere and get people to debate the stuff. So it's a mix.

Professor John Sinclair [Victoria University]

When we talk about "the global village" we have to remember that not everybody is a member of the global village. While cosmopolitanism might be part and parcel of everyday experience within Australia, it is not the case in India, where 75 percent of the population (nearly a billion people) are living in villages, and not a lot of those villages have television. There are something like 55 million television homes in India—that is a lot—but in terms of a billion people it's not really that great. Those people are also a very long way from a telephone [and cinema] . . . so their participation in the global village is really pretty marginal. So I think it's important that when we talk about globalization, [we recognize] that in actual fact it's not really a global movement. It is predominantly something which is happening within the Western societies and it's happening within the globalized sectors of societies like India . . . but the vast majority of people in the country are not [integrated].

Dipesh Chakrabarty [Indian academic teaching at the University of Chicago]

One obvious question that cuts across the tendency toward globalization is the question of privilege. Who has access, who doesn't, and interestingly, most of the studies of imagining the globe or moving between cultures, of hybridization, of global flows relate to more successful middle-class professional people. . . . So, when we talk about cultural homogenization, we can easily forget that not everybody experiences globalization in the same way. Not everybody participates in the same global culture, and not everybody is willing to be drawn into global culture anyhow. Above all, we need to realize that real people make regional, national and local cultures much more robust and adaptive than the rhetoric of globalization would have us believe.

Picture Gallery of Global Culture

The following picture gallery provides different examples of cross-cultural encounters in our increasingly interconnected global village. The sample photos come from a variety of nations, and they depict elements of cross-cultural exchange, adaptation, and innovation. But one needn't travel to far-off lands to see evidence of an ever-increasing global culture. Take a walk down the street of any American town or city and observe the many instances of cultural exchange and assimilation that exist today, ranging from the foods we eat to the clothing we wear and the music we listen to. As you view the photos in this section, and as

---

*One of the major cultural groups in India.

you witness the evolution of global culture in America, keep in mind the following questions.

QUESTIONS TO CONSIDER

1. What ideas or things tend to be the most adopted or imitated? Do you see any trends, and if so, how do you account for them?
2. What cultural ideas or objects seem to be more resistant to globalization? Again, do you witness any trends, and how might they be explained?
3. Some critics of globalization equate it with American cultural imperialism. Do you agree? Why, or why not?
4. What elements of global culture seem most prevalent in today's American society? How might you characterize current trends? In what areas are ideas and items most readily assimilated? Where are they most resisted?
5. Is evolution of a common global culture a "good" thing? Is there a danger inherent in uncontrolled and widespread cultural exchange? Do world cultures risk losing their unique and historical identities?

Figure 15.12 Guitarist in a cowboy bar in Tokyo, Japan.

Figure 15.13 Street scene in Bombay, India.

Figure 15.14 Outside an Iranian McDonald's Restaurant.

Figure 15.15 Poster for
*Crouching Tiger Hidden
Dragon* directed by
Ang Lee.

Figure 15.16 Shopping in Baghdad, Iraq.

NOTES

1. Estimates from Michael Kremer, "Population Growth and Technological Change," *Quarterly Journal of Economics* 108, no. 3 (1993): 681–716.

2. United Nations Population Division, *World Population Prospects: The 2002 Revision Population Database,* http://esa.un.org.unpp.

3. Estimates from Bradford J. DeLong, *Estimating World GDP, One Million B.C.– Present* (2000). At http://econ161.berkeley.edu/tceh/2000/world_gdp/estimating-world-gdp.html.

4. Data from McNeill, 15. Elaborated from Vaclav Smil, *Energy in World History* (Boulder, CO: Westview Press, 1994), 187.

5. Data from McNeill, 14. Elaborated from Smil, 185–87.

6. From M. Pemberton, *Managing the Future: World Vehicle Forecasts and Strategies to 2020,* Vol. 1: *Changing Patterns of Demand* (London: Autelligence, 2003).

7. Data from U.S. Department of Agriculture, *A History of American Agriculture 1776–1990.* At http://www.usda.gov/history2/text4.htm. Note that fertilizer figures are average annual consumption per decade, for the decade including the year shown.

8. Data from J. R. McNeill, *Something New Under the Sun: An Environmental History of the Twentieth-Century World* (New York: W. W. Norton & Company, Inc., 2000), 247.

9. Ibid., 213.

10. Ibid., 64.

11. Data from Bjorn Lomborg, *The Skeptical Environmentalist: Measuring the Real State of the World* (Cambridge University Press, 2001), 250. According to Lomborg, the rigorous requirements needed for documenting extinctions mean that these figures certainly underestimate its true number.

12. This refers to the contested 2000 presidential election.

CREDITS

	1880	1900	1910	1920	1930

ASIA

1880	1900	1910	1920	1930
Ottoman sultan Abd al-Hamid II (r. 1876–1908)	Russo-Japanese War (1904–1905)	Chinese revolution and establishment of republic (1911)	Mohandas Gandhi launches Non-Cooperation Movement (1920)	Mao Zedong develops guerilla tactics (1930)
Mustapha Kemal (1881–1938)	Young Turks revolt (1908)	Emperor Puyi abdicates throne (1912)	Jiang Jieshi unifies China (1927)	Long March (1934)
Indian National Congress founded (1885)		Battle of Gallipoli (1915)		Japanese invasions of Manchuria (1931) and China (1937)
Burma falls to Britain (1886)		Balfour Declaration (1917)		Rape of Naujing (1937)
Promulgation of the Meiji constitution (1889)		May Fourth Movement (1919)		
Sino-Japanese War (1894–1895)				
Hundred Days Reforms (1898)				
Boxer Rebellion (1899–1900)				

AFRICA

1880	1900	1910	1920	1930
British occupation of Egypt (1882)	Belgium takes control of Belgian Congo (1908)	Union of South Africa established (1910)	Harry Thuku establishes the Young Kikuyu Association in Kenya (1921)	Emperor Haile Selassie I assumes the throne of Ethiopia (1930)
Berlin Conference (1884–1885)		Italy invades Libya (1911)		Italy invades Ethiopia (1935)
Discovery of gold in South Africa (1886)		African National Congress created (1912)		
Battle of Omdurman (1898)		Revolution in Egypt (1919)		
Boer War (1899–1902)				

AMERICAS & OCEANIA

1880	1900	1910	1920	1930
Annexation of Tahiti (France), Fiji (Britain), and Marshall Islands (Germany)	Construction of Panama Canal	Mexican Revolution (1910–1920)	U.S. stock market collapses (1929)	Smoot-Hawley Tariff (1930)
Battle of Little Big Horn (1876)		Mexican Constitution of 1917	Great Depression begins	Implementation of New Deal legislation (1933–1938)
Northwest Rebellion (1885)		United States enters Great War (1917)		Lázaro Cárdenas, Mexican president (1934–1940)
Massacre at Wounded Knee (1890)		U.S. marines sent to Nicaragua		Program of land distribution
Spanish-American War (1898)		Evita Perón (1919–1952)		

EUROPE

1880	1900	1910	1920	1930
	Leonid Brezhnev (1906–1982)	Great War (1914–1918)	Lenin's New Economic Policy (1921)	Adolf Hitler becomes chancellor of Germany (1933)
		Battles of Verdun and the Somme (1916)	Benito Mussolini becomes leader of Italy (1922)	Spanish Civil War (1936–1939)
		Russian revolution (1917)	First Soviet Five-Year Plan (1929)	Munich Conference (1938)
		Treaty of Versailles (1919)		Nazi-Soviet pact (1939)
				German invasion of Poland (1939)
				World War II (1939–1945)